HANDBOOK ON THE GEOGRAPHIES OF REGIONS AND TERRITORIES

RESEARCH HANDBOOKS IN GEOGRAPHY

Series Editor: Susan J. Smith, *Honorary Professor of Social and Economic Geography* and *The Mistress of Girton College, University of Cambridge, UK*

This important new *Handbook* series will offer high quality, original reference works that cover a range of subjects within the evolving and dynamic field of geography, emphasising in particular the critical edge and transformative role of human geography.

Under the general editorship of Susan J. Smith, these *Handbooks* will be edited by leading scholars in their respective fields. Comprising specially commissioned contributions from distinguished academics, the *Handbooks* offer a wide-ranging examination of current issues. Each contains a unique blend of innovative thinking, substantive analysis and balanced synthesis of contemporary research.

Titles in the series include:

Handbook on Geographies of Technology
Edited by Barney Warf

Handbook on the Geographies of Money and Finance
Edited by Ron Martin and Jane Pollard

Handbook on the Geographies of Regions and Territories
Edited by Anssi Paasi, John Harrison and Martin Jones

Handbook on the Geographies of Regions and Territories

Edited by

Anssi Paasi
Geography Research Unit, University of Oulu, Finland

John Harrison
Department of Geography and Environment, Loughborough University, UK

Martin Jones
Executive and Department of Geography, Staffordshire University, UK

RESEARCH HANDBOOKS IN GEOGRAPHY

 Edward **Elgar**
PUBLISHING

Cheltenham, UK • Northampton, MA, USA

Published by
Edward Elgar Publishing Limited
The Lypiatts
15 Lansdown Road
Cheltenham
Glos GL50 2JA
UK

Edward Elgar Publishing, Inc.
William Pratt House
9 Dewey Court
Northampton
Massachusetts 01060
USA

Paperback edition 2020

A catalogue record for this book
is available from the British Library

Library of Congress Control Number: 2018931783

This book is available electronically in the **Elgar**online
Social and Political Science subject collection
DOI 10.4337/9781785365805

ISBN 978 1 78536 579 9 (cased)
ISBN 978 1 78536 580 5 (eBook)
ISBN 978 1 83910 441 1 (paperback)

Typeset by Servis Filmsetting Ltd, Stockport, Cheshire
Printed and bound by CPI Group (UK) Ltd, Croydon CR0 4YY

Contents

Figures

Tables

Contributors

John Agnew is Distinguished Professor of Geography and Italian at UCLA, Los Angeles, CA, USA.

Bjørn T. Asheim is Professor in Economic Geography and Innovation Theory at the University of Stavanger, Norway.

Sarah Ayres is Reader in Public Policy and Governance at Bristol University, UK.

Andrew Beer is Professor and Dean: Research and Innovation at the University of South Australia, Australia.

Irus Braverman is Professor of Law and Adjunct Professor of Geography at the University at Buffalo, The State University of New York, USA.

Gillian Bristow is Professor of Economic Geography at Cardiff University, UK.

John R. Bryson is Professor of Enterprise and Competitiveness, City-Region Economic Development Institute, at the University of Birmingham, UK.

Igor Calzada is Lecturer and Research Fellow in Urban Transformations at the University of Oxford, UK.

Rodrigo Castriota is PhD candidate at the Centre for Development and Regional Planning (CEDEPLAR) at the Federal University of Minas Gerais (UFMG), Brazil, and Researcher at the Singapore-ETH Centre.

Julian Clark is Reader in Political Geography at the University of Birmingham, UK.

Allan Cochrane is Emeritus Professor of Urban Studies at the Open University, UK.

Roberta Comunian is Reader in Creative Economy at King's College London, UK.

Kevin Cox is Emeritus Distinguished Professor of Geography at Ohio State University, Columbus, OH, USA.

Melisa Deciancio is Researcher Associate at the Latin American School of Social Sciences (FLACSO), Argentina.

Klaus Dodds is Professor of Geopolitics at Royal Holloway University of London, UK.

Michael Dunford is Visiting Professor at the Chinese Academy of Sciences, Beijing, China.

Lauren England is a PhD candidate in Culture, Media and Creative Industries at King's College London, UK.

J. Nicholas Entrikin is Professor of Geography (Emeritus) at UCLA, Los Angeles, CA, and Professor of Sociology (Emeritus) at the University of Notre Dame, IN, USA.

David Gibbs is Professor of Human Geography at the University of Hull, UK.

Michael R. Glass is Lecturer in the Urban Studies Program at the University of Pittsburgh, PA, USA.

John Harrison is Reader in Human Geography at Loughborough University, UK.

Alan D. Hemmings is Adjunct Associate Professor at the University of Canterbury, New Zealand.

Yoshiko M. Herrera is Professor of Political Science at the University of Wisconsin-Madison, USA.

Robert Huggins is Professor of Economic Geography and Director of the Centre for Economic Geography at Cardiff University, UK.

Bob Jessop is Distinguished Professor of Sociology at Lancaster University, UK.

Andrew E. G. Jonas is Professor of Human Geography at the University of Hull, UK.

Alun Jones is Professor of Geography at University College Dublin, Ireland.

Andrew Jones is Professor of Economic Geography and Vice-President (Research and Enterprise) at City, University of London, UK.

Martin Jones is Professor of Human Geography and Deputy Vice-Chancellor at Staffordshire University, UK.

Rhys Jones is Professor of Political Geography at Aberystwyth University, UK.

J. Miguel Kanai is Lecturer in Human Geography at the University of Sheffield, UK.

Dmitrii Kofanov is a PhD candidate in comparative politics at the University of Wisconsin-Madison, USA.

Dieter F. Kogler is Associate Professor in Economic Geography and Director of the Spatial Dynamics Lab at University College Dublin, Ireland.

John Loughlin is Emeritus Professor of Politics at Cardiff University and a Research Fellow at Blackfriars, University of Oxford, UK.

Frank Mattheis is Research Fellow at the Institut d'Etudes Européennes (IEE), Université Libre de Bruxelles, Belgium, and the Centre for the Study of Governance Innovation, University of Pretoria, South Africa.

Sami Moisio is Professor of Spatial Planning and Policy at the University of Helsinki, Finland.

Roberto Monte-Mór is Professor at the Centre for Development and Regional Planning (CEDEPLAR) and the School of Architecture (EAD) at the Federal University of Minas Gerais (UFMG), Brazil.

Cara Nine is Senior Lecturer in Philosophy at University College Cork, Ireland.

Anssi Paasi is Professor of Geography at the University of Oulu, Finland.

Michelle Pace is Professor in EU-MENA Politics at Roskilde University, Denmark, and Honorary Professor in Politics and International Studies at the University of Birmingham, UK.

Kimberley Peters is Lecturer in Human Geography at the University of Liverpool, UK.

Pia Riggirozzi is Associate Professor in Global Politics at the University of Southampton, UK.

Deusdedit Rwehumbiza is Lecturer in International Business and Trade at University of Dar es Salaam, Tanzania.

Seth Schindler is Senior Lecturer in Urban Development and Transformation at the Global Development Institute, University of Manchester, UK.

Anton Shirikov is a PhD student in comparative politics at the University of Wisconsin-Madison, USA.

Christophe Sohn is Senior Researcher in Urban Geography at Luxembourg Institute of Socio-Economic Research (LISER), Luxembourg.

David Storey is Principal Lecturer in Geography at University of Worcester, UK.

Ngai-Ling Sum is Reader in the Department of Politics, Philosophy and Religion at Lancaster University, UK.

Kees Terlouw is Assistant Professor in Political Geography at Utrecht University, the Netherlands.

Piers Thompson is Reader in Small Business and Local Economics at Nottingham Trent University, UK.

Ivan Turok is Executive Director at the Human Sciences Research Council, South Africa.

Luk Van Langenhove is Research Professor in the Institute of European Studies at the Vrije Universiteit Brussels, Belgium.

Weidong Liu is Professor in Economic Geography at the Chinese Academy of Sciences, Beijing, China.

Adam Whittle is a PhD candidate at the School of Geography, University College Dublin, Ireland.

Preface

The editors of this collection have shared for a long time a deep interest in theoretical and empirical questions related to changing socio-spatialities, particularly the concepts of region and territory, and their shifting roles in academic debates and social and governmental practices. During the last decade or so we have been particularly attentive to the theoretical and practical challenges that the gradual evolution of relational approaches, alongside more traditional territorial approaches, have provided to academic research, regional planning, politics and governance.

The structure of this cutting-edge Handbook has been developed to respond to these challenges and to further regional debates. The Introduction, written by the editors, provides readers with a broad overview of regional debates and an outline for responding to future challenges in regional research. It highlights the need for new approaches and argues for more consolidated regional geographies. The articles in Part I scrutinize the changing geographies of regions and territories from a historical and theoretical point of view, evaluating critically the existing wisdom and pushing debates further. Part II has an emphasis on the relations between the region and economy. Part III problematizes regions, politics and identity. Part IV examines urbanization and the emerging new forms of spatiality in general and in various circumstances. Part V scrutinizes regions and regionalism in context, that is, how these categories have been mobilized in various areal settings. Overall, our aim has been to make this collection a rich combination of chapters that both bring together cutting-edge debates and open scope for further conceptual and empirical examinations.

The compilation of this Handbook has been an exciting project that has taken, as usual, more time than we expected at the beginning. From the publishers, Edward Elgar, we wish to thank Matthew Pitman for his patience and his generous support to realize this project, Barbara Pretty and Sarah Cook. We are also very grateful to all authors that have contributed with their articles to this collection.

As editors we also wish to thank our institutions. Anssi Paasi extends his thanks to the University of Oulu and the Academy of Finland for their financial support to the RELATE (*Relational and Territorial Politics of Bordering, Identities and Transnationalisation*) Center of Excellence (2014-2019) (Grant 272168). Martin Jones would like to acknowledge the financial support of the Economic and Social Research Council (ESRC) for funding WISERD Civil Society (Grant ES/L0090991/1), work package on Spaces of New Localism, and Staffordshire University for supporting the Centre for City Region Dynamics. John Harrison wishes to acknowledge Loughborough University for providing support to realize this project.

All editors wish to thank warmly Mr. Mirko Honkavaara for his careful work in formulating the final manuscript to the publisher and for successful efforts to chase permissions and missing references!

In Oulu, Loughborough and Staffordshire, April 2018
Anssi Paasi, John Harrison and Martin Jones

1. New consolidated regional geographies
Anssi Paasi, John Harrison and Martin Jones

1.1 INTRODUCTION

Region and territory have been major keywords of geographical thinking, methodology and research practice since the institutionalization of geography as an academic discipline at the end of the nineteenth century. Even before this, region and territory were fundamental categories, with some authors tracing the roots of Regional Geography to classical Greece (Claval 1998). However, it is in the modern era where Regional Geography was, for a long time, presented in many states as the crown of the discipline and a critical subarea for Geography's disciplinary identity (Peet 1998; Agnew 2018). But what is a region? How are they constructed? How do regions relate to territory? Are regions and territories still relevant in today's modern world characterized by all kinds of flows and networks? How are regions and territories affected and shaped by social forces? What does it mean to study the geographies of regions and territories? What does the future hold for these spatial categories? These are just some of the key questions which have shaped the long intellectual history of regions and territories in geography, and are as relevant today as they have ever been.

This is not to say that region and territory have been the exclusive domain of Geography and geographers. Both concepts feature prominently in history, international relations theory, area studies, political science, philosophy, cultural anthropology, legal studies, organizational studies, and so on. They are, in modern parlance, interdisciplinary concepts but with this comes often stark differences in how regions are conceptualized and mobilized by scholars working from different disciplines and perspectives. While the idea of the region is most commonly associated with the subnational scale, the regional concept has since its inception been used to refer to all spatial scales, ranging from the very local to the international. You are just as likely to hear the term region applied to a subnational scale (e.g. the north-west region in England, the northern Ostrobothnia region of Finland) as you are to a supranational scale (e.g. the Middle East region, Barents region). With this comes an appreciation that region and territory have important utility across disciplines, scales and contexts. It also highlights how both concepts are mobilized differently by scholars – for example, international relations scholars and area studies specialists tend to associate regions with spatial units larger than an individual state, often referring to assemblies of several states (Söderbaum 2003) – but also by people in their everyday lives (Entrikin 2018; Terlouw 2018), and in places and settings which demonstrate the increased utility of region and territory in different social, political and cultural realms (Paasi and Metzger 2017).

1.2   REGIONS AND TERRITORIES: HISTORY, TRADITION, PROGRESS

To account for the changing geographies of regions and territories it is, as Thrift (1994) neatly put it, necessary 'to go back' before we can move 'forward'. History and tradition are integral to the study of regions and territory. To this end, we begin by tracing the evolving geographies of regions and territories through five distinct chronological phases. Yet we want to emphasize that the development of the conceptual basis in the research of regions and territories has by no means been an undisputed, straightforward evolutionary trajectory; such conceptual basis is a dynamic field characterized by theoretical struggles and ruptures. New concepts are invented incessantly. Some concepts have been used long-lastingly, some others abandoned permanently, while some others have been adopted once again after being rejected earlier from dominant discourses. It is also crucial to note that conceptual developments never occur *in vacuo* but in relation to wider economic and structural developments, societal interests of knowledge, and general philosophical and methodological developments. At times, these developments resonate with major societal upheavals like wars and ethnic conflicts (cf. Paasi 2011).

1.2.1   Traditional Regional Geography

This is the 'classical' period of regional geography, which existed during the long nineteenth century and continued into the early part of the twentieth century. It is important to remember that during this period regional geography was the crown of the geography discipline – *the* critical backbone for its academic identity. Integral to this in many national contexts was the link from regional geography to empire, the environment and maps. Rapid colonial exploration and the exploitation of continental interiors had placed a premium on acquiring regionally specific geographical knowledge. The foundations of regional geography thus came in surveying and mapping the features (topography, species, climate) of hitherto unexplored places to understand how imperial nations and merchants could establish and protect commercial and political interests there. Similar techniques were important in the nation-building processes of many emerging national states. It was in these traditions that regions were intimately connected to mapping and territory. Here, regions were typically regarded as absolute entities, with the surface of the Earth divided into distinct regions at various scales – be they 'climatic regions' (Herbertson 1902), '*paysages*' (regional landscapes) or '*genres de vie*' (regional lifestyles) (Vidal de la Blache 1918) or 'human regions' (Fleure 1919) – to create a world of different geographical types, and a framework through which geographical inquiry could be conducted.

Whereas the link to empire and the environment established the disciplinary foundations for regional geography, the decline of empire and the demise of environmental determinism in the early part of the twentieth century saw geography lose ground to emergent, widely regarded as more scientific and more relevant, subjects such as economics, sociology and meteorology. As the title indicates, in 1939, Richard Hartshorne's *The Nature of Geography – A Critical Survey of Current Thought in the Light of the Past* was an earlier forerunner to Thrift's (1994) mantra of 'go back' to move 'forward'. Critiquing earlier accounts which focused on climate, in the case of Herbertson, or culture, with Fleure, Hartshorne argued that none of these regional geographies on their own were sufficient for advancing regional study. Hartshorne proposed a more elaborate, all-encompassing, regional geography of 'areal differentiation', which was based on the synthesis of all types of regional knowledge. What made geography exceptional, Hartshorne argued, was that at its core it was a regional discipline, which through idiographic methods could comprehend local variations that saw the earth's surface subdivided into distinct unit areas.

1.2.2   Regional Science

The backlash to this came in the 1950s–1960s with the birth of regional science. Regional science killed off traditional regional geography as an idiographic discipline, arguing instead for a nomothetic (law-producing) approach. This owed much to the 'locational school' and the connection of economics, geography and planning that had been established in the wake of the Second World War. Assisted by the power of computation and a growing appetite for input-output techniques, linear modelling and gravity models, regional analysis centred on a quest to identify general ('scientific') laws to explain spatial behaviour. Seminal books by Walter Isard (1960) *Methods of Regional Analysis* and Peter Haggett (1965) *Locational Analysis in Human Geography* epitomized, on the one hand, a decline in place-based regional studies, yet, on the other hand, despite being often deployed in a discrete, bounded and uncritical way, regions provided the spatial backdrop also for this type of regional analysis because they continued to be 'one of the most logical and satisfactory ways of organizing geographic information' (Haggett 1965, p. 241). Regional geography as a subject has also continued its life in more or less traditional forms in geographic education and some themes of Northern American cultural geography, for example.

Until the 1960s the view on what a region is, was rather divided. As Minshull (1967, p. 13) observed, the region was either a 'mental device' needed in research or a 'real entity'. These views gave rise to questions such as how to discover regions, how to define regions, and how to describe regions. Most recent commentaries have suggested that the divide between mental device and real entities was simply false. This argument owes much to the new regional geography, which emerged in the 1980s.

1.2.3   New Regional Geography

Before the rise of new regional geography, regions were typically considered static and bounded territorial units, even if the representatives of regional science highlighted their functional nature (Haggett 1965). Current ways of thinking recognize that regions are produced and transformed through various forms of agency. Regions must be understood as social constructs based on social practice and discourse, and this is the real basis to evaluate their roles and functions. For what the new regional geography has done is to change the attitude towards regions from focusing on regions themselves, to social practices through which regions are constructed, gain their meanings, are reproduced, and ultimately destroyed or abandoned as part of wider socio-spatial transformations. This approach prerequisites that regions should be understood historically and their existence understood in relation to wider political, economic and governmental transformations as well as power relations. In general regions are now regarded as open or porous rather than strictly bounded *territories*, and such a relational point has become almost a new norm in regional thinking since the 1990s. As Allen et al. (1998, p. 2) encapsulate it:

> [Regional] studies are always done for a purpose, with a specific aim in view. Whether theoretical, political, cultural or whatever, there is always a specific purpose. One cannot study everything, and there are always multiple ways of seeing a place: there is no complete "portrait of a region". Moreover, we want to argue, "regions" only exist in relation to particular criteria. They are not "out there" waiting to be discovered; they are our (and others') constructions.

Aligned to this, Gilbert (1998) outlined how regions were variously the product of local responses to capitalist processes, the focus on cultural identification, and the medium for social interaction ('meeting points') for human agency and social structures. Characterizing the new regional geography was the coming together of previously isolated subdisciplines (economic, social, political, cultural, historical) and philosophical approaches (Marxism, humanism, critical social theory, realism) in geography through a shared interest and common ground in a (re)new(ed) geography of regions (MacLeod and Jones 2001).

As the case of the European Union and many other supra-state regions effectively display, regions are increasingly 'invented' in planning offices and political decision-making processes, thus moving from loose ideas to wider, often normative discourses, then appearing in maps and ultimately shaping wider spatial politics. Such regions may be labelled as new regions whereas old regions tend to institutionalize slowly as part of the unfolding socio-spatial divisions of labour. A further distinction can be made here, where 'old' refers to regions which are territorially embedded, historical, established parts of planning and governance (e.g. UK regions, German Länder), and 'new' identifies typically ad hoc, project-based regions operating across less-determinate geographies often aimed at developing or increasing the competitiveness of the region (Paasi 2009).

Integral to the new regional geography was the combination of space and time. One solution for understanding the dimensions of region-building processes, that is, how regions emerge, gain meaning, are reproduced, and eventually disappear, was the theory of regional institutionalization. This theory abstracted four stages of mutually constituting, reciprocal and recursive processes through which regions become institutionalized as a recognizable 'territorial unit' and spatial division of society: (1) *territorial shaping*: the formation of boundaries, which can vary from 'soft' to 'hard', practically open and insignificant to more or less closed; (2) *symbolic shaping*: the invention of power-laden cultural signifiers (naming, traditions, memorabilia) and narratives to develop a collective identity, differentiating what is internal from that which is external; (3) *institutional shaping*: the creation of vehicles or mechanisms, both formal and informal, to embed and entrench these processes; and (4) *region established*: the institutionalization of a region as a territorial unit in the spatial matrix and social consciousness of society, accompanying the de-institutionalization of some other regional – or other spatial – unit(s) (Paasi 1986).

1.2.4   New Regionalism

Overtaking these debates, the 1990s saw the rise to prominence of a new regionalism. Working hand-in-glove with globalization discourses, this new regionalism became the poster child for how, *contra* earlier globalist accounts documenting an era of global deconcentration and deterritorialization, geography still mattered. Not only this, regions – not nations per se – were presented by the chief protagonists of the new regionalism as *the* territorial platform for economic success, democratic legitimacy, and social life in twenty-first century global capitalism (Ohmae 1995; Storper 1997). It is important to note that at the same time IR scholars began speaking about a 'new regionalism', however, their spatial references were more often than not macro-regional – typically supra-state entities – and they were looking at various spatial forms of governance and the roles of civil society in shaping and building large-scale regional governance structures in a globalizing world (Söderbaum 2003; Fiaramonti 2014, Van Langenhove 2018).

At the centre of new regionalist debate in economic geography was a distinction between an economic and political logic for regionalism. Learning from the experiences of Silicon Valley (United States), Baden-Württemberg (Germany), and south-east England, among others, the economic logic drew on theories of agglomeration to explain why regions were emerging as competitive territories par excellence in this new era of globally oriented reflexive capitalism (Storper 1997). Fundamentally, information sharing and networking were seen to be replacing market-based competition, and regions – defined as localized economic agglomeration complexes – are the scale at which this occurs. The political argument centred on observations that a hollowing-out of the nation-state was taking place, with power being lost upwards through processes of Europeanization and internationalization, downwards through a resurgence in territorial identity, politics of assertion and devolution, and outwards through globalization and market forces challenging the very fabric of bounded entities (Keating 1998; Terlouw 2018).

During the mid- to late-1990s a new global policy discourse emerged around the new regionalism, linking the economic and political logic for regions in globalization (cf. Söderbaum 2003). Critics, however, argued that the new regionalism only offered a partial reading of unfolding patterns of regionalism and region-making. Lovering (1999) argued that the new regionalism told an 'attractive and persuasive story' but it was 'largely a fiction', while MacLeod and Jones (2001) drew attention to, among other shortcomings, a 'thin political economy' resulting from the absence of any sustained analysis of the state and the political economy of territory, scale and region-making. For Jones and MacLeod (2004) there was another problem: the economic and administrative geography of regions produces 'regional spaces', distinct from the political and cultural geography of regions which create 'spaces of regionalism'. Normative arguments saying that 'the region' is becoming the fundamental basis of economic, social and political life, or 'the region' is the ideal scale for policy intervention, were therefore challenged to consider 'which region?' The new regional geography taught us, regions are not out there waiting to be found; instead there are different ways of seeing 'the region' and their making such that it is more fruitful to talk about the 'geographies of regions' than a distinct 'regional geography'. As Ron Johnston (1991, p. 137) aptly put it, 'we do not need regional geography but we do need regions in geography'.

1.2.5   New Regional Worlds

Most recently, debate has centred on transitioning away from any one singular reading of region and territory, recognizing that these terms – as with most scientific terms – are perpetually transforming and subject to a growing plurality of philosophical, conceptual and methodological approaches in how they are developed, deployed and debated. As part of the evolution of the international, globalizing political landscape, academic scholars have launched many novel terms into the discussions on regions, territories and regionalism. New categories are doing much to broaden the spatial (city-region, cross-border region, megaregion, panregional, polycentric region), economic (learning region, competitive region, creative region, resilient region), political (NUTS regions, supranational regions, geopolitical regions) and environmental (sustainable region, bioregion) debate (see Table 1.1). This mushrooming of widely circulated regional-conceptual hybrids in both academic literature and in practical planning circles witness how intellectual debates about the character of regions are embedded in complex and contestable socio-spatial dynamics.

Aligned to this, rather than privileging one kind of regionalism over another, new conceptual frameworks increasingly prioritize the coming together of different perspectives to shape regions and regional thinking. The most obvious example of this new way of thinking is Jessop et al.'s (2008; Jessop 2018) TPSN framework, which grasps the polymorphic, multidimensional character of region-making through simultaneously deploying the lexicon of territorial, place-based, scalar *and* networked geographies.

A further extension of this is derived from broadening horizons in regional thinking. Amplified globalization, especially following the collapse of the sharp dividing line between communist east and capitalist west, has contributed to the crushing of old regional patterns of socio-economic or cultural life and given rise to diverging social movements that want to revive or create new forms of economic, cultural and political identities. There is increased awareness and recognition of regions, territories and regionalism beyond the neoliberal heartlands of Anglo-American geography. Regional development and governance is a global challenge and new regional thinking is increasingly likely to emerge in the context of developments occurring in the BRICS (Brazil, Russia, India, China, South Africa) and countries of the global South. Today, more than ever before, regional and territorial thinking is characterized by distinct regional worlds, diverse regional words, and decentred regional futures.

1.3   GLOBALIZATION AND THE REGIONAL RESURGENCE

1.3.1   Conceptualizing the Region – In What Sense Territorial?

As the previous section reveals, 'region' and 'territory' are integral to framing the world around us, but also to conceptualizing the other term. Moreover, the increasing economic, political and cultural complexities of the globalizing and networking world we live in mean that the geographies of places, regions and territories matter, now more than ever. At this moment, it is useful to briefly reflect on the difference conceptually between region and territory – the keywords of this collection.

There are significant dissimilarities between the connotations of the two terms, even if in the ordinary use of language – at times also in academic texts – they are oftentimes used as parallel terms. As with many other spatial terms, region and territory have several theoretical and practical undertones. Foucault (1980) once problematized spatial concepts and stated how territory is a geographical notion but first it is a juridico-political one. The Latin term *territorium* refers to specific land under the jurisdiction of a town or state. Region, for Foucault, was a fiscal, administrative and military notion, which stems from the Latin word *regio* that means direction. It is also derived from the Latin verb *regere*: to command or rule (Söderbaum 2003). In academic usage, both definitions are evidently in use.

A well-known theoretician of territory and territoriality Robert David Sack (1986) once suggested that all territories are regions but not all regions are territories. This argument is related to Sack's definition of territoriality which refers to the 'attempt by an individual or group to affect, influence, or control people, phenomena, and relationships, by delimiting and asserting control over a geographic area' (Sack 1986, p. 19). Sack reminds that:

> Circumscribing things in space, or on a map, as when a geographer delimits an area to illustrate where corn is grown, or where industry is concentrated, identifies places, areas, or regions in an ordinary sense, does not itself create a territory. This delimitation becomes a territory only when its boundaries are used to affect behaviour by controlling access. (Sack 1986, p. 19)

This control function and use of borders in control mean that such spatial entities or regions may be called the territory. An interesting question from the perspective of contemporary debates on relational spaces and open or porous borders is: how do we understand borders? Can the 'soft spaces' discussed by planning theorists have borders and, if they have, how should we understand them? Paasi and Zimmerbauer (2016) argue that the borders of regions must be seen not as mere lines but rather as spatio-temporal phenomena that can simultaneously be open and closed, depending on social practices and discourses that we are looking at.

Contrary to Sack's general ideas, for Elden (2013) territory is related above all to the State and state governance and he suggests that it consists of political-economic (land) and political-strategic (terrain) relations. Beyond these elements territory is also dependent on political-legal (law) and political-technical (calculative technologies) elements. He suggests that territory is thus part of a specific rationality that is a 'political technology' that is dependent on calculation as much as on control and conflict.

That territory is not merely a technocratic instrument of governance but is also related to social and individual identities becomes obvious in Hassner's (1997, p. 57) definition, covering a parallel element with debates on regional and place identities (see Entrikin 2018; Terlouw 2018). He notes that:

> Territory is a compromise between a mythical aspect and a rational or pragmatic one. It is three things: a piece of land, seen as a sacred heritage; a seat of power; and a functional space. It encompasses the dimensions of identity . . . of authority (the state as an instrument of political, legal, police and military control over a population defined by its residence); and of administrative bureaucratic or economic efficiency in the management of social mechanisms, particularly of interdependence. . . The strength of the national territorial state depends upon combination of these three dimensions.

While the Latin term *regio*(n) comes from *regere* 'to rule, direct' 'direction, district', these meanings are only one dimension of regions which are usually mobilized not only in governance but also in economy, culture and politics.

The link between globalization, regional resurgence, and territory is also very evident. It is no exaggeration to suggest that both categories, region and territory, have experienced a renaissance. Since the 1980s these terms and their applications have been widely in use across the social sciences, from IR studies to political science, from anthropology to archaeology and economics. Several edited collections on regions have been recently published, typically with the intention to trace the evolution and perpetual transformation of regional thinking (Keating 2004; Entrikin 2008; Jones and Paasi 2015; Riding and Jones

2017). Similarly, territory has been an object of both conceptual-genealogical analysis (Elden 2013) and several efforts have been made to identify diverging scalar, practical and political meanings of territories and territoriality (Sack 1986; Storey 2001; Delaney 2005; Kolers 2009).

Debates on territories and regions have not been just academic exercises. Innumerable governmental bodies, committees and planning offices around the world have been involved in such debates and state and quasi-state governance arrangements incessantly are the key context for both sub- and supra-state regionalization and region-building efforts (Paasi and Metzger 2017). Much of the resurgence in regional-thinking can be traced back to the work undertaken by political geographers and political scientists in the 1970s and 1980s documenting regionalism as a political movement and insurgency demanding greater territorial autonomy (Rokkan and Urwin 1982). Set against the backdrop of ever-deepening processes of neoliberalism, globalization, and transnationalism, the rise of regionalist parties (e.g. the Lega Nord in Italy, SNP in Scotland) and the European Commission's advocacy of a 'Europe of the regions' led to a renewed focus on regions as singular, bounded, relatively fixed, non-overlapping political-administrative-governmental units articulated through the spatial grammar of *territory* and territoriality. However, the fact that the EU is ultimately supporting the power of states rather than regions becomes evident in in the Catalonian plebiscite on 'independence' in autumn 2017. The EU supports the Spanish government rather than the Catalonian region, seemingly being worried about similar pro-independence tendencies in many European Union states.

During the 1980s, the conceptual link between region and territory was complicated as scholars became increasingly interested in *place* (and other terms such as locality). As Entrikin (2018) shows, place and related human experiences became prominent in the lexicon of regional geographers as social scientific thinking turned toward post-positivist approaches. Interpretative understanding of peoples and places (following Pred 1984) was integral to the development of the new regional geography and moves away from regions as static frameworks to regions as dynamic entities.

Likewise, a more controversial turn towards *scale* in 1980s and 1990s social scientific thinking was intimately linked to developments in regional thinking (Smith 1984; Herod 2011) and the new regionalism more precisely, both in geography and international relations studies. Attempts to understand the dynamics of how economic, social and political activity previously located at the national scale were increasingly being conducted at the regional (and other spatial) scale(s) was accompanied by a new vocabulary of geographical scale. Conceptual terminology, such as rescaling, multiscaled, politics of scale, scalar politics, multilevel governance, and global–local, became essential elements in attempts to account for the reterritorialization of capital and the state under conditions of deepening neoliberalism and globalization (Brenner 2004).

Multiscale territorial approaches were the cornerstone of the new regionalism and social scientific thinking in the late-1990s, but they faced a backlash in the early years of this century by the advance of *network* geographies. Seeing the world through the lens of relational thinking, front and centre of networked perspectives on the region was the insistence that regions, and space more generally, must be conceptualized as open, fluid and unbound; or to put it more bluntly, there is nothing useful in representing regions as 'territorially fixed in any essential sense' (Allen and Cochrane 2007, p. 1163). Relational thinking challenged the very essence of territorial regions and regionalism by attempting to decouple the two terms. No longer were region and territory seen as two sides of the same conceptual coin; instead regions were being conceptualized as breaking free from the perceived constraints of territory and territorial thinking. For advocates of relational approaches to region-making (1) regions have no automatic promise of territorial integrity, (2) they cannot be communities in the truest sense of the term if they attach themselves to territorially defined or spatially limiting arrangements, (3) the conceptual vocabulary associated with territorial approaches to regionalism (scalar hierarchy, boundaries, borders) is limiting whereas the language of relational thinking (assembling, flow, connectivity, folding, topology) is better equipped to capture the dynamism of contemporary capitalism, and (4) any attempt to 'fix' spatial identities through policy intervention over-simplifies and therefore fails to engage with the world as it is.

This approach, in turn, produced again its own backlash from scholars who wished to retain regions and territories in geographical thinking and instead of confronting territorial and regional approaches wanted to scrutinize in more detail the nuances, interfaces and conceptual limits of such confrontations. For the next decade, a series of back-and-forth exchanges occurred between what Varró and Lagendijk (2013) present as the 'radical relationalists' on the one side (those arguing to expunge regions, territories, and scale from the geographical lexicon) and the 'moderate relationalists' on the other side (those who concede that globalization and state restructuring are rendering regions more open and permeable, but counter that regionalism is also territorially defined and bounded in political space and we should never dismiss the role of territorial politics). Part of the problem in the first part of this century was the 'debilitating binary division' of territorial-scalar *or* networked-relational regionalism (Morgan 2007).

Today, the focus of regional and social scientific thinking is firmly centred on overcoming these binary divisions and reconciling regional geography within a territorial *and* relational world (Jessop et al. 2008; Jones 2009; Harrison 2013; Paasi and Zimmerbauer 2016; Cochrane 2018). This poses challenging questions for academic scholars and practitioners alike around the relations between spatial categories and processes, their relevance to regions and regionalism, and the implications for regional (as well as other forms of spatial) planning.

1.3.2 Regions as Competitive Economic Territories Par Excellence

Regional thinking has been forever linked to processes of economic development and related struggles over power. Students of regional change have long been drawn towards investigating the economic factors driving development. Throughout the era of traditional regional geography leading Anglophone scholars, from Halford Mackinder in *Britain and the British Seas* (1902) to D.E. Willington in *Economic Geography* (1927), attributed economic geography – or commercial geography as it was then often termed – to the influence of the physical environment on human activities in obtaining the life essentials and material goods. Industrial patterns were, in other words, seen as the result of regional geography. Through into the 1960s when regional science engaged closely with the locational school and economic thought, then the 1970s when Marxist inspired theorists drew attention to structural and strategic forces associated with the dynamics and contradictions of capitalism acting upon regions, regional thinking was for many years shaped by different phases of capital accumulation and the broader growth dynamic of capitalism. This led to the rise of some influential ideas on regions. Massey (1978), for example, argued that the analysis of uneven development should never begin from some pre-specified, fixed regionalization of space. Instead it would be of critical importance to scrutinize the patterns of capital accumulation, from which geographical analysis must then produce the concepts in the terms of the spatial divisions of labour. She also developed the well-known 'geological metaphor': the development of spatial structures can be seen as a product of the combination of 'layers' of the successive activity (Massey 1984, p. 118). More recently Ray Hudson (2002, 2007) has pushed Marxist political economy approaches further in the analysis of the production of places/regions.

This connection became more powerful in the 1980s and 1990s when economic and industrial geographers became caught up in attempts to account for the spatial implications of deindustrialization, globalization and transition towards a post-Fordist growth dynamic. New modes of production led to new geographies of production and with it ever more uneven patterns of economic growth and development. Emerging from this have been claims necessitating the mantra of competitiveness and a purported, almost universal need for learning and innovativeness – labels that were quickly attached to groupings of exemplary regional economies noted above (Silicon Valley, Baden-Württemberg, Emilia Romagna, Rhone-Alpes, south-east England) which were harbouring these key attributes for post-industrial regional economic growth.

In globalization, the economic logic for regions and regionalization has remained strong. Fuelled by the intellectual arguments put forward by the 'new economic geography' and related theories associated with agglomeration economies, technological innovation and relational proximity have often served to popularize regional thinking both within and beyond academic circles. If the underpinning economic logic for regionalism has ostensibly remained constant over the years, the same cannot be said for the spatial focus of regional economic thinking. Over the past 40 years, the focus has switched from debates oriented towards a 'new localism' in the 1980s, through into the 1990s and the 'new regionalism' (1990s), the 'new city-regionalism' of the 2000s, before most recently a renewed focus on 'megaregions' and 'megaregionality' has taken hold (Florida et al. 2008; Ross 2009). The significance of this is a trend towards a smaller number of increasingly larger regional units, each of which appears less territorially defined than its predecessor. The result has been a mushrooming of, to a lesser or greater extent, regional and territorial reference points and framings for economic development. For critics, questions remain as to the perceived dangers of 'reading-off' regionalism through an apparently new economic geography of globalization, something they are keen to argue requires more political and historical perspectives (Harrison and Hoyler 2015).

1.3.3   Regionalism, Devolution and the Territorial Restructuring of the State

If one of the fundamental drivers of regional change is economic then the other is political. While often presented in this binary way, political processes are never distinct from social and economic interests. These drivers come together in the fact that the production and reproduction of regions are social acts (Johnston 1991). In the post-war years, the territorial region assumed prominence as a key unit for policy development in the period known as 'spatial Keynesianism'. Spatial Keynesianism was a largely technocratic process that saw regional policies rolled-out with the aim of boosting the national economy and raising national welfare standards by supporting 'lagging regions' through redistributive programmes, a process which would then in theory benefit the 'wealthier regions' because there would be more consumers for their goods.

From the 1970s and into the 1980s, Europe became the focus for much of the work examining political regionalism. In large part, this was due to the manoeuvrings of – what is today – the European Union who created their own spatial map of territorial regions. First established in the early 1970s, NUTS (Nomenclature of Territorial Units for Statistics) regions served two purposes: a *technical* role in enabling the collection, development and harmonization of European regional statistics from which to develop policy; an *integrative* role because through this analysis the EU have pursued various policies and programmes with the intention of creating territorial, economic and social cohesion across Europe by providing financial assistance to weaker regions. Aligned to this formalized, hierarchical and technocratic process of political regionalism, Keating (1998) also identified six types of insurgent, bottom-up and citizen-led regionalism sweeping across Europe at the same time – conservative, bourgeois, progressive, social democratic, populist and national separatist.

Moving into the 1990s, a political logic for regionalism rooted in the ideals of enabling piecemeal democratic rights, greater civic engagement and encouraging progressive planning combined with a strong economic logic for competitive regionalism to provide, what for many was, an undeniable argument for understanding the resurgence of regions and territory in globalization (cf. Fiaramonti 2014). Enticed by this, political leaders and policymakers sought to put the new regionalism *into action* in what quickly became a global policy discourse of devolution and regionalization. For critics such as Lovering (1999), this was deeply problematic. He argued that the new regionalism quickly became nothing more than a 'theory led by policy' (Lovering 1999), while others pointed out that far from a total decline of state-led regional policy, the so-called resurgence of regions owed much to the role of the nation-state as a key orchestrator of how regionalization was being unfurled. To this end, the resurgence of regions was seen through the framework of a territorial restructuring and rescaling of the state, and an outcome of 'state spatial strategies' and 'state spatial projects' (Brenner 2004).

Most recently, Keating (2017) argues there are six competing dimensions in the social construction of territory and regions: integrative regionalism; competitive regionalism; welfare regionalism; identity regionalism; regions as government; and regionalism as a refraction of social and economic interests. Adopting a constructivist perspective, Keating argues that we must always consider the region as the outcome of political contestation over the definition and meaning of territory, because:

> Regions as vehicles for state policy are in tension with regions as a form of territorial autonomy. Regions are arenas for playing out some of the most important political issues such as the balance between economic competition and social solidarity. (Keating 2017, p. 16)

1.3.4 Regionalism in Context: Towards a World of Regionalism

Globalization has brought with it a growing awareness of regionalism beyond countries in the global North. As the chapters of this book display, from Africa to the Arctic, Australasia to Antarctica, regions and territories matter and various forms of regionalism are on the agenda. But with these global horizons in regional studies has come a series of methodological and conceptual challenges surrounding the need for more comparative analysis, balancing general theories with the particularity of individual cases, while avoiding both the dismissal of territory and territorial determinism (Hettne et al. 2001; Keating 2017). Today, regionalism is increasingly considered in a wider global horizon and the field of regional research is undeniably more global, but as Pike et al. (2017, p. 48) reveal:

> Such strands of work have tended to run in parallel with limited interaction and cross-fertilizations of theory, evidence and policy . . . [As a consequence] such fragmented conceptual, analytical and policy perspectives limit one's understanding of local and regional development in an increasingly globalized and interdependent world, constraining explanation, policy formulation and praxis.

Understanding regions and regionalism in context is one of, if not the, biggest single challenge facing scholars today. For this reason, in this Handbook, we dedicate a whole section to understanding how regionalism has unfolded and is conceptualized globally in different contexts. In effect, we reflect a world of regionalisms. This represents an important starting point for recognizing commonalities and differences in the geographies of regions and territories globally, but with this comes an appreciation that much work remains to be done if we are to achieve a truly global regionalism – taken to mean a global approach to the production of new regional knowledge and the practice of regional theory making. This is a common challenge for the regional researchers that has also been noted by IR scholars.

Appreciating regional context within the ever-expanding scope of globalizing regional research requires new tools and techniques for putting contextual accounts of the geographies of regions, territories and regionalism into conversation. This necessitates much more than recognition of a world of regionalisms – African, Chinese, Eurasian, Mediterranean, and so on – but an understanding that advancing global regionalism depends upon making these a more dominant part of the global narrative of regionalism.[1] Another important challenge is the recognition of the role of civil society organizations and local movements in the making of regionalisms – all too often regionalism has been seen as a process orchestrated by states and coalitions of states from above. This forces us to recognize how political and cultural come together with the economic.

For their part, Scott and Storper (2003, 2015) call for a 'common theoretical language' about the development of regions in all parts of the world vis-à-vis recognizing that 'territories are arrayed at different points along a vast spectrum of development characteristics' (Scott and Storper 2003, p. 582). Others, such as Roy (2009), have taken to arguing more strongly for 'new geographies' of imagination and epistemology in the production of regional theory; ideas which can debunk universal theories of regions and regionalism rooted in the EuroAmerican experience. Either way, there is an urgent task for scholars to engage with these different frames of reference – observations which are going to put more and more focus on the practice of how we go about 'doing' research into the changing geographies of regions and territories moving forward.

1.4   DISTINCT REGIONAL WORLDS, DIVERSE REGIONAL WORDS, DECENTRED REGIONAL FUTURES: FOUNDATIONS FOR CONSOLIDATED REGIONAL GEOGRAPHIES?

It hardly needs saying but the diversity of epistemological perspectives, geographical contexts and methodological approaches highlights the plurality within contemporary accounts showcasing the geographies of regions and territories. From the outset, the aim of this Handbook has been to bring together – through the contributions of high calibre experts – the cutting-edge knowledge and theoretical and empirical challenges related to these two categories and their contemporary conceptualizations, applications and challenges. In this final section, we take stock of the current state of debates on the theory and empirical dimensions of regions and territories, before making the argument for more consolidated – instead of fragmented – regional geographies.

Albeit necessarily selective, this introduction, alongside the list of contents, reveals the multiple geographies of regions and territories, in both theoretical debates and their mobilization in specific contexts in making sense of social, political and economic life. This has not always been the case, however; there is full recognition today that regional futures rely on moving beyond any singular conception of the region or territory, and investing in the plural of regions, regionalism and territories (Agnew 2013). Indicative of this is how Storper's (1997) conception of 'the regional world' has been replaced by recognition of multiple 'regional worlds' (Jones and Paasi 2015), and Storey's re-titling of *Territory: The Claiming of Space* (2001) to read *Territories: The Claiming of Space* by the time the second edition was published in 2012.

For all that these multiple ways of thinking about regions and territories has uncovered important knowledge, developed our understandings and stimulated debate, making sense of this complexity has presented researchers with a set of new challenges. To this end, contemporary debates are increasingly shaped by attempts to reconcile thinking around both the dynamically changing, as well as multiple, geographies of regions and territories. This is leading to work examining when, where and why different conceptions of regions and territories variously complement, contradict, overlap or compete with other regional, territorial and spatial imaginaries (MacLeod and Jones 2007, Harrison and Growe 2014).

Another consequence of the dynamically changing and multiple geographies of regions and territories is the observation that distinct regional worlds produce a diverse array of regional words (Jones and Paasi 2015). One indication of this can be seen in Table 1.1, which offers insight into some of the many regional words which are being currently used by academics and practitioners to comprehend new regional forms, new processes of regionalism, and new types of region. At one level, the explosion of new terms to go alongside some more established words in the vocabulary and lexicon of regional scholars reflects the dynamism and rapid change taking place within regional debate. But different regional words also reflect another increasingly important issue: the variegating meanings of such keywords in different languages.

It is clear that in different contexts geographical vocabularies may differ since they always reflect (even though are not determined) by social, cultural, political, economic and even physical geographic factors. Much of the contemporary, dominant conceptual basis of regional thinking – also discussed in this introduction – reflects largely the ideas

Table 1.1   150 concepts describing twenty-first century regions and regionalism

Names given to new regional forms	Names given to new processes of regionalism	Names given to new types of region
1 Bi-polar region	Aero-regionalism	Administrative region
2 City-region	Archipelagic regionalism	Ancestral region
3 Cross-border metropolitan region	Architectural regionalism	Anchor region
4 Cross-border region	Bourgeois regionalism	Autocratic region
5 Decentred region	City-regionalism	Autonomous region
6 Emerging mega economic region	Concentrated regionalism	Bioregion
7 Estuarial city-regional spaces	Conjoined regionalism	Border region
8 Fuzzy regions	Conservative regionalism	Capital region
9 Galactic region	Constellatory regionalism	Capitalist region
10 Global city-region	Cross-border regionalism	Civic region
11 Global metropolis	Cultural regionalism	Competitive region
12 Global region	De facto regionalism	Cosmopolitan region
13 Greater region	Economic regionalization	Creative region
14 In-between region	Environmental regionalism	Cultural region
15 Macro region	Extended urbanization	Devolved region
16 Mega-city region	Federalism	Ecological region
17 Mega-conurbation	Functional regionalism	Economic region
18 Megalopolis	Global suburbanism	Ecoregion
19 Megalopolis unbound	Identity regionalism	Fringe region
20 Megapolitan region	Insurgent regionalism	Geopolitical region
21 Megaregion	Integrative regionalism	Government region
22 Metro region	Interrregionalism	Green region
23 Metroplex	Localized regionalism	Growth region
24 Metropolitan region	Marine regionalism	Imagined region
25 Metropolitan scaled urban agglomeration	Metropolitan regionalism	Independent region
26 Monocentric urban region	Multi-city regionalism	Innovative region
27 Multi-city region	Nationalist separatist regionalism	Institutionalized region
28 Multi-nodal region	Networked regionalism	Learning region
29 Multi-polar region	New localism	Legal region
30 Networked metropolis	New regionalism	Made-up region
31 New megalopolis	Penumbral regional bordering	Military region
32 New metropolis	Planetary regionalism	Nationalist region
33 Non-metropolitan region	Political regionalism	Neoliberal region
34 Panregion	Polycentric regionalism	Non-capital region
35 Polycentric metropolis	Populist regionalism	Non-state space
36 Polycentric urban region	Pragmatic regionalism	Peripheral region
37 Polynucleated urban region	Progressive regionalism	Planning region
38 Post-metropolis	Reactionary regionalism	Political region
39 Post-suburban region	Real existing regionalism	Post-socialist region
40 Regional assemblage	Regional agglomeration	Productive region

Table 1.1 (continued)

Names given to new regional forms	Names given to new processes of regionalism	Names given to new types of region
41 Regional growth corridor	Regional assemblage	Resilient region
42 Regional network of cities	Regionalized urbanization	Rural region
43 Relational region	Relational regionalism	Semi-autonomous region
44 Soft space	Social democratic regionalism	Smart region
45 Stateless city-regional nation	Social regionalism	Supply chain region
46 Suburban region	Supply chain regionalism	Sustainable region
47 Supranational region	Supra-state regionalism	Technology region
48 Territorial region	Territorial regionalism	Transition region
49 World city-region	Transregionalism	Transport region
50 World super economic region	Welfare regionalism	Urban region

Source: Author's own, adapted from Taylor and Lang (2004).

outlined in the Anglophone world from where they have diffused elsewhere. As this introduction and the chapters by Agnew (2018) and Entrikin (2018) in this volume show, the origin of spatial ideas and concepts are much more diverse when we look at the evolution of these concepts historically. When geography became institutionalized, French and German geographers, for example, were in a critical position in outlining novel ideas. Since the Second World War and with the rise of quantitative revolution the situation has changed quite dramatically: Anglophone ideas associated with models, interaction and functional regions have spread extensively around the academic communities in various countries. While these ideas often had their background in the works of German economists and geographers such as Walter Christaller and August Lösch, new ideas were again travelling to other linguistic realms from the UK and US.

As we suggested at the beginning of this introduction, the development of the conceptual basis in the research of regions and territories has never been a straightforward evolutionary trajectory but a dynamic field of conceptual struggles and breaks. New concepts are continually invented, some concepts are in use long-lastingly, and some others are rejected permanently, while some others have been adopted once again after being aside from dominant discourses. It is also to be noted that conceptual developments never occur *in vacuo* but do so in relation to economic and structural developments, societal interests of knowledge, general philosophical and methodological developments, and at times these developments resonate with major societal upheavals like wars and conflicts (Paasi 2011).

There are also some new structural factors in the academia that need to be considered. Observations from science studies tell us that motives for research are both individual and institutional or 'systemic' (Becher and Trowler 2001). Current neoliberal pressures on institutional interests in the form of evaluations and assessments accentuate today more than ever publications and citations and claim for novelty and innovation. These systemic forces certainly help, in part, to understand the existing tendency to perpetually invent new keywords and attempts to attract attention. In the contemporary academia individual and systemic motives become fused in the fact that science is rapidly globalizing: ideas, concepts as well as students and researchers are increasingly mobile which very likely tends to homogenize the conceptual terrain. While knowledge is incessantly under negotiation, it is never made completely in one place and consumed elsewhere, and it tends to transform when it circulates (Agnew 2007). However, the regional world is uneven: ideas from linguistics power centres tend to flow to peripheries that are typically located outside of the Anglophone context.

At another level, one more recent observation in science studies has been the fragmentation of academic disciplines into federations of subdisciplines and sub-subdisciplines (Billig 2013). This certainly explains, partly, the mushrooming of new regional and territorial words and concepts in various subfields of Geography. Rather than being merely beneficial, such fragmentation points towards the need for a more *consolidated* approach towards regional thinking. The constant quest for new regional theories, concepts and words needs to halt and instead the field be reimagined in ways which allow them – taken to mean both new and existing – to be stress-tested and their explanatory veracity in accounting for the changing geographies of regions and territories. As Peck (2017, p. 332) has recently taken to arguing, the latter requires 'stretching and remaking received theoretical understandings, provisional conceptualisations, and working categories of analysis'.

In producing this Handbook our aim is not only to reflect the broad cross-section of current perspectives on the changing geographies of regions and territories, but for authors to explore the explanatory veracity of key theories, concepts, approaches and categories. For us as editors, the process has made us more aware of certain divides, challenges and trends which we feel need a new round of debate and broader engagement about the changing geographies of regions and territories. To spark such debate, we see this Handbook as highlighting the need for *consolidated regional geographies*. What follows is necessarily selective, but points towards a series of new horizons for regional and territorial thinking that go beyond both singular and 'business as usual' approaches.

Consolidating regional theories: a process of consolidation began ten years ago, marked by Jessop et al.'s (2008) plea for consolidating social scientific thinking around the multidimensional character of territory, place, scale and networks vis-à-vis the privileging of any one single dimension. Regional thinking has undoubtedly made significant strides forward in this regard; nevertheless, much remains to be achieved. First, developing holistic frameworks is, as with so many things, more easily constructed in theory than operationalized in practice – both empirically and in policy. Second, consolidating regional theories in a single discipline or approach is one thing; it is quite another to consolidate geographical theorizations with planning theories, IR theories, economic theories and so on. Extending this further, third, there is more work to be done in integrating the different processes and drivers of regional change and development – economic, political, historical, institutional – and better analysing the 'interplay' of geopolitics and geoeconomics (Moisio and Jonas 2018; Calzada 2018; Sparke 2018; Storper 2013).

Consolidating a world of regionalisms: the geographic expansion and territorial coverage reflected in this Handbook exemplifies how regional thinking has come to be shaped by understandings of how regions and territories evolve and adapt in different contexts. One consequence has been a growing demand to 'provincialize' dominant theories, and to move beyond the one-way diffusion of EuroAmerican theories, policies and practices to the world (Roy 2009). This raises important questions about the travel of concepts, theories and practices in regional and territorial thinking, but more than this, we need to consolidate our approaches in important ways. Beyond the important step of recognizing and adopting theories, concepts and ideas which emerge from beyond the global North, it is imperative that these different regionalisms (northern, southern, post-socialist, and so on) are put into conversation and not viewed as false opposites that are somehow always different and distinct. Consolidation of regional thinking, from this perspective, requires new tools, vocabularies, and frameworks that enable comparative regionalism: by this we mean, establishing mechanisms and networks, which promote greater engagement across contexts and territories. This said, we must also never lose sight of how these different perspectives are themselves not internally coherent, however much they might appear and be caricatured in this way.

Consolidating regional worlds: it goes without saying that there is an ever-increasing array of new regional imaginaries, new regional maps, and accounts documenting the unfolding of new processes of regionalism across a whole array of different geographical contexts and territories (see Table 1.1). Much endeavour goes into revealing these new and emerging geographies of regions and territories, but in and of itself what does this tell us about how meaningful these geographies actually are? Consolidating regional geographies would require less focus on documenting the rise of all new geographies, instead focusing more on how much significance we can attach to them by asking what makes these activities regional in any meaningful sense. To put it another way, following Metzger and Schmitt (2012), we see the need to focus on consolidating thinking around understanding which spatial imaginaries are likely to be short-lived and ultimately disappear, which are becoming stronger institutionalized forms, and which will remain 'soft' over time. Rather than spreading our attention across the full spectrum of new geographies, this sifting will enable intellectual energy to be devoted to those new geographies likely to develop the spatial integrity and deeper-rooted sense of regionalism necessary to become meaningful in significant ways.

Consolidating regional words: as noted above, there are many reasons for the mushrooming of regional concepts, words and terms but here we turn to the question of consolidation. Consolidation of regional terminology and conceptual refinement is important because to achieve consolidation across disciplines and contexts requires precision in how we deploy, define and distinguish regional concepts. All too often concepts and words are taken for granted, without the necessary conceptual scrutiny required of rigorous social scientific inquiry and public policy making. As a result, it is now commonplace for established concepts to be captured, glorified and reimagined in ways which create too much distance from the original intellectual claims. Add to this competing notions that are attempting to explain the same processes and examples, and new fashionable concepts, which are sometimes difficult to distinguish from more well-established ideas, and the result is an inevitable cocktail of complexity.

Consolidating regional methods: ultimately our argument for consolidating regional geographies rests and falls on how we 'do' regional research. Here we can again point to the plethora of different methodological approaches adopted by researchers to account for the changing geographies of regions and territories. Often these differing approaches reflect institutional and disciplinary tendencies – the economic-side of regional thinking adopting more quantitative methodologies whereas political perspectives generally adopt more qualitative approaches – but if we are to move beyond increased fragmentation, consolidated regional geographies will require more exchange, debate and deliberation between researchers working with different methodological tools and approaches. The trend towards interdisciplinary research, allied to a growing appreciation of the need to consider the interplay of economics, institutions, social interaction and politics in shaping regional and territorial development (e.g. Storper 2013), identifies the need for this type of research. The challenge if we are to genuinely consolidate approaches to regional and territorial thinking is to be more open to the explanatory veracity of different, often opposing, methodological approaches.

What this Handbook reveals is how regions and territories are multiple entities. Indeed, if the new regional geographies of the past generation have been characterized by investing in a plural logic that has seen regions, territories and regionalism as distinct, diverse, and different, a 'new' new regional geography is dawning where the emphasis is on consolidation, combination, and the conjunctural. As David Matless (2015, p. 8) recently instructed:

> Geographical description concentrates attention, gathers experience, observes and inscribes. To account for a region, move across its varieties.

1.5   NOTE

1. It should be noted that in recognizing these different world regionalisms, we must understand that they are not singular approaches to regionalism and it will be important to consider plurality within as well as beyond.

1.6   REFERENCES

Agnew, J. (2007), 'Know-where: geographies of knowledge of world politics', *International Political Sociology*, **1** (2), 138–148.

Agnew, J. (2013), 'Arguing with regions', *Regional Studies*, **47** (1), 6–17.

Agnew, J. (2018), 'Evolution of the regional concept', in A. Paasi, J. Harrison and M. Jones (eds), *Handbook on the Geographies of Regions and Territories*, Cheltenham, UK and Northampton, MA, USA: Edward Elgar Publishing, pp. 23–33.

Allen, J., D. Massey and A. Cochrane (1998), *Rethinking the Region*, London: Routledge.

Allen, J. and A. Cochrane (2007), 'Beyond the territorial fix: regional assemblages, politics and power', *Regional Studies*, **41** (9), 1161–1175.

Becher, T. and P. Trowler (2001), *Academic Tribes and Territories: Intellectual Enquiry and The Culture of Disciplines*, Buckingham: The Society for Research into Higher Education & Open University Press.

Billig, M. (2013), *Learn to Write Badly: How to Succeed in Social Sciences*, Cambridge: Cambridge University Press.

Brenner, N. (2004), *New State Spaces – Urban Governance and the Rescaling of Statehood*, Oxford: Oxford University Press.

Calzada, I. (2018), 'Political regionalism: devolution, metropolitanisation and the right to decide', in A. Paasi, J. Harrison and M. Jones (eds), *Handbook on the Geographies of Regions and Territories*, Cheltenham, UK and Northampton, MA, USA: Edward Elgar Publishing, pp. 231–242.

Claval, P. (1998), *An Introduction to Regional Geography*, Oxford: Blackwell.

Cochrane, A. (2018), 'Relational Thinking and the Region', in A. Paasi, J. Harrison and M. Jones (eds), *Handbook on the Geographies of Regions and Territories*, Cheltenham, UK and Northampton, MA, USA: Edward Elgar Publishing, pp. 79–88.

Delaney, D. (2005), *Territory – A Short Introduction*, Oxford: Blackwell.

Elden, S. (2013), *The Birth of Territory, Chicago*, Chicago: University of Chicago Press.

Entrikin, J.N. (ed.) (2008), *Regions – Critical Essays in Human Geography*, London: Routledge.

Entrikin, J.N. (2018), 'Geography of Experience: Place and Region', in A. Paasi, J. Harrison and M. Jones (eds), *Handbook on the Geographies of Regions and Territories*, Cheltenham, UK and Northampton, MA, USA: Edward Elgar Publishing, pp. 44–56.

Fiaramonti, L. (ed.) (2014), *Civil Society and World Regions*, Lanham: Lexington Books.

Fleure, H.-J. (1919), *Human Geography in Western Europe: A Study in Appreciation*, London: Williams and Norgate.

Florida, R., T. Gulden and C. Mellander (2008), 'The rise of the mega-region', *Cambridge Journal of Regions, Economy and Society*, **1** (3), 459–476.

Foucault, M. (1980), 'Questions on geography', in C. Gordon (ed.), *Power/Knowledge: Selected Interviews and Other Writings 1972–1977*, New York: Pantheon, pp. 63–77.

Gilbert, A. (1998), 'The new regional geography in English and French-speaking countries', *Progress in Human Geography*, **12** (2), 208–228.

Haggett, P. (1965), *Locational Analysis in Human Geography*, London: Edward Arnold.

Harrison, J. (2013), 'Configuring the new "regional world": on being caught between territory and networks', *Regional Studies*, **47** (1), 55–74.

Harrison, J. and A. Growe (2014), 'When regions collide: in what sense a new "regional problem"?', *Environment and Planning A*, **46** (10), 2332–2352.

Harrison, J. and M. Hoyler (eds) (2015), *Megaregions: Globalization's New Urban Form?*, Cheltenham, UK and Northampton, MA, USA: Edward Elgar Publishing.

Hartshorne, R. (1939), *The Nature of Geography – A Critical Survey of Current Thought in the Light of the Past*, Lancaster, PA: Association of American Geographers.

Hassner, P. (1997), 'Obstinate and obsolete: non-territorial transnational forces versus the European territorial state', in O. Tunander, P. Baev and V.I. Einagel (eds), *Geopolitics in Post-Wall Europe: Security, Territory and Identity*, London: Sage, pp. 45–58.

Herbertson, A. (1902), *Man and His Work*, London: A & C Black.

Herod, A. (2011), *Scale*, London: Routledge.

Hettne, B., A. Inotai and O. Sunkel (2001), *Comparing Regionalisms: Implications for Global Development*, Basingstoke: Palgrave.

Hudson, R. (2002), *Producing Places*, Oxford: Guilford Press.

Hudson, R. (2007), 'Regions and regional uneven development forever? Some reflective comments upon theory and practice', *Regional Studies*, **41** (9), 1149–1160.

Isard, W. (1960), *Methods of Regional Analysis*, New York, NY: John Wiley.

Jessop, B., N. Brenner and M. Jones (2008), 'Theorizing sociospatial relations', *Environment and Planning D: Society and Space*, **26** (3), 389–401.

Jessop, B. (2018), 'The TPSN schema: moving beyond territories and regions', in A. Paasi, J. Harrison and M. Jones (eds), *Handbook on the Geographies of Regions and Territories*, Cheltenham, UK and Northampton, MA, USA: Edward Elgar Publishing, pp. 89–101.

Johnston, R. (1991), 'The challenge for regional geography', in R. Johnston, J. Hauer and G. Hoekveld (eds), *Regional Geography: Current Developments and Future Prospects*, London: Routledge, pp. 122–139.

Jones, M. and G. MacLeod (2004), 'Regional spaces, spaces of regionalism: territory, insurgent politics and the English question', *Transactions of the Institute of British Geographers*, **29** (4), 433–452.

Jones, M. (2009), 'Phase space: geography, relational thinking, and beyond', *Progress in Human Geography*, **33** (4),487–506.

Jones, M. and A. Paasi (eds) (2015), *Regional Worlds: Advancing the Geography of Regions*, London: Routledge.

Keating, M. (1998), *The New Regionalism in Western Europe: Territorial Restructuring and Political Change*, Cheltenham, UK and Lyme, NH, USA: Edward Elgar Publishing.

Keating, M. (ed.) (2004), *Regions and Regionalism in Europe*, Cheltenham, UK and Northampton, MA, USA: Edward Elgar Publishing.

Keating, M. (2017), 'Contesting European regions', *Regional Studies*, **51** (1),9–18.

Kolers, A. (2009), *Land, Conflict, and Justice: A Political Theory of Territory*, Cambridge, UK: Cambridge University Press.

Lovering, J. (1999), 'Theory led by policy: the inadequacies of the "new regionalism" (illustrated from the case of Wales)', *International Journal of Urban and Regional Research*, **23** (2), 379–395.

Mackinder, H.J. (1902), *Britain and the British Seas*, London: Heinemann.

MacLeod, G. and M. Jones (2001), 'Renewing the geography of regions', *Environment and Planning D – Society and Space*, **19** (6), 669–695.

MacLeod, G. and M. Jones (2007), 'Territorial, scalar, networked, connected: in what sense a "regional world"?', *Regional Studies*, **41** (9), 1177–1191.

Massey, D. (1978), 'Regionalism: some current issues', *Capital and Class*, **6** (1), 106–126.

Massey, D. (1984), *Spatial Divisions of Labour*, Basingstoke: Macmillan.

Matless, D. (2015), *The Regional Book*, Axminster: Uniformbooks.

Metzger, J. and P. Schmitt (2012), 'When soft spaces harden: the EU strategy for the Baltic Sea Region', *Environment and Planning A*, **44** (2), 263–280.

Minshull, R. (1967), *Regional Geography: Theory and Practice*, London: Hutchinson & Co.

Moisio, S. and A.E.G. Jonas (2018), 'City-regions and city-regionalism', in A. Paasi, J. Harrison and M. Jones (eds), *Handbook on the Geographies of Regions and Territories*, Cheltenham, UK and Northampton, MA, USA: Edward Elgar Publishing, pp. 285–297.

Morgan, K. (2007), 'The polycentric state: new spaces of empowerment and engagement', *Regional Studies*, **41** (9), 1237–1251.

Ohmae, K. (1995), *The End of the Nation-State: The Rise of Regional Economies*, London: HarperCollins.

Paasi, A. (1986), 'The institutionalization of regions: a theoretical framework for understanding the emergence of regions and the constitution of regional identity', *Fennia*, **164** (1), 105–146.

Paasi, A. (2009), 'The resurgence of the "region" and "regional identity": theoretical perspectives and empirical observations on regional dynamics in Europe', *Review of International Studies*, **35** (S1), 121–146.

Paasi, A. (2011), 'From region to space, part II', in J. Agnew and J. Duncan (eds), *The Wiley-Blackwell Companion to Human Geography*, Oxford: Blackwell, pp. 161–175.

Paasi, A. and K. Zimmerbauer (2016), 'Penumbral borders and planning paradoxes: relational thinking and the questions of borders in spatial planning', *Environment and Planning A*, **48** (1), 75–93.

Paasi, A. and J. Metzger (2017), 'Foregrounding the region', *Regional Studies*, **51** (1), 19–30.

Peck, J. (2017), 'Transatlantic city, part 2: late entrepreneurialism', *Urban Studies*, **54** (2), 327–363.

Peet, R. (1998), *Modern Geographical Thought*, Oxford: Blackwell.

Pike, A., A. Rodríguez-Pose and J. Tomaney (2017), 'Shifting horizons in local and regional development', *Regional Studies*, **51** (1), 46–57.

Pred, A. (1984), 'Place as historically contingent process: structuration and the time-geography of becoming places', *Annals of the Association of American Geographers*, **74** (2), 279–297.

Riding, J. and M. Jones (eds) (2017), *Reanimating Regions: Culture, Politics, and Performance*, London: Routledge.

Rokkan, S. and D. Urwin (eds) (1982), *The Politics of Territorial Identity: Studies in European Regionalism*, London: Sage.

Ross, C.L. (2009), *Megaregions: Planning for Global Competitiveness*, Washington, DC: Island Press.

Roy, A. (2009), 'The 21st-century metropolis: new geographies of theory', *Regional Studies*, **43** (6), 819–830.

Sack, R.D. (1986), *Human Territoriality: Its Theory and History*, Cambridge: Cambridge University Press.

Scott, A.J. and M. Storper (2003), 'Regions, globalization, development', *Regional Studies*, **37** (6–7), 549–578.

Scott, A.J. and M. Storper (2015), 'The nature of cities: the scope and limits of urban theory', *International Journal of Urban and Regional Research*, **39** (1), 1–15.

Smith, N. (1984), *Uneven Development*, Oxford: Blackwell.

Söderbaum, F. (2003), 'Introduction: theories of new regionalism', in F. Söderbaum and T.M. Shaw (eds), *Theories of New Regionalism: A Palgrave Reader*, Basingstoke, Hampshire and New York, NY: Palgrave Macmillan, pp. 1–21.

Sparke, M. (2018), 'Globalizing capitalism and the dialectics of geopolitics and geoeconomics', *Environment and Planning A*, **50** (2), 484–489 .

Storey, D. (2001), *Territory: The Claiming of Space*, Harlow: Prentice Hall.

Storper, M. (1997), *The Regional World: Territorial Development in a Global Economy*, New York, NY: Guilford Press.

Storper, M. (2013), *Keys to the City: How Economics, Institutions, Social Interaction, and Politics Shape Development*, Princeton, NJ: Princeton University Press.

Taylor, P.J. and R.E. Lang (2004), 'The shock of the new: 100 concepts describing recent urban change', *Environment and Planning A*, **36** (6), 951–958.

Terlouw, K. (2018), 'Regional identities: quested and questioned', in A. Paasi, J. Harrison and M. Jones (eds), *Handbook on the Geographies of Regions and Territories*, Cheltenham, UK and Northampton, MA, USA: Edward Elgar Publishing, pp. 256–267.

Thrift, N. (1994), 'Taking aim at the heart of the region', in D. Gregory, R. Martin and G. Smith (eds), *Human Geography, Space and Social Science*, London: Macmillan, pp. 200–231.

van Langenhove, L. (2018), 'Comparing regionalism at supra-national level from the perspective of a statehood theory of regions', in A. Paasi, J. Harrison and M. Jones (eds), *Handbook on the Geographies of Regions and Territories*, Cheltenham, UK and Northampton, MA, USA: Edward Elgar Publishing, pp. 311–321.

Varró, K. and A. Lagendijk (2013), 'Conceptualising the region – in what sense relational?', *Regional Studies*, **47** (1), 18–28.

Vidal de la Blache, P. (1918), *Principles of Human Geography*, translated in New York: Holt & Co (1926).

Willington, D.E. (1927), *Economic Geography*, St Albans: Donnington Press.

PART I

HISTORY, THEORY AND KEY CONCEPTS

2. Evolution of the regional concept
John Agnew

2.1 INTRODUCTION

Within the social sciences and history as academic fields, thinking in terms of regions has come to be seen as an alternative to thinking entirely in terms of nation-states. But the term 'region' is not simply a technical one with little resonance in popular discussion. For example, the concept of region was intricately intertwined in discussion of one of the signal global events of 2016. On 23 June 2016 the UK electorate voted by referendum to leave the European Union (EU). Michael Gove, a former UK Minister of Education and prominent campaigner for the Leave side in the referendum, said: 'By voting to leave we can not only take back control of hundreds of millions of pounds we send to the European Union, we will also be detaching ourselves from the sinking ship that is the European Union economy' (quoted in Alphaville 2016). Britain had joined the precursor organization to the European Union in 1973. From then until 2016 it had been a somewhat reluctant member of the supranational enterprise, refusing to join the more ambitious projects such as the Schengen common passport zone and the common currency, the Eurozone. Thus, Britain's supra-regional geographies have never really overlapped that of the EU as a whole. Gove, of course, failed to mention that it has been the Eurozone and not the EU that has been in economic trouble. The vote revealed, however, deep geographical fractures between the regions of London, Scotland, and Northern Ireland, which net voted Remain, and large swathes of England and Wales beyond London, which voted net Leave. These differences reflect economic, cultural and political divisions across regions within a so-called nation-state over membership in a supra-national regional institution of which it was already only a reluctant and partial member. Regions of varying geographic magnitudes, then, were central to understanding what leaving the EU was all about and who supported it and who did not.

Thinking with regions is inherent in much academic and popular discourse about the world (e.g. Jones and Paasi 2013). Using such regional ideas as 'the Mediterranean World,' 'the Arctic' and 'the Caribbean' represents an effort to see the world in terms of macro-regions that have some internal physical, economic and political cohesion or homogeneity. When states get together on a world-regional basis, such as Europe or North America, supra-national organizations can result such as the EU, NAFTA (the North American Free Trade Agreement of Mexico, Canada and the USA) or ASEAN (the Association of South East Asian Nations). Concurrently, the term region is often also invoked to refer to smaller areal units such as cities and their hinterlands or sub-national territories that again have some degree of cohesion or homogeneity. It has such a wide register of meanings today that it can appear incoherent. Yet, usage reflects a desire to understand how the world works by privileging a specific geographic scale of region (mesoscale sub-national, city-region, supranational, macroscale and so on) in relation to a given phenomenon from economic transactions and political influence to legal and social practices that cannot be well captured by reference solely to states. Examining something of the intellectual history of the regional concept can potentially help explain the contemporary range of usage and how this has developed.

To this end, the chapter begins with a brief discussion of how the regional concept and the concept of the nation-state developed together in nineteenth-century Europe and North America. In the aftermath of the Second World War these concepts parted company. A second section details the dominant meanings of the regional concept that evolved thereafter, from sub-national regions to macro-regions, functional regions and supra-national regions. These usages have been subject to a number of critiques. A third section reviews these and how usage has changed as a consequence. The regional concept has been a significant but often vague category across the social sciences and particularly in geography. It is still understood in many different ways depending on the purpose at hand.

2.2 NATIONS AND REGIONS

The etymology of the word 'region' in English offers something of a beginning in pursuit of the more recent proliferation in its meanings. In medieval French it referred to a land or province. Later it was extended metaphorically into medicine (in the 'region' of the heart or other organ) and everyday idioms (the 'region' (suggesting the vicinity) of a meaning or activity). In its geographic meaning there never was much sense of a definite spatial limit or border unlike with such correlative terms as territory and place that have usually had a sense of boundedness. So, a region would have distinctive characteristics but not necessarily fixed boundaries. It is this aspect implicit in the word from the start that has given it such lability or slipperiness in meaning.

The usage that was most prevalent in academic debates about the regional concept from the nineteenth down until the mid-twentieth century was in fact much more specific, whatever the dictionary etymology might suggest. A strong case can be made that the dominant meaning to the regional concept as we know it today was born as the hand servant to nationhood in nineteenth-century Europe and North America. In brief, the emerging nation-states were made from mesoscale sub-national regions. If in Germany unification was famously achieved by binding together areas historically subordinate to Austria and Prussia with a number of independent principalities, local loyalties and national statehood were in fact reconciled by channeling local confessional and political identities into regional conceptions of *Heimat* that were viewed as intrinsic to the overall tapestry of the *Reich* or *Vaterland*. In Britain the very notion of British was constructed to re-identify people with pre-existing regional and national identities (from Irish and Scottish to Geordie (Tyneside) and Cockney (London)) with the larger state enterprise. As in Germany it coexisted well, at least until recently and for everyone save the Irish, with those local and regional identities.

Even in France, most significantly, since it was the model 'homogeneous' state following the French Revolution, peasants with limited local horizons had to be turned into citizens who looked to Paris. Regional 'ways of life' served to fertilize the overall national imagination. The very differences between the ways of life of different French *pays* served to define France as a 'unity' or rich amalgam among regional differences (Gascony and Burgundy and so on) just as the terroirs of vineyards were assimilated to a broader category of French wine as distinctive from any other national variety. This was the story of France told by Paul Vidal de la Blache followed a century later by the not all too different one of Fernand Braudel (1986). In Italy something similar happened following unification in 1871 to that in Germany around the same time. Unlike in Germany, geographic administrative divisions were devised following an older French model to cut across older regional affiliations. But these have never really succeeded in replacing older regional identities. In Italy regional differences have never been as easily assimilated into a national spatial imagination as in Germany.

Finally, in the United States, the co-existence of two incompatible labor systems, one in the south based on the enslavement of African Americans and the other, in the north, on free wage labor, came to a head in the civil war of 1861–65. The relations between these regions and the expanding frontier of settlement in the west came to define a basic regional structure (and internal divisions within these three macro-regions) that persists down to the present day. This arguably still both divides and unites US national identity around a set of themes (the aftermath of slavery, the frontier mystique and gun culture, the role of the federal government, etc.) that cannot be understood in purely 'national' terms. That the American and European cases are not entirely *sui generis* is suggested by the fact that in China provincial identities also bear a similar relation to 'Chineseness' as European and American regional identities do to their national ones (e.g. Oakes 2000).

Nineteenth-century anthropology, sociology and geography saw the axis of history as moving from *Gemeinschaft* (community) to *Gesellschaft* (society) with the former providing the source of legitimation for the latter in its 'grounding' in *Volk*, folklore and the mists of time. Thus, the claims of nations rested on claims about regions. This mesoscale or sub-national understanding of region became particularly important in the nascent field of geography. Unfortunately, in disciplinary debates about the concept the relationship to nation-statehood has been all but neglected. The 'classic' epoch of regional geography, to use Paul Claval's (1993, p. 15) phrase, was precisely that of the closing of the frontier of European expansion overseas and 'the leveling of traditional spatial hierarchies' (Kern 1983, p. 8) associated with Europe's multinational empires. Thus, the works of Paul Vidal de la Blache on France's regions and Alfred Hettner on Germany's coincide with, for example, German and Italian unification and the collapse of the Ottoman and Austro-Hungarian Empires. Dividing 'horizontal space' into regions out of which nation-states could be made was a powerful way for states (and their professional apologists) to show the natural attachment of regions, particularly peripheral ones, to those states. The famous essay by Vidal on *France de L'Est* was written right after the German conquest and occupation of Alsace-Lorraine but showed that the region was in fact a unique *pays* attached to France rather than to Germany (Gregory 1993). As institutionalized in school curricula, compulsory elementary education was also spreading at this time, thinking with regions became a way of identifying 'symbolic landscapes' and binding the nation together by identifying the character of its parts and how they related to the whole (Paasi 1986).

Drawing on Hettner's writings for his inspiration, the American geographer Richard Hartshorne offered one of the most famous justifications for the disciplinary focus on mesoscale regions. It missed the political context by solely emphasizing the scientific potential of the regional concept. In his *The Nature of Geography* (1939), Hartshorne argued that the region offered the means for realizing geography's integrative or synthesizing purpose. In this regard, it was not the uniqueness of the regions that was important as much as the way in which regions could be used to capture the differential co-variation of different physical, cultural and economic phenomena over space with the physical ones as foundational. Later critics of Hartshorne tended to associate him with the notion of regional uniqueness (e.g. Schaefer 1953). In my view, this claim misses his central argument that different regions arose as a result of the differential effects of similar causes (Agnew 1989). Be that as it may, assertions such as those of Hartshorne were significant in making regional geography at a mesoscale central to the field as a whole in the middle of the twentieth century. His lexical conservatism was based on tracing an essential meaning to the regional concept back to authorities such as Hettner (Agnew 2014).

This fixation on the mesoscale was to change rapidly in the aftermath of the Second World War. The term region quickly slipped out of the control of the regional geographers as scholars in other fields adopted it. As it did so the mesoscale monopoly also was cast aside. Some of this can be put down to reaction against the static or timeless definition of region that regional geography tended to prefer at a time when the world was changing rapidly. More important, perhaps, was the 'museum-like' genealogy for the term it proposed, to paraphrase Neil Smith (1989, p.92), freezing the term as defined by authorities such as Hettner and policing its meaning to discourage conceptual innovation (Barnes and Farish 2006, p.813). With the onset of the Cold War, both more expansive and more instrumental conceptions of region tended to emerge.

2.3   THE RECENT INTELLECTUAL HISTORY OF THE REGIONAL CONCEPT

Increasingly, some older pre-nineteenth-century usage reappeared covering vast tracts of land such as the continents or ocean basins alongside updated mesoscale regions such as major cities and their hinterlands as well as the now conventional meaning of regions as sub-national units. Much of this proliferation in type of usage is due to the borrowing of the term by scholars and intellectuals in fields such as political and economic history, sociology and international relations who put the regional concept to work for their own distinctive purposes. Some reflected the continuing indirect influence of geopolitical ideas about pan-regions and *Grossräume* (regional spheres of influence of the Great Powers) that contributed to the imperial rivalries that fractured the world between the late nineteenth century and 1945. The nation-to-region connection, if not completely severed, was increasingly only one use among many.

Broadly, four understandings of the regional concept came into common use during the period from the 1940s until the present day. The first is of looking at the world in terms of *functional regions* to examine such phenomena as urbanization and settlement distributions, industrialization, trade, class transformations and transformations of political rule. If in the nineteenth century the great socio-political theorists thought in terms of archetypical national cases, industrial England for Karl Marx, bourgeois France for Emile Durkheim, and so on, from the mid-twentieth century on the geographic context was much larger, reflecting the fact that the *Zeitgeist* was about global no longer about national capitalism (Thrift 1994). The regions now are spatial units unified and distinguished by the density of linkages and flows within them relative to those outside, irrespective of national boundaries. Sometimes these regions are construed at a smaller scale covering larger areas. Thus, for example, in Charles Tilly's *Coercion, Capital, and European States AD 990-1992* (Tilly 1992), logics of state coercion and private capital accumulation work differentially across Europe to produce different rates and degrees of territorial-state formation in Western as opposed to Central and Eastern Europe. It lagged most in those regions, such as what are now Italy, Switzerland and Germany, where capital accumulation and city-states tended to trump tax collection and the militarized coercion that this enabled. At a more fine-grained and sub-national scale, Gary Herrigel's study of German industrialization, *Industrial Constructions* (Herrigel 1996), shows how various physical-geographic factors and resource dependencies combined with prior histories of proto-industrialization to produce regional patterns of industrial development in the late nineteenth century. More recently, students of global urbanization (e.g. Scott 1998) have focused on how much agglomeration economies of scale now favor large metropolises over other regions in economic development. In all these cases what gives unity to the regional concept is the idea of regions as focal points for networks of relationships and flows both material and ideational (e.g. Harrison and Growe 2014).

The second usage consists of *macro-regions* as units for the pursuit of global or world-regional narratives about economic growth and cultural change. In the late 1940s two different approaches developed this regional concept. One, that later came to be associated with dependency and world-systems theories in sociology and political science, was the idea of the three worlds. The other was Braudel's idea of total history as expressed in his *The Mediterranean* (original French edition 1949). These approaches are related. They see the globe or a major chunk thereof as experiencing a long-term structural spatial differentiation as a result of persisting political-economic relations of dominance and subordination. In the former case this was down to the competition during the Cold War between the US and its allies on the one side (the First World) and the Soviet Union and its allies on the other (the Second World) in the Third World of unaligned countries that emerged with decolonization of the European overseas empires in the 1940s and 1950s. Ignoring the Second World, this mutated into the three zones of world-system theory: a core of developed states (beginning in Europe), a periphery of (former) colonialized countries and an in-between zone of semi-periphery countries, typically large countries with the potential to be upwardly mobile within the overall world-system (e.g. Taylor 1988). In Braudel's hands, the focus was rather on long-term functional linkages across the Mediterranean Basin, bringing into play flows of people and goods from the surrounding hinterlands as these developed over centuries. The nature and content of the flows tend to be as important as the areas of origin and destination in this version of the regional concept. These 'top-down' regions, and related ones such as Edward Said's (1978) discussion of 'imaginative geographies' at the level of global east and west, have become important if often implicit regionalizations in a wide range of academic and popular writing about colonialism and postcolonialism.

A very different understanding of the regional concept also emerged in the late 1940s and early 1950s. The Second World War was a truly global war. It made isolation of states a physical and political impossibility. In its aftermath Europe was the site of a number of efforts at creating *supranational regions*. Down the years similar efforts have occurred elsewhere from South and North America to SE Asia. So, even as the war provoked grand visions of a new global order it can also be credited with:

[U]shering in an unprecedented emphasis on supranational regions. Regional military theaters and postwar organizations like NATO, the Warsaw Pact, and the European Coal and Steel Community are the obvious examples, but regionalism was an important administrative problem in almost every international organization founded in the 1940s, and in many agencies regions became a crucial policy lever. (Rankin 2016, p. 69)

Geographic space itself was seen as undergoing a transformation into strategic and political-economic blocs because this space was *organized politically* not simply perceived or studied in terms of distinctive linkages and flows. Regional political-economic integration at the sub-continental or continental scale has been the leitmotif of this approach to the regional concept. Developmental regionalism, multi-level governance within supranational organizations, regionalism and the management of globalization and the emergence of regional security communities are among the subsequent topics of study stimulated by the real-world trend to supranational regions (e.g. Hettne and Söderbaum 2000, Hettne 2005).

Finally, partly as a result of the emergence of regional blocs and the diminished role of national governments, *sub-national regions* have re-emerged as an important recasting of the regional concept. Regions have become important political subjects in their own right from Scotland and Catalonia to Quebec and northern Italy (e.g. Keating 1995; Murphy 1993; Agnew 2001; Sorens 2008; Agnew 2015). There has been a massive increase in political demands from the populations of some regions, more especially peripheral ones, looking for greater say over their political and economic futures. This has been encouraged by the workings of supranational institutions, particularly in Europe, that have sanctioned offering funds and representation to sub-national regions. But this trend has been paralleled by and contributed to by the increased recognition of the economic role of regions in a more globalized economic world (Storper 1995; Agnew 2000). The historic sedimentation of agglomeration economies in some regions rather than others was seen as leading to the clustering of new industries and the creation of path dependencies for future economic growth. As a result, in the 1980s:

the [sub-national] region, long considered an interesting topic to historians and geographers, but not considered to have any interest for mainstream Western social science, was rediscovered by a group of heterodox political economists, sociologists, political scientists and geographers (Storper 1995, p. 191).

Rather than a secondary effect of 'more profound' socio-economic processes, the region was seen as fundamentally constitutive of economic growth as indicated by the successes of Silicon Valley, Toulouse, Hollywood, North East Italy, and Toyota City (e.g. Hopkins 2015).

These trends seemed to put new life into efforts at reviving 'regional geography', if now with the modifier 'new'. Little or no inspiration has come from the canons of Vidal's or Hettner's perspectives. Rather, while sharing the goal of trying to redefine the regional concept for the late twentieth century based loosely around sub-national regions, influence has come from very different directions. The first is that of a phenomenology in which 'being in the world' is associated with living in different places (Tuan 1974; Entrikin 1991). This humanistic geography has had persisting effects, particularly in Anglo-American cultural geography. The second is that of the uneven geography of capitalist development associated with the relative persistence and shifts in the spatial division of labor or ways in which different regions come to specialize in different types of production and consumption (Massey 1984). The third is rooted in efforts at combining sociological and spatial analysis by seeing regions as places or contexts in which different behavioral and social repertoires take root (e.g. Hägerstrand 1982; Pred 1984).

From one perspective, this could be seen as having come full circle. Certainly, the regional concept at issue – its scale and orientation, in particular – is not that different from that which dominated debates about the region in the late nineteenth century. But this would be a mistake. The new understandings differ in two ways in particular. The first difference is in the explicit attention to the broader spatial framing of particular regions. In this construction, regions cannot be construed as isolated or contained entities. Rather, they are tied into broader networks and connectivities well beyond national borders even as they retain their distinctiveness (Amin 2004; Paasi 2002). A second difference is that the regional differences do not rely in the last instance on some sort of physical or environmental determination. This was an important if recently little noted feature of Hettner's regional geography. If more muted in Vidal's preference for a 'possibilism' that limited the direct effects of the physical environment on human action, it was nevertheless part and parcel of a viewpoint that, after all, emphasized the lives of peasants whose daily and seasonal rhythms were more environmentally regulated than those of many other social groups. Recent efforts at breathing new life into an older regional concept, therefore, cannot be seen as simply reinventing the wheel (e.g. McKinnon and Hiner 2015).

One important part of this trend has been to challenge conventional territorial-bounded approaches with so-called relational thinking, which suggests that regions should be seen as non-fixed and open entities. In this way, regions 'stretch' across space so that their social contents and relations can be networked across borders. It is this networking that in fact constitutes the region. Thus, regional boundaries and identities need not to be exclusive to one another. In terms of politics, and following the writing of Doreen Massey, for example, seeing regions as bounded can be viewed as 'regressive' while seeing them as open is 'progressive' (Massey 2005). This relational thinking is also strongly implied in the ideas of scholars representing the so-called 'new mobility paradigm', emphasizing how much people move around rather than tie themselves to places (e.g. Sheller and Urry 2006). The question can arise as to how far this type of thinking can be pushed before regions dissolve into webs of networks and the stories of those in them go ungrounded in any conception of territorial space.

2.4   DILEMMAS OF THE REGIONAL CONCEPT

The regional concept, whatever the precise meaning given to it, has always been subject to criticism. One of the main problems with it has been that of adequate spatial definition: where does one end and another begin? This was raised most systematically for the dominant meaning the concept had had in geography at precisely the time when its monopoly was in question. In 1951 George Kimble (1951 [1996]) published a chapter laying out his objections to what he saw as the arbitrariness with which regions were often defined. He suggested that behind the absence of firm criteria for defining what makes a region the real problem was twofold: regions are in fact present-day fictions left over from a time when they may have existed (eighteenth-century Europe, he claims) and as such the stories told about them are drawn by the scholar and bear only a loose relationship to the actually existing reality the scholar claims for them. The dead hand of the past lay over the concept. In Kimble's (1951 [1996]), p. 507) words:

> We see, therefore, that the standard-model region is essentially a phenomenon of the European continent: that it was sired by feudalism and raised in the cultural seclusion of a self-sufficing environment, that it owed almost as much to history as to geography, and that it does not appear to thrive in the more turbulent atmosphere of modern times.

He goes on to advocate a view of human geography in which the concept has no role whatsoever.

Of course, you can defend any given region as reflecting popular 'convention' or administrative fiat and thus as not requiring any specific justification. Nevertheless, the larger question persists. A longstanding debate reflects Kimble's point about whether regions actually exist or are entirely in the eyes of the beholder. Recent philosophy of science suggests that these are not necessarily in opposition. Regions can reflect both differences in the world and ideas about the geography of such differences (Agnew 1999). Whatever the geographic scale at which they are invoked, regions are both potentially out there and in the mind of their proposer. Regionalizing, the act of dividing up a space into regions, is a type of classification. Regions

> [C]annot be reduced to one or the other. Observers and people in the world use regional designations to make sense of the world and these draw on real differences in the world but they cannot claim total fit to the world because they are based on ideas about regional differences that are not simply about those differences *per se* but also about ideas of how the world works. (Agnew 1999, p. 93)

Consequently, all regional schemas are inherently contestable. For example, given the importance of Europe or 'the West' to many macro-regional schemas based on opposing them to the rest of the world, it comes as no surprise that these are subject to contention. How inherently unified culturally and politically are these entities? Can they be usefully divided into sub-regions that have distinctive relationships to one another and to the rest of the world (east versus west or north versus south)? Is Europe as a supra-national enterprise (in the form of the European Union) a more realistic basis to defining 'Europe' than a quasi-mystical civilizational entity or a geographical region with a shared set of historical experiences entirely due to propinquity?

Such questions are not easily answered. But they need not paralyze usage of the regional concept. For one thing, it is usually when the search is for totalistic regions that presumably cover just about any aspect of human life – as macro-regions or totalistic sub-national regions – that the concept becomes most problematic. More typically, when regions are used to study industrialization or urbanization, for example, it is the features of the region in which the specific process is embedded that become relevant. From this viewpoint, the boundedness of the region is not the main point. Rather 'Overlapping and intersecting relationships define regions, not uniform attributes that "fill in" a definite space' (Agnew 2000, p. 107). Thus, the south-east of England as discussed in John Allen et al.'s *Rethinking the Region* (1998), is not just a bounded space on a map but a complex mix of representational projection on the part of various actors and a set of material-functional relationships:

Examining the case of London and the south-east of England, the authors argue that the south-east acquired a mythic status in the 1980s as the "growth region" par excellence in England, a product of its putative economic success in the heyday of the Thatcher government's experiment in neoliberalism. Investigating the claim to "success," the book weaves together a fascinating portrayal of the political uses of regional designations (such as the "successful south-east" as a model for other regions), the nature of the economic growth in the region and who benefited from it, and the specificities of localities (different economies, different social identities) within the region and their relationship to the economic path of the region as a whole. (Agnew 2000, p. 107)

Particularly in discussions of economic development and political participation, regions of various sizes are also often considered in relation to a temporal continuum that goes from backward at one end to modern at the other (Agnew 1996). This conversion of time into space has been important in historicizing certain macro-regions (the Third World or global South) or some sub-national regions (the Italian south, the American south) into a schema that locates regions on an idealized trajectory of historic progress (e.g. on Italy, see Putnam 1993). This of course endogenizes the temporal lag into the regions that are 'behind'. Their cultural or political characteristics are responsible for their lagging behind. That it could be spatial exploitation by the modern (richer) regions has been the riposte of some observers (e.g. Hechter 1976). Dependency and world-systems theories have this relation of dominance-subordination as their centerpiece. Whatever the response, however, the tendency to view regions in light of the backward-modern couplet reduces the possibility of viewing regions as more complex and even contradictory in their economic and political characteristics.

Finally, in much social science, at least until very recently, there has been a strong tendency to see regions, particularly sub-national ones, as fading in significance as settings for human behavior as nation-wide markets, common media of communication, national political parties and national cultures rob local and regional identities and interests of their specificity. This nationalization thesis rests on the presumption that social and political organization increasingly operates entirely at the national and no longer at the regional scale (see, e.g. Watkins 1991). The presumption is a shaky one. In fact, demographic, electoral and other indicators suggest that nationalization is not a one-way street and that a period of regionalization can follow on from one in which everywhere became more alike. Indeed, all sorts of behaviors may be mediated through the regionally specific routines and institutions of everyday life even as they become increasingly similar nationwide (Agnew 1987). The regional concept still seems to have much life in it as it is redefined for new purposes at different geographic scales in new circumstances.

2.5   REFERENCES

Agnew, J.A. (1987), *Place and Politics: The Geographical Mediation of State and Society*, London: Allen and Unwin.

Agnew, J.A. (1989), 'Sameness and difference: Hartshorne's *The Nature of Geography* and geography as areal variation', in J.N. Entrikin and S.D. Brunn (eds), *Reflections on Richard Hartshorne's* The Nature of Geography, Washington, DC: Association of American Geographers, pp. 121–139.

Agnew, J.A. (1996), 'Time into space: the myth of "backward" Italy in modern Europe', *Time and Society*, **5** (1), 27–45.

Agnew, J.A. (1999), 'Regions on the mind does not equal regions of the mind', *Progress in Human Geography*, **23** (1), 91–96.

Agnew, J.A. (2000), 'From the political economy of regions to regional political economy', *Progress in Human Geography*, **24** (1), 101–110.

Agnew, J.A. (2001), 'Regions in revolt', *Progress in Human Geography*, **25** (1), 103–110.

Agnew, J.A. (2014), 'By words alone shall we know: is the history of ideas enough to understand the world to which our concepts refer?', *Dialogues in Human Geography*, **4** (3), 311–319.

Agnew, J.A. (2015), 'Unbundled territoriality and regional politics', *Territory, Politics, Governance*, **3** (2), 119–123.

Allen, J., A. Cochrane and D. Massey (1998), *Rethinking the Region*, London: Routledge.

Alphaville (2016), 'If the EU is a sinking ship and the UK should leave, then most of the UK is a sinking ship and London should leave', *Financial Times*, June 30.

Amin, A. (2004), 'Regions unbound: towards a new politics of place', *Geografiska Annaler: Series B*, **86** (1), 33–44.

Barnes, T.J. and M. Farish (2006), 'Between regions: science, militarism and American geography from world war to Cold War', *Annals of the Association of American Geographers*, **96** (4), 807–826.

Braudel, F. (1949), *La Méditerranée et le Monde Méditerranéen a l'époque de Philippe II*, 3 volumes, Paris: Armand Colin.

Braudel, F. (1986), *L'identité de la France*, Paris: Armand Colin.

Claval, P. (1993), *Initiation à la géographie régionale*, Paris: Armand Colin.

Entrikin, J.N. (1991), *The Betweenness of Place: Towards a Geography of Modernity*, Baltimore MD: Johns Hopkins University Press.

Gregory, D. (1993), *Geographical Imaginations*, Oxford: Blackwell.

Hägerstrand, T. (1982), 'Diorama, path and project', *Tijdschrift voor Economische en Sociale Geografie*, **73** (6), 323–339.

Harrison, J. and A. Growe (2014), 'From places to flows? Planning for the new "regional world" in Germany', *European Urban and Regional Studies*, **21** (1), 21–41.

Hartshorne, R. (1939), *The Nature of Geography*, Lancaster PA: Association of American Geographers.

Hechter, M. (1976), *Internal Colonialism: The Celtic Fringe in British National Development*, Berkeley CA: University of California Press.

Herrigel, G. (1996), *Industrial Constructions: The Sources of German Industrial Power*, New York: Basic Books.

Hettne, B. (2005), 'Beyond the "new" regionalism', *New Political Economy*, **10** (4), 543–571.

Hettne, B. and F. Söderbaum (2000), 'Theorising the rise of regionness', *New Political Economy*, **5** (3), 457–472.

Hopkins, J. (2015), *Knowledge, Networks and Policy: Regional Studies in Postwar Britain and Beyond*, London: Routledge.

Jones, M. and A. Paasi (2013), 'Guest editorial: Regional world(s): advancing the geography of regions', *Regional Studies*, **47** (1), 1–5.

Keating, M. (1995), 'Europeanism and regionalism', in B. Jones and M. Keating (eds), *The European Union and the Regions*, Oxford: Clarendon Press, pp. 1–22.

Kern, S. (1983), *The Culture of Time and Space, 1880–1918*, Cambridge MA: Harvard University Press.

Kimble, G.H.T. (1951), 'The inadequacy of the regional concept', reprinted in J. Agnew, D. Livingstone and A. Rogers (eds), *Human Geography: An Essential Anthology* (1996), Oxford: Blackwell, pp. 492–512.

Massey, D. (1984), *Spatial Divisions of Labour*, London: Methuen.

Massey, D. (2005), *For Space*, London: Sage.

McKinnon, I. and C.C. Hiner (2015), 'Does the region still have relevance? (Re) considering "regional" political ecology,' *Journal of Political Ecology*, **23** (1), 115–122.

Murphy, A. (1993), 'Emerging regional linkages within the European Community: challenging the dominance of the state', *Tijdschrift voor Economische en Sociale Geografie*, **84** (2), 103–118.

Oakes, T. (2000), 'China's provincial identities: reviving regionalism and reinventing "Chineseness"', *Journal of Asian Studies*, **59** (3), 667–692.

Paasi, A. (1986), 'The institutionalization of regions: a theoretical framework for understanding the emergence of regions and the constitution of regional identity', *Fennia*, **164** (1), 105–146.

Paasi, A. (2002), 'Bounded spaces in the mobile world: deconstructing "regional identity"', *Tijdschrift voor Economische en Sociale Geografie*, **93** (2), 137–148.

Pred, A.R. (1984), 'Place as a historically contingent process: structuration and the time-geography of becoming places', *Annals of the Association of American Geographers*, **74** (2), 279–297.

Putnam, R. (1993), *Making Democracy Work: Civic Traditions in Modern Italy*, Princeton NJ: Princeton University Press.

Rankin, W. (2016), *After the Map: Cartography, Navigation, and the Transformation of Territory in the Twentieth Century*, Chicago: University of Chicago Press.

Said, E.W. (1978), *Orientalism*, New York: Vintage.

Schaefer, F.K. (1953), 'Exceptionalism in geography: a methodological examination', *Annals of the Association of American Geographers*, **43** (3), 226–249.

Scott, A.J. (1998), *Regions and the World Economy*, Oxford: Oxford University Press.

Sheller, M. and J. Urry (2006), 'The new mobilities paradigm', *Environment and Planning A*, **38** (2), 207–226.

Smith, N. (1989), 'Geography as museum: private history and conservative idealism in *The Nature of Geography*', in J.N. Entrikin and S.B. Brunn (eds), *Reflections on Richard Hartshorne's* The Nature of Geography, Washington, DC: Association of American Geographers, pp. 89–120.

Sorens, J. (2008), 'Regionalists against secession: the political economy of territory in advanced democracies', *Nationalism and Ethnic Politics*, **14** (3), 325–360.

Storper, M. (1995), 'The resurgence of regional economies, ten years later', *European Urban and Regional Studies*, **2** (3), 191–221.

Taylor, P.J. (1988), 'World-systems analysis and regional geography', *Professional Geographer*, **40** (3), 259–265.

Thrift, N.J. (1994), 'Taking aim at the heart of the region', in D. Gregory, R. Martin and G. Smith (eds), *Human Geography: Society, Space and Social Science*, London: Macmillan, pp. 200–231.

Tilly, C. (1992), *Coercion, Capital, and European States, A.D. 990–1992*, Oxford: Blackwell.

Tuan, Y-F. (1974), 'Space and place: humanistic perspective', *Progress in Geography*, **6**, 211–252.

Watkins, S.C. (1991), *From Provinces into Nations: Demographic Integration in Western Europe, 1970–1960*, Princeton NJ: Princeton University Press.

3. Territory and territoriality
David Storey

3.1 INTRODUCTION

In common usage 'territory' is a word frequently used to refer to an area of land claimed by a state, or to a 'homeland' claimed by a national grouping seeking self-determination. Territoriality is normally seen as the actions or behaviours used to control or exert power over a geographically designated space. Although territory might be seen as a central concept within geography, it has tended to be taken as a given and treated in a somewhat descriptive sense until comparatively recently. The pioneering work of Robert Sack (1986) drew attention to territoriality as a spatial expression of power. Subsequent textbooks (Delaney 2005; Storey 2012) have taken territory and territoriality as central concerns while others have identified territory as a key dimension of political geography (Cox 2003; Dahlman 2009). The heightened attention given to ideas of territory and territoriality was further reflected in the launch of the journal *Territory, Politics, Governance* in 2013.

While it might be tempting to regard territoriality as an innate feature of human beings, geographers tend to situate it in a social and political context in which territories are seen to be socially produced and territorial strategies can be viewed as mechanisms to achieve particular ends. In this way territory, and control over it, is bound up with the assertion or maintenance of power, or resistance to a dominant power. It is argued that, rather than being natural entities, territories reflect specific ways of thinking about geographic space and they are products of social practices and processes that link space and society (Delaney 2009; Elden 2013a). Territories and territorial strategies convey messages of political power which are communicated through various means including the creation and securing of borders. Territory is also intimately bound up with identity and can be used to instill and reproduce a sense of loyalty and affiliation. Territories can be seen to exist (with various degrees of control, contestation and bordering practices) across spatial scales and in a wide range of contexts and through various forms of what Sidaway (2007) has referred to as spatial enclaving. This can be seen through such things as the growing phenomenon of gated communities, controlled commercial and leisure spaces and other examples of the partial privatization of formerly public space (Bagaeen and Uduku 2010; Paasche et al. 2014). Following a discussion of ideas of territory and territoriality, this chapter limits the discussion to the overt political sphere focusing on the territorial nature of the state, considering both its territorial practices and the significance of territory in shaping identity.

3.2   THE CONCEPT OF TERRITORY AND TERRITORIAL STRATEGIES

In 1973 Jean Gottmann argued that territory confers security through the control of defensible space while also providing a range of opportunities through facilitating the economic organization of that space. This emphasis on security and opportunity points to a political and economic basis for territorial formations which make for a more efficient means of political organization than systems of overlapping jurisdictions. More recently, Stuart Elden has pointed to the failure to further explore the idea of territory, suggesting it has long been taken for granted so that 'strategies and processes toward territory ... conceptually presuppose the object that they practically produce' (Elden 2010, p. 803). He suggests that territories themselves, and their boundaries, reflect a distinctive mode of social and spatial organization linked to particular ways of thinking about geographic space and these ways reflect notions of power and control. Elden's (2013a) pioneering work traces the emergence of the concept of territory and he argues that our contemporary ideas of territory emerged alongside developments in cartography and spatial calculation; it is something that can be calculated, mapped and controlled. Territory has emerged through a series of social and political practices and territoriality, in allowing classification and differentiation, is an outcome of the ways in which space is imagined. In effect, territories are politicized space; mapped and claimed, ordered and bordered, measured and demarcated (Elden 2013a). Control of territory requires control of those within it while controlling people requires control of the land in which they reside. For Elden, territory 'is something shaped by, and a shaper of, continual processes of transformation, regulation and governance' (Elden 2013b, p. 17). Swiss geographer Claude Raffestin (2012) has also explored the emergence of territory and points to the ways in which spatial practices become solidified allowing for the utilization of territory in strategic ways (Murphy 2012).

If territories reflect a particular way of thinking about space, then this points to the importance of maps in solidifying and legitimizing these spatial units. Rather than neutral depictions of supposed geographical realities, a more critical analysis suggests that maps have always been useful weapons in larger political projects associated with territorial claims, and counter-claims (Harley 1988; Black 1998). Mapping of territory itself functions so as to enhance power sending out messages signifying control over portions of geographic space. Maps of the British Empire conventionally depicted Britain's overseas territorial possessions in pink, conveying geographic information while simultaneously proclaiming power over roughly one quarter of the planet's land area. Advances in cartography altered the ways in which space was considered, thereby facilitating attempts to apportion and control it. The military and political underpinnings of cartographic developments and the consequent role of mapping, in both practical and symbolic terms, in the creation of colonial territory was a key element in the imposition and maintenance of political control (Smyth 2006; Hewitt 2010).

Geographer Robert Sack's key work in the 1980s focused on territoriality as a geographic and political strategy through which individuals or groups endeavour to 'affect, influence, or control people, phenomena, and relationships, by delimiting and asserting control over a geographic area' (Sack 1986, p. 19). He emphasizes the instrumental nature of territoriality and draws attention to the means through which territorial strategies may be used to achieve particular ends so that control of geographic space can be used to assert or to maintain power, or, importantly, to resist the power of a dominant group. What this means is that territoriality is deeply embedded in social relations so that territories, far from being natural entities, are the result of social practices and processes and are produced under particular conditions in order to serve specific ends (Delaney 2005).

These perspectives are important in not only emphasizing the political context of territorial behaviour but also in highlighting how territoriality as a strategy operates at all spatial scales from the geopolitical strategies of global superpowers down to the micro-spaces of the home and the workplace. Sack also draws attention to the significance of territoriality in facilitating classification, communication and enforcement. Territoriality involves a classification by geographic area through which space is seen to be apportioned between states or between individuals. In this way a room, or an office, or a workstation becomes 'my' territory and others are discouraged from encroaching, except by invitation. Sack also argues that territoriality is easy to communicate via the use of boundaries which indicate territorial control and, hence, power over prescribed space (and of those within it). In this way there is a distinct separation between those who are 'inside' and those who are 'outside', thereby conveying clear messages about power and control. In this way territory, and associated border construction, in classifying space and communicating power, acts as a device for the enforcement of authority. Clearly, this has potentially important implications in constraining, restricting or limiting people's mobility. Territories and territorial ways of thinking link space and society and serve to convey clear meanings relating to authority, power and rights (Delaney 2009).

Another tendency of territoriality identified by Sack is that it functions as a means through which power is reified. Through the visibility of land (or a room or a desk) power can be 'seen' in a way which suggests that 'territory appears as the agent doing the controlling' (Sack 1986, p. 33). This reification is most obviously apparent in the deployment of the term 'the law of the land' whereby power appears to reside in the territory itself. Attention is thereby diverted away from the power relationships, ideologies and processes underpinning the maintenance of territories and their boundaries. In this way 'territory does much of our thinking for us and closes off or obscures questions of power and meaning, ideology and legitimacy, authority and obligation' (Delaney 2005, p. 18). This interpretation of territorial behaviour emphasizes the political functions of territoriality so that it can be seen as 'a primary geographic expression of social power' (Sack 1986, p. 5).

Once created, territories can become the spatial containers in which people are socialized through various social practices and discourses. Paasi (2008) suggests that the material and the symbolic are combined through territory. A material component, land, is something to be controlled while the symbolism associated with it feeds into people's social identity. In this way, the spatial is not simply a product of the social; rather the two are intimately bound together. Painter (2010) argues that territory is an effect or an outcome of a set of practices and networks of inter-connections and is (re)produced in seemingly mundane ways through such things as the collection and production of regional statistics and the devising of regional economic strategies. These confer and deepen a sense of regional delimitation, contiguity and coherence. Territories result from social practices and are solidified through an accumulation of administrative procedures.

3.3   THE TERRITORIAL STATE

The emergence and evolution of states and the construction of borders between them represent the most obvious political expression of territoriality. At its most fundamental level, territory is the functional space within which the state operates and wields power and it might be seen as a key and necessary feature of the state. Borders have traditionally been seen as the dividing lines where state control both begins and ends. However, while the territorial state is at the centre of the global political system, we need to be careful not to fall into what Agnew (1994) long ago termed the territorial trap whereby we naturalize states and their borders. Agnew argues that states are imagined as fixed sovereign entities with power over their territory, in turn suggesting a clear distinction between 'domestic' and 'foreign', whereby states are characterized as territorial containers of economy and society. However, Brenner and Elden (2009) point to the ways in which territory is continually reproduced through the actions of states and through various forms of political struggle. They argue that territory, rather than simply being a feature of the state, both facilitates and emerges from state action. Clearly sovereignty and the state system place a heavy emphasis on geographical borders that separate one territorial political entity from another. Borders are often seen as taken-for-granted features serving as political-cultural dividing lines. However, they might more accurately be seen as discursive constructs that serve to legitimize the state (Fall 2010; Newman 2010). The demarcation of territories and the bounding of space obviously bring with them issues of exclusion and control. Territories, and their boundaries, are frequently the centre of often violent disputes and the areal extent of particular territories, or even their very right to exist, may be regularly called into question. Rather than being fixed immutable entities, human territories and their boundaries are subject to periodic or continuous contestation, modification, transformation and destruction through the shifting spatialities of power (Paasi 2009).

Territory and borders are necessary features of the contemporary state but these are closely linked to ideas of sovereignty or the right of the state to control its people and its territory, concepts which have emerged and evolved alongside each other over recent centuries (Maier 2016). Agnew (2005) argues that sovereignty is highly complex and the sovereign power of an individual state is continually challenged, contested and modified. Processes associated with globalization (or linked together under that broad umbrella term) are seen by many as signalling a diminishing sovereignty for the territorial state. Borders are commonly depicted as increasingly porous in a world of trans-national flows of people, goods, finance and ideas. The emergence of regional economic alliances, epitomized by the evolution of blocs such as the European Union (EU) and the Association of South East Asian Nations (ASEAN) is heralded by some as the successor to the state system in an increasingly globalized world where state boundaries are assumed to have diminishing significance. The spatial diffusion of the financial crisis in recent years points to a diminishing ability of the state to maintain economic sovereignty.

Despite these predictions of the demise of the state and the supposed advent of a borderless world, the reality appears rather more complex. While a neoliberal economic orthodoxy (and its attendant crises) centred on trans-global economic flows seems to point towards the irrelevancy of borders, it simultaneously utilizes and reconfigures them in attempts to increase the returns to capital. In addition, there is the apparent paradox that while capital flows relatively freely across international frontiers, many people (depending on who they are, where they are from, and where they are trying to go) are faced with the intimidating paraphernalia of the state manifested at border crossing points. For the migrant confronted by a border fence or the security forces patrolling a frontier, power is unequivocally communicated. The 2016 United Kingdom vote to leave the European Union (EU) suggests a return to harder borders, a situation further epitomized by the erection and solidification of borders throughout central Europe designed to impede migration into the EU. United States (US) president Donald Trump's call for the construction of a wall between the US and Mexico is a stark example of the rhetoric surrounding borders and their control, though that rhetoric omits acknowledgement that sections of wall and fencing already exist along lengthy stretches of that frontier. In this sense, recent political developments seem to reflect an intensification of bordering practices rather than a new departure.

Geopolitically, Elden (2010) and others suggest that, far from disappearing, territory is continually being reconfigured and spatial political relations are constantly being re-shaped in ways suggestive of re-territorialization, rather than de-territorialization. Power is unequally distributed and some political–territorial formations exert significantly more than others. Some states display a willingness and ability to exert power well beyond their formal territorial boundaries while others (sometimes labelled 'failed' or 'rogue' states) become arenas for external intervention. The linkages between state sovereignty and territorial control are far from straightforward and lead to a consideration of effective sovereignty wielded by both states and quasi-state actors and deployed across a range of territorial contexts (Elden 2009; McConnell 2010). Sassen (2013) writes of the growing disjuncture between territory and state sovereignty in a heavily interconnected world. She sees territory as a capability that has a wider array of formats than simply the state.

Sassen suggests we need to think in terms of complex jurisdictions that cross borders creating holes in state sovereignty or what might be seen as a weakening of territoriality, when understood as legal control of geographic space. The creation and maintenance of military bases in other countries and the economic and political pressures exerted, both directly and indirectly, by major powers further highlight the contingent nature of state sovereignty through which some states might be said to possess the capacity to be considerably more sovereign than others through the exercise of military or economic muscle. US drone and other attacks in Pakistan and elsewhere represent asymmetrical interpretations of sovereignty whereby more powerful actors presume to act on a consid-erably more global stage than that permitted to others. Alongside this, the activities of major transnational corporations, with their highly complex geographies of production, distribution, marketing and taxation, serve to deepen the array of actors that wield forms of power within and across state borders.

Our sense of the world of states as being somehow 'natural' is clearly reinforced through political maps that display this territorial configuration of bordered spaces in a way that generates an impression of solidity. This state-centred view of the world means we tend to see territory as a mere canvas on which political processes play out (Kadercan 2015). However, the state system is a political and geographic construct that displays considerable dynamism. In recent decades the number of states has risen dramatically, consequent on state collapse (many associated with the fall of communism in the early 1990s) and secessionist nationalism. Clearly, secessionist ideologies (Basque, Kurdish or Scottish nationalism, for example) are premised on the construction of a territory, politically detached from the state(s) to which it currently belongs. Elsewhere, groups such as 'Islamic State' in Iraq and Syria and Boko Haram in Nigeria utilize the control of space in the pursuit of ideological objectives. The emergence of quasi-states such as South Ossetia (officially part of Georgia) and Transnistria (formally belonging to Moldova) reflect a means of territorial construction through opting out of larger spatial-political entities (Blakkisrud and Kolstø 2011; O'Loughlin et al. 2011).

Ultimately territorial sovereignty is relative, contingent and never complete. It may be more useful to think in terms of effective sovereignty wielded by both states and quasi-state actors and deployed across a range of territorial contexts where sovereign power does not necessarily stop at the border (Elden 2009; McConnell 2010; Kadercan 2015). The effective sovereignty of many states is reduced through various processes and global flows, and states operate alongside a widening range of non-state actors who might be seen to exert power across networks rather than over rigidly bordered territory. This, however, is not necessarily a completely new departure as Agnew (2009) suggests that political spaces have never been hermetically sealed and sovereign spaces have always been fragmented, overlapping and multi-scalar, a phenomenon exacerbated (but not created) through various strands of globalization. More broadly, some have begun to suggest that jurisdiction and sovereignty are not inextricably dependent on territory and boundaries, and the relationship between territory, property, assets and the law is becoming increasingly complex (Blomley 2016). As well as the jurisdictions of such bodies as the International Criminal Court, we also have the phenomenon of places such as London becoming a key arena for the settlement of legal cases involving non-domiciled business people. Nevertheless, as Paasi (2009) suggests, in spite of these increasingly complex and multifaceted interactions and networks, the state still acts as an organizer and regulator of territorial spaces, even if those spaces are becoming increasingly porous.

3.4   TERRITORY, PLACE AND NATION

While drawing attention to the emergence and functions of territories, it is clear that they are more than mere (sometimes leaky) spatial containers. Territories, and the ways in which they are imagined, can play an important role in the formation of peoples' self-identity and contribute to feelings of belonging or exclusion. Territory is quite central in many nationalist discourses and is habitually invoked in national conflicts where both generic territory and specific places may acquire enormous symbolism. At its most basic level is the idea of the national soil so that fighting for, or even dying for, the land are often seen as supreme acts of patriotism in times of national conflict. In the late nineteenth and early twentieth century notions of blood sacrifice in pursuit of national ideals were reflected in calls to defend the land (or national soil) and fight for it. In the struggle for Irish independence in the early twentieth century, rebel leader Pádraig Pearse once wrote of the need for the earth to be warmed by the blood of the battlefields. In a different context, formulations of *blut und boden* (blood and soil) formed part of Nazi ideology, reflecting a belief in an explicit link between territory and ethnicity. People fight (and die) for their country (or come to believe that they do), indicating how strong associations with territory may be utilized for political ends and how memories can be mobilized in support of the production and re-production of a national narrative (Paasi 2016). In the 1990s, land and territory were central in the Balkans conflict characterized by attempts to purify portions of land of those seen as 'other' (Toal and Dahlman 2011). While it is easy to portray such events as irrational, for some people in specific contexts strong attachments to territory may appear to make perfect sense. In colonial (and former colonial) societies, for example, where land has been appropriated, a strong sense of ownership and defence may persist through succeeding generations so that a collective memory of struggle for land ownership serves as a potent motivating force reflecting a material, and not simply sentimental, underpinning to an attachment to the land (Crowley 2006).

While history (actual or 'invented') is central to the nation's being, its right to exist usually rests on claims to a particular national space and, within this, particular places and landscapes often assume symbolic importance. There are numerous references to the 'generic' territory of the nation and allusions to the national soil even in what may appear quite banal ways (Billig 1995). Beyond the idea of the soil, particular parts of the national territory often acquire a significance as the presumed 'zone of origin' of the nation; its original heartland which remains the 'core' of the national imagination. These are often more remote and intrinsically rural places such as wilder more remote landscapes of northern Canada, the Scottish Highlands or the west of Ireland. The supposed 'taming' of the American west means that not just the 'pioneers' heading westwards, but also the landscapes through which they travelled and the land they 'conquered', assumed significance in the nation-building project. In some Welsh nationalist discourses the mountains are seen as the heart of the nation, symbolizing a Wales untainted by outside influences. More remote and less anglicized areas were seen to be the heartland of Welsh identity. This is reflected in the Welsh nationalist party, Plaid Cymru, choosing an idealized representation of mountains as the original symbol of the party at its foundation in the 1920s (Gruffudd 1995). The physical landscape is depicted as the embodiment of the nation.

The Balkans crisis of the 1990s and its lingering aftermath was underpinned by a series of claims to particular places seen as integral to specific ethnic identities (Storey 2002; Robinson and Pobrić 2006), claims underpinned through reference to historical myths and forms of boundary-making (Kolstø 2005). In this way, past Serbian occupation of present-day Kosovo serves as a useful justification for territorial control over an area almost exclusively occupied by ethnic Albanians. Kosovo's 2008 declaration of independence is a rupture of the territorial integrity of Serbia when seen through the lens of Serbian nationalism. It is clear that land and territory are utilized in conjunction with selective interpretations of history in forging and reproducing a sense of national identity. When seen through a somewhat inward-looking perspective, these ideas translate as 'our' land and this is reflected through strands of the UK referendum on leaving the EU and made apparent through some of the slogans used in that campaign such as 'we want our country back', premised on a simplistic notion of some homogenous sense of affinity to a geographical space. This sits alongside debates over material issues so that in the employment arena calls are made to prioritize jobs for nationals over migrant 'others' (Ince et al. 2015). In this somewhat xenophobic version of national identity, 'our' jobs are located in 'our' land and should be for 'our' people; the material, the symbolic and the geographic are intrinsically bound together.

Once again, the role of mapping in inculcating a sense of territorial identification needs to be emphasized here. The map of Turkey is a commonly reproduced logo and acts as a banal signifier of the nation (Batuman 2010), serving to ingrain the territory in the popular consciousness. Jim MacLaughlin (2001) writes about his father going to school in 1920s Ireland where an outline of the island of Ireland was nailed onto the school-room floor. Subsequently, Irish school exercise books had a map of Ireland displayed on the back cover as an everyday reminder of the outline of the nation, one territorially divided between an independent republic and a region within the UK. Mapping gives solidity to the state and portrays its territorial imprint thereby indelibly linking the state to its sovereign territory and giving it 'reality' in the minds of its citizens. In many seemingly banal ways the idea of the imagined community of the wider nation is linked to a delimited geographic space which is seen to be 'ours' and which may periodically need to be defended against 'others'.

3.5   CONCLUSION

Territories are political geographic entities that have emerged out of particular ways of conceiving geographic space. The most obvious version of this is the territorial state. Territory often constitutes a major component in shaping our everyday lives and in contributing to our senses of place, identity and belonging. Particular ideologies and social practices are manifested spatially and are reflected in struggles and territorial claims over the use and control of space. Territorial strategies are utilized in conflicts concerned with social power and identity at a range of spatial scales from the global down to the very local. These strategies may be to do with maintaining power or with resisting the imposition of power by a dominant group. States and their borders serve as exclusionary devices as well as a means through which people are classified as 'native' or 'alien'. While exclusionary ideologies may be consolidated and reinforced through territorial practices, they can also be resisted through similar means. Territoriality is a mechanism of power and territorial formation, control, resistance and transgression are all political phenomena. While it might be supposed that places and territorial boundaries are becoming less and less significant in an increasingly globalized world, the (re)production of territories and the associated creation and contestation of boundaries seem likely to continue to be important for the foreseeable future. Indeed, current developments suggest a further hardening of borders and a retreat into more exclusionary forms of territorial identity. Notwithstanding the evolution of a more globally interconnected world, territory continues to retain both an allure in terms of identity as well as a strategic value (Agnew 2010; Murphy 2013).

3.6   REFERENCES

Agnew, J. (1994), 'The territorial trap: the geographical assumptions of international relations theory', *Review of International Political Economy*, **1** (1), 53–80.

Agnew, J. (2005), 'Sovereignty regimes: territoriality and state authority in contemporary world politics', *Annals of the Association of American Geographers*, **95** (2), 437–461.

Agnew, J. (2009), *Globalization and Sovereignty*, Lanham, MD and Plymouth, UK: Rowman & Littlefield.

Agnew, J. (2010), 'Still trapped in territory?', *Geopolitics*, **15** (4), 779–784.

Bagaeen, S. and O. Uduku (eds) (2010), *Gated Communities: Social Sustainability and Historical Gated Developments*, London: Earthscan.

Batuman, B. (2010), 'The shape of the nation: visual production of nationalism through maps in Turkey', *Political Geography*, **29** (4), 220–234.

Billig, M. (1995), *Banal Nationalism*, London: Sage.

Black, J. (1998), *Maps and Politics*, London: Reaktion.

Blakkisrud, H. and P. Kolstø (2011), 'From secessionist conflict toward a functioning state: processes of state- and nation-building in Transnistria', *Post-Soviet Affairs*, **27** (2), 178–210.

Blomley, N. (2016), 'The territory of property', *Progress in Human Geography*, **40** (5), 593–609.

Brenner, N. and S. Elden (2009), 'Henri Lefebvre on state, space, territory', *International Political Sociology*, **3** (4), 353–377.

Cox, K. (2003), *Political Geography: Territory, State and Society*, Oxford: Blackwell.

Crowley, E. (2006), *Land Matters: Power Struggles in Rural Ireland*, Dublin: Lilliput Press.

Dahlman, C. (2009), 'Territory', in C. Gallaher, C. Dahlman, M. Gilmartin, A. Mountz and P. Shirlow (eds), *Key Concepts in Political Geography*, London: Sage, pp. 77–86.

Delaney, D. (2005), *Territory: A Short Introduction*, Malden: Blackwell.

Delaney, D. (2009), 'Territory and territoriality', in R. Kitchin and N. Thrift (eds), *International Encyclopedia of Human Geography*, Volume 11, Oxford: Elsevier, pp. 196–208.

Elden, S. (2009), *Terror and Territory: The Spatial Extent of Sovereignty*, Minneapolis: University of Minnesota Press.

Elden, S. (2010), 'Land, terrain, territory', *Progress in Human Geography*, **34** (6), 799–817.

Elden, S. (2013a), *The Birth of Territory*, Chicago: The University of Chicago Press.

Elden, S. (2013b), 'How should we do the history of territory?', *Territory, Politics, Governance*, **1** (1), 5–20.

Fall, J. (2010), 'Artificial states? On the enduring geographical myth of natural borders', *Political Geography*, **29** (3), 140–156.

Gottmann, J. (1973), *The Significance of Territory*, Charlottesville: University Press of Virginia.

Gruffudd, P. (1995), 'Remaking Wales: nation-building and the geographical imagination, 1925–1950', *Political Geography*, **14** (3), 219–239.

Harley, J. (1988), 'Maps, knowledge and power', in D. Cosgrove and S. Daniels (eds), *The Iconography of Landscape*, Cambridge: Cambridge University Press, pp. 277–312.

Hewitt, R. (2010), *Map of a Nation: A Biography of the Ordnance Survey*, London: Granta.

Ince, A., D. Featherstone, A. Cumbers, D. MacKinnon and K. Strauss (2015), 'British jobs for British workers? Negotiating work, nation, and globalization through the Lindsay oil refinery disputes', *Antipode*, **47** (1), 139–157.

Kadercan, B. (2015), 'Triangulating territory: a case for pragmatic interaction between political science, political geography, and critical IR', *International Theory*, **7** (1), 125–161.

Kolstø, P. (ed.) (2005), *Myths and Boundaries in South-Eastern Europe*, London: Hurst & Company.

MacLaughlin, J. (2001), *Reimagining the Nation-state: The Contested Terrains of Nation-building*, London: Pluto.

Maier, C. (2016), *Once Within Borders: Territories of Power, Wealth, and Belonging since 1500*, Cambridge, MA and London, UK: Belknap Press.

McConnell, F. (2010), 'The fallacy and the promise of the territorial trap: sovereign articulations of geopolitical anomalies', *Geopolitics*, **15** (4), 762–768.

Murphy, A. (2012), 'Entente territorial: Sack and Raffestin on territoriality', *Environment and Planning D: Society and Space*, **30** (1), 159–172.

Murphy, A. (2013), 'Territory's continuing allure', *Annals of the Association of American Geographers*, **103** (5), 1212–1226.

Newman, D. (2010), 'Territory, compartments and borders: avoiding the trap of the territorial trap', *Geopolitics*, **15** (4), 773–778.

O'Loughlin, J., V. Kolossov and G. Toal (2011), 'Inside Abkhazia: survey of attitudes in a *de facto* state', *Post-Soviet Affairs*, **27** (1), 1–36.

Paasche, T., R. Yarwood and J. Sidaway (2014), 'Territorial tactics: the socio-spatial significance of private policing strategies in Cape Town', *Urban Studies*, **51** (8), 1559–1575.

Paasi, A. (2008), 'Territory', in J. Agnew, K. Mitchell and G. Toal (eds), *A Companion to Political Geography*, Malden: Blackwell, pp. 109–122.

Paasi, A. (2009), 'Bounded spaces in a "borderless world": border studies, power and the anatomy of territory', *Journal of Power*, **2** (2), 213–234.

Paasi, A. (2016), 'Dancing on the graves: independence, hot/banal nationalism and the mobilization of memory', *Political Geography*, **54** (1), 21–31.

Painter, J. (2010), 'Rethinking territory', *Antipode*, **42** (5), 1098–1118.

Raffestin, C. (2012), 'Space, territory and territoriality', *Environment and Planning D: Society and Space*, **30** (1), 121–141.

Robinson, G. and A. Pobrić (2006), 'Nationalism and identity in post-Dayton accords: Bosnia-Hercegovina', *Tijdschrift voor Economische en Sociale Geografie*, **97** (3), 237–252.

Sack, R. (1986), *Human Territoriality: Its Theory and History*, Cambridge: Cambridge University Press.

Sassen, S. (2013), 'When territory deborders territoriality', *Territory, Politics, Governance*, **1** (1), 21–45.

Sidaway, J. (2007), 'Enclave space: a new metageography of development?' *Area*, **39** (3), 331–339.

Smyth, W. (2006), *Map-making, Landscapes and Memory: A Geography of Colonial and Early Modern Ireland c. 1530-1750*, Cork: Cork University Press.

Storey, D. (2002), 'Territory and national identity: examples from the former Yugoslavia', *Geography*, **87** (2), 108–115.

Storey, D. (2012), *Territories: The Claiming of Space*, London: Routledge, 2nd edition.

Toal, G. and C. Dahlman (2011), *Bosnia Remade: Ethnic Cleansing and its Reversal*, Oxford, UK and New York, USA: Oxford University Press.

4. Geography of experience: place and region
J. Nicholas Entrikin

4.1 INTRODUCTION: MULTIPLE REGIONALISMS

Two major political events in Europe and the United States have occurred before and during the writing of this chapter. One was the Brexit vote, a surprising-to-many referendum result in the United Kingdom in support of withdrawal from the European Union. The second was the 2016 American presidential election, in which the Republican candidate, Donald Trump, unexpectedly won the Electoral College vote over the popular-vote victor and favored Democratic candidate, Hillary Clinton. The reasons for the results are many and the unique circumstances of each make them difficult to compare, but they share certain similarities of relevance to the theme of this chapter.

In a broad sense, each may be seen as reflecting different forms of regionalism and place-based politics. In one sense, Brexit was a vote against regionalism, understood as an internationalist orientation toward greater economic and political cooperation among nation states, sometimes leading to a regional state organization, such as the European Union. A similar theme emerged in the American election, for example in the arguments of the winning candidate against the North American Free Trade Agreement (NAFTA), a regional, multinational trade agreement.

Regionalism was also evident in a different form, one related to the subnational scale and more closely associated with everyday experience. The regionalism of the European Union or NAFTA is a concept applied to international cooperation and is a staple of international relations theory. Regionalism at the subnational level refers to a sense of shared, collective experience and potential source of group identity. In these instances, regions within nations are set against one another, for example, in terms of perceived winners and losers of national and supranational policies allegedly imposed by internationalist elites in London or Washington DC.

Common arguments can be found within these two different national debates, most notably those related to trade and immigration. The winning side in each election employed rhetoric of economic nationalism and nativism. Both elections can be interpreted broadly as showing signs of growing appeal for an atavistic regionalism over a more progressive regionalism (Scott 1998), that is, support for a regionalism of grievance and retreat. The routines of everyday life bind social groups to areas and changes in these patterns contribute to a sense of loss of control that feeds the rhetoric of 'taking back' the local, which in turn often lends support to an atavistic regionalism and nationalism.

Place and region figure prominently on both sides of these debates, for example, in terms of the narratives of loss through globalization and those of regional gain associated with the relaxing the 'shackles' of the nation state on regional development (MacLeod and Jones 2007). Each relates to the topic of this chapter – the geographer's perspective on the experiential qualities of place and region. Both these concepts are at the center of academic geography and, as the above example illustrates, both share the benefits and weaknesses of having broad and imprecise definitions, a trait common to many of geography's core concepts. They are simultaneously part of two very different vocabularies, the scientific and the quotidian.

Geographers continue to grapple with the intellectual tension between theorizing about place and region and using them as descriptors of everyday life. Much has been written about place and region as academic and theoretical concepts, but how do these debates lend insight to understanding human experience? Humans have the experience of place and, more indirectly, region as existential facts; it is the meaning of such experience that is elusive, especially given the cumulative and erosive consequences of time.

4.2   GEOGRAPHY OF EXPERIENCE: WHAT IS IT?

> There is no doubt whatever that all our cognition begins with experience. (Immanuel Kant (1787 [1998], p. 136)

The geography of experience takes as its focus the existential fact of being-in-the-world and thus the everyday relationship of humans and the environment; it is the geography of everyday life. As David Lowenthal (1961, p. 241) wrote in his classic *Annals* article, 'Geography, Experience and Imagination',

> Beyond that of any other discipline. . . the subject matter of geography approximates the world of general discourse; the palpable present, the everyday life of man on earth, is seldom far from our professional concerns.

The contemporary origins of this form of study may be found in phenomenological underpinnings of humanistic geography, although scholarly interest in the topic dates to the origins of geography as an academic discipline. Carl Sauer wrote that the discipline of geography was based on the naïve experience of the differences among places and the desire to understand and explain those differences. For the French geographer, Vidal de la Blache, geography was the science of places. For the German geographer, Alfred Hettner, and his American disciple, Richard Hartshorne, geography was the science of areal differentiation and integration with the concept of the region at its center. They all pointed to the significance of place and region and to the ancient echoes of 'choros' and 'topos', but each of these disciplinary leaders was tied to a naturalist conception of geography that eschewed emphasis on the everyday and thus on matters of meaning and values (Agnew 2011; Berdoulay and Soubeyran 1991; Claval and Entrikin 2004; Curry 2005).

Humanistic geography and its immediate predecessors, for example, David Lowenthal (1961), Hugh Prince (1971), J.K. Wright (1947), J.B. Jackson (1984), and Eric Dardel (1952), offered various modes for making experience central to geographic study. Yi-Fu Tuan's (1977) monograph, *Space and Place: The Perspective of Experience*, offers one of the most explicit statements of this interest. Tuan describes the modes by which humans understand and construct reality. The modes are indeed many and the possibilities seemingly endless. However, the variety has structure, part of which comes from biological elements of perception, part from human cognitive capabilities, and part from language and communication, for example, social interaction.

Humanistic geography appeared to open a natural avenue of study for the discipline, the intellectual 'raw material' of which is drawn from immediately accessible aspects of the world, that is, human environments. Making sense of one's environment seems so intuitively important that the appeal of a geography of experience would seem without question. Yet, for many years the constraints of naturalism and a dominating scientism held back scholars, even those committed to a human or cultural geography (Claval and Entrikin 2004). That constraint weakened in the growing disciplinary pluralism of the late twentieth century, and explorations of the geography of everyday life have expanded in scope in the twenty-first century geography. Questions concerning everyday experiences lead to the exploration of a broad array of overlapping concerns related to the body, performance, representation, affect and emotion, each in its own way adding new dimensions to a geography of experience.

At its most elemental, the geographic perspective involves making sense of presence and absence, in the same way that historians engage remembering and forgetting. The work of these two groups of scholars intersects in the ways in which people spatialize the past and historicize place and region. For the geographer that means not only paying attention to the immediate experience of place and region but also leaving intellectual space for the sediments of meaning that remain a part of place long after the occurrence of the constitutive events. Cognitive understanding of place and region involves recognizing those present and past qualities of place that give character as well as those absent elements that similarly constitute difference.

The most fundamental geographical pedagogy, for example, in a primary school classroom, can be taught simply by asking students to pay closer attention to the world around them, to see and articulate what is there and, to a lesser extent, what is not. The geography teacher may ask students to notice elements of nature that intrude on the students' urban environments; to pay attention to the spaces in which they live their everyday lives; to question why schools and classrooms are different from other everyday spaces in their appearance and in terms of what is permitted to take place. Such experiential exploration at the micro scale resonates with the observations of professional geographers about the unique and accessible qualities of their scholarly efforts. It also resembles the professional craft of geography in terms of requiring judgments concerning selection and significance related to the basic components of place: nature, social relations and culture (Sack 1997).

To go beyond the descriptions of places and to ask why differences exist among them moves the inquirer from the world of experience to that of imagination. For American philosopher John Dewey (1916) this corporeal presence and imaginative absence are what make geography such a key part of civic education within democracies. In Dewey's philosophy of education, students use the experience of the immediate and local to help them imagine other worlds. Such imaginative engagement with unfamiliar environments is what for Dewey made geographical understanding so critical to the intellectual formation of democratic citizens.

Dewey (1916) used the analogy of lighted fence posts at the edges of early twentieth-century American towns and villages to serve as metaphorical beacons illuminating a world beyond the local. Such an analogy seems charmingly quaint to moderns who imagine worlds beyond the earth or spend part of their days in virtual reality. Technology has altered the meaning and experience of the local environment, but its impact is less revolutionary than expansive; less in need of a new ontology than a more extensive ontology; more remodeled than replaced.

   The geographic representation of experience has undergone numerous changes over the last half century, especially as geographers have increasingly engaged different theoretical traditions in the humanities and social sciences. During this period, a previously atheoretical discipline of geography has transformed itself into a hyper-theoretical one directly engaging with most of the prominent theoretical and meta-theoretical positions that have at various times gained currency in the human sciences. As a result of this shift, the vocabulary used by the geographer to describe place and region has broadened and the topics addressed have expanded exponentially to the point at which many current studies of place and region would be unrecognizable to practicing geographers of the mid-twentieth century.

   Such change should neither be surprising nor alarming. The same description would apply to many of the human sciences, although the changes appear to have been to a greater degree in geography than in its sister disciplines, in part because of its unusually broad subject domain (humans and the environment) and its relatively small size. Despite these shifts, some of the core issues of epistemology and ontology have remained the same, questions about culture/nature, mind/body, space/time, wholes/parts, subject/object, universal/particular, among others (Entrikin 1991). Pronouncements about the resolution of these core issues abound, but a quick look beneath the surface of such statements reveals that they are more asserted than argued.

   The most consequential change in the geographer's approach to place and region has been the attention to the active subject and to agency. The human actor as subject and the experience of place were of little concern in traditional regional geography. That neglect changed dramatically in the late twentieth century (Berdoulay and Entrikin 1998; Entrikin and Teeple 2005; Berdoulay et al. 2010; Entrikin 2010). Geography in the twenty-first century, however, has seen a reaction against the active subject through various emphases on non-representation theory, material agency, and the pre-cognitive that bypass the active, coherent subject. This push by some geographers toward anti-humanism precludes the most important functions of place and region as tools of engagement of humans and their environments and in so doing leave these concepts in a position of marginal theoretical utility or value. Before pursuing this theme further, it will be useful to continue to clarify terms and usages.

4.3   SPACE AND PLACE/PLACE AND REGION

> It is sensible, perhaps even irresistible, to assume that human experience begins with space and time and then proceeds to place. Are not space and time universal in scope, and place merely particular? Can place do anything but specify what is already the case in space and time? Or might it be that place is something special, with its own essential structures and modes of experience, even something universal in its own way? (Edward Casey 1996, p. 13)

The concepts of place and region overlap in meaning with other core geographic concepts, such as space, landscape, territory, environment, and nature. Despite their semantic overlap, each has had different and distinctive periods of prominence over the past approximately one hundred and fifty years of the discipline's history. As part of the chorological tradition in geography, the region has had a longer history in the discipline than has place. Place has gained greater attention in the late twentieth and early twenty-first centuries, as geographers moved away from a rigid naturalist conception of their field. Calls for a 'new' regional geography have appeared with regularity but have had uneven discipline-wide traction (Jones and Paasi, 2013).

In the twenty-first century literature, place is most often addressed in relation to space rather than region (Agnew 2011). For example, Yi-Fu Tuan (1977) describes place as involving bodily presence and a sense of being in an environment; in other words, it is experiential. Space is imaginative, a mental reflection on a world freed from the confines of place. Robert Sack (1997) writes of place being carved from space through human projects. It is the set of relations of subject and environment that creates a meaningful world out of the space of nature.

In contrast, space is derivative of place in Edward Casey's philosophy, as suggested above. Place is the intersection of social relations in space for Doreen Massey (1994), and thus to be seen more in terms of a network of social processes rather than a territory. Thus, space is general, place is particular; place is existential, space is conceptual; place is confining, space is liberating; place is gathering, space is extension, and so on. The list of oppositions can be extended, but for the purposes here, place incorporates the experiential; space the cognitive.

Region is also coupled with place but less frequently so. The primary distinction made between the two is that of spatial scale. The precise boundaries separating place and region are impossible to determine, but, like space, region is less experienced than it is imagined and conceived. The many definitions given to region have made it sometimes difficult to disentangle from space, place, territory, landscape (Entrikin 2008). Within geography's spatial tradition and in regional science, the region is a subunit of analysis, a means of areal classification that delimits areal units by means of one or several defining characteristics or functions (Agnew 2013). Territory and region may both be applied to an areal unit, but territory implies the sense of power or control that is not implicit to the concept of region.

Region, place and landscape have overlapped in usage throughout much of modern geography and indeed region and landscape are nearly synonymous in contemporary ecology. The subfield of landscape ecology may in many ways be understood as a science of natural regions. In human geography, the primary distinction has been the textual versus the visual (Entrikin 2011b). All three concepts imply a synthetic construction of drawing elements of the environment together into 'wholes'. Landscapes, like places and unlike regions, may be experienced directly but the experience is mediated through the visual.

As Casey (2002, p. 271; cited in Malpas 2011, p. 5) states:

> Landscapes are, in the final analysis, placescapes; they are congeries of places in the fullest experiential and represented sense. *No landscape without place*; this much we may take to be certainly true.

Landscape may be understood as the visible weave of the place order. Because it is viewed, it is often spectatorial and therefore detached, but as Malpas (2011, p. 21) argues, this need not be the only way we understand landscape:

> The problem of landscape is thus that landscape represents to us, not only our relationship with place, but also the problematic nature of that relationship – a relationship that contains within it involvement and separation, agency and spectacle, self and other.

The overlap of these core geographical concepts draws out specific elements of the geographic experience. Place is encompassing; region is imagined; space is ordered; territory is controlled or controlling, and landscape is seen and is a scene. Each does its conceptual labor at the geographer's primary intellectual intersection – where culture and nature meet.

Until the mid-twentieth century place, region, space, territory and landscape were *objects* of study by geographers. That an active subject is involved was only addressed in relation to a concern with the potential subjectivity of the geographer as a contaminating agent in the domain of objective science. For example, the study of place and region inevitably involved selection – what were the essential elements giving character to a region and place? Without theoretical criteria of significance and therefore of selection or some other verifiable standard, such objectivity remained an unattainable ideal. More recently, however, this boundary has eroded and the active engagement of the subject has played an increasingly prominent role in human geography, both in terms of understanding place and region and the reflexivity of the researcher.

4.4 MEANING, CULTURE AND PLACE

> I think there are two ways in which a place is known and cherished, two ways which may be complementary but which are just as likely to be antipathetic. One is lived, illiterate and unconscious, the other learned, literate, and conscious. (Seamus Heaney 1980, p. 131)

Heaney's first way is one of being, always being in place. It is the situatedness of being, associated most closely with the work of the German philosopher Martin Heidegger, that is the antecedent to thought. In the words of Heidegger scholar Jeff Malpas (2006, p. 39):

> In finding ourselves "in" the world, we find ourselves already "in" a place, already given over to and involved with things, with persons, with our lives. On this basis the central questions of philosophy, questions of being and existence, as well as of ethics and virtue, must themselves take their determination and their starting point from this same place.

This existential quality of being in the world is part of the inherent complexity in the study of place – as both a presence that is 'always there' and as a human construction. How can it be both? Its existential priority comes as Tuan suggested simply from the fact that human consciousness is embodied and as such has a locatable physical presence within an environment. That places are inevitably linked to subjects is evident when one considers how places come into existence through language. Simply the process of naming, of actors giving linguistic order to their environments, transforms the space of nature into the places of cultural worlds (Tuan 1991). That simple linguistic and cognitive act is a first step in the process by which humans continually transform nature and their environments in relation to their projects. Through the primordial tool of place making, humans give meaningful order to nature and thereby address their material and spiritual needs (Sack 1997).

The everyday experience of place as being-already-there gives place an apparent naturalness. Places create a fiction of security through the everyday rhythms that give the experience of place a perceived sense of stability and natural permanence. This comforting yet false perception of constancy is most dramatically challenged by natural disaster, war, toxic contamination that vividly expose the inherent fragility of places as a human construction (Entrikin 2011a). Place destruction through such events is often measured and accounted for solely in the material terms, for example, loss of buildings, destruction of infrastructure, and so on, but the loss of meaning, human projects and possibilities, and ways of life are of equal or greater significance (Till and Kuusisto-Arponen 2015).

Meaning and experience form the basis of culture, and therefore one would expect to find these concerns at the center of a cultural geography. However, a reading of the history of geographic thought suggests otherwise. Late nineteenth and early twentieth-century geography focused almost exclusively on material cultural as an object of study, especially in matters of distribution and diffusion (Claval and Entrikin 2004). The materialist focus has not disappeared, but certainly loosened its grip on the geographic imagination during the late twentieth century only to re-emerge in different guises in twenty-first century geography.

Geographers' interest in experience and meaning creation is not manifested in a unified approach but rather in ways that unfold in many directions. This variety is in part explained through the simple observation that experience does not divide without remainder into theoretical categories or analytic distinctions, but rather comes to the subject as a constant, undifferentiated stream. It is in the process of giving that experience meaning through language that the backcloth of culture becomes evident in the most fundamental way through naming. The influence of phenomenological philosophies in geography helped focus attention on the descriptions of these elemental processes.

4.5   PLACE, SUBJECT, BODY

> . . . as I have argued, emotions are continuous, that is, not contained in a place and in a moment; rather they move with an individual across contexts and mix with thoughts and feelings associated with other experiences. (Nancy Ettlinger 2004, p. 41)

The 'discovery' of the active subject is a distinctive feature of late twentieth and early twenty-first century geography, but it has not been a simple and unambiguous topic in geographic thought (Entrikin 2010). The interest developed unevenly over many different dimensions. The early signs were evident in the 1960s, for example, in Lowenthal's essay and J.B. Jackson's essays on landscape, and were brought to prominence in the 1970s with humanistic geography (Entrikin and Tepple 2006). These early developments were followed by the concern with a more politicized subject, one buffeted by the disciplining forces of societal power structures, for example, as expressed in feminist geographies (Massey 1994).

Following Laclau and Mouffe (1985), post-structuralist geographers turned the politicized subject, or decentered subject, into a 'subject position', a move that shifts emphasis from the active subject to the process of subjectification (Thrift 2007). Subject positions do not refer to individuals. Instead, individuals occupy and move in and out of subject positions. The individual subject then disappears in all but name in the materialized and agent-less or agent-full (depending on one's perspective) world of non-representational theory and the geography of affect (McCormack 2017). Agent-less because the active subject disappears, and agent-full because of material agency and the agency of things, which gives agency to all animate and inanimate objects, not only to bodies but also to things.

The irony of these developments is that part of the motivation appears to be the desire for a greater verisimilitude with the world of experience before thought. That is, they become attempts to approximate a closer description of experience, but one that diminishes the geographical in ways similar to Ettlinger's comment above. Emotions and the experience in which they occur are part of a holistic and continuous flow, altered and inevitably disassembled through the concepts scholars apply. In all neo-Bergsonian, process-oriented meta-theories, spatial concepts like place and region become artificial and distorting constructs, attempts to make static that which is dynamic and to hold as unchanging that which is constantly in the process of becoming. The recently revived interest by geographers in the philosophy of Maurice Merleau-Ponty, an earlier touch-stone for humanistic geography, shows another dimension of this shift, one that moves from a subject encountering the world through experience to a pre-experiential realm of a body in space.

Thrift (2011, p. 20) citing Toadvine (2009, p. 18) describes this shift in terms of a reformulated phenomenology:

> We can think of a number of comparatively recent ways of doing this. One is the later work of Merleau-Ponty. . . In particular, his account of space moves from one in which all orientation derives from the being of the human subject to a pre-experiential space which is formed at the confluence of body and world which is simultaneously a being's own orientation, its striving toward expression.

The experiential studies of early humanistic geography were of active, centered subjects giving meaning to their environments. The centered subject of humanistic geography is one who is actively interpreting and engaging the world. Such a subject is a relatively autonomous agent with the capability and power to create and interpret meaning in ways that affect the environment through either individual agency or collective action based on intersubjective communication and cooperation.

The signature studies of that time, interpreting landscape (Cosgrove 1984), seeing the social geography of the city (Relph 1976), giving symbolic significance to the natural environment (Tuan 1974), all involved active interpreters, subjects who both were shaped by and actively shaped their environments. In the politicization of the subject, this centered subject gave way to a decentered, fragmented subject, less an autonomous actor than a cipher shaped through the powerful interplay and contingent intersection of impersonal social forces. Power relations are the motor behind the creation of such subject positions and themes of domination, oppression, transgression become the primary focus in positing processes of subjectification.

Pile (2010, p. 7) describes such a shift in the move from humanist to feminist geographies:

> If humanistic geography offers a means to describe people's rich experiences of place and emotions, then feminist geographers politicised it. . . Where humanistic geography tended to posit a coherent, bounded, self-aware and universal human subject, feminist geography was illuminating the incoherences, permeabilities, opaquenesses and specificities of human subjectivity.

The decentered position followed from earlier, social reductionist arguments of those seeking to limit place to a nexus of social forces, from Bourdieu's habitus, to Giddens' locale and Massey's place/space (Entrikin 2007). It has been further explored by post-structuralists and post-humanists, who have transformed the subject from an active agent to a bio-physical presence through an emphasis on embodiment over subjectivity. In such arguments, the body itself shifts from being a material, natural object to becoming an 'experiencing agent' (Csordas 1994, p. 3). This shift has meant that geographers have blurred distinctions among terms such as, self, person, body. Both mind and body become subject and agent.

The consequences for geography of these meta-theoretical shifts are many, especially for the concepts of place and region. Advocates of non-representational theory empha-size the flow of experience and process and thereby transform spatial concepts into mere conceptual ciphers or abstract containers. Despite its name, non-representational theory neither eschews representation nor offers theoretical insight, but instead offers as a goal description of the flow of experience, description that opens itself to novelty and emergence (Pile 2010).

The flow of experience as process presents far too much to be captured through theory, and this excess is what is best understood in descriptions of emergence (Dewsbury et al. 2002, p. 437). Non-representational theorists are not invested in understanding the subject as the source of meaning creation, but rather conceive of a world of contingent relationships and encounters, seemingly faint echoes of what was once referred to as social physics, where all elements of the world human and nonhuman, subjects and objects, encounter each other as random particles intersecting in seemingly unpredictable ways. These intersections may be largely unpredictable, but proponents suggest that they are indeed also manipulable (Thrift 2011). The lack of an active subject in these studies appears to take geography back to an earlier era, when humans were conceptualized largely as geological agents interacting with other biophysical causal agents in transform-ing natural environments.

Place and region lose significance in such formulations in similar ways to their fate in the early stages of the positivist spatial analysis revolution in geography in the mid-1960s in which space and location reduced place and region to uni-dimensional locations and areal classifications. Places become moments of chance intersections and regions a larger scale variant of the same (Thrift 1999). The humanistic subject engaged in the continual process of meaning creation and interpretation becomes an object of romantic nostalgia, an unfortunate intellectual loss in the name of meta-theoretical reduction (Tomaney 2013).

This loss is clearly evident in the geography of affect. As Pile (2010, p. 11) notes:

> In affectual geography, the body is not seen as personal, but as transpersonal. More, the body is used to challenge the expression of emotions: the body, in this sense, is the location of the non-psychological. The body is not used to solicit telling testimony about people's lives, instead it becomes a device that enables the researcher to reveal the trans-human, the non-cognitive, the inexpressible, that underlies and constitutes social life – albeit unknowingly.

When disconnected from the active subject and individual agent, place, as an assemblage of animate and inanimate objects in dynamic, contingent and emergent relations becomes an object of seemingly infinite descriptive potential but of marginal theoretical importance. This diminished capacity is not unlike the status of the place concept in early twentieth-century geography, but, unlike that period, the view is shared by a subgroup supporting a particular meta-theoretical position and is not discipline-wide.

Tim Cresswell (2014, p. 20) has attempted to blend these various approaches in a synthetic concept of place based in a 'renewed practice of place writing' that takes the positives of the chorological tradition and incorporates them with the insights of the more theoretically informed geography of the present day. His advocacy for a non-reductive, synthetic, 'meso-theoretical interpretive framework for the analysis of place' (Cresswell 2014, p. 3) is inclusive but leaves open the same questions that have faced past generations of geographers. That is, what guides the geographer in determining criteria of significance and selection in terms of the presences and absences that determine the character and consequences of place and region? This question has been a primary motivation for theorizing place and region but has been a persistent challenge, not only for geographers but also for social theorists, for example, Henri Lefebvre (Entrikin and Berdoulay 2005).

4.6   PLUS ÇA CHANGE. . .

> Thus, regions appear to have persistent relevance and allure, both for academics and policy
> practitioners alike. Then again, understandings of what a region is and does have shifted
> considerably in the course of decades. (Anssi Paasi and Jonathan Metzger 2017, p. 27)

As the many meanings of place flood the broad fields of geography, the various interpretations of region remain largely channeled within economic and political geography. The persistence and viability of region as a research concept is no doubt due to both its semantic breadth and its practical utility (Entrikin 2008). Its continued rhetorical and social power stem from this ambiguity that gives it great capacity as a potential source of collective identity (Paasi 2003). The utilitarian value of regions has been an important part of the concept's legacy in geography and was well understood within geography's chorological tradition (Hartshorne 1959).

The multiple meanings of region are in keeping with its many different functions (Paasi and Metzger 2017). Like place, the region may be seen as a tool for human projects albeit at a larger scale. This pragmatic perspective on place and region reflects the fundamental humanism of geography that is captured succinctly and simply in the definition of geography as the study of how people make worlds out of nature. The region plays a role in this process, whether one is talking about the unique regions of chorology (e.g. Hart 1982), state planning regions (e.g. Keating 2017), regional consciousness and political identity (e.g. Paasi 2003), or regional biopolitics (Painter 2012).

As discussions of place have moved toward greater concern with processes, flows, and networks, so too have discussions of regions. Concerns of regional development, regional linkages in a global economy, and regional identity as a contributor to national and international (e.g. the EU) politics all involve ever-changing relationships that are increasingly described within a dynamic global framework (Jones and Paasi 2013). One consequence of this shift in framework has been definitional change from a territorial or cartographic concept of a region to a more relational concept that emphasizes connectivity of loosely bounded networks over cohesive, bounded areal units (Harrison 2013; Painter 2008;

MacLeod and Jones 2007). The choice between these different conceptions of the region appears to be less a matter of ontological rectitude and more a practical concern related to the topic under consideration, once again demonstrating persistence through flexible meaning (Jones and Paasi 2013; Paasi 2010).

Agnew (2013, p. 15) has succinctly summarized the various directions of regional research and the meta-theoretical and theoretical debates that have surrounded the concept of region and concluded that:

> The main lesson to be drawn from this analysis is that we should collectively invest in the plural of "regional logics," tailoring usage to the problems at hand, rather than in a singular logic that simply replaces the romance of the nation-state with an equally simple and one-size-fits-all alternative geographical unit of account such as the ocean basin, the civilization, the administrative region or the global city-region. All of these. . . have their place.

4.7   CONCLUSION

The experience of place and the imaginative utility of region have been fundamental themes of modern geography. The variety of ways in which these themes can be explored is quite extraordinary, and increasingly so as time passes. This variety is in large part a consequence of the semantic elasticity of the terms themselves, and, similar to other core geographic concepts, their application to the ever-negotiated and transforming culture/nature border.

These traditionally significant concepts in geography will continue to be semantically 'stretched' by the expanding theoretical and meta-theoretical smorgasbord that is twenty-first century geographical research. Despite the valiant efforts of many who write about this complexity and attempt to draw together the various competing formulations, there appears to be little hope for a sophisticated convergence of meaning and use; even less so for place than for region. A more likely path is one of the continued divergence of place studies into the humanistic realm in association with the research on the given cultural issues of the day, such as religious experience, environmental engagement, collective memory, and identity (e.g. Howe 2016; Tweed 2006; Till and Kuusisto-Arponen 2015; Puleo 2012). The region will likely continue to serve its pragmatic economic and political functions as noted above. Their fragmentation in use in professional geography will not diminish their key role in everyday language to describe individual and collective experience. As elemental spatial tropes, place and region are how humans see and narrate their worlds.

4.8   REFERENCES

Agnew, J. (2011), 'Space and place', in J. Agnew and D. Livingstone (eds), *The Sage Handbook of Geographical Knowledge*, London: Sage, pp. 316–330.
Agnew, J. (2013), 'Arguing with regions', *Regional Studies*, **47** (1), 6–17.
Berdoulay, V. and O. Soubeyran (1991), 'Lamarck, Darwin et Vidal: aux fondements naturalistes de la géographie', *Annales de Géographie*, **100** (561), 617–634.
Berdoulay, V. and J.N. Entrikin (1998), 'Lieu et sujet: perspectives théoriques', *L'Espace géographique*, **27** (2), 111–121.

Berdoulay, V., D. Laplace-Treyture and X. Arnaud de Sartre (2010), 'La question du sujet et la géographie', *Cahiers de géographie du Québec*, **54** (153), 397–418.
Casey, E. (1996), 'How to get from space to place in a fairly short stretch of time: phenomenological prolegomena', in S. Feld and K. Basso (eds), *Senses of Place*, Santa Fe, NM: School of American Research Press, pp. 13–52.
Casey, E. (2002), *Re-Presenting Place: Landscape Painting and Maps*, Minneapolis: University of Minnesota Press.
Claval, P. and J. Entrikin (2004), 'Place and landscape between continuity and change: perspectives on the cultural approach', in G. Benko and U. Strohmayer (eds), *Human Geography: A History for the Twenty-First Century*, London: Arnold, pp. 25–46.
Cosgrove, D. (1984), *Social Formations and Symbolic Landscapes*, Totowa, NJ: Barnes and Noble.
Cresswell, T. (2014), 'Place', in R. Lee, N. Castree, R. Kitchin, V. Lawson, A. Paasi, C. Philo, S. Radcliffe, S. Roberts, and C. Withers (eds), *The Sage Handbook of Human Geography*, London: Sage, pp. 3–21.
Csordas, T. (1994), *Embodiment and Experience: The Existential Ground of Culture and Self*, Cambridge: Cambridge University Press.
Curry, M.R. (2005), 'Toward a geography of a world without maps: lessons from Ptolemy and postal codes', *Annals of the Association of American Geographers*, **95** (3), 680–691.
Dardel, E. (1952), *L'Homme et la terre*, Paris: Presses Universitaires de France.
Dewey, J. (1916), *Democracy and Education: An Introduction to the Philosophy of Education*, New York: Macmillan.
Dewsbury, J.D., P. Harrison, M. Rose, and J. Wylie (2002), 'Enacting geographies', *Geoforum*, **33** (4), 437–440.
Entrikin, J.N. (1991), *The Betweenness of Place: Towards a Geography of Modernity*, Baltimore, MD: Johns Hopkins University Press.
Entrikin, J.N. and V. Berdoulay (2005), 'The Pyrenees as place: Lefebvre as guide', *Progress in Human Geography*, **29** (2), 129–147.
Entrikin, J.N. and J. Tepple (2006), 'Humanism and democratic place-making', in S. Aiken and G. Valentine (eds), *Approaches in Human Geography*, London: Sage, pp. 30–41.
Entrikin, J.N. (2007), 'Place destruction and cultural trauma', in J. Alexander and I. Reed (eds), *Culture, Society and Democracy: The Interpretive Approach*, Boulder, CO: Paradigm Press, pp. 163–179.
Entrikin, J.N. (ed.) (2008), *Regions: Critical Essays in Human Geography*, Aldershot: Ashgate.
Entrikin, J.N. (2010), 'Réintroduire le soi dans la subjectivité', *Cahiers de géographie du Québec*, **54** (153), 419–428.
Entrikin, J.N. (2011a), 'Regions and regionalism', in J. Agnew and D. Livingstone (eds), *The Sage Handbook of Geographical Knowledge*, London: Sage, pp. 344–356.
Entrikin, J.N. (2011b), 'Geographic landscapes and natural disaster', in J. Malpas (ed.), *The Place of Landscape: Concepts, Contexts, Studies*, Cambridge, MA: MIT Press, pp. 113–130.
Ettlinger, N. (2004), 'Toward a critical theory of untidy geographies: the spatiality of emotions in consumption and production', *Feminist Economics*, **10** (3), 21–54.
Harrison, J. (2013), 'Configuring the new "regional world": on being caught between territory and networks', *Regional Studies*, **47** (1), 55–74.
Hart, J. (1982) 'The highest form of the geographer's art', *Annals of the Association of American Geographers*, **72** (1), 1–29.
Hartshorne, R. (1959), *Perspective on the Nature of Geography*, Chicago: Rand McNally.
Heaney, S. (1980), *Preoccupations, Selected Prose, 1968–78*, London: Faber and Faber.
Howe, N. (2016), *Landscapes of the Secular: Law, Religion and American Sacred Space*, Chicago: University of Chicago Press.
Jackson, J. (1984), *Discovering the Vernacular Landscape*, New Haven, CT: Yale University Press.
Jones, M. and A. Paasi (2013), 'Regional world(s): advancing the geography of regions', *Regional Studies*, **47** (1), 1–5.
Kant, I. (1787), *Critique of Pure Reason*, P. Guyer and A. Wood (trans. and eds) 1998, Cambridge: Cambridge University Press.
Keating, M. (2017), 'Contesting European regions', *Regional Studies*, **51** (1), 9–18.
Laclau, E. and C. Mouffe (1985), *Hegemony and Socialist Strategy: Toward a Radical Democratic Politics*, London: Verso.
Lowenthal, D. (1961), 'Geography, experience and imagination: towards a geographical epsitemology', *Annals of the Association of American Geographers*, **51** (3), 241–260.
MacLeod, G. and M. Jones (2007), 'Territorial, scalar, networked, connected: in what sense a "regional world"', *Regional Studies*, **41** (9), 1177–1191.
Malpas, J. (2006), *Heidegger's Topology*, Cambridge: Polity.
Malpas, J. (2011), 'Place and the problem of landscape', in J. Malpas (ed.), *The Place of Landscape: Concepts, Contexts, Studies*, Cambridge, MA: MIT Press, pp. 3–26.

Massey, D. (1994), *Space, Place and Gender*, Minneapolis: University of Minnesota Press.

McCormack, D. (2017), 'The circumstances of post-phenomenological life worlds', *Transactions of the Institute of British Geographers*, **42** (1), 2–13.

Paasi, A. (2003), 'Region and place: regional identity in question', *Progress in Human Geography*, **27** (4), 475–485.

Paasi, A. (2010), 'Regions are social constructs, but who or what constructs them? Agency in question', *Environment and Planning A*, **42** (10), 2296–2301.

Paasi, A. and J. Metzger (2017), 'Foregrounding the region', *Regional Studies*, **51** (1), 19–30.

Painter, J. (2008), 'Cartographic anxiety and the search for regionality', *Environment and Planning A*, **40** (2), 342–361.

Painter, J. (2012), 'Regional biopolitics', *Regional Studies*, **47**, (8), 1235–1248.

Pile, S. (2010), 'Emotions and affect in recent human geography', *Transactions of the Institute of British Geographers*, **35** (1), 5–20.

Prince, H. (1971), 'Real, imagined and abstract worlds of the past', *Progress in Human Geography*, **3**, 1–86.

Puleo, T. (2012), *The Valtellina and UNESCO*, Lanham, MD, Lexington Books.

Relph, E. (1976), *Place and Placelessness*, London: Pion.

Sack, R. (1997), *Homo Geographicus: A Framework for Action, Awareness and Moral Concern*, Baltimore, MD: Johns Hopkins University Press.

Scott, A. (1998), *Regions and The World Economy: The Coming Shape of Global Production, Competition, and The Political Order*, Oxford: Oxford University Press.

Thrift, N. (1999), 'Steps to an ecology of place', in J. Allen and D. Massey (eds), *Human Geography Today*, Cambridge: Polity Press, pp. 124–151.

Thrift, N. (2007), *Non-Representational Theory: Space, Politics, Affect*, London: Routledge.

Thrift, N. (2011), 'Lifeworld Inc – and what to do about it', *Environment and Planning D: Society and Space*, **29** (1), 5–26.

Till, K. and A.-K. Kuusisto-Arponen (2015), 'Towards responsible geographies of memory: complexities of place and the ethics of remembering', *Erdkunde*, **69** (4), 291–306.

Toadvine, T. (2009), *Merleau-Ponty's Philosophy of Nature*, Evanston, IL: Northwestern University Press.

Tomaney, J. (2013), 'Parochialism – a defence', *Progress in Human Geography*, 37 (5), 658–672.

Tuan, Y.-F. (1974), *Topophilia: A Study of Environmental Perception, Attitudes and Values*, Englewood Cliffs, NJ: Prentice Hall.

Tuan, Y.-F. (1977), *Space and Place: The Perspective of Experience*, Minneapolis, MN: University of Minnesota Press.

Tuan, Y.-F. (1991), 'Language and the making of place: a narrative-descriptive approach', *Annals of the Association of American Geographers*, **81** (4), 684–696.

Tweed, T. (2006), *Crossing and Dwelling: A Theory of Religion*, Cambridge, MA: Harvard University Press.

Wright, J. (1947), 'Terrae incognitae: the place of imagination in geography', *Annals of the Association of American Geographers*, **37** (1), 1–15.

5. Scale and territory, and the difference capitalism makes
Kevin Cox

5.1 INTRODUCTION

Scale and territory as a couplet have a curious history in Anglophone human geography. They seem to have marched in tandem with changing awareness of globalization. The most recent interest is undoubtedly connected to the widespread publicity afforded the growth of trade and international investment in the world since the 1970s. There was an earlier phase associated with the first globalization that came to a halt with the First World War. This is the classical geopolitics of Mackinder and Bowman (Cox 2013). But then there was silence. As countries closed in on themselves, geographers seemed to lose interest in the topics. Earlier, power and space had been taken for granted. Later when the connection was rediscovered, it would be different. Human geography lost its innocence in a welter of self-questioning. This, of course, is to talk about globalization in an absolute sense. It is useful here, though, to think of it in relative terms: not of the local and the global, therefore, but of the *more* local and the *more* global, which is the meaning that seems to have caught on, if without explicit acknowledgement.

Since the 1970s, writing on the topic of scale and, often derivatively, if not explicitly, territory, has flourished. It has become a central preoccupation. It has also become a matter of some controversy. Clearing away the underbrush and identifying some stable mooring posts through which to navigate the topic therefore seems in order. The chapter commences with an historical résumé before moving on to the recent debates that scale and territory and their mutual imbrication have incited. This then paves the way for a discussion of some complementary windows on the topic with a view to deepening our understanding.

5.2 HISTORICAL BACKGROUND

The idea of scale has a long history in human geography; the idea of territory, less so, at least in terms that are explicit. Once territory made a serious appearance and its determinant conditions were understood, then the connection with scale was not far behind. By the last two decades of the twentieth century, the basic lineaments of a theorization of scale and territory were clear. This was a materialist understanding that saw geographic scales in relational terms – the global included in the local and the local in the global – and the tensions between them inherent in the contradiction between fixity and mobility that generated territoriality. Scale would assume institutional forms: multinationals, international currency exchange regimes, the scale divisions of labor of firms, state hierarchies. There would be scalar relations like those between neighborhood organizations and

57

city hall, and supplicant countries and the IMF. In other words, the connection forged between territory and scale took off from a recognition that questions of power could not be expunged from understanding in human geography. As the posts asserted themselves in human geography, this was a view of scale and territory that would be challenged.

Geographic scale has a long history in the field. It was at least implicit in country-studies where internal differentiation was handled by breaking the country down into regions. Regions would be divided into sub-regions and sub-regions divided still further (Haggett 1965, pp. 263–264). This would be the basis for the insight that the different conditions of variation over space had appropriately different scales of operation; climate operated at a different level than, say, soil type (for example, Bird 1956).

The spatial-quantitative work of the 1960s gave precision to the idea of scalar variation (Haggett 1965, pp. 265–269). Variance decomposition methods could then be, and were used to show how the total variation of, say population density, could be broken down into percentage 'contributions' from county, state or region level (Moellering and Tobler 1972). This was and remains particularly useful where there is a strong theory regarding the distribution of the variance (for example, Stokes 1965). But while there was advance in terms of precision, and that precision in turn raised important theoretical questions regarding scale, as in how scale entered into different location decisions, there were serious limitations. For example, with respect to questions of power, and since Mackinder and Bowman and the hey-day of classical geopolitics, human geography had shown a remarkable insouciance. Only with the critique of the spatial-quantitative work that took off after 1970 would this begin to change. The most analytically penetrating work of that period was Marxist. It should be no surprise, therefore, that a contribution heralding change in how geographic scale was viewed would come from that direction. This was Peter Taylor's paper of 1981, 'A Materialist Framework for Political Geography', which from the standpoint of scale was utterly revolutionary in how it viewed the question: a move away from the relative concepts of space that had dominated hitherto – a concern with the effects of scale as area or distance – to a more relational one; and a recognition of the central importance of social process.

Taylor's contribution had two points of departure. The first was Wallerstein's world systems theory, which in turn reflected the interest in Marxist geography initiated at the beginning of the 1970s. The choice of Wallerstein is highly significant since it represented recognition of the centrality of the global scale to what transpired at other scales, including that of the state which had, up to that point, been so prominent in the work of political geographers. The second condition for his intervention was the way in which political geographers had tended to organize their writings around three particular geographic scales: the global, the national and the urban. From this followed his suggestion that 'the threefold arrangement has an important general function within modern capitalism' and that 'we need a political economy of scale to unravel this situation.'

This is the background to his positing of relations between these scales starting with that of the world economy. He defined this as the scale of reality: 'real' because this is the scale at which accumulation and therefore production is organized, reflecting the Marxist priority accorded to the latter. The urban, on the other hand, is the scale at which accumulation is experienced since this is where people live their daily lives. So accumulation is experienced in the form of what people have to spend, whether or not they will be able to find work, pay the mortgage and the like. Finally, the national is the scale of ideology. This is the scale at which interpretations of experience at the urban level are dispensed, in nationalistic forms, for example, all with a view to justifying subordination to the accumulation process which is going on at the global scale.

Taylor's paper represented a major step forward in how geographers viewed geographic scale. Scale and scalar relations were conditioned by social organization. But for a view inscribed in a thoroughly relational view of space it was not quite there. This is because there is a functionalism about his argument that obscures the way in which scales and scalar relations are constructed: how they don't just come about because they happen to work but because people set about producing them and making them work; and they do this in virtue of particular sets of social relations like those defined by Wallerstein's world system. In addition, the close relation with territory now common in discussions of scale was absent and there are good reasons for this. Taylor's intellectual pedigree had been the world systems school of Marxism. This emphasized the sphere of circulation. Arriving at a materialist understanding of territory would require something different; the subordination of circulation to production that is the hallmark of classical Marxism. This would be the contribution of David Harvey in his 1985 paper, 'The Geopolitics of Capitalism.'

While it is unclear what influence Harvey had on it, by the 1990s there was certainly a common understanding of scale and territory and their mutual relationship. This emphasized relations of a vertical sort between higher and lower levels and a nested relation of differently scaled spaces. The way the state was organized territorially gave this idea concrete shape, as did the then current imaginary of relations between the global and the local. There may also have been some tendency, if only implicit, to put higher levels in a determinant role. This was a view that would then be subject to critique.

5.3   DEBATES

In the first decade of the new century there was a flurry of critical scrutiny, even attack. Papers by Amin (2002), Marston et al. (2005), and Allen both on his own (2010) and with Cochrane (2007, 2012) have been prominent. There are some common themes. They also seem to owe a lot in their understanding of the scale issue to Massey's work: in particular her view of how the construction of places is conditioned by the chance juxtaposition of a more extensive geography – actually *historical* geography – of relations (Massey 1999, 2005). A major focus of criticism has been the hierarchical understanding of scale: how scales are supposedly ordered in subordinate–dominant relations as in that between the local and the global or between local government and central government. A related one has been the territorial emphasis of scalar thinking. The power of the network then becomes the central consideration in destabilizing notions of scale and territory.

Scalar thinking is to emphasize vertical relations. The image of nested agencies of the state at different levels with those at higher levels constraining, even determining, what those at lower levels do is a common one. The contrast is with the horizontality of networks which interfere with top-down determination, opening up the possibility of resolutions of a more contingent, open character. Verticality also implies a very centered view of the world: the upper levels of the state are where the important things happen and decisions are then dispersed to lower levels. Networks, rather, are seen as a vehicle for the decentralization of decision-making; more democratic therefore. Similar arguments are made in the case of globalization and *its* politics of scale.

As far as the territorial frame of scalar thinking is concerned, networks, implicitly defined as horizontal, are seen as an agent of de-territorialization: as facilitating the dissolution of local attachments, the intimate local connections that firms often enter into and other forms of local or place dependence (Amin 2002). Territorial action, exclusion, inclusion, locally focused forms of development therefore dissolve away as dependence on the local, material and affective, is loosened. Firms become multinational; labor markets, at least for some, become continental, even of global proportions. Castells' space of flows (1983) is the most reductive of these arguments. In turn they have led to new claims about the relation between space and place: how place as a horizon of action in people's lives is being undermined by space.

Much of this critical literature has drawn impetus from post-structural and post-modern forms of thinking and this, as such, represents a rejection of the sort of political economy embraced by historical materialists. Scalar thinking is now seen as a particular form of discourse: a discourse for some and to the disadvantage of many; as a positioning for some sort of leverage. It is not, in other words, the way in which capitalist states, in virtue of the limits and possibilities of the capitalist space economy *have* to be organized. So too is it with territory. As Allen and Cochrane remark:

> It would seem that the language of territorial politics is not only stubborn, but equally that it cannot simply be wished away by some conceptual wand, since it is itself a powerful political construction. Assemblies, regional development agencies, and the like, are performed as territorial entities that try to hold down the fluid elements of global life in the general interest of their "regions" – seeking to generate fixity through "processes of government and governance." (Allen and Cochrane 2007, pp. 1162–1163)

As I have argued elsewhere, I believe these claims to be quite mistaken (see Cox 2013). Hierarchy is swept away in favor of networks; the vertical in favor of the horizontal. Necessity of a structural sort is replaced lock stock and barrel by contingency. But in a world where the domination of a particular social relation, that of capital is so evident, and to which the mass of the population is subordinated, and whose subordination has to be reproduced, this cannot be. If the critics had a point, it was that understandings of scale had hitherto been insufficiently relational. But to then argue that relationality was confined to the horizontal was a step too far. How therefore might we understand scale and territory in their mutual relations? It is to that question that we now turn by adumbrating some principles. These start, logically enough, with a brief discussion of social foundations.

5.4   SOME PRINCIPLES

5.4.1   The Capitalist Form of Development

In any discussion of scale and territory in the contemporary world, the capitalist form of development and its logics, including its spatial logics, has to be the point of departure. Fundamentally capitalism is a class relation: a relation between those who have the money to put the production process in motion by buying the necessary means of production and hiring the workers; and the vast majority comprising those who, stripped of the means of production, have to make themselves available for hire. It is also a contradictory relation, impelling capital to accumulate and, towards that end, to utterly revolutionize society in all its different aspects. This is mentioned at the outset since in many discussions of scale, particularly as they touch on globalization, it is competition rather than class that receives emphasis. This is mistaken. Competition cannot be treated as a *deus ex machina*. It, and its dominant form of competing in the form of costs of production is conditional on a very particular class relation. The drive to accumulate is crucial for everything else that happens but it is founded first and foremost on the confrontation between those with the money to buy the conditions of production and those without.[1]

5.4.2   Spaces of Circulation and Institutions

The historically unprecedented way in which capital has been able to develop the productive forces is registered by remarkable increases in the productivity of workers. Central to this has been the way in which production has been progressively socialized: the way, that is, in which production by individuals with limited forms of cooperation with others, producing for themselves, has given way to an all-round dependence of one worker on another. One key to this has been the development of the division of labor: between firms, between regions and so on. A second aspect of the socialization of production has then been the use of means of production in common: steel mills, container ports, assembly lines, railroad networks and cities with their shared physical and social infrastructures.

In consequence, the socialization of production assumes a geographic form in what might be called a space of circulation, albeit one where circulation is a moment of the production process. This is inevitably characterized by a certain geographic scale – urban, regional, national, for example – within which commodities, at various stages of their production circulate. The division of labor acquires a spatial form: a *geographic* division of labor as different places specialize in different products or perform different functions in a single labor process – from component producers to assemblers along with auxiliary functions like the headquarters one and research and development. Means of production-in-common, like railroads and highway networks, then facilitate this space of circulation.

Spaces of circulation have to be regulated: scale in the sense in which the idea is being developed here, always assumes institutional forms. We know that a metropolitan area has emerged as a unity of production and circulation when new, coordinating institutions, like regional chambers of commerce, public transit authorities, regional planning organizations and the like take shape. But this then raises the question of regulation (and implicitly of scale) for whom? In light of recent claims about globalization as a sphere of unfettered competition, this merits emphasis as we will see.

5.4.3   Scalar Differentiation and Territory

The recent talk has been of globalization. But as long as capital has existed it has been constructing more extensive spaces of circulation; new relations between more local configurations of activity and more global ones. New, more extended geographic divisions of labor emerge alongside the old, which then get transformed in their turn. Likewise, there have been new forms of agglomeration – new shared means-of-production, in other words – with their own transformed geographic divisions of labor: back offices and office parks in the suburbs, and a post-industrial downtown.

Alongside these developments there are new institutional dispensations; new regulatory practices, partly state initiatives, partly those of private agents, firms, labor movements, and often meshing in various ways – new distributions of powers and responsibilities creating new structures of governance. These institutional forms bear emphasis; arguments about globalization and tensions with those who are dependent on structures of relations at smaller geographic scales, often proceed as if the global is a sphere of unfettered market relations; an image of capital and commodities moving from country to country in an unregulated manner and challenging the reproduction of regulated spheres at national scales, as with labor laws; a sphere beyond human intervention, that is. But this is clearly incorrect. The more global is always a sphere of regulation: the Bretton Woods agreements were an obvious case in point, but while they disintegrated in the early 1970s, what succeeded them was far from an institutional void. There have always been mutually agreed-on ways of regulating international currency exchange going back to the gold standard to the current accepted practices of allowing values to be determined by forces of supply and demand or pegging them to that of a major international currency like that of the dollar. One could also argue that debate about capital controls has never gone away. One can certainly complain about the details of the regulations and the fact that they are always for some and not others, but to claim a sphere of market activity that is entirely lacking in any social constitution is absurd. Scalar relations are always about institutions and intervening in them. It is this that allows us to talk about a politics of scale. But this in turn is predicated on the idea of territory.

For as the new emerges alongside the old, the contradictions of capitalist development assume a geographic form: tensions between the more local and the more global, as David Harvey (1985) has made so clear. It is out of this tension that ideas of territory emerge. Production requires fixity in the form of physical and social infrastructures, including those of the individual firm. But accumulation also requires that the value extracted at a particular place be free to be laid out for the conditions of production regardless of location. The result is that value may no longer flow through those infrastructures threatening the amortization of investments in industrial plant, airports and the like; while removing the advantages of a particular ensemble of localized social relations. Labor faces its own challenges; certainly those of home ownership and the devaluation that can result as a local economic base implodes, but also the increasing irrelevance of local connections, with friends and kin, to finding work.

The upshot, as David Harvey has emphasized, has been the emergence of coalitions of forces behind attempts to protect and enhance values in place; to meet the challenges to 'our city, our country, the West Midlands, etc.' In other words, a discourse of territory can emerge in the context of plans to recapitalize, to refinance, and to restructure the local/regional/national economy, or whatever. And I use the word 'discourse' deliberately since the term can conceal more than it reveals and often quite intentionally. Interests get defined territorially, bringing different class forces behind a common banner. This can then lay the foundation for a distinct politics of scale.

5.4.4 Scale, Territory and Geographically Uneven Development

Differentially scaled institutional regimes create opportunity structures for territorially defined interests. This is a condition for a politics of scale that is widely acknowledged as in practices of scale 'jumping' (Cox 1998). But equally, if not more significantly, institutions specific to a particular scale become something to be challenged, disputed, reworked. Institutional regimes are always stakes for territorially defined interests. They work for some and not for others, or they can be transformed in order to provide an enhanced competitive advantage.

A graphic instance played out in the context of the East Asian financial crisis of the latter years of the 1990s (Wade 1996; Wade and Veneroso 1998). Commitment to a Japanese model of economic development led to short-term liquidity crises for firms and this in turn to financial shortfalls. This then led to IMF interventions which were, in effect, designed to impose a quite different model that was more congenial to American practice. American corporations had long chafed at the way in which adoption of the Japanese model made penetration of respective domestic markets more difficult, while increasing the competitive capacity of their firms in international markets. So the crisis provided a nice opportunity to do serious damage: a making of the global from the bottom-up, in other words, and an IMF which, while nominally an international organization, works to the advantage of some rather than all.

This example also underlines the way in which territory is not just defensive; it is also a base for geographic expansion and creating new spaces of circulation – new opportunities for American firms to dismantle the statist policies of countries like Thailand that had made it hard, among other things, for foreign takeovers of their banks. Geographic expansion via some strategic decentralization can be a means of protecting an existing territorial base: decanting the less skilled/de-skilled parts of the labor process elsewhere, while keeping the skilled parts which are less easy to move; in other words, a protective and selective hollowing out of part of the production process that is a form of vertical disintegration.

What this suggests is that scale and territory are always about uneven development: about protecting and enhancing some local advantage while forcing disadvantage on to others elsewhere. It is, in short, about struggles for local/regional/national hegemony in wider spaces of circulation. We can see this in current debates about London's dominant position within Great Britain (Massey 2007). The same occurs at metropolitan scales, where central cities in the US have been able to subordinate suburban peripheries to their purposes to quite variable degrees (Cox 2010; Cox and Jonas 1993). As David Harvey (2000) indicated, 'globalization discourse' tended to overlook this sort of relationship.[2] It also tended to encourage a view that the global was, causally, *the* crucial level; which brings us in turn to scale and territory as a discourse and the latter's ideological significance.

5.4.5   Scale and Territory as Discourse

The media, the politicians and the pundits don't talk about scale as such, or jumping scale, or territory, but they are replete with references to 'our country', 'what is good for Ohio', 'the challenges of globalization', 'federal neglect of our cities', struggles between older and newer suburbs played out at state level, and the grim reality of having to compete with cities and regions elsewhere. So on the one hand, a rhetoric of necessity imposed from without, some alien force of a more global political economy bearing down on the more local; and on the other, one of false social unities that advances political purposes while marginalizing, even silencing, what is really at stake; what is being reproduced and who is losing from that reproduction.

The globalization literature of the 1980s and even into the 1990s, fed a highly spatialized imaginary of competition between countries for inward investment: rhetorics of trickle down and raising all boats, the need to make concessions to mobile capital, and to loosen labor law. The contrast with the class framings of politics of capital's golden years of the 1950s and 1960s was striking. But class hadn't been evacuated from politics. It was just assuming new forms. The shift to international currency convertibility was emblematic, as Burnham (1997) and Notermans (1993, 1997) have pointed out. The problem confronted in the early 1970s was one of increasing wage demands that refused to buck a slowdown in productivity increases. The result was inflation. The external anchor provided by the adoption of convertibility that was already underway as a result of the collapse of Bretton Woods, emerged as a way of handling it. Henceforth, inflation would result in a decline in the value of the national currency as it was sold in favor of other currencies and balance of payments problems.[3] This would result in an increase in interest rates and a slowdown in the growth rate: all to be explained by a situation outside the control of the government in question. In other words, a government could dodge responsibility, all the while disciplining labor.[4] In such ways do scales get produced – or in this case, since there had been an earlier globalization with, in virtue of the gold standard, similar wage-repressing properties, rediscovered.

5.4.6   Bottom-up? Top-down? Or Irrelevant?

In talking about the construction of new spaces of circulation, and therefore new scales, a dominant sense in the chapter has been of a bottom-up motion. Capitals, supported by branches of the state working from the same territorial base, have expanded their markets and production spaces in a geographic sense, introducing new institutional supports as a necessary complement. Labor, in the form of the labor movement, has followed suit, trying to counter the advantages that capital's entry into labor markets yet to be organized can provide: the goal is always to take wages out of capital's competitive calculus through a common bargaining front (Cox 1997). This view, of course, is in sharp contrast to common criticisms of the politics of scale literature that it assumes a hierarchy in which upper levels are dominant; though the hierarchical form could prevail if the assumption is that the creation of those higher levels inevitably results in the alienation of power from the bottom-up forces; the creation, for example, of an anarchic, out-of-control, global scale.

But this in turn poses the question of just how should one envisage the relation between scales? Critical human geography has espoused notions of relationality and it is useful to see scales as related exactly in that way: how more local scales incorporate the more global and vice versa. What it tends to stop short of, though, is a conception of relationality between particular objects that is totalizing; that relates the relationality of scales to social formations *in toto* (Cox 2016). For a case can be made that scalar relations, a particular scalar division of state labor, among other things, cannot be understood outside of their relation to the social process as a whole. Given the way in which state forms vary, even while they are all capitalist states, the comparative provides a useful entrée into this set of relations.

The US has a highly decentralized set of scalar relations. To an unusually radical federation has been added the equally radical delegation of functions from state to local governments. These have certainly been the object of struggle but the decentralizing forces have tended to prevail so that more central branches function to a marked degree as resources to be turned to local advantage. The West European case is quite other: more evidently the hierarchical form attacked by critics of the politics of scale literature. Local governments are subordinated to a body of centrally defined law and are more reliant for their funding on central government. This sense of hierarchy can be a little deceiving, though, if one regards the national political parties as coalitions of locally based class forces. In both instances, therefore, local and central branches of the state internalize one another, if in different ways. Local government is what it is in virtue of a relation to the central state. The process through which the more global and more local scales have been formed has, accordingly, been a mutual one, structures at one scale conditioning the formative strategies which are possible at another.

This relationality then has its conditions in contrasting societies: contrasting in historically sedimented institutions, in class relations and in beliefs (Cox 2016, Chapter 8). Not least the US never had a centralizing absolutist state in its history and this created different sorts of opportunity structure for class forces and struggle over scalar relations. The fact that capitalist development started virtually on a tabula rasa in the US has also been important. In Western Europe significant pre-capitalist elements formed a background for different sorts of class alliance. Not least, labor movements found allies in elements of the ruling class absent in the US; without that configuration it seems unlikely that labor movements in Western Europe could have been as effectively centralizing as they have been, as in the formation of welfare states that are quite other than their US cousin.

5.4.7 Conclusion

We are now in a position to reassess the claims made by the critics of scalar/territorial understandings of politics. They counter claims of hierarchical scalar relations with an emphasis on networks; on horizontality rather than verticality. But while hierarchy has to be a necessary feature of social life in a capitalist society, where deep antagonisms have to be regulated, the fact of relationality in the vertical and not merely the horizontal, puts an additional blush on matters. So much so that in the US it appears that it is the tail that wags the dog. Moreover, verticality does not exclude horizontality and nor does hierarchy exclude networks. Scalar structures and their particular institutional regimes are fought over because of their significance for uneven development and for local/regional/national hegemony in more global contexts. This in turn requires the cementing of coalitions and alliances across space to secure and to impose particular scalar compromises that will inevitably be for some and not for all.

5.5 NOTES

1. Significantly this is the approach adopted in *Capital Volume I*: Marx proceeds as if competition did not exist. See also John Weeks (1981, Chapter 6).
2. 'That so many of us took the concept (of globalization) on board so uncritically in the 1980s and 1990s, allowing it to displace the far more politically charged concepts of imperialism and neocolonialism, should give us pause. It made us weak opponents of the politics of globalization particularly as these became more and more central to everything that US foreign policy was trying to achieve' (Harvey 2000, p. 13).
3. A common view is that a decline in the value of the national currency provides a fillip to exports while reducing imports. To the degree that exports depend on production using imported raw-materials and components, this may be problematic. Domestic producers may ultimately be able to substitute for imports, but that takes time. Likewise, expanding exports does not happen immediately; among other things, the necessary distribution networks elsewhere in the world have to be set up.
4. Thus Burnham (1997) who refers to the external anchor of currency convertibility as 'providing the strongest

possible public justification governments can muster for maintaining downward pressure on wages to combat inflation and thereby achieving price stability' (p. 154). And 'through depoliticization and externalization, states have found a novel (but not historically unique) way in which the mythical "national interest" can be brought to bear on wage settlements' (p. 157). See also Piven (1995) on globalization as ideology.

5.6   REFERENCES

Allen, J. and A. Cochrane (2007), 'Beyond the territorial fix: regional assemblages, politics and power', *Regional Studies*, **41** (9), 1161–1175.

Allen, J. (2010), 'Powerful city networks: more than connections, less than domination and control', *Urban Studies*, **47** (13), 2895–2911.

Allen, J. and A. Cochrane (2012), 'Assemblages of state power: topological shifts in the organization of government and politics', *Antipode*, **42** (5), 1071–1089.

Amin, A. (2002), 'Spatialities of globalization', *Environment and Planning A*, **34** (3), 385–399.

Bird, J. (1956), 'Scale in regional study: illustrated by brief comparisons between the western peninsulas of England and France', *Geography*, **41** (1), 25–38.

Burnham, P. (1997), 'Globalization, states, markets and class relations', *Historical Materialism*, **1** (1), 150–160.

Castells, M. (1983), 'Crisis, planning, and the quality of life: managing the new historical relationships between space and society', *Environment and Planning D: Society and Space*, **1** (1), 3–21.

Cox, K.R. and A.E.G. Jonas (1993), 'Urban development, collective consumption and the politics of metropolitan fragmentation', *Political Geography*, **12** (1), 8–37.

Cox, K.R. (1997), 'Globalization and workers' struggles in the late twentieth century', in R. Lee and J. Wills (eds), *Geographies of Economies*, London: Edward Arnold, pp. 177–185.

Cox, K.R. (1998), 'Spaces of dependence, spaces of engagement and the politics of scale, or: looking for local politics', *Political Geography*, **17** (1), 1–24.

Cox, K.R. (2010), 'The problem of metropolitan governance and the politics of scale', *Regional Studies*, **44** (2), 215–227.

Cox, K.R. (2013), 'Territory, scale, and why capitalism matters', *Territory, Politics and Governance*, **1** (1), 46–61.

Cox, K.R. (2016), *The Politics of Urban and Regional Development and the American Exception*, Syracuse, NY: Syracuse University Press.

Haggett, P. (1965), *Locational Analysis in Human Geography*, London: Edward Arnold.

Harvey, D. (1985), 'The geopolitics of capitalism', in D. Gregory and J. Urry (eds), *Social Relations and Spatial Structures*, London: Macmillan, pp. 128–163.

Harvey, D. (2000), *Spaces of Hope*, Berkeley and Los Angeles, CA: University of California Press.

Marston, S., J.P. Jones and K. Woodward (2005), 'Human geography without scale', *Transactions of the Institute of British Geographers*, **30** (4), 416–432.

Massey, D. (1999), 'Spaces of politics', in D. Massey, J. Allen and P. Sarre (eds), *Human Geography Today*, Cambridge: Polity Press.

Massey, D. (2005), *For Space*, London: Sage.

Massey, D. (2007), *World City*, Cambridge: Polity Press.

Moellering, H. and W.R. Tobler (1972), 'Geographical variances', *Geographical Analysis*, **4** (1), 34–50.

Notermans, T. (1993), 'The abdication from national policy autonomy: why the macroeconomic policy regime has become so unfavorable to labor', *Politics and Society*, **21** (2), 133–168.

Notermans, T. (1997), 'Social democracy and external constraints', in K.R. Cox (ed.), *Spaces of Globalization*, New York: Guilford Press, pp. 201–239.

Piven, F.F. (1995), 'Is it global economics or neo-laissez-faire?', *New Left Review*, **213**, 107–115.

Stokes, D.E. (1965), 'A variance components model of political effects', in J.M. Claunch (ed.), *Mathematical Applications in Political Science*, Dallas, TX: Arnold Foundation, pp. 61–85.

Taylor, P.J. (1981), 'A materialist framework for political geography', *Transactions of the Institute of British Geographers*, **7** (1), 15–34.

Wade, R. (1996), 'Japan, the World Bank, and the art of paradigm maintenance: the East Asian miracle in political perspective', *New Left Review*, **217**, 3–37.

Wade, R. and F. Veneroso (1998), 'The Asian crisis: the high debt model versus the Wall Street-Treasury-IMF complex', *New Left Review*, **228**, 3–24.

Weeks, J. (1981), *Capital and Exploitation*, London: Edward Arnold.

6. New regionalism
Gillian Bristow

6.1   INTRODUCTION

In her landmark book of 1961, *The Death and Life of Great American Cities*, Jane Jacobs defined the region as 'an area safely larger than the last one to whose problems we found no solution' (p. 410). For many urban and regional development scholars, the sentiment expressed by Jacobs will have considerable resonance. The importance of the regional scale in economic development thinking has certainly waxed and waned over the past 25 years, as has our appreciation of its economic problems and challenges. In the 1990s, 'New Regionalism' came to prominence in the economic development and innovation literature and strongly asserted that it was the regional scale, defined as the intermediate or 'meso' scale between the nation state and the local, that was critically important in terms of territorial governance and the nurturing of economic development activity. New Regionalism quickly became 'policy orthodoxy', aligning as it did with the contemporary trend towards territorial governance structures at a sub-national scale, and the re-scaling of economic development activities in a globalizing world (Lovering 1999).

Since then much has changed, not least with the rise of metropolitan city-regionalism and the increasing emphasis in theory and policy on the merits of governing economic activity around functional economic regions, increasingly defined as cities and their wider 'regional' hinterlands. As such, and some twenty years since the rise of New Regionalism, it is timely to reflect upon its legacy and impact, to consider what it has contributed both conceptually to our understanding of the 'region' and its role in economic development processes, and to reflect upon its influence on policy approaches. Critical questions include, has New Regionalism simply been rescaled and the boundaries of the region redrawn to embrace a slightly different (in the case of city-regions, smaller) geography at which the economic development problem is now defined and policy attention focused? How, if at all, has theorizing around the relationship between regional economic development fortunes and key aspects of the institutional landscape evolved over time? And, are the policy prescriptions of New Regionalism still valid and influential?

In seeking to address these questions, this chapter begins with a brief reminder of the core thinking underpinning New Regionalism and its rise to prominence. Following this, it will explore the main criticisms levelled against it and consider whether and how it has been remoulded and reshaped by considering how the theorizing and practice of regionalism has subsequently evolved. Finally, it will conclude by reflecting on the core tenets of New Regionalism namely the importance of inter-firm relationships and the relationship between regional economic development fortunes and institutional structures and consider where these sit within contemporary theoretical approaches to regional development and policy debates. In so doing, the chapter takes a broad, heterodox approach and synthesizes a range of perspectives and literatures for purposes of framing the complex contours of current regionalism debates.

6.2　NEW REGIONALISM'S RISE AND FALL

New Regionalism is the shorthand label used to describe the work of various Western European and North American scholars who, over the course of the 1980s and 1990s, played a key role in highlighting the significance of the region for steering economic development planning and political governance (for more detailed overviews see MacLeod 2001; Harrison 2006). This body of work was fundamentally driven by the success and dynamism of certain high profile regional economies and industrial districts in Western Europe and North America and coalesced around an understanding of the specific form of inter-firm relations and institutional and social conditions that characterized them. A key proponent, Michael Storper, argued that regions were critical to economic interaction, innovation and wealth creation in the global economy through their ability to foster traded (input–output) and untraded (institutional and social) interdependencies between firms. Where these interdependencies are localized, he argued, the region becomes the 'key, necessary element in the supply architecture for learning and innovation processes' (Storper 1997, p. 22). In so doing, Storper played a prominent role in promoting the rediscovery by many academics of the regional scale as a fundamental basis of economic and social life, and in propelling a research agenda focused on the role of specific regional rules, conventions, norms and trust in stimulating the innovation capacity critical to economic success (e.g. Morgan 1997; Malmberg and Maskell 2002).

At the same time, the regional state and sub-national governance was becoming a viable and forthright partner in policy design and delivery owing to the contemporary 'reshuffling of the hierarchy of spaces' associated with neoliberalism (Lipietz 1994, p. 36). Michael Keating (1998) argued that Western Europe had experienced a progressive new regionalism since the mid-1980s whereby the authority of the nation state had been increasingly challenged by the twin forces of internationalization from above, and the assertion of regions and civil society from below. In this regard, the nation state had been 'hollowed out' and its role as the prime regulator and controller of economic governance increasingly eroded (Jessop 1994). Thus, whereas throughout most of the post-war period governments intervened in the economy to promote balanced forms of territorial economic development, latterly these became less of a priority. As a result, regions became more exposed to international competition and became increasingly salient as economic and political actors in their own right.

New Regionalism quickly emerged as a fashionable banner for reifying the region as an object of study and creating a powerful but essentially normative narrative that the region had somehow attained a new authority in and of itself (Lovering 1999). Through its construction of the region as an economic project defined by its production systems, it also played a powerful role in sedimenting the view that the region was a key 'space for competitiveness' thereby embedding the concept of regional competitiveness firmly into policy discourse and practice (Bristow 2005, 2010). Regions and their production systems were deemed to be in competition with one another in a relational, zero-sum game. Using insights gained from endogenous growth theory, institutional economics and cognitive psychology, proponents of New Regionalism asserted that the critical propellants of competitive advantage in the globalized economy resided firmly within facets of the regional business environment – knowledge, relationships and motivation – that distant rivals could not easily imitate or match (Storper 1997; Porter 1998). Through a combination of the support of powerful interests and a timely dovetailing with political imperatives, the discourse of regional competitiveness arose and became ubiquitous. Its dominance was such that it pervaded the strategic policy ambitions for regions and encouraged a narrow policy focus on interventions and institutional forms aimed at enabling regional business environments to foster enhanced firm productivity and market advantage (Bristow 2005).

The appeal of New Regionalism lay in its seeming ability to offer both a convincing theoretical explanation for the success of fast growth regions such as Silicon Valley, Emilia-Romagna and Baden Wurttenburg, and to establish the regional scale as a new, effective arena for locating the institutions of post-Fordist political-economic governance (Harrison 2006). Yet this very appeal also provided the focus for much of its subsequent and most vehement criticism.

The critique of New Regionalism focused on a number of key issues. The first of these concerned its failure to adequately confront the conceptual definition of the 'region'. New Regionalists came under increasing attack for their tendency to both take the fundamental concept of 'the region' for granted (Oosterlynck 2010) and their overt attribution of agentic capacities to it, thereby displaying a kind of 'spatial fetishism' (MacKinnon et al. 2002; see also Paasi and Metzger 2017). In particular, it was argued that a lack of clarity surrounded whether and how the abstract notion of the 'region' used in much of New Regionalism and especially its discourse of competitiveness, corresponded to the actual regions in which people and firms lived and worked, and to the functional areas actually influencing competitive advantage (Lovering 1999). The result was the production of rather broad-brush policy prescriptions 'pursued on the basis of predefined administrative or political areas that may have little meaning as economically functioning units, and from which policy effects may "leak out" into other regions' (Kitson et al. 2004, p. 997).

A related criticism surrounded New Regionalism's tendency to focus narrowly on the processes of developing soft institutionalism and business growth *within* a region, thereby ignoring the constitutive outside influences, social networks and institutional relations impacting *upon* regions from elsewhere (Lovering 1999). This emanated from New Regionalism's assertion of a strongly bounded, territorial view of regions which led to a set of hypotheses around the critical importance of some of the key institutional features and inter-firm relationships which lay within them.

A further major criticism of New Regionalism was its inherent tendency to read off institutional developments from successful regions and assert their generic relevance. For Lovering, New Regionalism became a highly selective amalgam of 'all things good' in the world's regional economies, such that as a consequence it represented simply 'a set of stories about how "parts" of a regional economy might work, placed next to a set of policy ideals which "might" just be useful in "some cases"' (Lovering 1999, p. 384, original emphasis). Whilst various authors have usefully argued that this indictment may be overly harsh given the deeper reservoir of regional economic research evident in practice, powerful concerns were raised about the failure of New Regionalists to accurately represent their theoretical abstractions (with all their innate subtleties and nuances around context) to the policy-making community.

Finally, new Regionalism was criticized for its narrow focus upon manufacturing and export activities, and for its neglect of the service sector and, especially, the national and local state. According to Lovering (1999, p. 391), it thus represented 'a poor framework through which to grasp the real connections between the regionalization of business and governance and the changing role of the state'. As such, serious concerns were raised about the effectiveness of its policy prescriptions and their consequences. The significance of the 'region' and the role of factors endogenous to it in shaping firm performance were overstated and the key ingredients for success uniformly prescribed making for a 'one-size-fits-all' approach to regional economic development policy. The result was that policy-makers and economic development practitioners across very different regions ended up pursuing 'identikit' competitive strategies with limited tailoring to suit local circumstances (Bristow 2005).

This raises interesting questions about the legacy of New Regionalism and how, if at all, any of its key tenets have endured or evolved in contemporary thinking and policy-making in regional economic development. In seeking to address this question, this chapter now moves to outline three broad approaches to understanding the region in economic development which have emerged in scholarly debates since the heyday of New Regionalism namely: metropolitan new regionalism; critical regionalism; and evolutionary regionalism. These are broad categorizations which are neither mutually exclusive nor exhaustive but are discussed here in outline terms as a means of capturing some of the key trends in scholarly thinking around regional economic development which have emerged in the wake of New Regionalism, and to enable consideration of its evolution and legacy.

6.3   METROPOLITAN REGIONALISM

The legacy of New Regionalism, and particularly its association with sub-national interventions and agency in respect of the discourse of competitiveness, is most clearly evident in the emergence (or re-emergence) of interest in another territorial form – the city-region. City-regions are generally conceived as entities 'comprising two distinct but inter-related elements: the city (sometimes a regional or national metropolis), possessing some specified set of functions or economic activities; and a surrounding territory, which is exclusive to the city in question' (Parr 2005, p. 556). As such, city-regions often align to metropolitan regions and their functional economic relationships and patterns (such as travel to work areas) and are essentially territorial forms which sit beneath the 'meso' scale of regions emphasized by New Regionalism.

By the early years of the new Millennium, city regions were increasingly being upheld as the ideal scale at which economic competitiveness could be promoted and nurtured, with the task of devising city-regional policies becoming firmly established as a central institutional task throughout much of Western Europe, North America and beyond (Harrison 2007). For many scholars, particularly those inspired by a Marxist view of political economy, the resurgence of metropolitan or city-region governance was explained as reflecting the frenzied and ongoing trial and error search for new and durable spaces of accumulation and state regulatory activity (e.g. Brenner 2002). City-regions from this perspective were thus regarded as a product of the continued re-scaling of the geopolitical project of competitiveness and portrayed as the handmaiden of a neoliberal offensive 'to dismantle national redistributive structures' (Lovering 1999, p. 392).

The narrative of competitive city-regionalism – in which the city-region is portrayed as a relatively autonomous economic actor in the vanguard of creativity, innovation and development – has subsequently become one of the most seductive economic narratives in the world today, especially to business and political elites who have become mired in austerity capitalism (Morgan 2014). The compelling power of the competitiveness narrative has readily lent itself to being re-scaled and moulded to align with the emergent interest in metropolitan and city-regional governance. Indeed, many of the authors who so powerfully promoted the sub-national, regional territory as a key arena for economic success were increasingly claiming by the early 2000s that metropolitan city-regions were now the key motors of the global economy (e.g. Scott and Storper 2003). In this regard, the rise of city-regionalism can be understood in part at least as a deliberate process of scalar reorganization and crisis management by the state, reflective of its ongoing search for an appropriate scale to perform key economic growth functions in the midst of capitalism's inherent tendency towards uneven development.

A critical distinction in the competitiveness narrative as applied to city-regions lies in its iteration of the role of inter-firm relations. These relations retain a clear importance in competitive city-regionalism but contain a more specific emphasis upon the intense economic advantages and localized externalities that emerge from having spatial concentrations of firms. Thus, for Scott and Storper (2003, p. 581) city-regions have become the key territorial players in the global economy because they are 'the sites of dense masses of inter-related economic activities that also typically have high levels of productivity by reason of their jointly generated agglomeration economies and their innovative potentials' (Scott and Storper 2003, p. 581). City-regions provide economic advantages associated with their critical mass of workers and infrastructure, and their dense networks of suppliers and collaborators. Cities also help new ideas to form and flow, so that firms and workers can learn from each other.

Not surprisingly given their parallels, the rise of competitive city-regionalism has been subject to a similar critique as New Regionalism about the tendency for bad abstraction of the experiences of successful city-regions and all the attendant dangers of an amalgam of fashionable ideas being imitated from place to place (Harrison 2007). However, the tendency to assume that city-regionalism can entirely be explained as a product of a dominant competitiveness narrative or as some 'neoliberal plot' (Harding 2007) has also been criticized as essentially embodying a functional and economically reductionist view of city-regionalism. In practice, it is argued that the trend towards city-regionalism is uneven and best understood as representing an on-going, dynamic and conflict-ridden politics of and in space (Jonas and Ward 2004).

Politics is likely to be important in at least two key ways. First, issues concerning the structures of and relationships within governance are increasingly prominent in city-region debates, with city-region policies and institutions tending to layer over old, inherited landscapes and cultures of local and regional economic governance and spatial planning. Second, politics means that in practice the pursuit of competitiveness represents only one of a range of different rationales for city-regionalism. City-regionalism may emerge as a product of various social and environmental movements and in response to struggles and strategies around the effective management of social relations of production and matters of collective consumption around, for example, housing, education, investment, the environment and taxation (Brenner 2002; Jonas and Ward 2004). In short, whilst competitive city-regionalism abounds, there is now greater recognition of the plurality evident in regionalism and indeed, in the wider character, form and nature of regional development itself (Markusen 2006; Pike et al. 2007).

6.4   CRITICAL REGIONALISM

The increasing emphasis upon politics and plurality in regionalism links to a developing and wider body of critical work. The robust critique of New Regionalism spawned a developing literature seeking to place greater emphasis upon examining the political processes, actors and policies constructing the region not only from within its boundaries, but also from outside it. This literature, somewhat loosely labelled as 'critical regionalism' (Clark and Christopherson 2009), articulates two core and inter-related concerns: firstly, the need for a more critical stance towards the definition of 'the region', and secondly, for a more careful examination of who is using it and for what purposes (see Bristow 2013).

Fundamentally, critical regionalists assert that regions are not natural or self-evident entities. Instead, they are social constructions. Since there are multiple ways of seeing a region, there are many different approaches to defining it (see also Keating 2017). Over time, the New Regionalist bounded view of regions has been increasingly challenged by an alternative relational perspective. This sees regions as open, porous 'spaces of flows' constituted by an extended network of social relations and thus fundamentally shaped by their relations and connectivity with other scales and sites of economic organization (see Allen et al. 1998; Hudson 2007; Lagendijk 2007). The relational perspective sees patterns of regional development and prosperity as reflecting relations of power and control over space, where core regions tend to occupy dominant positions, and peripheral regions play marginal roles within wider structures of accumulation and regulation. In this regard, each regional economy is in a distinct position since each is a unique mix of relations over which there is some power and control, and other relations within which the region may be in a place of subordination (Massey 2004). This perspective posits that certain regions, such as the south-east of England in the UK, are likely to develop a hegemonic political and economic position which not only shapes their own development, but also impacts upon the development processes of other regions.

The relational perspective also asserts that regions are comprised of individual actors (e.g. workers, managers, consumers and politicians), as well as collective ones (such as firms, governmental bodies and other organizations). These actors are embedded in various structures of socio-institutional relations and actor-networks, which influence their decisions and actions and lead them to pursue multiple (economic and non-economic) goals and strategies. As such, the relational perspective also emphasizes the interdependencies between institutions, individuals and wider social structures, and the mutual constitution of the local and the global (Massey 2007).

This has important implications for policy. It implies that policies for regions need to be attuned to their international flows and connectivities and not simply relate to the exercising of territorial power. It also implies regions are not entirely autonomous entities capable of determining their own futures, although there is room for local initiative. Instead, it asserts that regions have to go beyond a narrow territorial basis and enter wider policy arenas to negotiate various arguments and claims. It also suggests the need to encourage local activation as a process of enrolment in, rather than protection against, the global (Bathelt, 2006). In short, it emphasizes the importance of situating regions and their development within a wider political economy which acknowledges the explicit and continuing influence of the nation state (Tomaney and Ward 2000).

Subsequent work has highlighted how the rise of the regional scale is deeply intertwined with the restructuring of the state, with a growing emphasis on understanding regional devolution in particular as part of a broader process of state reorganization (see, for example, Goodwin et al. 2005). Furthermore, Harrison (2006) has articulated the need to better understand the relationship between the region and the nation state and the complex way the national state produces, reproduces and articulates the scalar and spatial sites of economic governance. In particular, he has argued for deeper interrogation of the way in which the nation state is involved in meta-governance – or the government of governance – through the processes of democratic devolution, constitutional change and functional decentralization to regional institutions such as development agencies. This raises questions as to whether this results in the nation state building new capacity and steering the regions more effectively, or whether instead it retreats from support of the region and does less. It also brings into sharp focus the need to understand the agency of regions and the people within them in economic development policies and processes (Hudson 2007).

6.5   EVOLUTIONARY REGIONALISM

More recently, the attention of many urban and regional scholars, particularly within economic geography, has turned to exploring the enduring questions of how and why economic growth and transformation proceeds differently in different places over time, and particularly how and why cities and regions differ in their ability to adapt and exhibit resilience to economic shocks and change, and why spatial disparities and other institutional features tend to persist over time (e.g. Boschma and Martin 2010).

There is a broad and increasingly heterodox field of work addressing these questions. However, it is ostensibly characterized by an interest in understanding the nature and trajectory of evolution of the economic system, and, more specifically, the role played by geography in these evolutionary processes of economies, notably around innovation, resilience and structural renewal and change. A number of key evolutionary dynamics have come to the fore, each of which has spawned enhanced debate and developed further insight into both our understanding of the role the 'region' in economic development processes, and into appropriate policy approaches. As such, each of these has refined and enhanced New Regionalist thinking in a number of ways.

One key set of dynamic issues concerns the role of history in shaping processes of economic development and transformation. The economic development trajectories and processes of places are increasingly understood to be path-dependent. As Pike et al. (2007, p. 1258) observe, 'from Hackney to Honolulu to Hong Kong, each place has evolving histories, legacies, institutions and other distinctive characteristics that impart place dependencies and shape – inter alia – its economic assets and trajectories, social outlooks, environmental concerns, politics and culture'. In short, the choices made in the past around technologies, skills and business development, critically influence and shape the direction of subsequent pathways albeit in complex, non-linear ways (Martin and Sunley 2006). Critically, past and current evolutionary trajectories in terms of institutions are also vitally important. Whilst the 'first-nature' geography of a territory, or its innate physical and natural conditions, also has some influence, recent evidence suggests that in terms of regional economic growth, this is far outweighed by the influence provided by the quality of local and regional institutions (Ketterer and Rodriguez-Pose 2016).

Second, and following on from the above, the evolutionary dynamics of adaptability and innovation are also increasingly understood to be key determinants of differential patterns of regional development and change. It is the innovation capacity of regions, particularly their ability to reinvent themselves and break from their past, that is central to their dynamic capacity to develop new economic paths and change their industrial structure (Pike et al. 2007). Inter-firm relationships are again critical to this adaptability. A range of studies have demonstrated the importance played by the recombination of knowledge in overlapping technological fields – *related variety* – in long-term regional adaptability and new path creation (e.g. Boschma et al. 2013). Other studies have suggested that the development of new, *unrelated* activities is also critical for adaptability however, as regions with unrelated variety are more likely to produce technological breakthroughs (e.g. Boschma 2015). More broadly it is acknowledged that firms attain knowledge through pipelines to selected providers outside their territory, as well as via localized clusters within it (Bathelt 2006).

A further key set of dynamics relate to the systemic complexity of economies. Comparisons have long been made between cities and regions and organic systems (Jacobs 1961), but recent evolutionary approaches to local and regional economic systems have helped to define and assert salient features of this complexity and have produced a number of rich insights as a result. A critical insight is that regional systems are hugely diverse entities and comprised of collections of agents (principally businesses and institutions, but also households, workers and consumers), with important differences between the economic and technological trajectories of sectors, their path dependencies and vulnerabilities to shocks. An economy, at whatever scale, is a 'complex' of different activities that to some extent 'fit together' and need each other (Allen 1995). A further key insight is that the agency of and in regions is thus complex, distributed and contingent, yet also highly relational. These diverse agents interact with each other in complex ways, adapt and learn through trial and error, and create emergent patterns and waves of innovation and development through their contingent co-evolution with changes in the economic environment (Simmie and Martin 2010). In terms of regions, it is the interactions of economic agents through their social relationships and networks that become crucial in understanding how shocks play out, which regions exhibit resilience and how adaptation occurs (Bristow and Healy 2014, 2015).

A further insight provided from complex systems thinking is that regions sit within a nested hierarchy. This is indeed the very architecture of complexity (Simon 1962). They are embedded in rather than subordinate to multi-level spatial and institutional configurations which are constantly changing to meet new situations. As such, regional evolutionary dynamics are fundamentally shaped by, and intrinsically connected to, the wider national and global economic, political and social systems within which they operate (Martinelli et al. 2013).

6.6 CONCLUSIONS

So, what is the legacy of New Regionalism and where have the various different bodies of work on regions outlined here taken us in terms of our understanding of regional problems and how to address them? New Regionalism's legacy is undoubtedly strongest in the emergence of metropolitan or city-regionalism where there is clear evidence that its core concerns with competitiveness, governance and territoriality have been retained if re-scaled. New Regionalism's emphasis on the importance of inter-firm relationships for regional economic success has also been affirmed although distinctly sharpened through evolutionary thinking on how knowledge is acquired, combined and shared through the local and extra-local networks within which firms operate, and the importance of the absorptive capacity of firms. Institutions also still feature strongly in theorizing around regions and their development, although the nature of their role and significance has become more clearly circumscribed. Regions remain important containers for a range of state, quasi-state or non-state institutions and various coalitions of capital, labour and civil society. They also remain important sources for the growth of such institutions inasmuch as they appear to provide a convenient or appropriate scale for the organization and articulation of a range of economic, political, social and environmental interests. With the evolutionary turn however, the importance of the quality of institutions at the regional scale as opposed to simply their presence and type has become more salient, as has the nature of their relationships with the range of other agents within and outside the region that are understood to influence regional development processes and outcomes.

New Regionalism's assertion of the unassailable tour de force and significance of the regional scale for shaping development processes has undoubtedly been tempered however. With the emergence of new sub-national forms of governance, regions are now one of several, plausible sub-national tiers within increasingly polycentric systems of governance. Regions have also been re-conceptualized as broader social and material constructions, as products of both processes of territorial construction and their inherent relationships with other regions and scales, and thus as complex relational entities with an inherent variety and heterogeneity of interests. Critical regionalism has effectively challenged the notion that regions will be necessarily coherent entities with a pre-determined collective status and agency and suggests that the prioritizing of the region as the pivotal scale and tendential unit for development and policy purposes has to be based upon carefully grounded research rather than thin empirics (Hudson 2007).

In summary, regions are increasingly understood to be characterized by *variation, contradiction and complexity* (see e.g. Keating 2017). Regions are not necessarily characterized by some unified or notionally shared, collective interest or agency and are not univocal subjects of the policy decisions and mantras developed elsewhere. They are instead characterized by a continuous struggle for coherence between the competing demands of diverse and multiple interests and alliances, with varying values, aspirations and goals. Furthermore, these matters of struggle are rarely uniquely economic in nature or clearly pan-regional in coverage. Instead, they often emanate from localized debates around re-distribution and the material conditions of economic growth and uneven development. Regions are also understood to be hugely diverse in terms of their economic characteristics, institutional structures and social organization, and to evolve in various ways depending upon their histories, networks and nested hierarchies. In this ontology of complexity and change, place and context are hugely important in shaping critical networks, institutions and adaptive behaviours. However, the role and importance of the 'region' specifically cannot be assumed a priori (Hudson 2007).

This has significant, if challenging, implications for policy. New Regionalism's appeal lay, in part at least, with the simplicity and clarity of its policy implications. The turn towards variation, contradiction and complexity in our understanding of regionalism puts an end to the notion of off-the-shelf regional policy models or institutional blueprints. There is greater understanding that what works well in one set of circumstances may be unsuitable for another, and that broader 'design principles' for institutional arrangements (as proffered by Ostrom 2008) are preferable to universal panaceas. Similarly, there is a recognized need for regional policy interventions which are *place-based* rather than *place-bound* or which 'capitalise on region-specific assets rather than selecting them from a portfolio of policy recipes that owed their success in different environments' (Asheim et al. 2011, p. 900). This thinking has already influenced key areas of policy, notably the Smart Specialization approach to regional innovation policy in the European Union which is based upon building on a region's specific assets and potentials. This creates new sets of challenges however, particularly for less developed regions, in terms of the capacities and processes required to effect appropriate strategic analysis.

The bigger questions about the enduring challenges of uneven development also remain. One of the fundamental critiques of New Regionalism was its tendency to place too much attention on firm relationships and institutional structures within regions. The increasingly plural understandings of regionalism which have since emerged have provided greater awareness of the importance of the relationships between regional economies and the wider systems within which they are embedded. Regions are locked into increasingly complex inter-relationships and inter-dependencies which create particular vulnerabilities for them, especially where they are over-specialized in particular goods and services. These vulnerabilities are becoming ever more exposed in a world characterized by increasing economic instability as well as uncertainty over the availability and security of resources (Bristow 2010; Boschma, 2015). This implies the need to better understand regions as dynamic spaces of flows and to acknowledge the more complex political economy within which regions function and through which the uneven and path dependent nature of regional development proceeds. The national dimension in the form of the specific, historically constituted state and attendant social formation and political culture, remains critically important (Tomaney and Ward 2000). This poses significant challenges for those conceptualizing regions and regionalism, with a powerful argument emerging for a more integrative, holistic framework capable of bringing together the disparate theorizing and empirics around regional dynamics and political economy articulated broadly here (see Martin 2015). This also implies greater attention within regional policy debates to the influential interventions at the national scale which are likely to be critical to efforts at more fundamental spatial rebalancing (see, e.g. Martin et al. 2016).

6.7   REFERENCES

Allen, J., D. Massey and A. Cochrane (1998), *Rethinking the Region*, London: Routledge.
Allen, P.M. (1995), 'Cities and regions as evolutionary complex systems', *Journal of Geographical Systems*, **4** (1), 103–130.
Asheim, B., R. Boschma and P. Cooke (2011), 'Constructing regional advantage: platform policies based on related variety and differentiated knowledge bases', *Regional Studies*, **45** (7), 893–904.
Bathelt, H. (2006), 'Geographies of production: growth regimes in spatial perspective 3 – toward a relational view of economic action and policy', *Progress in Human Geography*, **30** (2), 223–236.
Boschma, R. and R. Martin (2010), 'The aims and scope of evolutionary economic geography', in R. Boschma and R. Martin (eds), *The Handbook of Evolutionary Economic Geography*, Cheltenham, UK and Northampton, MA, USA: Edward Elgar Publishing, pp. 3–39.

Boschma R., A. Minondo and M. Navarro (2013), 'The emergence of new industries at the regional level in Spain. A proximity approach based on product-relatedness', *Economic Geography*, **89** (1), 29–51.

Boschma, R. (2015), 'Towards an evolutionary perspective on regional resilience', *Regional Studies*, **49** (5), 733–751.

Brenner, N. (2002), 'Decoding the newest "metropolitan regionalism" in the USA: a critical overview', *Cities*, **19** (1), 3–21.

Bristow, G. (2005), 'Everyone's a "winner": problematising the discourse of regional competitiveness', *Journal of Economic Geography*, **5** (3) 285–304.

Bristow, G. (2010), *Critical Reflections on Regional Competitiveness: Theory, Policy and Practice*, Abingdon: Routledge.

Bristow, G. (2013), 'Changing state spatiality and the region: a critical regionalist perspective', *Geopolitics*, **18** (2), 315–327.

Bristow, G. and A. Healy (2014), 'Regional resilience: an agency perspective', *Regional Studies*, **48** (5), 923–935.

Bristow, G. and A. Healy (2015), 'Crisis response, choice and resilience: insights from complexity thinking', *Cambridge Journal of Regions, Economy and Society*, **8** (2), 241–256.

Clark, J. and S. Christopherson (2009), 'Integrating investment and equity: a critical regionalist agenda for a progressive regionalism', *Journal of Planning Education and Research*, **28** (3), 341–354.

Goodwin, M., M. Jones and R. Jones (2005), 'Devolution, constitutional change and economic development: explaining and understanding the new industrial geographies of the British state', *Regional Studies*, **39** (4), 421–436.

Harding, A. (2007), 'Taking city-regions seriously? Response to debate on "city-regions: new geographies of governance, democracy and social reproduction"', *International Journal of Urban and Regional Research*, **31** (2), 443–458.

Harrison, J. (2006), 'Re-reading the new regionalism: a sympathetic critique', *Space and Polity*, **10** (1), 21–46.

Harrison, J. (2007), 'From competitive regions to competitive city-regions: a new orthodoxy, but same old mistakes', *Journal of Economic Geography*, **7** (3), 311–332.

Hudson, R. (2007), 'Regions and regional uneven development forever? Some reflective comments upon theory and practice', *Regional Studies*, **41** (9), 1149–1160.

Jacobs, J. (1961), *The Death and Life of Great American Cities*, New York: Random House.

Jessop, B. (1994), 'Post-Fordism and the State', in A. Amin (ed.), *Post-Fordism: A Reader*, Oxford: Blackwell, pp. 251–279.

Jonas, A.E.G. and K. Ward (2004), 'Competitive city-regionalism as a politics of space: a critical reinterpretation of the new regionalism', *Environment and Planning* A, **36** (3), 2119–2139.

Keating, M. (1998), *The New Regionalism in Western Europe: Territorial Restructuring and Political Change*, Cheltenham, UK and Lyme, NH, USA: Edward Elgar Publishing.

Keating, M. (2017), 'Contesting European regions', *Regional Studies*, **51** (1), 9–18.

Ketterer, T.D. and A. Rodriguez-Pose (2016), 'Institutions vs. "first-nature" geography: What drives economic growth in Europe's regions?', *Papers in Regional Science*, published online first June 2016.

Kitson, M., R. Martin and P. Tyler (2004), 'Regional competitiveness: an elusive yet key concept?' *Regional Studies*, **38** (9), 991–999.

Lagendijk, A. (2007), 'The accident of the region: a strategic relational perspective on the construction of the region's significance', *Regional Studies*, **41** (2), 1193–1208.

Lipietz, A. (1994), 'The national and the regional: their autonomy vis-à-vis the capitalist world crisis', in R. Palan and B. Gill (eds), *Transcending the State-Global Divide*, Boulder, CO: Lynne Rienner, pp. 23–44.

Lovering, J. (1999), 'Theory led by policy: the inadequacies of the "New Regionalism" (illustrated from the case of Wales)', *International Journal of Urban and Regional Research*, **23** (1), 379–396.

MacKinnon, D., A. Cumbers and K. Chapman (2002), 'Learning, innovation and regional development: a critical appraisal of recent debates', *Progress in Human Geography*, **26** (3), 293–311.

MacLeod, G. (2001), 'New Regionalism reconsidered: globalization and the remaking of political economic space', *International Journal of Urban and Regional Research*, **25** (4), 804–829.

Malmberg, A. and P. Maskell (2002), 'The elusive concept of localisation economies: towards a knowledge-based theory of spatial clustering', *Environment and Planning* A, **34** (3), 429–449.

Markusen, A. (2006), 'Economic geography and political economy', in S. Bagchi-Sen and H. Lawton-Smith (eds), *Economic Geography: Past, Present, Future*, London: Routledge, pp. 94–102.

Martinelli, F., F. Moulaert and A. Novy (eds) (2013), *Urban and Regional Development Trajectories in Contemporary Capitalism*, Abingdon: Routledge.

Martin, R. and P. Sunley (2006), 'Path dependence and regional economic evolution', *Journal of Economic Geography*, **6** (4), 395–438.

Martin, R. (2015), 'Rebalancing the spatial economy: the challenge for regional theory', *Territory, Politics, Governance*, **3** (3), 231–272.

Martin, R., A. Pike, P. Tyler and B. Gardiner (2016), 'Spatially rebalancing the UK economy: towards a new policy model?', *Regional Studies*, **50** (2), 342–357.

Massey, D. (2004), 'The responsibilities of place', *Local Economy*, **19** (2), 97–101.

Massey, D. (2007), *World City*, Cambridge: Polity Press.

Morgan, K. (1997), 'The learning region: institutions, innovation and regional renewal', *Regional Studies*, **31** (5), 491–503.

Morgan, K. (2014), 'The rise of metropolitics: Urban governance in the age of the city-region', in N. Bradford and A. Bramwell (eds), *Governing Urban Economies: Innovation and Inclusion in Canadian City-Regions*, Toronto: University of Toronto Press, pp. 297–318.

Oosterlynck, S. (2010), 'Regulating regional uneven development and the politics of reconfiguring Belgian state space', *Antipode*, **42** (5), 1151–1179.

Ostrom, E. (2008), 'Institutions and the environment', *Economic Affairs*, **28** (3), 34–31.

Paasi, A. and J. Metzger (2017), 'Foregrounding the region', *Regional Studies*, **51** (1), 19–30.

Parr, J.B. (2005), 'Perspectives on the city-region', *Regional Studies*, **39** (5), 555–566.

Pike, A., A. Rodriguez-Pose and J. Tomaney (2007), 'What kind of local and regional development, for whom?', *Regional Studies*, **41** (9), 1253–1269.

Porter, M. (1998), *On Competition*, Harvard, MA: Harvard Business School Press.

Scott, A.J. and M. Storper (2003), 'Regions, globalization, development', *Regional Studies*, **37** (6–7), 579–593.

Simmie, J. and R. Martin (2010), 'The economic resilience of regions: towards an evolutionary approach', *Cambridge Journal of Regions, Economy and Society*, **3** (1), 27–44.

Simon, H.A. (1962), 'The architecture of complexity', *Proceedings of the American Philosophical Society*, **106** (6), 467–482.

Storper, M. (1997), *The Regional World*, New York: Guilford Press.

Tomaney, J. and K. Ward (2000), 'England and the "new regionalism"', *Regional Studies*, **34** (5), 471–478.

7. Relational thinking and the region
Allan Cochrane

7.1 INTRODUCTION

From the outside, it must sometimes seem very odd to see the ways in which academics and theorists scrabble around trying to understand words that most of us use most of the time without worrying too much about their meaning. And region is one of those words. Surely we all know what a region is when we use the term in everyday conversation. Yet, for very good reasons, debates around the ways in which the regional should be defined and mobilised conceptually have been among the most heated in contemporary human geography.

In some respects, of course, there can be little controversy or debate around the notion that regions have to be understood in relational terms. The very notion of 'region' is necessarily a relational one. Even if the starting point is the simplest hierarchy of apparently fixed geographical scales, regions are defined in terms of their relationship to other scales (local, urban, national, international, global and so on). And the fact that it is also possible to identify some spaces as global regions and others as megaregions surely confirms the extent to which the region is a malleable concept, which conjures up sets of social and economic relations as they are expressed in and across space. As Neil Smith reminds us, regions 'are as changeable' as 'the economic, political and social activity and relationships' through which they are defined (Smith 1995, p. 60).

Although there may be little disagreement when matters are set out in such broad terms, it is nevertheless very easy in any discussion of regions to start from some apparently accepted and taken for granted set of actually existing regions. In practice, the settling of administrative boundaries or the formation of government agencies with authority in (although rarely over) certain geographical areas (or territories) is often enough to frame discussion. In some countries (such as Germany and France) regions are clearly identified as having a particular position in government hierarchies. Even in England, it is possible to identify a series of administrative regions which have from time to time been given a status within public policy regimes focused on planning and development. So, for example, Regional Economic Planning Councils were introduced in the 1970s, only to be abolished under Thatcher, while Regional Development Agencies were set up in the first decade of the twenty-first century, only to be abolished in the first years of the Conservative led coalition that was formed in 2010. Nor is it only under Labour governments that regional initiatives are launched, it was Conservative governments that created regionally based Government Offices (now also gone) and it is a Conservative government that is currently seeking to foster the regionally based Northern Powerhouse and the Midlands Engine, as well as a series of Combined Authorities, nominally identified with city regions.

In practice the academic discussion of regions moves easily, perhaps too easily, between theoretical debate and particular expressions of the regional. Although often presented in terms which imply that arguments are focused on relatively abstract questions around how 'regions' or the 'region' should be understood (as reflected, for example, in a book which I co-authored which claimed to be *Rethinking the Region*, Allen et al. 1998) in practice the debates are deeply inflected by a series of more localised concerns (in the case of that book, the nature of the London city region as a growth region in the UK context). Much of the recent discussion of regions and the regional has had a European and UK inflection, as attempts have been made to capture and reflect the shifting political geographies of those spaces. So, in the context of the more than national project of the European Union Michael Keating has noted: 'The political, economic, cultural and social meaning of space is changing in contemporary Europe. . . new types of regionalism and of region are the product of a decomposition and recomposition of the territorial framework of public life, consequent on changes in the state, the market, and the international context' (Keating 1997, p. 383). This understanding has also helped to frame some of the UK based debates – it is almost as if the wider European experience can be seen to prefigure what is taking place in England and through devolution to Scotland, Wales and Northern Ireland. With the benefit of Brexit inspired hindsight, perhaps the European model is less easily transferred than might have been expected and even hoped for.

Elsewhere rather different (although not necessarily contradictory) sets of imaginaries are apparent. In the US, for example, although there is a substantial literature on regions, it tends to link urban and regional development and to focus on the metropolitan experience rather than to concern itself more broadly with 'regions' and their identities (Cox 2016; Rohe 2011; Soja 2000; Storper 2014). And a very different set of concerns emerges once the focus shifts to the globally uneven nature of globalisation, whether expressed in a language of global city regions or new mega regions (like the Pearl River Delta) (Castells 1998; Harrison and Hoyler 2015; Scott 2001).

What holds the various uses of the term together, however, is the way in which it is utilised to highlight and explore how changing forms of spatial organisation emerge in different contexts and at different times, in parallel to (sometimes beyond, sometimes within, sometimes across) conventional national boundaries. It is not hard to list an, admittedly incomplete, series of 'regions' which has been generated on this basis – global regions, megaregions, global city regions, city regions, sub-regions, mesoregions, learning regions, competitive regions, polycentric urban mega regions and so on. In other words, drawing on the language of regions offers a way of thinking geographically, a way of framing debates about the entanglement between spatial and other social relations. The question that follows is the extent to which particular regions can be identified as more or less settled condensations of those social relations. In a sense this is an empirical question, which can be answered by research and detailed investigation – presumably either somewhere is a 'region' in that sense or it is not. But that is precisely the issue that relational approaches bring into question.

7.2   DEBATING THE REGION

The debates that have taken place around what might be called the regional question have often seemed tortuous – and the arguments from different sides simply to pass each other by (Varró and Lagendijk 2013). The emphasis of some on fluidity and the uncertain process of region-making seems of little relevance to those whose prime focus is on the workings of the various institutions or planning structures, or to those eagerly looking for policy nostrums aimed at fostering growth through regional competitiveness (as reviewed by Kitson et al. 2004), or seeking to identify the possibilities associated with what have been identified as learning regions (Florida 1995; Morgan 1997; OECD 2007).

All this is understandable. After all there can be no doubt that 'regions' exist and that a wide range of political and policy processes runs through them, giving them life. So, perhaps it will help from the start simply to acknowledge that there currently are and historically have been institutional arrangements identified as regions or with particular regional inflections; that there are frameworks of regional planning in many national contexts; and – even – that it is sometimes (and in some places) possible to identify territories that may helpfully be (and in practice often are) labelled as regions. It is also necessary to recognise that the institutional settlements implied by such an acknowledgement may have a significant role in framing or shaping political and economic possibilities in particular areas. But it is equally important to question the rather simplistic ways in which territory and relational approaches are sometimes juxtaposed – insofar as territories (regional or otherwise) exist they have to be understood as the product of the social, economic and political relations that constitute them (Elden 2013).

From one perspective, regional structures, and indeed all forms of sub-central government (Rhodes 1988), might be interpreted as ways of deconcentrating power within nation-states, responding to the necessary complexities of contemporary governance which fit very uneasily with any simple visions of top-down hierarchy. But such institutional forms are almost always intertwined with a series of other possibilities – other regional imaginaries. So, for example, it is sometimes suggested that regions have their own cultural identities, or that they are defined through some shared economic formation. They may be global city-regions (Scott 2001) or post-Fordist ensembles (for a time Emilia-Romagna was presented as a model for the future, only to be replaced by Silicon Valley). They may be identified as representing a meso level or layer (between the local and the national or sometimes beyond the national), perhaps representing the most appropriate scale at which various forms of (active and informal) collective economic endeavour can be pursued, perhaps acting as a catalyst for economic development (Holland 1987; Paasi 2013; Storper 1997). In response to such wider shifts Michael Keating suggests that a regional or meso level of regulation/policy-making is emerging, at least in Europe (Keating 2017). In other words, as John Agnew puts it: 'Regions both reflect differences in the world and ideas about the geographies of such differences' (Agnew 2013, p. 13).

The existence of what might be thought of as 'real world' regions as policy objects or political foci makes the debates around how they should be understood particularly challenging. There is a continuing danger that each transient shift in the policy world also becomes imagined through the application of theory into a more significant and structural shift, rather than a particular expression of the continuing pressure on governance agencies to seek ways of managing the uncertain spatial politics of economic and social change. So, for example (and it is only one example of a wider phenomenon), in the English case it is hard to escape the extent to which each new initiative has been picked up as evidence of a new spatial settlement, even as each has also been overtaken in practice by a new one, which is introduced with little reflection on the previous one.

Peter Saunders confidently told us in the mid-1980s (1985) that regional agencies like the UK's water boards and health authorities reflected a corporatist structural inevitability, only to see the former disappearing with privatisation (often retaining regional names even as they became part of global enterprises) (Allen and Pryke 2013) and while the National Health Service and its management structures have been reshaped and remade in a series of apparently endless reforms over the last three decades. In the 1990s, it seemed as if the (now long forgotten) Training and Enterprise Councils presaged a decentralised local corporatism (Jones 1999); in the 1990s the introduction of Government Offices, Regional Assemblies and Regional Development Agencies was somehow seen as a necessary rescaling of the politics of development, although the weakness of their roots became apparent in the wake of their abolition after 2010 (Webb and Collis 2000; Deas and Ward 2000); trying to make sense of the post 2010 mish-mash around localism and Local Economic Partnerships proved more of a challenge to those looking for new settlements, but for some, at least, the local appeared to offer a new framework (Clarke and Cochrane 2013; Pike et al. 2015); but the arrival of governance deals after 2015 based on the identification of city-regions has reopened more or less confident assertions around regional rescaling as a governance strategy and the possibility of a new spatial settlement (Deas 2014; Harrison 2012). Meanwhile, of course, in the UK more widely the break-up of Britain moves apace with quite distinctive politics emerging in Scotland, Wales and Northern Ireland, and fitting uneasily into any straightforward rescaling message. It sometimes feels as if academic engagement with the changing world is always running fast to catch up with the latest development, and then eagerly explaining why it was logically necessary (perhaps as a particular expression of neoliberalism) and why it provides evidence of a structural shift (Lord 2009).

7.3   THINKING IN AND THROUGH SPACE

From a geographical perspective it is never enough to rely on pre-existing administrative divisions or electoral constituencies as a basis for thinking through the political economy of space. And that is what is at stake here. The ways in which regions are made up through interconnecting sets of social, economic and political relations highlight the significance of space as a powerful category – these are active processes rather than fixed categories. Geography is a dynamic process rather than something that is preordained and waiting to be uncovered through forms of mapping, cartographic and otherwise. Of course, that does not mean mapping is unimportant – but it highlights the challenge of seeking to capture something that is in motion (and even unpredictable) in a particular moment (Allen et al. 1998; Cochrane and Pain 2000, pp. 30–42). Some geographies are more stable than others, and some lines on maps may remain in place over long periods (even if their significance changes from time to time). But one of the tasks of those seeking to understand regions is to explore what animates them and defines them in practice, rather than to capture them like butterflies under glass.

   The active turn to a more explicit and direct engagement with regions in relational terms reflected a recognition of the break-up of the spatial as much as the economic and social settlements associated with the post-1945 Keynesian welfare states of the global North and the wider international settlements expressed in the language of the second (state socialist) and third (so-called underdeveloped or developing) worlds (Agnew 2013, p. 7). In other words, previously taken for granted spatial arrangements were called into question, in the context of the hollowing out of the nation-state, the rise of globalisation, the end of Bretton Woods, the collapse of the Soviet Union, the post-colonial moment and so on. The unravelling of the various international and national settlements that had emerged in the middle years of the twentieth century also brought the end of spatial Keynesianism, with its (never fully realised) commitment to smoothing out the effects of uneven development (Macleod and Jones 2007, p. 1180; Lobao et al. 2009). It was in this context that pioneering works like Doreen Massey's *Spatial Divisions of Labour* were published (Massey 1984) and that David Harvey developed the argument that the search for a spatial fix was endemic to the process of capitalist production, potentially generating a structured coherence reflecting regionalised economic and social relations (Harvey 1985). At the Open University, we sought to understand what was happening in our own backyard and produced a series of books as part of a course on restructuring Britain – aiming to explore the ways in which old spatial arrangements were being challenged and new ones were emerging (Allen and Massey 1988; Anderson and Cochrane 1989; Hamnett et al. 1989). As assumptions about wider state settlements were being questioned, so it was necessary to question assumptions about the spatial arrangements associated with them – if one aspect of this was to revisit assumptions about globalisation and its effects, another was to begin the process of rethinking the region (Allen et al. 1998).

One of the dangers of recognising not only that regions must be approached in relational terms, but also that the very notion implies a relational understanding, is that we may be left with no more than a tautology. If we are all relational now, how does that help? One response has been to seek to identify a post-relational moment (Anderson et al. 2012; Allen 2012). That may indeed offer one way forward, but here I want to take a rather different approach, one that highlights the extent to which what matters is the ability to think through the relations that matter to particular versions of the 'region' as well as to different theoretical approaches – we may all be relational now, but that does not mean that we all understand social and economic relations and their interconnection in the same ways. Nor does it mean that there is some overarching set of concepts which can define regions in some holistic and definitive fashion for everywhere and always.

Within an overall relational framework, it is possible to identify two distinct poles, although it is important not to assume that any individual author fully ascribes to either. On the contrary, what is apparent is the way in which theorists have sought more or less explicitly to work across the division, even as one or other tendency dominates. The first of these could be identified as the search for/belief in the emergence of a new settlement, in which there is a revised set of spatial arrangements – a scalar or spatial restructuring. The task of theorists becomes to explore the ways in which a new spatiotemporal fix may be achieved rather than to focus on fluidity and uncertainty, even if the complexity and uncertainty of the process is acknowledged, in subtle discussion of the interaction between territory, place, scale and network (Jessop et al. 2008). The second focuses rather more on the process itself, suggesting that outcomes are always in doubt, to the extent that the region in question can never be fully settled. As Anssi Paasi and Jonathan Metzger put it, regions always have to be understood as becoming rather than finding some fixed expression (Paasi and Metzger 2017, p. 26).

One way of responding to these questions has been to suggest that what is needed is some sort of accommodation in which the fixity of territory retains a significant status alongside relational approaches (Goodwin 2013) and such an approach has its attractions (see also Jonas 2012). However, once it is accepted that territory itself is a product of overlapping and intersecting economic, social and political relations then giving it such an autonomous status remains problematic particularly if a distinction is made between territory (as a bounded space) and territoriality as a process of political claims-making (Sassen 2013). John Allen highlights some of the uneasy ways in which borders shift, both through the imposition of forms of exclusion on particular populations (such as undocumented migrants) within state territories and the management of populations (such as refugees and asylum seekers) far away from those formally recognised territories (Allen 2016, pp. 128–148). In another context, Kevin Ward and I tried to capture the complexity of the issues at stake in contrasting territorial and relational approaches by suggesting that:

> [W]hat matters is to be able to explore the ways in which the working through of the tension serves to produce policies and places, policies in place. The conventional distinction that is often made between the two misses the extent to which each necessarily defines and is defined by the other – territories are not fixed, but the outcome of overlapping and intersecting sets of social, political and economic relations stretching across space, while the existence of identifiable territories shape and in some cases limits the ways in which those relations are able to develop (in other words relational space and territorial space are necessarily entangled). (Cochrane and Ward 2012, p. 12)

Here I would want to emphasise that because territorial space is itself necessarily a product of those relationships, territories themselves have to be understood relationally.

There is a real danger in presenting the various formulations as sharply defined alternatives. While for Doreen Massey, the focus may be on the 'throwntogetherness' of place (Massey 2005, p. 149), which implies an almost accidental coming together of social relations in the moment, and Harvey may seem concerned with identifying structured coherence, in practice the former explores long-term sets of relationships in and beyond places and regions, while the latter is concerned to explore the tendencies that point towards the possibility of a spatial fix, in practice he stresses the impossibility of any such settlement being achieved for any significant period (Harvey 1985). Both highlight the porosity and uncertainty of boundaries, recognising the extent to which they are politically produced (often through state projects of one sort or another) rather than being generated through necessary social or economic relations.

7.4   THINKING IN AND BEYOND THE REGION

In this context, it is possible to understand how apparently incompatible conceptions of the 'region' can (and must) exist alongside each other – there is no underlying and definitive set of structures waiting to be uncovered, no set of necessary (regional) relations that can be identified for the purposes of scientific study. Actively pursuing the insight of 'space as polymorphic and located beyond the realms of place and territory' (Jones 2016, p. 2) opens up new and exciting possibilities. As John Agnew argues, it is necessary to match 'regions' to particular purposes (and by implication focusing on particular sets of relations across space in different cases) rather than seeking to identify a 'singular' conception of regions (Agnew 2013). This means that there is, for example, no contradiction between approaches that focus on identifying the emergence of metropolitan (or city) regions and the ways in which they are held together, defined and imagined (Storper 2014) and those that highlight the importance of topology for understanding the ways in which social relations are stretched across space and folded back into place in uneven and uncertain ways (Cochrane 2012; Allen and Cochrane 2014).

It becomes possible both to identify the extent to which there are more or less settled identities for particular regions (or places) which generate political expressions (and may even be the product of state initiative) and to acknowledge the extent to which any such identities are necessarily provisional and may sit uneasily with the recognition that regional boundaries are always 'fuzzy' and that in practice the ways in which economic and social relations stretch beyond them are as important in shaping what is possible. This means, however, that it is important to be clear about the relations being explored, to spell out the concerns which provide the focus of debate and (above all) to recognise that any conclusion that may be drawn is necessarily incomplete. One of the strengths of the regional debate is the way in which it moves across (and at its best brings together) insights about changing economic activity spaces, emergent forms of political territory or governing spaces, and the shifting geographies of social relations (in terms of class, gender and race).

There are both theoretical and practical challenges to approaching matters in this way. Theoretically, it provides a release from even the most sophisticated attempt to find ways of definitively identifying regions, as expressed, for example, in the words of Martin Jones who suggests that: 'Regions are historical-geographical accomplishments, defined and delimited by shifting relationships' (Jones 2009, p. 499). Maybe some of them are at particular moments, but any such settlements are always provisional, even if they are sometimes long lasting. The challenge is always and everywhere to be committed to exploring and identifying the uneasy sets of relationships that make up and come to define actually existing regions, rather than seeking to uncover some underlying lattice of regional forms. Once regions are conceptualised relationally, it becomes possible to identify the tensions within them as well as between them and elsewhere. So, for example, in the case of a growth region like London and the south east, it is also important to identify the holes in the patchwork of growth, the places that are left over from previous rounds of growth (in the case, including the Fordist industrial legacies of Dagenham and Luton), as well as the significance of stretched relations to outposts of growth and privilege far beyond the administrative boundaries of the region (in parts of Manchester and as well as other global financial centres) (Allen et al. 1998).

From this perspective, as Anssi Paasi and Kaj Zimmerbauer note, the 'relational character and possible "boundedness" of regions is inevitably a phenomenon that is multilayered and complex as well as context and practice bound' (Paasi and Zimmerbauer 2016, p. 75). Regions are made up through their connections to elsewhere, but are also given meaning by the sets of relations that are generated in place. Conventional understandings of regions (and other institutional defined spaces) tend to identify borders of one sort or another between then and neighbouring jurisdictions (or territories). Any such distinction is, however, increasingly difficult to sustain either in theory or in practice. Paasi highlights the significance of what he calls penumbral borders as he emphasises the need to distinguish between the borders that appear in plans and the borders as they are imagined in planning practices (Paasi and Zimmerbauer 2016, p. 87) – for the purposes of preparing plans (particularly if they are to be presented to or are being developed on behalf of area-based government agencies or authorities) borders will appear on maps, but in thinking through development strategies in those plans, what Phil Allmendinger, Graham Haughton and others have identified as the fuzziness of the borders will play a greater part (Allmendinger et al. 2015). Haughton et al. develop a distinction between some of the hard spaces of formal government and the soft spaces of development practice, with which planners are seeking to engage (Haughton et al. 2010), and elsewhere I and others have sought to explore some of the attempts that have been made to govern these unbounded regional spaces (Cochrane et al. 2015). The complexity of the process and the way in which new spaces are incorporated into it are reflected in the mobilisation of a category of sub-regions through which it may be possible to develop a more informal, open and strategic planning process, relatively free from the more accountable and formal processes that Allmendinger et al. (2016) argue are captured in the work of regional agencies.

As the uneasy debates around how one might want to define 'the' region suggest, there is no simple answer to the apparently straightforward question – so, what is a region? The point is not to confirm the crystallisation of some new set of regional arrangements, but rather to highlight the importance of undertaking forensic analysis in exploring the ways in which the region is (or regions are) mobilised as part of a wider process of spatial politics, in which space has an active role in its own right. What matters is to explore and understand the ways in which regions are made up in practice for particular purposes. It is this that means focusing on the apparent dichotomy between territory and regions is ultimately unhelpful. Instead it is important to distinguish between the role of institutionally defined (or territorially defined) regions as government (as much as governing) spaces and the processes by which such spaces are made up in practice.

7.5 REFERENCES

Agnew, J. (2013), 'Arguing with regions', *Regional Studies*, **47** (1), 6–17.
Allen, J. and D. Massey (eds) (1988), *The Economy in Question*, London: Sage.
Allen, J., D. Massey and A. Cochrane (1998), *Rethinking the Region*, London: Routledge.
Allen, J. (2012), 'A more than relational geography?', *Dialogues in Human Geography*, **2** (2), 190–193.
Allen, J. and M. Pryke (2013), 'Financialising household water: Thames Water, MEIF, and "ring-fenced" politics', *Cambridge Journal of Regions, Economy and Society*, **6** (3), 419–439.
Allen, J. and A. Cochrane (2014), 'The urban unbound: London's politics and the 2012 Olympic Games', *International Journal of Urban and Regional Research*, **38** (5), 1609–1624.
Allen, J. (2016), *Topologies of Power: Beyond Territory and Network*, Abingdon: Routledge.
Allmendinger, P., G. Haughton, J. Knieling, and F. Othengrafen (2015), *Soft Spaces in Europe: Renegotiating Governance, Boundaries and Borders*, London: Routledge.
Allmendinger, P., G. Haughton and E. Shepherd (2016) 'Where is planning to be found? Material practices and the multiple spaces of planning', *Environment and Planning C: Government and Policy*, **34** (1), 38–51.
Anderson B., M. Kearnes, C. McFarlane and D. Swanton (2012), 'On assemblages and geography', *Dialogues in Human Geography*, **2** (2), 171–189.
Anderson, J. and A. Cochrane (eds) (1989), *Politics in Transition*, London: Sage.
Castells, M. (1998), *End of Millennium*, Oxford: Blackwell.
Clarke, N and A. Cochrane (2013), 'Geographies and politics of localism: the localism of the United Kingdom's coalition government', *Political Geography*, **34** (1), 10–23.
Cochrane, A. and K. Pain (2000), 'A globalizing society?', in D. Held (ed.), *A Globalizing World? Culture, Economics, Politics*, London: Routledge, pp. 5–45.
Cochrane, A. (2012), 'Making up a region: the rise and fall of the "South-East of England" as a political territory', *Environment and Planning C*, **30** (1), 95–108.

Cochrane, A. and K. Ward (2012), 'Researching the geographies of policy mobility: confronting the methodological challenges', *Environment and Planning A*, **44** (1), 5–12.

Cochrane, A., B. Colenutt and M. Field (2015), 'Governing the ungovernable: spatial policy, markets and volume house-building in a growth region', *Policy and Politics*, **43** (4), 527–544.

Cox, K. (2016) *The Politics of Urban and Regional Development: The American Exception*, Syracuse, NY: Syracuse University Press.

Deas, I. and K. Ward (2000), 'From the "new localism" to the "new regionalism"? The implications of regional development agencies for city-regional relations', *Political Geography*, **19** (3), 273–292.

Deas, I. (2014), 'The search for territorial fixes in subnational governance: city-regions and the disputed emergence of post-political consensus in Manchester, England', *Urban Studies*, **51** (11), 2285–2314.

Elden, S. (2013), *The Birth of Territory*, Chicago, IL: University of Chicago Press.

Florida, R. (1995), 'Toward the learning region', *Futures*, **27** (5), 527–536.

Goodwin, M. (2013), 'Regions, territories and relationality: exploring the regional dimensions of political practice', *Regional Studies*, **47** (8), 1181–1190.

Hamnett, C., L. McDowell and P. Sarre (eds) (1989), *The Changing Social Structure*, London: Sage.

Harrison, J. (2012), 'Life after regions? The evolution of city-regionalism in England', *Regional Studies*, **46** (9), 1243–1259.

Harrison, J. and M. Hoyler (eds) (2015), *Megaregions: Globalization's New Urban Form?* Cheltenham, UK and Northampton, MA, USA: Edward Elgar Publishing.

Harvey, D. (1985), 'The geopolitics of capitalism', in D. Gregory and J. Urry (eds), *Social Relations and Spatial Structures*, London: Macmillan, pp. 128–163.

Haughton, G., P. Allmendinger, D. Counsell and G. Vigar (2010), *The New Spatial Planning: Territorial Management with Soft Spaces and Fuzzy Boundaries*, London: Routledge.

Holland, S. (1987), *The Global Economy: From Meso to Macroeconomics*, London: Weidenfeld and Nicolson.

Jessop, B., N. Brenner and M. Jones (2008), 'Theorizing socio-spatial relations', *Environment and Planning D: Society and Space*, **26** (3), 389–401.

Jonas, A.E.G. (2012), 'Region and place: regionalism in question', *Progress in Human Geography*, **36** (2), 263–272.

Jones, M. (1999), *New Institutional Spaces: Training and Enterprise Councils and the Remaking of Economic Governance*, London: Jessica Kingsley.

Jones, M (2009), 'Phase space: geography, relational thinking, and beyond', *Progress in Human Geography*, **33** (4), 487–506.

Jones, M. (2016), 'Polymorphic political geographies', *Territorial, Politics, Governance*, **4** (1), 1–7.

Keating, M. (1997), 'The invention of regions: political restructuring and territorial government in Western Europe', *Environment and Planning C: Government & Policy*, **15** (4), 383–398.

Keating, M. (2017), 'Contesting European regions', *Regional Studies*, **51** (1), 9–18.

Kitson, M., R. Martin and P. Tyler (2004), 'Regional competitiveness: and elusive yet key concept?', *Regional Studies*, **38** (9), 991–999.

Lobao, L., R. Martin and A. Rodriguez-Pose (2009), 'Rescaling the state: new modes of institutional-territorial organization', *Cambridge Journal of Regions, Economy and Society*, **2** (1), 3–12.

Lord, A. (2009), 'Mind the gap. The theory and practice of state rescaling: institutional morphology and the "new" city regionalism', *Space and Polity*, **13** (2), 77–92.

MacLeod, G. and M. Jones (2007), 'Territorial, scalar, networked, connected: in what sense a "regional world"?', *Regional Studies*, **41** (9), 1177–1191.

Massey, D. (1984), *Spatial Divisions of Labour: Social Structures and the Geography of Production*, London: Macmillan.

Massey, D. (2005), *For Space*, London: Sage.

Morgan, K. (1997), 'The learning region: institutions, innovation and regional renewal', *Regional Studies*, **31** (5), 491–503.

OECD (2007), *Higher Education and Regions: Globally Competitive, Locally Engaged*, Paris: Organisation for Economic Co-operation and Development.

Paasi, A. (2013), 'Regional planning and the mobilization of regional identity: from bounded spaces to relational complexity', *Regional Studies*, **47** (8), 1206–1219.

Paasi, A. and K. Zimmerbauer (2016), 'Penumbral borders and planning paradoxes: relational thinking and the question of borders in spatial planning', *Environment and Planning A*, **48** (1), 75–93.

Paasi, A. and J. Metzger (2017), 'Foregrounding the region', *Regional Studies*, **51** (1), 19–30.

Pike, A., D. Marlow, A. McCarthy, P. O'Brien and J. Tomaney (2015), 'Local institutions and local economic development: the Local Enterprise Partnerships in England, 2010', *Cambridge Journal of Regions, Economy and Society*, **8** (2), 185–204.

Rhodes, R. (1988), *Beyond Westminster and Whitehall: The Sub-Central Governments of Britain*, London: Unwin Hyman.

Rohe, W.M. (2011), *The Research Triangle: From Tobacco Road to Global Prominence*, Philadelphia, PA: University of Pennsylvania Press.

Sassen, S. (2013), 'When territory deborders territoriality', *Territory, Politics, Governance*, **1** (1), 21–45.

Saunders, P. (1985), 'The forgotten dimension of central–local relations: theorising the "regional state"', *Environment and Planning C: Politics and Space*, **3** (2), 149–162.

Scott, A. (ed.) (2001), *Global City-Regions: Trends, Theory, Policy*, Oxford: Oxford University Press.

Smith, N. (1995), 'Remaking scale: competition and cooperation in prenational and postnational Europe', in H. Eskelinen and F. Snickars (eds), *Competitive European Peripheries*, Berlin: Springer, pp. 59–74.

Soja, E. (2000), *Postmetropolis: Critical Studies of Cities and Regions*, Oxford: Blackwell.

Storper, M. (1997), *The Regional World: Territorial Development in a Global Economy*, New York: Guilford Press.

Storper, M. (2014), 'Governing the large metropolis', *Territory, Politics, Governance*, **2** (2), 115–134.

Varró, K. and A. Lagendijk (2013), 'Conceptualizing the region – in what sense relational?', *Regional Studies*, **47** (1), 18–28.

Webb, D. and C. Collis (2000), 'Regional Development Agencies and the "new regionalism" in England', *Regional Studies*, **34** (9), 857–864.

8. The TPSN schema: moving beyond territories and regions
Bob Jessop

While geographers typically address the spatial aspects of social relations and other social scientists share this concern, this interest does not entail a specific account of sociospatiality or just one research method. On the contrary, questions about theories and methods provoke recurrent debates, often generating more heat than light. These are often one-sided, neglect the polymorphy of sociospatial relations, and create theoretical deficits, methodological hazards, and empirical blindspots. That analyses of territory and regions are not immune from these problems can be seen from the recent series of relatively isolated debates on territory, place, scale, and networks and their relevance to regions and regionalism. These problems inspired the TPSN schema, named after its mapping of possible relations among these moments (Jessop et al. 2008; Jones and Jessop 2010; Jessop 2016). This entry outlines the debates, introduces the schema, and then applies it.

8.1 SUCCESSIVE SOCIOSPATIAL 'TURNS' AND THEIR LIMITATIONS

Actors must reduce the complexity of the natural and social world to 'go on' within it, whether as participants or observers, by selecting some aspects as more meaningful or important than others. A fortiori, this holds for the complexity of geophysical and sociospatial relations with the result that actors are forced (usually unwittingly) to approach them through spatial imaginaries that frame their spatial understandings, projects, and experiences or, at least, through other kinds of social imaginary that have significant spatial presuppositions and implications (cf. Lefebvre 1991 on the dialectical relations among conceived, perceived, and lived space).

Space comprises socially produced grids and horizons of social action that divide and organize the material, social, and imaginary world(s) and orient actions in the light of such divisions. These grids and horizons typically function as *asymmetrical sites of social action* that factitiously privilege some kinds of action over others; as *objects of sociospatial ordering strategies* that aim to fix, manipulate, reorder, and relax material, social, and symbolic borders, boundaries, frontiers, and liminal spaces; and as *governmental technologies* used to steer action by sedimenting sites of action and establishing hegemonic spatial horizons of action.

In addition to their general spatial awareness, actors deploy more specific spatial grids and horizons of action. Critical geographers seek to reveal, explore, and explain the unstated, often problematic, spatial assumptions that underpin social action and/or sociospatial research and to trace their effects in the production of space. Among other sociospatial structuring principles, territory, place, scale, and network have attracted much attention along with their relevance to regions, region-building, and regionalism. Other principles exist, such as mobility (Sheller and Urry 2006) and positionality (Leitner et al. 2008), as do other analytical methods, such as multispatial assemblages (Anderson et al. 2012), topology (Weizman 2007), and phase-space (Jones 2009). But the TPSN quartet has been central to efforts to decipher major changes in sociospatial organization and provides the focus below.

8.2   TERRESTRIALITY, TERRITORIALITY, AND STATEHOOD

The significance of territorialization as a sociospatial structuring principle depends on the terrestrial–territorial distinction. The terrestrial refers to '*terra*,' or 'land,' in its broadest sense: land and the subterranean world; the sea, its depths and the seabed; the air above, and, nowadays, outer space. These supply the geophysical and socially appropriated 'raw materials' for territorialization. The terrestrial conditions state claims to sovereignty, underpins different kinds of territorial organization and political strategies, triggers different kinds of territorial disputes, influences the formation and development of land-based and maritime empires, and shapes international law. The main result of territorialization is to divide the landmass (and nearby waters) into delimited areas governed by a political authority (especially some kind of state) that makes binding decisions on residents and defends its authority against internal and external threats. This is reflected in a recent metaphor: 'power container.' Conversely, albeit for different reasons, the 'high seas' and some terrestrial areas (notably the Antarctic, currently legally defined as *terra nullius*, i.e. land without a sovereign) escape territorialization. Further, some forms of political power are only loosely related to distinct territories.

The historical significance of territory was side-lined for a time when its theoretical treatment was criticized on two grounds. First, the 'territorial trap' critique disputed three common assumptions: states are sovereign in their territory; the 'domestic-foreign' distinction is a fixed feature of the modern interstate system; and states are static, timeless, territorial power containers (Agnew 1994; Taylor 1994). Second, the 'methodological nationalism' critique argued that it was an error to delimit 'society' in terms of the territorial boundaries of national states, thereby conflating societies and nations. These criticisms led to lively debates on the changing territorialities of statehood, including regionalism and cross-border regions as well as new forms of sovereignty and governance (for a representative anthology, see Brenner et al. 2003) as well as a turn to other sociospatial themes.

8.3   PUTTING REGIONS IN THEIR PLACE

Grounded in studies of spatial divisions of labor and local or regional economic restructuring in the 1980s, geographers began to reject the notion that *place* (or locale) denotes fixed, areal, and self-contained building blocks of sociospatial organization. On the contrary, they claimed, its boundaries are contingent and relational and serve both to contain and connect interactions across places and spaces at diverse scales. They noted that the significance of place is usually closely tied to everyday life, has layered and differential temporal depth, and is tied to collective memory and social identity. The naming, delimitation, and meaning of places are contested and the coordinates of any given physical space can be linked with multiple places with different identities, spatiotemporal boundaries, and social significance. In other words, places were seen to emerge from relationally constituted, polyvalent processes that were embedded in broader sets of social relations (Cresswell 2004; Hudson 2002; Massey 1994, 1984; Pierce et al. 2011).

8.4   SCALAR TURNS

Scale was traditionally conceived as a nested hierarchy of bounded spaces of differing size and, in territorial terms, it was associated with different tiers of government. Such conceptions were challenged by a scalar turn in the 1990s (partly inspired by a Marxist analysis of uneven development conceived in scalar terms, Smith 1984) as part of efforts to discover how global, continental, national, regional and local relations were being recalibrated through capitalist restructuring, state transformation, and changes in 'civil society' and its mobilization. A useful distinction between dominant, nodal, and marginal scales was drawn by Collinge, who also noted that these may not be organized in a neat hierarchy from top to bottom (Collinge 1999). Scholars explored the (potentially tangled and divergent) processes of scale-making, rescaling, scale-bending, and upward and downward scale-jumping and how they affected the hierarchical relations among various intertwined forms of sociospatial organization such as market exchange, state institutions, urban forms, and citizenship regimes (Keil and Mahon 2009; Sheppard and McMaster 2004; Smith 1995; Swyngedouw 1997). The ensuing rich analyses of scalar relations had two contrasting results. One was a bandwagon that found scalarity and associated practices everywhere to the detriment of other sociospatial dimensions. The other was a 'flat ontology' that viewed scale as akin to horizontal networks assembled through diverse constitutive practices. This ignored how scales might also be linked: vertically or transversally, centripetally or centrifugally (cf. Leitner and Miller 2007).

8.5   THE NETWORK TURN

Focused on networking as a structuring principle, this turn studied *decentered* sets of social relations characterized by circular flows, functional interdependence, or *symmetrical connectivity* (Castells 1996). Scholars explored networks, stressing transversal, 'rhizomatic' forms of interspatial interconnectivity and studied network geographies in such fields as commodity chains, interfirm interdependencies, cross-border governance systems, interurban relations, and social movements (Grabher 2006). This fed interest in networks and their relation to territorial, place-based and scalar formations (Amin 2004; Marston et al. 2005). However, an emphasis on 'flat ontologies' risks neglecting the hierarchies that often exist within and among networks. Even if power relations inside all networks were egalitarian and symmetrical, asymmetries and inequalities might occur in network–network relations because of the uneven capacities of networked agents to pursue their own interests and strategies. This could arise from the place-based grounding of networks (global cities or marginal places), the scales at and across which they operate (e.g. dominant, nodal, or marginal), and their territorial (dis)embedding (e.g. colonies, empires, strong versus weak states). Such considerations highlight the importance of a broader TPSN approach.

All four turns were sometimes pushed too far and interpreted in one-dimensional terms. Some scholars fell into the metonymic trap of conflating a part (territory, place, scale, or networks) with the whole (the totality of sociospatial organization), whether this was due to conceptual imprecision, an overly narrow analytical focus, or ontological (quasi-)reductionism. Examples of this trap include: (1) *methodological territorialism*, which, as noted, subsumes all aspects of sociospatial relations under the rubric of [politicized] territoriality; (2) *place-centrism*, which treats places as discrete, largely self-contained, socio-ecological assemblages and/or relies excessively on the lexicon of place to interpret sociospatial relations; (3) *scale-centrism* treats scale as the axis around which other sociospatial dimensions are organized, or alternatively, subsumes ever more sociospatial relations under an increasingly sophisticated scalar rubric; and (4) a one-sided, *network-centric* focus on the horizontal, rhizomatic, topological and transversal interconnections of networks located in a frictionless space of flows and marked by accelerating mobility.

8.6   THE TPSN FRAMEWORK

Jessop et al. (2008) offered a distinctive metatheoretical response to such issues. Rather than making yet another turn to introduce yet another sociospatial moment, they proposed an overarching heuristic framework that, due to its focus on territory (T), place (P), scale (S) and networks (N), was termed the TPSN framework. It highlighted the existence of more complex, multidimensional sociospatial configurations without preempting future research. Table 8.1 cross-tabulates all four sociospatial dimensions regarded, first, as *structuring principles* and, second, as fields open to *structuration* through one or other principle. It shows that structuring principles apply not only to themselves – a route to mutually isolated forms of one-dimensionalism – but to other sociospatial fields too. The concepts given in each cell are illustrative, intended to spur fresh studies on the polymorphy of sociospatial relations. Serious polymorphic research must also overcome the two-dimensionalism of Table 8.1 to give a richer account of specific TPSN landscapes (for an example of how to do this, see Harrison 2013, on the new regionalism).

Taking territory to illustrate these points, this matrix shows that each sociospatial concept can be deployed in three ways:

- *in itself*, as a product of (re)bordering strategies that operated on the existing territorial landscape (this reads the matrix diagonally, hence territory ↔ territory);
- as a *structuring principle* (or causal mechanism) that impacts other already structured fields of sociospatial relations that may be undergoing restructuring in other respects too (this reads the matrix horizontally, hence: territory → place; territory → scale; territory → network), and
- as a *structured field*, produced in part through the impact of other sociospatial structuring principles on territorial dynamics (this reads the matrix vertically: place → territory; scale → territory; and network → territory).

Table 8.1   Towards a multidimensional analysis of sociospatiality

Structuring principles	Fields of operation			
	TERRITORY	**PLACE**	**SCALE**	**NETWORKS**
TERRITORY	States as power containers defined by their frontiers or boundaries	Integrating places into a territory, managing uneven growth in a state	Intergovernmental arrangements for coordinating different scales	Interstate alliances, consociational democracy, multi-area government
PLACE	Core–periphery relations, land-based empires, borderlands	Locales, milieux, cities, regions, localities, globalities	Glocalization, glurbanization (global–local and urban–global ties)	Local, urban, regional governance or partnerships
SCALE	Scalar division of political power (unitary versus federal state, MLG, etc.)	Local ↔ global articulations, areal (spatial) division of labor	Nested or tangled scalar hierarchies, scale jumping, rescaling, descaling	Parallel power networks, private international regimes
NETWORKS	Cross-border region, virtual regions, nomadic shadow empires	Global city networks, poly-nucleated cities, overseas trading companies	'Soft spaces,' networks of differently scaled places	Networks of networks, spaces of flows, maritime empires

The same points hold for the three other moments in this schema. It thereby suggests that sociospatial configurations can be interpreted as contingent expressions of efforts at strategic coordination and structural coupling in specific spatiotemporal contexts:

(1)   Different TPSN configurations could be the *site* for elaborating spatiotemporal strategies and fixes, that is, sites where strategies and fixes are elaborated and pursued (e.g. states, land-based empires, global city networks, or virtual regions such as the BRIC quartet of Brazil, Russia, India, and China).

(2)   They could be the *object* of spatiotemporal strategies and fixes, becoming objects of recalibration, reorganization, collibration, and so on – either as they currently exist (e.g. by rebalancing their structuring principles) or as potential objects (e.g. China's multispatial 'One Belt, One Road' project to reconnect the Eurasian heartland overland and by sea, see Sum, 2018).

(3)   They could have different roles *as means* in securing, modifying, or disrupting the coherence of spatiotemporal relations in social formations in different stages of development, historical contexts, and specific conjunctures.

(4)   The relative significance of these structuring principles is reflected in forms of sociospatial governance. Territorialization is associated with hierarchical rule by a sovereign state that governs a territory without being subject to external authority; place-based governance might sustain local democracy based on community and solidarity; interscalar articulation is appropriate to multilevel governance; and

networks relate to network governance. TPSN patterns also vary with institutional and spatiotemporal fixes.

(5)   These axes also provide reference points for spatial imaginaries and strategies. These could focus on one axis of spatial organization or involve two or more axes. For example, multilevel governance arrangements combine territory and scale; core-periphery relations are based on asymmetrical relations among places in a territory; polynucleated cities involve networked places; and cross-border regions are networked territories. In addition, multispatial metagovernance aspires to order and reorder three or more of these sociospatial dimensions (see below).

(6)   The TPSN schema also illuminates the potentially conflictual relation between (i) the territorial logic involved in governing states and interstate relations and (ii) the scalar and/or reticular logics of the governance of the space of flows (Arrighi 1994; Harvey 2003). The former concerns the territorialization of political power as instantiated in states as power containers and the use of state power to control territory to promote geopolitical interests. The latter concerns the balance between fixity and motion across continuous space–time, whether to promote capital accumulation or facilitate other border-crossing activities and interests (see below).

(7)   Crises and attempts at crisis resolution may both reorder the relative weight of the four principles and their institutional expressions and, hence, modify their respective roles in displacing or deferring crisis tendencies and contradictions in one or another spatiotemporal fix. They may also alter the prospects of sub- or counter-hegemonic projects (e.g. the social economy, the Occupy movement).

For its authors, the TPSN framework facilitates studies of spatial polymorphy because it elaborates useful concepts for (1) its four primary sociospatial dimensions and (2) their differential articulation or co-implication in specific spatiotemporal arrangements. As such, it allows – and encourages – sociospatial research to start from one or another single entrypoint and conclude with more complex analyses that give each moment its proper descriptive-cum-explanatory weight (Jessop et al. 2008, pp. 393–394). Such multispatial analyses do not assume the structured coherence of sociospatial arrangements and, depending on context, may reveal contradictions, dilemmas, crisis-tendencies, and points of conflict that limit the stability and durability of these arrangements. Moreover, as two of its proponents have argued (Jones and Jessop 2010), the TPSN approach can also highlight what they called '*geographies of compossibility.*' These arise because not every sociospatial arrangement that seems possible when judged in isolation can be combined in a relatively durable manner with all other individually feasible arrangements in a specific spatiotemporal context. In short, not everything that is possible is compossible. This opens several interesting fields of research on polymorphic spatiality that will now be illustrated in several ways relevant to this Handbook.

8.7   REGIONS AND TERRITORIES

The TPSN framework offers important insights into the problem of how best to define a region as a meaningful and feasible spatiotemporal matrix that both constrains and facilitates social action, institutional ordering, and their relation to broader sociospatial landscapes. One-dimensional regional imaginaries and practices include: the territorialization of political power in terms of subnational or supra-national regions, the propinquity of places as settings for action (e.g. city-regions), the regional scaling of instituted social systems (e.g. regional wage-bargaining, regional planning, and regional health or education systems), and network building to extend and reinforce spaces of flows in 'virtual cross-border regions' (e.g. the Four Motors cross-border region in Europe, comprising Baden-Württemberg, Rhône-Alpes, Lombardy, and Catalonia). These examples show how diverse definitions can influence regional strategies for economic development. More generally, the naming and mapping of regions are subject to discursive struggles (Jenson 1995; Paasi 2001, 2013) as well as more substantive struggles over their social, material, and spatiotemporal institutionalization. Thus seen, regions can have multiple boundaries and will be distinguished (or 'imagined' or simply 'imaged') in different ways in different discourses for different purposes and with different effects. The feasibility of this co-constitution (its compossibility) varies with historical legacies and how regions are embedded in economic, political, and social contexts (e.g. regions in centrally planned economies differ from those in decentralized, especially liberal market, economies).

Developing this relational approach to regional imaginaries and regional formation requires some geopolitical and geoeconomic reflections on how the interaction between competing territorial logics and spaces of flows transforms current terrestrial worlds and puts different spatial imaginaries and structuring principles into play. A useful synthetic analysis has identified a tangled hierarchy of contested regional spaces that also indicates the variable scope of the regional concept. The two contending peaks of the hierarchy comprise two broad geostrategic realms: first, a Maritime realm formed by Western Europe, North America, Maritime East Asia, Australia, and the Mediterranean littoral and, second, the Eurasian Continental realm, including the former Soviet Union and China (Mackinder, 1904, described the latter as the Eurasian heartland). Next come subordinate geopolitical regions (e.g. Europe, Japan, North America) and independent geopolitical regions outside the two main geostrategic realms (e.g. South Asia). Below these are individual national states followed by subnational and cross-border regions (Cohen 2003). We can complicate this schema further by distinguishing different kinds of territorial and maritime empire. There are changing forms of hegemony and hierarchy among these types of region, overlapping spheres of influence, national components and transnational influences, embryonic and dying regions, marginal spheres and areas of confrontation. There are continuing complex rearticulations of global–regional–national–local economies with uneven effects. Thus, we find mosaics of cross-border alliances organized within and across regions and continents, sometimes based on inter-governmental cooperation, sometimes on pooled sovereignty, sometimes on hidden forms of (neo-)imperial domination.

This is reflected not only in shifts in national economic fortunes but also in the rise and fall of regions, new 'north–south' divides, and so on. Thus, after the Soviet bloc split, space opened for new forms of rivalry in Europe and the wider world. The decline of US hegemony and the opening of China have reinforced these rivalries and created space for new forms of world market fragmentation, differentiation, and integration. For example, China's promotion, since 2013, of the One Belt, One Road project, aims to recreate the traditional land and maritime trade routes in the Eurasian heartland and link them to Africa. This project indicates how regions operate not only as containers but also as connectors through diverse cross-regional networks and therefore exist in a space marked by the tension between containment and connection, fixity and flow, imagined identity and actual connexity. This complicates regional dynamics and the prospects for regional strategies. Indeed, it would be more apt, if convoluted, to discuss plurispatial, multitemporal, and poly-contextual modes of imagining, constituting, and governing regional economies and their always relative, provisional, and unstable integration into more encompassing economic spaces, right up to the world market (for an interesting discussion of city-regions in this context, see Jonas and Moisio 2017).

8.8   THE RELATIVIZATION OF SCALE

An important context for regional shifts in this regard over the last 40 years has been the 'relativization of scale' that followed the loss of primacy of the national scale in advanced capitalist economies to the extent that no new primary scale emerged in place of the national level. The decline of a national spatiotemporal fix opened space for new kinds of regional strategy have become possible. These can be understood in TPSN terms. For example:

- Seeking to locate a given place or region within a vertical hierarchy to maximize the advantages accruing from its relations to each point in the scale.
- Developing horizontal linkages among places or regions of similar type, ignoring the vertical dimension in favor of network building (global city networks are one example, cross-border regions another).
- Building 'transversal' linkages, i.e. bypassing one or more immediately neighbouring scale(s) to link with processes on other scales. Examples are growth triangles, export processing zones, free ports, and regional gateways.
- Trying to escape from scalar or place-bound constraints by locating one's activities in a borderless space of networked flows or moving into 'cyberspace.'

These options may be combined in more complex strategies, which can be explored from three viewpoints: (1) the nature of the interscalar articulation involved – vertical (up and/or down), lateral (extraversion or introversion), transversal, etc.; (2) their primary carriers – private economic agents (e.g. firms, banks, chambers of commerce, private equity funds), public bodies (e.g. different tiers of government, local or regional associations, quangos), or social movements of various kinds (e.g. diasporas, civic associations, ethnic communities, nationalist movements, movements to assert the right to the city or proclaim cultural identities, etc.); and (3) the relative primacy of the logics of the de- and re-territorialization of political power – usually associated with state actors or forces dependent on the state – and the rescaling and reorganization of the space of flows – usually associated with economic actors seeking to optimize profits without regard to territorial boundaries. As these examples suggest, the choice of spatial scale for regional economic development is inherently strategic. It depends on the political, economic, and social specificities of an urban or regional context at a given conjuncture.

Seen in these terms, regional imaginaries could aim to strengthen regional political institutions and capacities to govern regional economic space and/or to find ways to capture flows through specific spatial fixes (e.g. infrastructure provision) or reducing frictions (e.g. deregulation, liberalization, flexibilization). This raises questions about how the logics of territorialization and flows are mixed in specific cases of regionalization and how to govern these sometimes complementary, sometimes antagonistic, logics. For these strategies are not mutually exclusive. Indeed, Harvey suggests that each logic generates contradictions that must be contained by the other. If territorial logic blocks the logic of capital, economic crises may occur; conversely, if capitalist logic undermines territorial logic, there is a risk of political crisis. Overall, this may generate a spiral movement of uneven development as contradictions are displaced from one logic to the other in a process of mutual adjustment and reaction (Harvey 2003, p. 140).

8.9   TERRITORIES AND REGIONS IN EUROPEAN UNION GOVERNANCE

Territory and regions are crucial issues for the European Union. First, viewed in TPSN terms, it has been described and approached strategically in various ways: territorially, as the Europe des *patries* (or nation-states); in place terms, as a Europe of cities or regions (including cross-border regions); in scalar terms, as a space of multilevel government or governance; and, finally, as a space of network governance oriented to a space of flows. Let us consider the last two mappings.

Multilevel government is a political regime based on imperative coordination through a territorial state (with a multilevel but unified hierarchy of command) that claims responsibility for managing relations among bounded areas under its exclusive control. This state can be a single territorial state (with at least two tiers of government) or a confederation of such states that has delegated at least some competences to one or more supranational political instances. The former pattern is typically analysed in terms of public administration and federalism. The latter has re-emerged as an analytical or strategic problem in two contexts: (1) the decomposition of the Soviet Union – *a multistate imperial regime dominated by Russia* – and its reorganization into a Commonwealth of Independent States that is seeking a new equilibrium of powers and competencies across economic spaces and states that were previously poorly integrated under central command; and (2) the expansion of the European Union as a *multitiered federal state in the process of formation*, in which the relationship among its political tiers (cities, regions, national states, and European institutions) is not yet settled and has evolved hitherto through a mix of incremental innovation in stable periods and crisis-induced radical integration in turbulent periods. Thus, whereas the Europe of Cities and the Europe of Regions are more incremental developments, recent proposals for tighter fisco-financial integration and centralized budgetary oversight are responses to the Eurozone crisis. The overall process of integration is a complex, hybrid process with different forms of government and governance in different policy fields and in different periods.

Theoretical and policy debates about multilevel government (hereafter MLG) range between two poles. One pole comprises arguments for multilevel government based on a commitment to subsidiarity, that is, maximum possible devolution of powers and competences to the lowest tier of government with higher tiers responsible for policy problems that cannot be settled at lower levels. The other pole comprises calls for a United

States of Europe with power concentrated in European-level institutions and lower tiers acting as relays for decisions made at the European level. Between these poles are many other proposals and, more importantly, competing tendencies or developmental trends. Interestingly, the MLG concept occupies just two cells in Table 8.1: those dealing with territorial ordering along scalar lines and the (re-)scaling of territorial relations. Likewise, the limited descriptive and explanatory power of the alternative concept of multiscalar metagovernance relative to the potential range of multidimensional sociospatial governance arrangements also shows the limits of this alternative concept. For, while it transcends government and governance, it merely substitutes scale for level as the site of metagovernance practices.

Network governance relies on a mix of well-ordered market relations (economic exchange), commitment to negotiation (consensus-oriented deliberation), and solidarity (credible commitments to cooperation). It can emerge spontaneously, in response to initiatives by key stakeholders, or from state initiatives to reduce the burdens of government by pooling sovereignty and/or sharing responsibilities for governing complex problems with diverse public, private, and third-sector partners. Network governance aims to secure the conditions for the flow of goods, services, technologies, capital, and people across different territories, for connecting different places in new divisions of labor (e.g. networks of cities, interdependent centers of production, different forms of center–periphery relation), over different scales of social organization (that may not coincide with territorial boundaries), and different sets of social bonds based on mutual trust. This pattern is less concerned to integrate government in an emerging supranational or federal state system than to create the conditions for integrated markets with agreed governance arrangements but no overall coordination. It is closer to the open regionalism model said to characterize East Asia and the wider Pacific Region. In the European Union, this governance pattern is seen in, inter alia, the Open Method of Coordination.

Multilevel government and network governance are prone to similar tensions and crisis-tendencies to those in the above-noted oscillation between territorial government and the governance of flows. The hybrid nature of EU government-cum-governance combines elements of both forms plus other transversal arrangements – further complicated by a new Franco-German political axis seeking to maintain the Eurozone through decisions imposed on weaker member states (notably Greece but also Portugal and Italy). We can also see attempts to secede from or split the EU (notably in the case of the British exit from the European Union under negotiation at the time of writing) as well as to develop new macroscales that go well beyond the territory and regions of the European Union and involve new kinds of governance.

8.10   MULTISPATIAL METAGOVERNANCE

This suggests that multilevel government and/or multiscalar governance and their respective agents should be put in their place in a broader multispatial context informed by the TPSN schema. In practice, much work occurring under the rubric of MLG (whether the third letter in the acronym is interpreted as government or governance) does consider some of these complexities, usually in presenting findings rather than in any prior theoretical analysis. Terminologically, then, MLG is a misleading and oversimplified self-designation of work in this field and this has triggered many efforts to clarify its different meanings and/or dimensions.

An alternative, drawing on the TPSN schema, is *multispatial metagovernance* (Jessop 2016). This is illustrated by the EU. Indeed, the latter is a major and, indeed, increasingly important, supranational instance of *multispatial metagovernance* in relation to a wide range of complex and interrelated problems. This is also relevant to other issues of governing complex social relations that exist in and across several spatiotemporal social fields. Multispatial metagovernance has four advantages over multilevel government, network governance, multilevel governance, and other widely used concepts. First, it affirms the irreducible plurality of territorial areas, social scales, networks, and places to be addressed in attempts at governance. It notes the complex interrelations between territorial organization, multiple scalar divisions of labor (and other practices), networked forms of social interaction, and the importance of place as a meeting point of functional operations and the conduct of personal life. Second, it recognizes the complex, tangled, and interwoven nature of the relevant political relations, which include important horizontal and transversal linkages – indicated in notions such as 'network state' or 'network polity' – as well as the vertical linkages implied in multilevel government and/or governance. Third, in contrast to a one-sided emphasis on heterarchic coordination, it introduces metagovernance considered as the reflexive art of balancing government and other forms of governance to create requisite variety, flexibility, and adaptability in coordinated policy-formulation, policy-making, and implementation. Two aspects of such collibration include (i) reliance on different scales and sites of action to address different challenges and/or to displace emerging problems to marginal or liminal territories, spaces, places, scales; and (ii) privileging one or two sociospatial moments until it becomes urgent to address hitherto neglected dimensions. Fourth, it stresses the plurality and heterogeneity of actors involved in such institutions and practices, which stretch well beyond tiers of government and the limits of any given administrative, political, or economic space.

Indeed, because the sources and reach of these problems go well beyond the territorial space occupied by its member states, the EU is an important, if confusing, point of intersection in the emerging, hypercomplex, and chaotic system of global governance (or, better, forms of multispatial metagovernance that have the planet and global society as their ultimate horizons of action). As such, it cannot be fully understood without considering its complex relations with other nodes above, below, and transversal to the European Union. Indeed, while one might hypothesize that the European scale is becoming increasing dominant within the EU's multispatial metagovernance regime, it is merely nodal in the emerging global multiscalar metagovernance regimes that are developing under the (increasingly crisis-prone) dominance of the United States. And, with the rapprochement between Russia and China and growing ties between Germany and these two counter-hegemonic regions, one might also see a new dominant Eurasian regional scale emerging.

8.11   CONCLUSION

The TPSN schema is one of several approaches to exploring the complexities of sociospatial organization. Its initial motivation was to offer a means to escape one-dimensional spatial turns and their associated theoretical, epistemological, and methodological traps. It has since been developed for other purposes, illustrated above. It emphasizes the variable significance of territory, place, scale, and network in different spatiotemporal configurations. It also indicates that crises arise when the dynamics associated with one dimension in one or another configuration undermine its previous structured coherence and strategic logic. Likewise, crisis resolution may depend on capacities to construct a new spatiotemporal fix that reorders the relative importance of territory, place, scale, and network. Lastly, the idea of compossibility is a valuable addition to the lexicon of sociospatial inquiry and highlights important features of four-planar topographies and topologies.

8.12   REFERENCES

Agnew, J. (1994), 'The territorial trap: the geographical assumptions of international relations theory', *Review of International Political Economy*, **1** (1), 53–80.

Amin, A. (2004), 'Regions unbound: towards a new politics of place', *Geografiska Annaler: Series B, Human Geography*, **86** (1), 33–44.

Anderson, B., M. Kearnes, C. McFarlane, and D. Swanton (2012), 'On assemblages and geography', *Dialogues in Human Geography*, **2** (2), 171–189.

Arrighi, G. (1994), *The Long Twentieth Century: Money, Power and the Origins of Our Times*, London: NLB.

Brenner, N., B. Jessop, M. Jones and G. MacLeod (eds) (2003), *State/Space: A Reader*, Oxford: Blackwell.

Castells, M. (1996), *The Rise of the Network Society*, Oxford: Blackwell.

Cohen, S.B. (2003), *Geopolitics of the World System*, Lanham, MD: Rowman and Littlefield.

Collinge, C. (1999), 'Self-organization of society by scale: a spatial reworking of regulation theory', *Environment and Planning D: Society & Space*, **17** (5), 557–574.

Cresswell, T. (2004), *Place: A Short Introduction*, Oxford: Blackwell.

Grabher, G. (2006), 'Trading routes, bypasses and risky intersections: mapping the travels of "networks" between economic sociology and economic geography', *Progress in Human Geography*, **30** (1), 1–27.

Harrison, J. (2013), 'Configuring the new "regional world": on being caught between territory and networks', *Regional Studies*, **47** (1), 55–74.

Harvey, D. (2003), *The New Imperialism*, Oxford: Oxford University Press.

Hudson, R. (2002), *Producing Places*, New York: Guilford Press.

Jenson, J. (1995), 'Mapping, naming, and remembering: globalization at the end of the twentieth century', *Review of International Political Economy*, **2** (1), 96–116.

Jessop, B., N. Brenner and M. Jones (2008), 'Theorizing sociospatial relations', *Environment and Planning D*, **26** (3), 381–401.

Jessop, B. (2016), 'Territory, politics, governance and multispatial metagovernance', *Territory, Politics, Governance*, **4** (1), 8–32.

Jonas, A.E.G. and S. Moisio (2017), 'City regionalism as geopolitical processes: a new framework for analysis', *Progress in Human Geography*, published online, doi/pdf/10.1177/0309132516679897.

Jones, M. (2009), 'Phase space: geography, relational thinking, and beyond', *Progress in Human Geography*, **33** (4), 487–506.

Jones, M. and B. Jessop (2010), 'Thinking state/space incompossibly', *Antipode*, **42** (5), 1119–1149.

Keil, R. and R. Mahon (eds) (2009), *Leviathan Undone? Towards a Political Economy of Scale*, Vancouver: University of British Columbia Press.

Lefebvre, H. (1991), *The Production of Space*, Oxford: Blackwell.

Leitner, H. and B. Miller (2007), 'Scale and the limitations of ontological debate: a commentary on Marston, Jones and Woodward', *Transactions of the Institute of British Geographers*, **32** (1), 116–125.

Leitner, H., E. Sheppard and K.M. Sziarto (2008), 'The spatialities of contentious politics', *Transactions of the Institute of British Geographers*, **33** (1), 57–72.

Mackinder, H. (1904), 'The geographical pivot of history', *Geographical Journal*, **23** (4), 421–437.

Marston, S.A., J.P. Jones III, and K. Woodward (2005), 'Human geography without scale', *Transactions of the Institute of British Geographers*, **30** (4), 416–432.

Massey, D. (1984), *Spatial Divisions of Labour*, Basingstoke: Macmillan.

Massey, D. (1994), *Space, Place and Gender*, Cambridge: Polity.

Paasi, A. (2001), 'Europe as a social process and discourse: considerations of place, boundaries and identity', *European Urban and Regional Studies*, **8** (1), 7–28.

Paasi, A. (2013), 'Regional planning and the mobilization of "regional identity": from bounded spaces to relational complexity', *Regional Studies*, **47** (8), 1–14.

Pierce, J., D.G. Martin and J.T. Murphy (2011), 'Relational place-making: the networked politics of place', *Transactions of the Institute of British Geographers*, **36** (1), 54–70.

Sheller, M. and J. Urry (2006), 'The new mobilities paradigm', *Environment and Planning A*, **38** (2), 207–226.

Sheppard, E. and R. McMaster (eds) (2004), *Scale and Geographic Inquiry*, Oxford: Blackwell.

Smith, N. (1984), *Uneven Development*, Oxford: Blackwell.

Smith, N. (1995), 'Remaking scale: competition and cooperation in prenational and postnational Europe', in H. Eskelinen and F. Snickars (eds), *Competitive European Peripheries*, Berlin: Springer, pp. 59–74.

Sum, N.L. (2018), 'The production of a trans-regional scale: China's "One Belt One Road" imaginary', in A. Paasi, J. Harrison and M. Jones (eds), *Handbook on the Geographies of Regions and Territories*, Cheltenham, UK and Northampton, MA, USA: Edward Elgar Publishing, pp. 428–443.

Swyngedouw, E. (1997), 'Neither global nor local: "glocalization" and the politics of scale', in K. Cox (ed.), *Spaces of Globalization*, New York: Guilford Press, pp. 137–166.

Taylor, P.J. (1994), 'The state as container: territoriality in the modern world-system', *Progress in Human Geography*, **18** (2), 151–162.

Weizman, E. (2007), *Hollow Land: Israel's Architecture of Occupation*, London: Verso.

PART II

REGION, TERRITORY AND ECONOMY

9. Economic regionalization
Andrew Jones

9.1 INTRODUCTION

After several decades of debate within human geography and other social sciences disciplines about the concept of globalization, in the second decade of the twenty-first century there has been a growing set of arguments developed that globalization is in retreat (Lund et al. 2013, Bodoni and Surgun 2017). Understood as the broad integration and growing interconnectedness of all aspects of social life at the planet-wide scale (Jones 2010), a large proportion of the globalization debate has focused on a narrow aspect – the globalization of economic activity. In fact, in popular debates in the media and politics, globalization is itself often equated with economic globalization – the power of transnational corporations, the shift of manufacturing production to different locations around the globe or the nature of globalized finance (Ritzer and Dean 2015). It is in that context also that more recent interventions have sought to suggest a retreat from (economic) globalization and a retrenchment towards the regional scale in the integration of economic activities. Over the last decade, therefore, the concept of economic regionalization has been widely associated as being in many senses in tension or even the opposite of the neoliberal economic globalization experienced across the global economy since the 1980s (Sunkel and Inotai 2016). Rather than the unbridled and unchecked integration of economic activities at the global scale as expressed in the hyper-globalization of the 1990s (cf. Held et al. 1999), economic globalization has diminished and reduced as a process and economic activity has receded to the regional scale (Cooper et al. 2007; Altman 2009). Economic regionalization in this sense is often defined as the intensification and focus of economic activities within regions at the expense of linkages and organizational arrangements of greater distances. In the current era of resurgent nationalism in the advanced industrial economies of Europe and North America (Cull 2016), along with political debates about increasing national economic protectionism (Greenaway et al. 2016), it would appear that economic globalization and economic regionalization are thus in tension and competing trends.

The key argument developed in this chapter, however, is that they are not and that a more sophisticated understanding of economic regionalization reveals how its development is entwined with wider globalization processes that have continued but evolved in the last fifty years. Despite widespread lack of clarity – as well as a tendency to counterpose these concepts as opposites – economic regionalization needs to be seen as another manifestation of economic integration across space that is entwined rather than in contradiction with more generalized globalization. That is not to say that regionalization and globalization amount to the same thing, nor that there are not countervailing tendencies where global scale integration has been superseded by intensifying integration at the regional scale. Rather the argument is that where globalization does appear to have been 'replaced' by stronger trends of regionalization, this intensification at the regional level remains strongly embedded in the wider context of simultaneous global scale integration.

To understand these arguments in more depth, the chapter first addresses some key conceptual issues of definition that also have not been clear in the social science debate about economic regionalization. In the next section, it briefly examines how economic globalization itself might be defined and the various facets to this process in the contemporary global economy. In the following section, it then uses this discussion to offer a definition of economic regionalization but also consider the significant challenges that exist in understanding the process and what is meant by 'a region' itself. The fourth part of the chapter moves on to develop the argument that counterposing economic globalization with economic regionalization amounts to a false dichotomy, elaborating the contention that there is a need to develop a more sophisticated conceptualization of the nature of economic regionalization. Finally, the chapter draws together some conclusions about how economic regionalization might be better understood in future theoretical and policy debates.

9.2   DEFINING ECONOMIC GLOBALIZATION

To understand the contemporary context of economic regionalization as a process, and what we might mean by that, we first need to frame this understanding around the broader idea of economic globalization. In this respect, if the concept of globalization itself refers to societal integration at the planetary scale (Jones 2006) in general, then undoubtedly the globalization of economic activity has and continues to play a very central role in this process. We can therefore define economic globalization as the growing integration and interconnectedness of a range of different dimensions to the capitalist world economy, and whilst this has been going on for many centuries, it is more the intense phase of economic globalization that has occurred since the end of the Second World War which has most concerned social scientists (Scholte 2005; Bisley 2007). Since the later part of the twentieth century, social scientists from a range of disciplines have argued that processes of economic globalization have made it increasingly appropriate to refer to one, integrated global economy (Dicken 2015). There are a number of factors that have led to this situation in the last forty or fifty years – the changing nature of international politics, deregulation, new information and communication technologies are just a few – but overall the degree to which economic activity in the twenty-first century is interconnected across the globe is greater than at any point in human history. For geographical thinkers and regional scientists, central to their analysis is to try to better understand and theorize how these processes have been *uneven* with very different impacts in different parts of the globe and between different regions (MacKinnon and Cumbers 2014). It is worth considering in more depth the historical development of this process. There are three key aspects I would suggest are important.

First, something that might be called world economy has existed throughout human history but, until relatively recently, economic activity was largely confined to the places and localities where it was undertaken (Held et al. 1999). In pre-industrial societies, economic activity entailed the production of food and various manufactured goods that were largely produced and consumed in the same local areas. However, notwithstanding this, the earliest form of what we might regard as economic globalization does have a long history in the form of trade between continents, regions and more recently (in the modern period) across national borders. In that sense, the integration of economic activity stretches back into antiquity, and human history over the last three millennia has seen a variety of different local regional, globally extensive trading systems (Held et al. 1999). Early processes of economic globalization are evident a surprisingly long way back with, for example, the Roman Empire organizing cross-continental economic activity around trade. The Chinese empire that existed for more than a thousand years in the middle ages also extended currencies, trade and other limited forms of economic activity at an inter-continental scale (Hobsbawm 2007). In that sense, in the medieval period we can talk about a world economy. However, and of particular importance to understand, its *degree* of global integration is very limited even if a few global-scale interconnections did exist (Held et al. 1999; Ritzer and Dean 2015). That is to say, whilst there were a surprising number of global scale linkages, their number, volume and intensity were very limited.

Second, what we mean by economic globalization in today's world is related to the nature of today's capitalist world economy that has developed since the sixteenth century, and which has been 'global in its scope' since the nineteenth century (Wallerstein 1974, 1979). Capitalism as a form of economic organization emerged in Western Europe and spread out through the globe through European colonial expansion and then later empires. During the twentieth century, an international system of nation-states gradually replaced these empires to cover the world map. However, early economic globalization was sporadic in nature. During the nineteenth century, there was considerable integration of many new parts of the world into the capitalist system, but the two world wars and their political consequences in the first half of the twentieth century interrupted and in fact reduced some of this economic integration (Hirst et al. 2015). The world that emerged in 1945 after the Second World War was divided between the capitalist first world, the communist second world and the developing third world. This 'tri-partite' world had a range of barriers to further economic integration with states regulating how much money and how many goods and services could be traded across national borders. A large part of the global map was communist and disconnected from the capitalist world economy altogether (Flint and Taylor 2007).

Third and finally, since the early 1970s this situation changed and the disconnected world economic system began to become more interconnected in a number of ways. During the 1970s, the degree of regulation of money exchange, flows and trade was progressively reduced as nation-states and international organizations removed restrictions (Garrett 2000; Holton 2001). In the advanced industrial first world, it became much easier to move money around the globe, for companies to invest overseas and for goods and services to be exported to new markets. This financial globalization was therefore an important basis for wider economic globalization because – when combined in the 1980s with new informational and communications technologies – it made it easier to move goods, people and services, for overseas investments to be made and for economic activity to be organized at the international level (Castells 2009). However, the extent and pace of these economic globalization processes accelerated dramatically during the 1990s. The central reason was the collapse of the Soviet Union and the re-integration of most of the communist second world into the global capitalist economic system. Even those states that remained communist – most notably China – largely sought to open their economies to the world capitalist economy. Combined with further deregulation and liberalization of international trade associated with an increasingly dominant neoliberal ideology and ongoing advances in information technologies, economic activity became increasingly interconnected across all national borders. It is therefore in the last 40 years that it has become meaningful to refer to a globalized economy since more or less most nation-states across the globe are integrated into the capitalist world economy (cf. Gilpin and Gilpin 2000; Wallerstein 2004).

The trajectory of this much more advanced integration of the world economy into one global capitalist economy in recent decades has been deeply uneven, and there are a range of social scientific theorists who have argued that integration has been strongest at a regional rather than a global level (e.g. Rugman 2001). In this respect, economic globalization in general has arguably been characterized by underpinning processes of economic regionalization occurring at the same time and as part of the wider process. There is, however, a considerable debate as to whether economic regionalization is just part of wider globalization, or represents a different process that cannot be subsumed into globalization in general. The next task of this chapter is therefore to examine the complexities around defining economic regionalization.

9.3   WHAT IS MEANT BY ECONOMIC REGIONALIZATION?

Economic regionalization in its simplest and intuitive sense can be understood as a process whereby economic activity becomes increasingly focused and concentrated within regional territorial space. An important implication underpins this idea which is that for economic regionalization to occur, economic activity must be diminishing in its focus or constitution across other scales. If economic activity is more regionalized, then it follows that it is becoming less localized or globalized (scales 'above' and 'below' that of the region respectively) (cf. Sheppard 2002). Regionalization thus often implies the prevalence of the regional scale as the increasingly important scale at which economic activity is organized in relation to others. An example might be where a group of firms that have global supply chain linkages with firms located across the planet replace those linkages with ones to firms within the sub-national region in which they are located. In this respect, by definition economic regionalization as a process largely presupposes the existence of a coherent thing that might be understood as a 'regional economy'.

However, the concept of the regional economy – as discussed elsewhere in this book – is not necessarily straightforward and is problematic around at least three interrelated aspects – first, whether regions are sub-national or supranational entities (or both); second is the question of what bounds the region or the regional scale (where does one region end and another begin?); and third, the extent to which economic activity located within a region is part of an economy that can be understood to be 'contained' in that territorial space (cf. Agnew 1994).

With regard to the first of these issues, the concept of the regional economy is widely used as both a description of global scale groupings of national economies (e.g. the Eurozone economy or the South American economy), and sub-national regions (e.g. the Californian economy, the Baden-Wurttenberg region in southern Germany or the 'coastal' regional economy of China). It is important to realize that there are thus important differences between these two types of regional economies. Supranational regional economies are essentially amalgamations of separate national economies (e.g. the Asian economy as

China, South Korea, Japan, and so on) that have clear national borders between them but which are (generally) adjacent in territorial terms. The internal and external boundaries of these supranational regions are usually straightforward to identify insofar as they follow the national borders of states. Yet these two different types of regional economies are often not clearly differentiated. Media discussion of regional economies, for example, often treats sub-national and supranational regional economies similarly, referring to the fortunes of the 'south Asian or east Asian economies' (supranational) in the same terms as the southern Indian economy or Chinese coastal regions (sub-national). The important issue is that the scale, boundaries, governance and coherence of these 'regional economies' in fact varies considerably.

Coming to the second issue, the boundaries of regional economies are ill-defined and used variably. Different nation-states are included in different supranational regional economies – for example, is Indonesia in the south-east Asian regional economy? There is often no definitive answer with different agencies, commentators or organizations including different sets of national economies in their understanding of a given supranational regional economy according to their purpose. This is further complicated by formal free-trade associations which overlap but do not fully incorporate all the national economies within a geographical region. Not all European countries are in the European Union, but the concept of the European (or even just west European) regional economy can be used either including or excluding non-EU member states. The boundaries of sub-national regional economies are even harder to demarcate, however, and used with greater inconsistency and lack of precision. Within the EU, for example, the European Union devised a set of standard territorial units (known as NUTS after the French *nomenclature d'unités territoriales statistiques*) based on administrative districts that government, policy-makers and research use. For policy purposes, the EU often defines regional economies around these NUTS units, but in wider usage by different government, policy, research and media sub-national regional economies are much more loosely and variably specified. Where in the UK the boundaries of East Midlands or north-east regional economies can be drawn is not universally recognized. Similarly, there are competing definitions of what represents the southern boundary of the northern Italian economy, or the economy of the southern United States. Such regional economies are generally understood in terms of the major areas they cover (Milan is part of the northern Italian economy and Rome is not), but there are not consistent uses and definitions of places that are more at the periphery of these regions. Clearly, classifications of regional economies based on administrative districts are more distinct (e.g. the economy of Galicia in Spain, the US state of Texas or Sichuan province in China), but frequently when a sub-national regional economy is referred to, there is imprecision, inconsistency or lack of agreement on boundaries.

Finally, and related to the third question, is the most difficult issue of all: the degree to which an economic activity can be understood to have occurred or exist *within* a given regional territorial space or scale (cf. Marston 2000). Whilst in a straightforward manner, firms have factories, offices and production facilities in given territorial places (in that sense the economy always happens somewhere), the contemporary production of goods and services is increasingly distributed across multiple locations. A great deal of the global economy's outputs are products accounted for by a relatively limited number of very large transnational firms, their subsidiaries and supply chains in most industries (UNCTAD 2016). This shift in recent decades – and with the internationalization of firms and production – means that many material goods are manufactured across multiple places with components (and their components) originating from different places. This significantly complicates what we might understand the economy of a region to 'be' which, if measured, restricts economic activity to a territorial container that in many senses it is constantly transgressing. Of course governments, policy-makers and researchers all seek to measure the economies of regions in terms of the wealth generated and the firms and jobs that exist in those territorial places, but in reality these measures are imperfect and need to account for how the economic activity within a region may be heavily embroiled and dependent upon lots of activity not occurring in that territory. A good example would be a car assembly plant whose operation relies on hundreds of components being manufactured by many different firms in many different places outside the region it was located in (Liu and Dicken 2006). In that sense a concept of the process of economic regionalization which is based on the development of economic activity in a given territory is often likely – in today's global economy – to still be heavily bound into economic activities not occurring within that territory.

Overall, therefore, the general definition of economic regionalization as a process of the concentration and greater focus of economic activity within a regional territory is broadly meaningful if the problematic issues identified above are taken into consideration. We can refer to this process in the abstract but it exists always in a scalar contrast that is also blurred at its boundaries and limits. Regionalization occurs at the expenses of larger or smaller territorial units (the nation above and localities below), and where regions 'start' and 'stop' in territory is inconsistent and arbitrarily defined in a way that the nature of economic activity does not necessarily respect. Most of all, however, in today's world, economic activity is only at best partially 'contained' within territorial space and this sits uncomfortably with the opposition of economic regionalization as a process that contrasts or counters economic globalization. It is therefore to this issue we turn next.

9.4 REGIONALIZATION VERSUS GLOBALIZATION? THE FALSE DICHOTOMY. . .

Much of the globalization debate of the last thirty years has only intermittently and often partially engaged with the complex spatialities of globalization processes and global societal integration (cf. Amin 2002). During the 1990s, debates about globalization were often framed around simplistic understandings of globalization as creating homogeneity and sameness (Bisley 2007) and the longstanding simplistic idea that this constitutes an 'end of geography' (cf. O'Brien 1991; Friedman 2007). Globalization was in this sense seen as a process by which places and their attributes became increasingly the same – manifest in arguments about the loss of local cultural difference, the presence of the same transnational corporations (TNCs) across the planet, selling similar products and creating a convergence of economies, cultures, politics and other aspects of society. Whilst the last decade has seen such perspectives strongly challenged and a more diverse and sophisticated approach to understanding what globalization 'is' (as a complex set of tendencies rather than a singular process or end state (Dicken 2015)), much discussion of globalization within a range of social science disciplines still does not foreground the intrinsic spatio-temporal nature of the transformations it is associated with (Jones 2010).

In considering both the debate about economic regionalization in relation to globalization, and its limitation, I want to argue that a conceptual understanding of the spatial and temporal aspects to economic integration that underpin *both* what is being often termed economic regionalization and economic globalization in the contemporary global economy provides a theoretical path through many of the challenges.

The starting point for understanding this debate is the way in which through the emerging globalization debate of the 1990s, the argument was developed that globalization was not as pervasive as some of the leading thinkers and commentators were arguing. A number of social scientific thinkers from different disciplines spanning sociology, geography, management studies, international business and anthropology countered the 'hyperglobalist' argument that saw globalization as an unstoppable force by empirically backed interventions that pointed to how economic activity continued to be heavily concentrated in regions, and that much of the argument about economic globalization rested on the increasing interlinkage of regional economies across the globe (e.g. Amin and Thrift 1995; Scott 1999). This argument was developed around both clusters of firms and industries in regions and in understanding how transnational corporations organized themselves across the global economy (Coe et al. 2004; Dicken 2015). A leading international business thinker, Alan Rugman, provided a significant intervention that exemplifies this in arguing that (economic) globalization was 'at an end' in the early 2000s. His argument was based on empirical analysis of leading TNCs in a wide range of sectors which he argued showed increased economic regionalization not economic globalization – firms activities were increasingly integrated at the supranational regional level but not at the 'truly' global scale (Rugman 2001). The globalization theorists were, in short, overstating the extent of global-scale integration, but the current period in fact represented an unprecedented period of economic regionalization. TNCs were not the harbingers of economic globalization, but deepened economic regionalization (Rugman 2001).

Another prong to this critique of economic globalization also came from political science (e.g. Boyer and Drache 2005) and management studies (e.g. Meyer et al. 2011) which examined patterns of global trade and foreign direct investment to make similar arguments to Rugman around growing regionalization rather than 'true' globalization. The contention in this strand of work is that most of the world's nation-states trade most with their near (supranational) regional neighbours (Hirst et al. 2015). To a lesser extent, the same is also true in relation to foreign direct investment (FDI) (Holton 2001). The extent, therefore, in recent decades of the development of a level playing field of global trade and investment, flowing relatively unrestricted across borders, was challenged on the grounds that much of the world's economic activity is focused around supranational regions. Whilst there has been the development of global-scale linkages, the counter argument was that this represents only a modest fraction of cross-national economic activity. In simple terms, such a point continues to be captured in the fact that most European economies do most trade with other European states, the US with Canada and Mexico and the south American states with each other (both those within and outside the Mercosur trading bloc) (Hirst et al. 2015). There has thus undoubtedly been an ongoing growth in the volume of trans-continental trade over the last few decades, notably as China and other Asian economies have grown substantially as well as more modest integration of some African states into patterns of global trade and investment, but supranational regional economic linkages still dominate numerically. In that respect it would seem there is considerable validity in the view that economic globalization has been overstated where in fact economic regionalization is the more dominant process. This has been amplified over the last five years or so through the debate about the apparent 'retreat of globalization' and era of increased trade protectionism (whether that be the challenges to the European Union or the dissatisfaction with NATFA in the USA).

However, in this final part of this chapter I want to elaborate the argument that to a large extent this debate is misconceived around a false division between two intertwined processes. The issues rest on the way in which several social science disciplines have developed theoretical understandings of the integration of economic activity using certain sets of data that do not fully capture all of the transformations to the global economy that have been occurring. To a large extent the conception of a (hyperglobalist) economic globalization – where global-scale economic integration occurs relatively easily and potentially equally everywhere – was premised on the evidence of new and unprecedented levels of relationships at the planetary scale. This was challenged with data on the volumes of trade and investment which are measured between nation-states, and the extent to which greater volumes occurred between states within supranational regions or which were more distant from each other. Similarly, within international business, the data used by Rugman (2001) and others to provide the empirical basis for arguing for regionalization over globalization is based on firm datasets collected around nationally registered firms or subsidiaries and based on the location of their registered activities. Whilst both approaches do offer insight into macro-level changes in the global economy, there are significant limitations around the theoretical arguments that can be developed using datasets of this nature. Trade data does not tell you about the nature of the economic relationship underpinning a transaction, for example, and increasingly captures different subsidiaries of the same TNC 'trading' with each other. Equally, location-based data for firm head offices and subsidiaries provides little insight into the nature of activities undertaken in certain places and their relation to others. This limits the understanding of the nature of economic activity in given territorial spaces and therefore the scope to differentiate whether these activities are actually well understood as being 'contained' within states, regions or part of global-scale activity.

In fact, and in contrast to this simple opposition of globalization and regionalization, other strands of firm-level work within economic geography and management studies have shown that the deepening of global-scale and regional-scale (both sub-national and supranational) economic integration are often interdependent. Research into the way that TNCs have constructed complex global production networks (GPNs) (Coe and Yeung 2015) reveals how manufacturing in many industries is now a global-scale activity orchestrated by firms involving sometimes hundreds of subsidiary and sub-contracting supply firms in dozens of locations around the globe (cf. Dunning and Lundan 2008). However, and importantly, these complex production networks are not evenly distributed across global economic space but also often incorporate regionalized concentrations around clusters of firms in certain industries or sub-sectors (Storper 1997). Good examples of this would be the aircraft industry, dominated by a small number of very large transnational firms such as Boeing and Airbus (cf. Ferdows 1997). Both have areas of historical assembly, research and development (the Pacific north-west of the US for Boeing, or the south-west of France for Airbus), but are drawing on supply chains where components are coming from clusters of firms in those and other regions. Similarly in electronics, Apple is famously centred on the Californian economy, but its manufacturing operations in China have produced both a regional concentration of supply firms and economic development in several of the southern coastal provinces and global-scale component production networks stretching across many continents (Coe and Yeung 2015).

The key point is that to a large extent economic globalization and economic region-alization are co-dependent processes occurring in synchrony. The concentration and development of certain types of firm clusters and industries in one region is related to global-scale linkages through multiple production networks and supply chains. This is not to over-simplify our understanding of these processes – there are certainly many cases of regionalization being less related to global-scale linkages, or global-scale linkages having less of an impact on the nature of a regional economy. Rather the argument is that with the increasing complexity of economic linkages between networks of large TNCs in the global economy, dividing our concept of economic integration between a regional and a global-level process is unhelpful and may conceal more than it reveals.

9.5   CONCLUSION

The aim of this chapter is to provide an overview of the concept of economic regionaliza-tion in relation to regional development, and in particular how it relates to the wider concept of economic globalization. It should be clear that the way regionalization has been discussed across social scientific thinking and research over the last thirty years is inextricably bound into the wider debate about economic globalization, and that it is important in considering what is meant by this process in the context of those wider debates. The analysis has considered how much of the surrounding conceptual debate has been framed around the idea that economic regionalization is in some way a countervailing process to wider economic globalization: in short that economic activity is becoming more regionally focused as opposed to either 'truly' globalized, or to a lesser extent more localized. The main argument that has been developed in relation to this is that the terms of this debate are misconstrued, and that to a considerable extent what we may understand as economic regionalization and economic globalization respectively are overlapping and entwined processes. Whilst in some contexts it might be relevant to see these as opposing trends in the spatial configuration of economic activity, a wider academic literature reveals the complexity of how these processes are often occurring not only simultaneously but as a consequence of each other. Furthermore, recent debates concerned with the apparent 'retreat' of (economic) globalization in light of apparently increased protectionism and the fracturing of free trade agreements (e.g. Brexit in the EU), need to be informed by a more sophisticated conception of what regionalization might be. The reconfiguration of regional trade alignments, or new institutional barriers emerging in the global economic landscape, should not simply be equated with some kind of deglobalization and a re-emphasis on the region.

This is not to argue that there is no value in either the concept of economic regionaliza-tion nor that researching this process is not important. In drawing some conclusions for the future development of research and thinking, I would end by arguing that there is a need to develop a much more sophisticated theoretical understanding of how regional economies are bound into activities of proximate and distant actors. People still live and work in regions, and economic activity always takes place somewhere, so the concept of the regional economy (definitional issues notwithstanding) and the idea of regionalization have considerable utility. Social scientific research and thinking around global production networks (GPNs) and transnational firms have provided a powerful basis for a more spatially sophisticated understanding of the nature of regional economic space, but there is considerable scope for developing these ideas further. Such approaches have, for example, not pushed the understanding of the role of trans-regional institutional or socio-cultural linkages and their influence on regional economic trajectories to the same degree as that around firms or supply chains. In that respect, future theories of economic regionalization could begin to better understand the complex interaction of economic and non-economic factors that 'perforate' (cf. Amin 2002) regional economic space from within and outside of territorial boundaries. This should move the debate beyond simplistic either/or understandings of regionalization and globalization, and it is in this direction that it seems likely future thinking on the process of economic regionalization will continue to evolve.

9.6   REFERENCES

Agnew, J. (1994), 'The territorial trap: the geographical assumptions of international relations theory', *Review of International Political Economy*, **1** (1), 53–80.
Altman, R. (2009), 'Globalization in retreat: further geopolitical consequences of the financial crisis', *Foreign Affairs*, **88** (2), 1–6.
Amin, A. and N. Thrift (1995), *Globalization, Institutions, and Regional Development in Europe*, Oxford: Oxford University Press.
Amin, A. (2002), 'Spatialities of globalization', *Environment & Planning A*, **34** (3), 385–399.
Bisley, N. (2007), *Rethinking Globalization*, Basingstoke: Palgrave Macmillan.
Bodoni, C. and B. Surgun (2017), 'The sunset of globalization, the sunrise of alterglobalization', *International Scientific Conference "Strategies XXI"*, **2**, 62–67.
Boyer, R. and D. Drache (eds) (2005), *States Against Markets: The Limits of Globalization*, London: Routledge.
Castells, M. (2009), *The Rise of the Network Society: The Information Age: Economy, Society and Culture, vol. I*, Oxford: Blackwell, Second Edition.
Coe, N.M., M. Hess, H. Yeung, P. Dicken and J. Henderson (2004), '"Globalizing" regional development: a global production networks perspective', *Transactions of the Institute of British Geographers*, **29** (4), 468–484.
Coe, N.M. and H. Yeung (2015), *Global Production Networks: Theorizing Economic Development in an Interconnected World*, Oxford: Oxford University Press.
Cooper, A.F., C.W. Hughes and P. De Lombaerde (eds) (2007), *Regionalisation and Global Governance: The Taming of Globalisation?*, London: Routledge.
Cull, N.J. (2016), 'Engaging foreign publics in the age of Trump and Putin: three implications of 2016 for public diplomacy', *Place Branding and Public Diplomacy*, **12** (4), 243–246.
Dicken, P. (2015), *Global Shift: Mapping the Changing Contours of the World Economy*, London: Sage, Sixth Edition.
Dunning, J. and S. Lundan (2008), *Multinational Enterprises and the Global Economy*, Cheltenham, UK and Northampton, MA, USA: Edward Elgar Publishing.
Ferdows, K. (1997), 'Made in the world: the global spread of production', *Production and Operations Management*, **6** (2), 102–109.
Flint, C. and P. Taylor (2007), *Political Geography: World-economy, Nation-state, and Locality*, Basingstoke: Pearson Education.
Friedman, T. (2007), *The World is Flat: The Globalized World in the Twenty-First Century*, New York: Penguin, Second Edition.
Garrett, G. (2000), 'The causes of globalization', *Comparative Political Studies*, **33** (6–7), 941–991.
Gilpin, R. and J. Gilpin (2000), *The Challenge of Global Capitalism: The World Economy in the 21st Century*, vol. 5, Princeton, NJ: Princeton University Press.
Greenaway, D., R.C. Hine, A.P. O'Brien and R.J. Thornton (eds) (2016), *Global Protectionism*, New York: Springer.

Held, D., A. McGrew, D. Goldblatt and J. Perraton (1999), *Global Transformations: Politics, Economics and Culture*, Cambridge: Polity.

Hirst, P., P. Thompson and S. Bromley (2015), *Globalization in Question*, Oxford: Wiley, Third Edition.

Hobsbawm, E.J. (2007), *Globalisation, Democracy and Terrorism*, London: Little Brown.

Holton, R. (2001), *Globalization and the Nation-State*, Basingstoke: Palgrave Macmillan, Second Edition.

Jones, A. (2006), *The Dictionary of Globalization*, Cambridge: Polity.

Jones, A. (2010), *Globalization: Key Thinkers*, Cambridge: Polity.

Liu, W. and P. Dicken (2006), 'Transnational corporations and "obligated embeddedness": foreign direct investment in China's automobile industry', *Environment and Planning A*, **38** (7), 1229–1247.

Lund, S., T. Daruvala, R. Dobbs, P. Härle, J. Kwek and R. Falcón (2013), 'Financial Globalization: Retreat or Reset', *McKinsey Global Institute*, https://www.mckinsey.com/global-themes/employment-and-growth/financial-globalization (accessed 21 February 2018).

MacKinnon, D. and A. Cumbers (2014), *Introduction to Economic Geography: Globalization, Uneven Development and Place*, London: Routledge.

Marston, S.A. (2000), 'The social construction of scale', *Progress in Human Geography*, **24** (2), 219–242.

Meyer, K.E., R. Mudambi and R. Narula (2011), 'Multinational enterprises and local contexts: the opportunities and challenges of multiple embeddedness', *Journal of Management Studies*, **48** (2), 235–252.

O'Brien, K. (1991), *Global Financial Integration: The End of Geography*, New York: Council on Foreign Relations Press.

Ritzer, G. and P. Dean (2015), *Globalization: A Basic Text*, Oxford: John Wiley & Sons.

Rugman, A. (2001), *The End of Globalization*, London: Random House.

Scholte, J.A. (2005), *Globalization: A Critical Introduction*, Basingstoke: Palgrave Macmillan.

Scott, A.J. (1999), *Regions and the World Economy: The Coming Shape of Global Production, Competition, and Political Order*, Oxford: Oxford University Press.

Sheppard, E. (2002), 'The spaces and times of globalization: place, scale, networks, and positionality', *Economic Geography*, **78** (3), 307–330.

Storper, M. (1997), *The Regional World: Territorial Development in a Global Economy*, London: Guilford Press.

Sunkel, O. and A. Inotai (2016), *Globalism and the New Regionalism*, vol. 1, New York: Springer.

UNCTAD (2016), 'World investment report', Geneva: UNCTAD.

Wallerstein, I. (1974), *The Modern World-System, vol. I: Capitalist Agriculture and the Origins of the European World-Economy in the Sixteenth Century*, New York/London: Academic Press.

Wallerstein, I. (1979), *The Capitalist World-Economy*, Cambridge: Cambridge University Press.

Wallerstein, I. (2004), *World-systems Analysis: An Introduction*, Durham, NC: Duke University Press.

10. Regional innovation and growth theory: behavioural and institutional approaches
Robert Huggins and Piers Thompson

10.1 INTRODUCTION

A perennial question in the field of regional studies is why some regions, cities and territories are better able to foster innovation – broadly defined as the introduction of new products, services and ways of doing business and working – and economic growth than others. A myriad of factors relating to the availability of capital in the form of investment and resources, the skills of the workforce, the availability and capability of entrepreneurs and other agents of innovation, as well as the cooperation and collaboration achieved through ecosystems, are all offered as explanatory factors (Capello and Nijkamp 2009; Cooke et al. 2011; Stimson et al. 2011; Shearmur et al. 2016). Undoubtedly, each is likely to matter; however there is little understanding of how these factors are related or connected.

As a means of seeking to better understand these connections and to consider the deeper and less transparent drivers of regional development, this chapter examines the behavioural and institutional determinants of the innovation and growth capability and capacity of regions. From the institutional perspective, regions are portrayed as growth systems whereby the availability of a range of capital forms and the quality of institutions play a key role in promoting innovation and growth. This capital and associated institutions, however, may lack effectiveness unless a region contains significant numbers of individuals, especially entrepreneurs, with the behavioural traits that allow them to act as agents of innovation.

These more behavioural aspects can be considered to underpin the functioning of regional growth systems and subsequent innovation and growth. The chapter argues that regional innovation and growth are contingent upon two key behavioural traits, namely: socio-spatial culture; and personality psychology. Behavioural action will result in a range of activities, and from the perspective of innovation it is important to pinpoint actions in the form of human agency that may impact on the development of a particular region.

In general, the approach adopted here echoes the notion of regions as 'Schumpeterian hubs' for recombining capital in order to generate innovation. The chapter, however, argues that merely investing in such capital may not be enough to secure innovation and economic growth. In summary, the overall model the chapter presents is illustrated by Figure 10.1, which highlights the inter-connection of regional growth systems and regional behavioural systems as the drivers of innovation and economic growth.

10.2 REGIONAL INNOVATION AND GROWTH THEORY

Theoretical perspectives on regional innovation and growth predominantly come in two related forms. First, those that seek to understand the processes and organizational

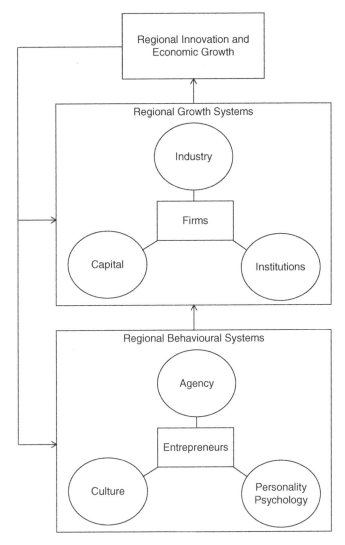

Figure 10.1   *The determinants of regional innovation and economic growth: the inter-*
connection of regional growth and behavioural systems

factors relating to the innovation process within regions, that is, regional innovation
theories. Second, a theoretical strand focused on understanding the role of innovation
in facilitating regional economic growth, that is, innovation-based theories of regional
growth. As shown by Figure 10.2, the conceptual frameworks employed by both theoretical approaches broadly consist of either a resource-based view or an interaction-based
view. The resource-based view largely concerns the assets and endowments within a
region, and from the perspective of regional innovation theories this relates to the types
of industries, industrial mix and the capacity of these industries to foster regional innovation. From the innovation-based growth perspective, the focus is very much on the notion

	Regional Innovation Theories	Innovation-Based Theories of Regional Growth
Resource-Based Frameworks	Industrial structure, (smart) specialisation, diversity, relatedness, path dependency, absorptive capacity, knowledge economy, entrepreneurship	Endogenous growth, agglomeration, human capital, creative class, entrepreneurship capital, knowledge capital and research capital
Interaction-Based Frameworks	Regional innovation systems, innovative milieu, technopoles, industrial districts, local production systems, networks, buzz, knowledge pipelines, learning regions, clusters and open innovation	Network-based view of regional growth, knowledge accessibility, network capital, social capital and spillovers

Figure 10.2   Theoretical perspectives on regional innovation and growth

of endogenous growth and the accumulation of the forms of intangible capital associated with triggering and sustaining long-term growth.

The interaction-based view is complementary to the resource-based view, focusing on the nature the relationships, linkages and networks that exist between regional actors engaged in innovation. Most prominently conceptualized as regional innovation systems, innovation milieu and clusters, the interaction-based view considers these modes of connectivity to provide diffusion channels allowing the knowledge required for innovation to flow within and across regions. With regard to innovation-based growth theories, there is a growing discourse that conceptualizes these channels and flow mechanisms as a form of capital – for example, network capital and social capital – that are part of the mix of 'capitals' that can be accumulated as part of endogenous growth processes. Similarly, these growth processes are a component of a wider theoretical canvass that focuses on the 'success' of regions, broadly related to their economic development trajectories.

Regional economic development principally concerns the capacity and capability to achieve economic growth, and understanding how and why such growth occurs is central to a number of research streams beyond innovation-based theories. For instance, research in spatial economics seeks to understand the role of agglomeration effects, trade costs, and other regionalization and urbanization factors (Storper 2013). More generally, contributions from economic geography and spatial economics have become increasingly concerned with understanding and demonstrating the regional micro-foundations of macroeconomic growth models.

Endogenous growth theory, in particular, has focused on the role of human capital, knowledge and innovation in regional growth processes, with a need to better understand the mechanisms underlying regional growth patterns identified as a key priority in aiding effective economic development policy (Stimson et al. 2011). Innovation and endogenous growth models make clear that growth is driven by technological change arising from intentional investment decisions made by profit-maximizing agents (principally firms), with the stock of human and knowledge capital – and investments in such capital – determining the rate of growth (Romer 1990). Knowledge capital refers to the cumulative stock of information and skills concerned with connecting new ideas with commercial values, developing new products and processes, and doing business in a new way. Therefore, whereas innovation is a process, knowledge consists of the recipes and the ingredients to be processed.

Endogenous capital accumulation models are to some extent allied to contributions related to the New Economic Geography, which like antecedents such as models of circular and cumulative causation, emphasize the notion of increasing returns from capital investment (Storper and Scott 2009). Similarly, work on regional competitiveness has sought to pinpoint the 'territorial capital' of regions, which covers the wider set of assets underpinning economic growth (Camagni and Capello 2013, Huggins et al. 2014).

10.3   THE EMERGENCE OF INSTITUTIONAL THEORIES

Alongside the endogenous model of growth, an emerging field of study has sought to cut into the growth debate at a different level by placing the concepts of institutions as the central source for understanding growth differentials (Farole et al. 2011; Rodríguez-Pose 2013; Tomaney 2014). Somewhat contrary to the capital accumulation model of regional growth, institutional theorists argue that differences in growth and prosperity across regions are more fundamentally related to the type, stage of development and efficiency of the economic and political institutions that underpin economic systems (Acemoglu and Robinson 2012; Rodríguez-Pose 2013; Tomaney 2014). Institutions, therefore, relate to the incentives and constraints concerning the organization of production. Within this institutional paradigm, the prevailing view is that differences in 'the rules of the game' across economic systems are a key driver of growth differentials, with more efficient institutions facilitating the development of the conditions that allow the forms of capital accumulation associated with innovation-led growth to flourish (Huggins 2016).

In general, institutions are defined as the humanly devised constraints that structure interaction covering both formal (de jure – rules, laws, constitutions) and informal (de facto – norms, behaviour, conventions) constraints and their enforcement, which then define the incentive structure of societies and their economies (North 2005). Institutions, especially those of a more formal nature, can be further categorized as: (1) economic institutions, such as individual property rights, contracts, patent laws and the like; or (2) political institutions, which generally refer to the extent to which democratic political rules underlie the nature of territorial governance. Institutions can also be categorized according to whether they are innately 'extractive' or 'inclusive', with extractive institutions tending to be those which result in rent-seeking behaviour (Acemoglu and Robinson 2012).

In effect, institutions, in the shape of both the tangible and intangible characteristics constituting the political economy of regions are either enablers of, or constrainers on, growth. Institutional enablers are the conditions and factors that facilitate growth by creating an environment conducive for firms to operate at their highest level. These enablers principally encompass institutions that support economic actors in taking advantage of perceived opportunities.

Although some of these institutions are fixed across nations – such as law, regulation and property rights – others may be subject to regional-level differentiation. In this sense, regional-level institutions can be considered to consist of the underlying rules of the game relating to factors such as the incentives to: save and invest; embrace competition, undertake innovation and technological development; engage in education, learning, and entrepreneurship; participate in networks; along with the presence and structure of property ownership and the provision of public services. Regions with institutions conducive to enabling economic development are likely to increase their growth by attracting investment, skills and talent. Some examples include: local business regulations that allow commercial activity to be efficient; the ease of doing business; local government initiatives; and ultimately, the perceptions of businesses and individuals in a region (Huggins 2016). In general, institutional theories analyse regional growth from quite a different perspective to capital accumulation approaches, but as the following section argues, this does not prevent the theoretical streams from complementing one another.

10.4   REGIONAL GROWTH SYSTEMS

The key argument of regional endogenous growth theory is that long-term differentials in growth across regions will emerge as a result of differences in the structure of their economic systems, especially their endowment of assets and the preferences of economic actors (Capello and Nijkamp 2009; Stimson et al. 2011). Whilst endogenous capital accumulation theories of growth are based on preferences, endowment, resource allocation and intentional investment decisions (Romer 1990), institutional theories of growth are based on constraints, incentives and organizational arrangements (North 2005; Acemoglu and Robinson 2012).

Although these two theoretical positions are usually considered as distinctive explanations of economic growth differences, it is interesting to consider the extent to which they may interact, given that both theories can be considered to be endogenous in nature (Farole et al. 2011). For example, preferences and investment decisions may be shaped by prevailing institutions, whilst the availability and accumulation of capital may shape incentive structures and organizational arrangements. Furthermore, an institutional approach facilitates a consideration of the ownership structure of stocks of capital.

Recent work on regional and urban development has sought to develop a more transparent link between institutional and capital accumulation theories of growth whereby regional economies are conceptualized as growth systems through which different forms of institutions are associated with different forms of capital accumulation (Huggins 2016). In this model, the capital drivers of growth are not merely the result of preferences and existing capital endowments, but are mediated by a set of institutional factors.

As shown by Figure 10.3, such a model builds on the existing acknowledgement that both capital and institutional factors influence the nature, quality and performance of: (1) firm-level growth dynamics – which concerns the role of human capital and knowledge capital and the learning and innovation institutions that constrain or incentivize the accumulation of these forms of capital; (2) inter-firm-level growth dynamics – which concerns the transactions and interactions between firms through the markets and networks they form, and the role of entrepreneurship capital and entrepreneurial institutions in market processes, as well as network capital and associational institutions in network formation; and (3) regional-level growth dynamics – which relates to the overall governance of

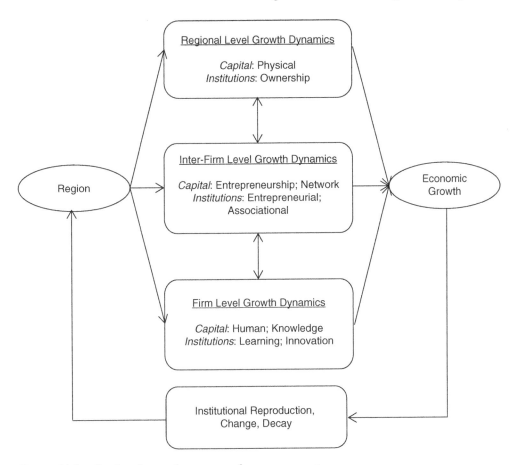

Figure 10.3   Regional growth systems – key components

regional political economies, especially with regard to the institutions of ownership and physical capital (Huggins 2016).

Although each growth dynamic will help shape and determine rates of economic growth, the firm level is clearly central with regard to the dynamics of knowledge creation. Firms are dependent on the role of human capital and knowledge capital and, therefore, the learning and innovation institutions that constrain or incentivize the accumulation of these forms of capital (Glaeser 2011). In the case of human capital, learning institutions, such as intra-regional and inter-regional labour markets, create incentives and constraints as to the type of human capital formed in a particular region, as well as conventions in relation to workforce development and regional education systems.

Institutions in the form of labour markets enable human capital to take advantage of the benefits of specialization, encouraging economic growth. Therefore, there is likely to exist a recursive relationship between the nature of firms in a region, as typified by patterns of economic specialization, and the institutions and human capital available. Similarly, institutions influence firm behaviour and subsequently patterns of industrial specialization, with the relationship being bidirectional in nature, that is, firm behaviour also impacts upon relevant institutions. Conversely, regions may have a more diversified portfolio of firms that are either related or unrelated in their 'variety', with institutions again playing a role in determining these patterns (Boschma and Capone 2015).

With regard to knowledge capital, there is a need to consider innovation institutions in the form of the incentives and constraints to creating and/or embracing new technology, as well as conventions in relation to the financing of innovation and norms regarding the 'restriction' or 'freedom' of ideas (Storper 2013). For example, where innovative opportunity exploitation is encouraged through greater rewards (e.g. lower effective tax rates) or at the very least are not discouraged (as might be the case where high administrative burdens are present), the marginal latent innovator is more likely to pursue innovation opportunities. Although conventions in relation to the financing of innovation, and incentives and constraints with regard to undertaking differing forms of innovation, are likely to stem from national and supra-national level institutions, more localized formal and informal institutions also play a role.

Less formal institutions in the shape of the nature of competition are also likely to be a factor in shaping the knowledge capital capacity of a region. Furthermore, the competition conditions under which firms in a region operate are likely to shape the rate and character of innovation, with those firms operating in the most sophisticated and demanding markets tending to be those that are most likely to possess the highest levels of innovation.

10.5   INNOVATION AND INTER-FIRM GROWTH DYNAMICS

Alongside firm-level dynamics, it is increasingly argued that the inter-firm level has grown in importance, the flow and diffusion of created knowledge determining long-run rates of innovation. Both the concepts of 'open' and 'interactive' innovation acknowledge that innovation processes are now rarely linear or independent activities, but rely on the markets and networks that firms operate through in order to connect themselves to the most important sources of knowledge.

Inter-firm level growth dynamics concern the transactions and interactions across economic agents, with the effectiveness of firms to enter and successfully compete in their respective markets likely to rely on the accumulation of entrepreneurship capital. Such capital refers to the capacity of a region to generate entrepreneurial activity, whereby entrepreneurs are alert to market opportunities and subsequently contribute to economic growth (Audretsch and Keilbach 2004).

Entrepreneurship capital encompasses not only the available entrepreneurial talent that allows firms to operate in high value and tradable markets, but also the capability to access the finance entrepreneurs may require to invest in the resources necessary to engage in these markets. Entrepreneurial institutions come in the form of incentives and constraints to engaging in entrepreneurial activity, including property rights, tax codes, social insurance systems, labour market legislation, competition policy, trade policies, capital market regulation, and the enforcement of contracts and law and order (Henrekson and Sanandaji 2011).

Alongside markets, research has identified the role of both inter- and intra-regional networks as a type of capital shaping regional growth processes, that is, network capital, in the form of investments firms make in cooperation and collaborative relationships with other firms and organizations in order to gain access to economically beneficial knowledge (Huggins and Thompson 2014). In this case, the capital value of networks within and across regions is likely to be regulated by a series of 'associational institutions' in the form of conventions with regard to inter-organizational collaboration and cooperation, especially associational business behaviour and the norms of trust and collective action. Urban regions, in particular, are considered to be key locations for high rates of network formation due to the high density of actors and high frequency of human interactions (Glaeser 2011; Florida et al. 2017). An institutional perspective on these networks and flows suggests that firms are incentivized to engage in networked activity through the availability of formal associational institutions, such as chambers of commerce, business and trade associations, as well more informal institutions in the form of the geographic clustering of firms within which networked cooperation and collaboration is fostered through embedded institutional norms and customs.

10.6   BEHAVIOURAL ECONOMIC GEOGRAPHY

As indicated above, explanations of innovation and growth differences across regions are generally rooted in factors based on the structure, dynamics and organization of firms, industries and capital. Contemporary economic geography theory, however, is moving toward a (re)turn to addressing the role of individual and collective behaviour in determining regional development outcomes (Obschonka et al. 2013; Huggins and Thompson 2017). A number of concepts relating to the behaviour of individuals and groups have taken an increasingly central role in shaping an understanding of why some places are better able to generate higher rates of development and growth (Tabellini 2010; Tubadji 2013).

A behavioural approach is not strictly 'new' in either comparative economics or what we now term economic geography. Myrdal (1968), for instance, takes a behavioural and cultural approach to understanding economic development across Asian economies, in particular the role of religious and social (caste) systems. From the 1960s there was also an emerging school of behavioural geography largely concerned with identifying the cognitive processes that lead to individuals and communities codifying, reacting to, and recreating their environments. Pred (1967), in particular, argued that economic geographic and locational distribution patterns are a consequence of the aggregate manifestation of decisional acts made at the individual, group and/ or firm level. This provoked a significant behavioural 'turn' in the field of location studies and economic geography. However, subsequent cultural turns in the wider field of human geography triggered the demise of behavioural geography.

Given the range of theoretical developments in recent years, it would appear time to reconcile behavioural, cultural and agentic turns as a means of better-understanding regional innovation, growth and development. Based on thinking from behavioural economics, some economic geographers suggest that individual decision-making results from local influences experienced through situations. Such 'situations' equate to the dominant cultural traits embedded within the local communities where these 'influences' are formed (Storper 2013). Behavioural economics concerns the integration of psychological theories of behaviour as a means of explaining economic action (Cartwright 2014). Such theories have increasingly shown the limits of rational-choice theories in explaining economic, as well as social, action and the underlying decision-making processes of individuals in determining such action (Hodgson 2013).

Drawing on Simon's (1982) notion of 'bounded rationality', behavioural economics suggests that the minds of individuals are required to be understood in terms of the environmental context in which they have evolved, resulting in restrictions to human information processing, due to limits in knowledge and computational capacity (Kahneman 2003). Similarly, the rise in importance given to cultural values in regional development theory has led to the emergence of a 'new sociology of development' entwining the role of geography with factors relating to individual and collective behaviour. As Clark (2015) argues, human behaviour is fundamental to the social sciences in terms of understanding what people do, where and why they do it, and the costs and benefits of this behaviour. In order to understand the 'aggregate' differences in socio-economic activities and performance there is a need to explore how these stem from the experiences and actions of individual actors (Storper 2013).

10.7   SOCIO-SPATIAL CULTURE AND PERSONALITY PSYCHOLOGY

As Mokyr (2015) suggests, once institutions are accepted as an important factor in explaining development differences, cultural explanations – in the form of the beliefs and values upon which institutions are founded – are unlikely to be far behind. The issue of how cultural factors impact on regional development has been increasingly debated in recent years (Tubadji 2013). In particular, recent work on socio-spatial culture and the spatial nature of personality psychology has sought to address knowledge gaps relating to the role of context and environment in shaping behaviour (Huggins et al. 2018).

From the psychological perspective, Obschonka et al. (2015), for example, draw on the Five-Factor Theory of Personality – or the *Big Five* traits – to explain differences in behaviour across regions. This theory is the predominant personality psychology model in contemporary psychological science (Benet-Martinez et al. 2015), and within studies of geographical personality, the measures normally associated with the Big Five framework of personality traits consist of: (1) openness – the tendency to be open to new aesthetic, cultural or intellectual experiences; (2) conscientiousness – the tendency to be organized, responsible and hardworking; (3) extraversion – an orientation of one's interests and energies toward to the outer world of people and things rather than the inner world of subjective experience, characterized by positive affect and sociability; (4) agreeableness – the tendency to act in a cooperative unselfish manner; and (5) neuroticism (emotional stability) – neuroticism is a chronic level of emotional instability and proneness to psychological distress, whilst emotional stability is largely the opposite and concerns predictability and stability in emotional reactions, with an absence of rapid mood changes (Credé et al. 2012).

Alongside personality psychology, the concept of culture generally refers to the way in which people behave as a result of their background and group affiliation. Rather than concerning individual behaviour, it relates to shared systems of meaning within and across ascribed and acquired social groups (Hofstede 1980). Culture can be defined by the values, beliefs and expectations that members of specific social groups come to share. Socio-spatial culture refers to the broader societal traits and relations that underpin places in terms of prevailing mindsets and the overall way of life within particular places (Huggins and Thompson 2016). Therefore, it principally constitutes the social structure and features of group life within regions that can generally be considered to be beyond the economic life of such places. Fundamentally, socio-spatial culture consists of the overarching or dominant mindsets that underlie the way in which regions function; that is, the ways and means by which individuals and groups within communities interact and shape their environment.

Huggins and Thompson (2016) have established a model of socio-spatial (or what they also term 'community') culture whereby five component factors are argued to be of principal importance, namely: (1) engagement with education and work – partly drawing on Max Weber's enduring notion of the work ethic and attitudes to economic participation; (2) social cohesion – relating to Emile Durkheim's notion of mechanical and organic solidarity social cohesion, whereby trait similarities and interdependence among individuals result in a perceived unity, togetherness, and less likelihood of exclusion; (3) femininity and caring attitudes – relating to Hofstede's (1980) typology of national cultures and the notion of the femininity or masculinity of these cultures, with masculine cultures considered to be more competitive and materialistic than their feminine counterparts; (4) adherence to social rules – referring to the acknowledged role of such adherence for coordination purposes, but also noting that it may constrain creative and innovative behavioural intentions; and (5) collective action – referring to the extent to which regions adopt an equality-driven cooperative action approach as opposed to a more individualistic action approach.

10.8 PSYCHOCULTURAL BEHAVIOUR

Both personality and cultural traits have been found to be factors influencing rates of innovation, entrepreneurship and growth across regions (Huggins and Thompson 2016; Obschonka et al. 2015; Lee 2016). In particular, individualism, diversity and more masculine cultures have been found to be associated with such outcomes, and a group of studies have found that open tolerant cities and regions grow faster (Florida et al. 2008; Boschma and Fritsch 2009). This allows access to more ideas, but can also help exploit the knowledge held and developed within a region as more diverse skill sets become available.

Unlike cultural norms, which are formed at the group level, personality traits are based on the individual, and when a region has a relatively larger proportion of particular personality types, this is likely to affect innovation and growth. Using a cluster analysis approach, Rentfrow et al. (2013) identify three psychological profiles of regions in the US: friendly and conventional; relaxed and creative; and temperamental and uninhibited. They find that in terms of economic prosperity, a positive link exists with openness and extraversion, whilst conscientiousness displays a negative association.

Although personality psychology represents a potential powerful means of explaining the uneven development of regions, it is important to highlight that personality traits in the form of the Big Five are defined without reference to any context, that is, situation or socio-spatial culture. Indeed, a long-term perspective on development should acknowledge that the genetic – encompassing personality psychology – evolution of humans and their cultural evolution are ultimately interactive, that is, positive and negative interactions between cultural and biological evolution may occur and give rise to cultural-genetic co-evolution (Van den Bergh and Stagl 2003). Such co-evolutionary forces can be related to theories of 'generation' and 'collective memory', or what Lippmann and Aldrich (2015) refer to as 'generational units', in the form of meaningful collectives that move through time with high degrees of self-awareness. In this sense, the interaction between culture and psychology forms part of the complex adaptive systems that are considered to explain economic outcomes in the form of innovation and growth.

10.9   HUMAN AGENCY

Together, culture and personality psychology form the key component of the psychocultural behaviour of a region, and it is the co-evolution of cultural and personality traits that may best explain the role of behaviour on regional-level growth and innovation (Huggins et al. 2018). Culture and personality traits underlie the reasoning why individuals, or collectives of individuals, ultimately behave in particular ways, which in the long-term influence regional development. In other words, macro-level outcomes are retraceable to individual decision-making agents, suggesting a link between the extent to which individual agents are motivated to achieve and the ensuing rates of development of the regions in which they operate.

In this sense, to be an agent is to intentionally make things happen by one's actions. Psychologist Albert Bandura (2001) proposes three modes of agency: personal agency in the form of the power to originate actions for given purposes; proxy agency, which relies on others to act on one's behest to secure desired outcomes; and collective agency exercised through socially coordinative and interdependent effort. From the perspective of regional theory, it is instructive to build further upon this typology in order to identify with more precision the types of agent, agency and action that are likely to achieve desired (or undesired) results and outcomes. Although a multiplicity of overlapping forms of agency at differing scalar levels can be considered, a starting point is to examine three meta-forms of localized agency that clearly impact on regional development outcomes, namely: entrepreneurial agency, political agency and labour agency. Although all three will influence the growth and development of a region, entrepreneurial agency is likely to be most the important in terms of innovation-led growth (Huggins and Thompson 2017).

Entrepreneurs are increasingly depicted as agents of economic and social change that develop communities, often enacting a collective identity that facilitates and shapes development. From both a spatial and temporal perspective, entrepreneurs have been conceived as 'generational units' in the sense that they are agents who mould collective memories through space and time (Lippmann and Aldrich 2015). Crucially, they are highly heterogeneous agents possessing a wide range of personality traits including extraversion, openness to experience, conscientiousness, and the ability to bear risk.

Studies have repeatedly found that autonomy and independence, rather than pecuniary reasons, are cited as motivations for engaging in entrepreneurial activities. Furthermore, the opportunity to use the creative side of our personalities may also feature in motivations for entrepreneurship expressed through innovative attributes, flexibility and adaptability to change (Huggins and Williams 2011).

Overall, the entrepreneurial agency fuelling regional innovation can be considered to operate across the personal-proxy-collective continuum. Most prominently, there is the personal agency of individual entrepreneurs, but also the networks and collaborations they form are the basis of a collective agency that will impact on regional development outcomes. Furthermore, their connections with other economic agents such as investors in the form of venture capitalists and the like take the form of a proxy agency, whereby entrepreneurs are empowered to achieve the outcomes of this wider group of stakeholders.

10.10 CONCLUSION

This chapter has sought to provide an introduction to some contemporary theoretical perspectives on regional innovation and growth, in particular the concepts of regional growth systems and institutions, as well as behavioural theories concerning both cultural and psychological explanations. It has been suggested that both behavioural and institutional-based conceptual frameworks can usefully complement existing theories of regional innovation and growth. For example, although existing conceptual frameworks such as the regional innovation systems literature note the importance of entrepreneurship as a feature of such systems, they are not formally incorporated into these models. Indeed, even though the legacy and prevalence of Schumpeterian discourse has led to 'entrepreneurship' and 'innovation' more often than not being uttered in the same breath the connection between the two is usually implicitly, rather than explicitly, formulated. This suggests the need for further theoretical integration, particularly through the deployment of a behavioural conceptual lens.

As outlined by Figure 10.4, behavioural-based frameworks incorporating cultural and psychological aspects help us understand why particular agents within a region, especially entrepreneurial agents, may possess a proclivity towards fostering innovation, as well as how the interaction between cultural and psychological factors result in regional behavioural systems with a higher or lower tendency to sustain long-term economic growth.

Behavioural economic geography, encompassing culture, psychology and agency, potentially provides new insights into the persistence of the long-term unevenness of innovation, growth and development across regions. Psychocultural behavioural

	Regional Innovation Theories	Innovation-Based Theories of Regional Growth
Behavioural-Based Frameworks	Socio-spatial culture, personality psychology, and entrepreneurial agency	Regional behavioural systems, psychocultural behaviour, and agency
Institutional-Based Frameworks	Rules of the game, constraints/incentives, and the institution-capital interface	Regional growth systems, growth dynamics, and innovation institutions

Figure 10.4 New theoretical perspectives on regional innovation and growth

patterns, and their evolution, provide a basis for understanding the type and nature of human agency that exist within regions. Such agency is likely to be one of the key rooted drivers associated with more traditional explanatory causes underlying uneven regional development.

Institutional-based frameworks allow us to consider how both informal and formal institutions are likely to moderate the behaviour of regional actors, with institutions forming part of the broader growth systems and growth dynamics that ultimately determine regional economic growth. By identifying the connection between types of institutions and forms of 'growth capital', it is possible to consider distinct varieties of economic growth systems at play across regions. In summary, through the prevailing forms of culture, personality psychology and institutions, it can be suggested that regions themselves produce a spatially bounded rationality that determines the nature of human agency and subsequently the rate and nature of innovation and growth.

10.11   REFERENCES

Acemoglu, D. and J.A. Robinson (2012), *Why Nations Fail? The Origins of Power, Prosperity and Poverty*, London, UK and New York, NY, USA: Profile Books and Crown.

Audretsch, D.B. and M. Keilbach (2004), 'Entrepreneurship and regional growth: an evolutionary interpretation', *Journal of Evolutionary Economics*, **14** (5), 605–616.

Bandura, A. (2001), 'Social cognitive theory: an agentic perspective', *Annual Review of Psychology*, **52** (1), 1–26.

Benet-Martinez, V., M.B. Donnellan, W. Fleeson, R.C. Fraley, S.D. Gosling, L.A. King, R.W. Robins and D.C. Funder (2015), 'Six visions for the future of personality psychology', in M. Mikulincer, P.R. Shaver, M.L. Cooper and R.J. Larsen (eds), *APA Handbook of Personality and Social Psychology: Personality Processes and Individual Differences*, vol. 4, Washington, DC: American Psychology Association, pp. 665–690.

Boschma, R.A. and M. Fritsch (2009), 'Creative class and regional growth: empirical evidence from seven European countries', *Economic Geography*, **85** (4), 391–423.

Boschma, R. and G. Capone (2015), 'Institutions and diversification: related versus unrelated diversification in varieties of capitalism framework', *Research Policy*, **44** (10), 1902–1914.

Camagni, R. and R. Capello (2013), 'Regional competitiveness and territorial capital: a conceptual approach and empirical evidence from the European Union', *Regional Studies*, **47** (9), 1383–1402.

Capello, R. and P. Nijkamp (2009), 'Urban economics at a cross-road: recent theoretical and methodological directions and future challenges', in M. Sonis and G.J.D. Hewings (eds), *Tool Kits in Regional Science*, Dordrecht, Netherlands and Heidelberg, Germany: Springer, pp. 273–291.

Cartwright, E. (2014), *Behavioral Economics: Second Edition*, Abingdon, UK and New York, NY, USA: Routledge.

Clark, G.L. (2015), 'Behavior, cognition and context', mimeo, Smith School of Enterprise and the Environment, Oxford, UK: Oxford University.

Cooke, P., B. Asheim, R. Boschma, R. Martin, D. Schwartz and F. Tödtling (eds) (2011), *Handbook of Regional Innovation and Growth*, Cheltenham, UK and Northampton, MA, USA: Edward Elgar Publishing.

Credé, M., P. Harms, S. Niehorster and A. Gaye-Valentine (2012), 'An evaluation of the consequences of using short measures of the big five personality traits', *Journal of Personality and Social Psychology*, **102** (4), 874–888.

Farole, T., A. Rodríguez-Pose and M. Storper (2011), 'Human geography and the institutions that underlie economic growth', *Progress in Human Geography*, **35** (1), 58–80.

Florida, R., C. Mellander and K. Stolarick (2008), 'Inside the black box of regional development – human capital, the creative class and tolerance', *Journal of Economic Geography*, **8** (5), 615–659.

Florida, R., P. Adler and C. Mellander (2017), 'The city as innovation machine', *Regional Studies*, **51** (1), 86–96.

Glaeser, E. (2011), *Triumph of the City: How Our Greatest Invention Makes Us Richer, Smarter, Greener, Healthier and Happier*, London: Macmillan.

Henrekson, M. and T. Sanandaji (2011), 'The interaction of entrepreneurship and institutions', *Journal of Institutional Economics*, **7** (1), 47–75.

Hodgson, G.M. (2013), *From Pleasure Machines to Moral Communities: An Evolutionary Economics without Homo Economicus*, Chicago, IL: University of Chicago Press.

Hofstede, G. (1980), *Culture's Consequences: Internal Differences in Work Related Values*, London, UK and Beverly Hills, CA, USA: Sage.

Huggins, R. and N. Williams (2011), 'Entrepreneurship and regional competitiveness: the role and progression of policy', *Entrepreneurship and Regional Development*, **23** (9–10), 907–932.

Huggins, R. and P. Thompson (2014), 'A network-based view of regional growth', *Journal of Economic Geography*, **14** (3), 511–545.

Huggins, R., H. Izushi, D. Prokop and P. Thompson (2014), *The Global Competitiveness of Regions*, Abingdon, UK and New York: Routledge.

Huggins, R. (2016), 'Capital, institutions and urban growth systems', *Cambridge Journal of Regions, Economy and Society*, **9** (2), 443–463.

Huggins, R. and P. Thompson (2016), 'Socio-spatial culture and entrepreneurship: some theoretical and empirical observations', *Economic Geography*, **92** (3), 269–300.

Huggins, R. and P. Thompson (2017), 'The behavioural foundations of urban and regional development: culture, psychology and agency', *Journal of Economic Geography*, DOI: 10.1177/0308518X18778035.

Huggins, R., P. Thompson, and M. Obschonka (2018), Human behaviour and economic growth: A psycho-cultural perspective on local and regional development, *Environment and Planning A: Economy and Space*, DOI:10.1093/jeg/lbx040.

Kahneman, D. (2003), 'Maps of bounded rationality: psychology for behavioral economics', *American Economic Review*, **93** (5), 1449–1475.

Lee, N.D. (2016), 'Psychology and the geography of innovation', *Economic Geography*, http://dx.doi.org/10.1080/00130095.2016.1249845.

Lippmann, S. and H. Aldrich (2015), 'A rolling stone gathers momentum: generational units, collective memory, and entrepreneurship', *Academy of Management Review*, **41** (4), 658–675.

Mokyr, J. (2015), 'Intellectuals and the rise of the modern economy', *Science*, **349** (6244), 141–142.

Myrdal, G. (1968), *Asian Drama: An Inquiry into the Poverty of Nations*, London, UK: Allen Lane.

North, D.C. (2005), *Understanding the Process of Economic Change*, Oxford, UK and Princeton, NJ, USA: Princeton University Press.

Obschonka, M., E. Schmitt-Rodermund, R.K. Silbereisen, S.D. Gosling and J. Potter (2013), 'The regional distribution and correlates of an entrepreneurship-prone personality profile in the United States, Germany, and the United Kingdom: a socioecological perspective', *Journal of Personality and Social Psychology*, **105** (1), 104–122.

Obschonka, M., M. Stuetzer, S.D. Gosling, P.J. Rentfrow, M.E. Lamb, J. Potter and D.B. Audretsch (2015), 'Entrepreneurial regions: do macro-psychological cultural characteristics of regions help solve the "knowledge paradox" of economics?', *PLoS ONE*, **10** (6), http://dx.doi.org/10.1371/journal.pone.0129332.

Pred, A. (1967), *Behavior and Location: Foundations for a Geographic and Dynamic Location Theory*, Lund: C.W.K. Gleerup.

Rentfrow, P.J., S.D. Gosling, M. Jokela, D.J. Stillwell, M. Kosinski and J. Potter (2013), 'Divided we stand: three psychological regions of the United States and their political, economic, social, and health correlates', *Journal of Personality and Social Psychology*, **105** (6), 996–1012.

Rodríguez-Pose, A. (2013), 'Do institutions matter for regional development?', *Regional Studies*, **47** (7), 1034–1047.

Romer, P.M. (1990), 'Endogenous technological change', *Journal of Political Economy*, **98** (5), S71–S102.

Shearmur, R., C. Carrincazeaux, and D. Doloreux (2016), 'The geographies of innovations: beyond one-size-fits-all', in R. Shearmur, C. Carrincazeaux, and D. Doloreux (eds), *Handbook on the Geographies of Innovation*, Cheltenham, UK and Northampton, MA, USA: Edward Elgar Publishing, pp. 1–21.

Simon, H.A. (1982), *Models of Bounded Rationality: Empirically Grounded Economic Reason*, London, UK and Cambridge, MA, USA: MIT Press.

Stimson, R., R.R. Stough and P. Nijkamp (eds) (2011), *Endogenous Regional Development: Perspectives, Measurement and Empirical Investigation*, Cheltenham, UK and Northampton, MA, USA: Edward Elgar Publishing.

Storper, M. and A.J. Scott (2009), 'Rethinking human capital, creativity and urban growth', *Journal of Economic Geography*, **9** (2), 147–167.

Storper, M. (2013), *Keys to the City: How Economics, Institutions, Social Interaction and Politics Shape Development*, Oxford, UK and Princeton, NJ, USA: Princeton University Press.

Tabellini, G. (2010), 'Culture and institutions: economic development in the regions of Europe', *Journal of the European Economic Association*, **8** (4), 677–716.

Tomaney, J. (2014), 'Region and place I: institutions', *Progress in Human Geography*, **38** (1), 131–140.

Tubadji, A. (2013), 'Culture-based development – culture and institutions: economic development in the regions of Europe', *Society Systems Science*, **5** (4), 355–391.

Van den Bergh, J.C. and S. Stagl (2003), 'Coevolution of economic behaviour and institutions: towards a theory of institutional change', *Journal of Evolutionary Economics*, **13** (3), 289–317.

11. Learning regions – a strategy for economic development in less developed regions?
Bjørn T. Asheim

11.1 INTRODUCTION: WHAT IS A 'LEARNING REGION'?[1]

In the book *The Learning Region: Foundations, State of the Art, Future* by Rutten and Boekema (2007) four articles are reprinted as representing the foundations of the concept of learning regions: Storper (1993) Florida (1995); Asheim (1996); and, finally, Morgan (1997). This demonstrates that the concept of 'learning regions' is a product of the 1990s. Theoretically, the concept reflects the definition of post-Fordist societies as learning economies, where innovation is seen as basically a socially and territorially embedded, interactive learning process, which cannot be understood independent of its institutional and cultural contexts (Lundvall and Johnson 1994). Empirically, the changes from Fordism to post-Fordism in the 1980s highlighted the potentials of achieving endogenous regional economic development based on flexible specialization and small and medium-sized firms, taking advantage of new computerized technology to combine semi-customized production with high productivity. The central and north-eastern regions of Italy – the so called 'Third Italy' (Toscana, Emilia-Romagna and Veneto being the largest) – were the paradigmatic regional examples, which drew the attention towards the importance of co-operation between SMEs in industrial districts and between firms and local authorities at the regional level in achieving international competitiveness (Asheim 2000). Policy-wise a change occurred in regional policies in the 1970s and 1980s from a model of national welfare redistribution to a more growth-oriented policy of stimulating endogenous regional development, where the new ideas of regional innovation systems fitted perfectly. Later in the 1990s and in the 2000s this was boosted even more by the diffusion and use of the cluster approach, which in many ways built on some of the same theoretical perspectives.

Even if these contributions in many ways have a common view on how to understand 'learning regions', underlining the important role of innovation, understood as context-ualized social processes of interactive learning, they also disclose interesting differences. One such difference can be found between the American and European approaches (Rutten and Boekema 2007). In North American context learning regions are associated with the importance of the quality of the knowledge infrastructure of leading universities and research institutions in a knowledge-based, high-tech economy, producing, attracting and retaining highly skilled workers (e.g. Silicon Valley) (Florida 1995). On the contrary, in a European context of learning economies the focus is much more on the role informal institutions such as social capital and trust play in promoting formal and informal inter-firm networks and the process of interactive learning (e.g. industrial districts in the Third Italy) (Asheim 1996; Morgan 1997). The broadness in the different interpretations of learning regions clearly also demonstrates that the concept can be fuzzy and the use of the concept both theoretically and practically rather flexible.

At least one could say that the concept of 'learning regions' has been used in three different ways (Asheim 2001). The concept was originally introduced by economic geographers in the mid-1990s, and was used to emphasize the role played by co-operation and collective learning in regional clusters and networks in order to promote the innovativeness and competitiveness of firms and regions (Asheim 1996; Morgan 1997). The second approach expressing the idea of learning regions originates from the writings of evolutionary and institutional economics on the learning economy, where innovation is seen as a socially and territorially embedded, interactive learning process, making knowledge the most fundamental resource and learning the most important process (Lundvall and Johnson 1994). The third approach conceptualizes learning regions as regional development coalitions. It was developed by action-oriented, socio-technical organizational researchers taking their knowledge of how to form intra- and inter-firm learning organizations based on broad participation out of the firm context and applying it at the regional level as a bottom-up, horizontally based co-operation between different actors in a local or regional setting (Ennals and Gustavsen 1999).

According to this third perspective learning regions should be looked upon as a strategy for the formulation of long-term partnership-based development strategies initiating learning-based processes of innovation and change. In the promotion of such learning regions the inter-linking of learning organizations ranging from work organizations inside firms via inter-firm networks to different actors in the community, understood as 'regional development coalitions' (Ennals and Gustavsen 1999), is highlighted. Of strategic importance in this context is the capacity of people, organizations, and networks in a regional setting to learn (Lundvall 2008). The concept of a learning region can, thus, be used to describe a region characterized by innovative activity based on localized, interactive learning, and co-operation promoted by organizational innovations in order to exploit learning-based competitiveness (Asheim 2001).

Planners and politicians find the concept of learning regions attractive as it at one and the same time promises economic growth and job generation as well as social cohesion. As such, learning regions may be analysed as an answer and opportunity at the regional level, especially for less developed and lagging regions with weak territorial competence bases, to contemporary changes in the global economy. The approach underlines the strategic role played by social capital's emphasis on the social and cultural aspects of regions facilitating collective action for mutual benefit (Woolcock 1998), which Piore and Sabel (1984) described as the fusion of society and economy with reference to industrial districts in the Third Italy. Thus, it is not accidental that this approach to learning regions was used by the Regional Innovation Strategies pilot actions of the EU Commission as part of new policy developments in Europe since the 1990s to promote economic development through innovation in less developed regions within the EU (Bellini and Landabaso 2007).

11.2 THE RELEVANCE OF LEARNING REGIONS FOR WHICH REGIONS?

When learning regions are defined as regional development coalitions they resemble a regional innovation system broadly defined, which includes the wider setting of organizations and institutions affecting and supporting learning and innovation in a region with an explicit focus on competence-building and organizational innovations (Asheim 2007; Asheim and Gertler 2005; Lundvall 2010). This wider setting refers to organizations and institutions contributing to competence-building such as found in the educational system of non-university HEIs and the labor market, as well as formal institutions that represent framework conditions for promoting innovation, such as macroeconomics, access to finance, public policy stimulating innovation and various demand-side drivers of innovation (Lundvall 2010). This type of system is less systemic with respect to university–industry relations than the narrowly defined types of innovation systems (Asheim 2007). Firms mainly base their innovation activity on interactive, localized learning processes stimulated by geographical, social and cultural/institutional proximity, without much direct contact with knowledge-generating organizations (R&D institutes and universities) (Asheim and Gertler 2005). Due to its broadness it can, however, play a very important role in establishing a 'culture of innovation' in a region, and, thus, reach out to more 'ordinary', low-tech firms than the other types of innovation systems. Knowledge and innovation should not simply be equated with R&D. Innovative activities have much broader knowledge bases than just science-based R&D, which implies that a region's knowledge base is larger than its science base. Thus, being part of an increasingly more knowledge intensive globalizing economy does not necessarily mean that innovation and competitiveness is only dependent on R&D.

The importance of defining learning regions as regional development coalitions resembling a broadly defined regional innovation system lies in the linking up with the innovation system approach (Asheim et al. 2016). This expands the political usefulness of the learning regions approach, which is underlined by the use of it in the Regional Innovation Strategies pilot actions of the EU Commission mentioned above.

Thus, for which regions would the learning region's approach be a viable strategy for economic development? Above we have referred to less developed or lagging regions. Using the Regional Innovation Scoreboard from 2014, which benchmarks innovation performance at the regional level, regions in Europe can be divided into four categories based on their relative performance. Innovation leaders are those regions performing 20 per cent or more above the EU average. Among the key strengths of innovation leaders are business R&D and higher education. Innovation followers are regions at levels between 90 per cent and 120 per cent of the EU average. They are performing well on indicators measuring SMEs' co-operation in innovation activities and share of SMEs innovating in-house but less well on indicators related to the performance of their business sector. Moderate innovators are performing between 50 per cent and 90 per cent of the EU average and modest innovators perform below 50 per cent of the EU average, the latter with low scores on all indicators except being equipped with a relatively well-educated population (72 per cent of the EU average).

Thus, some of the moderate and all the modest innovators could be used as examples of regions, where the learning region approach would be a useful strategy to promote economic development. The regions belonging to the modest innovators are largely to be found in the post-socialist transition economies. Others are to be found in Croatia and the islands off the Mediterranean coast of Spain. Moderate innovators are more broadly distributed across Europe, with significant groupings in the southern member countries (Spain, Portugal, Italy and Greece) the Czech Republic, and parts of Slovakia, Hungary and Poland.

The features that characterize these modest and moderate innovators vary across regions and national contexts, and provide the basis for identifying at least two main categories of relevance for the learning region approach: first, regions and countries experiencing post-socialist transitions; and second, regions and countries located in southern Europe.

In a comparison of the initial performance levels and the change in performance between 2004 and 2010 for all regions in the Regional Innovation Scoreboard, most regions have improved their innovation performance during the observation period even though there is no 'catching-up' process taking place. In regions located in southern Europe a decrease in innovation performance is seen in some regions such as the east coast of Spain, and in regions experiencing post-socialist transitions innovation performance growth is more divergent, most notably with groups of decreasing regions in eastern Poland, Croatia and western Romania. Here we find a number of less-performing regions experiencing a relative decline of innovation performance over time.[2]

11.3 WHAT CHARACTERIZES MODERATE AND MODEST INNOVATIVE REGIONS?

As we have seen from the Regional Innovation Scoreboard moderate and modest innovative regions are characterized by economic activities that are less innovative than the average in Europe. This implies that they have a traditional industrial structure dominated by medium-low and low-tech industries, that is, industries using between 1 per cent and 2 per cent of turnover on R&D (e.g. manufacturing of refined petroleum products, rubber and plastic products, basic metals products, and building of ships and boats) and less than 1 per cent (e.g. textiles and clothing, leather products, wood and furniture, and food and beverages). Such regions, especially modest innovators, have a less developed knowledge infrastructure (universities and research institutes), and, thus, a low capacity of generating new knowledge, but also a low exploitation capacity due to a weak absorptive capacity in firms, which is caused by a low educational level of the employees and less developed R&D activities of firms and regions. These characteristics often co-exist with a low quality of regional government and weak (formal) institutions (Rodríguez-Pose and Di Cataldo 2015).

11.3.1 Mode of Innovation

The industries in these regions, using small resources on R&D, basically depend on an experience-based mode of innovation, what Lorenz and Lundvall (2006) call the D(oing), U(sing) and I(nteracting) mode of innovation. The distinction between non-R&D and R&D-based (regional) economies implies the use of different modes of innovation. On the one hand we can talk about a broad definition of the mode of innovation as DUI relying on informal processes of learning and experience-based know-how. The DUI mode is a user- or market-driven model based more on competence-building and organizational innovations and producing mostly incremental innovations. On the other hand one finds a narrower definition of the mode of innovation as STI based on the use of codified scientific knowledge, which is a science push/supply-driven high-tech strategy able to produce radical innovations. These two modes of innovation will also be differently manifested with regard to regional specialization and clustering. The broadly defined regional innovation system, referred to earlier and which resembles learning regions, is characterized by the DUI mode of innovation.

Referring to Lorenz and Lundvall, 2006 the STI mode of innovation, based on the use of codified scientific knowledge, could broadly be associated with the analytical knowledge base, while the DUI mode, relying on informal processes of learning and competence-building and experience-based know-how, would mostly resemble the synthetic and symbolic knowledge bases.

11.3.2   Knowledge Bases

The distinction between 'synthetic', 'analytical', and 'symbolic' types of knowledge bases partly transcends the tacit-codified dichotomy arguing that the two forms of knowledge always co-exist but in different combinations, and partly emphasizes that all types of economic activity can be innovative but that the modes of innovation differ, thus, transcending the high-tech–low-tech dichotomy. As this threefold distinction refers to ideal-types, most economic activities are in practice comprised of more than one knowledge base. However, one knowledge base will represent the critical knowledge input which the knowledge creation and innovation processes cannot do without (Asheim 2007). This approach also implies that no type of knowledge should a priori be classified as more advanced, complex, and sophisticated than other types of knowledge, or to consider science-based (analytical) knowledge as more important for innovation and competitiveness of firms, industries and regions than engineering-based (synthetic) knowledge or art-based (symbolic) knowledge. This is important to keep in mind when the potentials of economic development in learning regions are discussed. In these regions the synthetic knowledge base dominates in contrast to innovation leaders, where the analytical knowledge base is more prevalent.

An analytical knowledge base refers to economic activities where scientific knowledge based on formal models and codification is highly important. Examples are biotechnology and nanotechnology. University–industry links and respective networks are more important than in the other types of knowledge bases. Knowledge inputs and outputs are in this type of knowledge base more often codified than in the other types. The workforce, as a consequence, needs more often some research experience or university training. Knowledge creation in the form of scientific discoveries and (generic) technological inventions is more important than in the other knowledge types, and, consequently, innovations are science-driven. Many of these inventions lead to patents and licensing activities. Knowledge application is in the form of new products or processes, and there are more radical innovations than in the other knowledge types. An important route of knowledge application is new firms and spin-off companies which are formed on the basis of radically new inventions or products.

A synthetic knowledge base refers to economic activities, where innovation takes place mainly through the application or novel combinations of existing knowledge. Often this occurs in response to the need to solve specific problems coming up in the interaction with customers and suppliers, and, thus, innovations are user-, market-, and demand-driven. Industry examples include plant engineering, specialized advanced industrial machinery, and shipbuilding. University–industry links are also important for this knowledge base, but more in the field of applied research and development than in basic research. Tacit knowledge is more important than in the analytical type, in particular due to the fact that knowledge often results from experience gained at the workplace, and through learning by doing, using and interacting. Compared to the analytical knowledge base, there are more concrete know-how, craft and practical skills required, which is provided by technical universities, polytechnics, or by on-the-job training. Overall, this leads to a rather incremental way of innovation, dominated by the modification of existing products and processes.

Symbolic knowledge is related to the creation of meaning and desire as well as aesthetic attributes of products, such as designs, images and symbols, and to its economic use. The increasing significance of this intangible type of knowledge is observed by the OECD (2013) mentioning, for example, design as a new source of growth as part of firms' knowledge-based capital as well as through the dynamic development of cultural production such as media (film making, publishing, and music), advertising, design, brands and fashion. In cultural production the input is aesthetic rather than cognitive in quality. This demands rather specialized abilities in symbol interpretation and creativity. This type of knowledge is often narrowly tied to a deep understanding of the habits and norms and 'everyday culture' of specific social groupings. Due to the cultural embeddedness of interpretations this type of knowledge base is characterized by a distinctive tacit component and is usually highly context-specific. The acquisition of essential creative, imaginative and interpretive skills is less tied to formal qualifications and university degrees than to practice in various stages of the creative process; however, this knowledge base has become increasingly more knowledge-intensive.

11.3.3 Types of Work Organization

Research on types of work organization also shows a clear north–south divide with regard to the dominating forms of work organization, corresponding to the picture of where moderate and modest innovating regions are located. Northern Europe is dominated by learning forms of work organization, while southern and eastern Europe have work organizations characterized by either Taylorist or simple forms. This study distinguishes between four main forms of work organization: 'learning', 'lean', 'Taylorist' and 'simple' structures. It shows that not only does the learning work organization result in less job stress and greater worker satisfaction, it also implies more labour market flexibility, superior conditions for learning and innovation, and even a larger propensity for patenting (Lorenz and Valeyre 2006).

11.3.4 Organizational and Institutional Structures

Recently, an attempt has been made to elaborate on the notions of thickness and thinness of RIS. Based on a comprehensive review and critical discussion of the respective literature, Zukauskaite et al. (2017) advocate a clear distinction between the organizational and institutional dimension of thinness. Organizational thickness (thinness) refers to the presence (absence) of a critical mass of firms, universities, research bodies, support organizations, unions, associations, and so on. Institutional thickness (thinness) is defined as the presence (absence) of both formal institutions (laws, rules, regulations) and

Table 11.1   Organizational and institutional thickness/thinness of RIS[3]

	Organizational thickness	**Organizational thinness**
Institutional thickness	Metropolitan/city regions in northern and western Europe	Industrial districts in the Third Italy, Nordic peripheral regions
Institutional thinness	Larger cities in southern and eastern Europe; old industrial regions in western Europe (moderate innovators)	Southern and eastern peripheral regions (modest innovators)

Source: Trippl et al. (2016).

informal institutions (such as an innovation and co-operation culture, norms and values) that promote collective learning and knowledge exchange (Trippl et al. 2016).

Based on this clear-cut distinction, one can argue that regions may suffer from institutional thinness, organizational thinness or a combination of both dimensions of thinness. This leads to a distinction between three types of less-developed regions, of which we in this chapter have focused on the two latter ones as we consider institutional thinness to be the key weakness to be addressed in promoting economic development in less-developed regions. Consequently, the learning region approach is seen to be most applicable and useful here (see Table 11.1):

- Organizationally thick but institutionally thin regions: This type of region can often be found in larger cities in southern and eastern Europe but also some old industrial areas in western Europe may fall under this category. These places are characterized by the existence of a critical mass of firms as well as research, educational and other supporting organizations (organizational thickness). In these regions the knowledge generation subsystem predominates, especially due to EU's innovation policy which has been directed towards increasing the R&D capacity of universities and public research organizations. However, innovation activities are seriously curtailed by the absence of an innovation and co-operation culture as well as a low quality of government institutions and weakly developed institutions (institutional thinness).
- Institutionally and organizationally thin regions: Such constellations tend to prevail in peripheral regions located in southern and eastern Europe. More often than not, these areas are poorly endowed with innovation-relevant organizations (organizational thinness) as well as a business sector with a low absorptive capacity and suffer from an institutional set-up that is not conducive to innovation due to a low quality of government and weak institutions (institutional thinness).

11.4   WHAT CAN BE DONE IN LEARNING REGIONS TO PROMOTE ECONOMIC DEVELOPMENT?

For a long time an innovation-based strategy of economic development was thought of as being identical with promoting high-tech, R&D-intensive industries in accordance with the linear view of innovation, and, thus was out of scope for most of what we have here called less-developed, learning regions in southern and eastern Europe. More and more, however, the recognition has evolved that a broader and more comprehensive view of innovation has to be applied to retain and develop competitiveness in a heterogeneity of countries and regions. This implies that all drivers of innovation (both supply and demand side (user, market, demand (including social innovation)) as well as employee-driven innovation) have to be integrated into an overall approach to innovation policy. This requires a differentiated knowledge-based approach, distinguishing between analytical, synthetic and symbolic knowledge, as well as a broad perspective on modes of innovation making a distinction between the STI and DUI modes, to be fully accommodated (Asheim and Gertler 2005; Asheim 2007; Lorenz and Lundvall 2006). Such a broad-based innovation policy is in line with the innovation system approach of defining innovation as interactive learning.

The DUI mode of innovation is characterized by its focus on experience-based knowledge and the recombination of knowledge from various internal and external sources. Thus, it involves numerous actors and agencies in flexible forms of organizations and networks, and generates knowledge that may be highly tacit and specialized with respect to its context of development and application.

However, it is important to understand that the STI mode is not only limited to an analytical knowledge base, but must also include synthetic (and symbolic) knowledge bases. Moreover, the DUI mode is not limited to industries based on synthetic or symbolic knowledge as also predominantly analytical-based industries (e.g. pharmaceutical and biotech industries) make use of synthetic knowledge in specific phases of their innovation processes (Herstad et al. 2008; Laursen and Salter 2004; Moodysson et al. 2008). This can be illustrated by reference to applied research undertaken at (technical) universities, which clearly must be part of the STI mode, but mainly operates on the basis of synthetic (engineering) knowledge.

The main problem of traditional industries with respect to promoting economic development and making them more innovative and competitive is a low education and competence level and a lack of investment in R&D. This implies that these firms and industries have a low absorptive capacity, which limits their capacity of accessing and acquiring new and often external knowledge from outside the region, making use of new production equipment and penetrating new markets, especially international ones. It also handicaps them in approaching universities to make their knowledge more research-based and/or informed, which would extend their mode of innovation to also including the STI type. What is needed is to build absorptive capacity of DUI-based firms by increasing their research-based competence (Isaksen and Nilsson 2013). This is an important strategy for the upgrading of traditional industries, as research has demonstrated that combining DUI and STI makes firms perform better by utilizing both analytical and synthetic knowledge bases (Lorenz and Lundvall 2006). Examples of such unrelated knowledge-based combinations would be traditional textile or shoe industries moving into technical textile or shoes by adding nanotechnology (analytical knowledge base) to the traditional (synthetic) knowledge base of the industry, or the food industry starting to produce functional food using biotechnology (analytical knowledge base).

Another strategy of upgrading of traditional industries is to move into high value-added niches. This is a strategy that most efficiently can be realized by mobilizing the symbolic knowledge base, often in combination with synthetic knowledge, and by applying a platform approach, that is, transcending traditional sectors, in the concrete design and implementation. This would normally imply that the firms continue to rely on the DUI mode of innovation, but are able to climb the value-added ladder in sectors such as textile and clothing, food and beverages and tourism by introducing new products with a high element of symbolic knowledge. This may accomplish product differentiation through branding and marketing and, thus, create a unique product at the high-end of the global market.

Finally, the relatively high educational level found in eastern and southern European regions, even in regions which are modest innovators, should enable an upgrading of the dominant form of work organization from Taylorist and primitive work organizations to at least a lean form of work organization. This would also enhance the innovative capacity of firms by supporting employee-driven forms of innovation.

11.5 CONCLUSION: SMART SPECIALIZATION AND LEARNING REGIONS AS A DEVELOPMENT STRATEGY

Smart Specialization is probably the single largest attempt ever of an orchestrated, supra-national innovation strategy to boost economic growth through economic diversification. It has been launched by the European Commission and is a strategic approach to an industrial policy for national and regional economic development, pursuing a high-road strategy of innovation-based competition as the sustainable alternative to a downward spiral of cost competition (i.e. the low-road strategy), which dominates in the majority of regions in southern and eastern Europe. As such, smart specialization represents a new industrial policy that aims to promote new path development and economic diversification. Furthermore, for the first time in the EU, smart specialization provides a policy framework or platform for promoting and implementing a broad-based innovation policy.

Smart specialization is not about 'specialization' as known from previous regional development strategies, that is, a Porter-like cluster strategy, but about diversified specialization. What this means is that countries should identify areas – or 'domains' – of existing and/or potential competitive advantage, where they can specialize in a different way compared to other countries and regions. Countries and regions should diversify their economies primarily based on existing strengths and capabilities by moving into related or unrelated sectors.

'Smart' in the smart specialization approach refers to 'entrepreneurial discovery', which is the way these domains of competitive advantage should be identified. However, 'entrepreneurial' should be understood broadly as an entrepreneurial mindset to encompass all actors (including individual entrepreneurs), organizations (including firms and universities) and public agencies, as well as the civic society, that have the capacity to discover domains for securing existing and future competitiveness. Such a broad interpretation of 'entrepreneurial discovery' avoids the pitfall of ignoring the systemic nature of innovation. The systems approach to innovation policies also highlights the role of government in driving innovation, as well as the balance between exploration and exploitation (Asheim and Gertler 2005; Asheim et al. 2016). A learning-region approach represents a realistic alternative for implementing such public–private partnership-based, broad innovation policy.

The 'entrepreneurial discovery' approach is a bottom-up strategy relying on mobilizing people in a region with an entrepreneurial mindset from all sectors of the community or society. Thus, it represents a potential viable strategy for learning regions in eastern and southern Europe that suffer from a traditional business sector with low absorptive capacity as well as a low-quality government and weak formal institutions. The strategy of building broad local or regional development coalitions would be a way of activating the entrepreneurial discovery process in these less-developed learning regions and starting a process of economic development. In initiating these processes, there might still be something to be learnt from the way action researchers transformed intra- and inter-firm learning organizations based on broad participation to regional development coalitions as a bottom-up, horizontally based co-operation between different actors in a local or regional setting (Ennals and Gustavsen 1999). Likewise looking at the EU's Regional Innovation Strategies pilot actions, which were inspired and informed by this approach, could prove helpful.

11.6 NOTES

1. The introduction is an adapted version taken from my article in *Regional Studies* (2012) on 'The Changing Role of Learning Regions in the Globalizing Economy: A Theoretical Re-examination', **46** (8), 993–1004.
2. The Regional Innovation Scoreboard suffers from several shortcomings. Most notable in our context is a bias towards measuring R&D-driven innovation activities and even though non-R&D activities are targeted (for example through non-R&D expenditure as a percentage of turnover in SMEs), it remains unclear what is covered in this regard. While some indicators are broad and can include a wide variety of innovations, most are narrower and targeted towards measuring analytical knowledge, the S(cience) T(echnology) I(innovation) mode of innovation and narrowly defined RIS. For more details on the Regional Innovation Scoreboard, please see Trippl et al. (2016), which these paragraphs are extracted and adapted from.
3. This matrix is based on an idea by Bjørn Asheim, outlined in a project application for the Marianne and Markus Wallenberg Foundation in 2013.

11.7 REFERENCES

Asheim, B.T. (1996), 'Industrial districts as "learning regions": a condition for prosperity?' *European Planning Studies*, **4** (4), 379–400.
Asheim, B.T. (2000), 'Industrial districts: the contributions of Marshall and beyond', in G. Clark, M. Feldman and M. Gertler (eds), *The Oxford Handbook of Economic Geography*, Oxford: Oxford University Press, pp. 413–431.
Asheim, B.T. (2001), 'Learning regions as development coalitions: partnership as governance in European workfare states?', *Concepts and Transformation, International Journal of Action Research and Organizational Renewal*, **6** (1), 73–101.
Asheim, B.T. and M. Gertler (2005), 'The geography of innovation: regional innovation systems', in J. Fagerberg, D. Mowery and R. Nelson (eds), *The Oxford Handbook of Innovation*, Oxford, UK: Oxford University Press, pp. 291–317.
Asheim, B.T. (2007), 'Differentiated knowledge bases and varieties of regional innovation systems', *Innovation – The European Journal of Social Science Research*, **20** (3), 223–241.
Asheim, B.T., M. Grillitsch and M. Trippl (2016), 'Regional innovation systems: past – presence – future', in D. Doloreux, R. Shearmur and C. Carrincazeau (eds), *Handbook on the Geography of Innovation*, Cheltenham, UK and Northampton, MA, USA: Edward Elgar Publishing, pp. 45–62.
Bellini, N. and M. Landabaso (2007), 'Learning about innovation in Europe's regional policy', in R. Rutten and F. Boekema (eds), *The Learning Region: Foundations, State of the Art, Future*, Cheltenham, UK and Northampton, MA, USA: Edward Elgar Publishing, pp. 231–251.
Ennals, R. and B. Gustavsen (1999), *Work Organisation and Europe as a Development Coalition*, Amsterdam: John Benjamin's Publishing Company.

Florida, R. (1995), 'Towards the learning region', *Futures*, **27** (5), 527–536.

Herstad, S.J., C. Bloch, B. Ebensberger and E. van den Velde (2008), 'Open innovation and globalisaton: theory, evidence and implications', Report, *VISION Era-Net*.

Isaksen, A. and M. Nilsson (2013), 'Combining innovation policy: linking scientific and practical knowledge in innovation systems', *European Planning Studies*, **21** (12), 1919–1936.

Laursen, K. and A. Salter (2004), 'Searching high and low: what types of firms use universities as sources of knowledge?', *Research Policy*, **33** (8), 1201–1215.

Lorenz, E. and B.-Å. Lundvall (eds) (2006), *How Europe's Economies Learn: Coordinating Competing Models*, Oxford: Oxford University Press.

Lorenz, E. and A. Valeyre (2006), 'Organisational forms and innovative performance', in E. Lorenz and B.-Å. Lundvall (eds), *How Europe's Economies Learn: Coordinating Competing Models*, Oxford: Oxford University Press, pp. 140–161.

Lundvall, B.-Å. and B. Johnson (1994), 'The learning economy', *Journal of Industry Studies*, **1** (2), 23–42.

Lundvall, B.-Å. (2008), 'National innovation systems – analytical concept and development tool', *Industry & Innovation*, **14** (1), 95–119.

Lundvall, B.-Å. (2010), 'Post script: innovation system research – where it came from and where it might go', in B.-Å. Lundvall (ed.), *National Systems of Innovation: Towards a Theory of Innovation and Interactive Learning*, London: Anthem, postscript.

Moodysson, J., L. Coenen and B.T. Asheim (2008), 'Explaining spatial patterns of innovation: analytical and synthetic modes of knowledge creation in the Medicon Valley life science cluster', *Environment and Planning A*, **40** (5), 1040–1056.

Morgan, K. (1997), 'The learning region: institutions, innovation and regional renewal', *Regional Studies*, **31** (5), 491–504.

OECD (2013), *OECD Reviews of Innovation Policy: Sweden*, Paris: OECD.

Piore, M. and C. Sabel (1984), *The Second Industrial Divide: Possibilities for Prosperity*, New York: Basic Books.

Rodríguez-Pose, A. and M. Di Cataldo (2015), 'Quality of government and innovative performance in the regions of Europe', *Journal of Economic Geography*, **15** (4), 673–706.

Rutten, R. and F. Boekema (eds) (2007), *The Learning Region. Foundations, State of the Art, Future*, Cheltenham, UK and Northampton, MA, USA: Edward Elgar Publishing.

Storper, M. (1993), 'Regional "Worlds" of Production', *Regional Studies*, **27** (5), 433–455.

Trippl, M., B.T. Asheim and J. Miörner (2016), 'Identification of regions with less developed research and innovation systems', in M.D. Parrilli, R.D. Fitjar and A. Rodríguez-Pose (eds), *Innovation Drivers and Regional Innovation Strategies*, London: Routledge, pp. 23–44.

Woolcock, M. (1998), 'Social capital and economic development: toward a theoretical synthesis and policy framework', *Theory and Society*, **27** (2), 151–208.

Zukauskaite, E., M. Trippl and M. Plechero (2017), 'Institutional thickness revisited', *Economic Geography*, **93** (4), 325–345.

12. Divisions of labour, technology and the transformation of work: worker to robot or self-employment and the gig economy?

John R. Bryson

Work, or the experience of work, shapes or defines individuals. Work is one of the basic building blocks, perhaps the most basic building block, of regional economic activity. The individual's experience of work may be good or bad; work may be all consuming shaping an individual's identity or just a means to support everyday living. Work is at the centre of everyday living and influences how an individual thinks about themselves and is considered by others. Work contributes to establishing routines of everyday living constructed around the cycle of the working day, week, month and annual holidays. Work influences where people live, how well they live and whom they socialise with. It also shapes consumption patterns and plays an important role in how children are educated. Work is often taken for granted – as a given that supports individual well-being but it is also a vehicle for taxation that contributes to wider societal welfare.

Within economic geography there is a danger that 'work', or the experience of work, is subsumed into a concern with firms, organisations or commodity chains; individuals and their everyday experiences are replaced with a concern for understanding the activities of representative firms or networks. The use of these different terms – individuals, firms and chain-based metaphors – reflects the defined object of study that dominates a particular approach to a research area. This is to highlight the importance of exploring the relationship between geographic scale – from the interaction between an employee's place of work and home to understanding the role relationships play in contributing to the development of careers and the competitiveness of firms (Moretti 2013). This is to argue that one of the pillars of economic geography must be a person-centric approach that explores individuals, the development of careers and everyday living. Other key pillars include understanding organisations or firms (firm-centric), exploring relationships between firms as well as people (relationship-centric) and the relationships between place, firm and people (place/regional-centric). This latter pillar emphasises the importance of region or territory in shaping the life changes and lifestyles of individuals and the competitiveness of firms. Geography matters in the ways in which 'place' provides the micro-frameworks for supporting everyday living, but also the ways in which places engage with meso or regional processes and more macro (national/international) processes. Nevertheless, the micro-geographies of everyday living are predominantly a local place-bounded experience.

Firms are in a constant state of becoming as the wider framework condition that supports economic activity alters. The drivers of change include new forms and sources of competition, new technologies that destroy existing production processes and the evolution of the global economic geography of production – in other words what is produced, where it is produced, how it is produced, and where it is traded? These drivers of change alter and sometimes transform employment; existing jobs are destroyed and new forms of work created. Thus, work, like firms, is a continual state of change as new technologies and processes emerge. It is important to understand the drivers behind these changes. Research on skills and individual capabilities tends to be the focus of a specialist niche within economic geography (Lowe 2015) whilst the wider research agenda on work tends to be dominated with a concern with gender (Bryson et al. 2004). Economic geographers must return the nature of work, the experience of work and skills to the centre of academic debate. This is to ensure that a balanced economic geography emerges that is place-centric, firm-centric, person-centric and very much concerned with a focus on scale and the relationships between different places.

This chapter explores the relationships between work and firms in the context of regional economies. The concern is to identify drivers of change as they apply to the experience of work. These drivers can be traced back to the emergence of capitalism but their impacts alter as macro-economic processes are transformed. Labour markets are experiencing a particular moment of transformation as mobile technologies, combined with developments in artificial intelligence (AI), are creating new jobs, often forms of precarious employment, as well as transforming and in some cases destroying existing work. The focus is on exploring the changing relationship between work and organisation as new ways of organising production emerge in response to process and technological innovations.

12.1   PLACE, SPACE, FIRMS AND LABOUR

The relationship between firms and labour is being continually challenged as firms experiment with new forms of employment relationship that shift employees from inside the boundary of the firm to some type of more informal relationship in which the firm's responsibilities and liabilities are limited. This attempt to redefine the role labour plays within organisations reflects what can be termed a 'timeless process' in which firms try to reduce variable costs within their business. The most important variable cost is the cost of labour. One solution is to either replace people with machines that represent a known fixed capital cost or to transfer employment to other organisations. The latter includes the establishment of a new contractual relationship with other firms to provide goods and services at an agreed cost.

A focus on understanding interactions between workers and firms draws attention to the need to define the firm. For many economic geographers, the firm is an ambiguous concept that is much used, seldom defined and often obfuscated in empirical analysis. Firms are too often a shadowy presence in studies of regional economies with a focus, for example, on international business, foreign direct investment and the activities of transnational corporation or an analysis of small and medium sized enterprises (SMEs). In much research, the firm is taken to be a 'phenotype' or the smallest unit of analysis that is considered to be the site for timeless processes. These processes include profit maximisation, decision-making under uncertainty, rules, rituals, habits and routines and a site for learning, innovation and knowledge transfer. A simple definition of a firm is that it is a boundary-maintaining, socially contracted system of routines that are mechanisms for co-ordinating and motivating the activities of individuals (Grossman and Hart 1986, p. 692; Holmstrom and Roberts 1998, p. 75; Nooteboom 2000, p. 71).

There are many different types of firms. On the one hand, there are SMEs and even much larger firms that are grounded in particular places. These are firms whose origins and operations are in some way bounded by place. This may include cluster-based relationships with co-located firms. Such local firms may have established relationships with local families that can be traced back generations. In the West Midlands, UK, the manufacture of locks was heavily localised and was supported by large complex family networks in which children followed their parents into the industry (Bryson et al. 2008; Greene et al. 2001, p. 214). It was not uncommon for employees to have immediate family members working with them and for employees to have married one another. Kinship networks were identified as key to the recruitment and retention of workers and more importantly 'skill thus becomes something that is kin-defined, with the family possessing substantial resources within certain employment contexts' (Greene et al. 2002, p. 281). This reflects an older form of relationship between firm and family that was at one time important, but has been undermined by the increasing mobility of people, limited access to avoidable housing combined with gentrification and the shift from labour markets that were predominantly local or regional to labour markets that operate nationally and sometimes internationally.

On the other hand, there are transnational corporations (TNCs) that engage in precarious place-based investment; precarious as it is often temporary and is part of a wider international strategy. Such investment decisions are made on the basis of 'market-based drivers' including gaining access to protected markets and 'asset-based drivers', for example, access to skilled labour or inexpensive labour, government subsidies and a location's connectivity. This division between assets and drivers should be based within an historical, sector and geographical context. Different industrial sectors, at different times, will make decisions that emphasise one of these processes over the other. A good example of this is Arthur Price of England, a family owned, manufacturer of cutlery, which was established in 1902. In the 1940s and 1950s Arthur Price was a 'factory-led company' based on the management of assets, but in the 1960s began to alter to become a 'consumer-led company' and the strategy was 'to shed the factory-led element and direct resources and effects to the consumer' (Price 1997, p. 160). This highlights the importance of a focus on product, consumers, quality and price and marketing. Up to 1992, all Arthur Price products had been manufactured in the UK, but competitors had been importing product and 'no leading cutler in Europe was without a lower end of imports' to supplement their home-produced products (Price 1997, p. 212). The problem was that many consumers only wanted to spend up to £100 for a six-person cutlery set and British manufactured cutlery could not compete in this market segment. Arthur Price began an import or outsourcing and offshoring programme under the branding 'Arthur Price International' to distinguish this cutlery from product branded 'Arthur Price England' and manufactured in England. The decision to go ahead with Arthur Price International was made once the company's managing director 'was satisfied . . . that it wouldn't rob Sheffield of a single knife, fork or spoon' (Price 1997, p. 212). The decision eventually led to limited differentiation between cutlery sold by Arthur Price that was manufactured in the UK or imported. Arthur Price survived as a family firm, but now production has been outsourced and offshored as the company's focus has shifted from manufacturing to designing, sourcing and marketing cutlery.

The distinction between SMEs that are grounded in a place and TNCs that are grounded in many places reflects a key divide in the economic geography literature between research that focuses on understanding geographies of entrepreneurship (Nijkamp 2003; Delgado et al. 2010) and that which explores international business (Dicken 2014). There is an important point to make here; organisational size might not be important in differentiating between different types of economic activity. Larger firms might be considered to be more important than SMEs, but combined SMEs employ more people. Perhaps organisational size does not matter as similar endogenous and exogenous processes are at work in both large and small firms. It is to these processes that we now turn our attention.

12.2   FLEXIBLE FIRMS AND DIVISIONS OF LABOUR

Organisations are the basic vehicle through which collective action occurs. In this context, organisations are goal-directed groupings of individuals that come together for a period of time to co-ordinate and control a set of assets. Establishing a boundary between members and non-members includes the creation of a recruitment process designed to select some people for inclusion in to the organisation and to exclude others. The boundaries of organisations are being continually challenged as new ways of producing goods and services emerge. Here it is important to distinguish between different types of organisational employment relationship. In 1984, Atkinson explored the development of a 'flexible' firm model in which a new form of polarisation was identified between a 'core' and a 'peripheral' workforce; the former providing functional flexibility and the latter numeric flexibility. These forms of flexibility enabled firms to adapt to changing market demands for their products and services. In the periphery, workers may experience insecurity and irregular employment and may not have a direct relationship with their employer, being, for example, self-employed of sub-contracted.

The concept of the 'flexible firm' reflects UK employment law. Under UK law there are three types of employment relationship: 'employees', 'self-employed' and 'workers'. The majority of people are 'employees' under a contract of employment and are entitled to minimum employment rights with an obligation by law for the employer to deduct Income Tax and National Insurance contributions. A 'self-employed' individual does not have a contract of employment, but will be contracted to provide services or some form of work for a certain period of time for a fee. The self-employed pay their own tax and National Insurance and do not have employment rights. 'Workers' represent any individual who works for an employer, under a contract of employment or any other contract, where someone undertakes to provide work or services. 'Workers' are mostly casual workers, temporary workers and some freelancers and have rights to the National Minimum Wage, rest breaks, paid holiday and some other benefits. These three categories provide different types of protection in the labour market. The ongoing transformation of the organisation of production reflects attempts by firms to alter the balance in their business between 'employees', 'self-employed' and 'workers' reducing risks and liabilities and enhancing profit and flexibility.

The history of capitalist firms is one in which there is a continual search to increase profitability and to control uncertainty or to increase certainty by strategies designed to remove risk. The emergence of various types of flexibility in the organisation of firms plays an important role in the process of increasing certainty. There are a number of processes at work here including the ongoing evolution of a social and technical division of labour, replacement of people by machines including deskilling and finally altering the boundaries of organisations to include outsourcing of production tasks to other firms and offshoring tasks to other countries. There is a balance between the advantages that are derived from territorial agglomeration, some type of regional clustering, with organisational strategies that rely on the substitutability of labour between many different locations (Christopherson 2006; Bryson 2007).

Fundamental to understanding the relationship between firms, labour and place is the division of labour (Sayer and Walker 1992). David Harvey (2014, p. 112) has recently noted that 'the division of labour should, by rights, be positioned as one of the funda-mental features of what capital is all about'. The division of labour is arguably a timeless process that is fundamental to the functioning of capitalism. This concept describes the process by which complex productive and reproductive activities can be disaggregated into simpler tasks. This process is implicated in the deskilling of labour and a reduction in the cost of undertaking production tasks. Specialised sub-divided tasks are reunited through a process of organised co-operation that can occur within a family, firm, between co-located or clustered firms or across global production networks. It is worth stating that all other labour processes commence with the division of labour. A division of labour precedes the substitution of labour by machines as well as the outsourcing of production tasks to other firms and to offshoring tasks. The division of labour is an ongoing process which is continually reshaped by capitalism in response to process innovations, including the development of new geographies of production tasks, and technological innovations. Three distinctions are important to make regarding the division of labour. First, a techni-cal division of labour occurs when a task is divided into subtasks that anyone can do. Second, a social division of labour occurs when a specialised task emerges that can only be undertaken by someone with adequate training and perhaps social and cultural capital and interpersonal skills. Third, the relationship between place and space and the division of labour results in a spatial division of labour in which specialist tasks can be identified and labour located in one place substituted for labour located in another place. The devel-opment of a more advanced division of labour goes hand-in-hand with developments in contract law that are intended to regulate more complex relationships between people and organisations (Bryson and Taylor 2010). The threat of contract enforcement is more important than actual enforcement with the contract providing an agreed specification of the roles, responsibilities and expectations of those involved in a relationship that is regulated via the law of contract.

The division of labour was applied by Richard Walker in an important paper published in 1985 to explain the decline in manufacturing employment and the rapid growth of service. He argued that the concepts of 'services' and 'service economy' had entered the literature with surprisingly little critical examination. He noted that the arguments for the emergence of a service economy rested on the distinction made between the output of goods and services and on the form of labour involved in the production process. In Walker's view, this distinction was a simplification and the focus of the analysis should instead be on the production system and the division of labour. Walker's argument rests on the simple proposition that 'services' such as banks and hotels are not new, and consequently service functions can be explained by drawing upon existing theoretical frameworks. There was also too much emphasis placed on information and knowledge, to the extent that some theorists claim that we have entered a new information or knowledge age. Walker noted that information is not free floating and that much of it is directly related to the practical business of production and consumption. Thus, the growth of services reflects not the development of a 'new' economy, but rather 'the revolutionary force of capital has generated dramatic shifts in the division of labour in society' (Walker 1985, p. 239). Thus, the outsourcing of service functions by clients and the creation of new types of service occupations represent an increase in, or extension of, the division of labour. An expanding division of labour reflects both increasing specialisation of activity with a resultant increase in the complexity of production, and alterations in the way in which production is organised. Here the important point is the *extended labour process* (Sayer and Walker 1992; Walker 1985), which is the work that occurs before and after goods and services are physically produced. Thus, research and development, design, market research, trial production, product testing, marketing, customer care and sales are all essential parts of the production process. The fact that they can be separated in both time and space from actual production, does not necessarily imply that they are not an integral part of the manufacturing sector of the economy. Ultimately, this means that the dramatic growth in service employment, for example, reflects alterations in the way in which manufacturing production is organised.

The development of the concept of an extended division of labour highlights the relevance of this concept for understanding more recent developments. In 2017, the current media and political debate is on the emergence of the 'sharing economy', the rise of the 'gig economy' and the application of AI to work. These new types of work can be explained as part of an ongoing tendency for capitalism to develop more complex divisions of labour and to reduce variable costs in production processes. Thus, the technology and the labels might be new, but the drivers behind these new forms of work can be traced back to the origins of capitalism.

12.3   GIG JOBS AND THE GIG ECONOMY

Since the early 2000s one of the defining features of the UK has been the growth in self-employment. Between 2008 and 2015 the level of self-employment in the UK increased from 3.8 million to 4.6 million. This absolute change in self-employment was evenly divided between part- and full-time employment, but part-time self-employment grew by 88 per cent between 2001 and 2015 compared to 25 per cent for the full-time self-employed. Much of this work is concentrated in finance and business services and in higher occupational groups with full-time self-employment being particularly more concentrated in London. Much of the growth in self-employment appears to reflect older workers managing their careers as they shift from full-time employment to part-time self-employment and then retirement (Wales and Agyiri 2016). There is a problem with this category of employment in that it only reflects one type of employment relationship ignoring the category of 'worker'.

The label 'gig economy' emerged in the media in early 2009 as one response to the ongoing financial crisis. The term 'gig' was first used by jazz musicians in the 1920s to describe a temporary one-night musical engagement. The application of this musical term to other forms of work during this century draws attention to the growth in part-time and temporary forms of work in which individuals undertake a number of part-time jobs/

gigs but in the capacity as 'self-employed' with limited employment rights compared to 'employees' or 'workers'. There is no official definition of the 'gig economy', but a gig describes a single task, activity or project for which someone is hired to perform for a temporary period. Some gigs represent short-term temporary jobs while others are a form of self-employment.

This type of short-term self-employment is not new. What differentiates the world of the musicians' gigs from the gig economy is the development of business models that are based on linking workers with temporary jobs through websites or mobile applications, known as apps (Torpey and Hogan 2016). This has led to the development of new business models based on employing 'workers' to undertake tasks on a relatively unregulated and temporary basis. The new technology uses apps to link providers with consumers enabling access to services including fast food delivery and taxis. Apps and Internet-based platforms have also been created that have led to the development of a sharing economy. Individuals and households with assets that provide them with use rather than exchange values are able to create exchange values by providing strangers with access and use of these assets in exchange for payment. The rise of Airbnb is part of this process in which a spare room can occasionally be let to others via an online platform. Private assets that are also commodities that can be purchased and sold outright are being converted into commodities that can be rented for a fixed period.

The relationship between the sharing and gig economy is all about the temporary nature of these economic relationships. Airbnb and the sharing economy provide another source of income that unlocks some of the exchange values temporarily locked in fixed capital investments, but the gig economy or gig-style employment is about another form of precarious employment in which the power in the employment relationship shifts towards employers and away from employees. But not in all cases, for some this type of employment relationship fits with their lifestyles. The gig economy is just another reflection of the operation of the division of labour in which new forms of technology enable new forms of work to emerge. Temporary work has been a feature of capitalism for some considerable time, and one can argue that there is nothing new about 'gig-style' employment apart from the name and the use of technology.

The gig economy provides alternative employment opportunities reflecting the management of labour inputs by the application of technology that has the potential to co-ordinate and control many part-time 'employees' or self-employed contractors. Gig-style work is being challenged by trade unions and by the legal system. The unions are concerned with the transfer of work from 'employee' to 'worker' status reducing employment rights, but also removing employees from the trade union movement. Uber, the alternative provider of taxi services, uses a smartphone app to transform a private vehicle into a taxi with the owner of the vehicle being defined as 'self-employed' rather than as a 'worker'. In 2016, a UK court case explored the employment status of Uber drivers. This case transformed Uber taxi drivers from 'self-employed' drivers to 'workers' with benefits including the national living wage and holiday pay (Osborne 2016). This court case revolved around employment status, employment rights and responsibilities.

New forms of working relationship challenge established methods of organising labour including undermining the role trade unions play in representing and protecting the interests of their members. In 2016, another case involving a gig economy employer emerged. The Independent Workers Union of Great Britain (IWGB) wrote to the chief executive of Deliveroo, a fast food delivery service that is accessed via an app, requesting that the company formally recognised it as the union representing Deliveroo riders in Camden, north London (Foot 2016). This request for collective bargaining challenged the Deliveroo business model that is based on self-employment limiting the company's exposure to financial liabilities linked to 'workers' or 'employees' and maximising organisational flexibility.

Self-employed contractors are unable to engage in formal collective bargaining. A reclassification to worker status and collective bargaining would enable the riders to negotiate pay and terms and conditions whilst automatically acquiring rights to holiday pay and sick leave and all the other rights that come with 'worker' status. This request was rejected by Deliveroo and in November 2016 the IWGB submitted an application for trade union recognition to the Central Arbitration Committee, a government-backed body that deals with disputes between workers and employers.

The gig economy challenges existing employment relationships. The Uber court case and the request for collective bargaining from the IWGB for Deliveroo riders working in Camden reflects attempts to bring the gig economy in to line with established labour market practices. The legal definition of work needs to be reconsidered. The category of 'self-employed' emerged to cover a particular type of employment relationship and often this category of worker is advantaged as they control and regulate their conditions of employment including pay. The category of self-employment has been used in the UK to define gig-style employment in which this form of employment comes with no ability to regulate the terms of engagement with work. There is an important debate regarding how employment is categorised and the rights and responsibilities associated with particular types of work/employer relationship. For geographers it is important to recognise that these employment regulations reflect locally based institutional practices that emerge during the construction of the relationship between a national legal system and the regulation of nationally constructed labour practices. At the moment the boundary between 'gig-style' employment and work is blurring, but this blurring will become more focused as trade unions and workers challenge the ongoing transformation of work that is emerging with technological innovation.

12.4   ARTIFICIAL INTELLIGENCE AND THE TRANSFORMATION OF WORK

The application of AI, including robotics and autonomous systems (RAS), to some types of labour represents the most recent reworking of the relationship between an evolving division of labour and technological innovation. RAS are combinations of physical and software systems that can perceive their environments, reason, adapt and control their actions. Developments in RAS are making it possible to automate tasks that previously could only be undertaken by people. There is much media discussion about RAS and its impact on work, but very few studies have assessed the potential impacts RAS will have on labour markets. The difficulty is that there is no rigorous and robust technique for forecasting such impacts. RAS is just another stage in the application of machines to labour and could potentially increase productivity, destroy some forms and employment, but create new forms of work. It might be that RAS increases unemployment, by creating jobs with high barriers to entry based around capabilities in computer programming and mathematics or highly developed social skills. At the moment, any assessment of RAS impacts is based on speculation and prediction.

It is possible to explore the impacts of former technological changes on today's labour market. Between 1980 and 2012 per capita world output increased, on average, by 1.7 per cent corresponding to cumulative growth of just over 60 per cent. This represented a major transformation in lifestyles, consumer behaviours, in technology and in labour markets. A relatively modest annual growth rate over a thirty-year period involved transformational technological changes including the Internet, mobile computing, smartphones, health-care, transport and creative and digital services. It led to the emergence of cybercrime and also employment in cyber security or policing. According to Piketty:

> These changes have also had a powerful impact on the structure of employment: when output per head increases by 35 to 50 percent in thirty years that means that a very large fraction – between a quarter and a third – of what is produced today, and therefore between a quarter and a third of occupations and jobs, did not exist thirty years ago. (Piketty 2014, pp. 95–96)

The implication of this analysis is that a per capita growth rate of between 1 per cent and 1.8 per cent represented rapid transformational change in the economy and in labour markets. There is no reason for assuming that this type of transformation will not continue to occur over the next thirty years. Perhaps between 25 per cent to 30 per cent of all jobs will be destroyed as they are substituted by various forms of RAS; from robots that are designed to look like humans to small black boxes that run complex computer science algorithms. But, other jobs will be created.

It is important to conceptualise this transformation as a continual process as organisations try to enhance productivity, profitability and competitiveness. This process begins with the division of labour and then has a number of stages including:

1.   Replacing some tasks by mechanically operated machine tools.
2.   Outsourcing some tasks, but to firms located in the same country.
3.   Offshoring some tasks through foreign direct investment.
4.   Outsourcing and offshoring tasks to companies located elsewhere.
5.   Replacing some full-time with part-time employees.
6.   Standardising tasks as a process of deskilling and also delivering tasks by employees guided by computer-aided scripts.
7.   Repatriation of some tasks that were offshored. The repatriated tasks will have been transformed by the application of technology. Reshoring of tasks does not imply a simple direct substitution of tasks from one location to another.
8.   Replacing employees with 'temporary workers' or 'self-employed' workers.
9.   Replacing some tasks with RAS either in part or completely.

This is partly a linear process, but many firms will include a blend of all these strategies. The ultimate driver is to increase certainty in the creation of a product or service and to maximise profitability combined with enhancing competitiveness.

There is considerable uncertainty regarding the application of RAS to production tasks including the pace of transformation and whether RAS will lead to a net decrease or increase in employment. Companies are experimenting with RAS. The Henn-na

Hotel, Nagasaki, Japan, has three robots at reception who deal with the check-in and check-out process, a robot porter and a robot cloak room. The Beam Store, Palo Alto, California, is staffed by employees located in remote locations in the US and elsewhere who interact with potential customers through non-autonomous robots equipped with screens, speakers and wheels. These are high profile examples that have been covered in the mainstream press, but they hide more important applications of RAS to production tasks. These include the rise of automated factories and warehouses. Robotic surgical systems were approved for use in the US in 2000 to facilitate complex surgery using a minimally invasive approach. Nevertheless, these systems are not based on an autonomous robot but are controlled by a surgeon from a console.

Two influential studies have tried to calculate the impact of RAS on labour markets. The Frey and Osbourne (2014) study estimated that 35 per cent of jobs that existed in the UK in 2013 had a greater than 66 per cent chance of being automated in the coming decades. A more recent study by Arntz et al. (2016) explored 2012 data and estimated that for 10 per cent of UK jobs it would be possible to automate 70 per cent of their component tasks over the next decade and that another 25 per cent of jobs could have at least 50 per cent of their tasks automated. The difficulty with these studies is that they say nothing about new tasks and jobs that might be created through the application of RAS. This is the known, unknown of the implications RAS will have on future labour markets.

Jobs that might be protected from RAS appear to have similar characteristics to those service jobs that were identified as being relatively immune to offshoring and the second global shift (Bryson 2007). The literature on services and offshoring identified service tasks that would be difficult to standardise and offshore. The ability to standardise tasks also applies to RAS applications. Thus, it will be difficult to apply RAS to activities that require emotional labour (Wellington and Bryson 2001; Bryson et al. 2004), well-developed social skills, persuasion, empathy and negotiation, artistic and intellectual capabilities, programming and maintaining digital systems and tasks that involve dealing with high levels of unpredictability. The Frey and Osbourne (2014) study identified jobs in sales, transport, logistics and administration as being particular suitable to automation. This list is unsurprising as many of these jobs have already been transformed by the application of technology. Jobs that were considered to be less likely to be affected were in health-care, education and financial and management services. The difficulty is that no one yet knows how ongoing developments in RAS will impact on specific jobs and the experience of work and worker.

12.5 CONCLUSIONS

The chapter is based around the identification and application of what are defined as timeless processes that continue to transform economic relationships. The ongoing revolutionary forces that shape capitalism continue to create dramatic shifts in the division of labour redefining the relationships between work and worker. The locus of competitive advantage has shifted from direct employment to various forms of indirect relationship. This includes outsourcing tasks to other firms, offshoring tasks from one country to another and in the process substituting labour located in one place with labour located in another. It also includes replacing full-time employees with self-employed workers and the self-employed with 'workers' with very limited employment benefits. This reflects a long-term process based on substituting people with machines. It makes no difference if the machine is a relatively simple mechanical device or a more complex form of RAS; the outcome is the same the replacement of a variable cost with a fixed.

Central to capitalism is a tension between firms and labour. Firms require workers and workers require firms. Nevertheless, a key challenge for firms is to reduce or control variable costs; the activity that accounts for most of these variable costs is labour. For firms, there are many different solutions to this tension including deskilling labour by replacing expensive skilled labour with less expensive unskilled labour, replacing employees with machines or relocating production processes to countries with lower labour costs. In 2017, it is possible to argue that firms and employees are at the beginning of a major transformation or revolution in the relationship between labour and production. There are two possible futures for work. The first is a more efficient or productive version of work based on process innovations and the continued application of technology. The second future involves a radical transformation in work with the application of innovations in RAS that have the potential to replace people with robotic workers and/or computer algorithms. Developments in RAS represent a radical approach to deskilling labour and substituting variable costs with fixed capital investments. This new world of work means that jobs that require face-to-face interactions and activities that cannot be easily undertaken by RAS will continue to be performed by people. But, it may also mean greater unemployment. The only known is that the division of labour will continue to transform work as companies try to reduce variable costs and the legal system will continue to try to balance the interests of worker and firm. There is a fundamental contradiction here (Harvey 2014); for capitalism to survive and grow, consumers need to be able to afford to consume. And, at the moment, robots are not consumers. There will always have to be a balance between the efficiency of production systems and the ability of workers to consume.

12.6   REFERENCES

Arntz, M., T. Gregory and U. Zierahn (2016), *The Risk of Automation for Jobs in OECD Countries*, Paris: OECD.

Atkinson, J. (1984), 'Manpower strategies for flexible organisations', *Personnel Management*, August, 28–31.

Bryson, J.R., P.W. Daniels and B. Warf (2004), *Service Worlds: People, Organizations, Technologies*, London: Routledge.

Bryson, J.R. (2007), 'The "second" global shift: the offshoring or global sourcing of corporate services and the rise of distanciated emotional labour', *Geografiska Annaler: Series B, Human Geography*, **89** (s1), 31–43.

Bryson, J.R., M. Taylor and R. Cooper (2008), 'Competing by design, specialization and customization: manufacturing locks in the West Midlands (UK)', *Geografiska Annaler: Series B, Human Geography*, **90** (2), 173–186.

Bryson, J.R. and M. Taylor (2010), 'Mutual dependency, diversity and alterity in production: cooperatives, group contracting and factories', in D. Fuller, A.E.G. Jonas and R. Lee (eds), *Interrogating Alterity*, Farnham: Ashgate, pp. 75–94.

Christopherson, S. (2006), 'Behind the scenes: how transnational firms are constructing a new international division of labor in media work', *Geoforum*, **37** (5), 739–751.

Delgado, M., M.E. Porter and S. Stern (2010), 'Clusters and entrepreneurship', *Journal of Economic Geography*, **10** (4), 495–518.

Dicken, P. (2014), *Global Shift: Mapping the Changing Contours of the World Economy*, London: Sage.

Foot, T. (2016), 'Deliveroo rejects union's "Camden Zone" pay plea', *Camden New Journal*, 25 November 2016, accessed 1 March 2017 at http://archive.camdennewjournal.com/news/2016/nov/deliveroo-rejects-union%E2%80%99s-%E2%80%98camden-zone%E2%80%99-pay-plea.

Frey, C. and M.A. Osbourne (2014), *Agiletown: The Relentless March of Technology and London's Response*, London: Deloitte.

Greene, A., P. Ackers and J. Black (2001), 'Lost narratives? From paternalsim to team-working in a lock manufacturing firm', *Economic and Industrial Democracy*, **22** (2), 211–237.

Greene, A., P. Ackers and J. Black (2002), 'Going against the historical grain: perspectives on gendered occupational identity and resistance to the breakdown of occupational segregation in two manufacturing firms', *Gender, Work and Occupations*, **9** (2), 266–285.

Grossman, S. and O. Hart (1986), 'The costs and benefits of ownership: a theory of vertical integration', *Journal of Political Economy*, **94** (4), 691–719.

Harvey, D. (2014), *Seventeen Contradictions and the End of Capitalism*, London: Profile Books.

Holmstrom, B. and J. Roberts (1998), 'The boundaries of the firm revisited', *Journal of Economic Perspectives*, **12** (4), 73–94.

Lowe, N. (2015), 'From skills mismatch to reinterpretation: challenges and solutions for manufacturing worker retention and recruitment', in J. Bryson, J. Clark and V. Vanchan (eds), *Handbook of Manufacturing Industries in the World Economy*, Cheltenham, UK and Northampton, MA, USA: Edward Elgar Publishing, pp. 474–488.

Moretti, E. (2013), *The New Geography of Jobs*, Boston, MA: Mariner Books.

Nijkamp, P. (2003), 'Entrepreneurship in a modern network economy', *Regional Studies*, **37** (4), 395–405.

Nooteboom, B. (2000), *Learning and Innovation in Organisations and Economies*, Oxford: Oxford University Press.

Osborne, H. (2016), 'Uber loses right to classify UK drivers as self-employed', *The Guardian*, 28 October 2016, accessed 1 March 2017 at https://www.theguardian.com/technology/2016/oct/28/uber-uk-tribunal-self-employed-status.

Piketty, T. (2014), *Capital in the Twenty-First Century*, Cambridge, MA: Harvard University Press.

Price, J. (1997), *The Cutler Tale*, Lichfield: Arthur Price of England.

Sayer, A. and R. Walker (1992), *The New Social Economy: Reworking the Division of Labour*, Oxford: Blackwell.

Torpey, E. and A. Hogan (2016), 'Working in a gig economy', United States Department of Labor, accessed 23 December 2012 at https://www.bls.gov/careeroutlook/2016/article/what-is-the-gig-economy.htm.

Wales, P. and A. Agyiri (2016), *Trends in Self-employment in the UK: 2001 to 2015*, London: Office for National Statistics.

Walker, R. (1985), 'Is there a service economy? The changing capitalist division of labour', *Science and Society*, **49** (1), 42–83.

Wellington, C.A. and J.R. Bryson (2001), 'At face value? Image consultancy, emotional labour and professional work', *Sociology*, **35** (4), 933–946.

13. The geography of knowledge creation: technological relatedness and regional smart specialization strategies
Dieter F. Kogler and Adam Whittle

13.1 INTRODUCTION

The production of economically valuable knowledge has taken center stage as one of the most critical dimensions of regional development and economic growth, and is considered a significant determinant of the varying levels of prosperity that persist among territories (Schumpeter 1942; Asheim and Gertler 2005). Considering the recent economic crisis, there is a growing awareness among regional scientists and policy-makers that the fortunes of regions, and by extension the firms embedded within them, are intrinsically related to a set of localized capabilities and regionally embedded know-how (Maskell and Malmberg 1999). More broadly, these region-specific capabilities function as an economic roadmap guiding the future development of regions, as new products (Hidalgo et al. 2007), industries (Neffke et al. 2011) and technologies (Kogler et al. 2013) emerge from the existing knowledge base of the region (Boschma and Frenken 2012).

That regions/firms/industries diversify into activities related to their current specialization should come as no great surprise, and has broadly been confirmed by several recent studies (Boschma 2017). Despite this insight, what remains unclear are the complex geocentric processes that lie at the heart of technological change and regional diversification (Kogler 2017). Thus, while considerable focus has been directed towards the processes of knowledge production in a spatial context, significantly less attention has been directed towards the actual types of knowledge produced within regions and how the properties of this knowledge impact future regional development. This is a significant research gap with far reaching policy implications given that most advanced economic development theories, as well as innovation policies, stress the importance of 'local knowledge' as a source of jurisdictional competitive advantage.

The realization regarding the importance of knowledge production and diffusion processes for innovation and subsequent economic development and growth is certainly nothing new (Feldman 1994; Bathelt et al. 2011). However, it is only recently that the relevant literatures have started to consider the properties of local knowledge rather than mainly focusing on absolute measures in terms of output and quality. Building on older ideas in geography, for example, Tobler's first law of geography that states that 'everything is related to everything else, but near things are more related than distant things' (Tobler, 1970, p. 236), and in economics, for example, input–output analysis (Simpson and Tsukui 1965), the concept of 'technological relatedness' has risen to the forefront, constituting a framework with the potential to depict past and future regional technology trajectories.

Following the contribution of Hidalgo et al. (2007), economic geographers have begun redirecting their attention towards the role of knowledge creation and its impact on regional diversification. Here the concept of relatedness, how related two economic activities are to one another, has been particularly influential, as it moves beyond absolute values in terms of economic concentration and industrial composition to explain 'distance' between technologies as a key factor of future regional development (Essletzbichler 2015). Indeed, the ability to accurately capture relatedness between economic activities opens up a platform for understanding future regional diversification as a branching process grounded in 'geographical biases' (Penrose 1959; Boschma 2017; Rutten 2017). More precisely, this enables us to quantify the emergence of new industries from how related that new industry is to the existing technological portfolio of the region (Teece 1982; Engelsman and Van Raan 1991; Teece et al. 1994).

Armed with this rationale, the purpose of this chapter is to synthesize the literatures of evolutionary economic geography (Boschma and Martin 2007, 2010; Martin and Sunley 2007; Kogler 2015) and the geography of innovation (Feldman and Florida 1994; Asheim and Gertler 2005; Feldman and Kogler 2010) to demonstrate the path-dependent and evolutionary logic inherent to knowledge creation. Critically, this synthesis reaffirms the importance of geography as a palpable medium to organize economic activity. Making explicit use of the 'knowledge space' methodology developed by Kogler et al. (2013), Rigby (2015) and Boschma et al. (2015) this chapter provides detailed insights on how regional knowledge trajectories are shaped by path-dependent, recombinant, and co-evolutionary network dynamics. We do this by examining the knowledge space of regions in Ireland over the time period 1981–2010.

13.2   THE GEOGRAPHY OF KNOWLEDGE CREATION

Innovation exhibits a particular geography (Feldman 1994). Although the past few decades have provided detailed accounts of the underlying process of knowledge production in a spatial context, the nexus between geography and innovation remains a bit of a mystery, whereby neither geographers nor economists have managed to fully open the 'black box of innovation' (Rosenberg 1994). In attempting to deconstruct this black box several authors have postulated that different types of 'space' produce different sources of knowledge as their competitive advantage (Bunnell and Coe 2001). Here, recent enquires have engaged in a debate whether it is specialized places, characterized by economies of scope and scale, or those that exhibit a more diverse sectoral structure, that facilitate the cross-fertilization of ideas between previously unconnected knowledge bases, that are more conductive to knowledge production and thus higher levels of innovation activities (Beaudry and Schiffauerova 2009).

Marshall (1920) already stressed the importance of concentrating related industries at a particular place to maximize comparative advantages in the market, but it was Jacobs (1969) who rightfully pointed out the role of diversity for innovation and economic growth, a process now commonly referred to as 'development through diversification'. For Jacobs, it is the addition of new work and the resulting division of labor that cause regions to expand and continually develop. Comparing the failures of Manchester with the successes of Birmingham, Jacobs remarks that it was the addition of many little industries with fragmented working patterns, some of which went on to form large organizations, that resulted in Birmingham becoming the center of industrial development within the United

Kingdom at the time. By the same token, Manchester's over-specialization in the once dominant textiles industry resulted in it being ill-equipped to engage in other (related) sectors of the economy. Even today, it is possible to identify those regions that were once prosperous but have since declined. Detroit, the Rust Belt in general, or the Ruhr region are all examples of once thriving economies which have since stagnated. As Jacobs herself puts it, they are 'economies that did not add new kinds of goods and services, but continued only to repeat old work' (Jacobs 1969, p. 49). In a geographic context, they are regions that became locked-in due to institutional insolvencies, outdated manufacturing techniques and an inability to look outwards (Grabher 1993; Hassink 2010; Martin and Sunley 2006).

In addition to its economic functions, Jacobs also claims that cities enact important social processes, not just by bringing many people together but also by bringing together a wide variety of ideas from which potentially new knowledge can be created. In this regard, Jacobs' conceptualization of the city as being the locus for innovation draws extensive parallels with Schumpeter's (1942) 'creative destruction' thesis. As a foundation to this chapter the writings of Jacobs (1969) and Schumpeter (1912, 1942) provide two important insights into the underlying capabilities of regions and their capacity to generate new types of knowledge.

First and foremost, innovation is a fractured and complicated process whose effects are not evenly distributed throughout space (Rigby 2015). Ironically, innovations' only certainty is the uncertainty associated with trial-and-error (Essletzbichler 2015). Further, the majority of innovations in the past decades have occurred in cities. In their study of the US knowledge space, 90 percent of all patent applications are concentrated within 366 metropolitan statistical areas (Kogler et al. 2013). Large diversified cities embody a functioning urban network ecology, frequently well-developed political and institutional systems, research facilities as well as global knowledge linkages, all of which are conducive to knowledge creation (Gertler 2003; Bathelt et al. 2004). With regards to their creative potential, cities are places where the division of labor is greatest and where new work rapidly replaces older work.

Second, in an evolutionary context the creation of new knowledge is not a random or exogenous process as neo-classical interpretations would suggest. It is in fact, both highly stylized and path dependent. Once again, this line of argument draws inference from both Jacobs' (1969) theories of diversity and cross-fertilization of ideas, and from Schumpeter's (1912) 'neue Kombinationen' thesis. Essentially, the creation of new knowledge is recognized as a fundamentally recombinant process whereby 'old ideas are reconfigured in new ways to make new ideas' (Weitzman 1998, p. 333). Since this cross-fertilization of ideas is greatest in diversified cities, it is cities that hold the most potential for knowledge creation and regional diversification (Beaudry and Schiffauerova 2009).

Notwithstanding, the aforementioned studies have recently been criticized on a number of theoretical and methodological grounds, given their tendency to ignore the evolutionary paradigm inherent to firms and regions. Inspired by the methodology developed by Hidalgo et al. (2007) a growing body of empirical literature has begun analyzing the branching capabilities of regions, industries and technologies, as a process grounded in local capabilities. It has become common to refer to this division of the literature as the 'relatedness literature'. The point of departure is where the geography of innovation primarily asks 'where does innovation take place?' The relatedness literature asks, 'why does a particular innovation take place here and not elsewhere?' Accordingly, this perspective shifts from a static to a dynamic understanding of regional diversification and technological change, with a concise appreciation of the role history plays in shaping regional development (Kogler 2015). However, while the recent evolutionary resurgence in economic geography has brought with it its own theories and methods, the role of history in explaining economic growth vis-à-vis path dependence is again not entirely new. In this vein Dosi (1997, p. 1531) states that any historical perspective or explanation of 'why something exists intimately rests on how it became what it is' – a point that will be revisited below.

13.3 RELATED VARIETY AND TECHNOLOGICAL RELATEDNESS

Moving beyond the categorical (dichotomy) classification of places and activities into Marshallian specialization or Jacobian diversification externalities (Beaudry and Schiffauerova 2009) recent insights point to the necessity to develop a more nuanced and continuous way of describing the relationships between different knowledge and technology domains. Essentially, both patterns of specialization as well as the cross-fertilization of ideas between sectors, are important aspects that shape regional economic development patterns (Caragliu et al. 2016). Following this line of argument, recent advances in the relevant literature, in particular in the field of Evolutionary Economic Geography, have begun to focus on the role of relatedness in driving regional development (Boschma and Frenken 2012).

Here, in addition to the spatial proximity, it is increasingly also cognitive proximity that is considered necessary to facilitate knowledge absorption and learning processes that result in the creation of new and economically valuable products and processes, that is, innovations (Cohen and Levinthal 1990). The insight is that co-location alone does not automatically result in knowledge recombination or creation processes, but that it also needs a common framework of understanding among the agents and sectors that engage in knowledge exchange processes. This assumption does not necessarily undermine the importance of geography in mediating knowledge flows as cognitive proximity has always been a consideration, if not direct but implicit, in the methodologies applied in earlier relevant studies concerning knowledge flows and spillovers (Jaffe et al. 1993; Audretsch and Feldman 2004; Paci et al. 2014). One could even argue that the concept of relatedness foremost demonstrates how geography facilitates knowledge exchange and learning processes, but also indicates how in turn spatial proximity enforces other relevant dimensions of proximity, that is, social, organizational, institutional, as well as cognitive (Nooteboom 2000; Boschma 2005). Fornahl et al. (2011) define cognitive distance as knowledge that is neither identical (hence it can be usefully exchanged) nor too distant (therefore it can still be effectively absorbed). Related variety achieves this delicate combination by balancing similarity with dissimilarity (Frenken et al. 2007).

But what is technological relatedness? How would one measure it? What does it measure, and why would one want to measure it to begin with? For the past decade or so economic geographers have been grappling with these types of questions to better understand the branching patterns of industries, technologies, regions and even countries

(Penrose 1959; Hidalgo et al. 2007; Neffke et al. 2011; Kogler et al. 2013). The logic underpinning the relatedness framework is that future diversification is grounded in a series of path-dependent processes, whereby new knowledge branches out from existing or related pieces of knowledge. As described by Neffke (2009, p. 125), 'regional economies have coherent portfolios of industries that expand into related industries and contract by getting rid of unrelated industries'. These ideas parallel both the resource-based view (RBV) of the firm (Penrose 1959) and the evolutionary theory of the firm (Nelson and Winter 1982). Thus, the relatedness literature reinforces the evolutionary processes of selection, variety and retention, and demonstrates that the accumulation and production of knowledge is embedded in region-specific patterns which have been developed slowly over time (Frenken and Boschma 2007).

Evolutionary analogies within economic geography are uniquely positioned to address these questions, given that over the past two decades or so a vast and flourishing literature has emerged stressing that the foundations for long term sustainable economic growth rested on the ability of regions to produce knowledge that is both spatially sticky and non-ubiquitous (Gertler 2003; Hidalgo and Hausmann 2009). In their writings on 'localized capabilities' Maskell and Malmberg (1999) explain that the resources available to the firm are both tangible (machinery and technologies) and intangible (organizational practices, skills and cultural norms) but since they have been developed slowly over time are not easily reproducible by others. Conversely, this firm-specific knowledge is largely tacit in nature, hence continuing to infer an advantage onto those firms that produced it in the first place (Balland and Rigby 2017). Over time, this type of knowledge, often embedded in individuals (skills) and in firms (routines) transcends the boundaries of the individual firm and, thereafter, becomes embedded in the economic ecology of a region. These processes result in the production (accumulation) of knowledge being a path dependent phenomenon, whereby regions (firms) leverage their place specific assets to recognize and thereafter exploit new economic paths. From an evolutionary standpoint, it makes sense that regions (firms) employ practices that have proven successful in the past as it reduces the opportunistic risk and trial and error characteristics associated with technological change (Schumpeter 1942; Nelson and Winter, 1982; Romer, 1990). For regions, the gradual layering of 'successful' knowledge contributes to both the place specific and path dependent processes of knowledge creation and diffusion. Ultimately, this layering ensures that imitation by non-local actors is highly unlikely because geographical distance, among other things, forms a barrier to knowledge transfer and learning processes.

Region-specific capabilities, or the knowledge space of a region, contain a multitude of information on both the opportunities for the *likely* future diversification, but also a *realistic* expectation on the innovative capacity of that region. This is because, at least in the short run, the industrial composition of regions can be considered relativity stable as technologies or routines do not change rapidly.[1] Hidalgo et al. (2007) tested these claims utilizing export data, and demonstrated how a countries current industrial structure significantly affects its potential for future diversification possibilities. In doing so, the authors developed the product space framework and argue that two products are considered related if two countries have a comparative advantage in both products. Similarly, Hausmann and Klinger (2007) also found that those countries that populate denser sections of the product space, that is, countries with a comparative advantage in multiple products, have a greater opportunity to diversify into new products. Intuitively this makes sense as more developed countries have increased opportunities (capabilities) to expand their industrial portfolios, while less developed countries would struggle to meet these demands. Kogler et al. (2013) adapt the same general principles in their portrayal of the US knowledge space. Employing information on the co-occurrence of technology classes listed on patent documents, these authors discern the distance (relatedness) between individual inventions by calculating how related each patent technology class is to each other, and more importantly how this changes over several decades of technology evolution. Furthermore, by analysing levels of relatedness between products, technologies and industries it is possible – albeit imperfectly – to predict what areas of the knowledge space a region is most likely to diversify into relative to its current position.

Notwithstanding the significant theoretical advances in the study of the geography of knowledge, innovation and technical change that have been made recently, empirics have significantly lagged behind theorizing mainly due to the lack of available micro-level data required for detailed investigations. This shortcoming resulted in a series of rather top level descriptive statistics, but significantly less empirical validation, especially across countries/regions. Fortunately, many of these concerns are now being addressed as previously underutilized information in several databases is exploited. In terms of investigating the evolutionary patterns of regional technological change it is most notably the United States Patent and Trademark Office (USPTO) and the European Patent Office (EPO) which provide valuable data inputs to empirically validate some of the theoretical advances that have been made in the past decade.

Patent data provide a wealth of information pertaining to the creation and diffusion of technical knowledge in regions (Usai 2011). Contained within a patent document is information regarding inventors' names, addresses, dates, external affiliations, technological classification codes and patent as well as scientific literature citations. This level of detail gives researchers the tools needed to trace the technological development of regions, industries and knowledge typologies over space and time. Most importantly for the current chapter are the technological classification codes listed on patent documents. Mapping the co-occurrence of these classification codes generates the 'knowledge space', a topic to which we will turn now.

13.4   THE KNOWLEDGE SPACE

The concept of the product space (Hidalgo et al. 2007) provided the initial idea for the knowledge space developed by Kogler et al. (2013). Essentially, the product space is a network-based representation that captures the levels of cognitive proximity (relatedness) based on how often two specific products are co-exported by each country (Hidalgo et al. 2007). In this network, the individual nodes are product categories and the links between them indicate the degree of relatedness. Making use of international trade data this approach aimed to analyze whether a country would develop a comparative advantage in a specific product category on the condition that this new product was related to the country' existing export portfolio (Hidalgo et al. 2007; Hausmann and Hidalgo 2010).

Moving down the geographical scale, Kogler et al. (2013) develop a knowledge space to analyze the technological evolution of US cities. The key distinction is that instead of focusing on the co-production of exports, the knowledge space is created using information on the co-occurrence of classification codes listed on patent documents. In this study, the authors establish a link between technological relatedness and the pace of invention in US cities. They also found that some cities maintain their technological coherence, while the technological trajectories of others fracture and dissipate, yet in other cities new technologies develop. In a follow up study, Rigby (2015), found that technologies that were related to the region's pre-existing knowledge base had a higher probability to enter that particular region than technologies that were unrelated. Boschma et al. (2015) have also demonstrated that the probability of gaining a new technology class in a metropolitan area increases by 30 percent if the level of relatedness with existing technologies in the city increases by 10 percent, while the exit probability of an existing technology in a city decreases by 8 percent.

Complementary to the above, are the contributions of Neffke (2009), Boschma et al. (2013) and Essletzbichler (2015) who found that it was the regional structure, opposed to the national structure, that mattered most for regional diversification and knowledge creation. These findings give primacy to the claim that certain resources are less mobile than others, suggesting that capabilities need to be developed at a regional level to enable the development of new specialization patterns (Maskell and Malmberg 1999). Throughout the geography of innovation literature the significance of regions as drivers of technological change is well documented (Feldman and Kogler 2010), and well-known regional success stories include ICT in Silicon Valley (Saxenian 1994), fuel cell technology in the Baden-Wuerttemberg region (Tanner 2014, 2016), speciality wine in Piedmont (Morrison and Rabellotti 2009), or the media cluster in Leipzig (Bathelt 2005).

Following the methodology outlined in Hidalgo et al. (2007), the knowledge space is operationalized in the following manner:

$$\varphi_{i,j,t} = \min\{P(RTAx_{i,t}|RTAx_{j,t}), \{P(RTAx_{j,t}|RTAx_{i,t})\}\} \tag{13.1}$$

where technological relatedness $\varphi_{i,j,t}$ between technologies i and j is computed as the minimum pair-wise conditional probability of citing technology i while also patenting in technology that j at time t. As has become commonplace, we only focus on those regions that are a substantial producer of a given technology, whereby we restrict our sample to include only those regions with a regional technological advantage, $RTA_{r,t}(i)=1$ if:

$$\frac{patents_{r,t}(i)/\Sigma_i\,patents_{r,t}(i)}{\Sigma_c\,patents_{r,t}(i)/\Sigma_c\Sigma_i\,patents_{r,t}(i)} > 1 \tag{13.2}$$

With these specifications in mind, Figure 13.1 shows the knowledge space for Dublin for the years 1981–85 and 2001–05. The knowledge space is an intuitive way to model the process of technological specialization/diversification in a regional economy. More specifically, it shows the growth (entry) and decline (exit) of certain technological domains and the relationships between them. In doing so, it corroborates the key principles in the relatedness literature and demonstrates that the geography of knowledge production is not a random phenomenon, but is both highly stylized and path dependent. Critically, it demonstrates that technology and associated industry sectors do not simply diversify into any direction, but rather branch out into related technologies (Kogler et al. 2017).

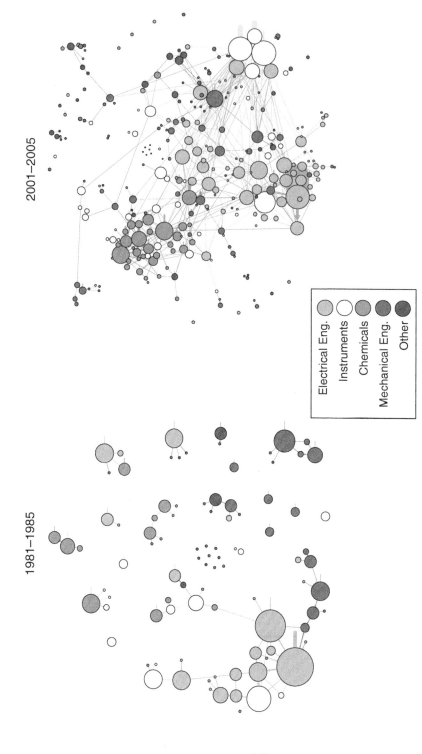

2001–2005

1981–1985

Electrical Eng.
Instruments
Chemicals
Mechanical Eng.
Other

Figure 13.1 Dublin knowledge space

Following Schmoch (2008), the knowledge space has been aggregated into the five main technology classes: Chemistry, Instruments, Electrical Engineering, Mechanical Engineering and Other. The assumption is that nodes that appear in the same broad technology class also share a similar knowledge base, or that the competencies used in the production of one technology class can be easily reconfigured to develop another related one. The nodes in the networks in Figure 13.1 correspond to one of the 629 international patent classification codes listed in patent documents published by the European Patent Office (EPO), and the size of the node illustrates the number of patents in a particular technology class. In terms of descriptive statistics, instrument-based patents have shown the greatest increase in applications increasing from 14 percent in the period 1981–85 to 31 percent by the end of 2010. Similarly, Electrical Engineering has increased from 13 percent to 26 percent over the same period.

Since the early to mid-1980s Dublin's knowledge space has evolved in ways that we might have anticipated. There have been clear signs of clustering of patents associated with Chemistry and Electrical Engineering indicating a high degree of relatedness between those classes. Following an evolutionary logic that new knowledge branches out from related and previously existing types of knowledge, it is worthwhile noticing that the development of the Instrument sector (optical instruments, medical technologies, measurement instruments) lies between the areas of Electrical Engineering and Chemistry. Boschma and Frenken (2012, p. 5) have previously pointed out that, 'we understand the emergence of a new industry in a region from the level of technological relatedness between the new industry and the existing industries in a region'. Similarly, Hausmann and Klinger (2007, p. 6) have demonstrated that these networks are extremely heterogeneous whereby if technologies 'require highly similar inputs and endowments, then they are "closer" together, but if they require totally different capabilities, they are "farther" apart'.

Next, we need to discern how relatedness between technologies shapes technological change at a regional level. To do this we generate a relatedness density index which captures how close a potentially new technology (specialization) is to the knowledge base of the region. Augmenting the density index outlined in Hidalgo et al. (2007) and accounting for the differences in data and technical specifications, relatedness density is operationalized as follows. The density for a specific technology i in region r at time t is calculated using the corresponding relatedness index of technology i to the technologies in region r that have an RCA in time t, divided by the sum of technological relatedness of technology i to all the other technologies in Ireland in the t:

$$RelDen_{i,r,t} = \frac{\sum_{j \in r, j \neq i} \varphi_{ij}}{\sum_{j \neq i} \varphi_{ij}} \times 100 \qquad (13.3)$$

By design, relatedness density takes a value between 0 percent and 100 percent. A density value equal to 0 percent would indicate that there is no technology related to technology i in region r at time t. As such, is it unlikely that this technology would be adopted in the region because it cannot build on related expertise. Conversely, a value of 100 percent would indicate that all the technologies related to i are present in the region r knowledge space. With this in mind, Table 13.1 provides information on the

Table 13.1　Relatedness density for Irish NUTS 3 regions, 1981–85

Region	Technology Class				
	Electrical Engineering	Instruments	Chemistry	Mechanical Engineering	Other
Border	68	36	36	1	64
Dublin	67	82	89	44	60
Mid-East	19	55	21	86	18
Mid-West	19	55	21	86	18
Midlands	42	27	64	14	55
Southeast	2	18	11	57	1
Southwest	13	27	54	71	18
West	87	73	46	29	82

relatedness density values of Irish NUTS3 regions for the time period 1981–85. To further illustrate this point, the density value around 'Chemistry' in Dublin was equal to 89 percent during the period 1981–85. Similar to Figure 13.1, you can see that Dublin's specialization in Chemistry enabled it to successfully build on related technologies. In the following period (2001–05), Chemistry became the most dominant patented technology sector in the Dublin knowledge space. A similar trend is also observed for Dublin's other specializations in 'Electrical Engineering' and 'Instruments', which had relatedness density values of 67 percent and 82 percent respectively, and which later became key technologies in Dublin's knowledge space.

The above studies demonstrate the potential of the relatedness framework to anticipate future regional technology trajectories. Indeed, the relatedness literature stresses that the production of new knowledge exhibits a strong path dependency whereby new knowledge branches out from an existing piece of knowledge (Boschma 2017; Kogler 2017). These are without a doubt serious claims that have important bearings on both the capacity of regions to create new knowledge, but also for policy-makers who aim to enhance investment strategies for future regional development pathways. Therefore, it is not by coincidence that the literature on relatedness and regional diversification is increasingly used as a point of reference in many policy initiatives, including the European Union's cohesion policy framework (McCann and Ortega-Argilés 2013, 2015), or more recently in the Smart Specialization thesis which aims to provide a regional development framework for Europe for the coming decade (Foray et al. 2009; Morgan 2015; Foray 2015).

13.5　SMART SPECIALIZATION STRATEGIES

Very few development strategies have gained as much political traction as the Smart Specialization Strategy thesis (Morgan 2015). Popularized by Dominique Foray and colleagues in 2009, the concepts' immediate popularity came at a time when the industrial composition of regions ranked high on almost every political agenda. Although not a direct outcome of the crisis itself,[2] the concept has had, and will continue to have, a significant impact on the economic re-structuring of regions in the future.

At its core, smart specialization strategies are the European Union's innovation policy for the coming decade, and admittedly its approach is relatively straightforward (McCann and Ortega-Argilés 2015). The strategy aims to enhance regional competitiveness by identifying and enabling those regions that have particular 'strengths' in certain industries (technologies). Accordingly, the strategy has two goals. First, by focusing on their relative strengths, it is envisioned that regions will be able to identity future development avenues through which they can thereafter build a relative competitive advantage against other jurisdictions. This process underpins the entrepreneurial discovery part of the strategy, which is expected to result in structural change. Second, it is envisioned that these regional specialization patterns will also prevent the duplication of efforts and exhaustion of resources in the common market. Adhering to the Research and Innovation Strategy for Smart Specialization is currently a prerequisite by the EU Commission for regions to receive further funding from the European Regional Development Fund (ERDF).

Intuitively this approach seems perfectly logical and in line with the theories concerned with regional economic development, which is a compounding factor contributing to the Smart Specialization Strategies concept's success. However, as rightfully pointed out by Foray et al. (2011, p. 1) this has resulted in the concept itself becoming a 'policy running ahead of theory'. The closing segments of this chapter seek to demonstrate how the relatedness literature in general, but the knowledge space framework more specifically, has the capacity to address a number of these key concerns.

One could argue, the greatest strength of the Smart Specialization Strategy is its reversal in protocol, and more specifically in its empowerment of individual regions as champions of their own destiny. From a geographic standpoint is it easy to see how the relatedness literature has increasingly been linked up with the Smart Specialization Strategy. Returning to the theory outlined above, regions are repertoires of history, reflecting the path dependent (Martin and Sunley 2006) and place dependent (Hassink 2010) characteristics of knowledge production, often referred to as local capabilities (Maskell and Malmberg 1999). From this perspective, the assemblage of knowledge in a region provides certain opportunities in terms of future diversification, but it also functions as an indicator of potential limitations to the future innovative capacity that can be developed assuming that regional, industrial, and technical configurations remain relatively constant in the immediate term. Similarly, Markkula (2015, p. 50), states that 'smart specialisation and societal innovation can only work if choices are based on real knowledge of local potential and if the right actors are involved'. This reorientation from a traditionally top-down to a more bottom-up policy approach indicates that regions no longer must prescribe to some predefined example of innovative excellence, frequently referred to as the 'Silicon Valley Model' (Saxenian 1991). Instead, the entrepreneurial backbone of the entire Smart Specialization thesis should be geared towards the relative strengths and capabilities present in a given region. This would deter spurious investments in the 'fashionable fields' of biotechnology and nanotechnology, among others, as most regions do not have the capacity nor knowledge infrastructure to diversify into these industry sectors.

Operationalizing an approach capable of capturing regional development pathways throughout the entire European Union has proven to be a difficult task. Until recently, the lack of evidence was due to the shortage of appropriate data required for such large-scale detailed investigations. Fortunately, the increased digitalization of many datasets, as well as the merging of existing ones, along with more advanced methodological toolsets, have equipped researchers with the necessary means to tackle this task. The knowledge space methodology and the analysis of regional knowledge spaces provide unique insights into the branching capacities of regions through the process of related diversification. The ultimate objective is to provide regions with clear directions regarding where they should invest today in order to maximize their local knowledge base in the future, which is really the key question we still lack an answer for in the widely discussed Smart Specialization framework.

Boschma and Frenken (2012) and Kogler (2015), put forward the idea that the sectoral evolution of regions can be predicted, albeit imperfectly, through understanding the processes of technological relatedness underlying structural change. Since then a number of follow-up studies have confirmed that regions/firms/technologies diversify into activities that are technologically proximate to their current specialization (Hidalgo et al. 2007; Neffke et al. 2011, Kogler et al. 2013, 2017; Rigby 2015; Boschma et al. 2015; Essletzbichler 2015). Based on the relatedness-index between technologies, recent attempts to map the knowledge space of US cities have shown that some cities maintain their current specialization, while others develop entirely new technological regimes (Rigby 2015). In a more European context, Kogler et al. (2017), extend their original methodology to account for the impact of entry and exit on patterns of regional specialization. Initial efforts in this direction indicate that by analysing the evolution of knowledge cores of regions it is possible to predict the most likely diversification pathways of specific regional economies. Furthermore, it also indicates that it is possible to show where regions are lacking specialization and should withdraw engagement, and finally, where it would be possible to bridge the gap between two distinct technologies to generate new technology trajectories through the recombination of existing ones.

Based on the evolutionary logic that the production of new technological capabilities exhibits a strong path dependency whereby new knowledge branches out from existing pieces of knowledge, it indicates that regions cannot rapidly switch between economic activities and that radical technological jumps are an exception. All of this demonstrates that regional strategies that do not adequately take into consideration the knowledge base of the region are destined to fail, and warns of the dangers of a 'one size fits all' policy.

13.6   CONCLUDING REMARKS AND FUTURE RESEARCH DIRECTIONS

Much has been written about the localized dimension of knowledge production and its impact on regional diversification (Boschma 2017; Kogler 2017). Such discussions have increasingly pointed towards the evolution of regions' economic structure in terms of their underlying knowledge base and specifically the path- and place-dependent characteristics guiding their evolution (Kogler 2016). Throughout this chapter, we adopted an evolutionary discourse of technological change to reaffirm the continued importance of geography as a palpable medium to organize economic activity. Following a series of studies (Kogler et al. 2013, 2017) concerning the technological relatedness at a given place the principle assumption is that technological advances build on, and derive from, existing pieces of knowledge expertise present at a place.

To further investigate and map local evolutionary technology trajectories, we introduced the knowledge space framework, which is a network-based representation that captures the underlying technological structure of regional economies (Kogler et al. 2013). More precisely, we examined the technological evolution of Ireland's capital city Dublin and provided new insights on how regional knowledge trajectories are shaped by path-dependent, recombinant, and co-evolutionary network dynamics. Critically, we demonstrated how Dublin's knowledge space provided certain opportunities for its future diversification. To further illustrate this point, we introduced a relatedness density index to quantify how close an emerging technology is to the existing knowledge base of the region. Essentially, we established how the density of technologies located around Dublin's knowledge space provided a series of likely diversification options, which then became key sectors for Dublin's economy at a later point in time.

Looking ahead, and in terms of future research directions, this chapter briefly concluded by theorizing how the proposed knowledge space methodology has important bearings for the recently proposed Smart Specialization Strategies framework. By taking an evolutionary look at regions in terms of their underlying knowledge structure the expectation is that it is possible to direct investments into realistic development pathways, while also providing advice on where to retract engagement due to the lack of regional specialization competencies. Further, the knowledge space methodology also holds the potential to provide insights into the areas of regional knowledge spaces where it is most likely possible to bridge the gap between two distinct technologies that have previously been unconnected by means of recombination activities. (Feldman et al. 2015). These are undoubtedly serious claims with far reaching implications for academics, practitioners, and policy-makers alike, and should serve as a blueprint for future research directions in this field of inquiry and policy-making.

13.7 NOTES

1. Following Neffke et al. (2011), Kogler et al. (2013, 2017) demonstrate that over longer periods of time, that is, decades, the level of relatedness between technologies can – and does – change. With this in mind, an important question then is, how can we understand the emergence of a new industry (technology) in a region from how related that new industry (technology) is to the existing composition of the region.
2. The Smart Specialization Strategy was developed because of recommendations put forward by the Knowledge for Growth Expert Group in 2005; see here for further information: http://ec.europa.eu/invest-in-research/monitoring/knowledge_en.htm.

13.8 FUNDING ACKNOWLEDGEMENTS

We are grateful to two anonymous referees for comments, and would like to acknowledge funding from the European Research Council under the European Union's Horizon 2020 research and innovation programme (grant agreement No 715631); and the Irish Research Council, Postgraduate Government of Ireland Scholarship in Science Policy and Innovation. Project ID GOIPG/2015/2957.

13.9   REFERENCES

Asheim, B. and M. Gertler (2005), 'The geography of innovation: regional innovation systems', in J. Fagerberg, D. Mowery and R. Nelson (eds), *The Oxford Handbook of Innovation*, Oxford: Oxford University Press, pp. 291–317.

Audretsch, D. and M. Feldman (2004), 'Knowledge spillovers and the geography of innovation', *Handbook of Regional and Urban Economics*, **4**, 2713–2739.

Balland, P.A. and D. Rigby (2017), 'The geography of complex knowledge', *Economic Geography*, **93** (1), 1–23.

Bathelt, H., A. Malmberg and P. Maskell (2004), 'Clusters and knowledge: local buzz, global pipelines and the process of knowledge creation', *Progress in Human Geography*, **28** (1), 31–56.

Bathelt, H. (2005), 'Cluster relations in the media industry: Exploring the "distanced neighbor" paradox in Leipzig', *Regional Studies*, **39** (1), 105–127.

Bathelt, H., M.P. Feldman and D.F. Kogler (eds) (2011), *Beyond Territory: Dynamic Geographies of Knowledge Creation, Diffusion, and Innovation*, London: Routledge.

Beaudry, C. and A. Schiffauerova (2009), 'Who's right, Marshall or Jacobs? The localization versus urbanization debate', *Research Policy*, **38** (2), 318–337.

Boschma, R. (2005), 'Proximity and innovation: a critical assessment', *Regional Studies*, **39** (1), 61–74.

Boschma, R. and R. Martin (2007), 'Constructing an evolutionary economic geography', *Journal of Economic Geography*, **7** (5), 537–548.

Boschma, R. and R. Martin (2010), 'The aims and scope of evolutionary economic geography', in R. Boschma and R. Martin (eds), *The Handbook of Evolutionary Economic Geography*, Cheltenham, UK and Northampton, MA, USA: Edward Elgar Publishing, pp. 3–39.

Boschma, R. and K. Frenken (2012), 'Technological relatedness and regional branching', in H. Bathelt, M. Feldman and D. Kogler (eds), *Beyond Territory: Dynamic Geographies of Knowledge Creation, Diffusion and Innovation*, London: Routledge, pp. 64–81.

Boschma, R., A. Minondo and N. Mikel (2013), 'Related variety and regional growth in Spain', *Papers in Regional Sciences*, **91** (2), 241–256.

Boschma, R., P.A. Balland and D.F. Kogler (2015), 'Relatedness and technological change in cities: the rise and fall of technological knowledge in US metropolitan areas from 1981 to 2010', *Industrial and Corporate Change*, **24** (1), 223–250.

Boschma, R. (2017), 'Relatedness as driver of regional diversification: a research agenda', *Regional Studies*, **51** (3), 351–364.

Bunnell, T.G. and N.M. Coe (2001), 'Spaces and scales of innovation', *Progress in Human Geography*, **25** (4), 569–589.

Caragliu, A., L. de Dominicis and H. de Groot (2016), 'Both Marshall and Jacobs were right!', *Economic Geography*, **92** (1), 87–111.

Cohen, W. and D. Levinthal (1990), 'Absorptive capacity: a new perspective on learning and innovation', *Administrative Science Quarterly*, **35** (1), 128–151.

Dosi, G. (1997), 'Opportunities, incentives and the collective patterns of technological change', *The Economic Journal*, **107** (444), 1530–1547.

Engelsman E. and A. Van Raan (1991), 'Mapping of technology, a first exploration of knowledge diffusion amongst fields of technology', *The Hague: Policy Studies on Technology and Economy* (BTE) Series No. 15.

Essletzbichler, J. (2015), 'Relatedness, industrial branching and technological cohesion in US metropolitan regions', *Regional Studies*, **49** (5), 752–766.

Feldman, M. (1994), *The Geography of Innovation, vol. 2*, Amsterdam: Springer.

Feldman, M. and R. Florida (1994), 'The geographic sources of innovation: technological infrastructure and product innovation in the United States', *Annals of the Association of American Geographers*, **84** (2), 210–229.

Feldman, M. and D. Kogler (2010), 'Stylized facts in the geography of innovation', in H. Bronwyn and N. Rosenberg (eds), *Handbook of the Economics of Innovation*, Oxford: Elsevier, pp. 381–410.

Feldman, M., D. Kogler and D. Rigby (2015), 'rKnowledge: the spatial diffusion and adoption of rDNA methods', *Regional Studies*, **49** (5), 798–817.

Foray, D., P. David and B. Hall (2009), 'Smart specialization – the concept', *Knowledge Economists Policy Brief Number 9*, June, European Commission, Brussels: DG Research.

Foray, D., P.A. David and B.H. Hall (2011), 'Smart specialization. From academic idea to political instrument, the surprising career of a concept and the difficulties involved in its implementation', *MTEI Working Paper*.

Foray, D. (2015), *Smart Specialization: Opportunities and Challenges for Regional Innovation Policy*, Abingdon: Routledge.

Fornahl, D., T. Broekel and R. Boschma (2011), 'What drives patent performance of German biotech firms? The impact of R&D subsidies, knowledge networks and their location', *Papers in Regional Science*, **90** (2), 395–418.

Frenken, K. and R. Boschma (2007), 'A theoretical framework for evolutionary economic geography: industrial dynamics and urban growth as a branching process', *Journal of economic geography*, **7** (5), 635–649.

Frenken, K., F. Van Oort and T. Verburg (2007), 'Related variety, unrelated variety and regional economic growth', *Regional Studies*, **41** (5), 685–697.

Gertler, M. (2003), 'Tacit knowledge and the economic geography of context or the undefinable tacitness of being (there)', *Journal of Economic Geography*, **3** (1), 75–99.

Grabher, G. (1993), 'The weakness of strong ties; the lock-in of regional development in the Ruhr area', in G. Grabher (ed.), *The Embedded Firm: On the Socioeconomics of Industrial Networks*, New York: Routledge, pp. 255–277.

Hassink, R. (2010), 'Regional resilience: a promising concept to explain differences in regional economic adaptability?', *Cambridge Journal of Regions, Economy and Society*, **3** (1), 45–58.

Hausmann, R. and B. Klinger (2007), 'The structure of the product space and the evolution of comparative advantage', *Working Paper no. 146*, Cambridge, MA: Centre for International Development, Harvard University.

Hausmann, R., and C. Hidalgo (2010), 'Country diversification, product ubiquity, and economic divergence', *HKS Faculty Research Working Paper Series RWP10-045*, John F. Kennedy School of Government, Harvard University.

Hidalgo, C., B. Klinger, A. Barabassi and R. Hausmann (2007), 'The product space conditions the development of nations', *Science*, **317** (5837), 482–487.

Hidalgo, C. and R. Hausmann (2009), 'The building blocks of economic complexity', *Proceedings of the National Academy of Sciences of the United States of America*, **106** (26), 10570–10575.

Jacobs, J. (1969), *The Economy of Cities*, New York: Random House.

Jaffe, A., M. Trajtenberg and R. Henderson (1993), 'Geographic localization of knowledge spillovers as evidenced by patent citations', *Quarterly Journal of Economics*, **108** (3), 577–598.

Kogler, D.F., D. Rigby and I. Tucker (2013), 'Mapping knowledge space and technological relatedness in US cities', *European Planning Studies*, **21** (9), 1374–1391.

Kogler, D.F. (2015), 'Editorial: Evolutionary economic geography – theoretical and empirical progress', *Regional Studies*, **95** (5), 705–711.

Kogler, D.F. (ed.) (2016), *Evolutionary Economic Geography – Theoretical and Empirical Progress*, New York, Routledge.

Kogler, D.F. (2017), 'Relatedness as driver of regional diversification: a research agenda – a commentary', *Regional Studies*, **51** (3), 365–369.

Kogler, D.F., J. Essletzbichler and D. Rigby (2017), 'The evolution of specialization in the EU15 knowledge space', *Journal of Economic Geography*, **17** (2), 345–373.

Markkula, M. (2015), *The Parliament Magazine's Regional Review: Europe's Regions and Cities*, Brussels: European Commission.

Marshall A. (1920), *The Principles of Economics*, London: Macmillan, eighth edition.

Martin, R. and P. Sunley (2006), 'Path dependence and regional economic evolution', *Journal of Economic Geography*, **6** (4), 395–437.

Martin, R. and P. Sunley (2007), 'Complexity thinking and evolutionary economic geography', *Journal of Economic Geography*, **7** (5), 573–601.

Maskell, P. and A. Malmberg (1999), 'The competitiveness of firms and regions: "ubiquitification" and the importance of localized learning', *European Urban and Regional Planning Studies*, **6** (1), 9–25.

McCann, P. and R. Ortega-Argilés (2013), 'Transforming European regional policy: a results-driven agenda and smart specialization', *Oxford Review of Economic Policy*, **29** (2), 405–431.

McCann, P. and R. Ortega-Argilés (2015), 'Smart specialization, regional growth and applications to European Union cohesion policy', *Regional Studies*, **49** (8), 1291–1302.

Morgan, K. (2015), 'Smart specialisation: opportunities and challenges for regional innovation policy', *Regional Studies*, **49** (3), 480–482.

Morrison, A. and R. Rabellotti (2009), 'Knowledge and information networks in an Italian wine cluster', *European Planning Studies*, **17** (7), 983–1006.

Neffke, F. (2009), 'Productive places. The influence of technological change and relatedness on agglomeration externalities', PhD thesis, Utrecht: Utrecht University.

Neffke, F., M. Henning and R. Boschma (2011), 'How do regions diversify over time? Industry relatedness and the development of new growth paths in regions', *Economic Geography*, **87** (3), 237–265.

Nelson, R. and S. Winter (1982), *An Evolutionary Theory of Economic Change*, Cambridge: The Belknap Press.

Nooteboom, B. (2000), *Learning and Innovation in Organizations and Economies*, Oxford: Oxford University Press.

Paci, R., E. Marrocu and S. Usai (2014), 'The complementary effects of proximity dimensions on knowledge spillovers', *Spatial Economic Analysis*, **9** (1), 9–30.

Penrose, E. (1959), *The Theory of the Growth of the Firm*, Oxford: Oxford University Press.

Rigby, D. (2015), 'Technological relatedness and knowledge space: entry and exit of US cities from patent classes', *Regional Studies*, **49** (11), 1922–1937.

Romer, P. (1990), 'Endogenous technological change', *Journal of Political Economy*, **98** (5, Part 2), 71–102.

Rosenberg, N. (1994), *Exploring the Black Box: Technology, Economics, and History*, Cambridge: Cambridge University Press.

Rutten, R. (2017), 'Beyond proximities. The socio-spatial dynamics of knowledge creation', *Progress in Human Geography*, **41** (2), 159–177.

Saxenian, A. (1991), 'The origins and dynamics of production networks in Silicon Valley', *Research Policy*, **20** (5), 423–437.

Saxenian, A. (1994), *Regional Advantage: Culture and Competition in Silicon Valley and Route 128*, Cambridge, MA: Harvard University Press.

Schmoch, U. (2008), 'Concept of a technology classification for country comparisons', *Final report to the World Intellectual Property Organisation (WIPO)*.

Schumpeter, J. (1912), *Die Theorie der Wirtschaftlichen Entwicklung*, Leipzig: Duncker & Humblot.

Schumpeter, J. (1942), *Capitalism, Socialism and Democracy*, New York: Harper.

Simpson, D. and J. Tsukui (1965), 'The fundamental structure of input–output tables: an international comparison', *Review of Economics and Statistics*, **47** (4), 434–446.

Tanner, A. (2014), 'Regional branching reconsidered: emergence of the fuel cell industry in European regions', *Economic Geography*, **90** (4), 403–427.

Tanner, A. (2016), 'The emergence of new technology-based industries: the case of fuel cells and its technological relatedness to regional knowledge bases', *Journal of Economic Geography*, **16** (3), 611–635.

Teece, D. (1982), 'Towards an economic theory of the multiproduct firm', *Journal of Economic Behavior and Organization*, **3** (1), 39–63.

Teece, D., R. Rumelt, G. Dosi and S. Winter (1994), 'Understanding corporate coherence. Theory and evidence', *Journal of Economic Behaviour and Organization*, **23** (1), 1–30.

Tobler, W.R. (1970), 'A computer movie simulating urban growth in the Detroit region', *Economic Geography*, **46**, 234–240.

Usai, S. (2011), 'The geography of inventive activity in OECD regions', *Regional Studies*, **45** (6), 711–731.

Weitzman, M. (1998), 'Recombinant growth', *The Quarterly Journal of Economics*, **113** (2), 331–360.

14. Creative regions: from creative place-making to creative human capital
Roberta Comunian and Lauren England

14.1 INTRODUCTION

Discourses on the importance of creativity in regional economic development have now been around for two decades (Florida 2002; Bianchini and Landry 1995; Hall 2000). Indeed, in the United Kingdom, we can trace many of these economic arguments to the first Department for Culture, Media and Sport mapping which aimed to capture the economic dimension (industry GVA and employment) of the creative industries (DCMS 1998). Nevertheless, critics were quick to point out that an emphasis on creativity in regional development was not a one-size-fits-all solution and that it did not address issues of regional disparity. For example, Oakley (2004) highlights how:

> It appears that everywhere needs a university, some incubators and a 'creative hub', with or without a cafe, galleries and fancy shops [. . .] In other words, all regions are pursuing the same culture/knowledge-based economic development strategy despite the evidence that their human capital stock cannot support it and they will have difficulty in the short and medium term in attracting or retaining the kind of workers on which these economies depend. (Oakley 2004, p. 73)

Meanwhile, far from addressing issues of regional disparity, new forms of divide between creativity-rich and creativity-poor locations were highlighted (Jayne 2004, 2005; Chatterton 2000). The result, in the UK at least, is that despite numerous policy interventions, the latest figures do not suggest any major change has taken place in the last two decades, with the geography of creativity still very much a London-centred industry.

While Glückler (2005) warns against attempting to identify objective outcomes because the embeddedness of social and organizational structures within the creative industries and creative activity leads to heightened uncertainty in determining trajectories for creative economy development, we suggest that complexity thinking enables us to explore the development of creative regions and frameworks for locally embedded creative activity by taking into account their fluid and multifaceted construction. For despite this complexity and uncertainty, and a fairly static picture in overall geographical change, the creative economy (as it is now more often defined, to include both industries and creative occupations) has grown and exceeded expectations. In 2014, the Creative Economy (CE) was worth up to £133.3bn to the UK economy and accounted for 8.2 per cent of GDP (DCMS 2015). Its definition was also expanded in 2015 to include not only the creative industries (Advertising, Antiques, Architecture, Crafts, Design, Fashion, Film, Leisure Software, Music, Performing Arts, Publishing, Software and TV and Radio) but also creative occupations (e.g. designers, publishers) in other industries. Since 2011 CE output has grown by a quarter (24.9 per cent), significantly faster than the UK economy as

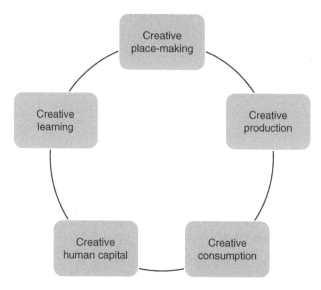

Figure 14.1   The complex creative ecology of creative regions

a whole (12.1 per cent) over the same period. This trend highlights the importance of workers equipped with requisite creative skills and education to long-term employment and GDP growth.

As with the changing definition of creative industries and the creative economy, in this chapter we review the evolution of academic and policy understanding of the concept of 'creative regions' (Chapain et al. 2013; Clifton et al. 2015). In particular, we aim to highlight how the definition of 'creative region' needs to take into consideration five key interconnected elements (Figure 14.1). We will also explore their role in defining a 'creative region' and examine the limitations of adopting a single perspective to define this concept. In the conclusion, we will outline the value of using a creative ecology perspective and complexity thinking to take forward the research agenda on creative regions.

14.2   CREATIVE PLACE-MAKING: INVESTING IN IMAGE AND PLACE

Perhaps the earliest understanding of creative regions (or cities) was a response to urban decline and a need to regenerate areas in disuse after the industrial period (Evans and Shaw 2004). From the late 1980s into the 1990s the focus of much of the research and policy was on the role that creativity can play in re-shaping urban and regional territories for new economic activities or simple re-housing (Smith 1996; Ley 2003). Creativity here is often associated with artistic and cultural interventions from informal artist's occupations to more structured regeneration plans and investments around new cultural flagship projects.

Creative regions in this context have been associated with an investment – often policy-led – in the built-environment and image of a region (Griffiths 1995). However, there has been quite a lot of criticism of this form of urban intervention which has tended to adopt a one-size-fits-all tactic and favour internationally renowned architects and approaches instead of promoting local distinctiveness (Evans 2003). Furthermore, others have criticized the disconnection between some of these interventions and the opportunity to develop strong creative and cultural production sectors. Interventions of this kind have also tended to push creative producers and artists out of cities or quarters and cause gentrification and displacement in the long term (Comunian and Jacobi 2015; Comunian and Mould 2014).

However, from an economic development perspective, many have highlighted that investment and policy-led intervention can be successful in attracting new resources, investments, elites and visitors to a region (Shearmur 2006). In this respect, the success of investment in cultural infrastructure, tourism and general image have been measured and evaluated positively by many economic geographers and economists (Herrero et al. 2006; Richards and Wilson 2004). Nonetheless, criticisms of short-term strategies have also been shared (Richards 2000; Mooney 2004). This approach to intervention also has strong connections with dynamics of cultural consumption and cultural tourism which have become a growing global trend (Richards 1996) and strongly connects with consumption and production within the creative economy.

Pine and Gilmore's (1998) concept of the experience economy is also useful in understanding the development of creative place-making in that regions can develop cultural tourism through events such as open-studios, workshops and demonstrations (Smith 2009; Glinkowski 2003). Such events enable regions to capitalize on both their heritage and the current presence of local CI organizations (Comunian and England 2018). Industrial heritage in particular has been reframed within a new CE context to preserve and build tourism based on local tradition and legacy (Jonsen-Verbeke 1999). The preservation, marketing and reforming of legacies into new forms of creative production not only embeds regional associations with cultural and creative practices but develops new markets for producers and consumers.

More recently the concept of 'creative place-making' has entered planners' and geographers' vocabulary. This has been positively summarized by Markusen and Gadwa (2010, p. 3):

> In creative place-making, partners from public, private, non-profit, and community sectors strategically shape the physical and social character of a neighbourhood, town, city, or region around arts and cultural activities. Creative place-making animates public and private spaces, rejuvenates structures and streetscapes, improves local businesses, viability and public safety, and brings diverse people together to celebrate, inspire and be inspired.

However, others have more critically acknowledged that rather than being a new trend, this policy approach bears strong similarities with pre-existing cultural policy and fits with other arts-based economic and community development activities (Nicodemus 2013). Consistent key elements of these interventions appear to be the aesthetic improvement of an area or city and the consumption of public and private space, which remain a constant from 1980s regeneration strategies to the contemporary 'creative place-making' rhetoric of today. Within the current context of cultural industries and the creative economy, this concept is primarily used as a stimulus for urban regeneration – spatially, economically and socially.

In creative place-making and urban regeneration community engagement is also used as a strategy for audience attraction and attitude change. As a result, it sometimes functions in the context of the marketing activities of local bodies, organizations and institutions in order to create activism but with a focus on relationship building which benefits the community. Glückler (2001, p. 241) also suggests that economic action evolves not between isolated actors, but through embedded social action and systems of social relations. This would suggest that embedding community engagement within regeneration strategies is advantageous in deriving economic benefits in addition to building relationships, although socio-economic context is an important consideration here (Glückler 2001).

While community engagement is often about the process of building a grassroots movement involving community members, in a creative economy and creative regions context it has primarily been considered for the value of repositioning specific social contexts and improving them. It is also important to distinguish between those initiatives which take a truly grassroots approach to local/regional development and those which take a primarily top-down approach with a community engagement element included either as an afterthought or as an instrumental method of public promotion. Jones and Wilks-Heeg (2004, p. 341) note the potential for conflict between local residents and event-based cultural regeneration strategies that are marketed as community-based in that they have the potential to exacerbate rather than improve social division and inequality. Further argument has been presented around the potential for flagship cultural projects to intensify precarious labour conditions and expedite gentrification (Comunian and Mould 2014; Comunian and Jacobi 2015).

The development of place-making strategies therefore cannot be considered in a vacuum. As noted by Oakley (2004, p. 73) the pursuit of 'culture/knowledge based economic development' strategies without consideration for local capacity – production–consumption systems for CIs, extant human capital or the potential to attract and retain human capital – is unsustainable and unlikely to lead to long-term benefits. This is supported by further critiques of the European Cultural Capital (ECC) initiative where creative place-making and cultural tourism generation are central to the agenda (Mooney 2004; Richards 2000). According to Mooney, hype generated around such bids and flagship cultural events, far from forming or contributing to sustainable regeneration strategies, 'do little but gloss over and divert attention away from the major structural problems which characterise many ex-industrial cities' (Mooney 2004, p. 327). Richards further indicates that while tourism and spending may increase in the short-term, there is little evidence that event-based cultural strategies such as the ECC generate long-term benefits (Richards 2000, p. 159). This highlights the importance of considering the complexity, capacity (Oakley 2004), socio-economic context (Glückler 2001), and extant consumption–production systems (Pratt 2008) of locations in the development of strategies for sustainable creative economic development.

The importance of place and place-making has been distinctly studied and considered in relation to the creative economy. However, it is important to consider how the creative economy itself has been studied in a very fragmented way, favouring the role of production (in the forms of cultural quarters and creative clusters) rather than aiming to provide a holistic understanding of its relationship with cultural and creative consumption and markets. It is the role and interdependency of cultural production and consumption that we turn to next in understanding the complexity of creative regions.

14.3 CREATIVE INDUSTRIES: LINKING PRODUCTION AND CONSUMPTION

Although the connection between production and consumption is often implied and taken for granted, there is a clear distinction between research investigating cultural production on one side and research concerned with the role of cultural consumption and its fruition in the regional context on the other. There is a large corpus of literature concerned with the way cultural production is developed within urban and regional contexts and how it is linked to certain areas and scenes (Mould and Comunian 2015). Meanwhile, many economic geographers and urban geographers have focused on the system of cultural production in attempts to identify what the relationship is between specific urban sites and their cultural production systems (Pratt 2004).

Many 'creative clusters' researchers adopt a common approach and study the relationship between local creative industries and urban space and qualities. In most related studies, there is a strong emphasis on locality, trust and place-based networks, local institutions and the larger local cultural scene (Banks et al. 2000; Ettlinger 2003). Most of this literature refers to or adopts a cluster perspective inspired by Porter (1998) highlighting the role of local connection, competition and cooperation dynamics, public sector support and business strategy. However, the role of demand, one of the pillars of Porter's Diamond model, is rarely taken into consideration.

Outside of a clusters perspective, Brown (2014) has noted a growing consumption–production relationship where a demand for authenticity, derived through an association with place and local production, enables provenance to translate into value. It is further suggested that this is a reaction to the ubiquitous presence of mass-produced wares, driving an added-value market for 'personalised, exclusive and original objects with a genuine local connection' (Brown 2014, p. 9). This demand for authentic, locally embedded cultural products thrives within a UK context where the 'Made in Britain' label remains a prominent marketing tool (Davis 2011; Ewins 2013). It has also been noted that, in a UK context, 'Making and provenance are inexorably linked' (Greenlees 2014), with British design historically seen as both symbolic of nationhood and as a means of conveying tradition and quality (Huygen 1989), in some instances linked with a particular region, that is, Staffordshire and the ceramics industry (Ewins 2013). More broadly, growing environmental concerns and market interest in ethical, sustainable production (Brown 2014) enable a futher production–consumption link within the creative economy, strengthening consumer relationships with locally produced goods.

It is therefore important to consider how consumption and production are linked with place-making in the development (and decline) of regional creative ecologies. Examples of creative place-making that have developed enhanced consumer-producer relationships in recent years based on locality include the establishment of Hay-on-Wye as a literature hub and Craft Town initiatives in Farnham and West Kilbride which build on distinctive local traditions to attract consumers and develop markets for local producers (Brown 2014). Such strategies indicate how place-making and creative consumption and production come together to establish regional CE growth.

There is an argument that in a globally connected world, every country, city and region are positioned in competition and that globalized markets, the Internet and new technological developments have established a single market (Anholt 2007). On the other hand, such systems and developments can be seen as increasing opportunities (Glückler 2005) and enhancing the capacity for situated production, promotion and export, thereby supporting the regional embededdness of creative production (Brown 2014). Glückler (2005, p. 1727) does however warn that accelerated technology, internationalized production and globalized markets 'increase the complexity and uncertainty of firm decisions and future developments', which given the existing complexity and somewhat unpredictable nature of creative industries activity (Potts et al. 2008) may pose a further challenge in accurately mapping future trajectories for CE growth.

It may also be the case that regionally situated consumer-producer realtionships vary within sectors of the creative economy. Jacobi (2016) indicates that while creative production and painting in particular retains a strong regional connection, it is also mediated by a globalized art market, and this may result in the regional connection being lost at a consumer level due to the market's focus on major capital cities. In contrast, other creative markets such as craft may retain stronger relationships with their local systems of cultural production (Brown 2014). However, there is a tendency within existing literature to amalgamate sectors within the broad category of CIs and therefore understanding of sector variations in localized consumption–production systems remains limited and unclear.

Contrastingly, alongside economic geography studies on local systems of cultural production, there is a vast literature that looks at how cultural provision and consumption affect urban contexts. In particular, many authors suggest an underlying connection between urban regeneration and public investment in culture and the possibility to develop and foster cultural and creative activities and attendance (Bianchini and Landry 1995; Griffiths 1995; Bailey et al. 2004). As mentioned in the introduction, within the UK context there remains an issue with a London-centric approach to cultural and creative industries funding which drives greater disparity within regional CE development (NESTA 2009). According to a report by GPS Culture (2014, p. 3) an excessive funding bias towards London as England's champion creative city prevents the country 'from realising the potential of the arts and the cultural and creative industries for the economy'. There remains however limited discussion of how this disparity impacts consumer-producer relationships at a regional level.

A more recent approach to creative regions that is connected with discourses of creative production and consumption is the understanding of creative regions as locations or concentrations of creative human capital and creative learning. It is that we consider next in developing our understanding of creative regions as complex systems.

14.4   CREATIVE HUMAN CAPITAL AND CREATIVE LEARNING

A key feature of the development of creative regions discourses and interventions is the role and importance of creative employment. The emphasis on work and employment has also been connected with the attention of policy towards measuring the role of CCIs as a new employment sector – in many regions and countries which had previously been affected by unemployment and restructuring – as well as with the popularity of the creative class (Florida 2002) theory in the mid–early 2000s.

In the UK there has been a strong trajectory of growth in employment in the sector. The positive projection of cultural and creative work as a new panacea to support regional development, even for lagging regions, has also generated a fierce battle for the attraction and retention of these jobs and workers. However, the regional breakdown of CE employment further highlights a London and south-east dominated market – in 2015 London accounted for 28.8 percent of all CE employment and the south-east for a further 15.9 percent in comparison with 2.3 percent in the north-east (DCMS 2015). This highlights a need for enhanced regional support for CE development, particularly in northern regions.

Nevertheless, many acknowledge that creative work in particular is a crucial part of knowledge-intensive employment and that graduates with a creative background constitute an important subset of this group. Research has been conducted on connections between educational institutions, industries and localities, with recent studies showing an increased emphasis on the role of Higher Education (HE) providers in the support and development of local economies in weaker regions (Goddard and Vallance 2013). However, recent policy interventions by NESTA have highlighted our limited understanding of the interconnections between HE and the creative economy. Amin and Roberts have nevertheless suggested that local creative economies and their component networks are heavily influenced by 'the nature of local institutions, labour markets, infrastructures, capital markets [and] research environments' (Amin and Roberts 2008, p. 366), suggesting that HE institutions can have a significant positive impact through the development of market awareness, the provision of infrastructure, research dissemination and the integration of graduates within the creative labour market. This is extended by Comunian and Gilmore (2015) who argue that HE providers contribute to the creative economy through cultural production and preservation in addition to the generation of creative human capital. For example, the concept of 'Creative Human Capital' is being used to demonstrate the link between graduates and creative workers on the one side, and university academics and researchers on the other.

In this, institutions can be seen as facilitating the production and development of locally embedded tacit knowledge, which in turn supports 'the creation of unique capacities and products' (Gertler 2003, p. 79) by facilitating knowledge flow between a region's human capital and its local actors and institutions. Tacit knowledge is context-specific which makes it spatially 'sticky' and dependent on interaction or 'learning through doing' in order to evolve (Bathelt et al. 2004). It therefore relies on the creation of a common social context and socially organized learning in order to produce and disseminate knowledge at a local level that could contribute to the development of a creative region. The importance of embedded knowledge and skills within specific locations and institutions has been highlighted in particular within the literature on industrial and post-industrial clusters (Asheim and Isaksen 2002) and regional craft economies (Comunian and England 2018).

In understanding the ecological relationship between place-making, production–consumption and creative human capital and creative learning, we highlight that the retention and attraction of a human capital stock (Oakley 2004) capable of generating and supporting creative production–consumption through tacit knowledge 'are social processes in that they rest on the social (and physical-environmental character)' (Gertler 2003, p. 81). Furthermore, knowing in action can also be linked with community engagement as discussed in relation to creative place-making in that learning and knowing are linked to three dimensions of community: mutual engagement, a sense of joint enterprise, and a shared repertoire of communal resources (Amin and Roberts 2008). To this end, there has been a growing recognition of communities of practice (CoPs) as drivers of learning and knowledge formation.

There are however challenges in considering the role of tacit knowledge and situated learning within creative regional development. First, there is limited understanding regarding the management of tacit knowledge and the potential for it to be transferred between sites or from a social to a private context (Gertler 2003). Second, there are significant challenges in measuring such knowledge and its potential scalability alongside uncertain definitions of the proximity requirements for knowledge transfer. Finally, in the context of regions building a CE based on extant tacit knowledge and/or regional expertise, the retention of creative human capital becomes crucial in order to preserve a competitive advantage and, in turn, to attract a greater stock of human capital for the region (e.g. creative graduates, Florida 2002).

However, we still do not know the extent to which CE growth is powered by graduates with creative credentials, although the perpetual feeding of the creative graduate market has arguably resulted in an oversupply (Sunley et al. 2010). Previous research has also demonstrated the difficulties faced by 'Creative Graduates' who pursue a degree in what is traditionally seen as a 'creative subject' such as music, design or architecture, but are subsequently unable to enter the creative industries occupations, or even to access graduate-level opportunities (Comunian et al. 2015; Comunian and Faggian 2014). The saturation of the creative employment market could be seen as the HE system contributing to increased resource competition beyond a sustainable level for creative economies at both a regional and national level. This can be particularly problematic in regions or localities with a lack of alternative community support and infrastructure for creative industries or creative graduates and could lead to issues with local graduate retention (England and Comunian 2016).

Human capital is obviously a complex concept, which incorporates an individual's stock of knowledge, training and skills, their personality and experiences, and the extent to which this enables them to perform a job that produces economic value. In a creative context this issue is made more complex by the perceived importance of 'innate' ability over schooling, and the apparent weakness of the link between formal training and creative occupation (Towse 2006). There has also been increased interest in the development of instrumental approaches to graduate employment in the creative sector through UK policy incentives and HE marketization (Oakley 2013). This growing body of academic research considers tensions surrounding the employability agenda in arts HE (Comunian and Gilmore 2015; Turner 2011), bringing to the forefront issues surrounding the capacity of creative learning to prepare students for creative occupations (Ball 2003; Bridgstock 2011; Oakley 2013) and the extent to which creative HE provides a sufficient degree of authenticity (Ashton 2016) for creative learning.

It is acknowledged that current literature only 'hints to the possibility that these graduates enter the labour market not equipped with the right kind of skills' (Faggian et al. 2013, p. 197) as empirical studies on developing employability in creative HE are currently limited. However, the importance of HE in obtaining creative employment can be observed within the measurements of creative economy employment which indicate that in 2015, 59.9 percent of CI workers in the UK had a degree or equivalent (compared with 32.7 percent of all UK jobs) and 62.5 percent of all creative occupations were held by individuals with a degree or equivalent (DCMS 2016). This shows an increase from earlier research by NESTA in 2003 which indicated that 43 percent of CI workers had a tertiary qualification or higher degree (compared with an average of 16 percent for the total workforce), further indicating a growing importance of obtaining degree qualifications in the sector, and employment market overall. So, although we share Towse's reservations (2006) regarding the suitability of more generic human capital definitions for CE study, we nonetheless believe that HE degrees constitute an important gateway to creative employment.

14.5 CONCLUSIONS: COMPLEX ECOLOGIES AND CREATIVE REGIONS

In articulating the current knowledge and understanding of 'creative regions' it is important to consider the complex ecologies that connect place image, cultural production and consumption, human capital and local learning. All of the perspectives presented here coexist and interact within the concept of a creative region. However, what has been missing so far in our understanding is a way to account for the complexity of these interactions and consider such phenomena holistically. For this reason, the use of complexity thinking and creative ecologies (Hearn et al. 2007; Stankevičienė et al. 2011) is advantageous (cf. Martin and Sunley 2007 on complexity thinking in economic geography more broadly). Pratt (2008, p. 107), meanwhile, has noted the importance of understanding and accounting for complex systems and interrelated components of 'cultural industries as an object that links production and consumption, manufacturing and service' within regeneration policies, and we would add to this creative human capital and creative learning.

We suggest that the complexity/ecological perspective is relevant in relation to creative regions at different levels: looking at interactions between creative practitioners in designing products and processes (micro), interactions between creative industries within local clusters or the role of cultural infrastructure within regions (meso), and the interaction between creativity, place image and its global reach and connections (macro). It is also particularly relevant to the understanding of the links between creative regions as connecting nodes between local and global communities from both a production and a consumption perspective. Despite challenges, we argue that this ecological approach offers the possibility to explore and understand these interconnections across different levels of understanding of creative regions (micro, meso and macro) as well as the possibility to integrate different disciplinary understandings and findings. As such, the application of this approach would help to establish a more coherent framework for defining and understanding how creative regions work, but also further explore the boundaries of the creative economy and its interconnection with communities, labour markets and social values. The main agents considered in this complex system would be ideas, peoples and practices (representing the agents and sets of relations and interactions taking place at the micro, meso and macro levels of the creative economy), with a focus on the interconnection of these different sets of agents across levels as set out below:

- By micro we refer to understanding creativity and creative practice by focusing on creative individuals (cognitive and practical skills, creative expression), creative processes and methods (how ideas are generated, theories of creativity, methods for generation of solutions), as well as creative outcomes and products (understanding artefacts and their characteristics).

- By meso we refer to the dynamics and connections which link across individuals (creative practitioners) and companies in the creative industries and beyond. In particular, we are interested in how they are interconnected (collaborations, knowledge sharing, networks), the motivations behind these interconnections (economic, social, cultural) and the platforms that are created as meso-structures to support such collaboration (online platforms, local clusters and others).
- By macro we review and consider the trends and dynamics which emerge at the summative level. These can refer to cities, national systems or the global economy. These physical as well as immaterial structures (for example fashion trends) emerge as a result of the interactions at micro and meso levels and are always evolving and in relation to previous structures, new adaptations and feedback mechanisms.

One of the main perspectives of complexity thinking which is key to our research (and social science in general) is that it accounts for dynamics and changes which are non-linear and affect the system as a whole rather than simply considering the singular linear trajectories of single units (individuals/organizations) which are part of this system. Complexity theory can capture these dynamics and understand emerging patterns across the system and across micro meso and macro levels. While having a better understanding of how agents, networks, events and performances come together can provide us with new tools to argue for their impact or improve their work, complexity theory implies abandoning a causal prescriptive view. In this it is non-deterministic and suggests that we cannot predict intervening changes or how the system will behave and respond as a whole.

Nevertheless, the advantage of complexity thinking in relation to research on the CE is that it provides a mind-map from which different strands can be drawn in developing research frames for studying the Creative Industries. Rather than being static, the components we discuss here – place making, consumption, production, creative human capital and creative learning – represent adaptive and interrelated perspectives from which to consider creative regional development. At different stages of the research process these perspectives could be considered independently in order to drill down into the micro processes occurring within creative economies while keeping in mind what bearing this has on meso and macro structures and processes, and vice versa how the micro is influenced by the meso and macro.

The research on creative regions has certainly moved forward in the last two decades but many research questions remain open for future investigation and more coherent research again will enable the development of a stronger understanding of these dynamics. In particular, we highlight three key areas of future work that need to be explored further. First, how we might reconcile the notions of the cultural, the social and the economic within the context of creative regions as they remain profoundly intertwined and need to be valued for their own merit, but also understood in the way they feed and support each other. Second, how we re-connect the notion of the individual with social and community talent. Against the notion of the individualized genius, we know that context, communities of practice and collaboration play an important role in ensuring creative regions are recognized internationally. The openness to co-production and a collective vision of creativity therefore needs to be explored within regional contexts. Finally, what role does the region play as a physical space in relation to its producers and community in a globalized economy where nodes are becoming increasingly interconnected. As the dialogue between rural and urban and from urban to international to global increases in speed and volume, exploring the balance between real spaces and virtual connections will become more important in the next decade. We suggest that complexity theory will enable this exploration in developing an understanding of the dynamics and changes taking place and in identifying the emergence of patterns and connections between regional, national and global creative economies.

14.6 REFERENCES

Amin, A. and J. Roberts (2008), 'Knowing in action: beyond communities of practice', *Research Policy*, **37** (2), 353–369.
Anholt, S. (2007), *Competitive Identity*, London: Palgrave Macmillan.
Asheim, B.T. and A. Isaksen, (2002), 'Regional innovation systems: the integration of local "sticky" and global "ubiquitous" knowledge', *The Journal of Technology Transfer*, **27** (1), 77–86.
Ashton, D. (2016), 'From campus to creative quarter: constructing industry identities in creative places', in R. Comunian and A. Gilmore (eds), *Higher Education and the Creative Economy: Beyond the Campus*, Abingdon: Routledge, pp. 21–40.
Bailey, C., S. Miles and P. Stark (2004), 'Culture-led urban regeneration and the revitalisation of identities in Newcastle, Gateshead and the North East of England', *International Journal of Cultural Policy*, **10** (1), 47–65.
Ball, L. (2003), 'Future directions for employability research in the creative industries', ADM (The Higher Education Academy Subject Centre for Arts, Design and Media). York: The Higher Education Academy.
Banks, M., A. Lovatt, J. O'Connor and C. Raffo (2000), 'Risk and trust in the cultural industries', *Geoforum*, **31** (4), 453–464.
Bathelt, H., A. Malmberg and P. Maskell (2004), 'Clusters and knowledge: local buzz, global pipelines and the process of knowledge creation', *Progress in Human Geography*, **28** (1), 31–56.
Bianchini, F. and C. Landry (1995), *The Creative City*, London: Demos.
Bridgstock, R. (2011), 'Skills for creative industries graduate success', *Education Training*, **53** (1), 9–26.
Brown, J. (2014), *Making it Local: What Does This Mean in the Context of Contemporary Craft?*, London: Crafts Council.
Chapain, C., N. Clifton and R. Comunian (2013), 'Understanding creative regions: bridging the gap between global discourses and regional and national contexts', *Regional Studies*, **47** (2), 131–134.
Chatterton, P. (2000), 'Will the real Creative City please stand up?', *City*, **4** (3), 390–397.
Clifton, N., R. Comunian and C. Chapain (2015), 'Creative regions in Europe: challenges and opportunities for policy', *European Planning Studies*, 23 (12), 2331–2335.
Comunian, R. and A. Faggian (2014), 'Creative graduates and creative cities: exploring the geography of creative education in the UK', *International Journal of Cultural and Creative Industries*, **1** (2), 19–34.
Comunian, R. and O. Mould (2014), 'The weakest link: creative industries, flagship cultural projects and regeneration', *City, Culture and Society*, 5 (2), 65–74.
Comunian, R. and A. Gilmore (2015), 'Beyond the creative campus: reflections on the evolving relationship between higher education and the creative economy', London: King's College London.
Comunian, R. and S. Jacobi (2015), 'Resilience, creative careers and creative spaces: bridging vulnerable artist's livelihoods and adaptive urban change', in H. Pinto (ed.), *Resilient Territories: Innovation and Creativity for New Modes of Regional Development*, Cambridge: Cambridge Scholars, pp. 151–166.
Comunian, R., A. Gilmore and S. Jacobi (2015), 'Higher education and the creative economy: creative graduates, knowledge transfer and regional impact debates', *Geography Compass*, **9** (7), 371–383.
Comunian, R. and England, L. (2016), 'Creative clusters and the evolution of knowledge and skills: from industrial to creative glassmaking', *Geoforum*.
Davis, E. (2011), *Made In Britain: How the Nation Earns its Living*, London: Hachette.
DCMS (1998) 'Creative industries mapping document', London: DCMS.
DCMS (2015), 'Creative industries economic estimates', London: DCMS.
DCMS (2016), 'Creative industries: focus on employment', London: DCMS
England, L. and R. Comunian (2016), 'Support or competition? Assessing the role of HEIs in professional networks and local creative communities: the case of glass-making in Sunderland', in R. Comunian and A. Gilmore (eds), *Higher Education and the Creative Economy: Beyond the Campus*, Abingdon: Routledge, pp. 145–163.
Ettlinger, N. (2003), 'Cultural economic geography and a relational and microspace approach to trusts, rationalities, networks, and change in collaborative workplaces', *Journal of Economic Geography*, **3** (2), 145–171.

Evans, G. (2003), 'Hard-branding the cultural city – from Prado to Prada', *International Journal of Urban and Regional Research*, **27** (2), 417–440.

Evans, G. and P. Shaw (2004), 'The contribution of culture to regeneration in the UK: a review of evidence', London: DCMS.

Ewins, N. (2013), 'UK ceramic manufacturing strategies, marketing and design, in response to globalization c.1990–2010', *Mobility and Design: 22nd Annual Parsons/Cooper-Hewitt Symposium on the Decorative Arts and Design*, New York.

Faggian, A., R. Comunian, S. Jewell and U. Kelly (2013), 'Bohemian graduates in the UK: disciplines and location determinants of creative careers', *Regional Studies*, **47** (2), 183–200.

Florida, R. (2002), *The Rise of the Creative Class*, New York: Basic Books.

Gertler, M.S. (2003), 'Tacit knowledge and the economic geography of context, or the undefinable tacitness of being (there)', *Journal of Economic Geography*, **3** (1), 75–99.

Glinkowski, P. (2003), 'Open studios – a gem worth polishing', London, UK: Arts Council. Technical Report.

Glückler, J. (2001), 'Zur Bedeutung von Embeddedness in der Wirtschaftsgeographie', *Geographische Zeitschrift*, **89** (4), 211–226.

Glückler, J. (2005), 'Making embeddedness work: social practice institutions in foreign consulting markets', *Environment and Planning A*, **37** (10), 1727–1750.

Goddard, J. and P. Vallance (2013), *The University and the City*, Abingdon: Routledge.

GPS Culture (2014), 'Hard facts to swallow', available online at: http://www.gpsculture.co.uk/downloads/hardfacts/141120HardfactstoswallowGPSmain.pdf, accessed 29 March 2017.

Greenlees, R. (2014), 'The importance of place', available online at: http://www.craftscouncil.org.uk/articles/out-and-about-july-2014/, accessed 5 April 2017.

Griffiths, R. (1995), 'Cultural strategies and new modes of urban intervention', *Cities*, **12** (4), 253–265.

Hall, P. (2000), 'Creative cities and economic development', *Urban Studies*, **37** (4), 639–649.

Hearn, G., S. Roodhouse and J. Blakey (2007), 'From value chain to value creating ecology: implications for creative industries development policy', *International Journal of Cultural Policy*, **13** (4), 419–436.

Herrero, L.C., J.A. Sanz, M. Devesa, A. Bedate and M.J. del Barrio (2006), 'The economic impact of cultural events: a case-study of Salamanca 2002, European Capital of Culture', *European Urban and Regional Studies*, **13** (1), 41–57.

Huygen, F. (1989), *British Design: Image & Identity*, London: Thames & Hudson.

Jacobi, S. (2016), 'Painting and the regional', http://www.post-creativecity.com/painting-and-the-regional, accessed 5 April 2017.

Jayne, M. (2004), 'Culture that works? Creative industries development in a working-class city', *Capital & Class*, **28** (3), 199–210.

Jayne, M. (2005), 'Creative industries: the regional dimension?', *Environment & Planning C: Government & Policy*, **23** (4), 537–556.

Jones, P. and S. Wilks-Heeg (2004), 'Capitalising culture: Liverpool 2008', *Local Economy*, **19** (4), 341–360.

Jonsen-Verbeke, M. (1999), 'Industrial heritage: a nexus for sustainable tourism development', *Tourism Geographies*, **1** (1), 70–85.

Ley, D. (2003), 'Artists, aestheticisation and the field of gentrification', *Urban Studies*, **40** (12), 2527–2544.

Markusen, A. and A. Gadwa (2010), 'Arts and culture in urban or regional planning: a review and research agenda', *Journal of Planning Education and Research*, **29** (3), 379–391.

Martin, R. and P. Sunley (2007), 'Complexity thinking and evolutionary economic geography', Journal of *Economic Geography*, **7** (15), 573–601.

Mooney, G. (2004), 'Cultural policy as urban transformation? Critical reflections on Glasgow, European City of Culture 1990', *Local Economy*, **19** (4), 327–340.

Mould, O. and R. Comunian (2015), 'Hung, drawn and cultural quartered: rethinking cultural quarter development policy in the UK', *European Planning Studies*, **23** (12), 2356–2369.

NESTA (2009), The Geography of Creativity, London: NESTA.

Nicodemus, A.G. (2013), 'Fuzzy vibrancy: creative placemaking as ascendant US cultural policy', *Cultural Trends*, **22** (3–4), 213–222.

Oakley, K. (2004), 'Not so cool Britannia: the role of the creative industries in economic development', *International Journal of Cultural Studies*, **7** (1), 67–77.

Oakley, K. (2013). 'Making workers: higher education and the cultural industries workplace', in D. Ashton D. and C. Noonan (eds), *Cultural Work and Higher Education*, New York: Palgrave Macmillan, pp. 25–44.

Pine, B.J. and J.H. Gilmore (1998), 'Welcome to the experience economy', *Harvard Business Review*, **76**, 97–105.

Porter, M.E. (1998), 'Clusters and the new economic competition', *Harvard Business Review*, **76** (6), 77–90.

Potts, J., S. Cunningham, J. Hartley and P. Ormerod (2008), 'Social network markets: a new definition of the creative industries', *Journal of Cultural Economics*, **32** (3), 167–185.

Pratt, A. (2004), 'The cultural economy: a call for spatialized "production of culture" perspectives', *International Journal of Cultural Studies*, **7** (1), 117–128.

Pratt, A. (2008), 'Creative cities: the cultural industries and the creative class', *Geografiska Annaler: Series B Human Geography*, **90** (2), 107–117.

Richards, G. (1996), 'Production and consumption of European cultural tourism', *Annals of Tourism Research*, **23** (2), 261–283.

Richards, G. (2000), 'The European cultural capital event: strategic weapon in the cultural arms race?', *International Journal of Cultural Policy*, **6** (2), 159–181.

Richards, G. and J. Wilson (2004), 'The impact of cultural events on city image: Rotterdam, cultural capital of Europe 2001', *Urban Studies*, **41** (10), 1931–1951.

Shearmur, R. (2006), 'The new knowledge aristocracy: the creative class, mobility and urban growth', *Work Organisation, Labour and Globalisation*, **1** (1), 31–47.

Smith, D.K. (2009), 'Open studios – regional promotion of art tourism', *OR Insight*, **22** (3), 153–164.

Smith, N. (1996), *The New Urban Frontier: Gentrification and the Revanchist City*, London: Routledge.

Stankevičienė, J., R. Levickaitė, M. Braškutė and E. Noreikaitė (2011), 'Creative ecologies: developing and managing new concepts of creative economy', *Business, Management and Education*, **9** (2), 277–294.

Sunley, P., S. Pinch and J. MacMillen (2010), 'Growing design? Challenges and constraints facing design consultancies in three English city-regions', *Regional Studies*, **44** (7), 873–877.

Towse, R. (2006), 'Human capital and artists' labour markets', in V. Ginsburgh and D. Throsby (eds), *Handbook of the Economics of Art and Culture*, Oxford, North Holland, pp. 865–894.

Turner, G. (2011), 'Surrendering the space: convergence culture, cultural studies and the curriculum', *Cultural Studies*, **25** (4–5), 685–699.

15. Sustainable regions
David Gibbs

15.1 INTRODUCTION

A growing awareness of the environmental damage caused by economic development has been a key feature within international and national policy making over the past 30 years. Although awareness predated these, the 1987 Brundtland Report and the Rio Earth Summit in 1992 popularised the concept of sustainability and led to the incorporation of sustainable development aims into international, national and local policy frameworks. In the much-quoted words of the World Commission on Environment and Development, sustainable development is defined as 'development that meets the needs of the present without compromising the ability of future generations to meet their own needs' (WCED 1987, p. 8). Sustainable development appeared to offer the prospect of continued economic growth, but combined with social equity and ecological protection. The notion of 'thinking globally, acting locally' embodied in sustainable development led policy makers, academics and activists to posit that sustainability was best developed at the local scale. This received formal recognition through the Rio declaration's Local Agenda 21 (LA21) programme and was promoted by non-governmental organisations such as the International Council for Local Environmental Initiatives (ICLEI) as a key initiative that local authorities could sign up to and subsequently implement (ICLEI 2012). This promotion of sustainability at the local scale extended to arguments that regions should also be made more sustainable. Some scholars have suggested that the urban and regional scales have a particular importance as key sites to combine environmental and economic policies and have a particular capacity to act within the overall politico-administrative system (Diamantini 2001; Lafferty and Narodoslawsky 2003). Within these debates, however, there was rarely any consideration of what was actually meant by the terms 'local' or 'regional'. Although there was some discussion of the need to delineate these on the basis of watersheds or bioregions (see for example McGinnis, 1999), using natural criteria, a more common response was to work on the basis of existing administrative divisions into local and regional government areas.

Despite this initial enthusiasm, sustainable development subsequently became open to criticism as a 'fuzzy concept' that could be interpreted in multiple ways and LA21 largely disappeared without any real evaluation of what it achieved (Graute 2016). However, the legacy of the environmental awareness its adoption engendered continues to be of salience. If anything, the continued catalogue of environmental degradation and, particularly, a focus on climate change and sea level rise since 1996 has re-enforced the need for both global and local policy responses. For example, at the international scale UN member states adopted Sustainable Development Goals (SDGs) in 2015 (UN 2015) which require implementation at the local scale, albeit there has been criticism that member states retain control of the process at the expense of greater involvement by local and regional stakeholders (Graute 2016).

However, much of the policy debate has shifted away from the generalities of sustainable development towards a more pragmatic emphasis on reducing carbon emissions in recognition of their role in enhanced global warming and to a focus on limiting a rise in global temperatures (While et al. 2010). Following on from the Kyoto Protocol of 1997 which required signatories to reduce greenhouse gas emissions by 5.2 per cent over the 2008–12 period (from a 1990 baseline), the UN Paris agreement on climate change in 2016 subsequently aimed to limit global temperature rises to 'well below' 2°C and 'endeavoured to limit' them to 1.5°C. The agreement reached was for legally binding requirements from 2020, which meant achieving a balance between anthropogenic emissions by sources and removals by sinks of greenhouse gases in the second half of this century (Clémençon 2016). As with the shift in international policy focus, there has been a parallel move towards exploring new directions for regional development and a continued focus on the local and regional scale as a key site for action. In particular, local and regional development strategies have increasingly focused on the concept of the green economy as a source of both a response to environmental problems, such as carbon emissions, and as a new source of development for regional economies (Christopherson 2011). Thus although there are a range of responses and policy areas (e.g. transport, buildings, natural resource use) that could be considered as part of a move towards sustainable regions, this chapter takes as its main focus the development of the green economy at the regional level.

The structure of the chapter is as follows. The next section considers the varying definitions and interpretations of the sustainable region that have been used, and then examines the shift away from sustainable development to low carbon and green economies, drawing on the concept of 'eco-state restructuring'. Following this, the chapter considers the rise of the green economy and then briefly outlines the geography of the green industry in the USA and the European Union, from secondary source material. The chapter then turns to the ways in which local areas and regions have sought to develop their own green economy initiatives. A recent strand of research has sought to conceptualise this through notions of sustainability transitions, drawing on socio-technical transitions theory and the chapter outlines the ways in which this has been used to develop the concept of 'transition regions'. A final section concludes the chapter and points to questions for further investigation.

15.2   FROM SUSTAINABLE REGIONS TO ECO-STATE RESTRUCTURING

Compared to research on the role of regions in economic development, the literature on how regional activities contribute to sustainable development is much more limited (Haughton and Morgan 2008). Haughton and Morgan (2008, p. 1220) argue that the value of taking a regional approach is not to reify the region as a necessary scale, but in 'thinking about regions as a prism for understanding how ideas about sustainable development work through at a variety of scales and across a range of sectors'. Certainly there has been a lack of clarity about what is meant by a sustainable region and whether regions can be sustainable. Given the interconnectedness of the global economy, the potential for greater autarky at the regional scale seems an improbable option. McManus (2008) builds on Ravetz's (2004) definition of regional sustainable development to suggest that it involves a regional identity based on interrelationships between economic, sociocultural and ecological practices based on the principles of sustainability, notably living within the region's resources. A sustainable region is:

> [O]ne that is continuously becoming more sustainable. This means improving the sustainability of individual industries where possible, closing and replacing industries that cannot be made more sustainable, encouraging sustainable lifestyles within the region, and repairing ecological damage caused by previous economic activities. Regions that embark on this process will soon be distinct from regions that are laggards, thus enabling the term "sustainable region" to be applied in the relative sense and to recognise the achievements of moving towards sustainability. (McManus 2008, p. 1278)

A key focus of past work on sustainable regions has been to investigate the policy processes at work, 'these contributions are primarily concerned with policy-led initiatives for sustainable regional development, emphasising the role of governance experimentation and public-private coordination' (Truffer and Coenen 2012, p. 8). However, despite the fact that environmental concerns have had an impact on policy and practice at the local and regional scales, in general past attempts to green regional economies have met with mixed success and a preference for promoting economic development over environmental and social aims (Jonas et al. 2011b).

An attempt to provide a better conceptualisation of the processes at work has been undertaken by While et al. (2010) who divide the period since the mid-1960s as comprising various waves of what they term 'eco-state restructuring' (ESR). This is defined as:

> [T]he reorganisation of state powers, capacities, regulations and territorial structures around institutional pathways and strategic projects, which are (at least from the vantage of state interests at a given moment in time) viewed as less environmentally damaging than previous trajectories.

This means that the state becomes involved in directing and regulating environmental concerns, as well as organising and mobilising actors, projects and interests in order to be consistent with strategic environmental aims. Thus 'the concept of ESR draws attention to the ways in which states are struggling with growing pressures to reduce or manage global warming, cut carbon emissions and promote economic development in less harmful ways' (Jonas et al. 2011b, p. 284). An initial wave of ESR was concerned with pollution prevention and control up until the mid-1980s, when the logics of sustainable development became dominant. This period saw the promotion of a new round of accumulation based around ideas of ecological modernisation, at the heart of which is a belief in technology, innovation and progress to solve environmental problems (Roberts and Colwell 2001; Mol 2002). A subsequent wave from the late 1990s onwards focused on carbon control measures and the development of a low carbon economy. In the process, city-regions:

> [H]ave been subjected to a . . . process of eco-state restructuring whereby the reduction of reliance on fossil fuels – or what can be called the politics of carbon control – has emerged alongside, or even replaced altogether, sustainable development as the principal discourse and rationality underpinning new modes of societal regulation. (Jonas et al. 2011a, p. 2542)

An overarching theme across these various waves (particularly the second two) is the extent to which environmental governance has become neo-liberalised and dominated by marketisation, to the detriment of a focus on equity and environmental protection, and where sustainability goals have often been secondary to concerns over economic competitiveness (Castree 2008; Jonas et al. 2011b). Despite the supposed ability of sustainable development to consider economy, environment and society in a holistic manner and to establish trade-offs between these three elements, sustainability was frequently seen as a threat to economic activity and remained secondary to economic competitiveness in many localities (Jonas et al. 2011b). Reframing climate change as an economic opportunity through the specific form of a green or low carbon economy has allowed governments to set demanding targets for decarbonisation, yet at the same time to present these as measures designed to increase economic competitiveness (Bailey et al. 2011). In this manner, 'although presented as a response to socio-ecological crisis, low-carbon restructuring is perhaps more accurately read as a political-economic fix enacted through the domain of state environmental regulation' (While et al. 2010, p. 83). This form of 'ecological fix' has been strongly influenced and shaped by the larger context of neoliberal environmental governance, which has constrained what it is politically possible to implement.

The aim here though is not to provide a detailed theoretical analysis of state theory and the environment, important though this is. Rather, the concept of eco-state restructuring and its various 'waves' provides a useful contextual background against which to situate regional responses and policy initiatives. In particular, both ecological modernisation and carbon control have encouraged a response based around the development of a low carbon or green economy, 'creating new opportunities for eco-innovation and green growth' (Healy and Morgan, 2012, p. 1048).

15.3   THE GREEN ECONOMY

Recent years have therefore seen a growing interest by policy makers in the development of what is variously termed a 'green', 'low carbon' or 'clean tech' economy. For example, the United Nations Environment Programme (UNEP 2011, p. 16), using a definition that encompasses all three terms, sees it comprising an economy that is 'low carbon, resource efficient, and socially inclusive [where] growth in income and employment should be driven by public and private investments that reduce carbon emissions and pollution, enhance energy and resource efficiency, and prevent the loss of biodiversity and ecosystem services'. However, it is not clear how such an economy can be mainstreamed and there is considerable debate over the extent to which current green economy policy measures will substantially address global environmental problems, such as global warming and rising greenhouse gas emissions. For example, Bina (2013) categorises green economy policies on a spectrum from 'business-as-usual' to 'all change', reflecting the extent to which environmental issues are simply seen as an economic opportunity, or whether they call for substantive changes in the organisation of the economy and society. Such divergent views would appear to reflect the political stance of authors rather than any disciplinary differences. Thus while some authors, such as the geographer Caprotti (2012) and economist Gendron (2014), believe that the most likely scenarios involve mild reform along the lines of ecological modernisation with limited environmental benefits, others, such as geographer Davies (2013) and anthropologist Shear (2014), suggest that green economy developments can engender more substantive and radical change.

From a policy maker's perspective, the green economy is increasingly seen as a source of new growth and jobs and the basis of a new round of capital accumulation. At the local scale, 'regions and cities see the challenge as an opportunity to take our societies out of the global economic crisis transformed into more sustainable, low carbon, less resource intensive and inclusive communities' (Bonsinetto and Falco 2013, p. 126). Nations, regions and cities have begun to try and position themselves as leaders in the green economy and as destinations for new forms of investment (Gibbs and O'Neill, 2014). In such cases 'regional governments have continued to assume greater responsibility for environmental policy implementation and this has had to be factored into economic development strategy' (Jonas et al. 2011b, p. 287). However, from a geographical perspective, we have a limited understanding of how these developments are occurring over space, nor do we have much purchase on the ways in which local and regional governments are promoting the development of the green economy or the related institutional and governance shifts that are taking place. Moreover, space is important here, not just in terms of providing 'containers' for the green economy, but also in order to explore how such developments in turn affect particular regions and cities. By investigating the processes of transition towards a green economy in particular places, we can not only explore how specific places aim to affect, or bring about, such transitions, but also how the processes of transition can in turn affect those places. Thus green economic development may also change the nature of particular places, through, for example, widespread adoption of renewable energy technologies, the development of community-based initiatives or through their self-promotion as key green economy locations. This then goes back to debates around what constitutes a sustainable region – is it just that the region contains green industries or should there be a broader shift towards greater self-reliance, more sustainable lifestyles and constraints on living within regional resources? In addition, we need to see such local activities in a broader context and examine spatial change in relational terms, in order to understand how the actors involved transcend the local and operate at multiple scales.

15.4   GEOGRAPHIES OF THE GREEN ECONOMY

Exploring the geography of the green economy at a regional scale, however, is an exercise fraught with problems given the lack of available definitions and data – for example, green jobs do not form a specific sector under current industrial classifications and may be found across many sectors. Research by ESPON (2014) in Europe and the USA by Muro et al. (2011) has begun to map out where such activity is taking place in these two continents. Both studies are heavily focused on an approach which sees the green economy as a source of future economic development. Thus Muro et al. (2011) compiled a comprehensive national database for the USA and define the green economy as comprising the following sectors:[1] agricultural and natural resources conservation; education and compliance; energy and resource efficiency; greenhouse gas reduction, environmental management and recycling; and renewable energy. The report indicates that the US green economy is predominantly located in metropolitan areas – which accounted for 84 per cent of total green industry jobs in 2010 – and that those areas where firms are clustered together experienced faster job growth. Key locations include city-regions in the north-eastern

US (e.g. Boston, Albany) and on the west coast (e.g. Seattle, San Jose, Los Angeles, San Diego). Within these regions, Christopherson (2011, p. 379) claims that:

> [G]reen economy manufacturers choose green field sites and locations where they can pay relatively low wages while still providing for high-quality homes and amenities for their management. The concentrated structure and location patterns of these green industries replicates that in other advanced manufacturing industries. . .Because of their location pattern, green advanced manufacturing plants are likely to contribute to regional inequality rather than reduce it.

Correspondingly, in Europe, ESPON (2014) identifies clusters derived from an analysis of European Cluster Observatory data relating to a similar set of green economy sectors (Environmental Technology, Bioenergy, Hydrogen and Fuel Cells, Recycling, Solar Energy, Wind Energy, Eco-construction, Renewable Energy, Sustainability, Water and Green Technology). Relative to population, regions in north Sweden, Hungary, southern Finland, and eastern Austria all had green economy clusters, while an analysis based on environmental technology patents added German and Danish regions to the list of prominent green economy locations. Based on a range of factors and indicators, ESPON (2014) identifies a number of regions with a 'high green economic development potential', mainly located in Germany, Scandinavia and Austria. The ESPON report argues that regions have a key role in translating national and supranational sustainability visions into realities. The region and actors within it, are particularly significant in larger, more decentralised EU nation states such as Spain, Germany and Italy, whereas in those with a weaker regional structure, such as Sweden, municipalities are more important actors. Overall, then, both the US and EU studies indicate that certain regions are becoming dominant for the development of new green economy sectors. In the next section, the chapter turns to sustainability transitions theory as a means of explaining why this may be the case and how such developments might challenge existing unsustainable economies.

15.5 SUSTAINABILITY TRANSITIONS

A useful perspective from which to explore the rise of the green economy in regions is provided by research into sustainability transitions and, in particular, the multi-level perspective (MLP) of innovation (Rip and Kemp 1998; Smith 2003; Geels 2005). The MLP identifies three synergistic levels: the socio-technical *landscape*, which encompasses social values, cultural norms, the natural environment and the macro political economy etc.; a meso-level of socio-technical *regimes* (such as fossil fuel-based energy systems), that include interconnected systems of existing technologies, institutions, rules, norms and practices (Berkhout et al. 2004); and a micro-level of protected *niches*, which act as test-beds for innovative ideas and technologies and the potential emergence of new socio-technical constellations that challenge the existing regime (Späth and Rohracher 2010).

In transitions research a key focus has been on experimentation with new ideas and technologies in niches and the lessons for policy that this provides (Smith 2003). Niche developments are seen as the source of new socio-technical configurations which can grow, and perhaps eventually displace, incumbent unsustainable regimes (Berkhout et al. 2004). These tensions are a product of changing circumstances in the wider socio-technical landscape acting as a driver for regime transitions, where new imperatives, such as policy measures to address the impact of climate change and accelerated global warming, carbon reduction targets, and targets for energy generation from renewable technology sources, act as a challenge to existing technological regimes (Smith et al. 2010). From a policy perspective, one advantage of utilising socio-technical transitions research is that it focuses attention upon the networks and institutional structures that support the green economy (Smith 2003). This indicates that broader changes are necessary to develop a green economy beyond the simplistic focus on the formation and expansion of new firms and economic sectors advocated in some government initiatives (see for example HM Government 2008).

For a study of the green economy, socio-technical transitions theory provides a useful conceptual framework for the institutional and governance shifts that are involved, as well as for the development of innovative and entrepreneurial activities. However, within the theory little attention has been paid to *where* niche development or transitions are taking place. As McCauley and Stephens (2012, p. 214) comment 'the framework remains centrally focused on describing the trajectory of technological change, without sufficient consideration of the ways in which transitions are embedded in local regions and, indeed, remake those regions'. In cases where space *has* been explicitly addressed, the main focus has been on national scale transitions (Hodson and Marvin 2010). This lack of spatial context has come to be recognised as an important shortcoming in socio-technical transitions research, where an inattention to space hinders it from adequately capturing the evolution and development of networks of institutions, entrepreneurs and innovations into stable forms that can challenge and replace existing regimes. Research which has begun to focus on the role of space and place in transitions research suggests that the sub-national scale is important and that regions and cities are key locations from which green economy transitions may develop. 'The scope for unilateral action at the sub-national scale may be extremely modest, but it is not unimportant . . . a whole series of eco-innovations are being trialled at the sub-national level all over the world' (Healy and Morgan 2012, p. 1049). Niches are likely to develop in these locations, which subsequently play an important role in upscaling these experiments to wider spatial scales (Coenen et al. 2010).

Similar conclusions are reached by ESPON (2014) and Badinger et al. (2016) where European regions and cities are identified as key actors encouraging sustainability transitions. Such locations have been classified as 'transition regions' defined as constituting sub-national administrative areas, with policies and support mechanisms in place to support green industries, especially for regional innovation processes (Cooke 2011). Such transition regions will have clusters of related green industries and a platform of related variety sectors and sub-sectors (see Box 15.1). What is important about the regional and urban scales is not just that they provide opportunities for niche experimentation, but that they also 'appear to bridge the niche-regime divide and provide "social contexts" (actor networks, institutions, complementary technological structures) "to integrate" and implement socio-technical configurations which differ from the dominant regime and may be important for long-term transition processes' (Späth and Rohracher 2012, p. 475). In moving beyond a view of regions and cities as simply places for experimentation and demonstration, we need to link together the niche with the regime and landscape. Hence some of the factors at work in a region or area will not be specifically 'local' and of importance is how actors adapt or adopt national and international factors and how these

---

BOX 15.1   EXAMPLES OF GREEN ECONOMY REGIONS

Eco World or the 'Green Tech Valley' has been developed by the Austrian province of Styria. Eco World is one of Europe's leading green economy locations with over 170 companies involved in biomass, solar energy, photovoltaics and energy efficiency. The initiative has its origins in an initial project in 1998 and was formally established in 2005. Eco World is a provincial and city (Graz) government supported initiative, but also involves a range of institutions in a triple helix research-industry-government approach. While Eco World encourages firm location, new start-ups and innovation, it is not solely focused on economic development, with a major shift towards renewable energy use in the province and support for local, community and local energy initiatives. At the same time, Eco World uses the Green Tech Valley appellation and its designation as the world's leading green tech cluster (by Clean Edge in 2010) to represent itself externally. This has promotional value, with Eco World staff giving presentations and study tours to representatives from overseas local and regional government staff, but also the recent development of a Green Tech Service Alliance, with partners in ten countries (6 in the EU, plus Singapore, South Korea, Canada and the USA) to enable Styria's companies to access business opportunities in other green business clusters.

The East of England region has aspirations to become the UK's leading centre for the green economy. The New Anglia Local Enterprise Partnership (LEP), covering Norfolk and Suffolk, has been designated the UK Government's 'Green Economy Pathfinder', with the aim of achieving 'sustainable, low-carbon growth, skills development and employment'. There is a substantial focus on economic development issues, notably through developing the offshore renewable energy sector and establishing Low Carbon Business Zones, with incentives for inward investment. The strategy is also linked with other East of England developments in the Greater Cambridge area in clean energy technologies in Cambridge Cleantech and Peterborough's EnviroCluster, which are also focused on the economic opportunities offered by the green economy. Thus Cambridge Cleantech builds upon the area's existing reputation as a location for high tech industry and represents a 'triple helix' partnership to develop Greater Cambridge as a leading European cleantech location. The EnviroCluster is linked with other EU clean tech locations through the EU-funded EcoCluP project, including Eco World Styria. However, the focus is not solely on economic development, with the LEP strategy aiming to have a positive environmental impact by reducing greenhouse gas emissions ahead of UK and EU targets, as well as having a community impact, through linking with Transition Town initiatives in the area and community-owned renewable energy projects.

---

come to be configured locally. In MLP terms, while socio-technical landscapes provide the broad context of opportunities and constraints for green business developments and their supporting institutions, they do not (despite sometimes being seen as 'external pressures') determine outcomes or mechanically impact niches and regimes (Hodson and Marvin 2010). Actors within a region need to perceive and translate these external landscape developments in order to have purchase (Geels and Schot 2007). The role of purposive actors and institutions is therefore important in this process, not just within the local area, but also to help transcend the regional and urban scale.

Drawing on transitions research suggests that the development of the green economy will be unevenly distributed in space and that sustainability transitions will depend on the interplay of actors, networks and institutions available in some regions and not others. The incorporation of space and place into MLP research helps to explain why it is that niches can emerge in certain localities rather than others (Raven et al. 2012). Some regions or places may offer greater opportunity both for niches to develop and operate and for the formation and development of green economy activities. Healy and Morgan

(2012, p. 1050) argue that there is a need for political alliances committed to sustainable development in such areas:

> [W]ithout such alliances it is difficult to fashion the collaborative governance arrangements – for commercializing knowledge in new and existing firms, for cultivating clusters, for crafting supply chains, for nurturing new skill sets and so forth – to deliver the kinds of "smart, sustainable and inclusive growth" envisaged by European Union policy-makers.

Similar conclusions are reached for the USA by Chapple et al. (2011, p. 23) who argue that US state actors are important in promoting green economy growth such that 'the more proactive local governments will likely emerge as the winners, at least initially, in the green economy'. However, exactly *why* certain locations have a favourable confluence of institutions and structures is unclear and needs empirical investigation to ascertain how this has arisen. In future more empirical research is needed in order to help address the criticism of socio-technical transitions research that it lacks any real sense of the politics and power relations involved between the different actors and institutions that may facilitate or hinder transitions. As Bailey and Caprotti (2014, p. 1800) argue, we need to focus

> attention on the politics of the green economy as regions, cities, and companies compete to host emerging sectors or to emulate others' successes. Such processes will inescapably produce winners, losers, and uneven development as regions specialise or are outcompeted in the factors of green economic production. Conflicting visions of the green economy – stressing global or local issues and social, economic, and environmental benefits in different measures – will also surface as regional governments, businesses, and communities decipher the concept.

15.6   CONCLUSIONS

This chapter has focused on shifting approaches to, and interpretations of, sustainable regions. While initially the local and regional scales were seen as important by both academics and policy makers as key sites to implement international environmental agreements such as the Earth Summit, the concept of sustainable regions was largely ill-defined and vague in nature. The rise of low carbon and green economy strategies has given a new impetus to policies for, and studies of, sustainability in regions. It has been argued in this chapter that drawing on research into sustainability transitions provides a clearer conceptual background and a rationale as to why the local and regional scale are important for these new developments. This work proposes that regions and urban areas act as niches for the development of new socio-technical formations, but also act as a link between these niches and the broader regime. This helps to move away from earlier formations which saw sustainable regions as self-contained and helps to see sustainable regions in more relational terms. The shift towards a green economy focus has also helped to move towards a more concrete approach to sustainability, with a growth in green economy and transition regions being seen as key drivers for wider change at the national level (Cooke 2011, 2015).

Despite this renewed interest, key questions remain in both regional research and that on sustainability transitions as to what the outcomes of a shift to a more sustainable future or a green economy would entail. As the examples provided in this chapter indicate the explicit or implicit assumption is that this will involve a heavy reliance on technologically led solutions and the development of new low carbon sectors. Certainly these form the major policy focus in the two examples outlined in Box 15.1, albeit that both have wider aims, with Eco World encouraging renewable energy use within the region and both Eco World and the East of England region including a range of community initiatives. However, such approaches have been criticised for focusing on the green economy as 'a new motor for economic development' (Kenis and Lievens 2016, p. 217) and neglecting social and environmental issues in the same way that occurred with sustainable development. A consequence of this is that policies to develop green economies often appear to be a thinly veiled version of business-as-usual, rather than a shift to a more sustainable economy where social and environmental aspects have parity with economic aspects, epitomising a process of paradigm *fixing* rather than paradigm *shifting* (Bina 2013). This means 'environmental problems come to be framed as issues that are politically, economically and technologically solvable within the context of existing institutions and power structures and continued economic growth' (Bailey et al. 2011, p. 683). In reality, rather than being a clear or stable end point and an unproblematic shift to some form of idealised 'eco state' (Meadowcroft 2005), the green economy is 'a disaggregated and contested discourse' (Ferguson 2015, p. 26) and an ongoing contest between different economic visions of the future (Bailey and Wilson 2009; Bailey and Caprotti 2014).

Critiques of this approach to the green economy offer alternative pathways for economic development, based around ideas of degrowth and post growth (see for example Latouche 2006, 2010; Kallis 2011). Such alternatives are often disjointed and small-scale including Transition Towns (Hopkins 2008), localised currencies (North 2014; Seyfang 2003; Longhurst 2015), voluntary simplicity (Alexander 2013), diverse economies (Gibson-Graham 2008; Roelvink et al. 2015), solidarity purchasing groups, solidarity economy districts, Slow Food (Grasseni 2014) and Slow Cities (Mayer and Knox 2008). As yet, these are largely incipient and do not form the basis for strategies for sustainable regions, but offer a radical challenge to policy makers and to lifestyles within regions. As Hodson et al. (2016, p. 145) argue this calls 'for more work on better understanding the range of alternatives and an examination of the interconnections and possible interconnections between alternative initiatives and formal priorities'. Thus, while the hegemonic form of green economy and transition regions may draw heavily on eco-modernising discourses, there is a set of alternative practices and activities that point to ways in which sustainable regions could be thought of, and constructed, in alternative forms.

15.7 ACKNOWLEDGEMENTS

David Gibbs acknowledges the support of a Regional Studies Association Fellowship Research Grant for the research on which his chapter is based.

15.8 NOTE

1. Note that Muro et al. (2011, p. 14) use the term clean economy rather than green economy. This is defined as 'economic activity – measured in terms of establishments and the jobs associated with them – that produces goods and services with an environmental benefit or adds value to such products using skills or technologies that are uniquely applied to those products'.

15.9   REFERENCES

Alexander, S. (2013), 'Voluntary simplicity and the social reconstruction of law: de-growth from the grassroots up', *Environmental Values*, **22** (2), 287–308.
Badinger, H., D. Bailey, L. De Propris, P. Huber, J. Janger, K. Kratena, H. Pitlik, T. Sauer, R. Thillaye and J. van den Bergh (2016), *New Dynamics for Europe: Reaping the Benefits of Socio-ecological Transition, Part II Model and Area Chapters*, WWWforEurope Synthesis Report, Final Version, Vienna, Brussels.
Bailey, I. and G. Wilson (2009), 'Theorising transitional pathways in response to climate change: technocentrism, ecocentrism, and the carbon economy', *Environment and Planning A*, **41** (10), 2324–2341.
Bailey, I., A. Gouldson and P. Newell (2011), 'Ecological modernisation and the governance of carbon: a critical analysis', *Antipode*, **43** (3), 682–703.
Bailey, I., and F. Caprotti (2014), 'The green economy: functional domains and theoretical directions of enquiry', *Environment and Planning A*, **46** (8), 1797–1813.
Berkhout, F., A. Smith and A. Stirling (2004), 'Socio-technological regimes and transition contexts', in B. Elzen, F.W. Geels and K. Green (eds), *System Innovation and the Transition to Sustainability: Theory, Evidence and Policy*, Cheltenham, UK and Northampton, MA, USA: Edward Elgar Publishing, pp. 48–75.
Bina, O. (2013), 'The green economy and sustainable development: an uneasy balance?', *Environment and Planning C: Government and Policy*, **31** (6), 1023–1047.
Bonsinetto, F. and E. Falco (2013), 'Analysing Italian regional patterns in green economy and climate change: can Italy leverage on Europe 2020 strategy to face sustainable growth challenges?', *Journal of Urban and Regional Analysis*, **5** (2), 123–142.
Caprotti, F. (2012), 'The cultural economy of cleantech: environmental discourse and the emergence of a new technology sector', *Transactions of the Institute of British Geographers*, **37** (3), 370–385.
Castree, N. (2008), 'Neoliberalising nature: the logics of deregulation and reregulation', *Environment and Planning A*, **40** (1), 131–152.
Chapple, K., C. Kroll, T.W. Lester and S. Montero (2011), 'Innovation in the green economy: an extension of the regional innovation system model?', *Economic Development Quarterly*, **25** (1), 5–25.
Christopherson, S. (2011), 'Green dreams in a cold light', in A. Pike, A. Rodríguez-Pose and J. Tomaney (eds), *Handbook of Local and Regional Development*, London: Routledge, pp. 371–380.
Clémençon, R. (2016), 'The two sides of the Paris climate agreement: dismal failure or historic breakthrough', *Journal of Environment and Development*, **25** (1), 3–24.
Coenen, L., R. Raven and G. Verbong (2010), 'Local niche experimentation in energy transitions: a theoretical and empirical exploration of proximity advantages and disadvantages', *Technology in Society*, **32** (4), 295–302.
Cooke, P. (2011), 'Transition regions: regional-national eco-innovation systems and strategies', *Progress in Planning*, **76** (3), 105–146.
Cooke, P. (2015), 'Green governance and green clusters: regional and national policies for the climate change challenge of Central and Eastern Europe', *Journal of Open Innovation: Technology, Market and Complexity*, **1** (1), DOI: 10.1186/s40852-015-0002-z.
Davies, A.R. (2013), 'Cleantech clusters: transformational assemblages for a just, green economy or just business as usual?', *Global Environmental Change*, **23** (5), 1285–1295.
Diamantini, C. (2001), *The Region: Approaches for a Sustainable Development*, Trento: Temi Editrice.
ESPON (2014), 'GREECO: Territorial Potentials for a Greener Economy', Final Report, ESPON/Tecnalia.
Ferguson, P. (2015), 'The green economy agenda: business as usual or transformational discourse?' *Environmental Politics*, **24** (1), 17–37.
Geels, F.W. (2005), *Technological Transitions and System Innovations: A Co-evolutionary and Socio-technical Analysis*, Cheltenham, UK and Northampton, MA, USA: Edward Elgar Publishing.
Geels, F. and J. Schot (2007), 'Typology of socio-technical transition pathways', *Research Policy*, **36** (3), 399–417.
Gendron, C. (2014), 'Beyond environmental and ecological economics: proposal for an economic sociology of the environment', *Ecological Economics*, **105**, 240–253.
Gibbs, D. and K. O'Neill (2014), 'The green economy, sustainability transitions and transition regions: a case study of Boston', *Geografiska Annaler: Series B, Human Geography*, **96** (3), 201–216.
Gibson-Graham, J.K. (2008), 'Diverse economies: performative practices for "other worlds"', *Progress in Human Geography*, **32** (5), 613–632.
Grasseni, C. (2014), 'Seeds of trust. Italy's *Gruppi di Acquisto Solidale* (Solidarity Purchase Groups)', in B.J. Burke and B.W. Shear (eds), 'Non-capitalist political ecologies', *Journal of Political Ecology*, **21**, 127–221.
Graute, U. (2016), 'Local authorities acting globally for sustainable development', *Regional Studies*, **50** (11), 1931–1942.
Haughton, G. and K. Morgan (2008), 'Editorial: sustainable regions', *Regional Studies*, **42** (9), 1219–1222.
Healy, A. and K. Morgan (2012), 'Spaces of innovation: learning, proximity and the ecological turn', *Regional Studies*, **46** (8), 1041–1053.

HM Government (2008), *Building A Low Carbon Economy: Unlocking Innovation and Skills*, London: DEFRA.

Hodson, M. and S. Marvin (2010), 'Can cities shape socio-technical transitions and how would we know if they were?', *Research Policy*, **39** (4), 477–485.

Hodson, M., E. Burrai and C. Barlow (2016), 'Remaking the material fabric of the city: "alternative" low carbon spaces of transformation or continuity?', *Environmental Innovations and Societal Transitions*, **18**, 128–146.

Hopkins, R. (2008), *The Transition Handbook*, Totnes: Green Books.

International Council for Local Environmental Initiatives (ICLEI) (2012), *Local Sustainability 2012: Showcasing Progress Case Studies*, Bonn: ICLEI.

Jonas, A.E.G., D. Gibbs and A. While (2011a), 'The new urban politics as a politics of carbon control', *Urban Studies*, **48** (12), 2537–2554.

Jonas, A.E.G., A. While and D. Gibbs (2011b), 'Carbon control regimes, eco-state restructuring and the politics of local and regional development', in A. Pike, A. Rodríguez-Pose and J. Tomaney (eds), *Handbook of Local and Regional Development*, London: Routledge, pp. 283–294.

Kallis, G. (2011), 'In defence of degrowth', *Ecological Economics*, **70** (5), 873–880.

Kenis, A. and M. Lievens (2016), 'Greening the economy or economizing the green project? When environmental concerns are turned into a means to serve the market', *Review of Radical Political Economics*, **48** (2), 217–234.

Lafferty, W.M. and M. Narodoslawsky (2003), *Regional Sustainable Development in Europe: The Challenge of Multi-level Cooperative Governance*, Oslo/Graz: ProSus.

Latouche, S. (2006), *Le pari de la décroissance*, Paris: Fayard.

Latouche, S. (2010), 'De-growth', *Journal of Cleaner Production*, **18** (6), 519–522.

Longhurst, N. (2015), 'Towards an "alternative" geography of innovation: alternative milieu, socio-cognitive protection and sustainability experimentation', *Environmental Innovations and Societal Transitions*, **17**, 183–198.

Mayer, H. and P. Knox (2008), 'Slow cities: sustainable places in a fast world', *Journal of Urban Affairs*, **28** (4), 321–334.

McCauley, S.M. and J.C. Stephens (2012), 'Green energy clusters and socio-technical transitions: analysis of a sustainable energy cluster for regional economic development in Central Massachusetts, USA', *Sustainability Science*, **7** (2), 213–225.

McGinnis, M.V. (1999), *Bioregionalism*, London: Routledge.

McManus, P. (2008), 'Mines, wines and thoroughbreds: towards regional sustainability in the Upper Hunter, Australia', *Regional Studies*, **42** (9), 1275–1290.

Meadowcroft, J. (2005), 'From welfare state to ecostate', in J. Barry and R. Eckersley (eds), *The State and Global Ecological Crisis*, Boston, MA: MIT Press, pp. 3–24.

Mol, A.P.J. (2002), 'Ecological modernisation and the global economy', *Global Environmental Politics*, **2** (2), 92–115.

Muro, M., J. Rothwell and D. Saha (2011), *Sizing the Green Economy: A National and Regional Green Jobs Assessment*, Washington DC: Brookings Institution.

North, P. (2014), 'Ten square miles surrounded by reality? Materialising alternative economies using local currencies', *Antipode*, **46** (1), 246–265.

Raven, R., J. Schot and F. Berkhout (2012), 'Space and scale in socio-technical transitions', *Environmental Innovation and Societal Transitions*, **4**, 63–78.

Ravetz, J. (2004), 'Editorial: Evaluation of regional sustainable development – mapping the landscape', *Journal of Environmental Assessment Policy and Management*, **6** (4), v–xxi.

Rip, A. and R. Kemp (1998), 'Technological change', in S. Rayner and E. Malone (eds), *Human Choices and Climate Change*, Volume 2, Columbus, OH: Batelle, pp. 327–399.

Roberts, P. and A. Colwell (2001), 'Moving the environment to centre stage: a new approach to planning and development at European and regional levels', *Local Environment*, **6** (4), 421–437.

Roelvink, G., K. St. Martin and J.K. Gibson-Graham (2015), *Making Other Worlds Possible: Performing Diverse Economies*, Minnesota, MN: University of Minnesota Press.

Seyfang G. (2003), 'Growing cohesive communities one favour at a time: social exclusion, active citizenship, and time banks', *International Journal of Urban and Regional Research*, **27** (3), 699–706.

Shear, B.W. (2014), 'Making the green economy: politics, desire, and economic possibility', *Journal of Political Ecology*, **21**, 193–209.

Smith, A. (2003), 'Transforming technological regimes for sustainable development: a role for alternative technology niches?', *Science and Public Policy*, **30** (2), 127–135.

Smith, A., J.-P. Voß and J. Grin (2010), 'Innovation studies and sustainability transitions: the allure of the multi-level perspective and its challenges', *Research Policy*, **39** (4), 435–448.

Späth, P. and H. Rohracher (2010), '"Energy regions": the transformative power of regional discourses on socio-technical futures', *Research Policy*, **39** (4), 449–458.

Späth, P. and H. Rohracher (2012), 'Local demonstrations for global transitions – dynamics across governance levels fostering socio-technical regime change towards sustainability', *European Planning Studies*, **20** (3), 461–479.

Truffer, B. and L. Coenen (2012), 'Environmental innovation and sustainability transitions in regional studies', *Regional Studies*, **46** (1), 1–21.

United Nations (UN) (2015), *Transforming Our World by 2030: A New Agenda for Global Action*, A/RES/70/1, 25 September, New York: UN.

United Nations Environment Programme (UNEP) (2011), *Towards a Green Economy: Pathways to Sustainable Development and Poverty Eradication – A Synthesis for Policy Makers*, accessed 8 March 2018 at http://drustage.unep.org/greeneconomy/sites/unep.org.greeneconomy/files/field/image/green_economyreport_final_dec2011.pdf

While, A., A.E.G. Jonas and D. Gibbs (2010), 'From sustainable development to carbon control: eco-state restructuring and the politics of urban and regional development', *Transactions of the Institute of British Geographers*, **35** (1), 76–93.

World Commission on Environment and Development (WCED) (1987), *Our Common Future*, Oxford: Oxford University Press.

PART III

REGION, POLITICS AND IDENTITY

16. Territory and governance
John Loughlin

16.1 INTRODUCTION

Territory and systems of governance are closely related but the meaning of the concepts and their relationship has changed over time. The primary meaning of territory is to denote a physical space, marked by recognizable boundaries within which societies exercise control. For both human and animals, this control is connected to food gathering and providing security for themselves and their off-spring against competitors, whether from their own species or others. Human beings also have the capacity to reflect on the meaning of territory and to change it according to circumstances both within their own societies and in their relations with other societies. This is true from the most primitive societies of hunters and gatherers to the most advanced and sophisticated civilizations of the ancient and modern worlds.

Human beings' understanding of their territory is closely related to their wider understanding of their place in the world, that is, to the mythological framework of their culture (Elden 2013, Chapter 1). The development of this understanding in the West draws on two principal sources: (1) Greco-Roman mythology, philosophy and law and (2) Judaeo-Christian religion and values which also incorporated some of the ideas of classical authors such as Plato, Aristotle and Cicero. It is impossible to understand modern conceptions of territory and governance without at least some awareness of these sources as Elden has shown.

Greek mythology often depicted human beings as the off-spring of mating between the earth itself (Gaia) and the sky (Uranus). There was thus an intimate relationship between Mother Earth and human beings, earth's off-spring (Elden 2013). It was this connection that led human beings to love the piece of territory on which they were born and to be willing to fight and die for it. This theme of the sacred nature of one's own piece of earth came to the fore in modern nationalism during the nineteenth century.

Territory, then, for human beings became more than a piece of earth but was imbued with religious and symbolic importance by the societies that developed on it. The Greeks and Romans reflected on how these societies should be organized and governed. Plato identified five different types of government – aristocracy, timocracy, oligarchy, democracy, and tyranny (*Republic*, Book VIII). Aristotle thought there were three main types – monarchy, oligarchy and democracy each of which could be good or bad although he favoured monarchy (*Politics*). The Romans were of a less philosophical bent than the Greeks but they too thought of territory in a mythological fashion similar to the Greeks from whom they borrowed much of their mythology. They also thought of the earth as a mother – *Tella Mater* or *Terra Mater*. But they had the notion of 'Father' as in *patria* referring to their society, that is, the community descended from their fathers. The famous phrase *dulce et decorum est pro patria mori* ('it is sweet and pleasant to die for the fatherland') is a line from a poem by the lyrical poet Horace and is used in modern times to refer to patriotism or nationalism. The Roman Republic and Empire however contained many peoples marked by different languages and religions and this diluted the link between territory, governance and identity.

The other primary source of Western thought about territory and governance comes from the synthesis the early Fathers of the Church made of the Bible and Greco-Roman philosophy and law (Ramsey 1993). Although the ancient Hebrews of the Old Testament shared some of the mythological conceptions of the surrounding peoples such as the Babylonians and Egyptians, they interpreted them in quite distinct ways (Day 2013). The key difference was that they believed that the earth was created from nothing (*creatio ex nihilo*) by a single God (monotheism). The Bible tells the story of a people – the Hebrews – specially chosen by Yahweh who gave them a piece of earth after he delivered them from bondage in Egypt. After many centuries, including exile in Babylon, this became Israel, still called the Holy Land. But there was a tension, especially in Prophets such as Isaiah, between this exclusive notion of a particular people, chosen by God, and rooted in a specific piece of the earth, and God's universal message of salvation that was destined for all of mankind (Rivers 2009).

Christianity at first shared this ambiguity but, under the influence of St Paul, the universalism prevailed. Thus began the long and complex history of Christianity spreading out into the Roman Empire and other parts of the world and gradually replacing the old pagan religions. St Augustine describes this process in the *City of God* published in AD 426 which became the standard influence on thinking about territory and governance for the next thousand years.

These introductory reflections show the importance of history, religion and culture for understanding governance and territory. Although the modern Western world has undergone three centuries of secularization, its culture is rooted in historical developments not just of institutions but also of religion and culture. This chapter will outline in a somewhat summary form these historical developments before analysing contemporary developments in governance and territory.

16.2   HISTORICAL DEVELOPMENT OF GOVERNANCE

16.2.1   The Post-Classical and Mediaeval Periods

The Roman Empire was united by a common system of law, a vast communications system of roads and administration, an expanding Roman citizenship (Beard 2016). In AD 330 the Emperor Constantine moved the seat of the Empire from Rome to the newly named city of Constantinople, and the Pope became effectively the governor of Rome. The Western part of the Empire, from the fifth to the sixth centuries AD, disintegrated under the attacks of Barbarian tribes and gradually broke up into distinctive kingdoms. During this period, territory was fluid and it was at times difficult to know where one kingdom ended and the next began. The Christians of the East, known as Byzantines who were under the authority of the Byzantine Emperor, gradually drifted apart from those of the West both theologically and spiritually, until, in 1054, there was a breach that has never been healed.

But it is developments in the West that interest us here. First, the Roman system of administration was replaced by 'feudalism' whereby powerful patrons protected clients and received in turn loyalty and goods in kind such as the produce of land or service in the lord's military forces replaced Roman law (Bloch 1940 [2014]). Second, some of these societies developed into kingdoms whose rulers claimed sovereignty over defined territories although the state was still quite primitive (Spruyt 1994). Third, was the founding of the Holy Roman Empire by the Frankish King Charlemagne who was crowned by Pope Leo III in AD 800 (Wilson 2016). After the death of Charlemagne, however, the Empire was divided among his sons and the title passed to what was in effect the Germanic Empire. Fourth (unlike in the Byzantine East) the Church under the leadership of the Pope became a territorial as well as spiritual ruler and the Church's relationship with the Emperor and the other secular powers in Europe came to determine the course of European history. The fifth development was the revival and growth of cities from the eleventh century and the emergence of a new burgher class (Berman 1983). This led to the formation of city leagues, such as the Hanseatic which was itself a kind of state but not confined to a particular territory, the emergence of city states such as Florence, Venice and Milan mainly on the Italian peninsula, and 'free' cities within the Empire (Spruyt 1994).

By the late Middle Ages, therefore, territory and governance were marked by an extraordinary complexity with different, overlapping orders of law and sovereignty, in which a piece of territory could be subject to several different 'governors' – the Pope, the Emperor, the local bishop or abbey, the monarch, the city authorities and the feudal baron (Berman 1983). The overarching entity was the Catholic Church and there was division of labour between canon law and the different systems of secular law. From about 1050 onwards, however, under Pope Gregory VII, Rome began a process of centralization and standardization of canon law with the aim of withdrawing the Church from the control of the secular powers. Harold Berman called this the 'Papal Revolution' and he claimed that the Western Church was the world's first 'nation-state' (Berman 1983, pp. 85–120). At the same time, the other powers, especially the Emperor, while still recognizing the spiritual authority of the Pope, contested his right to secular authority. The history of Europe from the eleventh century until the sixteenth century Reformation was that of struggle and shifting alliances between these entities of governance (Spruyt 1994).

In summary, pre-Reformation Europe was marked by different systems of governance each of which claimed some role over the same pieces of territory or rather over those who lived on these territories. The two major systems were the Church, especially the Papacy but also bishops and abbeys, and the Empire who collaborated sometimes but were often in conflict with each other. The spiritual authority of the Pope reached to every corner of Christendom. The boundaries of the Empire itself shifted considerably throughout the 1,000 years of its existence and, at times, it covered most of Germany and the Low Countries, expanded into the Italian peninsula and included the Iberian Peninsula (Wilson 2016). Then there were the emerging monarchies or, as Spruyt calls them, 'territorial states'. Finally, came the cities which were sometimes found within the other systems, sometimes they aspired towards becoming city-states as in Italy or had more or less degrees of autonomy as in the Empire, sometimes forming 'leagues' such as the Hanseatic League.

Each of these systems made claims over the inhabitants of a particular territory. All were under the spiritual authority of the Church but they were also grouped according to their place of birth or language. These groupings were called 'nations' (from the Latin *natus*) and there were certainly stereotypes of national or ethnic characteristics (Smith 1986). But they were not 'nations' in the modern sense of the word. There were also 'states' and there were, already from about the tenth or eleventh centuries, governance entities corresponding to our modern 'states' but they lacked the resources or control over territories characteristic of their modern successors (Poggi 1978).

16.2.2   The Protestant Reformation and Catholic Counter-Reformation

All this would change with the Reformation that began in 1517 when Martin Luther challenged the authority of Rome and questioned several key aspects of the teaching of the Church. Probably without intending to, Luther sparked off a series of events that would change the history of Europe forever and, in the process, redefine the nature of governance and its relationship to territory. Harold Berman dubbed this the 'German [i.e. Lutheran] Revolution' (Berman 2003, pp. 29–198). The following developments may be noted.

Luther was backed by some of the German Princes who sought greater autonomy within the Empire and this led to the bitter conflict known as the Wars of Religion. In effect, the states of the Holy Roman Empire divided into Lutheran Protestant and Catholic States. The 1555 Peace of Augsburg formulated the principle of *cuius regio, eius religio* – the religion of the ruler (Protestant or Catholic) would be the religion of the state. But it was only in 1648 with the Treaty of Westphalia that this principle was finally put into practice. This is the origin of the modern system of international relations usually described as 'Westphalian'. Borders had always existed between territorial entities but now they became even 'harder'.

The second key development was the new link between the nation and (Christian) confessional identity (Greenfeld 1992). The old multidimensional identities of the pre-Reformation period gave way to more exclusive and totalizing identities of Protestant or Catholic. The old overarching ecclesial system that transcended all the particular languages and identities of European peoples was now replaced by national Churches: the Church of Sweden, the Church of Scotland, and so on. Although the Papacy resisted this 'nationalization' of the Church, the Catholic Church too was influenced by it. In France (Gallicanism), Spain, Ireland, and Poland, Catholicism became core elements of national identity. Leah Greenfeld argues thus that there were five 'paths' to the modern nation closely linked to a particular brand of Christianity: England (Protestant); France (Catholic); Germany (Protestant/Catholic); Russia (Orthodox); and the United States (originally Protestant). Of course, 'state' and 'nation' were still not completely aligned. This would have to wait some time yet.

The different theological traditions led to different conceptions of church-state relations and also of the nature of the state itself. This led to the development of distinctive state traditions in Europe and those countries influenced by European states (Dyson 2011). These different state traditions developed distinctive ways of conceptualizing the state, state-society relations and forms of territorial organization (Loughlin and Peters 1997).

16.2.3   The Enlightenment

During the eighteenth century, many European and American intellectuals responded to the Wars of Religion of the previous two centuries by a growing rejection of religion and its link with the state and the nation. This was the period of scientific discovery and the application of science to ever widening domains of daily life that was transforming economic production, work practices and opening up the world of travel. During the nineteenth century, steam ships and railways transformed the understanding of territory and people's relations with one another. This facilitated 'the great transformation' by which the market system replaced older systems of barter and social relations (Polanyi 1945 [2001]). The crucial development during this period was the growing alignment between the state, the nation and the market. The state itself was becoming ever more secular and the close link between Church and state that had existed since Westphalia was broken.

These vast shifts were some of the unintended consequences of the Reformation (Gregory 2012). The colonization of North America was, in part, a consequence of religious minorities fleeing persecution in Britain. The colonists revolted against rule by Britain and thus founded the United States of America, first as a confederation, then as a federation. Although federalism had existed before, the US was the first modern federation based on the principles of democracy, the separation of powers and the separation of church and state. It would become a model for subsequent states, especially those in Latin America (Hueglin and Fenna 2006). The American understanding of territorial governance was dominated by the idea of unlimited space and room for expansion towards the West and, right up to the twentieth century, new states were being added to the federation.

But the eighteenth-century Enlightenment produced another model of governance and territory. The French Revolution, begun in 1789, occurred in a France where the monarchy had been centralizing for several centuries although it co-existed with a system of provincial organization that recognized the great variety of customs and even languages that characterized the French territory (Hayward 1987; Loughlin 2007a). After the abolition of the monarchy, the more extreme Jacobin revolutionaries, in line with the scientific developments of eighteenth-century Europe, sought to impose a 'rational' and 'scientific' model of territorial organization based on grids. This was not adopted but the departmental system was a deliberate attempt to undermine the old territorial organization of provinces. Napoleon I consolidated this system with the creation of prefects appointed by the state who represented the central state at the local level and were supposed to represent local interests at the level of the national state (Machin 1977).

The French Revolution was also important in that it invented the notion of the nation-state, that is, the idea that nations should have states and states should coincide with nations. This became important as there was thus established a close link between national identity and territory (Rokkan and Urwin 1983). The French model of the nation-state also produced nationalism as a political ideology and movement. In the nineteenth century, the French model was often seen as being 'progressive' and 'modern' and was adopted by many states who won independence from imperial powers: Greece in 1832 after more than a decade of struggle with the Ottomans; Italy in 1870; Finland in 1917; Ireland in 1921; and many new states following decolonization in Africa after the Second World War.

Thus, by the end of the nineteenth century, there were two principal models of territorial governance: US federalism and French unitary centralism. Both models were nation-states but each organized its territory differently. Other models also existed (Loughlin et al. 2013).

The above is true of Western states, but we should also remember that from the fifteenth century onwards, empires developed as these states used newly developed means of travel (steam ships and railways) and more sophisticated weaponry to conquer lands in Asia and Africa. England, France, Spain, Portugal and the Netherlands all established empires from this period. In the nineteenth century, there was a renewed bout of imperial creation or expansion as France conquered North Africa and Germany founded colonies in Africa. Italy tried to do the same but was defeated in Abyssinia (modern Ethiopia) although it did occupy some Greek islands such as Rhodes and established a presence in Albania. The imperialist mode of governance over vast territories was made possible by the enlistment of local elites who governed on their masters' behalf, the most striking example of which was the Indian Raj. The end of the nineteenth and first half of the twentieth century was a period when these empires became rivals for hegemony over trade routes and control over the primary resources of industrialization. This led to military clashes including two world wars which almost destroyed most of the nations involved.

16.3   POST-SECOND WORLD WAR, NATIONS AND REGIONS

The Second World War was an attempt by the Axis powers of Germany, Italy and Japan to create new empires involving the direct enslavement of the subject peoples. Their defeat by the Allies led to dramatic changes in international relations and in the shape of Western states. First, the war was the death knell of the old empires of Britain, France and Portugal and these rapidly decolonized. Second, the United States emerged from the war more powerful economically and politically than ever and had to assist those European allies who were seriously damaged in both senses. Third, the recovery of the European states, assisted by US Marshall Funds, also took the form of the creation of welfare states which adopted different forms in different states.

16.3.1   The Welfare State

It has been argued that the welfare state was the final stage of nation-state building (Flora 1999). Previously, the nation-state, at least in its democratic form, provided a link between nation, state and citizenship giving citizens the right to participate politically in the affairs of the state through representative elections. The welfare state added social citizenship to political citizenship by creating a number of social rights to welfare. During this period, roughly between 1945 and 1975 (what the French call *Les Trente Glorieuses*), Western states expanded as they recovered from the Second World War thanks to the Marshall Funds.

The founding of welfare states profoundly affected their systems of governance and relationship to their territories (Loughlin 2007b). First, to deliver the expanding policy programmes, the states expanded in numbers of personnel, became more centralized as well as bureaucratic. Second, in both federal or unitary states power concentrated in central governments at the expense of subnational governments. The latter were important in the delivery of services but their autonomy was constrained by the parameters established by the centre. The emphasis was on standardization, symmetry and the inclusion of peripheral territories into the national polity. During the 1950s, regionalization did take place but it was almost always for economic development within the context of the nation as a whole rather than because of any recognition of regional and local identities, languages or cultures. Indeed, this was a period when many of those who possessed such identities and languages abandoned them to adapt to the national culture.

The institutions of the European Communities were established during this period but they were rather residual to the growing consolidation of the nation-states of their members. Nor did the EEC develop a significant regional policy until much later as we shall see below (Nugent 2010).

16.3.2   Crisis of the Welfare State, Neo-Liberalism, and Globalization

In the late 1960s, there were a number of crises of the welfare state partly because of the difficulties it had in financially sustaining its policies (the fiscal crisis) and partly because of events in international politics with the oil crises of 1973 and 1979 related to the Arab–Israeli conflict, and the collapse of the Bretton-Woods system of external exchange agreements (Joppke 1987). These developments also led to social unrest as unemployment rose thus putting even more strain on the welfare systems.

The most significant development in reaction to these crises was the emergence of what came to be known as 'neo-liberalism', an economic approach and ideology that had been in existence since the 1950s but which had been almost an underground movement buried by the dominant Keynesianism and welfare statism which it systematically opposed (Plant 2009; Harvey 2005). In fact, this was a survival of classical economic theory that sought a greater role for markets and a diminution in the role of the state in both society and the economy. UK Prime Minister Margaret Thatcher and US President Ronald Reagan applied this approach to public and especially economic policy.

In practice, this meant a reduction of subsidies to regions and local authorities and a shift away from top-down regional aid packages to an approach which encouraged regions to fend for themselves and mobilize their own resources rather than relying on the state. During this period, from the early 1980s onwards, new paradigms of regional development were developed: concepts such as the 'learning region' (Asheim 2018) or the 'innovative region' became popular among political elites and academics (Cooke and Morgan 1998). At the same time, 'neo-liberalism' became a dominant policy framework that encouraged 'competition' and 'fiscal federalism', seeking to apply market-based approaches also to territorial organization. 'Competitive regionalism', both within nation-states and with other regions internationally began to become a new way of thinking about relationships among regions (Burroni 2014).

Finally, the new neo-liberal policy approach, combined with the collapse of the Bretton-Woods systems of controls over international monetary exchanges led to a loosening of the rigid borders of the Westphalian state and could be seen as important factors in leading to the 'new globalization' that developed from the 1980s (Held et al. 1999; Steger 2009). 'Globalization' is a complex phenomenon which affected many different policy areas especially financial transactions with the creation of global financial markets that increasingly escaped from the controls of national governments and were allegedly self-regulating. But the systems of self-regulation were increasingly inadequate as banks and other financial institutions developed new and more sophisticated financial instruments such as derivatives. There was also globalization in the 'real' economy as new markets developed that transcended national economies which had been the traditional locus of economic activities. In this new world of global markets, subnational regions and even local authorities were meant to compete with each other by mobilizing their resources to attract inward investment (Amin and Thrift 1994). Furthermore, new technological developments such as the Internet and electronic banking meant that 'hard' territory was less important as a factor of investment. Previously, physical location near towns, railways, or ports was important. Now it was thought that other factors such as quality of life would become more important. Some authors spoke of 'deterritorialization' but also of 'reterritorialization' or 'supraterritoriality', that is, new ways of thinking about territory (Scholte 2000, p. 16).

16.3.3   European Integration

After its initial founding phase after the Second World War, European integration stagnated during the period of the *Trente Glorieuses* but then found a new lease of life at the end of the 1970s and early 1980s (Nugent 2010). This was, in large part, a response by European administrative, business and political elites to the above challenges of the crisis of the welfare state and Keynesian economic system, the emergence of neo-liberalism as a dominant paradigm and the new globalization. European leaders realized that their countries risked being dominated by the economic powers of the US and (the then powerful) Japanese bloc in the Far East. They realized that they could compete more successfully together rather than as individual states. This led to the 'relaunch' of Europe by French and German leaders Giscard d'Estaing and Helmut Schmidt in 1974, the declaration of the European Round Table of Industrialists in favour of integration in 1983, and the draft Treaty Establishing the European Union (the Spinelli Declaration) adopted by the European Parliament in 1984 (Cowles 1995). Finally, Jacques Delors, a convinced European federalist, became President of the European Commission in 1985 and launched the almost completely successful drive to complete the European internal market by 1 January 1993.

The accelerated pace of European integration had a profound impact on both the conceptualization and practice of governance and territory. Nation-states did not disappear as some of the more ardent European federalists desired, nor were they replaced by a federalist 'Europe of the Regions' (Loughlin 1996). Nevertheless, the nature and role of governments at different levels and their relations with each other were profoundly modified. First, the increasingly dominant European institutions, although not becoming a 'super-state' or a federation, as those hostile to the project claimed, did exercise control over many aspects of law, public policy and economic development. This constrained the room for manoeuvre of the member states. Second, subnational authorities, while still forming part of the governance system of their national states, could now relate directly to the European institutions, and especially the Commission, through the creation and increasing development of European Regional Policy and the Structural Funds from the mid-1980s (Loughlin 1996). The principles governing these funds were 'subsidiarity' and 'partnership' – not in opposition to national governments but usually in collaboration with them and the European institutions. This system of governance was dubbed 'multi-level governance' by Marks and Hooghe and others in several influential works (Hooghe and Marks 2001; Piattoni 2009). Subnational authorities, both regions and local authorities, nevertheless found new opportunities to escape the constraints of their own states, sometimes forming alliances with similar entities in other member states and, in some cases, even developing a kind of 'paradiplomacy', a term coined by Soldatos, by establishing in other countries even those outside the EU (Soldatos 1990).

All these developments led to new ways of conceptualizing 'territory' in Europe. Nation-states still existed with their national governments and traditional systems of territorial governance – federal, unitary and 'union' states. But there was now a new awareness of the wider European setting in which they were situated. Planners began to conceptualize planning on this Europe-wide scale and 'territory' was no longer confined to the land found within national borders (Adams et al. 2012). Geographical dimensions that transcended these borders were now recognized: coastal regions, mountain regions, cross-border regions, and so on. Some authors even claimed, with some justification, that features of the older pre-modern system before the nation-state were re-emerging (Zielonka 2007). Regions were becoming more prominent like the old provinces, world cities such as London, Paris and the Randstadt were similar to city-states, and even new city leagues were being recreated. It would be a mistake to think of this as a 'return' to the Middle Ages, despite its being dubbed 'neo-mediaevalism' (Bull 1977 [2012]). A better term might be 'post-modernism' although this suggests a leaving behind of modernity. Perhaps the best way of thinking about this is 'hybridity'. Some features of the pre-modern nation-state have re-emerged and, in some respects, we are developing new systems that are different from the nation-state (Loughlin 2013). Nevertheless, the modern nation-state has not disappeared but it now co-exists with the re-emerged regions and local authorities and with qualitatively different systems of governance thanks to the new technological developments. The concept of 'governance' attempts to capture this complexity (Rhodes 1997).

16.4   CONCLUDING REMARKS: THE 2008 FINANCIAL AND ECONOMIC CRISIS AND THEIR IMPACT ON EUROPEAN INTEGRATION

The narrative outlined largely concerns the emergence of the nation-state as the quintessential modern form of territorial governance which replaced the complex overlapping and multifarious systems of governance and law of the pre-modern and early modern periods. Nation-states basically divided into unitary and federal states with a few anomalous states such as the United Kingdom which can be characterized as 'union' states. The key concept of this system was the Westphalian notion of national sovereignty over a defined piece of territory with 'hard' borders. Within these borders sovereign national governments were free to organize their territories as they wished. The post-Second World War welfare states were the culmination of this process of nation-state building which had begun at the French Revolution almost two hundred years before.

A series of crises and developments such as globalization and, in Europe, the relaunch of integration quite significantly reconfigured this system by undermining the central role of national governments and introducing a much more complex system of different actors such as international organizations, including multinational corporations, the institutions of the European Union, but also regions and local authorities that became actors in their own right alongside their national governments. From the 1990s onwards, these processes seemed unstoppable. In 2007/8, however, they did quite considerably slow down and even, in some ways, went into reverse with the financial and economic crises of those years. Once again, national governments tried to regain control over financial global developments that were spinning out of control and menacing the stability of societies, at least in the developed Western states. One of the consequences of this has been the tightening up of central control over subnational authority borrowing and spending and of fiscal rules. Another has been the reversal of the tendency towards open borders and transmigration of labour. This was the case even before the devastation caused in the Middle East and the wars which followed the Arab Spring leading to vast migratory movements from that region to Western countries. Already, in the mid-2000s, the EU enlargement led to an influx of migrants especially to the UK and Ireland. But it was local authorities which had to cope with the consequences of this in areas such as housing and education. The more recent developments have exacerbated this. This has led to a rise of populist resentment and, in the UK, to Brexit thus strengthening the move towards the re-establishment of national sovereignty. Similar developments can be seen in the US and in other European countries. We are still in the middle of these developments but it would seem that we are witnessing a return to the status quo ante.

16.5   REFERENCES

Adams, N., G. Cotella and R. Nunes (2012), *Territorial Development, Cohesion and Spatial Planning: Building on EU Enlargement*, London: Routledge.
Amin, A. and N. Thrift (eds) (1994), *Globalization, Institutions and Regional Development in Europe*, Oxford: Oxford University Press.
Aristotle ([2000]), *The Politics* [translated by Trevor J. Saunders], London: Penguin.
Asheim B. (2018), 'Learning regions – a strategy for economic development in less developed regions?, in A. Paasi, J. Harrison and M. Jones (eds), *Handbook on the Geographies of Regions and Territories*, Cheltenham, UK and Northampton, MA, USA: Edward Elgar Publishing, pp. 130–140.
Beard, M. (2016), *SPQR: A History of Ancient Rome*, London: Profile Books.
Berman, H.J. (1983), *Law and Revolution: The Formation of the Western Legal Tradition*, vol. 1, Cambridge, MA: Harvard University Press.
Berman, H.J. (2003), *Law and Revolution II: the Impact of the Protestant Reformations on the Western Legal Tradition*, Cambridge, MA: Harvard University Press.
Bloch, M. (1940 [2014]), *Feudal Society*, Routledge Classics (first published in French in 1940), London: Routledge.
Bull, H. (1977 [2012]), *The Anarchical Society: A Study of Order in World Politics*, Basingstoke: Macmillan Palgrave, fourth edition.
Burroni, L. (2014), 'Competitive regionalism and the territorial governance of uncertainty', *Transfer: European Review of Labour and Research*, **20** (1), 83–97.
Cooke, P. and K. Morgan (1998), *The Associational Economy: Firms, Regions and Innovation*, Oxford: Oxford University Press.
Cowles, M.G. (1995), 'Setting the agenda for a new Europe: the ERT and EC 1992', *Journal of Common Market Studies*, **33** (4), 501–526.
Day, J. (2013), *From Creation to Babel: Studies in Genesis 1-11*, London: Bloomsbury.
Dyson, K. (2011), *The State Tradition in Western Europe: A Study of an Idea and an Institution*, Colchester: ECPR Press.
Elden, S. (2013), *The Birth of Territory*, Oxford: Oxford University Press.
Flora, P. (1999), 'Introduction and interpretation', in P. Flora, S. Kuhnle and D. Urwin (eds), *State Formation, Nation-Building and Mass Politics in Europe: The Theory of Stein Rokkan*, Oxford: Clarendon Press, pp. 1–91.
Greenfeld, L. (1992), *Nationalism: Five Roads to Modernity*, Cambridge, MA: Harvard University Press.
Gregory, B.S. (2012), *The Unintended Reformation: How a Religious Revolution Secularized Society*, Cambridge MA: Harvard University Press.

Harvey, D. (2005), *A Brief History of Neoliberalism*, Oxford: Oxford University Press.

Hayward, J.E.S. (1987), *Governing France: The One and Indivisible Republic*, London: Weidenfeld & Nicolson, second edition with 1986 postscript.

Held, D., D. Goldblatt, A. McGrew and J. Perraton (1999), *Global Transformations: Politics, Economics and Culture*, Cambridge: Polity Press.

Hooghe, L. and G. Marks (2001), *Multi-Level Governance and European Integration*, Lanham, MD and Oxford, UK: Rowman & Littlefield Publishers.

Hueglin, T.O. and A. Fenna (2006), *Comparative Federalism: A Systematic Inquiry*, Peterborough, ON: Broadview Press.

Joppke, C. (1987), 'The crisis of the welfare state, collective consumption, and the rise of new social actors', *Berkeley Journal of Sociology*, **32**, 237–260.

Loughlin, J. (1996), '"Europe of the Regions" and the federalization of Europe', *Publius: The Journal of Federalism*, **26** (4), 141–162.

Loughlin, J. and B.G. Peters (1997), 'State traditions, administrative reform and regionalization', in M. Keating and J. Loughlin (eds), *The Political Economy of Regionalism*, London: Frank Cass, pp. 41–62.

Loughlin, J. (2007a), *Subnational Government: The French Experience*, Basingstoke: Palgrave Macmillan.

Loughlin, J. (2007b), 'Reconfiguring the state: trends in territorial governance in European states', *Regional and Federal Studies*, **17** (4), 385–403.

Loughlin, J. (2013), 'Reconfiguring the nation-state: hybridity vs. uniformity', in J. Loughlin, J. Kincaid and W. Swenden (eds), *The Routledge Handbook of Regionalism and Federalism*, London: Routledge, pp. 3–18.

Loughlin, J., J. Kincaid and W. Swenden (eds) (2013), *The Routledge Handbook of Regionalism and Federalism*, London: Routledge.

Machin, H. (1977), *The Prefect in French Public Administration*, London: Croom Helm.

Nugent, N. (2010), *Government and Politics of the European Union*, Basingstoke: Palgrave Macmillan, seventh edition.

Piattoni, S. (2009), 'Multi-level governance: a historical and conceptual analysis', *European Integration*, **31** (2), 163–180.

Plant, R. (2009), *The Neo-Liberal State*, Oxford: Oxford University Press.

Plato ([2017]) *The Republic of Plato*, vol. 8 (Classic Reprint), London: Forgotten Books.

Poggi, G. (1978), *The Development of the Modern State: A Sociological Introduction*, London: Hutchinson.

Polanyi, K. (1945 [2001]), *The Great Transformation: The Political and Economic Origins of Our Time*, Boston, MA: Beacon Press.

Ramsey, B. (1993), *Beginning to Read the Fathers*, London: Student Christian Movement.

Rhodes, R.A.W. (1997), *Understanding Governance: Policy Networks, Governance, Reflexivity, and Accountability*, Buckingham, UK and Philadelphia, PA: Open University Press.

Rivers, J. (2009), 'The nature and role of government in the Bible', in N. Spencer and J. Chaplin (eds), *God and Government*, London: Society for the Propagation of Christian Knowledge, pp. 40–60.

Rokkan, S. and D.W. Urwin (1983), *Economy, Territory, Identity: Politics of West European Peripheries*, London: Sage.

Scholte, J. (2000), *Globalization: A Critical Introduction*, Basingstoke: Palgrave Macmillan.

Smith, A.D. (1986), *The Ethnic Origins of Nations*, London: Basil Blackwell.

Soldatos, P. (1990), 'An explanatory framework for the study of federated states as foreign-policy actors', in H.J. Michelmann and P. Soldatos (eds), *Federalism and International Relations: The Role of Subnational Units*, Oxford: Clarendon, pp. 34–53.

Spruyt, H. (1994), *The Sovereign State and its Competitors: An Analysis of Systems Change*, Princeton, NJ: Princeton University Press.

Steger, M. (2009), *Globalization: A Very Short Introduction*, Oxford: Oxford University Press.

Wilson, P.H. (2016), *The Holy Roman Empire: A Thousand Years of Europe's History*, London: Allen Lane.

Zielonka, J. (2007), *Europe as Empire: The Nature of the Enlarged European Union*, Oxford: Oxford University Press.

17. Territorial rights and justice
Cara Nine

> How can a man or a people seize an immense territory and keep it from the rest of the
> world except by a punishable usurpation, since all other are being robbed, by such an act, of
> the place of habitation and the means of subsistence which nature gave them in common?
> (Rousseau 1920, p. 20)

Any philosophical theory of territorial rights must include an account of Who and
What. Who is qualified to hold territorial rights? What is a territorial right? In addition
to conceptual analysis, a *theory* of territorial rights will tell us Why. Why are territorial
rights justified, if at all?

This chapter articulates the concept of territorial rights (the What), and also sets up a
framework for addressing the kind of agent that may hold territorial rights (the Who). In
the final section, I defend a particular set of values that set the framework for a theory of
territorial rights (the Why).

17.1   WHAT – THE PARTS OF TERRITORIAL RIGHTS

A territorial right includes the following component rights:

(A)   Jurisdictional rights over persons within the territory;
(B)   Jurisdictional rights over resources within the territory;
(C)   Ownership rights over resources; and
(D)   Control of borders.

There is a difference between, for example, a right to establish justice regarding the civil
liberties of persons within a region (part of (A), jurisdictional right over persons) and a
right to declare the nationalization of domestic oil reserves (part of (B), jurisdictional
right over resources). The direct object of the former right is persons within a certain
region, and the direct object of the latter is (non-human) resources within the same
region. The holder of a territorial right has the authority to legislate rights regarding only
persons, like freedom of speech, and rights regarding goods, like property or resource
rights. Jurisdictional authority in persons and resources encompasses powers and rights
such as legislative power to determine systems of rights over persons and goods within the
region; adjudicative power to interpret these rights; and enforcement power to enforce the
rights (Simmons 2001). Jurisdictional authority over resources (B) includes these powers
regarding resources, most importantly the powers to determine property rights over
resources. Together these powers comprise the necessary elements of a territorial right.

A benefit of this definition is that it separates the necessary from the contingent elements of the territorial right. On this definition, (A) and (B) are necessary elements of a

territorial right, and (C) and (D) are only contingently part of the right. As necessary elements, a territorial right exists only if both (A) and (B) hold. By contrast, a territorial right may exist even if (C) and (D) do not hold. The distinction between (B) the jurisdictional right over resources, and (C) the ownership rights over resources, is significant. Each includes a distinct set of incidents of rights over resources, and each is justified by a different kind of theory. (B) captures the incidents of territorial rights that convey jurisdictional powers of legislation, adjudication and enforcement to the holder of the right. Conversely, ownership rights include incidents of the right to access resources, to manage resources, to value retention from the sale of resources, and so on. For instance, jurisdictional rights over resources include powers to legislate, adjudicate, and enforce rights over goods in the region, including rules of taxation and the (limited) power to determine, through rule of law, the use of goods in that region. In comparison, the incidents of ownership rights over resources include a set (and not necessarily a full set) of the following incidents that includes rights of access, management, extraction, alienation (to sell something to another party), and to obtain proceeds from those sales. To illustrate, ownership may be entirely held by individual members, like Texan property owners owning the oil beneath their land. This property is not held by the entire collective, as the collective holds all of Texas as a territory. But rather, the personal property is governed by the collective.

Authority to control borders, (D), is a contingent, not a necessary, part of a territorial right, because the right to control borders is not necessary for jurisdictional control within a region. In fact, it is not clear that eliminating border control would undermine any of the other rights. It is coherent that collectives hold rights of jurisdictional authority over territory and at the same time to maintain that the same collectives do not have the right to control their borders (Fine 2010; Macedo 2007, pp. 63–68).

In sum, the component parts of a territorial right are normally understood as including, to some extent, all four component rights: jurisdictional authority over persons and resources, ownership of resources, and control of borders. Unlike resource ownership and border control, jurisdictional authority is *essential* for territorial rights, and therefore theoretical justifications of territorial rights focus here.

17.2 WHO – COLLECTIVES WITH RIGHTS OF SELF-DETERMINATION

Since territorial rights should be understood primarily as jurisdictional rights over persons and resources, the 'who' of territorial rights must be agents who demonstrate the capacity to establish legitimate rule of law. For the most part, these agents will be collectives whose members share a general interest in or desire to be collectively self-determining. This position runs contrary to three alternative positions: (1) that *individuals* hold territorial rights, (2) that *states* hold territorial rights, and (3) that collectives hold territorial rights only in virtue of some *ascriptive* feature of the collective, such as cultural identity.

First, individuals, such as monarchs, should not be understood as the holders of territorial rights. Yet in places like Saudi Arabia, we have examples of monarchical rule, and they seem to have territorial rights. The point here is that the monarchy does not have territorial rights. But rather, the people of Saudi Arabia (for example) hold these rights. The assertion that the people, instead of a monarch or leader, should hold political authority within a territory is a fairly recent development, marked by the end of colonialism after the Second World War (Cassese 1995, pp. 48–56). As is true of many historical political shifts, such as the end of slavery, the importance of self-determination is not merely a matter of historical contingency; it is also supported by important normative considerations. Former colonies threw off colonial rule in the name of 'self' rule, or self-determination. Self-determining collectives have a unique fit with territorial rights because these collectives are capable of establishing a *legitimate* rule of law. Given the nature of territorial rights in establishing jurisdictional authorities, these rights are properly held by those collectives that are capable of establishing legitimate rule of law. Because territorial rights are jurisdictional rights, the exercise of these rights establishes rule of law that coerces persons. Only an agent with the legitimate authority to coerce those particular persons can hold territorial rights. A self-determining collective fits this description, because this collective rules itself – it is not dominated by foreigners or other powerful agents. The introduction of the liberal idea of legitimate jurisdictional authority compels the conclusion that only collectives with a right to self-determination are candidates as holders of territorial rights.

Second, it is problematic to say that states are the holders of territorial rights. Here, 'state' refers to the set of functioning institutions that effectively make, adjudicate, and enforce law within the region. By contrast, the 'collective' mainly refers to the collective of persons that consists of the enduring, trans-generational membership of that collective. In the case of a failed state, for example, it is fair to say that the state as a set of functioning institutions is practically non-existent. The collective, however, continues to exist. The Republic of Sierra Leone went through a period of extreme turbulence in the 1990s. The war, displacement, and corruption during this decade brought about an extensive breakdown of the rule of law resulting in widespread suffering and human rights violations. During this time Sierra Leone was a failed state. However, it does not seem that Sierra Leone lost its full set of territorial rights during this time. Imagine that a foreign occupying force established functioning state institutions there. This foreign force would not have the liberty to enforce any laws, but rather it will be bound by the establishment of a rule of law that would be legitimate for Sierra Leoneans. Moreover, the foreign force would not acquire jurisdictional rights in perpetuity in the form of annexing the territory. Instead, they would be bound to transfer their powers back to the Sierra Leoneans after a time. Finally, a foreign occupying force would not have ownership rights to sell off and reap the benefits of Sierra Leonean resources like diamonds. The case of a failed state demonstrates the benefits of distinguishing between the collective and the state. The collective signifies the agent that holds rights when the state no longer exists.

Even more, the collective is the normative source of territorial rights. The collective is normatively important because it is comprised of individuals, and their decisions and interests are the normative source for legitimizing political power. A state, by contrast, is merely a set of institutions. It is a tool to establish jurisdictional authority. As a tool, it is not itself the holder of the relevant rights. The right-holder is the wielder of the tool, that is, the collective. This is why the state institutions may fail to exist, as in the case of Sierra Leone, while the territorial right is still in place; the individuals remain and they are the locus of moral concern. The right is held by the collective, because the members' moral importance provides the reasons for the territorial right in the first place. And the individual members exist even when state institutions do not.

This position requires that there is a way to identify the collective without the existence of a state. Theorists disagree about how to identify the qualities that characterize a collective as having a right to self-determination, but there is consensus about the fact that all of these collectives share one crucial feature: the members of the collective have a significant interest in or will that the collective be politically autonomous; they desire/have an interest in making significant social and political decisions for their collective that are respected by outsiders (Margalit and Raz 1990; Miller 2007; Philpott 1995). The Sierra Leoneans are an example of such a group in that they desire to be politically autonomous, and, further, in the period before state failure, they demonstrated a capacity to organize themselves to be self-determining.

Third, it is important to examine the view that a collective may hold resource rights merely in virtue of an ascriptive feature of that collective, such as cultural, ethnic, or national identity (Buchanan 2003). The ascriptive characteristic of the collective is not a sufficient condition for the collective to be a potential holder of a resource right; the collective must also demonstrate an interest in being or a desire to be self-determining and a capacity for the establishment of a legitimate rule of law over itself. In order to be a candidate for a right, the holder must be capable of fulfilling the function of the right. In the case of territorial rights, if a right holder is not the type of agent that can fulfil the function of the right, that is, in establishing legitimate rule of law, then necessarily injustice ensues from this right holder having the right to resources. The effects of this injustice are devastating for many persons inside and outside of the territory. Because the function of a territorial right is the establishment of the rule of law, it is the collective's capacity to fulfill this function that fits with the right and not an ascriptive feature of the collective, such as culture or nationality.

17.3 WHY – JUSTIFYING TERRITORIAL CLAIMS

In the above sections, the concept of territorial rights (the What and, to a certain extent, the Who) is explained. The Why remains. This section sketches a collectivistic Lockean framework for explaining particular territorial rights. A particular right to territory is a right to a specific portion of the Earth. This is in contrast with a general right to territory, or a claim to be self-determining over some territory, even if the particular territory is not yet identified. Ireland has a particular right to (most of) the island of Ireland. It does not, for example, have a particular territorial right to the island of Hispaniola.

Territorial rights theories that utilize John Locke's philosophy have the strongest potential to explain particular territorial rights, because Locke's theory justifies rights over things in the absence of any government or society with the moral authority to assign rights. This reasoning avoids circular argumentation in justifying territorial rights. The circular worry goes like this: Assume that exclusive rights over goods require a government or other moral authority to assign those rights. But territorial rights constitute, in part, the political authority that assigns rights by giving the government form and domain. To justify the territorial right itself would need to reference an even higher political authority, one that would have the authority to distribute rights globally. But since there seems to be no such authority, then territorial rights must be justified on some other grounds (Brilmayer 1989).

Locke argued that persons could acquire rights over goods by having certain interactions with those goods. Not just any interaction will do – the interaction has to be value-generating. When a person invests her labour in the land, the land becomes more valuable. The owner of the labour deserves the product of her labour, because it is her labour that made the product valuable (Locke 2003, book 2, chapter 5). When an agent acquires a right over a good, that right is exclusionary; that good belongs to her and to nobody else. Applied to territory: if a territory is made more valuable by a collective, then that collective has an exclusionary claim to the territory. A collective acquires a territorial right by working particular resources in that geographical area, including agricultural land, aquifers, mountains, valleys and minerals. The geographical location of these resources fixes the territorial right on the map; the collective claims territory over those specific lands, aquifers, and minerals, and not over similar resources in a different location.

This strain of territorial rights theories identifies three relevant values: material value, symbolic value, and the value of justice. David Miller defends territorial rights as based on material and symbolic values. Regarding material value, a collective's coordinated efforts under the guidance of social and political institutions are the source of value-creation in its resources. These actions include cross-generational technological advances and conservation efforts coordinated by communities and enforced by rule of law that engender beneficial material results ranging from real estate value to the fundamental values of providing food, clothing and shelter to individuals. Symbolic value, by contrast, picks out the cultural, religious, or social meanings that a group attributes to certain places or features. The site of an historical battle, the sacred river, and the mythological skyline illustrate the symbolic meaning of territory (Meisels 2009; Miller 2012). Symbolic value emerges out of deep connections – the collective's values and ways of life are shaped by the territory, and the territory, in concord, reflects them. Through these connections, the territory becomes an emblem of the collective itself, representing their identity and culture. On Miller's theory, territorial rights can be justified indirectly over particular resources, because jurisdictional authority is necessary to secure collective claims to the material and symbolic values embodied there.

The third conception of value, the value of justice, justifies territorial rights on the basis of the collective's capacity to establish legitimate rule of law. When the collective uses the resources within that territory to achieve the value of justice, a right is acquired over a particular territory. Because the function of a territorial right is the establishment of the legitimate rule of law, when a collective interacts with territorial resources to create just institutions, it comes to deserve a territorial right over those resources (Nine, 2013).

The value of justice seems most fitting for establishing territorial rights, because many groups and individuals can create material and symbolic value within a certain place. Chinese corporations working on foreign land create significant increases in material resource value, for example. And non-territorial religious collectives construct symbolic value in specific locations. The role of justice, however, uniquely fits territorial rights as rights of jurisdictional authority. Jurisdictional authority is important for the ways that it affects individual rights and interests. Most importantly, jurisdictional authority solves the coordination problem, and this is an important means for creating other kinds of value. The 'coordination problem' signifies the obstacles undermining rational pursuits that arise from lack of coordination between persons. The problem can be expressed in terms of both its negative, harmful effects and its solution's positive, constructive effects. The negative effects occur when existing pursuits or interests are thwarted or harmed as a result of the lack of coordination. For example, I cannot safely drive to visit my mother if drivers in my society have not agreed on certain road rules, like driving on the left-hand side of the road. The positive effects occur when coordination creates an avenue for the creation of new pursuits and goods which would not be available without coordination. A group of persons may develop a cure for a type of cancer, but only by relying on the coordinated efforts that produced the education system that collected and dispensed certain kinds of knowledge to the young scientists.

Additionally, territorial jurisdictional authority is important for the coordination of geographically dependent common goods. A common good is, 'a set of conditions which enables the members of a community to attain for themselves reasonable objectives, or to realize reasonably for themselves the value(s), for the sake of which they have reason to collaborate with each other' (Finnis 2011, p. 155). Geographically dependent common goods such as potable water, sewers, public education, healthcare, and public order are necessary for meeting individual basic needs. Each requires (among other things) reconciling competing values and the management of resources. Decisions regarding these prior issues (negotiating competing values and resource management) must be made in order to coordinate action effectively that brings about the common good. Because several different decisions can be made that sufficiently achieve these various ends, an authority is often required in order to determine a course of action between the alternatives. Likewise, the same authority is often required to provide the coercive force that imposes obligations necessary for solving the coordination problem. With political authority inevitably comes the coercive structures of political institutions, compelling those living under the institutions to live according to institutional rules. Enforcement of rules creates a stable environment which is crucial for individuals to reliably access the objects of their basic needs.

Because the jurisdictional authority over territory is a crucial means to solving important coordination problems, such as the provision of potable water, sewers, property rights, public order, and so on, attributing the right of jurisdictional authority over territory to an agent that solves the coordination problem serves basic individual interests. This is the moral mandate of territorial rights – that the right only exists if the exercise of the right functions to meet individuals' basic needs. Thus only an agent capable of solving the coordination problem may claim authority over territory.

Since there are many different adequate solutions to many different coordination problems, we cannot hold an authority to any particular solution. Rather, for the purposes of justifying a collective right to jurisdictional authority over territory, the authority must only demonstrate that it has the capacity to adequately solve the coordination problem to the extent that it secures the objects of its members' basic needs. One familiar way to articulate this condition is that the agent must demonstrate the capacity to meet minimal standards of justice. From the above analysis, and in accordance with other theories of political legitimacy, I identify the 'minimum standards of justice as the adequate protection and respect for human rights of both members and non-members' (Altman and Wellman 2009, p. 13; Buchanan 2004, p. 234), where human rights are understood in terms of securing access to the objects of basic individual needs. Minimum standards of justice also include standards of non-aggressive behaviour towards other self-determining groups, and similar standards of good conduct in the international sphere (such as honouring treaties, accepting refugees, and so on). Meeting the minimum standards of justice importantly establishes a base for political legitimacy upon which a group can justify coercive political structures that are necessarily a part solving the coordination problem. Further, political authority must be legitimate. That is, to meet minimal standards of justice, the authority must be able to secure access to basic needs without undermining basic liberties, such as the right of self-rule.

The value of justice-creation matches the purpose and form of territorial rights and is strengthened by examining the way that acquisition of territory is justified. Three normative concepts play a role in further justifying territorial rights: desert, efficiency, and autonomy.

17.4   THE PRINCIPLE OF DESERT

The desert principle applied to rights to land has considerable intuitive appeal. It is the influence behind many legal instantiations of property acquisitions, such as squatter's rights (when a trespasser acquires title to another's land through adverse possession and use of the land). On a Lockean theory of desert claims to territory, collectives can come to deserve territorial rights over particular geographical regions. The Lockean principle of desert applied to territory can be stated as: If the value of the territory T is significantly attributable to an agent X, then agent X has a weak rights claim to T. The rights claim generated by the Lockean principle of desert is weak because it may be defeated by other considerations, most importantly by another agent's prior rights claim to T.

Locke appeals to desert as a justification for particular property rights. When a person invests her labour in the land, the land produces valuable products. The value of those products and of the land is attributed mostly to the labour. The owner of the labour, then, deserves the product of her labour, because it is her labour that made the product valuable (Locke 2003, chapter 5; Schrader-Frechette 1993).

On the principle of desert, if the value of a territory is significantly attributable to the collective, then the collective has a weak rights claim to the territory. The collective is a unique and significant author of the land's value in several different ways. The collective's governance of land use creates stable systems of agriculture and other forms of production that create value in land (and air and water) at any particular time and over long periods of time. Much of the value of the lands occupied by the members of a collective is due to the coordinated efforts of those members under the guidance of collective institutions, coordinated by communities and enforced by rule of law. Even in cases of foreign ownership, where Chinese corporations mine resources in Australia, for example, the Australian government and social rules determine by whom and how resources should be used and extracted. These actions engender many kinds of valuable results ranging from real estate value to the fundamental value of providing food, clothing and shelter to individuals.

The activity that generates a right to jurisdictional authority on the basis of desert is the creation of justice. When a musician performs beautifully, we do not say that the musician deserves an Olympic gold medal for competitive diving. There is a fit between what an agent deserves and which values they have created. A collective comes to deserve jurisdictional authority over territory by interacting with the territory in such a way that demonstrates that they have the capacity to establish legitimate rule of law. This conception of desert fits with the particular right. For a system of jurisdictional authority over territory, the value of providing justice – through institutions necessary for the provision of basic individual needs – is served only if a collective with the capacity to establish justice is in possession of the right to establish rule of law.

It is unusual to apply the desert principle to territorial rights, because this seems to create counter-intuitive incentives for colonization. If a group seizes an area and enforces the rule of law there, then on the principle of desert, it seems like they would have a claim to territorial rights over the unjustly seized lands. However, the principle of desert grants only a weak claim to territorial authority. This claim does not become an entitlement unless it is consistent with the overall system of territorial rights. As David Schmidtz explains:

> A just system works to minimize the extent to which people's entitlements fly in the face of what they deserve, but not at a cost of compromising people's ability to form stable expectations regarding their entitlements, and thus to get on with their lives in peaceful and productive ways. (Schmidtz 2006, pp. 69–70)

Desert claims may be trumped by other considerations, such as a previous entitlement, especially if that entitlement continues to be deserved by the collective that holds it. This does not entail that desert claims are never successful against conflicting entitlements. But it does require that desert claims leading to entitlement and existing legitimate entitlements must be made consistent under an overall system that balances the competing claims in ways that allow for the functions of the rights to be fulfilled.

Additionally, the principle of desert has a distinct benefit in that it explains how a collective of people can have a right to a homeland without relying on market, nationalist or cultural accounts of that land's value. The Lockean theory of territory articulates why a collective has a claim to territory over land with which it has a deep, historical connection. The right is a right to a particular piece of land affected by a relationship with the collective over time; it takes time to establish justice and efficient patterns of land use. This relationship can be described as a deeply felt relationship because members of the collective have worked hard to make the collective successful in its attempts to establish a just and fair use of resources within the territory. Further, this historical rights connection cannot be overridden by alternative external attempts to 'mix their labour' with the land.

17.5   THE PRINCIPLE OF EFFICIENCY

The principle of efficiency explains territorial rights in two ways. One is from the institutional perspective, and one is from the particular rights perspective. From the institutional perspective, the principle of efficiency states that, all other things being equal, a system of rights to land that makes most efficient use of the land is to be preferred. From the institutional perspective, we're not justifying that the US should have territorial rights to the Hawaiian Islands, for example. Instead, we're justifying the international set of institutions that endorses and perpetuates particular territorial rights, as opposed to an international system that denies territorial rights.

For Locke, efficiency is a key motivation for the original members of the social contract to enter political society. Political society provides a common judge to which citizens can appeal for jurisprudence. The presence of a common judge and of the mechanisms to enforce law is what stabilizes a social system. As argued above, territorial jurisdictional authority is essential for achieving a solution to the coordination problem which allows for individuals to meet their basic needs.

At the particular rights level, principles concerning the efficient use of land are spelled out in comparative terms. An agent is said to have a better claim to land if they use that land more efficiently. Like with the principle of desert, controversy follows the principle of efficiency, and in this case targets the ambiguous and perhaps culturally relative nature of value. Margaret Moore argues that an efficiency principle applied to territorial rights would be impossible to implement because each collective of people values their land and its use in different ways. 'Efficient use of' and 'wasted' land will mean different things for different peoples. One people will value old, untouched wilderness while another values the economic development (such as logging) of wilderness (Moore 1998).

We can overcome this objection by focusing, again, on the value of territorial rights. It is important to remember that the primary function and value of a territorial right is the establishment of justice through the creation of institutions that provide individuals with secure access to the objects of basic needs. Efficiency in territorial rights should be measured in the capacity of collectives to establish justice. Because justice is measured on this theory in terms of universal values (the meeting of individual basic needs including things that make it possible for a people to be politically organized), 'justice' is a value that arguably transcends cultural difference (Nussbaum 2000). The list of basic needs can help us to articulate universal meanings of 'wasted' and of 'used efficiently'. If a land is not utilized, but is capable of providing goods like food, shelter, and a place to assemble, and there is a people who has no food, shelter or place to gather, then there is a reason from efficiency to allow the people access to the unutilized land. Similarly, we can say that a land is wasted if political authorities use this land in unjust ways – ways that prevent individuals from meeting their basic needs.

Additionally, once land has been acquired, it cannot be acquired by a different party merely because they are using it more efficiently. That is, you can't take somebody else's stuff just because you might be able to use it better (Bishop 1997, pp. 316–317). The reason behind this rule, especially regarding territorial rights, is that a system of territorial rights that protects historical rights is most efficient in achieving territorial justice. Security and stability in the institution of territorial rights are essential background features of the collective's ability to establish just institutions. This analysis supports a system of territorial rights where collectives hold these rights in perpetuity, over a region where they have demonstrated the capacity to establish just rule of law within and over the territorial domain.

17.6   THE PRINCIPLE OF AUTONOMY

With respect for the justification of *property* rights, autonomy plays two important roles. First, respect for individual autonomy is a crucial premise in the argument for property from self-ownership. Locke states that, 'the natural liberty of man is to be free from any superior power on earth, and not to be under the will or legislative authority of man' (Locke 2003, chapter 4, paragraph 22). Because we are not inferior to any other creature (on Earth) our natural liberty gives us a claim to self-ownership, including ownership over our own bodies and labour. Through our natural liberty, we have the capacity to mix our labour with other things, thereby extending our ownership rights to the things that are laboured upon (Locke 2003, chapter 5, paragraph 27). In other words, we are able to own things because we are autonomous beings.

Second, respect for individual autonomy provides a trigger for the Lockean Proviso. That is, if an agent's personal liberties are severely curtailed because they lack access to property, then property rights should be changed so as to alleviate this burden. Property rights are justified only under conditions where agents do not need those particular goods in order to meet their basic individual needs.

Each of these arguments can be adapted for collective territorial rights. Territorial rights are necessary for autonomy, because they are a prerequisite for the realization of a right of self-determination (Margalit and Raz 1990; Young 2007, pp. 47–48). Most instances of self-determination require a physical space where the people's values can be brought to bear. Assemblies need places to gather, values in land use need plots for application, and civil rights, like the right of privacy, need protected spaces in order to be realized. The right of self-determination, as derived from respect for individual autonomy, is best realized if the collective has a territory where it has the opportunity and capacity to express those values.

Analogous to the arguments for particular property rights, respect for autonomy plays an essential role in two arguments for particular rights to territory. First, respect for individual autonomy is a crucial premise in the argument for territory from 'self-ownership'. A self-determining collective, by definition, is free from domination by any other self-determining collective. This does not mean that the self-determining collective is not restricted by the rule of (international) law. Rather, it means that the self-determining collective has the power to determine its actions without arbitrary interference by others (Young 2007, p. 48). Territorial rights are integral to this autonomy because territorial rights designate a space within which a people, in forming a state, has the freedom to act on its own decisions. Without such a designated zone of control, a people is not insulated from coercion by others. This autonomy equips a self-determining collective with the capacity to determine a course of action and to act accordingly. Self-determining collectives have the capacity and legitimate authority to change the spaces around them, thereby securing valuable results and earning rights over territory by the arguments from desert and efficiency, above.

Second, respect for autonomy provides a trigger for the Lockean Proviso adapted for territorial rights. If persons are denied basic liberties because their political collectives do not have access to territorial rights, then there is a reason to limit the territorial rights of existing states in order for the disenfranchised collective to claim 'surplus' territorial rights. In cases where the people without access to land or water are either figuratively dying (the self-determination of the people is endangered) or literally dying or disenfranchised (the people are subjected to institutionalized basic human rights violations) because they do not have territory of their own, then existing states should be compelled to carve out from existing territories a new territory for these people (Nine 2012).

17.7 CONCLUSION

Rousseau asked how a territorial right – exclusive control over a vast space full of valuable resources – could ever be justified. This chapter presented a set of universal values: justice in meeting basic needs, desert, efficiency, and autonomy. Because everybody has a reason to value these principles, then everybody has a reason to believe that territorial rights are, in principle, justified, even though they may exclude outsiders from an immense territory. Territorial rights are justified as a system of international rights, when this system creates more political justice than alternatives. Particular territorial rights are justified when self-determining collectives demonstrate the capacity to use the geographical domain and its resources to rule themselves justly. These values are best realized in a system of territorial rights where collectives can exercise political jurisdictional authority over their territory in perpetuity.

17.8 REFERENCES

Altman, A. and C.H. Wellman (2009), *A Liberal Theory of International Justice*, Oxford: Oxford University Press.

Bishop, J.D. (1997), 'Locke's Theory of Original Appropriation and the Right of Settlement in Iroquois Territory', *Canadian Journal of Philosophy*, **27** (3), 311–337.

Brilmayer, L. (1989), 'Consent, contract, and territory', *Minnesota Law Review*, **74** (1), 1–35.

Buchanan, A. (2003), 'The making and unmaking of boundaries: what liberalism has to say', in A. Buchanan and M. Moore (eds), *States, Nations, and Borders: The Ethics of Making Boundaries*, Cambridge: Cambridge University Press, pp. 231–261.

Buchanan, A. (2004), *Justice, Legitimacy, and Self-Determination: Moral Foundations for International Law*, Oxford: Oxford University Press.

Cassese, A. (1995), *Self-Determination of Peoples: A Legal Reappraisal*, Cambridge: Cambridge University Press.

Fine S. (2010), 'Freedom of association is not the answer', *Ethics*, **120** (2), 338–356.

Finnis, J. (2011), *Natural Law and Natural Rights*, Oxford: Oxford University Press.

Locke, J. (2003), 'The second treatise of government', in I. Shapiro (ed.), *Two Treatises of Government and a Letter Concerning Toleration*, New Haven, CT: Yale University Press.

Macedo, S. (2007), 'The moral dilemma of US immigration policy: open borders versus social justice?', in C.M. Swain (ed.), *Debating Immigration*, Cambridge: Cambridge University Press, pp. 63–68.

Margalit, A. and J. Raz (1990), 'National self-determination', *Journal of Philosophy*, **87** (9), 439–461.

Meisels, T. (2009), *Territorial Rights*, Dordrecht: Springer, second edition.

Miller, D. (2007), *National Responsibility and Global Justice*, Oxford: Oxford University Press.

Miller, D. (2012), 'Territorial rights: concept and justification', *Political Studies*, **60** (2), 252–268.

Moore, M. (1998), 'The territorial dimension of self-determination', in M. Moore (ed.), *National Self-Determination and Secession*, Oxford: Oxford University Press, pp. 134–157.

Nine, C. (2012), *Global Justice and Territory*, Oxford: Oxford University Press.

Nine, C. (2013), 'Resource rights', *Political Studies*, **61** (2), 232–249.

Nussbaum, M.C. (2000), *Women and Human Development: The Capabilities Approach*, Cambridge: Cambridge University Press.

Philpott, D. (1995), 'In defense of self-determination', *Ethics*, **105** (2), 352–385.

Rousseau, J.-J. (1920), *The Social Contract, and Discourse*, London: J.M. Dent & Sons.

Schmidtz, D. (2006), *Elements of Justice*, Cambridge: Cambridge University Press.

Schrader-Frechette, K. (1993), 'Locke and limits on land ownership', *Journal of the History of Ideas*, **54** (2), 201–219.

Simmons, A.J. (2001), 'On the territorial rights of states', *Noûs*, **35** (s1), 300–326.

Young, I.M. (2007), *Global Challenges: War, Self-Determination and Responsibility For Justice*, Cambridge: Polity.

18. Regional governance and democracy
Sarah Ayres

18.1 INTRODUCTION

The aim of this chapter is to explore the relationship between regional governance and democracy. Enhancing local democracy is often cited as one of the motivations behind regionalism, alongside efforts to boost economic development and transform public services. Many scholars associate regional governance with improving the legitimacy and accountability of political institutions and fostering political participation (Escobar-Lemmon and Ross 2014; Wills 2016), promoting the growth of regional economies (Krugman 2011) and increasing the efficiency of public services (Channa and Faguet 2016). Global nations have, therefore, been implementing regional reforms in distinct and unique ways.

Governance theorists such as Hooghe et al. (2016), for example, note that there has been a global trend towards regionalisation over recent years. Of the 52 countries they examined two-thirds have witnessed an increase in their levels of regional authority. This work built on their previous analysis in which they employed an 'Index of Regional Authority' to illustrate a marked increase in the level of regional authority over the last half-century (Hooghe et al. 2010). They tracked 'regional authority' through a combined measure of regional-level democracy, policy competences, tax-raising powers and roles in co-determining central government policy. However, while the direction of change towards more regional authority is clear, the pattern has not been uniform. Marks (2015) refers to 'differentiated' multi-level governance to describe the various approaches to regionalism in terms of policy and territorial scale in different parts of the world. He suggests that the term 'region' often refers to different geographical scales, including localities (Jones and Woods 2013), metropolitan areas, cities or city regions (Harrison and Hoyler 2015). The conception of the regional scale is not the same in various languages and traditions. It carries meanings and connotations that are not always easy to translate without losing their contextual relevance and specific histories. This chapter acknowledges the differentiated and contested nature of the regional tier. As such, it defines the 'region' in its broadest sense – as the intermediate or 'meso' level 'between the state and the local level' (Keating 2017, p. 2).

The decentralisation of state functions to the regional tier is viewed by some as a response to a variety of pressures including managing distinct national identities and cultures, relieving the political and bureaucratic burden associated with centralisation and changing political views on the contribution of decentralisation to achieving economic and social policies (Pike et al. 2016). Yet, while many national governments put regions and regionalism at the forefront of the policy agenda, a regional approach often remains contested and can be criticised for lacking distinctiveness and vision (Huggins et al. 2015). Regional governance is often hamstrung by the continued dominance of the Centre and tensions between multi-level governance tiers (Ayres and Stafford 2014). So, while there may be compelling evidence of a global trend towards regionalisation, there is far less agreement about whether it has delivered on key objectives, such as enhancing democracy. In the absence of concrete evidence, Bucek and Ryder (2015, p. 2) suggest that 'the reorganisation of administrative regions and the reallocation of power, driven by economic and administrative necessity, may be one of the greatest public administration experiments ever undertaken'.

This chapter will examine three areas that are often used to demonstrate the link between regional governance and democracy, namely (1) enhanced civic engagement, (2) effective local leadership, and (3) reducing spatial disparities. The presentation of material is intended to be objective in identifying global evidence of both success and failure. These competing accounts provide an insight into the potential and limitations for regional governance to deliver better democratic outcomes. The chapter concludes by arguing that there is huge variation in prospective outcomes. Regional governance is shown to enhance civic engagement, local leadership and lead to a reduction in spatial disparities when the right subnational conditions are in place. However, outcomes across the globe are variable and measurement is prone to distortion (Davoudi et al. 2015). In short, there is no optimal spatial scale for success and regional governance cannot be assumed to automatically enhance democracy. Much depends on the contextual factors shaping, and constantly reshaping, regional governance structures and practices.

The following section highlights research that explores the link between regional governance and enhanced civic engagement.

18.2   REGIONAL GOVERNANCE AND ENCHANCED CIVIC ENGAGEMENT

Regional governance can serve to promote civic engagement and territorial identity in a number of ways (Malloy 2013). Regionalism is often linked with an improvement of democracy, popular participation and empowerment of local people (Mehrotra 2005). It suits the principle of subsidiarity (World Bank 2008), promotes responsiveness and enhances accountability (Van Dijk 2008). In the field of political science, Jeffery (2008) suggests that in relation to 'bottom-up' calls for subnational identity and autonomy, most attention has been given to the ways in which shared social identity can sustain a sense of the distinctiveness of the political community. Jeffery refers to a number of 'usual suspects' in this kind of analysis: in particular Catalonia, Quebec and Scotland, but also the Basque Country, Bavaria, Flanders and Wales. All have been territorial sources of demands and movements for constitutional change that have challenged and recast the constitutional structures of the state to establish more decision-making authority at the regional level.

Others emphasise the advantages derived from the proximity between the governed and governors (Treisman 2007). By bringing policy making 'closer to the people', regionalism has been credited with improved responsiveness, better oversight and disciplining of public officials, intensified grassroots participation and, ultimately, increased legitimacy. In addition, by disjoining regional authorities from the choices made at the centre, devolution is considered to allow room for policy innovation (Ayres 2017). These effects can result in improved civic engagement, democratic quality, state capacity and allocative efficiency. Other political scientists like Baldersheim et al. (2013), for example, identify the positive link between regional governance, civic engagement and democracy in Post-Communist Europe, including East Germany, Czech Republic, Poland, Hungary, Baltic Countries, Slovenia, Croatia, and Russia. Their research draws the following conclusions:

- Decentralisation brings government nearer to the citizens, creating conditions for the democratisation of governance and for increasing its efficiency.
- It provides opportunities for large segments of the population to participate directly in government through elective offices or more indirectly through regional elections and through watching how government works at close quarters.
- It provides the opportunity for the development of new elites at subnational levels who learn new political skills and the roles required to participate eventually in national political life.
- Subnational government acts should be considered at least as a check or a counter-vailing force to national government.
- Decentralisation activates regional actors to become involved in local and regional economic and social development.
- Devolution of competencies to regional and local government prevents overload developing at the centre.

Coulson and Campbell (2013) also compare and contrast what is happening in different Eastern European countries regarding transparency and accessibility to their inhabitants. They conclude that what was occurring in Central and Eastern Europe was not simply the democratisation of one level of government, nor the direct transfer of institutional models from Western Europe. Rather it was the rediscovery and reinvention of the purpose and rationale of regional government, seen as playing a central role in the political and social life of the country. Regional governance helped to bridge the divide between the State and civil society. They argue that the link between regional governance and enhanced democracy depends on historical factors and context specific relationships. In this view, regionalism is not a value in itself. It is promoted as an institutional prerequisite to democratic and efficient government and is justified only to the extent that it serves this purpose. Democracy and efficiency are seen as the potential outcomes of regional governance not an inevitable outcome.

The benefits of regional autonomy and civic engagement have also been felt in developing countries, such as India, Brazil, Mexico and the Philippines. In the field of political economy, Faguet and Poschl (2015) suggest that when public policies are physically brought closer into the territory they become more accessible to more people and arguably more locally responsive. Likewise, Speer (2012) argues that subnational control over public policies in the developing world have brought about several benefits, including increased civic participation, higher government responsiveness and better public services. Speer suggests that evidence on these claims is positive, but limited and variable. A key challenge is enabling and motivating citizens and public officials to make inclusive governance arrangements work, especially in parts of the world where regional structures are less developed (Mollel and Tollenaar 2013). Regional governance offers the potential for policies tailored to local circumstances and citizens' needs. However, while this is advantageous for those areas that thrive, the public, in particular, are often nervous about a so-called 'postcode lottery' and different levels of quality in service delivery around the country. A lack of national consistency can be seen to undermine standards and threaten social justice and equity. Henderson et al. (2013) refer to a 'devolution paradox': citizens want their regional governments to do more and yet seem reluctant to embrace the logical consequences of regional control, namely inter-regional policy variation and limited state-wide intervention in policy provision.

This issue is emphasised in Yu's (2013) research on the devolution of social welfare services in the Philippines. Findings revealed the fragmentation of welfare support across municipalities and citizen concerns about rising inequality in the system. Devolution in the Philippines was informed by global debates about devolved power and its ability to increase local decision-making and control (World Bank 2009). The objective was to increase local democracy and the independence of communities and enhance innovation, accountability and responsiveness. Newly created regional agencies were given the power to independently shape responses to local conditions and find localised solutions to policy problems. Nonetheless, Yu's (2013) study confirms that innovation and responsiveness in local welfare were *not* achieved. Instead, the initiative resulted in the 'widening of policy differences across localities and this compromised the protection of the rights of vulnerable populations' (Yu 2013, p. 204).

This evidence shows that the link between regional governance and enhanced democracy is not automatic and much will depend on how territories manage their governance structures and engender a spirit of engagement and inclusiveness. A number of potential barriers are noted in the literature. The first relates to whether regional bodies have the required capacity to respond to and manage regional institutions. They may not necessarily be able to respond adequately to the needs and aspirations of citizens in a post-industrial and global age. Indeed, Arnold and Cole (1987, p. 133) summarise that 'the beguiling themes of "participation", "responsiveness" and "democracy" have been interwoven into programmes for decentralisation in such a way that many initiatives have been launched under a shadow of ambiguous, vague and often contradictory objectives'.

Second, economic geographers like Peck and Theodore (2015) suggest that nation-states may seek to decentralise responsibility but not the necessary resources required for regional implementation. This is a particular concern during times of austerity when nation-states seek to do 'more for less' in difficult financial climates. Lowndes and Gardner (2016) argue that subnational tiers face particular challenges in engaging communities and territories in an era of financial crisis and austerity. Based on their analysis of decentralisation in England in the United Kingdom (UK), they argue that the regional tier confronts 'super-austerity', where new cuts come on top of previous ones, compounding original impacts and creating dangerous (and unevenly spread) multiplier effects. Finally, some fear that a place-focused politics, if it emerges strongly, would fall into what has been described as 'the localist trap', creating an introverted, and sometimes exclusionary, political community that ignores connections and responsibilities to neighbouring places and to wider relations (Davoudi and Madanipour 2015). Increased parochialism can undermine attempts to coordinate across regional jurisdictions to achieve economies of scale.

The next section explores the relationship between regional governance and the potential for more effective local leadership.

18.3   REGIONAL GOVERNANCE AND EFFECTIVE LOCAL LEADERSHIP

In the regional studies literature, there has been a recent abundance of academic and policy interest in place-based approaches for promoting economic productivity, harnessing civic engagement and generating creative policy responses (Beer and Clower 2014). Part of this interest has involved a growing literature on so-called 'place-based' solutions to policy issues and problems. Much attention has been paid to the extent to which intervention should be either place-based or place-neutral (Garcilazo et al. 2010). Whilst place-neutral advocates promote the role of aspatial 'people-based' policies, place-based approaches highlight the importance of the interactions between place-based communities, institutions and geography for developing policies, requiring researchers and policy makers 'to explicitly consider the specifics of the local and wider regional context' (Barca et al. 2012, p. 140).

Local government scholars like Hambleton (2015) argue that imaginative place-based leadership can shape more inclusive, democratic and sustainable cities. Drawing on detailed 'innovative stories' from around the globe, Hambleton describes how effective place-based leadership can lead to policy innovation, effectiveness and greater responsiveness to citizens' needs. Examples include advances in the use of Information and Communication Technology in Chicago, dealing with troubled families in the UK, housing in South Africa and city development in Aukland, New Zealand, to name but a few. Eminent sociologist Anthony Giddens (2015) also agrees that the city level is the most effective scale for leaders to tackle challenging issues, such as climate change and environmental policy. He asserts that civic interest, engagement and action can be garnered and coordinated by local leaders and that global city leaders can work together more readily than nation-states. In this view, regional leaders are more effective than nation-states in tackling difficult global and local challenges (Yoder 2015).

This view is supported by a recent OECD (2015) report that highlights the importance of local leadership in a comparative analysis of four European cities: Amsterdam, Hamburg, Manchester and Stockholm. It finds that robust city leadership is essential in promoting economic productivity and policy entrepreneurship. It refers to a 'leadership dividend' in ensuring positive outcomes, including growth and investment readiness and locally responsive policy solutions. Nonetheless, successful local leadership is seen to require a particular set of skills. Greasley and Stoker (2008, p. 722) suggest that the traditional bureaucratic leader is inappropriate at the beginning of the twenty first century because this requires 'the leader to have very high access to and control over the resources of finance, authority, organisation, networks, and patronage'. High levels of control over these policy leavers is not always a feature of modern democracies and instead local leaders have to work with multiple parties at different levels of governance to secure policy outcomes. They draw on the work of Svara (2003, p. 157) in noting the emergence of a type of elected urban political leader who is 'a facilitator who promotes positive interaction and a high level of communication among officials in city government and with the public and who also provides guidance in goal setting and policy making'. In their view, this style of 'facilitative leadership' is emerging as the de facto style of governing in many regional arenas.

Political scientist Benjamin Barber (2013) agrees with this assertion and suggests that in the face of considerable global challenges, the nation-states of the world are paralysed.

He claims that cities, and the mayors that run them, offer the best new forces of good governance. According to Barber, cities are home to more than half of the world's population, a proportion which will continue to grow. They are the primary incubator of the cultural, social, and political innovations which shape our planet. Most importantly, they are unburdened with the issues of borders and sovereignty which hobble the capacity of nation-states to work with one another. Drawing on case studies from around the globe, including Korea, the United States (US) and Singapore, Barber demonstrates that regardless of city size or political affiliation, local executives exhibit a non-partisan and pragmatic style of governance that is lacking in national and international halls of power. Through these qualities of leadership, mayors are able to retain the trust of citizens in their office, help cities become beacons of good governance, and spearhead city-to-city collaborations in order to better address shared problems.

Barber's boldest proposal is a 'World Parliament of Mayors', established on a voluntary basis to enable cities to have a stronger voice in global affairs, provide a worldwide platform for the sharing and transfer of urban best practices and establish a more democratic basis for addressing global priorities. Ryšavý (2013) also argues that mayors are hugely important in promoting democracy and citizenship and suggest that directly elected mayors, in particular, have strong and unchallenged legitimacy. Beal and Pinson (2014) agree that mayors can have an active and successful role in urban international relationships policy (e.g. city twinning, participation in cities networks, study trips). These activities provide resources for building up political legitimacy and for electoral control, which are crucial in accessing the resources required for local policy solutions to urban problems.

However, by contrast, Sancino and Castellani (2016) note that directly elected mayors do not necessarily equate with strong leadership. Based on their analysis of Italy they conclude that more than 20 years after their introduction, directly elected mayors are key players in Italian urban governance, but the effectiveness of their leadership is variable. Governance scholars like Denters and Kloka (2013) also raise the point that strengthened institutional arrangements to promote local democracy can actually act as a barrier between local leaders and citizens. They found that the stronger the regional democratic institutions, the less local leaders maintained contact with citizens and local stakeholders. In a similar vein, Lackowska and Mikula (2015) draw on a case study of Poland to describe an environment where city region governance is both developed and effective. Yet, public support remains low. This research evidence shows that even when regional institutions and leadership are effective, there are barriers to engaging the public in an administrative tier in which they may have little affiliation. This underscores the importance of regional and local identity as a route to enhanced engagement and democracy.

In the field of politics and European studies, Loughlin et al. (2010) also highlight the importance of regional and local identity in their analysis of 27 member states of the European Union (EU) plus Norway and Switzerland. They focused on the practice of democracy, including the roles of leaders, political parties and interest groups and also how subnational political institutions relate to the ordinary citizen. Their research reveals a wide variety of practices across Europe in this regard. Among the challenges identified were citizens' disaffection and switch-off from politics. Some countries have confronted this challenge more successfully than others but all countries face it. Differentiation in the quality of democratic ideals lies, therefore, in the specific circumstance, history, definition and context of regional governance.

The next section explores the third and final theme often used to justify the link between regional governance and democracy, namely reducing spatial disparities.

18.4   REGIONAL GOVERNANCE AND REDUCING SPATIAL DISPARITIES

Reducing spatial socio-economic disparities has been one of the key drivers behind the process of regionalisation over recent years. This is seen as beneficial in boosting the over-all economic productivity of nation-states while also engendering greater spatial equity and social justice between territories. This motivation has been particularly prominent in the EU where there is evidence of some success. Regional studies scholars Bodor and Grunhut (2015), for example, argue that one of the most significant trends of the past thirty years in regional governance has been the reduction in socio-economic disparities between the developed and the less developed regions of the EU. This process began at the beginning of 1989 when the Cohesion Policy was launched and the first cycle of Structural Funds resources allocated (1989–93). To pursue the aim of bridging regional disparities, vast sections of the European 'periphery', that included the regions in southern Europe, Ireland and the north and west of the UK, were below the EU mean of 75 per cent in terms of the average GDP per capita.

Yet, by the end of the third programmatic cycle (2000–2006) of the Structural Funds most of the less developed regions had moved beyond that 75 per cent threshold. Ireland exited completely from this category, Spain's original thirteen less developed regions were cut to one for the new planning cycle of 2014–20; Portugal's original seven regions requiring special assistance have been reduced to three; in 1989 Italy had eight less developed regions and now that number has been whittled down to four; Greece began participating in the Cohesion Policy with the entire country (i.e. thirteen regions) eligible for socio-economic assistance and in the 2014–20 cycle the total of eligible regions will have been cut by nine leaving four with special assistance; and in the UK only the western part of Wales continues to receive special consideration by the Cohesion Policy. A similar trend emerged in the eastern part of Germany and in the new member states in Central and Eastern Europe during and immediately after their accession to the EU in 2004. This evidence points to the success of regional governance and EU regional policy in reducing spatial disparities across Europe.

This position is also supported by Maynou et al. (2016) who argue that ever since the launch of the European integration process, the EU has endeavoured to facilitate economic convergence across Europe by providing funds to its poorer regions and countries. Their paper analyses whether the Structural and Cohesion Funds have contributed towards convergence between the Eurozone countries during the past two decades, 1990–2010. The results illustrate that these funds have positively contributed to the gross domestic product per inhabitant of receiving regions, thus allowing them to reach greater convergence. Kyriacou et al. (2017) extend this argument beyond Europe in their analysis of 23 Organisation for Economic Co-operation and Development (OECD) countries. They suggest that a process of fiscal decentralisation accompanied by measures to improve the quality of regional government is an effective strategy for reducing spatial inequalities.

Other scholars cite the importance of geographical scale and the 'relational' features of regional governance (Goodwin et al. 2012) as a route to promoting economic productivity. For example, in political science the concept of 'social capital' (Putnam 1993) and in geography the concept of 'institutional thickness' (Amin and Thrift 1994) place great weight on the wider terms, trust, cooperation and reciprocity in boosting economic productivity and reducing spatial disparities. Putnam (1993, p. 167) defined social capital as those 'features of social organisation, such as trust, norms and networks that can improve the efficiency of society by facilitating co-ordinated actions'. Hence, at the regional level, social capital is broadly perceived in terms of norms of civic engagement and cooperation. Civic associations, chambers of commerce, business promotion and community groups can all facilitate communication and foster shared norms. In regions where social relationships are more horizontal, based on trust and shared values, participation in social organisations is higher and social capital is higher. Putnam asserts that regions with high levels of social capital have higher economic performance and more effective regional governance.

In this argument, the region is the optimal level at which institutional networks and institutional thickness may be developed – it is small enough to allow for face-to-face contact upon which trust and cooperation are built but large enough to permit economies of scale and scope. This perspective highlights how spatial scale can be linked to the promotion of a vibrant local democracy, which, in turn, can offer tangible economic and social advantages. For example, Putnam's (1993) analysis of Italian regions indicated that active citizenship and social capital can have a significant impact on economic development and regeneration. Moreover, Amin and Thrift's (1994) notion of 'institutional thickness' draws on engaged and connected communities in the United States and Europe as a basis for economic productivity.

Beugelsdijk and Schaik (2005) present an index measuring social capital at the regional level in Europe. It shows that there are large regional differences on this social capital index. Their research explored whether higher scores on this social capital index correlated with higher levels of economic development and regional economic growth in 54 Western European regions. The preliminary empirical results suggest that (1) there are significant regional differences in scores on our social capital index in Europe, and (2) social capital is positively related to the level of economic development and growth at the regional level in Europe. Regional leaders who can harness the potential of their localities by working across sectors and governance tiers – facilitative leadership – are able to benefit from the social capital and institutional thickness that Putnam (1993) and Amin and Thrift (1994) describe. This asset can then utilise this to boost productivity and reduce spatial disparities to promote greater equity and social justice.

However, some of the assumptions about a positive relationship between regional governance and economic productivity have been disputed. Emerging evidence has questioned the 'economic dividend of regionalism' (Morgan 2006) and the lack of progress made in meeting national targets to reduce economic disparities between regions (Burch et al. 2008). For example, Torrisi et al. (2015) argue that previous research that suggested a link between regionalism and a reduction in regional disparities in Italy is refutable. They argue, instead, that the decline in regional disparities in Italy between 1996 and 2006 was driven by population dynamics and, to some extent, by the loss of competitiveness and consequent poor relative performance of northern regions. They conclude that links between regionalism and the reduction of spatial disparities is unproven and its benefits are temporally and geographically uneven.

Likewise, Dąbrowski (2014) assessed the capacity of the EU cohesion policy to promote inclusive regional governance and cooperation in regional development initiatives in Central and Eastern European countries. EU cohesion policy is often credited with improving cooperation and coordination in the delivery of the regional development policy through the principle of partnership working. By imposing a close partnership among a variety of actors, cohesion policy has the capacity to alter domestic relations between the centre and the periphery, and to create a broader scope for regional and bottom-up involvement in economic development policy. However, a lack of tradition of decentralisation and collaborative policy making, as well as a limited capacity of subnational actors, can result in uneven outcomes of the application of the partnership principle and its effectiveness. This raises questions about the transferability of the partnership approach to new member states characterised by weak regional institutions, a legacy of centralised policy making and limited civic involvement. Indeed, this issue is also pertinent to parts of the developing world, such as India, where the concept of partnership working and citizen involvement is less developed (Asthana 2013).

Promoting inclusive and cooperative regional development remains a challenge in all parts of the world. Economic geographers Martin et al. (2015) suggest that in the UK, for example, there is a need for a fundamental rethink to spatially rebalance regions. They identify entrenched and persistent spatial disparities in economic and social conditions in the UK. They assert that 'the growth gap between the South and the North (and indeed between most of the cities in the South and most of those in the North) is long-standing and cumulative' (Martin et al. 2015, p. 58). Their research indicates that the problem is rooted in the spatially biased nature of the national political economy. In this view, decentralisation to regional tier (cities or city regions) will lead to differential benefits, whereby the richest and most productive parts of the country continue to thrive, while the less favoured areas fall further behind. In this view, decentralisation leads to enhanced competition between places for central government funds and inward investment and, in these situations, the most powerful or largest cities are most likely to prosper at the expense of more peripheral areas (Tomaney 2016).

Outside Europe, the potential for inter-regional competition is also identified by Jeffery (2006, p. 87) who claims that there 'is a growing tendency for richer regions to seek to limit any need to share resources with economically weaker regions in the same state'. The demand for regional authority in such cases is about reducing obligations to inter-regional solidarity. Grumbles of the rich about transfers to the less well-off have appeared in Canada, with oil-rich Alberta leading the way and Australia, where Victoria periodically protests about the rigours of the Australian fiscal equalisation process. This evidence proves that regional governance and policy can be both a tool for reducing and also widening spatial disparities.

18.5   CONCLUSIONS

Jeffery and Schakel (2013, p. 299) indicate the tendency within political science to focus on the nation-state as the main unit of analysis in studying social and political life, and, in consequence, to neglect the region as a unit for political analysis. This tendency has been criticised as a 'methodological nationalism'. Indeed, social scientists, from a variety of disciplines, all too easily reproduce un-reflected, 'naturalised' assumptions that the nation-state, as Martins (1974, p. 276) put it in an early critique, is 'the terminal unit and boundary condition for the demarcation of problems and phenomena for social science'. This means that the regional tier as a unit of analysis receives less attention and there is, therefore, less evidence on which to draw conclusions. Nonetheless, a number of observations are drawn from the international evidence presented in this chapter.

First, political scientist, Michael Keating (2017), suggests that the task of exploring the relationship between regional governance and democracy is complicated by the contested nature of 'the region' as a concept and a lack of comparable indicators and global data. It is difficult to develop operationalised definitions across national contexts, access high quality and consistent data and compare across national contexts to disentangle and isolate the effects of regionalisation on democratic processes. Second, there is no 'one' correct model in efforts to promote democracy at the regional tier. There are big discrepancies in global case studies regards regional governance arrangements, configurations of institutional structures and processes and their impact on democracy. Outcomes are determined by a complex mix of macro political, economic and social traditions, the quality of subnational leadership and levels of civic support.

Finally, sociologist, Bob Jessop (2016, p. 14), argues that 'the territorial organisation of political authority is the essential feature of modern statehood'. It has different forms and rests on specific political, economic and relational attributes that result in different kinds of governance arenas. He suggests that regional territories serve as policy laboratories to experiment in government and governance with implications for redesigning institutions, policies and politics in response to policy failures and other crises. The evidence identified in this chapter epitomises this process of trial and error, experimentation and reinvention through which nation-states and regional institutions continue to (re)design structures and processes in pursuit of policy objectives. The relationship between regional governance and democracy is, therefore, in a constant state of flux and adaptation and is dependent on how regional strategies are pursued across and within nation-states in different parts of the world.

18.6 REFERENCES

Amin, A. and N. Thrift (1994), 'Living in the global', in A. Amin and N. Thrift (eds), *Globalisation, Institutions and Regional Development in Europe*, Oxford: Oxford University Press, pp. 1–22.

Arnold, P. and I. Cole (1987), 'The decentralisation of local services: rhetoric and reality', in P. Hoggett and R. Hambleton (eds), *Decentralisation and Democracy*, Bristol: School for Advanced Urban Studies, pp. 133–155.

Asthana, A.N. (2013), 'Decentralisation and supply efficiency: evidence from a natural experiment', *International Development Planning Review*, **35** (1), 67–86.

Ayres, S. and I. Stafford (2014), 'Managing complexity and uncertainty in regional governance networks: a critical analysis of state rescaling in England', *Regional Studies*, **48** (1), 219–236.

Ayres, S. (2017), 'Assessing the impact of informal governance on political innovation', *Public Management Review*, **19** (1), 90–107.

Baldersheim, H., M. Illner and H. Wollmann (2013), *Local Democracy in Post-Communist Europe*, London: Springer.

Barber, B. (2013), *If Mayors Ruled the World: Dysfunctional Nations, Rising Cities*, London: Yale University Press.

Barca, F., P. McCann and A. Rodríguez-Pose (2012), 'The case for regional development: place-based versus place-neutral approaches', *Journal of Regional Science*, **52** (1), 134–152.

Beal, V. and G. Pinson (2014), 'When mayors go global: international strategies, urban governance and leadership', *International Journal of Urban and Regional Research*, **38** (1), 302–317.

Beer, A. and T. Clower (2014), 'Mobilizing leadership in cities and regions', *Regional Studies, Regional Science*, **1** (1), 5–20.

Beugelsdijk, S. and T.V. Schaik (2005), 'Differences in social capital between 54 Western European regions', *Regional Studies*, **39** (8), 1053–1064.

Bodor, A. and Z. Grunhut (2015), *Cohesion and Development Policy in Europe*, Institute for Regional Studies, Center for Economic and Regional Studies, Hungarian Academy of Sciences, pp. 67–71.

Bucek, J. and A.C. Ryder (eds) (2015), *Governance in Transition*, New York: Springer.

Burch, M., A. Harding and J. Rees (2008), 'Unequal regions: a growing imbalance?', *English Regions Devolution Monitoring Report*, January 2008 Constitution Unit, London.

Channa, A. and J.P. Faguet (2016), 'Decentralization of health and education in developing countries: a quality adjusted review of the empirical literature', *The World Bank Research Observer*, **32** (2), 199–241.

Coulson, A. and A.C. Campbell (eds) (2013), *Local Government in Central and Eastern Europe: The Rebirth of Local Democracy*, London and New York: Routledge.

Dąbrowski, M. (2014), 'EU cohesion policy, horizontal partnership and the patterns of sub-national governance: insights from Central and Eastern Europe', *European Urban and Regional Studies*, **21** (4), 364–383.

Davoudi, S., G. Harper, J. Petts and S. Whatmore (2015), 'Judging research quality to support evidence-informed environmental policy', *Environmental Evidence*, **4** (9), 39–60.

Davoudi, S. and A. Madanipour (eds) (2015), *Reconsidering Localism*, London, Routledge.

Denters, B. and P.J. Kloka (2013), 'Citizen democracy and the responsiveness of councillors: the effects of democratic institutionalisation on the role orientations and role behaviour of councillors', *Local Government Studies*, **39** (5), 661–680.

Escobar-Lemmon, M. and A.D. Ross (2014), 'Does decentralisation improve perceptions of accountability? Attitudinal evidence from Columbia', *American Journal of Political Science*, **58** (1), 175–188.

Faguet, J.P. and C. Poschl (2015), *Is Decentralisation Good for Development?*, Oxford: Oxford University Press.

Garcilazo, J.E., J. Oliveira, C. Martins and W. Tompson (2010), *Why Policies May Need to be Place Based in Order to be People-Centred*, Paris: OECD Regional Development Policy Division.

Giddens, A. (2015), 'The politics of climate change', *Policy & Politics*, **43** (2), 155–162.

Goodwin, M., M. Jones and R. Jones (2012), *Rescaling the State: Devolution and the Geographies of Economic Governance*, Manchester: Manchester University Press.

Greasley, S. and G. Stoker (2008), 'Mayors and urban governance: developing a facilitative leadership style', *Public Administration Review*, **68** (4), 722–730.

Hambleton, R. (2015), *Leading the Inclusive City*, Bristol: Policy Press.

Harrison, J. and M. Hoyler (2015), *Megaregions: Globalization's New Urban Form?*, Cheltenham, UK and Northampton, MA, USA: Edward Elgar Publishing.

Henderson, A., C. Jeffery, D. Wincott and R. Wyn Jones (2013), 'Reflections on the "devolution paradox": a comparative examination of multilevel citizenship', *Regional Studies*, **47** (3), 303–322.

Hooghe, L., G. Marks and A. Schakel (2010), *The Rise of Regional Authority: A Comparative Study of 42 Democracies*, London: Routledge.

Hooghe, L., G. Marks, A.H. Schakel, S. Niedwiecki, S. Chapman Osterkatz and S. Sharir-Rosenfield (2016), *Measuring Regional Authority: A Postfunctionalist Theory of Governance, Volume 1*, Oxford: Oxford University Press.

Huggins R., B. Morgan and N. Williams (2015), 'Regional entrepreneurship and the evolution of public policy and governance', *Journal of Small Business and Enterprise Development*, **22** (3), 473–511.

Jeffery, C. (2006), 'Devolution and social citizenship: which society, whose citizenship?', in S. Greer (ed.), *Territory, Democracy and Justice*, London: Palgrave Macmillan, pp. 67–91.

Jeffery, C. (2008), 'The challenge of territorial politics', *Policy & Politics*, **36** (4), 545–557.

Jeffery, C. and A.H. Schakel (2013), 'Editorial: towards a regional political science', *Regional Studies*, **47** (3), 299–302.

Jessop, B. (2016), 'Territory, politics, governance and multispatial metagovernance', *Territory, Politics, Governance*, **4** (1), 8–32.

Jones, M. and M. Woods (2013), 'New localities', *Regional Studies*, **47** (1), 29–42.

Keating, M. (2017), 'Contesting European regions', *Regional Studies*, **51** (1), 9–18.

Krugman, P. (2011), 'The new economic geography, now middle aged', *Regional Studies*, **45** (1), 1–7.

Kyriacou, A.P., L. Muinelo-Gallo and O. Roca-Sagalés (2017), 'Regional inequalities, fiscal decentralization and government quality', *Regional Studies*, **51** (6), 945–957.

Lackowska, M. and L. Mikula (2015), 'How metropolitan can you go? Citizenship in Polish city-regions', *Journal of Urban Affairs*, **35** (1), 12–36.

Loughlin, J., F. Hendriks and A.C. Lidström (eds) (2010), *The Oxford Handbook of Local and Regional Democracy in Europe*, Oxford: Oxford University Press.

Lowndes, V. and A. Gardner (2016), 'Local governance under the Conservatives: super-austerity, devolution and the "smarter state"', *Local Government Studies*, **42** (3), 357–375.

Malloy, T.H. (2013), 'Nordic (minority) autonomies and territorial management in Europe: empowerment through regionalisation?', *International Journal on Minority and Group Rights*, **20** (1), 85–106.

Marks, G. (2015), 'A quiet revolution: multilevel governance since 1950', presentation to the World Forum, Milan, October.

Martin, R., A. Pike, P. Tyler and D. Gardiner (2015), *Spatially Rebalancing the UK Economy: The Need for a New Policy Model*, London: Regional Studies Association.

Martins, H. (1974), 'Time and theory in sociology', in J. Rex (ed.), *Approaches to Sociology*, London: Routledge, pp. 246–294.

Maynou, L., M. Marc Saez, A. Kyriacou and J. Bacaria (2016), 'The impact of structural and cohesion funds on Eurozone convergence, 1990–2010', *Regional Studies*, **50** (7), 1127–1139.

Mehrotra, S. (2005), 'Governance and basic social services: ensuring accountability in service delivery through deep democratic decentralization', *Journal of International Development*, **18**, 263–283.

Mollel, H.A. and A. Tollenaar (2013), 'Decentralization in Tanzania: design and application in planning decisions', *International Journal of Public Administration*, **36** (5), 344–353.

Morgan, K. (2006), 'Devolution and development: territorial justice and the north–south divide', *Publius*, **36** (1), 189–206.

OECD (2015), *Local Economic Leadership*, Paris: OECD.

Peck, J. and N. Theodore (2015), *Fast Policy: Experimental Statecraft at the Thresholds of Neoliberalism*, Minneapolis, MN: University of Minnesota Press.

Pike, A., L. Kempton, D. Marlow, P. O'Brien and J. Tomaney (2016), *Decentralisation: Issues, Principles and Practice*, Newcastle: Newcastle University.

Putnam, R. (1993), *Making Democracy Work*, Princetown, NJ: Princetown University Press.

Ryšavý, D. (2013), 'European mayors and councillors: similarities and differences', in B. Egner, D. Sweeting and P.J. Klok (eds), *Local Councillors in Europe*, Fachmedien Wiesbaden: Springer, pp. 161–180.

Sancino, A. and L. Castellani (2016), 'New development: directly elected mayors in Italy-creating a strong leader doesn't always mean creating strong leadership', *Public Money and Management*, **36** (2), 153–156.

Speer, J. (2012), 'Participatory governance reform: a good strategy for increasing government responsiveness and improving public services?', *World Development*, **40** (12), 2379–2398.

Svara, J. (2003), 'Effective mayoral leadership in council-manager cities: reassessing the facilitative model', *National Civic Review*, **92** (2), 157–172

Tomaney, J. (2016), 'The limits of devolution: localism, economics and post-democracy', *Political Quarterly*, **87** (4), 546–552.

Torrisi, G., A. Pike, J. Tomaney and V. Tselios (2015), '(Re-)exploring the link between decentralization and regional disparities in Italy', *Regional Studies, Regional Science*, **2** (1), 123–140.

Treisman, D. (2007), *The Architecture of Government: Rethinking Political Decentralisation*, Cambridge: Cambridge University Press.

Van Dijk, M.P. (2008), 'The impact of decentralization on poverty in Tanzania', in G. Crawford and C.H. Hartmann (eds), *Decentralization in Africa: A Pathway Out of Poverty and Conflict?*, Amsterdam: Amsterdam University Press, pp. 145–168.

Wills, J. (2016), *Locating Localism*, Bristol: Policy Press.

World Bank (2008), *Decentralization in Client Countries: An Evaluation of World Bank Support 1990–2007*, Washington, DC: World Bank.

World Bank (2009), *Systems of Cities: Harnessing Urbanisation for Growth and Poverty Alleviation*, Washington, DC: World Bank.

Yoder, J.A. (2015), *Crafting Democracy: Regional Politics in Post-Communist Europe*, Lanham, MD: Rowman and Littlefield.

Yu, N.G. (2013), 'Devolution: discontinuity and dissonance', *International Social Work*, **56** (2), 193–207.

19. Political regionalism: devolution, metropolitanization and the right to decide
Igor Calzada

19.1 INTRODUCTION: RESCALING NATION-STATES IN THE AGE OF DEVOLUTION IN EUROPE

Regions and city-regions are neither static territorial entities nor isolated geographical areas inside *pluri*national-states (Harrison 2017; Paasi and Metzger 2017). Nation-states – which are responsible for regions and city-regions, whether actively or passively, voluntarily or involuntarily, sceptically or acceptingly, alone or with others – end up playing the game of interdependence and entering into agreements on common goods with them (Innerarity 2016). Therefore, in this era of politics beyond nation-state borders, despite intimate relations between nation-states and regions/city-regions (Calzada 2015), the hegemonic idea that regions/city-regions are predominantly just sub-national entities nestled within singular nation-states (e.g. Agnew 2015, p. 120) has been superseded by growing claims for self-determination and independence in some small stateless city-regional nations such as Scotland, Catalonia (Colomb et al. 2014) and the Basque Country (Calzada and Bildarratz 2015) (see Table 19.1). Some argue that this change towards devolution in certain nation-states is caused by a new political equilibrium regarding regional identity confrontations in an evolutionary step of political re-scaling (Keating 2014; Khanna 2016).

Two main intertwined explanations can be presented. First, a new political regionalism is emerging characterised by devolution (Goodwin et al. 2012; Khanna 2016) and self-determination claims (Guibernau 2013), which is expressed and embodied via geo-democratic practices such as the 'right to decide' (Barceló et al. 2015, Cagiao y Conde and Ferraiulo 2016). Secondly, driving these changes could stem from 'metropolitanisation' (Sellers and Walk 2013) insofar as these small stateless nations are advocating a new socially progressive political agenda around 'civic nationalism' appealing to universal values (notably freedom and equality), and in contrast to 'ethnic nationalism' which is seen to be zero-sum, aggressive and draws on race or history to set the nation apart. Thus, this chapter suggests that an increasing metropolitan drive can be connected to the willingness for a bottom-up democratic experimentation towards the 'right to decide'.

To set this in context it is important to, first, understand how the Westphalian interstate system made up of sovereign territorial nation-states is being re-scaled, in the aforementioned cases, by a 'civic nationalism'. This is particularly relevant in a European context increasingly characterised by multi-level governance (e.g. Jones 2016, p. 3; Alcantara et al. 2016; Benson 2015) and a polymorphic political geographic recognition of city-regions becoming increasingly important 'sub-national', 'third' or 'meso'-level political actors. More specifically, as we will observe later, this chapter reinforces the 'Europe of regions' thesis (see Keating 2014) by adding two new dimensions: first, metropolitanisation as the geoeconomic (Harrison 2012) and geo-political (Guibernau 2013; Requejo 2015; Moisio and Paasi 2013) basis for emergent small stateless city-regional nations; and, second, the 'right to decide' as the geo-democratic basis for small stateless city-regional nations.

In the 1990s, many hyper-globalist scholars forecast the imminent demise of national state power because of the purportedly borderless, politically uncontrollable forces of global economic integration (Ohmae 1995). In contrast, a growing literature on state-rescaling provided a strong counterargument: namely, that national states are being qualitatively transformed – not eroded or dismantled – under contemporary capitalist conditions (Brenner 2004). In a longer historical perspective, Keating (2014) argues for the re-scaling of nation-states as the politicisation of regional space, which in some cases coincides with strong historical identities and national diversity, such as in the cases selected for this chapter (Scotland, Catalonia and the Basque Country). Connecting these together, Goodwin et al. (2012, p. 64) examine the devolved structures and strategies of economic development that have been put in place across the UK in an attempt to increase global economic competitiveness while tackling entrenched social inequalities, recognising cultural and identity politics, and enabling piecemeal democratic rights.

It seems remarkable that the current recentralisation vs. devolution debate (see Calzada 2016) in each nation-state implies a different starting point from the perspective of political regionalism. This perspective requires including the demands of some small stateless city-regional nations that claim to hold plebiscitarian referenda on full devolution – understood as secession – and to be included *automatically* as member states in the EU. In this regard, and contrary to general perception, according to Muro and Vlaskamp (2016), the prospects of EU membership have had only a limited effect on support for the creation of a sovereign state. Moreover, their study concludes that the impact was strongly mediated by the participants' previous degree of nationalism and their attitudes with respect to the EU. This observation provokes reflection on the potential dysfunctionalities in the way *communication* and *negotiation* are implemented between small stateless city-regional nations and their respective nation-states (for example, see the case of Catalonia in Forcadell 2017).

In the year 2014, two pluri-national states, the United Kingdom and Spain, faced debates about re-scaling their nation-states and similar turning points in their relationships with some of their city-regional small nations: albeit in different ways. While the United Kingdom (UK) witnessed a Scottish Independence referendum in September 2014, agreed upon by the then Prime Minister of the UK, David Cameron, and the former Scottish First Minister, Alex Salmond, Spain's central government upheld the territorial unity of the Spanish nation-state and refused any expression of self-determination as demanded by a considerable population in Catalonia (Crameri 2015; Guibernau 2013). A further important difference is the political landscape in the Basque Country over the past 40 years has been dominated by attempts to overcome political violence. At present, a hopeful peace process is being fuelled by civic society and avoiding confrontational inertia between ETA (Euskadi Ta Askatasuna or Basque Country and Freedom: the armed Basque nationalist and separatist organisation) and the Spanish state. To this end, there is some progress being made, or at least an interest in leveraging self-government and implementing the 'right to decide' in the Basque country (Barceló et al. 2015; Calzada and Bildarratz 2015).

Nevertheless, the Scotland, Catalonia and the Basque Country cases could be depicted in different ways. This is the point of the departure for this chapter, which aims to address the rapidly changing balance between 'small nations' (Kay 2009) and their referential pluri-national states. This chapter outlines the political history of each small nation and the status and achievements of political negotiation with their pluri-national states. This is important because it demarcates power relationships and establishes the preconditions for the future negotiations of the power devolution between the regional and state levels.

19.2 PERVASIVE CITY-REGIONAL METROPOLITANISATION: GEO-ECONOMICS, GEO-POLITICS AND GEO-DEMOCRATICS

Brexit and the soon-to-be end of the UK's continued membership of the EU has triggered a much wider debate about the organisation and legitimisation of nation-state power, both institutionally and territorially. After the plebiscites on Scottish independence (Calzada 2014), this debate includes the growing push for regional devolution within existing nation-states in Europe (Keating 2017).

However, the established and simplistic state-centric vision for the research of city-regions, focused on geo-economic processes, no longer suffices (see Harrison and Hoyler 2014, 2015; Jonas and Moisio 2016; Moisio and Jonas 2018). Instead, geo-political and geo-democratic dynamics must be included to articulate and enrich a systematic analysis of devolution that goes beyond a focus on re-territorialising an existing nation-state to match it to relationally defined diversifying (regional) ideas of nationality, identity, representation and devolutionary ambitions as new geo-political global 'connectographies' (Khanna 2016).

While the world is continuously urbanising, it has also rapidly metropolitanised. At present, complex processes of city-regional metropolitanisation (Sellers and Walk 2013; Clark and Moonen 2016) are altering the nature of the relationship between city-regional small nations, which are pushing ahead in pursuing greater devolution deals, and their respective nation-states, which are *obsessed* with maintaining territorial unity (Ruiz and Fernández 2003). Metropolitanisation stands out, as this distinction between a more visible, articulate and dominant 'metropolitan class' and those in the more peripheral, less articulated, non-metropolitan areas, has developed into a formidable struggle for influence on national politics and policies. This conflict is evident not only in the recent Brexit plebiscite in the UK (especially in Scotland and Northern Ireland), but also in Spain, where the Catalan regional election of 2015 was framed as a proxy for an independence referendum (Generalitat de Catalunya 2014) and resulted in the appointment of a new mayor in Barcelona, Ada Colau, who is not in favour of independence but advocates the 'right to decide'. Thus, pro-referendum does not mean pro-independence; the 'right to decide' resonates as a democratic, rather than a merely nationalistic, practice.

As such, metropolitanisation may show that identities and related political agendas are no longer expressed in territorially homogeneous units circumscribed by clearly demarcated boundaries or borders. Instead, identities develop a more explicit metropolitan versus non-metropolitan dichotomy (Brenner 2003; Sellers and Walk 2013), with clear implications for defining, articulating and claiming the 'right to decide' regardless of the possible outcomes of an independence referendum (Barceló et al. 2015). Another common metropolitan fact in Glasgow (Pattie and Johnston 2016), Barcelona (Martí and Cetrà 2016) and Bilbao (Calzada 2014, 2015, 2016, 2017) refers to citizens' political behaviour regarding devolution and their position in favour of the 'right to decide'.

In the UK, although Scotland voted in the end to remain part of the UK, the independence referendum and the broad political discussions within and outside the Scottish Parliament have encouraged calls for further re-organisation of the UK state (Keating and Harvey 2014): through extension of powers to the 'national territories' – Scotland, Wales and Northern Ireland – and new regional representation for England to disentangle the English and joint parliamentary representations and politics. In the case of Spain, the way out of the territorial crisis that threatens the integrity of the nation-state itself is even less clear (Moreno 2015). Thus, the inability or unwillingness of the Spanish political class to accommodate these desires for greater self-determination has resulted in an increasingly confrontational and centrifugal dynamic that undermines the very state that is to be protected in its status quo (Martí and Cetrà 2016; Requejo 2015; Serrano 2013).

As such, Moreno (2015) argues that interdependence in the old continent goes beyond internal boundary building and the establishment of self-centred compartments of governance, as occurred with the old Westphalian nation-states. Catalonians, like Scots and Basques, have reiterated their support for further Europeanisation, a process that many aim to make congruent with territorial subsidiarity and home rule. That the three metropolitan-civic nationalisms rooted in the city-regional small nations embrace and try to preserve the European social model is opposite the position of the pro-Brexit 'ethnic nationalism' (Breuilly 2016). This demonstrates the connection between devolution claims, metropolitan inclusiveness as a social value and a politically and socially progressive agenda, as shown in the political programmes of the main parties (Gillespie 2016; Sage 2014).

Likewise, these three cases underpin the debate about multi-level governance, the changing nature of the nation-state in the EU, and the relative power of central state governments. This theme is often presented as a debate about whether the nation-state's political authority and capacity to act are being eroded 'from below' by the demands of territorially based city-regional groups, and 'from above' by the logic of economic and political integration among European nation-states. However, we can also observe in the three cases how nation-states are eroding their 'particular' sovereignty by disempowering their endogenous capacity for democracy and implementation of multi-level governance as follows: (a) In post-Brexit Scotland, diminishing the 'right to decide' to remain part of the EU or to be present in the negotiations; (b) In Catalonia, prosecuting the president of the Catalan parliament for allowing debate on a potential referendum (Crameri 2015); and (c) In the Basque Country, the continual attacks of autonomy's *concierto económico* economic agreement with Spain as the contemporary political and symbolic taxation devolution formulae used as the principal asset of the Basque self-government (Bourne 2008; Uriarte 2015).

In parallel, metropolitan governance has been found to re-scale nation-states (Sellers and Walk 2013) by evolving from the initial territorial competitiveness agenda (geo-economic argument; Harrison 2012), moving towards articulating quests of self-determination (geo-political argument; Moisio and Paasi 2013) and reaching the 'right to decide' on their own futures (geo-democratic argument, Harvey 2008; Crameri 2015). As a consequence, three inter-related dimensions of pervasive city-regional metropolitanisation affecting political regionalism may be identified:

1. The *geo-economic argument* refers to new forms of city-suburban cooperation, regional coordination, region-wide spatial planning and metropolitan institutional organisation promoted in Western European city-regions (Brenner 2003; Harrison and Hoyler 2015). Growing tensions between nation-states and 'their' city-regions have resulted in either political rescaling via pervasive devolution (e.g. Khanna 2016, p. 63) or resistance to such centrifugal pressures. The financial crisis of 2008 has called into question the suitability of the 'one-size-fits-all' orchestration of state territoriality (Harrison and Hoyler 2015) through hierarchical, top-down, asymmetric relationships between the centre and subordinated, peripheral spaces (Brenner 2003). Instead, for example Khanna (2016, p. 75) argues that 'the more peripheral areas witness – but don't partake in – the success of the centre, the more they will push to seize control of their own affairs'. However, does this mean political dissolution of nation-states per se (Stanic 2016)? The increasing visibility and dominant economic position of the main cities vis-à-vis the state (Herrschel and Newman 2017) have yielded headlines about 'cities going independent', such as the provocatively titled 'Devo Met' (*The Economist* 2014). To some, particularly in conventional 'realist' International Relations debates, this is heresy; states are fixed and whole geographic entities. The growing focus on the economic dimension of statehood (geo-economic argument) and its territorial and institutional manifestation, however, questions the validity of such familiar assumptions as overly simplistic.
2. This leads to the second argument, the *geo-political argument*, which seeks to capture the continuing struggle within nation-states around new emerging centres of political identity and agency – whether they are metropolitan or, indeed, based on small nations. For city-regions, this has provoked both a more explicit and conscious sense of *belonging* and an update of the propagated 'right to the city' as 'individual liberty to access urban resources' (e.g. Harvey 2008, p. 23). This builds the third argument: geo-democratics.
3. As globalisation has added impetus to questions about the role and purpose of borders and territorialities of identities and competitiveness, presumed contiguous state territories have become increasingly brittle. State territorial cohesiveness and continuity are no longer a given. This opens the way to new *geo-democratics*. Democratic experiments such as direct democracy and plebiscites exercise the 'right to decide'. Thus, just as urbanisation played a crucial role in the absorption of capital surpluses (Harvey 2008), currently, metropolitanisation favours further devolution towards governing self-responsibly at different scales and within different boundaries than the established 'nation-states', whether for cities themselves or for city-regions or regions with strong notions of identity or 'self-ness'. New territorialities in democratic representations seem to be a matter of course.

These three inter-related dimensions of pervasive city-regional metropolitanisation affect political regionalism in terms of going beyond established notions of the region as a 'natural' subdivision of the state by pointing to claims by cities for self-rule, as they are deemed to no longer require their national capitals and states to filter their (mainly economic) relations with the world (Herrschel and Newman 2017; Khanna 2016; Barber 2013). Discussions about the metropolitanisation of the multi-level governance in Europe during the 1990s (Benson 2015) thus should extend to cities and city-regions as distinct entities in an 'age of devolution' (Calzada 2016), an age that establishes a new geo-political relationship with the respective nation-state, which will entail new ways to agree and implement geo-democratic experiments connected to the original meaning of the right to the city.

This resulting 'fused' 'civic nationalism' with the city as its centre may suggest that strategic nationalist ambitions in small stateless city-regional nations could, in essence, be considered an updated and expanded version of a metropolitan-based 'right to the city', as Lefebvre coined the term (see Purcell 2003). Are the two 'rights' comparable and, based on their sub-national scale and from a conventional international relations perspective, possibly mutually subordinate to established nation-states? According to Harvey (e.g. 2008, p. 40), 'Lefebvre was right to insist that the revolution has to be urban, in the broadest sense of that term'. Is the 'right to decide' a potential 'democratic' extension of the 'right to the city'?

19.3   FROM THE RIGHT TO THE CITY TO THE RIGHT TO DECIDE: POLITICAL REGIONAL AGENDA IN SCOTLAND, CATALONIA AND THE BASQUE COUNTRY

To capture how geo-democratics is taking place differently based on how each small stateless city-regional nation is setting its political regional agenda driven by devolution, this chapter compares three cases as outlined in Table 19.1.

Instead of providing a comprehensive taxonomy of city-regions (Calzada 2015), in this chapter, the term 'small, stateless city-regional nations', as shown in Table 19.1, refers to the Basque Country, Scotland, and Catalonia. They are defined as politically-entrepreneurial, socio-territorial entities nurtured by blending two dimensions: first, the urban dimension that is characterised through the interaction of their network of cities and their hinterlands in a particular regional context in pursuing 'internationality'; and second, the political dimension that is fuelled by community-driven, diverse, and plural metropolitan identity – clearly an opposition to an inward-looking, homogeneous, ethnopolitical view. This heterogenous metropolitan identity articulates a strategic socially progressive policy vision through devolution, agreed or not, in reference to its nation-state. Regardless of the particular pathway, hindrances and, last political achievements; although by always emphasising as the ultimate goal, democratic experimental and entrepreneurial activist practices based on inclusive social values.

Much of the question of self-determination, or the 'right to secede', seems closely linked to economic opportunity – actual and/or perceived (e.g. Khanna 2016, p. 68; Guibernau 2013). There is an evaluation of 'costs' and 'benefits' and a desire to self-manage and use such perceived opportunities to one's own advantage (Sage 2014): 'can we afford full independence economically' and 'which way are we better off – independently or as part of the UK or Spain?' These questions produce very different responses from the political regionalism perspective, as shown in Table 19.1.

In the case of the Basque Country, after suffering from the lack of peace caused by a spiral of political violence between the organisation ETA and the Spanish state, there is evidence that this era is being left behind. After the ceasefire announced by the organisation ETA in 2011, political parties have been pursuing a normalised context in

Table 19.1   *Political regional agenda in Scotland, Catalonia and the Basque Country*

Small Stateless City-Regional Nations	Basque Country	Scotland	Catalonia
(Pluri) Nation(al)-States	SP & FR	UK	SP
Network of cities and their hinterlands/outlying areas	Bilbao San Sebastian Vitoria Pamplona Bayonne	Glasgow Edinburgh Inverness Aberdeen Dundee	Barcelona Tarragona Girona Lleida
Devolution dimensions	Fiscal, Policy and Political devolution	Policy and Political devolution	Political devolution
Devolution strategies	Fixed by institutions	Fuelled by the government	Driven by civic society
Devolution deal	Economic Agreement (*Concierto Económico*)	After the Independence Referendum in 2014, Scotland Act 2016	In 2010, the Spanish Constitutional Court invalidated the democratically achieved 2006 Statute of Autonomy
Right to Decide implementation	Unilateral or Bilateral Consultation/ Referendum agreed by the Spanish Government and Basque autonomy potentially in 2017 or beyond	After Brexit vote, potential 2nd Referendum of Independence (presumably) between autumn 2018 and spring 2019	Since 2015, several mechanisms used for the referendum seem to be constitutionally illegal: Consultation in 2014 and Plebiscitarian Elections in 2015. The independence referendum took place on 1 October 2017.
Political innovation processes	Post-violence politics	Rationalised Dialectic	Antagonistic Dialectic

which they can express projects (independence included) without the threat of political unrest and violence. There is an intensive and committed effort from institutions and civic society to cure wounds. In this context, devolution claims may not be radicalised insofar as the self-government policy driven by the Economic Agreement (*Concierto Económico*; Uriarte 2015) shows wide support from Basque society as a source of the social and economic well-being of the last 30 years. Self-government, understood as total tax policy devolution and some capacity to act with policy and political devolution, is legitimised both in the Basque Autonomous Community and the Statutory Community of Navarra, which are the only two regions in Spain with such unique historic 'privilege' (for those Spanish nationalists/unionists against it) or 'responsibility' (mainly the entire Basque Society, according to surveys; Ruiz and Fernández 2003). A key role has been played by Bilbao's transformation, in just a few decades since the late 1980s/early 1990s, from being the city of iron symbolised by large, polluting steel furnaces into an international place of culture and urbanity characterised by the iconic and world-renowned Guggenheim Museum opened in 1997.

Scotland is recognised as a constituent nation of the United Kingdom, unlike the Basque Country and Catalonia, which are named simply as 'nationalities' in the Spanish Constitution. This issue of 'nation' versus 'nationality' reinforces the 'indivisibility unity of the Spanish nation' and is the principal source of conflict in the case of Catalonia with Spain. Scottish autonomy is new and was conferred in a referendum in 1997. It was established by the Scotland Act passed by the New Labour government in 1998, which led to the election of the first Scottish Parliament in May 1999 and the formation of a new Scottish devolved government in charge of a wide-ranging set of policy fields, including health care, education and energy. Thus, Scotland has been gaining political and policy devolution fuelled solely by the new Scottish Government (2013). This is the same government that held the independence referendum in 2014 and obtained votes from 56 out of 59 MPs from Scotland in the 2015 UK General Elections. The Scottish public has greater levels of trust in Holyrood than in Westminster and, we could argue, in the SNP than in the Labour Party (at least clearly in Glasgow), whose sentiments go beyond the claim for further fiscal devolution. Glasgow has gained a metropolitan and an international visibility that goes along with a sharper political profile and a distinct democratic standing (Clark and Moonen 2016). In both referenda for independence and EU membership, Glasgow set the main trend. To summarise, even though independentists were defeated by the small margin of 45 per cent versus 55 per cent, the rational way in which the independence debate was run showed constructive pros and cons which were not seen in Catalonia. However, after the Brexit vote, in the age of devolution, there is a question of how to respect the people of Scotland's vote to remain part of the EU.

Finally, in Catalonia, the 27 September 2015 Catalan regional election was framed as a proxy for an independence referendum by the pro-independence parties (Martí and Cetrà 2016). Since then, the new government has explicitly expressed the goal of holding a referendum in 2017. The controversial turning point occurred in 2006, when a new Statute of Autonomy was approved by the Catalan Parliament but was immediately banned by the Spanish Constitutional Court. This event led to massive demonstrations in Catalonia calling for the 'right to decide' their own future as a 'nation'. This phenomenon has been studied by scholars from diverse ideologies who advocate various solutions to the territorial tension, either from the federalist or secessionist side of the debate (Cagiao y Conde and Ferraiulo 2016; Barceló et al. 2015; Requejo 2015; Moreno 2015; Guibernau 2013). The hegemonic Catalan feeling that used to be driven by pragmatism has turned secessionist because of lack of faith in a federal agreement given the re-centralist, defensive, uncommunicative strategy of the Spanish government (Serrano 2013). The 'right to decide' thus became the motto (Calzada 2014).

Since then, the goals in Catalonia have been to reinforce the majority of votes in parliament and to design an operative plan to 'disconnect' from Spain after the referendum in 2017, which has recently provoked the prosecution of the President of the Catalan parliament, Ms Forcadell (2017). In this set of tumultuous events, Barcelona plays a unique pivotal role insofar as the newly elected activist mayor, Ada Colau, representing the new radical left party, 'Barcelona In Common', has revitalised her municipal powers by embracing global initiatives of cities exactly in the way Barber (2013), Corijn (2009) and Sassen (2002), among many authors, suggest. As such, Colau shows an ambivalent 'metropolitan'-based strategy regarding the tension between Catalonia as a small stateless nation and Spain as a nation-state with a re-centralist approach: although Colau does not favour secession as influenced by municipally based federal political principles, she does support a referendum and the application of the 'right to decide' not only as the representative of the internationalised capital city of the city-region, Barcelona, but also as a relevant part of Catalonia, the small stateless city-regional nation. In fact, in 1998, as a sign of its growing empowerment, Barcelona approved the Municipal Charter, which provided the framework for devolution of institutional powers in urban planning, infrastructure, education, social services and culture and offered greater financial resources to cover those responsibilities. Thus, as Serrano (2013, p. 541) argues, opposition by the Spanish central government to delivering greater fiscal powers to Catalonia as a region has effectively been bypassed. As in its metropolitan form, the scenario of independence has gained 'realness' and more political acceptability.

19.4   FINAL REMARKS: 'EUROPEANISING' POLITICAL REGIONALISM IN THE AGE OF DEVOLUTION?

In this chapter, a comparative description of three small stateless city-regional nation cases has been presented to better understand how metropolitanisation and the 'right to decide' are setting up the devolution-driven political regional agenda in Europe. As such, in the context of eventful years for secessionist movements both in the UK and Spain since 2014, we can conclude that metropolitan areas and major cities such as Glasgow, Barcelona and Bilbao as urban centres are strongly fuelling the democratic debate between the community-based city-regions and their respective nation-states. Furthermore, from the political regionalism perspective, geo-economic arguments claiming devolving powers are important, but in the event of being allowed the ability to hold a referendum by nation-states, however likely or unlikely, geo-political and geo-democratic manifestations count even more.

Regarding the European political regional dimension, authors such as Bourne (2014), Muro and Vlaskamp (2016) and Moreno (2015) have investigated the role of the future EU membership of these three cases' potential new states in debates about the advantages and disadvantages of devolution, secession or even independence. However, paradoxically, the EU's structure may stimulate support for an independent state while discouraging the act of secession. In fact, insofar as the EU could provide a complex web of opportunities and constraints for approximately 20 significant pro- and anti-independence or devolution movements, it is also likely to remain implicated in secession processes, according to Bourne (e.g. 2014, p. 95). These arguments can be considered arguments about 'Europeanisation' or the ways in which European integration affects politics, policies and institutions within European nation-states and small stateless city-regional nations.

In Table 19.2, an analysis of the potential EU positions regarding various political regionalist devolution strategies is presented.

In the current context, the EU's regional policy and multi-level governance provide an important *instrumentarium* and a platform for the international outreach of subnational actors in the pursuit of their own, increasingly more articulate, interests and

Table 19.2   'Europeanising' political regionalism in the age of devolution?

Impact	How integration affects city-regional power	Source of city-regional power affected
Disempowerment	Bias of the EU's decision-system against (city-)regions	Legal-constitutional
Empowerment	Supranational institutions are potential allies for regional governments	Relational
	Emergence of multi-level process of interest aggregation where others may depend on city-regions' resources	Possession of valued resources
	Supranational institutions promote ideas that affect the legitimacy of city-regional actors	Legitimacy
No effect	Domestic processes of interest aggregation are more salient for city-regional influence, and nation-states' governments can dominate state relations with the EU	Relational

Source: Adapted from Bourne (2008, p. 11).

priorities (Herrschel and Newman 2017). This is the case for Scotland, Catalonia and the Basque Country, whose strategic positions within the regional political arena have been empowered by the EU through their active economic sectorial leadership, their influential 'lobbying' and networking and their construction of their 'own' metropolitan space with a clear European dimension. However, whereas the domestic argument of legitimacy often works to mobilise the support base, the international dimension seems crucial to those who want to join a 'society of states' in the EU. In this respect, the current context requires the adoption of an anticipative and active role of the EU. However, as Connolly argues (Connolly 2013, p. 12), devolution and the 'right to decide', currently understood as the right to self-determination or secession in international law, provide little guidance for addressing separatist claims of stateless nations in Europe (Friend 2012) or other parts of the world. Thus, in Europe, devolution claims will increasingly be shaped by the institutions of the EU as part of the ongoing push and pull of having 'more say' in the EU, as its current member states and small stateless city-regional nations are fueled by an increasing metropolitan drive and a bottom-up exercise towards the 'right to decide'.

19.5   REFERENCES

Agnew, J. (2015), 'Unbundled territoriality and regional politics', *Territory, Politics, Governance*, **3** (2), 119–123.
Alcantara, C., J. Broschek and J. Nelles (2016), 'Rethinking multilevel governance as an instance of multilevel politics: a conceptual strategy', *Territory, Politics, Governance*, **4** (1), 33–51.
Barber, B.R. (2013), *If Mayors Ruled the World: Dysfuntional Nations, Rising Cities*, New Haven, CT: Yale University Press.
Barceló, M., M. Corretja, A. González, J. López and J.M. Vilajosana (2015), *El derecho a decidir: Teoría y práctica de un nuevo derecho*, Barcelona: Atelier.

Benson, D. (2015), 'Policies within the EU multi-level system', *Regional and Federal Studies*, **25** (3), 323–325.

Bourne, A.K. (2008), *The European Union and the Accommodation of Basque Difference in Spain*, Manchester: Manchester University Press.

Bourne, A. (2014), 'Europeanization and secession: the cases of Catalonia and Scotland', *Journal on Ethnopolitics and Minority Issues in Europe*, **13** (3), 94–120.

Brenner, N. (2003), 'Metropolitan institutional reform and the rescaling of state space in contemporary Western Europe', *European Urban and Regional Studies*, **10** (4), 297–324.

Brenner, N. (2004), *New State Spaces – Urban Governance and the Rescaling of Statehood*, Oxford: Oxford University Press.

Breuilly, J. (2016), 'Nationalism and Brexit', *Oxford University Press's Blog*, 12 December, accessed 24 April 2017 at http://blog.oup.com/2016/12/nationalism-brexit-identityreferendum/?utm_source=twitter&utm_medium =oupacademic&utm_campaign=oupblog.

Cagiao y Conde, J. and G. Ferraiulo (eds) (2016), *El encaje constitucional del derecho a decidir: un enfoque polémico*, Madrid: Catarata.

Calzada, I. (2014), 'The right to decide in democracy between recentralisation and independence: Scotland, Catalonia and the Basque Country', *Regions*, **296** (4), 7–8.

Calzada, I. (2015), 'Benchmarking future city-regions beyond nation-states', *Regional Studies, Regional Science*, **2** (1), 351–362.

Calzada, I. and J. Bildarratz (eds) (2015), *Political Innovation: Constitutional Change, Self-Government, The Right To Decide & Independence*, Donostia: TransLoKal – Academic Entrepreneurship for Policy Making Publishing.

Calzada, I. (2016), 'Between independence and re-centralisation: political innovation in an age of devolution', *OxPol, The Oxford University Politics Blog*, 24 February, accessed 24 April 2017 at http://blog.politics.ox.ac. uk/between-independence-and-re-centralisation.

Calzada, I. (2017), 'The techno-politics of data and smart devolution in city-regions: comparing Glasgow, Bristol, Barcelona, and Bilbao', *Systems*, **5** (1), 18.

Clark, G. and T. Moonen (2016), 'The business of cities: the role of metropolitan areas in the global agenda of local and regional governments for the 21st century', *Working Paper for the Preparation of the 4th Global Report on Local Democracy and Decentralization (GOLD)*.

Colomb, C., K. Bakke and J. Tomaney (2014), 'Shaping the territory in Scotland, Catalonia and Flanders: analysing contemporary debates on devolution and independence from a spatial planning and territorial cohesion lens', *UCL European Institute, Working Paper No. 5*.

Connolly, C.K. (2013), 'Independence in Europe: secession, sovereignty and the European Union', *Duke Journal of Comparative and International Law*, **51**, 1–51.

Corijn, E. (2009), 'Urbanity as a political project: towards post-national European cities', in L. Kong and J. O'Connor (eds), *Creative Economies, Creative Cities: Asian-European Perspectives*, GeoJournal Library, 98.

Crameri, K. (2015), 'Do Catalans have 'the right to decide'? Secession, legitimacy and democracy in twenty-first century Europe', *Global Discourse*, **6** (3), 423–439.

The Economist (2014), 'Devo met: big English cities are pushing for more power', accessed 10 January 2017 at http://www.economist.com/news/britain/21627697-big-english-cities-are-pushing-more-power-devo-met.

Forcadell, C. (2017), 'Defending freedom in Catalonia', *New York Times*, 30 January, accessed 24 April 2017.

Friend, J.W. (2012), *Stateless Nations: Western European Regional Nationalisms and the Old Nations*, London: Palgrave Macmillan.

Generalitat de Catalunya – Government of Catalonia (2014), 'White paper on The National Transition of Catalonia', Barcelona: Generalitat de Catalunya – Government of Catalonia, Department of the Presidency.

Gillespie, R. (2016), 'The contrasting fortunes of pro-sovereignty current in Basque and Catalan nationalist parties: PNV and CDC compare', *Territory, Politics, Governance*, **5** (4), 1–19.

Goodwin, M., M. Jones and R. Jones (eds) (2012), *Rescaling the State: Devolution and the Geographies of Economic Governance*, Manchester: Manchester University Press.

Guibernau, M. (2013), 'Secessionism in Catalonia: after democracy', *Ethnopolitics: Formerly Global Review of Ethnopolitics*, **12** (4), 368–393.

Harrison, J. (2012), 'Towards the new regional world?', in A. Growe, K. Heider, C. Lamker, S. Paßlick, T. Terfrüchte (eds), *Polycentric Urban Regions – The Region as Planning Space*, Dortmund: Academy for Spatial Research and Planning, pp. 9–21.

Harrison, J. and M. Hoyler (2014), 'Governing the new metropolis', *Urban Studies*, **51** (11), 2249–2266.

Harrison, J. and M. Hoyler (eds) (2015), *Megaregions: Globalization's New Urban Form?*, Cheltenham, UK and Northampton, MA, USA: Edward Elgar Publishing.

Harrison, J. (2017), 'Constructing alternative paths to city-region policy and governance', in I. Deas and S. Hincks (eds), *Territorial Policy and Governance: Alternative Paths*, London: Routledge, pp. 53–70.

Harvey, D. (2008), 'The right to the city', *New Left Review*, **53**, accessed 24 April 2017 at http://newleftreview. org/II/53/david-harvey-the-right-to-the-city.

Herrschel, T. and P. Newman (2017), *Cities as International Actors – Urban and Regional Governance Beyond the Nation State*, Basingstoke: Palgrave Macmillan.

Innerarity, D. (2016), *Governance in the New Global Disorder: Politics for a Post-Sovereign Society*, New York: Columbia University Press.

Jonas, A.E.G. and S. Moisio (2016), 'City regionalism as geopolitical processes: a new framework for analysis', *Progress in Human Geography*, online first, 1–21.

Jones, M. (2016), 'Polymorphic political geographies', *Territory, Politics, Governance*, **4** (1), 1–7.

Kay, J. (2009), *The Economics of Small States*, Edinburgh: David Hume Institute.

Keating, M. (2014), 'Rescaling the European state: the making of territory and rise of the meso', *Oxford Scholarship Online*, **52** (1), 1–38.

Keating, M. and M. Harvey (2014), *Small Nation in a Big World: What Scotland Can Learn*, Edinburgh: Luath Press.

Keating, M. (2017), 'Contesting European regions', *Regional Studies*, **51** (1), 9–18.

Khanna, P. (2016), *Connectography: Mapping the Global Network Revolution*, London: Weidenfeld & Nicholson.

Martí, D. and D. Cetrà (2016), 'The 2015 Catalan election: a de facto referendum on independence?', *Regional & Federal Studies*, **26** (1), 107–119.

Moisio, S. and A. Paasi (2013), 'From geopolitical to geoeconomic? The changing political rationalities to state space', *Geopolitics*, **18** (2), 267–283.

Moisio, S. and Jonas, A. E. G. (2018), 'City-regions and city-regionalism', in A. Paasi, J. Harrison and M. Jones (eds), *Handbook on the Geographies of Regions and Territories*. Cheltenham, UK and Northampton, MA, USA: Edward Elgar Publishing, pp. 285–297.

Moreno, L. (2015), 'Catalonia's in(ter)dependence and Europeanization', *Instituto de Políticas y Bienes Públicas (IPP) CSIC*, Working Paper published July 2015.

Muro, D. and M.C. Vlaskamp (2016), 'How do prospects of EU membership influence support for secession? A survey experiment in Catalonia and Scotland', *West European Politics*, **39** (6), 1115–1138.

Ohmae, K. (1995), *The End of the Nation State*, New York: Simon & Schuster.

Paasi, A. and J. Metzger (2017), 'Foregrounding the region', *Regional Studies*, **51** (1), 19–30.

Pattie, C. and R. Johnston (2016), 'Sticking to the Union? Nationalism, inequality and political disaffection and the geometry of Scotland's 2014 independence referendum', *Regional & Federal Studies*, **27** (1), 83–96.

Purcell, M. (2003), 'Citizenship and the right to the global city: reimagining the capitalist world order', *International Journal of Urban and Regional Research*, **27** (3), 564–590.

Requejo, F. (2015), 'National pluralism, recognition, federalism and secession (or Hegel was a clever guy)', in G.-A. Gagnon, S. Keil and S. Mueller (eds), *Understanding Federalism and Federation*, Farnham: Ashgate, pp. 157–176.

Ruiz, C. and P.M. Fernández (2003), '¿Aprobaron los vascos la Constitución?', *Revista de Estudios Políticos (Nueva Época)*, **122**, 167–178.

Sage, D. (2014), 'The Scottish National Party: transition to power', *Regional & Federal Studies*, **24** (4), 532–533.

Sassen, S. (2002), 'Towards post-national and denationalized citizenship', in E.F. Isin and B.S. Turner (eds), *Handbook of Citizenship Studies*, London: Sage, pp. 277–291.

Scottish Government (2013), *White Paper. Scotland's Future: Your Guide to An Independent Scotland*, Edinburgh: Scottish Government.

Sellers, J.M. and R.A. Walks (2013), 'Introduction: the metropolitanisation of politics', in J.M. Sellers, D. Kübler, M. Walter-Rogg and R.A. Walks (eds), *The Political Ecology of the Metropolis*, Colchester: ECPR Press, pp. 3–36.

Serrano, I. (2013), 'Just a matter of identity? Support for independence in Catalonia', *Regional and Federal Studies*, **23** (5), 523–545.

Stanic, A. (2016), 'Preparing for independence: lessons learned from newly born states', *Centre Maurits Coppieters*, accessed 10 January 2017 at https://vimeo.com/163375542.

Uriarte, P.L. (2015), *El Concierto Económico Vasco: Una visión personal*, Bilbao: Concierto Plus.

20. Regions and cultural representation
Rhys Jones

20.1   INTRODUCTION: CULTURAL REGIONS IN FOCUS

Regions exist or are formed for a variety of reasons, as the various chapters in this edited volume show. They can be formed, first, as a means of addressing some of the socio-economic challenges associated with capitalism. The creation of regions, in this sense, can be part of a 'spatial fix' that seeks to allow the individuals, firms and corporations located within a particular location to compete on a global scale or, as policy elites often put it, to 'punch their weight in the global economy' (quoted in Jones 2001, see also Bristow 2010). A second logic for the creation of regions revolves around the need to reflect some kind of functional reality or unity. Regions, in this sense, are created, merely, as a means of reflecting what is actually going on on the ground as it were, whether in terms of the movement of goods or people. The recent emphasis on city regions in policy fits in with this general model of regions being created to reflect some kind of functional unity (e.g. Harrison 2007). While these two academic and policy motors for the creation of regions can be viewed as part of a largely 'top-down' process of state restructuring, a third logic centres on the more 'bottom-up' calls made by particular groups of people for greater political and cultural representation. Such regions, as Keating (2001) has argued, often exist 'against the state', coming about as a result of the 'political contestation over the definition and meaning of territory' (Keating 2017, p. 9). They also possess a vision of a regional future, which is often based on greater autonomy and self-determination (Keating 1998, p. 187; Cole and Pasquier 2015). The line of demarcation between regional forms of cultural representation and examples of what have been described as minority or ethnic nationalisms is, of course, blurred.

Different themes are, of course, enrolled into this more cultural process of region-building. As Paasi (1991) has famously argued, there are many aspects to the process whereby regions are institutionalised. The most significant in the context of the present discussion, perhaps, is the notion of the symbolic shape of the region or, in other words, how things such as a language, traditions, customs and other symbols come to be connected with a particular region and help to define it. These cultural symbols become key markers of the 'groupness' (Brubaker 2004) of the region in question. But, of course, institutions are also required in order to promote and give permanence and weight to this symbolic shape. One of the key institutions, in this respect, is an education system that can help to inculcate in young members of the region or nation an awareness and appreciation of these cultural norms. Institutions can also allow regional and national cultures to be communicated to outsiders. Work has explored, in this context, how culture can be used to market or sell particular regions, thus showing how different cultural symbols can help a region to become or be institutionalised in quite instrumental ways (Thomas et al. 2013).

While this chapter, of necessity given its title, focuses explicitly on cultural forms of regionalism, it is important to realise that this kind of discourse and practice of regionalism interacts in complex ways with the other kinds of logics discussed in the opening paragraph of this chapter (see Haughton and Allmendinger 2015). To be sure, there are examples of regions in which these three logics positively reinforce each other (indeed, the empirical discussion below shows how important connections can exist between them) but it is significant that they have often been in conflict or tension with one another. One can extend Keating's arguments by stating that culturally or ethnically informed visions of region, as well as existing 'against the state', often exist in opposition or in tension with state-sanctioned or defined regions. Jones and MacLeod (2004) have illustrated the existence of such tensions in their valuable study of the different logics helping to define regions in the south-west of England. Drawing on Lefebvre's writings, they illustrate the contestation that exists between the 'regional spaces' of state-sanctioned regions, such as RDAs, and the 'spaces of regionalism' associated with the more culturally informed regions being promoted by Cornish nationalists and Wessex regionalists. We should consider, equally, how a functional logic associated with city regions, for instance, articulates with more culturally informed regional identities and entities (Harrison and Heley 2015).

I seek to develop three lines of argument in this chapter. First of all, I will add empirical weight to the conceptual framework developed by Jones and MacLeod (2004) by demonstrating the tensions that can exist between more cultural, and more economic or political forms of regionalism. But, in discussing these ideas, I also seek to develop, extend and critique Jones and MacLeod's (2004) work in two ways. My second aim is to problematise the conception of cultural regionalism and to show that it is far from being a unitary or homogeneous thing. This second aim – something that Jones and MacLeod (2004) hint at but do not fully explore – centres on showing that there are different versions of the cultural 'spaces of regionalism' that can exist or can be promoted within a particular region. My third aim is to show that the duality between top-down 'regional spaces' and more bottom-up 'spaces of regionalism' is never straightforward. A complex dialogue can exist between them. They are, undoubtedly, sometimes in conflict with one another but, at certain times, they can complement and reinforce one another.

My empirical focus in this chapter is, unashamedly, on Wales, the region within which I live and work. The empirical themes discussed in the chapter derive from a series of projects that I have conducted on different aspects of Welsh regional and national identity. But before accusing me of either laziness or parochialism, I would like the opportunity to justify my focus on this region. It is a region, for one thing, that possesses a complex and contested history, and one that has been characterised by long-running debates about the alleged characteristics of its regional (or national) culture, not least in relation to the role that should be played by the Welsh language within debates about Welsh identity (Johnes 2012). It is also a region that has been characterised by numerous territorial configurations and geographical imaginations, with these, in many respects, reflecting the aforementioned contested versions of Welshness, the Welsh culture and the Welsh language (Jones and Fowler 2007). Wales is, arguably, therefore, an ideal region within which to examine debates concerning cultural representation and its connection to processes of region formation.

20.2   CONSTRUCTING AND CONTESTING THE WELSH CULTURAL REGION

Wales, as an administrative and territorial entity, first emerged, arguably, during the sixteenth century, as the result of the so-called Acts of Union that took place between England and Wales. Although the Acts led to an increased administrative homogeneity between England and Wales, most clearly with regard to the extension of the shire system throughout the whole of Wales, it also helped to bring a greater territorial shape to Wales as a region through the precise definition of the boundaries of the English and Welsh shires. The formal incorporation of Wales into the English state during the sixteenth century also had far-reaching – and contradictory – impacts on all aspects of Welsh culture, not least the Welsh language. The Acts of Union stipulated that the Welsh language should be extirpated from public life in Wales but, some fifty years later, the English state, somewhat perversely, supported the translation of the Bible into Welsh. Similarly, while the British state of the nineteenth century could lay claim to the fact that the Welsh language was a hindrance to the economic and moral progress of the Welsh people, it created a Welsh Board of Education a little later with a view to increasing the prevalence of the Welsh language within schools. In other words, a convoluted relationship has existed between the British state and Welsh culture for the past four to five hundred years. It is this tangled relationship, too, which has underpinned much of the growth in Welsh nationalism since the nineteenth century, a nationalism that has been defined largely in opposition to the British state. This nationalist or regional discourse has, historically, been promoted by a few key institutions and groups, most notably Plaid Cymru (the Welsh Nationalist Party, formed in 1925) and the Welsh Language Society, a pressure group formed in 1963 to seek greater support and status for the Welsh language in Wales (Johnes 2012). At the same time, this form of cultural or ethnic nationalism has not unfolded in a straightforward manner. A convoluted and contradictory relationship has existed between a Welsh cultural region and a Wales defined in more political and administrative terms. It is this tangled relationship between an administratively and politically defined Welsh region, on the one hand, and a more culturally defined one, on the other, that forms the substance of the discussion on the following pages of this chapter.

20.3   IMAGINING THE WELSH CULTURAL REGION: 'LE PAYS DE GALLES' AND 'Y FRO GYMRAEG'

Much of the basis of dominant geographical imaginations of a Welsh culture region can be traced to academic and political debates, which emerged during the 1950s and 1960s. The first contribution, arguably, came in the form of Emrys Bowen's (1959) presidential address to the Institute of British Geographers, in which he explored different ways of imagining the region of Wales. Using linguistic, historic, geomorphic and climatic themes, his paper illustrated the contested geographic character of Wales as a political and cultural entity (see Figure 20.1). At one level, Wales was a straightforward political or administrative entity, which had first begun to emerge as a result of the Acts of Union. This was a region that was about to be further reinforced through an administrative devolution of power to the Welsh Office in 1965. Reflecting his adherence to the French regional school, Bowen was able, nonetheless, to conceive of another kind of Welsh region. This was a

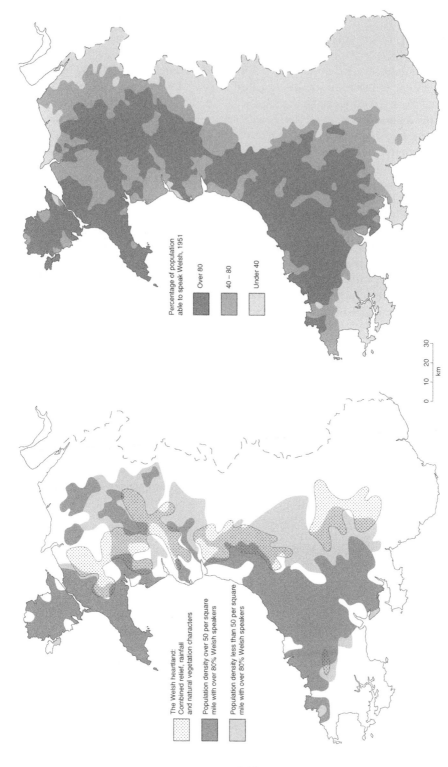

Percentage of population
able to speak Welsh, 1951

Over 80

40 – 80

Under 40

0 10 20 30
km

The Welsh heartland:
Combined relief, rainfall
and natural vegetation characters

Population density over 50 per square
mile with over 80% Welsh speakers

Population density less than 50 per square
mile with over 80% Welsh speakers

Figure 20.1   The contested geographical imaginations of Wales during the 1950s and 1960s

246

Wales constituted as a 'pays' or a region characterised by specific 'physical or cultural endowments' (Bowen 1959, p. 1). The main signifier of the Welsh pays for Bowen was the particular cultural endowment of the Welsh language. For Bowen, the Welsh language, culture and identity, were intimately intertwined in his definition of the cultural region of Wales.

Nor was this merely an academic understanding of a more culturally defined Welsh region. Similar geographical imaginations had been prevalent among some political groups since the 1920s and 1930s. Gruffudd (1994, 1995), for instance, has shown how Plaid Cymru argued during the interwar period that the Welsh people would have to 'return to the land' – and specifically, the land of the north and west of the country – if they were to regain their rightful place as a moral people. Welsh people would need to live and work in rural areas so that they could avoid Anglicised metropolitan values. Such ideas were further reinforced in political and public debate during the 1950s among certain members of the Welsh intelligentsia. Syr Ifan ab Owen Edwards, the leader of Urdd Gobaith Cymru – Wales' Guild of Hope, a youth movement set up in the 1920s as an alternative to the Scouts and Guides – sought to exhort the movement's members to work tirelessly to defend the Welsh-speaking heartlands in the north and the west of the country from the English incursions associated with electrification, forestation, holiday camps and the creation of reservoirs (Jones et al. 2016).

Two different versions of the Welsh region existed during the 1950s and 1960s, therefore: a regional space associated with the creation of Wales as an administrative unit of the British state, alongside a space of regionalism linked to an alternative, culturally defined region. The tension between these different visions of the Welsh region has, arguably, been reinforced in recent years. An executive devolution of power to Wales took place in 1999, with a newly elected National Assembly for Wales taking responsibility for, inter alia, education, health and transport policy; something, which, at face value, has helped to give additional weight to a Welsh region defined in administrative and political terms. The devolution of power to a Welsh region, defined in this way, represents what has been termed a 'filling in' of the UK state through the sedimentation of new organisations and practices of governance at a Welsh scale (Jones et al. 2005). At the same time, further efforts have been made following devolution to promote the need to protect a Welsh region defined in cultural and, specifically, linguistic terms. Some civil society groups have advocated such a view. Cymuned – literally Community – was created in 1999 with the sole aim of protecting the Welsh-speaking heartland or, as it has described it, 'y Fro Gymraeg'. The significance of 'y Fro Gymraeg' – as the fundamental basis of a Welsh cultural region – is made clear in the literature produced by Cymuned (see Figure 20.2) and has been reinforced in interviews conducted by members of the organisation:

> I think that it's necessary for us to try to keep the 'Fro Gymraeg'. . . unless there are communities and areas where Welsh is the natural language of the community, I don't feel that there is a future for Welsh . . . that is, it will become a minority language in all areas and in the end it won't be very different from the Cornish, for example.

As one can see from the above quote, two interrelated themes inform understandings of 'y Fro Gymraeg'. At one level, the organisation promotes a familiar argument about the need to protect the Welsh language within the Welsh-speaking heartland of 'y Fro Gymraeg'. At the time, there is a recognition that 'y Fro Gymraeg' does not exist solely as a large-scale territory but is also made up of a series of Welsh-speaking communities. A mutually

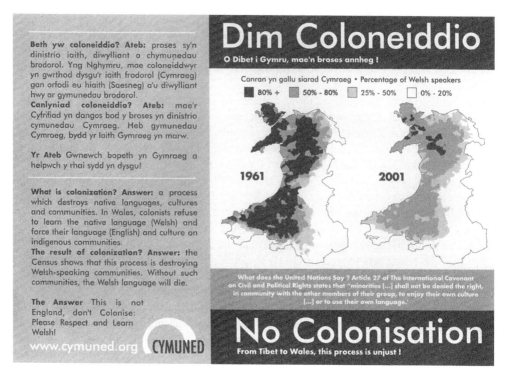

Figure 20.2   Defending the Welsh cultural region

reinforcing relationship is said to exist between these two scales; the Welsh-speaking heartland is made up of a number of Welsh-speaking communities but the existence of 'y Fro Gymraeg' provides these communities with a larger, territorial frame of reference.

So far, so familiar, therefore. We witness in Wales the existence of two kinds of regional imaginations, with some reflecting an administrative and political entity and others being based more on a culturally informed take on Wales and Welshness. And yet, politics in Wales in the period since the devolution of power in 1999 has been characterised by a significant attempt to forge a closer dialogue between regional spaces and spaces of regionalism. Attempts to forge a closer relationship between a Welsh cultural region and the political and administrative entity of Wales have taken place in two contrasting ways. First, an effort has been made to re-scale the cultural region of Wales – particularly in its linguistic form – so that it applies to the whole of the administrative and political entity of Wales. Certain civil society actors, for instance, have queried the tendency to view the Welsh language as something that is pertinent only to 'y Fro Gymraeg'. One language activist in Wales put it to me in the following way:

> I see it as problematic when people compartmentalise Wales, and say that this is a more Welsh area, and this area isn't . . . And to what extent can you tie it down to one small, restricted area. I understand that there are differences. But I believe that what we mustn't do is alienate ourselves from the non-Welsh speaking Welsh people [in south-east Wales] to start with, an industrial area where there is massive potential for us to expand on Welshness. Yes, it will be totally different

from the Welshness of Bethesda [in north-west Wales], for example. But I believe you have to, like, embrace it as a country.

Such statements allude to the fact that many view the whole of Wales as being the cultural region that is of most significance, rather than a particular portion of it that lies to the north and west of the country. This kind of viewpoint has been reinforced – at least in part – by the Welsh government since 1999. It has published a number of documents in recent years, which have sought to outline specific policies and strategies that can enable Wales to remain a bilingual country (e.g. Welsh Assembly Government [WAG] 2002, 2003; WG 2012). Many of these statements have asserted the need for the Welsh language to become a cultural asset that is relevant and important for the whole of the region. Particular policies – most notably associated with state education, and the policies associated with the Welsh Language Act of 1993 – have, arguably, recast the geographical frame of reference for the Welsh language and culture so that they extend throughout the whole of the territory of Wales.

A second way in which a closer dialogue now exists between a regional space of Wales and a more cultural space of regionalism is in the context of the Welsh governments' emerging attempts to recognise the significance of 'y Fro Gymraeg' in political and policy contexts. A key consideration within the various Welsh language strategies and policies that it has published in recent years is the need to deal with the preservation of Welsh as a community language within 'y Fro Gymraeg'. A key strand with the Welsh Government's policy statement concerning the Welsh language, entitled *Dyfodol Dwyieithog/A Bilingual Future*, outlined the Welsh Government's key role in invigorating Welsh as a community language. The document maintains that 'the reduction in the number of primarily Welsh-speaking communities is clearly one of the most serious threats to the future of the Welsh language' (WAG 2002, p. 11). In order to address this threat two main policy solutions are advocated. This first is to create economically and socially sustainable communities. The second policy solution is to encourage planning and housing policies and decisions to take account of the linguistic character of communities. Subsequent documents have reiterated the same commitment to preserving Welsh as a community language within 'y Fro Gymraeg' (e.g. WAG 2003; WG 2012). While the most recent consultation document published by the Welsh Government (WG 2016) is suggestive of a more nuanced take on the linguistic significance of 'y Fro Gymraeg' (see below for further detail), much political and public discourse in Wales still reinforces the need to protect the Welsh-speaking heartland (and the Welsh-speaking communities that lie within it).

The discussion in this subsection illustrates the conflict that can exist between different versions of the same region, with one being defined in more political and administrative terms, and the other being more overtly linguistic and cultural in nature. Importantly, there have been attempts to develop a closer articulation between these two versions of the region.

20.4 CONTESTATION AND THE CREATION OF MULTIPLE WELSH CULTURAL REGIONS

The above narrative, focusing as it does on the relationship between Welsh regional spaces and Welsh spaces of regionalism represents somewhat of a well-worn theme within studies of regions and cultural representation. At the same time, however, one is aware of the fact that the 'group-making' process associated with all kinds of group identities – national and regional – are, ultimately, variegated and contested in nature (Brubaker 2004). One cannot speak, therefore, of a singular, more cultural form of regionalism that exists in opposition to a state-sponsored regionalism. Certainly, when one focuses on Wales, one becomes aware all too quickly of the existence of many 'Waleses' and many cultural regions within Wales. The existence of these multiple regions, of necessity, complicates a simply binary relationship between regional spaces and spaces of regionalism.

In this respect, Wales is, arguably, an ideal context within which to examine the existence of multiple cultural regions. It has been suggested that Wales, as a region, is even more fractured and subdivided than other regions. Wales has been described by one sociologist as a 'community of communities' (Day 1998) and work by geographers and others has demonstrated the fact that there are 'many different ways to be Welsh' (Cloke et al. 1998; Bowie 1993). At a broad level, one needs to be aware of the fact that the Welsh-speaking identity associated with the cultural region of y Fro Gymraeg merely represents one particular interpretation of what it means to be Welsh. Labour historians, largely based in south Wales, have been keen to contest the Welsh-speaking identity associated with the Welsh-speaking and rural heartland, seeking instead to promote an alternative version of Welshness – and an alternative Welsh cultural region – that can be found in the more industrialised parts of Wales (e.g. Smith 1988). For these academics, Welshness should be viewed as something that is connected with heavy industry and the particular kinds of socialist communities located in the south Wales coalfield. The ways of living in these communities have, it is argued, helped to generate a different kind of Welsh culture, based on communitarianism and socialism, and expressed most obviously today in a love of the sport of rugby. But this is just the beginning of the story. Others have questioned the partial nature of these two dominant geographical imaginations of Welshness. North-east Wales and the more coastal parts of south-east Wales are doubly marginalised, it has been argued (e.g. Evans 2007). They are excluded from both a cultural region in the north and west, defined primarily in linguistic terms, as well as from an alternative cultural region centred on an urbanised and industralised south Wales. Calls have been made to interrogate and celebrate the other kinds of Welshness that exist in these, often 'forgotten' Welsh cultural regions.

The existence of these different interpretations of Welshness – and of alternative Welsh cultural regions – has also been played out in more political and public contexts. One of the most significant conflicts arising from these different conceptions of Welsh culture and Welsh cultural regions occurred in the context of the campaign that was fought by many Welsh nationalists during the 1960s and 1970s to change the monolingual English road signs dotted throughout the region into bilingual ones (for an account, see Merriman and Jones 2009; Jones and Merriman 2009). While the campaign attracted a variety of different actors – including Plaid Cymru, the Welsh Language Society, and the Friends of the Language (a more middle-class, middle-aged and respectable group of professionals) – it is also significant for the ire it drew from other Welsh people, who saw the campaign as an unwelcome distraction from the more pressing issues facing Wales during that period. As Dafydd Iwan, leader of the Welsh Language Society at the height of the campaign, put it in a recent interview (quoted in Jones and Merriman 2009), the road sign campaign succeeded in polarising opinion in Wales with a 'large number of non-Welsh speakers wondering what the fuss was all about'. Key figures in the Welsh Office were also opposed to the notion of bilingual road signs, most notably George Thomas, the one-time Labour Secretary of State for Wales. He described the Welsh Language Society's campaign as the antics of a 'lunatic fringe' and maintained that the issue of road signs had the potential to enflame anti-Welsh-language sentiments within Wales. The resentment that the campaign generated also spilt over into violence. A report published in the *Western Mail* (1969) detailed the confrontation that had taken place between a coach-load of language activists and the local residents of the town of Rhaeadr in mid-Wales. A number of individuals had decided to daub monolingual English road signs in the town but were apprehended and confronted by a group of the local townspeople. The townspeople forced entry onto the coach before verbally and physically abusing the students. The local townspeople in Rhaeadr objected to the students' behaviour and to their 'general attitude *towards the rest of Wales*' (*Western Mail* 1969, emphasis added). Here, we witness how certain groups of people could contest the discourse that underpinned the road sign campaign and could, significantly, draw upon alternative geographical imaginations to do so (Jones and Merriman 2009). Bilingual road signs, according to the townspeople of Rhaeadr, were, at best, an issue for those areas of Wales containing the highest percentages of Welsh speakers. It was irrelevant for people living in the more Anglicised areas of mid and east Wales. We get a flavour, here, of the different kinds of opinions being aired about the road sign campaign and the way in which these reflected different popular imaginations of the Welsh cultural region at the time.

The above discussion shows how we need to appreciate the existence of multiple cultural regions; even within the same regional space. At the same time, recent work on relational regions has also illustrated the benefits accruing from thinking about the territorial shape of regions in more sophisticated ways; ways that possess implications, necessarily, for how we think about cultural regions. Debates about a relational region (Varró and Lagendijk 2013) and the need for regions to engage with a 'politics of connectivity' (Amin 2004) signal a potential re-evaluation of the significance of cultural regions defined purely in territorial terms. A territorial imagination is still significant for cultural regions but one also needs to consider how these regional territories come into being through networked connections between people, infrastructures and things of different kinds (Merriman and Jones 2017). Whereas some of these may well be located within the cultural region in question, others may exist outside it (while still being connected to it in various ways).

I shall discuss two brief examples, which illustrate the value of adopting such an approach. The first relates to how the Welsh government, in its most recent consultation document concerning the Welsh language, is beginning to develop new conceptualisations of a Welsh cultural region, defined in linguistic terms. It has attempted to backtrack significantly from its commitment to securing the future of Welsh as a community language in the Welsh heartland. Specifically, it has begun to think the unthinkable by asking whether, in an age of movement and flow, a focus on protecting Welsh as a community language – understood in territorial, enclosed and parochial terms – is practical or realistic:

We recognise that the meaning of 'community' now includes networks of common interest and digital networks, which not only connect people scattered in cities or in the countryside, but which also bridge continents. That being so, we need to consider to what extent the emphasis on 'community' as a residential, geographical entity is still important? (WG 2016, p. 15)

The import of such a statement cannot be underestimated since it reflects a revolution, not just in terms of government policy relating to the Welsh language, but also – more significantly – with regard to geographical imaginations of Wales and Welshness. Instead of viewing a Welsh cultural region as a static and purely territorial entity, such a statement opens the door to more flexible, relational and even topological understandings of the Welsh language and culture and, by extension, the Welsh cultural region (for similar, fuzzy, interpretations of regions in Wales, see Heley 2013).

A second way in which a Welsh cultural region is being reconsidered in more relational and topological ways revolves around attempts to interrogate the relationship between the Welsh language and social media. Debates about the role that minority languages, such as Welsh, should play in relation to computing, the Internet and social media have been ongoing ever since the invention of these new technologies (e.g. Jones and Uribe-Jongbloed 2013). While English remains the most popular language for minority language speakers when using these new means of communication, it is also evident that a small and active minority have sought to use minority languages in creative ways, when using these new technologies. One of the most interesting ways of approaching this issue is in relation to the use of Welsh on Twitter. The map in Figure 20.3 shows the location of Welsh-medium tweets and conveys a very different kind of geographical imagination of the Welsh language and of the Welsh cultural region to that which appeared in Figures 20.1 and 20.2. As well as drawing more attention to the significance of a young and technologically skillful class of Welsh speakers in Cardiff, the capital of Wales, than a more conventional map of Welsh-language ability would, it also hints at particular kinds of mobility that are associated with Welshness; witness the Welsh-language tweets happening on the Severn Bridge as Welsh speakers either arrive in or leave Wales, and those taking place on ferries in the middle of the Irish Sea. We see here how a focus on social media enables one to develop an understanding of an alternative geographical configuration of the Welsh language and new topological interpretations of a Welsh cultural region.

The map also reinforces the fundamental argument of this subsection: namely that there are many different ways of engaging with Welsh culture, and the Welsh language as a specific marker of it. These different engagements with Welshness, of necessity, lead to different geographical configurations of a Welsh cultural region. Some of these configurations, being more comprehensible or palatable to the state, have greater scope to be articulated positively with the regional spaces being promoted by the Welsh government, while others may well remain as perpetual spaces of regionalism, existing in conflict or tension with more officially designated regions. The challenge for scholars of the region, as well as policy makers, is to appreciate this fluidity and the implications that it has for notions of sociocultural inclusion and exclusion within the region.

20.5 CONCLUSIONS: CULTURAL REGIONS IN PROSPECT

My aim in this chapter has been to examine the relationship between culturally defined regions and more administratively and politically defined ones, and to do so through reference to the various institutionalisations of regions that have taken place in Wales over the past fifty or so years. While tensions can exist between these different kinds of regions, it is also evident that it is possible to develop more productive dialogues

Figure 20.3   A map of Welsh-medium tweets

between them. At the same time, one also needs to recognise the multiplicity of cultural regions that can exist within the same place. The growing academic and public policy recognition of the significance of relational and topological regions has only served to complicate further this picture. There is rarely a straightforward interaction, therefore, between a singular cultural region and the regional spaces within which it is located.

Besides using the conclusion as a way of providing a recap of the main arguments made in the chapter, I also wanted to discuss briefly some possible challenges arising in relation to the future trajectories of cultural regions (see Paasi and Metzger 2017). It is clear, in this context that the future roles of regions, including cultural regions, may well become even more pertinent and pressing – especially in Europe – in relation to the fundamental questions that are being asked about the European Social Model, notions of territorial justice and political and cultural representation. For instance, to what extent do high degrees of cultural distinctiveness require high levels of political and administrative autonomy? To what extent can a perceived failure of the European Social Model within many 'peripheral' regions be addressed by higher levels of regional autonomy? When viewed as a whole, these current academic and policy debates highlight the continued – and, quite possibly – growing saliency of the need to consider the fluid and contested interactions between political and cultural regions. As well as being crucial academic questions, they also, patently, have the potential to affect the opportunities available to cultural groups living and working in various regions throughout Europe.

It may be that some recent developments in Wales provide a potential way of contributing to broader re-evaluations of the kinds of governmental roles that regions – including cultural regions – might play in the future. As part of a national conversation that has taken place in Wales over the past few years, the people of Wales have been encouraged to determine 'the Wales we want/*y Gymru a garwn*' (Sustain Wales 2015, p. 2) or, in other words, the Wales that they would like to see in existence in the year 2050. There are many significant aspects to this process, not least the attempt to connect the trajectories of the Welsh region or nation to the principles of sustainable development (Jones and Ross 2016). For the purposes of this chapter, what we witness here is an attempt to enrol the people of Wales into a conversation about the future that they would like to see for their children and grandchildren. Seven 'foundations of the well-being of future generations' in Wales formed the basis of the conversation including, significantly, the fact that 'celebrating success, valuing our heritage, culture and language will strengthen our identity for future generations' (Jones and Ross 2016, p. 5). In many respects, such an exercise represents an effort to draw together different individuals, organisations and communities in Wales in order to map out the future of both the Welsh political region and the Welsh cultural region and, more importantly, to imagine a productive association between the two. I apologise to the reader if I am a little too optimistic and partisan when I suggest that the approach taken in Wales might well provide one way of addressing the broader challenges facing both political and cultural regions, elsewhere, in the present and the future; but I do so to stimulate policy and academic debate concerning their possible futures.

20.6   REFERENCES

Amin, A. (2004), 'Regions unbound: towards a new politics of place', *Geografiska Annaler: Series B*, **86** (1), 33–44.
Bowen, E.G. (1959), 'Le Pays de Galles', *Transactions and Papers of the Institute of British Geographers*, **26**, 1–23.
Bowie, F. (1993), 'Wales from within: conflicting interpretations of Welsh identity', in S. Macdonald (ed.), *Inside European Identities*, Oxford: Berg, pp. 167–193.
Bristow, G. (2010), *Critical Reflections on Regional Competitiveness: Theory, Policy and Practice*, London: Routledge.
Brubaker, R. (2004), *Ethnicity Without Groups*, Cambridge, MA: Harvard University Press.
Cloke, P., M. Goodwin and P. Milbourne (1998), 'Cultural change and conflict in rural Wales: competing constructs of identity', *Environment and Planning A*, **30** (3), 463–480.

Cole, A. and R. Pasquier (2015), 'The Breton model between convergence and capacity', *Territory, Politics, Governance*, **3** (1), 51–72.

Day, G. (1998), 'A community of communities? Similarity and difference in Welsh rural community studies', *The Economic and Social Review*, **29** (3), 233–257.

Evans, D. (2007), 'How far across the border do you have to be to be considered Welsh? National identification at a regional level', *Contemporary Wales*, **20** (1), 123–143.

Gruffudd, P. (1994), 'Back to the land: historiography, rurality and the nation in interwar Wales', *Transactions of the Institute of British Geographers*, **19** (1), 61–77.

Gruffudd, P. (1995), 'Remaking Wales: nation-building and the geographical imagination. 1925–50', *Political Geography*, **14** (3), 219–239.

Harrison, J. (2007), 'From competitive regions to competitive city-regions: a new orthodoxy, but some old mistakes', *Journal of Economic Geography*, **7** (3), 311–332.

Harrison, J. and J. Heley (2015), 'Governing beyond the metropolis: placing the rural in city region development', *Urban Studies*, **52** (6), 1113–1133.

Haughton, G. and P. Allmendinger (2015), 'Fluid spatial imaginaries: evolving estuarial city-regional spaces', *International Journal of Urban and Regional Research*, **39** (5), 857–873.

Heley, J. (2013), 'Soft spaces, fuzzy boundaries and spatial governance in post-devolution Wales', *International Journal of Urban and Regional Research*, **37** (4), 1325–1348.

Johnes, M. (2012), *Wales Since 1939*, Manchester: Manchester University Press.

Jones, E.H.G. and E. Uribe-Jongbloed (eds) (2013), *Social Media and Minority Languages: Convergence and the Creative Industries*, Bristol: Multilingual Matters.

Jones, M. (2001), 'The rise of the regional state in economic governance: partnerships for prosperity or new scales of state power', *Environment and Planning A*, **33** (7), 1185–1211.

Jones, M. and G. MacLeod (2004), 'Regional spaces, spaces of regionalism: territory, insurgent politics and the English question', *Transactions of the Institute of British Geographers*, **29** (4), 433–452.

Jones, R., M. Goodwin, M. Jones and K. Pett (2005), '"Filling in" the state: economic governance and the evolution of devolution in Wales', *Environment and Planning C: Government and Policy*, **23** (3), 337–360.

Jones, R. and C. Fowler (2007), 'Where is Wales? Narrating the territories and borders of the Welsh linguistic nation', *Regional Studies*, **41** (1), 89–101.

Jones, R. and P. Merriman (2009), 'Hot, banal and everyday nationalism: bilingual road signs in Wales', *Political Geography*, **28** (3), 164–173.

Jones, R., P. Merriman and S. Mills (2016), 'Youth organizations and the reproduction of nationalism in Britain: the role of Urdd Gobaith Cymru', *Social and Cultural Geography*, **17** (5), 714–734.

Jones, R. and A. Ross (2016), 'National sustainabilities', *Political Geography*, **51**, 53–62.

Keating, M. (1998), *The New Regionalism in Western Europe*, Cheltenham, UK and Lyme, NH, USA: Edward Elgar Publishing.

Keating, M. (2001), *Nations Against the State: The New Politics of Nationalism in Quebec, Catalonia and Scotland*, Basingstoke: Palgrave.

Keating, M. (2017), 'Contesting European regions', *Regional Studies*, **51** (1), 9–18.

Merriman, P. and R. Jones (2009), '"Symbols of Justice": the Welsh Language Society's campaign for bilingual road signs in Wales, 1967–1980', *Journal of Historical Geography*, **35** (2), 350–375.

Merriman, P. and R. Jones (2017), 'Nations, materialities and affects', *Progress in Human Geography*, **41** (5), 600–617.

Paasi, A. (1991), 'Deconstructing regions: notes on the scales of spatial life', *Environment and Planning A*, **23** (2), 239–256.

Paasi, A. and J. Metzger (2017), 'Foregrounding the region', *Regional Studies*, **51** (1), 19–30.

Smith, D. (1988), *Wales: A Question for History*, Bridgend: Seren.

Sustain Wales (2015), *The Wales we Want: A Report on Behalf of Future Generations*, Cardiff: Sustain Wales.

Thomas, N.J., D. Harvey, H. Hawkins (2013), 'Crafting the region: creative industries and practices of regional space', *Regional Studies*, **47** (1), 75–88.

Varró, K. and A. Lagendijk (2013), 'Conceptualizing the region: in what sense relational?', *Regional Studies*, **47** (1), 1–11.

WAG (2002), *Dyfodol Dwyieithog/A Bilingual Future*, Cardiff: Welsh Assembly Government.

WAG (2003), *Iaith Pawb: A National Action Plan for a Bilingual Wales*, Cardiff: Welsh Assembly Government.

Western Mail (1969), 'Ten scuffle with daubers', 17 February 1969.

WG (2012), *A Living Language: A Language for Living – Welsh Language Strategy 2012 to 2017*, Cardiff: Welsh Government.

WG (2016), *Consultation on a Welsh Government Draft Strategy: A Million Welsh Speakers by 2050*, Cardiff: Welsh Government.

21. Regional identities: quested and questioned
Kees Terlouw

21.1 INTRODUCTION

The study of sub-national regions was central to geography until the 1960s. The goal was to determine the individual character for each demarcated region based on a unique combination of spatial and social elements. For each region, geographers studied the interaction between physical layers – e.g. soil and climate – and the social, cultural and political aspects of human activities. The specific configuration of these interactions formed the essence or identity of that region. This academic quest for regions with a deeply rooted identity was questioned in the 1960s by a new generation of geographers who wanted to modernize geography and turn it into a spatial science. The focus in geography therefore shifted from regional synthesis to thematic specialization. Geography then split into many sub-disciplines, each seeking to generate knowledge that was more generally applicable and policy-relevant to the expanding welfare state (Holmén 1995; Johnston and Sidaway 2004).

Towards the end of the twentieth century the current validity of this national regulatory framework was challenged by proponents of globalization and especially its neoliberal acolytes. The ensuing debate helped to put the region and identity back into the limelight. Political regionalism became a potent force in regions like Scotland, Catalonia, Flanders, Northern Italy and Croatia. Their claims for autonomy, which were partly based on strong regional identities, rekindled academic interest in regions and regional identities. Regional identity became more important in politics but also in economic geography and economic policies. Many academics and policy makers now claim that through globalization the nation-state has given way to (urban) regions as the provider of an adequate framework for firms to be competitive. They link the competitiveness and innovative capacity of a region with the strength and type of its regional identity. While the location decisions of firms are increasingly based on soft factors related to regional identity, regional administrations and stakeholders try to project an attractive regional identity. Competitive regional identities emulating those of successful regions like Silicon Valley are quested by many regional administrations but are questioned by many academics (Jones and MacLeod 2004; Keating 2013; Brenner 2004; Paasi 2013). The rising tide of anti-globalization populism also brings these forward-looking regional identities into question and might spur a quest to strengthen more traditional regional identities (Turok et al. 2017, p. 2). These shifting conceptualizations of regions and their identities suggest that these are social constructions quested by many different stakeholders, but whose fetishizing and objectification is questionable (Paasi and Metzger 2017, p. 24). Regions and their identities are constantly evolving social constructions which give meaning to the spatial existence of humans and are linked to changeable political processes. The borders and the size of what people regard as a meaningful region are often contested. Not only the spatial form but also what characterizes the identity of a region are frequently questioned especially during political conflicts over which territory is the most suitable for people to determine their own future.

This point is clearly illustrated by the referenda held in 2014 in Scotland and 2016 in the United Kingdom. That Scotland has a distinct identity is hardly disputed, whereas the character of Scottish identity is contested. Is it a regional identity within an overarching British national identity? Is it one of the four nations which are united in the United Kingdom? Is it a nation without a state protecting its interests? Does the medieval 'Braveheart' embody the true Scottish identity? Or is its identity based on 'Scotland's future' as decided upon by the people of Scotland? These and other conceptualizations of Scottish identity are quested and questioned. The debate on Scottish independence was initially focused on what bounded or separated Scotland in relation to the rest of the United Kingdom. But it also resulted in a discussion on whether the people in regions within Scotland with a distinct identity, like the Shetland and Orkney islands, should also get more autonomy (Cartrite 2012). Their population voted, unlike the rest of Scotland, overwhelmingly against Scottish independence. They voted, like the rest of Scotland, by a large majority to remain in the EU but on one of these islands, Whalsay, 82 per cent of the inhabitants voted to leave (Kay 2016). People on Whalsay have a strong collective identity. 'It's a very small island and we're just all together – we are one big family' (Gall 2012). The island of Whalsay is a region with clear borders and its identity is based on a shared history and livelihood. Most of the inhabitants have worked till recently in its flourishing fishing industry (EC 2013; Cardwell and Gear 2013). They form 'a community which has faced and weathered crises whose outcome might have been disastrous. It is in precisely these respects that the fishery and Whalsay are identified with each other in people's minds' (Cohen 1987, p. 166).

The premise that regional identity plays a key role in such referenda is undisputed, but what the relevant region is and what constitutes its identity is contested. It is not only the spatial form and character of regional identities that are disputed but also the importance that different groups attach to a specific regional identity. Horizontally, regional identities compete with other, sometimes overlapping, regional identities. Vertically, the relations between regional identities and spatial identities at other scales are also subjected to political debate (Bauman 2004; Confino 1997). Time also affects these identity discourses. They change by adapting to changing political, social or economic circumstances. In addition, the positive or negative attitudes to changes over time are important elements of regional identity discourses (Terlouw 2017).

This chapter seeks to clarify the disputed and constructed character of regional identities by examining ways in which regional identity discourses are linked to other spatial identity discourses. The focus is on the different ways in which regional identities are used as arguments for or against particular developments, in effect creating different regional identity discourses in relation to other regional, local and national identities. Analysing these scalar linkages, the chapter shows the different ways in which regional identities are used in constantly evolving debates on spatial identity and societal change. But before delving into the cross-scalar relations of regional identities, it is pertinent to discuss how identities are formed and transformed in order to make sense of shifting notions of belonging and difference.

21.2   FROM INDIVIDUAL IDENTITY TO DIFFERENT IDENTITY DISCOURSES ON REGIONAL DEVELOPMENT

Identity conceptualizes which elements $(n-1)$ characterize an entity (n) and how this relates to others $(n+1)$. Individual identity gives meaning to the relation between the individual (n) and the communities to which one belongs $(n+1)$ in relation to the different character traits a person possesses $(n-1)$. These identities are not fixed; they are fluid. Life experiences shape and change an individual's identity, especially while he or she is acquiring new characteristics and has to deal with new challenges in maintaining relations with others. People adapt their identity to make sense of this strained and changing relation between their individual uniqueness and their collective sameness. Individuals try to comprehend these frictions by constructing a more or less coherent life story (n) which tries to make sense of their acquired characteristics $(n-1)$ and their changing relations with others $(n+1)$. These life stories or identity discourses not only change over time but also incorporate visions of change. Besides individual characteristics $(n-1)$ and the relation with others $(n+1)$, past $(t-1)$ and future $(t+1)$ changes of identity are also part of a given identity discourse at a specific moment in time. Identities are based on life stories about who I was, who I am, and who I want to become. Identity is a story created, told, revised and retold throughout life. Identity is not only about sameness and difference but also about stability and change (Verhaeghe 2014; Ricoeur 1991; Bauman 2004). Groups (n) also have identities which likewise make sense of the even more strained and changing relation with yet larger entities $(n+1)$ based on a selection of their components $(n-1)$. '"identity" is revealed to us only as something to be invented rather than discovered; as a target of an effort, "an objective"; as something one still needs to build from scratch or to choose from alternative offers and then to struggle for and then to protect through yet more struggle' (Bauman 2004, pp. 15–16). Regional identity is not a fact but a

> social construct that is produced and reproduced in discourse. The discourses of regional identity are plural and contextual. They are generated through social practices and power relations both within regions and through the relationship between regions and the wider constituencies of which they are part (Paasi 2013, p. 3).

Like any other kind of identity, regional identities not only position a certain region with reference to other ones but also in time, to the past and the future. A regional identity discourse is also a kind of life story about the formation of a regional identity through history and about its hoped or feared future development. Laments about the 'good old days' and the perceived decline of spatial identities are pervasive elements of the discourse (Terlouw 2017). Paradoxically, the sense of loss propels identity into the political debate. The current phase of liquid modernity undermines established identities and thereby, ironically, enhances the importance attached to these threatened identities (Bauman 2004, pp. 13–46). The intergenerational continuity of communities is an important aspect of their identity. Anthony Giddens (1991) has stressed the importance of the reflexive awareness and discursive consciousness of identities in dealing with existential anxiety. This results in the continuous incorporation of how one has to deal with new threats into their identity discourses.

Diminishing identity and the fear of its further decline constitute a widespread

Table 21.1 Aspects of regional identity discourses

ASPECT	Ranging from traditional *thick*:	**to future-oriented** *thin*:
Spatial form	Closed	Open
	Territorial	Network
Organization	Institutionalized	Project
Participants	General population	Administrators and specific stakeholders
Purpose	Broad and many	Single
	Culture	Economy
Time	Defensive	Offensive
	Historically oriented	Future-oriented
	Stable	Change
	Old	New
Scale focus	Local and National	Global

Source: Terlouw (2009).

narrative in the regional identity discourses of the population in well-established regions. These discourses of fear and decline contrast with those of administrations which hope to improve the economic performance of their region. Many of these policy discourses focus on regional competitiveness and stress the importance of specific characteristics of the region for its success. The administration thus creates new future-oriented and externally directed identity discourses. These are, however, difficult to align with the well-established traditional regional identity discourses which are common among the population. These old types of regional identity have been institutionalized and thickened over generations in a territory. On the other hand, these new forms of regional identity are much thinner; they are more susceptible to changes and challenges through their relations with the outside world. Table 21.1 gives an ideal-typical overview of the types of elements used in thick and thin spatial identity discourses. Elements of thick spatial identity tend to be backward-looking, placing value on the whole region and its population. They focus more on bonding within a region. Elements of thin identity focus more on bridging between regions. Thin spatial identities are more forward-looking and place value on the effectiveness of specific, mostly economic policies. Thin spatial identities are more functional and linked to sectoral policies, special interests and stakeholders, while thick spatial identities are more integrative. Thin spatial identities are thus created around a few – often economic – characteristics, while thick spatial identities embrace a broad range of cultural, social, political, landscape and economic characteristics. Thin spatial identities are more changeable. Their spatial form and meaning can be adapted to changing circumstances. They are less grounded in static territories with a fixed meaning but more responsive to the changing position of a region in larger networks (Terlouw 2009; Antonsich 2011, Sack 1997; Jones and MacLeod 2004; Bauman 2004, pp. 13–46).

21.3   REGIONAL IDENTITY DISCOURSES RELATED TO OTHER SPATIAL IDENTITIES

A key characteristic of regional identity discourses is that they position a region in space. A region is positioned horizontally with respect to other regions and vertically with reference to the nation to which they belong (n+1) and the localities which they enclose (n−1). These horizontal and vertical relations can be based on positive associations or on negative oppositions. Identities are always linked to processes of inclusion and association ('us') and processes of exclusion and distancing ('them'). Table 21.2 depicts the positive and negative associations between spatial identities. It shows six different ways in which regional identity discourses are linked to other spatial identities. These are discussed in the rest of this chapter.

Table 21.2   Positive and negative relations in regional identity discourses across scales

Positive \ Negative	Nation (n+1)	Region (n)	Local (n−1)
Nation (n+1)		Regional identity against national identity	
Region (n)	Regional identities as part of a national identity	Conflicts Similarity complementarity	Local resistance identities against regional identity
Local (n−1)		Regional identities protecting local identities	

21.4   LOCAL RESISTANCE IDENTITIES AGAINST REGIONAL IDENTITY

Regional identities tend to compete with local identities. People identify more easily with the local community they live in than with the more abstract and distant region (Terlouw 2017). The local community has a strong basis in the shared interests of living close to other people (Amin and Thrift 2002; Massey 2005). Sharing a local space in daily life generates more shared interests and experiences than living in a region could do. Although the daily life of almost all individuals extends beyond the place where they live, reaching into the wider region, their activities and networks intersect more often in their place of residence than in a region. Members of a local community share a residential setting, but many of them commute to different workplaces in the wider region. The same is true for recreational trips and visits to family and friends. All these networks and experiences fan out from the same place but do not create a clear delimited region. Not only what the relevant region for identification is, but also what characterizes it are less clear for a region than for a place. Regional and local identities also consist of various elements. Social characteristics of the local community are the key ingredients of local identity discourses, while regional identity discourses tend to focus more on spatial elements like buildings and the landscape (Terlouw 2017). Local identities are based largely on shared experiences in daily life, while regional identities depend more on forms of organization and communication linked to political processes (Paasi and Metzger 2017).

Local identity discourses are frequently used when local autonomy is threatened by regional cooperation or municipal amalgamation. The incompatibility and uniqueness of their local identity is stressed by accentuating the thick identity elements which set them apart from others, notably their territorial borders, history and cultural differences. Their local identity thus thickens into a local resistance identity discourse (Zimmerbauer and Paasi 2013; Zimmerbauer et al. 2012). The local population tends to protect the thick local identity. Meanwhile many administrations and business interests want to promote a thinner regional identity discourse in order to strengthen the economic competitiveness of the region. Those fearing the loss of local autonomy question these kinds of regional identity discourses. While local resistance identity discourses emphasize the differences between their local and the regional identity, they also question the importance of this thin regional identity. The population's weak identification with the region is frequently cited and compared with the strength of its local identification. Also questioned is the relative importance of the planned administrative region compared to other, sometimes competing and partially overlapping regions (Terlouw 2017).

For example in the Netherlands the vast majority of the inhabitants of Goedereede opposed the amalgamation of their municipality with three others into a large regional municipality uniting the whole island of Goeree-Overflakkee. They feared losing their local autonomy and their ability to protect some key characteristics of their local identity, mainly touristic entrepreneurialism and religious sentiments. They associated these characteristics with their distinct history. Opponents of amalgamation denied that the island was a region with a distinct identity. Some even went so far as to suggest that a centuries-old dam connecting the two parts of the island should be cut through, thereby restoring the medieval situation of two separate islands. Another way they questioned the regional identity of the island was by disputing its relevance as a relevant region compared to other regions. They stressed that they had more in common with other coastal touristic places on other islands than with the rural inland communities on the island of Goeree-Overflakkee (Terlouw and Hogenstijn 2015).

21.5 REGIONAL IDENTITIES PROTECTING LOCAL IDENTITIES

Regional and local identity discourses can also reinforce each other. The identity discourses of well-established regions tend to value the regional mosaic of similar local identities. The Dutch province of Brabant, for example, has a strong and widely recognized regional identity. Its small towns and snug villages are important elements of its regional identity discourse (van Gorp and Terlouw 2017). On the other hand, local identity discourses also place value on being part of Brabant. For instance, in a radio interview with the mayor of Tilburg, which was scheduled to host the official festivities to celebrate the King's birthday in 2017, the mayor invited people from the rest of the Netherlands to visit Tilburg while it was such a nice Brabantian town, with Brabantian hospitality and Brabantian conviviality

(NPO 2016). In this interview he mentioned the name of the region, Brabant or its adjective Brabantian, more often than the name of his town itself, Tilburg.

The formation of new regions does not have to result in the formation of local resistance identities that bond the local population against the outside world. Regional identity discourses can also be used to bridge local differences and collectively promote their interests. Especially when the local administration is not seen to effectively protect local identity and promote local interests, local support can grow for stronger regional cooperation or municipal amalgamation. The region is then used as a vehicle to protect local interests and identities (Terlouw and Weststrate 2013). Especially when the gap between the population and the administration is already wide and the dominant spatial identity discourses and administrative borders are divergent, a regional identity discourse linked to the scaling-up of the administration can gain support. Contrary to local resistance identity discourses, the local identity discourses do not thicken. Rather they become thinner and focus more on those similar or complementary elements in other identity discourses which are regarded as important for the future development of the region in its relations with others. These new regional identity discourses tend to be thin but can become more rooted by incorporating elements of thicker and more established local identity discourses through the layering of these different identities (Terlouw and van Gorp 2014).

To return to the example of municipal amalgamation on Goeree-Overflakkee, whereas the measure was opposed locally by the population and administration of Goedereede, it was strongly supported by the business community. This emanated from a growing awareness that the lagging island economy can only be improved by concerted action. The business community took the lead in formulating economic policies and promoting and communicating a new regional identity through island marketing. They used the attractive characteristics of the landscape and some thick identity elements linked to the local communities on the island to project a new and appealing regional identity to the outside world (Terlouw and Hogenstijn 2015; Terlouw 2016).

21.6 SIMILARITY AND COMPLEMENTARITY BETWEEN REGIONS

The identity discourses of different regions can strengthen each other. This is the case for new regions with a thin regional identity but also for well-established regions with a thicker regional identity. Regional administrators and politicians compare themselves with institutionalized regions, often to legitimize their claims for similar rights and privileges. Sometimes administrators from different regions even cooperate to collectively promote their interests. Through organizations like the Committee of the Regions, the Conference of European regions with legislative power, the four motors for European associates, regions cooperate to collectively promote their interests in the European Union. Within countries such organizations abound.

Stakeholders in well-established regions frequently use very similar regional identity discourses. Having a distinct history visible in their regional heritage and a distinct landscape within stable borders are important elements of most regional identity discourses. Regional historical associations and regional heritage agencies propagate these elements in similar ways in conjunction with regional administrations. Their publications echo the old-fashioned way in which regional identity was conceptualized in human geography until the 1960s. Previously regional identities were seen as facts to be uncovered by systematic study of the kind of livelihoods humans had developed over time by using their physical environment in their very own way, thus creating a mosaic of distinct regions (Holmén 1995; Johnston and Sidaway 2004).

The stakeholders in new regions frequently engage in similar regional identity discourses. For new regions emphasizing economic development, stakeholders tend to develop regional identity discourses which include associations with successful regions. The success of Silicon Valley in California has generated a multitude of regional identity discourses projecting the idea that they are or will be similarly successful, given a similar clustering of industries and knowledge institutions in their region (Brenner 2004; Keating 2013). The Netherlands now has a several such clusters: a Health, Shipping, Food, Energy and Metal Valley. The basis for these new Dutch 'valleys' lies in cooperation between municipalities, research institutions and the private sector. Their regional identity discourses focus on stimulating regional development by creating linkages similar to those on which the success of Silicon Valley is based. Their similarity – be it real, potential or imagined – with successful regions is a point frequently raised by the stakeholders to attract outside resources from private investors and especially from the central government.

Complementarity is also used to position a region as part of a mosaic of regions, whereby unique individual qualities are considered part of a larger whole. For instance, the regional identity discourses of these Dutch 'valleys' revolve not just around their regional strength based on their specialization but also around their complementarity, which strengthens the competitiveness of the Dutch economy as a whole (VDM 2016).

21.7   CONFLICTS BETWEEN REGIONS

Competition with other regions is another common theme in regional identity discourses (Boisen et al. 2011; Terlouw and van Gorp 2014). Many of the conflicts between new regions that are embedded in regional identity discourses may be traced to the overlap between competing regions and rival claims for which region and regional identity discourse is the best way to represent the identity and interests of regional stakeholders. Regions compete with each other on who is, or will be, the most successful in promoting the interests of their members. New regions with new borders and new regional identity discourses constantly emerge in reaction to the perceived shortcomings of older regions (Brenner 2004; Frey 2003). One example is the western urbanized core of the Netherlands, which has successively been conceptualized as a world-city, four city regions, two metropolitan regions and part of a larger Delta-metropolis (VDM 2016).

Regional identity discourses frequently stress the differences from neighbouring regions. Besides ascribing negative characteristics to the 'other', regional identity discourses of established regions also refer to their borders. Over time people living in the border areas can shift their affiliation from one region to the other. In the Netherlands, for example, the border between Twente and Salland has shifted. Twente, the more urbanized of the two, has developed a regional identity discourse based on its record of industrial innovation and its residential and landscape qualities, while Salland has remained a declining traditional agricultural region. The villages just over the border from Twente profit from the economic

collective path to a better future. Regional identities based on 'naturally bounded' historical regions can then be used to cultivate active national citizens (Paasi 2013, p. 6). In these
discourses regional identities are linked to the past while the nation is linked to the future.
The nation and the region are not conceptualized as competing but as complementary.

The emergence of a strong German national identity in the late nineteenth century can
be linked to the simultaneous ascendancy of regional identity discourses hinging on the
concept of 'Heimat'. Germany was an amalgamated territory uniting states with very
diverse political, economic and social histories. Its unification coincided with the transformation of society through industrialization and urbanization. That was the context
of the local identity discourse based on Heimat, which articulated the historical roots
of everyday local life. The German nation was conceptualized as a mosaic of different
Heimats and the general German culture as rooted in historically grown, specific local and
regional identities. This notion of Heimat was used to lay out a distinct national path to
modernity in opposition to the direction taken by other, especially West European nations
(Confino 1997; Applegate 1990; Cremer and Klein 1990). 'As one of Germany's responses
to modernity, the Heimat idea was a memory invented just when German society was
rapidly changing, as a bridge between past and present that looked uniquely dissimilar'
(Confino 1997, p. 98). The discourses on Heimat and local and regional identities have
taken various forms since the end of the nineteenth century. During the Nazi regime
Heimat was reformulated in terms of race, blood and soil. As part of this fascist legacy,
the Heimat idea was discredited in the first decades after the Second World War. Then in
the 1960s Heimat was adopted by left-leaning identity discourses criticizing West German
society for its renewed nationalism, American consumerism and environmental pollution
(Confino 1998, p. 193).

Not only well-established traditional regions but also new regions can strengthen
their identity discourses by linking up with national policy discourses. The focus would
then shift from the traditional, historical regional roots of national development to the
contribution that economically strong new regions could make to the nation as a whole.
The effectiveness of the relatively thin identity discourses of new regions depends to a
large extent on their association with national policy discourses. This is illustrated by the
regional identity discourses of metropolitan regions in the Netherlands. Their economic
competitiveness is promoted not only in terms of each region's individual characteristics
but also in terms of how they collectively, through interrelatedness and complementarity,
advance competitiveness in the Dutch economy as a whole (VDM 2016).

21.10 CONCLUSION

Besides being social constructions, regional identities incorporate many other kinds of
identity. Regional identities are best understood in relation to other identity discourses
and the different interests and power relations which drive these discourses. To understand regional identities it is necessary to position them in the wider debates on sometimes
competing and sometimes complementary spatial identity discourses. This chapter
has contextualized regional identities by relating them to local and national identities.
The overview of the various relations between spatial identity discourses highlights the
changing and disputed nature of regional identity discourses. As circumstances change,

regional identity discourses and the support for them can also change. This point has been elaborated in this chapter by discussing a wide variety of regional identity discourses of both well-established and newer regions linked in positive or negative ways to other spatial identity discourses.

In light of the examples given throughout the chapter, it is clear that regional identity is not a fixed fact linked to a stable territory but a dynamic discourse linked to other discourses on spatial identities. There is ample room for adapting regional identity discourses to different situations and interests. The borders, character, positive associations with others – both horizontally and vertically – are subject to different and changeable interpretations by different actors. As those interpretations are based on different valuations, they are either attracted to or repelled by particular regional identity discourses. Thus the regional identity quested by one is frequently questioned by another. In that sense regional identities should not be seen as a stable rock on which legitimate policies can be built but rather as a slippery slope of inconsistencies and shifting intentions. Although human geographers are frequently asked for advice on these kinds of political conflicts, the 'true' identity of a region cannot be determined. The most useful way to study regional identity is to analyse why some quest a particular identity discourse while others question it. Although its malleability prevents regional identity from becoming a key academic concept in geography, its indeterminate and inherently disputed nature pushes it to the foreground of the increasingly messy politics that characterize the faltering nation-state in search of legitimacy.

21.11   REFERENCES

Amin, A. and N. Thrift (2002), *Cities: Reimagining the Urban*, Cambridge: Polity.
Antonsich, M. (2011), 'Grounding theories of place and globalization', *Tijdschrift voor Economische en Sociale Geografie*, **102** (3), 331–345.
Applegate, C. (1990), *A Nation of Provincials: The German Idea of Heimat*, Berkeley, CA: University of California Press.
Bauman, Z. (2004), *Identity: Conversations with Benedetto Vecchi*, Cambridge: Polity.
Béland, D. and A. Lecours (2008), *Nationalism and Social Policy: The Politics of Territorial Solidarity*, Oxford: Oxford University Press.
Boisen, M., K. Terlouw and B. van Gorp (2011), 'The selective nature of place branding and the layering of spatial identities', *Journal of Place Management and Development*, **4** (2), 135–147.
Brenner, N. (2004), *New State Spaces: Urban Governance and the Rescaling of Statehood*, Oxford: Oxford University Press.
Cardwell, E. and R. Gear (2013), 'Transferable quotas, efficiency and crew ownership in Whalsay, Shetland', *Marine Policy*, **40**, 160–166.
Cartrite, B. (2012), 'The impact of the Scottish independence referendum on ethnoregionalist movements in the British Isles', *Commonwealth & Comparative Politics*, **50** (4), 512–534.
Cohen, P. (1987), *Whalsay: Symbol, Segment, and Boundary in a Shetland Island Community*, Manchester: Manchester University Press.
Confino, A. (1997), *The Nation as a Local Metaphor*, Chapel Hill, NC: University of North Carolina Press.
Confino, A. (1998), 'Edgar Reitz's Heimat and German nationhood: film, memory, and understandings of the past', *German History*, **16** (2), 185–208.
Cremer, W. and A. Klein (eds) (1990), *Heimat: Analysen, Themen, Perspektiven*, Bielefeld: Westfalen Verlag.
EC (2013), *Shetland: Whalsay Case Study Report*, Brussels: European Commission.
Flint, C. and P. Taylor (2007), *Political Geography: World-Economy, Nation-State and Locality*, Harlow: Pearson.
Frey, B.S. (2003), 'Functional, overlapping, competing jurisdictions: redrawing the geographical borders of administration', *European Journal of Law Reform*, **5** (3–4), 543–555.
Gall, C. (2012), 'Black fish scandal: how fishing quota scam saw tiny isle of Whalsay earn "Millionaires Island"

nickname', *Daily Record*, 25 September, accessed 11 September 2017 at http://www.dailyrecord.co.uk/news/scottish-news/black-fish-scandal-how-fishing-1117298.

Giddens, A. (1991), *Modernity and Self-Identity: Self and Society in the Late Modern Age*, Cambridge: Polity.

Holmén, H. (1995), 'What's new and what's regional in the new regional geography', *Geografiska Annaler: Series B*, **77** (1), 47–63.

Johnston R.J. and J.D. Sidaway (2004), *Geography and Geographers: Anglo-American Human Geography Since 1945*, London: Routledge.

Jones, M. and G. MacLeod (2004), 'Regional spaces, spaces of regionalism: territory, insurgent politics and the English question', *Transactions of the Institute of British Geographers*, **29** (4), 433–452.

Kay, J. (2016), 'Why Whalsay voted out?', *Shetland Times*, 29 June, accessed 11 September 2017 at http://www.shetlandtimes.co.uk/2016/06/29/why-whalsay-voted-out-joseph-kay.

Keating, M. (2013), *Rescaling the European State: The Making of Territory and the Rise of the Meso*, Oxford: Oxford University Press.

MacLeod, G. (1998), 'In what sense a region? Place hybridity, symbolic shape, and institutional formation in (post-) modern Scotland', *Political Geography*, **17** (7), 833–863.

Massey, D. (2005), *For Space*, London: Sage.

NPO (2016), 'De ochtend', accessed 20 October 2016 at http://www.nporadio1.nl/gemist/2016-09-02.

Paasi, A. (2013), 'Regional planning and the mobilization of "regional identity": from bounded spaces to relational complexity', *Regional Studies*, **47** (8), 1206–1219.

Paasi, A. and J. Metzger (2017), 'Foregrounding the region', *Regional Studies*, **51** (1), 19–30.

Ricoeur, P. (1991), 'Narrative identity', *Philosophy Today*, **35** (1), 73–81.

Sack, R. (1997), *Homo Geographicus*, Baltimore, MD: Johns Hopkins University Press.

Smith, A. (1983), 'Ethnic identity and world order', *Millennium: Journal of International Studies*, **12** (2), 149–161.

SSE (2013), *Streekeigen nieuwbouw in Salland*, Holten: Stichting Sallands Erfgoed.

Terlouw, K. (2009), 'Rescaling regional identities: communicating thick and thin regional identities', *Studies in Ethnicity and Nationalism*, **9** (3), 452–464.

Terlouw, K. and J. Weststrate (2013), 'Regions as vehicles for local interests: the spatial strategies of medieval and modern urban elites in the Netherlands', *Journal of Historical Geography*, **40**, 24–35.

Terlouw, K. and B. van Gorp (2014), 'Layering spatial identities: the identity discourses of new regions', *Environment and Planning A*, **46** (4), 852–866.

Terlouw, K. and M. Hogenstijn (2015), *Eerst waren we gewoon wij en nu is het wij en zij: gebruik slijtage en vernieuwing van regionale identiteiten*, Den Haag: Ministerie van Binnenlandse Zaken en Koninkrijksrelaties.

Terlouw, K. (2016), 'Territorial changes and changing identities: how spatial identities are used in the up-scaling of local government in the Netherlands', *Local Government Studies*, **42** (6), 938–957.

Terlouw, K. (2017), *Local Identities and Politics: Negotiating the Old and the New*, London: Routledge.

Turok, I., D. Bailey, J. Clark, J. Du, U. Fratesi, M. Fritsch, J. Harrison, T. Kemeny, D. Kogler, A. Lagendijk, T. Mickiewicz, E. Miguelez, S. Usai and F. Wishlade (2017), 'Global reversal, regional revival?', *Regional Studies*, **51** (1), 1–8.

van Gorp, B. and K. Terlouw (2017), 'Making news: newspapers and the institutionalisation of new regions', *Tijdschrift voor Economische en Sociale Geografie*, **108** (6), 718–736.

VDM (2016), *Agenda voor metropoolvorming in Nederland*, Rotterdam: Vereniging Deltametropool.

Verhaeghe, P. (2014), *What About Me? The Struggle for Identity in a Market-Based Society*, London: Scribe.

Yack, B. (2012), *Nationalism and the Moral Psychology of Community*, Chicago: University of Chicago Press.

Zimmerbauer, K., T. Suutari and A. Saartenoja (2012), 'Resistance to the deinstitutionalization of a region: borders, identity and activism in a municipality merger', *Geoforum*, **43** (6), 1065–1075.

Zimmerbauer, K. and A. Paasi (2013), 'When old and new regionalism collide: deinstitutionalization of regions and resistance identity in municipality amalgamations', *Journal of Rural Studies*, **30** (1), 31–40.

22. Military-to-wildlife geographies: bureaucracies of cleanup and conservation in Vieques

Irus Braverman

22.1 INTRODUCTION

This chapter examines the interplay between territory, law and legal geographies through an exploration of the intricate relationship between militarism and conservation as it has played out in Vieques: a municipality island in the unincorporated US territory of Puerto Rico, located about seven miles southeast of the mainland. The chapter is strongly situated in the legal geography literature – namely, it seeks to expose the reciprocal relationship between law and spatiality, discovering the ways in which law is 'worlded' and the world is 'lawed.'

The Expanding Spaces of Law: A Timely Legal Geography (Braverman et al. 2014) identifies three modes of legal geography research: the first mode includes disciplinary work in law or geography and an import and export between the two disciplines; the second consists of an interdisciplinary bridge between law and geography, whereby a common project emerges; and the third mode represents a shift from inter-, to trans-, and even to post-disciplinary scholarship (Braverman et al. 2014, pp. 2–10). This latter mode is characterized by an engagement with third disciplines such as cultural anthropology, and with an integration of broader social and humanities concerns into the traditionally bi-disciplinary focus of law and geography (Braverman et al. 2014, p. 10).

It is precisely at the third mode of post-disciplinary legal geography that this chapter is situated. It engages in traditional geographical inquiries about the relationship between territory and power, military and nationhood, periphery and center, privatization and globalization and, perhaps most importantly, landscape and contamination. At the same time, the chapter is also concerned with legal questions about the role of law, bureaucratization, and shifting regulatory regimes and about how these both constitute and perpetuate the contaminated geographies in Vieques. In this sense, the chapter promotes a pluralistic understanding of law that not only moves away from the assumption that law is an exclusive project of the state (Von Benda-Beckmann et al. 2009), but also shows the fragmentation of this state and its inner contradictions. Finally, the chapter ties in broader humanities issues such as the relationship between nature and imperialism and the interconnections among the contaminated body of the human, nonhuman plants and animals, and the physical landscape. In this way, territory becomes a dynamic project that weaves together complex conceptions of law and an understanding of the interrelatedness of human and nonhuman ecosystems.

During the 1940s, the US Navy acquired about 25,000 acres on the eastern and western ends of Vieques. These lands were used for naval gunfire support and air-to-ground training from the 1940s until 2003, when as a result of insistent protests the Navy ceased all military operations on the island and transferred its property on the eastern side (and to a smaller extent, also on the western side) to the Department of the Interior's (DOI) US Fish and Wildlife Service (USFWS). The land was designated as a wildlife refuge upon transfer (Figure 22.1). In 2005, the US Environmental Protection Agency (EPA) added portions of Vieques to the Superfund National Priorities List: a list of the most heavily contaminated sites in the US (EPA 2013). Many military relics, including tanks, are still scattered around the island's landscape.

Vieques is but one of numerous 'Military-to-Wildlife' (M2W), or 'bombs to birds' (Krupar 2016, p. 122), sites in the US. Specifically, since the late 1980s, 'nearly two-dozen major military sites have been closed and [subsequently] reclassified [as wildlife refuges], adding more than one million acres to the US National Wildlife Refuge System' (Havlick 2011, p. 183). 'Paradoxically, military installations include the most contaminated as well as the most biodiverse lands managed by the federal government' (Havlick 2011, pp. 183–184; see also Sanders 2009; Wilcox 2007). Such contaminated yet wild sites challenge the ideal of pristine wilderness. Coates et al. suggest along these lines that, 'What makes the relationship between sites of biodiversity and toxicity on military lands particularly intriguing is that, far than being distant from one another, they are often adjacent and sometimes interdependent' (Coates et al. 2011, p. 468).

The hybrid nature of M2W lands has also presented new challenges to conservation managers, as the lands are often riddled with explosives or chemical contaminants (Havlick 2011). Furthermore, conversion into wildlife lands often conceals military impacts as these sites emerge with new names, new managers and new management goals without necessarily requiring a full military cleanup (Havlick 2011). These sites are therefore subject to a form of 'double erasure,' in Sasha Davis's phrasing. What is erased, he argues, is both the 'social life that existed in the place prior to its takeover by the military' and 'the history of the military's use' (Davis 2007, p. 131). Havlick asks along these lines: 'Will these places provide scientists and federal managers with new opportunities to critically examine the relationship between technology, militarism, and the environment . . . or will long-standing policies of exclusion and secrecy remain in place despite the change in land managers?' (Havlick 2011, p. 191). Finally, in her work on postnuclear landscapes, Shiloh Krupar highlights how the waste's repositioning into the realm of external wilderness makes for a 'refuge fix,' calling for an ethics attentive to the radioactive legacies of the Cold War era (Krupar 2011, p. 269). Since the presence of endangered species indicates 'a healthy rather than terminally polluted landscape . . . military-to-wildlife conversions supposedly demonstrate that military activities have not just destroyed nature but actively conserved it' (Krupar 2011, p. 122).

This chapter will study the relationship between militarism and the environment through the perspective of Commonwealth and federal officials involved with the cleanup in Vieques, and particularly through the perspective of USFWS officials who manage the majority of the contaminated land on the island. I am especially interested in the formal and informal regulatory mechanisms that connect (post)military and conservation landscapes. Such regulatory mechanisms expose both the centrality of the state for contaminating and purifying the colonial landscapes (Peluso 1993) as well as its simultaneous decline through privatization (Woodward 2014). The chapter is situated at the nexus of the scholarships on critical military geography, legal geography, and green imperialism.

The last few decades have witnessed a sharp increase in scholarship on critical military geography and post-military landscapes (Davis 2007, 2011; Havlick 2011; Krupar 2011,

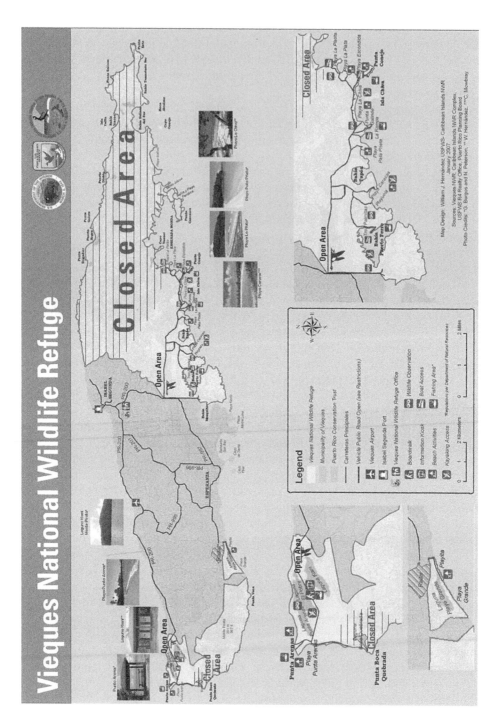

Figure 22.1   Map of Vieques' national wildlife refuge

2016; Woodward 2005, 2014). A prominent voice in this scholarship, Rachel Woodward highlights that: 'Post-military landscapes arguably demand different interpretative frames which take as their starting point the continuity of military imprint despite the removal of military power and control, and require us to look to their present and future particularly when re-use is orientated towards tourism and heritage' (Woodward 2014, p. 46). My chapter draws on this literature to understand the presence-absence of military bureaucracy in Vieques, namely how 'the global apparatus touches the ground' (Woodward 2014, p. 51).

My methodology for this chapter is predominantly ethnographic and, as such, draws on in-depth and recurring interviews and participatory observations with nine conservation officials who have been involved in the cleanup of Vieques. These interviews and observations were carried out from late 2014 until early 2015, especially during my visit to Vieques in January 2015. I have concealed the identity of some of my interviewees by using pseudonyms and by obscuring their affiliation. The Navy has not responded to my interview requests so I was unable to include their perspective here.

Sasha Davis' grounded work, too, has taken him to Vieques, mostly to document the local community's perspective (Davis et al. 2007). Unlike Davis' work, however, my chapter will study the perspective of conservation officials. My chapter thus adds another layer to the existing grounded scholarship on critical military geography: it offers a *legal* geography of military landscapes. Specifically, this project explores the administration of ordnance cleanup in Vieques: the laws, regulations, guidelines, and (in)formal practices exercised by various agencies in their efforts of removing contamination, or lessening it, and the complex interactions between these agencies.

22.2   VIEQUES: COLONIAL CONTAMINATION

Puerto Rico's ambiguous political status as an unincorporated territory of the US – with no voting rights but a non-voting delegate in Congress and a limited application of the Constitution – and Vieques's even more ambiguous status as a 'colony within a colony,' as the locals often refer to it, makes this place into a productive site for documenting the relationship between colonialism, militarism, and conservation. So while in many ways this island is no different than many other M2W and Superfund sites across the US, its colonial status creates a unique situation. It is from this particular status of the island, for example, that the complex role of the USFWS as both a colonizer and a benefactor emerges. Inheriting the contaminated military landscape of Vieques, the USFWS is assigned to monitor the Navy's cleanup while also shielding the existing natural resources from human development. This situation readily evokes the concept of ecological imperialism: the strategic imposition of Western environmental ideals on developing countries (Dreissen 2005; see also Braverman 2013; Martinez-Alier 2003). The traditional form of ecological imperialism, whereby Western forms of conservation are imposed on non-Western countries, is more extreme in Vieques in light of the ongoing marginalization of Puerto Rico. The controversial redesignation of federal lands in Vieques from M2W makes for one of the largest national wildlife refuges in the Caribbean.

In his book *Green Imperialism*, Richard Grove argues that 'modern environmentalism, rather than being exclusively a product of European or North American predicaments and philosophies, emerged as a direct response to the destructive social and ecological conditions of colonial rule' (Grove 1995, p. 489). Grove sees tropical islands as critically important geographies in modern environmentalism's coming of age, highlighting the complex interrelations between center and periphery and the radical form of conservation that has emerged by specialists and scientists in the periphery. In his words: 'it is perfectly clear that the motivations of those specialists who proposed controls (and who were critical of the ecological degradation which they saw happening) were by no means always identical to those of the state. On the contrary, they were sometimes actively anti-colonial' (Grove 1995, p. 479).

The bombing of Vieques was an essential aspect of its colonization and became even more intense when the Navy withdrew from Culebra, Vieques's smaller sister-island, in the 1970s. 'The Navy dropped a trillion pounds of explosives on Vieques, including napalm and everything in the US arsenal from the Second World War to 2003,' recounts Roberto Rabin, an outspoken leader in the fight against the Navy. Surveys of environments subjected to such weapons suggest, accordingly, that 'contaminants of the land and water resulting from these activities may include mercury, lead, copper, magnesium, lithium, perchlorate, TNT, napalm, depleted uranium, PCBs, solvents, and pesticides' (Porter et al. 2011, p. 74). Moreover, certain studies indicate that Vieques has 27 percent higher cancer rates than the rest of Puerto Rico (Navarro, interview) and many locals believe this to be the direct result of the military toxins in the environment. From the perspective of the locals, then, the contamination of the land has translated into the contamination of their bodies, for whom a cleanup would entail an entirely different process than the one being instigated in the landscape.

The devastating effects of the bombings formed the basis for a powerful resistance to the Navy, which reached its peak in the 1990s. Rabin describes: 'I remember grandmothers and grandfathers and little kids participating in protests and being arrested – priests, pastors, ministers, bishops – being arrested with us, in totally nonviolent actions. There was this immense power; the community was empowered.' The accidental death of David Sanes, a local employed in the Live Impact Area, by a Navy bomb in 1999 became the catalytic event that catapulted the struggle and finally led to the Navy's pulling out of Vieques in 2003. From this point, the material impact of nearly 70 years of routine bombing had to be dealt with. This process is referred to as the 'cleanup.'

22.3   THE CLEANUP AND USFWS

'Even the cleanup is controversial,' Gary Machlis tells me. Machlis is Science Advisor to the Director of the National Park Service and an expert on military landscapes. 'From a Viequense point of view,' he explains, 'if you really wanted the island cleaned up, you would put a hospital every 5 to 10 kilometers. But a wildlife refuge requires much less. . . . The cleanup continues at about 2 per cent a year, so it will be 50 years before it's done.' For this reason, community leader Roberto Rabin tells me, the USFWS 'has been used as a trashcan for military damaged lands in the US.' As a result of the partiality and the slow pace of the cleanup, some of the locals have been feeling that 'they were taken in twice: once when the land was expropriated and they were bombed for close to 70 years, and the second [time] when they finally got the Navy base out, and none of it was given back to them' (Machlis, interview). Rabin explains the local community's point of view:

> We had hoped that the decontamination process would involve a lot of community participation, that our scientists' [who are in] solidarity with Vieques from the universities here and [in] other places, would be able to take a part, and that it would be an important element to the economic development of Vieques as well.

Instead, Rabin tells me, the military brought in a multimillion dollar company: the CH2M Hill.

According to Rabin, the decontamination phase merely perpetuates the occupation and reifies Vieques' marginalization. 'These are the processes that I believe are again continuing to violate the basic needs and rights of the people of Vieques to have a real, genuine cleanup done,' he tells me. 'If left to the Navy,' Rabin continues, 'they would blow all that stuff up right in place, destroying whatever – they don't care. And the company would like to do that too so that they can make all their money quickly.' Indeed, the open detonation of unexploded ordnances has been going on for a decade or so. Rabin says: 'I would hope that there's some good influence from some nice people in the Fish and Wildlife, but they don't have the power, the control is really in the hands of the Navy.'

Rabin's portrayal of the USFWS as an agency with good intentions but little power to counter the colonial legacy of the Navy is the more positive perspective in this context. Many others, local Viequenses in particular, see the USFWS as part and parcel of the same military regime that reigned earlier, only concealed in green. 'There are very bad relations between Viequenses and USFWS,' Machlis tells me. Nonetheless, he emphasizes, 'this was not something that the USFWS sought. Vieques was forced upon them.'

Mario (pseudonym) is a USFWS employee in Vieques' natural wildlife refuge. He tells me: 'I was involved in clearing the protesters [out of the Live Impact Area] once this [became] Fish and Wildlife [land].' It was the same set of protesters who previously protested against the Navy, he explains. 'Same people, different cause. This time: kick the Fish and Wildlife out.' The USFWS is thus in a paradoxical position in Vieques. On the one hand, it performs policing missions typically assigned to the state, such as that of clearing out protestors. On the other hand, it finds itself disagreeing with the Navy on many issues, and in these cases it is politically aligned with the local community.

22.4 SUPERFUND BUREAUCRACY

Although the Navy is formally long gone from Vieques, military names and acronyms are still alive in the landscape: they are marked as such ostensibly in order to identify and document the cleanup process. The center of Vieques is designated as the 'civilian zone,' while the two opposite sides are defined as 'impact zones.' Mario of the USFWS explains that:

> the very tip where the [Navy] did most of their bombing is the Live Impact Area, the LIA. The next section is the SIA, the Secondary Impact Area. And the rest is the EMA [Eastern Maneuver Area]. The LIA is where they concentrated all their heavy power – that's the area with the most contaminations. Whatever they missed went into the SIA. (interview)

For the most part, the three military areas are still closed to the public. However, some of the beaches – named Red, Blue, Green et cetera by the Navy – have been cleaned, made

¡Peligro de Explosión!
Por su Seguridad
Permanezca
en la Vereda

Explosive Hazard!
For Your Safety
Stay on Marked Trail

Source: Photo by author, January 2015.

Figure 22.2   *Signs warn visitors from picking up suspicious objects serving as a reminder of the not-so-distant military occupation of Vieques*

accessible, and renamed according to their local, pre-military name. For instance, the famous beach of *La Chiva* – the goat – has replaced the Blue Beach, and Caracas replaced the Red Beach. Such renaming practices again speak to the ways in which the landscape is reimagined and reinvented, highlighting the double erasure of military history discussed in Davis's work. But the erasure of military presence in Vieques is far from complete: signs scattered along the beaches that warn visitors from picking up suspicious objects (for example, Figure 22.2) serve as constant reminders of the not-so-distant military occupation of the island. These signs contribute to the making of a hybrid tourist-military landscape.

Alongside the visible military traces, the landscape of Vieques is also highly determined by much less visible legalities. In 1980, the US Congress passed the Comprehensive Environmental Response Compensation and Liability Act (CERCLA), commonly referred to as the Superfund Act. Sites eligible for cleanup through Superfund are additionally listed by the US Environmental Protection Agency (EPA) on the National Priorities List (NPL) (NAVFAC, n.d.). At the request of the Governor of Puerto Rico, in 2005 the EPA designated large areas of Vieques and nearby waters, officially known as the Atlantic Fleet Weapons Testing Facility (AFWTF), as a Superfund Site (Porter et al. 2011). 'Because of its assignment to the NPL, most observers expected that cleanup of both terrestrial and marine environments [in Vieques] would start immediately,' ecologist James Porter writes (Porter et al. 2011, p. 110). 'This did not happen. Although the

Department of Defense had been held accountable under the EPA laws pertaining to CERCLA/Superfund Sites since 1985, in 2002, the Pentagon successfully sought exemption from almost all environmental laws and regulations, citing preparedness needs in a time of heightened national security concerns' (Porter et al. 2011, p. 110). The official superfund law was thus stripped of much of its power.

Notwithstanding, at least five Commonwealth and federal agencies have been involved in the Vieques cleanup: the Navy, the EPA, the USFWS, Puerto Rico's Environmental Quality Board (the equivalent of the EPA on the state level), and Puerto Rico's Department of Natural Environmental Resources (DNER). Craig Lilyestrom is director of marine resources at the DNER and the Natural Resources Trustee of both land and water in Puerto Rico. Lilyestrom explains that: 'CERCLA is the legal framework under which we have to work to perform the cleanup. That's why we have all these meetings with all these agencies: we go over there and approve the [cleanup plans] and make comments in the process.' Because of the prohibition of federal agencies from suing each other, 'we are the only agency that has the power to sue the Navy for noncompliance with the Superfund requirements,' he adds.

Under the legal geographies of CERCLA, the cleanup is configured first and foremost as a bureaucratic process. How much needs to be cleaned and to what degree, who will do the cleaning and how, who monitors the process and under what timeline – these questions and others are continually negotiated between multiple agencies, producing a massive number of documents, reports, reviews, court cases, and more reports. The complex technicalities of the Superfund process were highlighted by all my interviewees. Daniel Rodríguez, EPA's Remedial Project Manager in Vieques, told me:

> This is a very slow process. The thing is [that] to do your work you need to develop a work plan, we need to review the work plan, and from the work plan you create a report, we need to review a report and then we need to make sure you're complying with all the regulations that apply so that [we determine] that you are using sound science. And it has to be documented: every single decision that we make on this site it is backed up with data. It's not make-believe science. . . . I keep the exact original copy of the final draft here [points to library shelf].

The EPA website contains the following updated cleanup numbers for January 2016 (EPA 2016):

> Surface Clearance: Over 2,531 acres cleared of munitions; over 38,000 munitions items removed and destroyed; Sub-surface Clearance: A total of 9.5 miles of roads cleared (includes a 25-foot buffer on either side) and 10.7 miles of beaches cleared (includes sandy beach areas and a turtle nesting habitat); Scrap metal: Over 16.9 million pounds processed and over 13.2 million pounds recycled.

The intensified bureaucratization of the cleanup process serves to highlight both the control and the containment that government agencies exercise over hazardous military matter. Indeed, the manageability of the site becomes front and center of the cleanup project (Krupar 2011, p. 269). During a tour of the beaches of Vieques, Mario and his colleague Anna tell me that 'they're supposed to be done on land by 2023, which is another eight years, but then they've got the underwater zone. The underwater is supposed to be done by 2028.'

The cleanup process is also not consistent across the landscape. Lilyestrom explains that rather than removing every bomb from the island, the military looks for 'high density anomaly areas.' This search technique is good for finding where ordnance is common, 'but not as good at finding out where they're less common.' 'You're never going to be able to clean it completely,' Lilyestrom continues. 'So there's no way you're ever going to be able to tell someone that it's absolutely safe. . . . That's why they turn it over to Fish and Wildlife. . . . They hope that the wildlife isn't going to blow itself up . . . [but] if they do, it's less of a problem than if a person on a bulldozer gets blown up.' Such biopolitics of contamination spell out the differential treatment of bodies and the particular usefulness of nature and wilderness in the cleanup process. In Krupar's words: 'Essentially, that which has been liquidated is repackaged as ecological improvement and 'peace dividends'. . . . However, such military-to-wildlife conversions are also utopian projects of the nation-state, which propagate the idea that such lands are now demilitarized and safe for public recreation and observation of nature' (Krupar 2016, p. 122).

In Vieques, the superfluous and meticulous planning and paperwork, as well as the redundancies, contradictions, and delays inherent to the documentation and planning of the cleanup, reiterate that the Navy is far from leaving the island. In fact, its practices may well be impacting the landscape as much as during the bombing phase. Hence, not only the naturalization of the landscape but the bureaucratization of the cleanup process, too, serves as a form of erasure: it redirects attention to the (micro)technicalities and away from the (macro)politics of colonial contamination.

22.5   BOMBS VERSUS WILDLIFE: NEOLIBERAL INTERPRETATIONS

The USFWS officials I interviewed have suggested that if not for the military zones, the wild areas of Vieques would have already been developed, resulting in a variation on the nearby highly developed island of St. Thomas. But while the USFWS is the formal manager of the land in its new designation as a national wildlife refuge, this agency's officials in fact have to constantly negotiate their operations with the civil contractors who perform the physical clearing and cleaning in these areas. At this juncture, the carefully laid out plans to protect the habitat of the island's twenty-five endangered species, and its other wildlife, are being reinterpreted and redirected.

The everyday practices of ordnance cleanup on the part of the military and USFWS' wildlife conservation result in numerous conflicts. Lilyestorm recounts: 'you tell them to leave all the trees of diameter greater than 3 inches, the contractors say: "well, that tree was leaning against another one that we had to take down." This kind of stuff.' 'It's much more expensive for them to go cherry-picking and trimming rather than just cutting everything down and getting it out of the way,' Lilyestorm explains, adding that:

> Every now and again they'll run into a situation where they'll have to do a detonation. And [with] certain kinds of munitions, when you detonate them they send out incendiary materials, [so] they'll start a fire and you'll end up with 400 burned acres. You know, it's tough; it's tough to protect things when they're under that condition.

'"The budget is for cleanup, it's not for restoration," the [Navy] keeps telling us,' Lilyestrom continues. 'But there seems to be some way of getting around that [to] require [that] if you cut down a tree, you plant a tree. This way, [the Navy] may be made to pay for a restoration of some areas. It gives us a standing, in any case, to demand it.' Such checks and balances can be introduced precisely because of the complex bureaucratic layering of this project, which paradoxically enables malleable legalities to emerge.

In addition to their legal manifestations, the ongoing tensions between military and conservation interests are evident in the physical landscape. When we travel through the southwestern parts of the refuge, for example, Anna and Mario direct my attention to clear-cut areas and, within them, to tall piles of dead branches. 'They just pile everything together,' Mario explains. 'And nobody takes it away. That's an ongoing controversy that we have with the Navy.' These huge piles of cleared brush are a fire hazard, Mario complains. In the area's climate, they can set the entire area on fire, with devastating results for wildlife.

Another controversy between the USFWS and the Navy pertains to the land crab habitats scattered along Vieques' beaches. Land crabs are protected species in the Commonwealth of Puerto Rico and are managed carefully on Vieques, Mario tells me. He drives me to a particular site, where he explains: 'This is one of the primary land crabbing areas where we did all the studies. So we told the Navy: you treat that area like it was a baby, you go in there with a laser and just do the bare minimum. [But] they destroyed them.' Mario's frustration is evident. 'The Navy still doesn't know, but we'll file a report about this,' he comments.

On another day, Mario takes me to visit the closed military zone. After a long drive over rough dirt paths, we finally arrive at the LIA's Central Processing Center (Figure 22.3). 'This is where the Navy does their cleanup,' he tells me, pointing to the scrap metal,

Source: Photo by author, January 2015.

Figure 22.3   Live Impact Area's Central Processing Center, Vieques

the incinerator that burns off the residues, the drums for storing the scrap metal, and the containers which 'get shipped off the island to a metal scrap yard, and they get sold. This is how the cleanup goes. They're very organized, they're very methodical in their process' (interview).

Vieques' local residents are no longer allowed into the LIA, which used to be accessible to them (except during bombing times) when the Navy owned the land. USFWS personnel, too, are now formally required to coordinate with the Navy before they enter the LIA. Because live ordnance is still scattered in the area, the USFWS are prohibited from conducting a variety of management operations. Yet despite this official prohibition, USFWS personnel and other volunteers dig nests in the LIA for endangered hawksbill turtles to lay their eggs in, as part of their conservation management. While military regulations and policies continue to override and hinder the everyday conservation work on the island, the relevant agencies and nonprofits perform small acts of resistance through their insistence on practicing conservation even in the face of contrary military orders.

Keeping in mind that the USFWS is a federal agency, the turtle example, like many others, illuminates the underlying complexity of colonial power. Specifically, such examples demonstrate how the imperial center can lose control over its periphery. The complex and convoluted bureaucracy of the M2W conversion in Vieques means that conservation efforts – the initial purpose of the land's reclassification as a national wildlife refuge – are rendered semi-illicit. Richard Grove observes similarly that 'the sheer tyranny of physical and mental distance from the centre contributed to the growth of peripheral or even sectarian sympathies. Even colonial governments became peripheral in their attitudes' (Grove 1995, pp. 482–483). In this case, the center is not only the US Navy and its headquarters in the mainland, but also the central headquarters of the USFWS, which undermine the conservation operations in Vieques by understaffing and underpaying their Vieques constituents.

To complicate the picture, the presence of the USFWS on the island as well as its prioritizing of endangered species over human needs are perceived by many locals as a form of ecological imperialism. As Rabin's earlier quote emphasizes, the choice to turn the vast majority of the island into a wildlife refuge was anything but a local choice. Performed in the name of locals and proclaimed as enacted for their benefit, the locals were in fact never consulted about this move. The cleanup operations in Vieques thus provide a backdrop for ongoing clashes between different forms of colonialism.

22.6 RADIOACTIVE CONTAMINATION

While officials struggle to sort out the conflicting policies and regulations regarding the ongoing cleanup, both humans and nonhumans continue to be exposed to contaminants. 'We are almost wholly ignorant of the effects that high explosives and heavy metals have on ecosystem health and ecosystem function,' James Porter et al. write (2011, p. 103). James Porter is an ecologist with particular expertise in coral ecosystems. He explains in our interview that this ignorance is especially true for the underwater environment. 'Out-of-sight, out-of-mind thinking prevails,' Porter writes, 'but as most ecologists know, it rarely, if ever, works' (Porter et al. 2011, p. 110).

The question of radioactive contamination demonstrates the extent of the Navy's development in Twente and attract its residents. To protect their regional identity, municipalities along the border in Salland have drawn up policies that encourage building new houses in a style befitting the Salland region. To facilitate this new housing policy, they provide a style guide with modern versions of the traditional Salland farmhouse (SSE 2013). In other cases it is not the fluidity but the stability of the regional border that strengthens regional identity. The distinctiveness of Scotland is symbolized by the borderland heritage of castles whose narratives are part of Scottish identity discourses (MacLeod 1998).

21.8   REGIONAL IDENTITY AGAINST NATIONAL IDENTITY

Sometimes the 'other' in regional identity discourses is not a neighbouring region but the nation-state to which it belongs. The main opposition is then not directed horizontally at other regional identities but vertically against the national identity. The most conflictual spatial identity discourses question having 'only' a regional identity and stress that they also have a national identity. This 'nation without a state' narrative is widely used by those who appeal for secession of their region from their nation-state (Flint and Taylor 2007). In peripheral regions many associate nation-state formation with economic, political and cultural subordination. The perceived injustices have fed the regional identity discourses of decline and loss of thick identity elements. Many regionalist movements were started to defend their traditional regional culture and especially their language rights against national homogenization. Later, as in Flanders, the discourses promoting cultural and language rights were extended with arguments initially promoting political and eventually socio-economic autonomy (Béland and Lecours 2008). In Flanders, as in Scotland and Catalonia, regional identity discourses have shifted over the past few decades. The goal of preserving thick identity elements has given way to promoting thinner elements, particularly their own regional economic development potential, bringing the region into direct competition with the nation-state.

   The national identity is sometimes questioned by regional actors, but national identity discourses also question the importance and character of regional identities. Traditionally most academics and nationalists see the rise of national and the decline of regional and local identities as two sides of the same coin. The decline of regional identities since the nineteenth century was welcomed as a step toward breaking down the legacy of medieval society. Those traditional bonds were seen as posing constraints on individuals in their pursuit of modernity, individual freedom, democracy and economic development. Urban and regional identities were seen as relics of the divisive medieval past, which was finally being supplanted by future-oriented modern and integrative nationalisms. Modern individuals were presumed to identify predominantly with their national community (Smith 1983; Paasi 2013; Yack 2012).

21.9   REGIONAL IDENTITIES AS PART OF A NATIONAL IDENTITY

National and regional identity discourses can also strengthen each other. The national identity then crowns the traditional regional identities and unites them by providing a 'out-of-sight, out-of-mind' mentality and its secretive and exclusionary operations. In addition to the chemical ordnance, 'the Navy admitted to strafing the eastern end of the island with 267 rounds of armor-penetrating depleted uranium ammunition,' Porter et al. write (2011, p. 71). In their words:

> Because the use of radioactive munitions required special permission from the US Nuclear Regulatory Commission (which had not been obtained), the Navy attempted to recover the material. Although approximately half of the depleted uranium shell casings were located (only from land sites), none of the radioactive material contained in them was found, leading to concern that radioactive materials from this depleted uranium ordnance may also have spread into the marine environment. (Porter et al. 2011, p. 71; see also Vera, interview)

The risk of radioactive contamination on Vieques is further indicated by the presence of the sunken USN Killen, a Navy ship launched in 1941 and used as a target during the atomic bomb tests in the Marshall Islands. The Navy claims that the Killen underwent a water wash after the atomic blasts to remove as much of the radioactivity as possible (Porter et al. 2011, p. 70). In 1975, the Killen was towed to Vieques and scuttled just across from the LIA. Seven years later, a survey conducted by both the DNER and the Navy concluded that the ship's wreckage is 'an important marine habitat and that no action should be taken to remove the remaining hulk because it would be ecologically damaging to attempt to do so' (quoted in Porter et al. 2011, p. 113–114).

According to Porter, corroding bombs on Vieques' coral reefs spill and leach out onto the surrounding reef, contributing to the chemical contamination of the area. The area surrounding the Killen in particular was found to be chemically contaminated. However, Porter found no indication of radioactive contamination 'that would have been associated with [the Killen's] participation in nuclear testing on the US Marshall Islands in 1958' (Porter et al. 2011, p. 115).

22.7 CONCLUSION

Military interests and procedures still shape ex-military spaces even in the absence of formal control (Woodward 2005, 2014). Vieques exemplifies this disjuncture between presence and absence: while on paper the Navy is responsible for cleaning the island from military contamination, it has in fact delegated the everyday cleanup operations to private companies. Governmental agencies such as the USFWS, EPA, DNER, as well as nonprofit and community groups, monitor the situation to ensure that the Navy and its contractors perform their job with the least damage to the environment. This chapter has examined the bureaucracies of this cleanup, highlighting the complex interrelations between the different agencies, personalities, and interests that operate in this place.

The original colonial narrative underlying the historical designation of Vieques as a bombing range and the continued military presence on the island is straightforward, some may even say banal (Davis 2011). 'There were developed countries and underdeveloped countries,' Porter explains in our interview. 'Puerto Rico wasn't a main concern to the [United] States, and Vieques was even less of a concern than Puerto Rico. So if you want to do some testing, [you say] "Hey, let's do it in Bikini [atoll], let's do it in Vieques! . . . Let's keep our house clean. We can dirty somebody else's [house] with the stuff we have to do"' (interview). Davis writes in this regard: 'It should be emphasized that the colonialisms on these islands hosting military facilities are very enduring and consistent. Changes in American political administrations, including to the current Obama administration, have had very little effect on either military planning or questions of political status' (Davis 2011, p. 2; citations omitted).

But while this traditional form of colonialism may not be new, the ongoing geopolitical militarism in Vieques is newly obscured behind heaps of bureaucratic documents and complex legal geographies. This highly bureaucratic militarism is in turn privatized by the state. Alongside the old-fashioned colonialism, then, an extensive bureaucracy and a new form of cleanup have emerged that feed on the prevailing neoliberal order and that result in the outsourcing, privatization, and subcontracted management of military functions and actions (Woodward 2014, p. 45). As this chapter has documented, the privatization of the cleanup has added several layers of operational conflicts to restoration efforts in Vieques. Colonialism in Vieques thus takes on different shapes, both traditional and transformed.

In the military legal geographies of Vieques, environmental cleanup is trapped between conflicting colonial and neoliberal interests, necessitating complex navigations among multiple agencies. The USFWS in particular is in a difficult bind: perceived as an arm of the Navy by the people of Vieques, the USFWS' office on the island is underfunded and understaffed. The words of Richard Grove are highly pertinent in this context. 'At some periods,' he writes in *Green Imperialism*, 'departments or agents of the colonial state have themselves taken on a sectarian or peripheral role in countering the complacency of a metropolitan centre unable or undisposed to be sensitive to the environmental risks perceived in the peripheral colonial state' (Grove 1995, p. 485). Indeed, the USFWS in Vieques is engaged in multiple forms of peripheral conservation projects, which seem to go against the colonial state. Simultaneously, in imposing certain environmental ideals on the local communities without executing democratic decision-making processes, the USFWS exercises a form of ecological imperialism.

22.8   INTERVIEWS

Mario (pseudonym), Vieques Refuge, USFWS. In-person, Vieques, PR. In-person, January 12–13 and 16, 2015.
Craig Lilyestrom, Director, Marine Resources Division; Natural Resources Trustee, PR's DNER. Telephone, November 12, 2014.
Gary Machlis, Professor of Environmental Sustainability, Clemson University; Science Advisor to the Director, National Park Service. Telephone, September 28, 2014.
Cruz Navarro-Delgado, Biostatistics and Epidemiology, School of Public Health, University of San Juan. Telephone, September 18, 2014.
James W. Porter, Meigs Professor of Ecology, Odum School of Ecology, University of Georgia. Telephone, September 24, 2014.
Roberto Rabin, Director, Fortin Conde de Mirasol Museum. January 19, 2015. In-person, Esparanza, Vieques, PR.
Daniel Rodríguez, Remedial Project Manager (Vieques Field Office), US EPA. In-person, Isabelle Segundo, Vieques, PR. January 16, 2015.
Anna (pseudonym), Caribbean National Wildlife Refuge Complex, USFWS. Telephone, August 24, 2014. In-person, January 12–13, Vieques, PR.
Juan Vera, State Underwater Archaeologist, Puerto Rico. In-person, Isabelle Segundo, Vieques, PR. January 16, 2015.

22.9 REFERENCES

Braverman, I. (2013), 'Animal frontiers: a tale of three zoos in Israel/Palestine', *Cultural Critique*, **85**, 122–162.

Braverman, I., N. Blomley, D. Delaney and A. Kedar (2014), *The Expanding Spaces of Law: A Timely Legal Geography*, Stanford, CA: Stanford University Press.

Coates, P., T. Cole, M. Dudley and C. Pearson (2011), 'Defending nation, defending nature? Militarized landscapes and military environmentalism in Britain, France, and the United States', *Environmental History*, **16** (3), 456–491.

Davis, S. (2007), 'Introduction: military natures: militarism and the environment', *GeoJournal*, **69** (3), 131–134.

Davis, S., J. S. Hayes-Conroy and V. M. Jones (2007), 'Military pollution and natural purity: seeing nature and knowing contamination in Vieques, Puerto Rico', *GeoJournal*, **69** (3), 165–179.

Davis, S. (2011), 'The US military base network and contemporary colonialism: power projection, resistance and the quest for operational unilateralism', *Political Geography*, **30** (4), 1–10.

Dreissen, P. (2005), *Eco-Imperialism: Green Power, Black Death*, New Delhi: Academic Foundation.

EPA (2013), *Region 2 Superfund*, accessed March 21, 2014 at http://www.epa.gov/region02/vieques/history.htm.

EPA (2016), *Site Information for AFWTA*, accessed March 21, 2014 at http://cumulis.epa.gov/supercpad/cursites/dsp_ssppSiteData1.cfm?id=0204694.

Grove, R. (1995), *Green Imperialism: Colonial Expansion, Tropical Island Edens, and the Origins of Environmentalism, 1600–1860*, Cambridge: Cambridge University Press.

Havlick, D. (2011), 'Disarming nature: converting military lands to wildlife refuges', *Geographic Review*, **101** (2), 183–200.

Krupar, S. (2011), 'Alien still-life: distilling the toxic logics of the Rocky Flats National Wildlife Refuge', *Environment and Planning D: Society and Space*, **29** (2), 268–290.

Krupar, S. (2016), 'The biopolitics of spectacle: salvation and oversight at the post-military refuge', in B. Magnusson and Z. Zalloua (eds), *Spectacle*, Seattle, WA: University of Washington Press, pp. 116–153.

Martinez-Alier, J. (2003), *The Environmentalism of the Poor: A Study of the Ecological Conflicts and Valuation*, Cheltenham, UK and Northampton, MA, USA: Edward Elgar Publishing.

NAVFAC (undated), *Comprehensive, Environmental Response Compensation and Liability Act (CERCLA)*, accessed February 25, 2015 at http://www.navfac.navy.mil/products_and_services/ev/products_and_services/env_restoration/installation_map/navfac_atlantic/vieques/site_descriptions/regulatory_overview/cercla.html.

Peluso, N.L. (1993), 'Coercing conservation? the politics of state resource control', *Global Environmental Change*, **3** (2), 199–217.

Porter, J.M., J.V. Barton and C. Torres (2011), 'Ecological, radiological, and toxicological effects of naval bombardment on the coral reefs of Isla de Vieques, Puerto Rico', in G. Machlis, T. Hanson, Z. Špirić and J. McKendtu (eds), *Warfare Ecology: A New Synthesis for Peace and Security*, in 65 NATO Science for Peace and Security Series C: Environmental Security, Dordrecht, the Netherlands: Springer, pp. 65–122.

Sanders, B. (2009), *Green Zone: The Environmental Costs of Militarism*, Oakland, CA: AK Press.

Von Benda-Beckmann, F., K. von Benda-Beckmann and A. Griffiths (eds) (2009), *Spatializing Law: An Anthropological Geography of Law in Society*, Farnham: Ashgate.

Wilcox, D.A. (2007), *The Modern Military and the Environment*, Government Institutes, accessed March 7, 2018 at https://safetybuecher.science/pub/review-the-modern-military-and-the-environment-the-laws-of-peace-and-war-pdf-by-william-a-wilcox-william-a-wilcox.html.

Woodward, R. (2005), 'From military geography to militarism's geographies: disciplinary engagements with the geographies of militarism and military activities', *Progress in Human Geography*, **29** (6), 718–740.

Woodward, R. (2014), 'Military landscapes: agendas and approaches for future research', *Progress in Human Geography*, **38** (1), 40–61.

PART IV

URBANIZATION AND NEW FORMS OF SPATIALITY

23. City-regions and city-regionalism
Sami Moisio and Andrew E.G. Jonas

23.1 INTRODUCTION

Today, the terms city-region and city-regionalism are widely used by urban managers, planners, representatives of business associations and international organizations, real estate and property developers and state officials and politicians. These terms are not only catchwords in urban policy practices but also disclose the complex intertwining of contemporary urbanization, world economy and world politics. As such, they reveal much about the diverse ways in which the state and the economy are being spatially reconfigured, and also about the production of new state territorial formations at the city-region scale (Brenner 2004). As Harrison and Hoyler (2015a, p. 2) indicate, there is a great deal of 'buzz and appetite' amongst academics as well as state policymakers, consultants and planners about the rise of city-regions and, in particular, megaregions (major agglomerations comprised of several metropolitan areas) as the primary sites of economic growth, planning and governance in the contemporary global economy. This new spatial policy imaginary manifests itself in, for instance, recent books suggesting that a world of 'connectography' (Khanna 2016) – metropolitan and regional formations – has replaced the world of nation-state territories. This is a new world in which cities and their mayors are supposed to be better equipped to solve 'global problems' than is the case for the nation-state and sub-national state governments (Barber 2013).

Following a brief discussion of the global dimensions of city-region growth, we examine a range of academic interpretations of this phenomenon. We suggest that city-regions should not be understood as discrete spatial units that operate as 'agents' or 'actor-scales' in themselves. Nor should city-regions be considered as passive backdrops on which economy, politics or social reproduction simply happen. Rather city-regions may be conceptualized as dynamic sites of policy experimentation and political struggle, which are produced from various political processes operating within and around the national state and its institutions. Such processes highlight ongoing geopolitical tensions around capital accumulation, which take the form of struggles around social distribution, environment, culture, security, and suchlike. Our emphasis, therefore, is on exposing the geopolitics of city regionalism alongside contingently manifested problems of social distribution, uneven development, and environmental sustainability; contingencies that nevertheless are important for understanding the social and political construction of city-regionalism in different geopolitical settings.

23.2 CITY-REGION: THE EMERGENCE OF A CONCEPT

The concept of the city-region first appeared in regional planning in the early twentieth century at a time when the rapid growth of metropolitan-scale urban centres posed a range of new societal challenges relating to housing, social provision, and nationally balanced economic growth. It is often associated with the writings of influential regional planners and urban reformers, such as Patrick Geddes in the UK and Lewis Mumford in the USA, for whom ideas of the 'region-city' or 'regional city' provided useful devices for discussing and debating the mounting social ills of the industrial city. Later on in the twentieth century, as cities spread further outwards and merged with the surrounding suburbs, villages and rural communities, the 'city-region' served both as a planning construct and a statistical unit for measuring and debating urbanization trends in different national settings (Hall 2009).

In the meantime, statistical definitions of the city-region have evolved along with the size and population of these putative urban-cum-regional agglomerations. Today, urbanization trends are frequently measured at the global scale, being characterized by the explosive growth of city-regions of all sizes. Globally, the United Nations (UN) has estimated that in 2014 there were 28 city-regions with more than 10 million inhabitants, 43 with population between five and ten million, 417 between one and five million inhabitants, and more than 500 hundred city-regions which fall into a category between 500,000 and 1 million (UN, 2014). Nevertheless, more than half of the world's urban population live in approximately 2,000 city-regions having less than 500,000 residents (UN, 2014).

In the past two decades, urbanization has spread far beyond the political boundaries of the central city and its suburbs, and even those of the sub-state administrative regions and state borders. With regard to the latter case, scholars have identified 'megaregions' or 'megacity-regions' as functional economic entities with the potential to challenge the taken-for-granted power and authority of the nation-state. These megacity-regions are manifested as a series of cities that are 'functionally networked' and 'clustered around one or more larger cities' (Hall and Pain 2006, p. 3). The resultant 'stretching' of urbanization has challenged received notions of 'the city' conceived in the narrow sense as the most appropriate spatial entity to understand social organization and community stability in the modern era.

Of course, the 'urban' itself is a focus of ongoing theoretical debate in the literature (see Scott and Storper 2015). It therefore would perhaps be foolish to propose a totalizing and universal definition for the concept of the city-region. Indeed, the concept's meaning and usage has shifted throughout the course of the twentieth century. In the 1950s and 1960s, the city-region concept was often used in planning and regional science to denote the interaction and division of labour between cities and their surrounding rural areas. One intervention originating around this time in particular stands out from pack. Building on her earlier insights about the importance of the street for urban economic growth (Jacobs 1961), Jane Jacobs subsequently extended her critical gaze to the wider city-region. In *Cities and the Wealth of Nations* (Jacobs 1984), she argued that the economic success of cities depends on their ability to substitute imports from outside the city-region with locally produced commodities; an intervention that has since served as a benchmark for the revival of the city-region concept in the 1990s and 2000s.

To this day, the city-region concept remains a useful term for describing and measuring different forms of regionalization around central cities. This has involved inter alia measuring the spatial extent of functional city-region interactions (for example, labour markets, commuting fields, and so on), estimating the economic benefits of spatial agglomeration, or mapping the emergence of new structures of regional collaboration.

Indeed, the city-region concept is often to be found in the kitbox of techniques used by professional planners and policy consultants throughout the world. As such, the concept is deployed in multiple city-regional policy imaginaries which are designed to inform and influence public opinion and national policymakers in many different countries.

23.3   CITY-REGIONS, STATE TERRITORY, AND THE 'GLOBAL'

From the vantage point of the present volume, the usefulness of the concept of the city-region further stems from its potential to deconstruct a persistent binary between the external and internal processes of territories, not least those of national state territory. For example, it has appeared as one of the keywords to characterize the replacement of Fordist and Keynesian national economic and political institutions (Jessop 2000) by conceivably new relational and transnationalizing spatial imaginaries and material structures (Jonas and Ward 2007). These new city-regional territorial structures, in turn, potentially challenge systems of democracy, social reproduction and governance which are premised upon the twentieth-century ideal of the territorially integrated nation-state operating within an inter-state system. In the process, the concept of the city-region has been transformed from a planning category into a powerful theoretical construct, one which has been redesigned better to fit the dynamic processes and patterns of urban development and spatial organization associated with globalization (Rodríguez-Pose 2008). Scott (2001, pp. 813, 817) has expressed the connection between globalization, city-regions and the new world order as follows:

> Indeed, as globalization proceeds, an extended archipelago or mosaic of large city-regions is evidently coming into being, and these peculiar agglomerations now increasingly function as the spatial foundations of the new world system that has been taking shape since the end of the 1970s . . . These city-regions form a global mosaic that now seems to be overriding in important ways the spatial structure of core-periphery relationships that has hitherto characterized much of the macro-geography of capitalist development.

This process – recently dubbed as 'regional urbanization' (Soja 2011) – signals how capital accumulation in the age of globalization takes place around large urban agglomerations rather than nation-states having fixed internal and external borders. The implicit message here is that capitalist globalization is to a great extent mediated through the international archipelago of city-regions rather than the system of sovereign territorial states.

It has also become almost axiomatic to argue that the rise of the political-economic significance of city-regions discloses a pivotal moment in the territorial organization and rescaling of the competition state and underpins the neoliberal spatial constitution of globalization more generally (Brenner 2004). However, critiques of this state-theoretical interpretation of the rise of city-regions have suggested that there is nothing inevitably 'neoliberal' about the concept and that an interrogation of the processes of city-regionalism can better assist in disclosing progressive politics than somehow representing a neoliberal plot (Harding 2007). In this regard, the literature on state rescaling often fails to disclose the nature of political interests shaping urban development and collective consumption around city-regions (Ward and Jonas 2004). Since factions of capital have different stakes in how city-regions – as well as the spaces within and between them – develop, studying such differences might be crucial for explaining potential conflict and resistance to new territorial structures of the state (Cox 2011).

Scholars have further highlighted the rise of city-regions in a global context. The concept of the global city-region – an interesting spatial marker in itself – does not entail the demise of the territorial state but rather seeks to mark a qualitative shift towards intensive inter-city region interactions, collaboration and rivalries. The literature on global city-regions generally deals with major urban agglomerations – places dominated by some combination of finance and producer services, high technology industries, and the creative economy – as key spaces of capital accumulation and spaces within which human capital and productivity increasingly concentrate. Drawing on an earlier work of 'world cities' and 'global cities', Scott et al. (2001, pp. 11–12) argue that 'global city-regions have emerged of late years as a new and critically important kind of geographic and institutional phenomenon on the world stage'. Such statements might have prompted somewhat tautological claims to the effect that global city-regions are 'global' precisely because they represent highly productive regions which are centred upon 'global cities' and contain transnational corporations and other command posts of the world system. Moreover, it is often argued that global city-regions are not only centres of growth, accumulation and innovation but also 'liveable' spaces within which enlightened 'global' subjects and citizens are made. Notwithstanding the resurgence of nationalism throughout much of the world, it seems that global city-regions are to be viewed as beacons of innovation and progressive politics, which somehow exist in stark contrast to antediluvian or 'territorialist' processes seemingly operating elsewhere especially in the so-called 'periphery' (see Morgan 2007).

Indeed, an increasing autonomy of political action is one of the defining features of such global city-regions. As such, they are often treated in the literature as spatial exceptions within the national fabric of the state and, as such, function as the (trans)national champions of economic growth, which demand special treatment in respect of state expenditures on research and development, infrastructure and collective social provision. As an outgrowth of pre-existing large metropolitan areas that might have benefitted disproportionately from earlier rounds of state expenditure and prior phases of national economic planning, the rise of global city-regions is not simply a quantitative change in levels of urbanization; instead city-regions need to be understood qualitatively as relational and political constructs, which can be identified and delimited not so much by population or geographic size per se as by irreducibly territorial processes. Before we examine such processes, we consider three dominant ways in which city-regions and city-regionalism have been investigated in the literature.

23.4 CITY-REGIONALISM AS A SOCIETAL PROCESS

City-regionalism is, essentially, a socially mediated process of producing, maintaining and transforming space. In this section, we make a distinction between city-regionalism as a set of, respectively, geo-economic, political-administrative and/or geopolitical processes, which overlap to a greater or lesser degree (Figure 23.1). As a set of processes, moreover, city-regionalism can be comprehended both as a spatial formation which is constituted in and through the dynamics of capital accumulation (or, following Jane Jacobs, the emergent economics of city-regions), and as a particular societal and regulative response

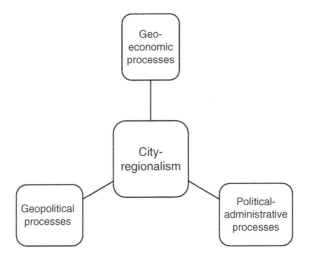

Source: Authors.

Figure 23.1   The three dimensions of city-regionalism as a societal process

to these emergent city-regional economies as well as to the challenges that political communities are more generally perceived to face (in other words, the political-administrative and the geopolitical readings). In the latter meaning, city-regionalism is tied up with the ongoing political struggles and historically contingent forms of capitalist development and associated discursive formations. We begin with briefly reviewing the economic geographical literature on city regionalism, before interrogating city regionalism as a set of political-administrative and/or geopolitical processes in more detail.

23.4.1   Geo-economics of City-Regionalism

In the work of urban economics, city-regions are often treated as statistical areas which can be compared against each other in order to analyse their differences in, for instance, per-worker productivity, and thus assist in mapping the possible operation of agglomeration economies (Glaeser and Resseger 2010). In such an analysis, 'city-regions' are individualized and largely detached from the political and regulatory structures of the state. City-regions emerge around large cities as economically diverse spaces that are well connected and attractive to rationally behaving workers and employers, who perceive these economic spaces to be ideal locations in their efforts to maximize life chances and business opportunities. Storper (2013) offers an extensive critical review of the neo-classical urban economists' explanations for the rise of city-regions, highlighting the important role played by the co-presence of institutional, social, cultural and, tellingly, political processes.

The work of urban economists has nonetheless important policy implications. The complementarity between skills and large and dense city-regions, as well as the related link between skills and productivity, has been so widely debated that national governments have faced pressures to tailor policies that would concentrate skills and firms in their most dynamic city-regions (Peirce 1993). The presumed link between metropolitan agglomeration economies and national economic growth plays an increasingly important political function in contemporary state strategies (see, for example, OECD 2015).

In economic geography, the emergence of the literature on city-regions can be traced back to writings on the rise of new industrial spaces and a new post-Fordist societal order in the late 1980s and 1990s. The emphasis was often placed on the geo-economic resurgence of city-regions. In this literature, city-regions are understood as engines or locomotives of national economies, a sort of intensive economic spaces with dense masses of interconnected economic activities (Scott and Storper 2003). In such a view, a city-region is a spatial concentration of economic activities, consumers, firms and services: a sort of functional economic territory which is tightly connected to corresponding territories through the interaction between economic agents.

Economic geographers have been at pains to explain the emergence of city-regions as particular concentrations of economic activities. It is often suggested that the rise of city-regions has to do with the presence of agglomeration economies and associated measures of productivity. Accordingly, city-regionalism signals the intensifying gathering together of many types of productive economic activities ranging from services to manufacturing (Scott 2001). The Porterian idea of spatial clustering (Porter 2001) – and the related emergence of regional production complexes or urban superclusters which partially stem from the need to minimize multifaceted transaction costs in the post-Fordist economy – has been a widely debated factor of city-regional growth. On the other hand, research on the social conventions underpinning regional economic development (Storper 1997) has sought to understand the ways in which the city-regions emerge on the threshold of economy and society. According to the so-called 'new regionalism,' particular regional worlds of production (city-regions as 'regional economies') can be understood as growing out of the technological and organizational worlds that produce regions more generally (Storper 1997, p. 48).

The rise of city-regions and the economic processes of 'learning' have also been knitted together. Major city-regions are understood to emerge as concentrations of innovation potentials and skilled work force which dynamic firms are able to harness effectively. City-regions are thus 'learning regions' (see Morgan 1997; Asheim 2018) which function both as 'repositories' and 'collectors' of ideas, as well as providing a unique environment which 'facilitates the flow of knowledge, ideas and learning' (Florida 1995, p. 527). This dimension of city-regionalism is arguably particularly pertinent in the context of the contemporary 'cognitive cultural' economy (Scott 2007) which comprises high-tech sector, cultural industries and a neo-artisan manufacturing, and which underscores the foundations of localized innovative energy.

23.4.2 City-Regionalism and Political-Administrative Processes

The institutions of local government and governance might coincide with the borders of city-regions but often in practice this territorial correspondence between the state and institutionalization around 'functional regions' has not been realized. In some national contexts, such as in Finland, city-regionalism has emerged as a spatial policy strategy to blur the stark line between cities and their surrounding 'rural' areas. The key idea has been to recognize and map 'functional regions' (such as labour market areas) and gradually to develop political governance matching the borders of these putative city-regions.

Often these new city-regional governance arrangements are designed to be 'flexible' and explicitly recognize the importance of the 'interstitial' or 'soft' spaces existing between formal and functional administrative regions (see Allmendinger and Haughton 2009).

It is very difficult to say to what *extent* the spatial consequences of material city-regional growth have informed or are impacted by the processes of city-regional governance. What can be said, however, is that the bringing together of systems of governance and city-regions is often characterized by political struggles and heated contestation. The same applies to the tailoring of city-regional spatial planning systems which would deal with issues such as land use, transportation, housing or economic development. In other words, 'functional' city-regions seem to effectively escape and disturb the world of political governance and regulation which is often rooted in historically construed borders and material interests (in, for example, land, property or markets) that can have long-lasting impacts on local political institutions and processes (Cox and Jonas 1993).

It is widely assumed that the contemporary political expression of city-regionalism discloses the ways in which capitalism has been territorially re-shaped: the growing importance of city-regions as economic territories and the emergence of metropolitan city-regions as sites of policy experimentation have been closely interconnected processes (Brenner 2004). Yet even a cursory examination of the literature on city-regions suggests that questions of state territoriality and territorial politics generally have been much lower on the research agenda than those of economic growth and competitiveness (Cox 2009; Harrison 2007; Jonas 2011). If economic geographers and urban economists have delved insightfully into the constitutive economic processes and features of city-regions, urban political geographers have increasingly sought to trace the political dynamics and regulatory structures and institutions of city-regions and city-regionalism. According to such political-geographic interpretations, city-regions are both outcomes and mediums of politics. Attention is now turning to the political construction of city-regions and the ways in which different city-regional formations have been made visible by the state as well as regional and local actors. At the heart of this thematic is the organization and management and governance of city-regions as both territorializing and de-territorializing spatial units.

In a series of contributions that are indicative of political-geographic investigations of city-regions, John Harrison has sought to unpack the relationship between the territorial politics of city-regionalism and underlying economic and political interests. His research addresses inter alia the relationship between city-region political imaginaries and geographies of investment and uneven development (Harrison 2010, 2014), the degree to which city-regionalism is centrally orchestrated by the state or, conversely, regionally orchestrated by growth coalitions (Harrison 2008), and the manner in which national coalitions representing certain economic sectors have sought to propagate the idea of the megaregion (Harrison and Hoyler 2015a, 2015b). In the latter case, the recent excitement surrounding the megaregion concept in the USA is closely tied to the lobbying activities of the Regional Plan Association of America and the US Department of Transportation, which have used the concept to promote high-speed rail projects (Harrison and Hoyler 2015b) as well as commuter and light rail systems (Jonas et al. 2014). Whilst Harrison (2007) has expressed cautious optimism about the growth of serious intellectual interest in city-regions, he nevertheless urges more work on its links to territorial politics (see also Jonas 2012).

23.4.3   Geopolitics of City-Regionalism

An inquiry into the political construction of city regions inevitably discloses the contested and often contradictory geopolitical interests and strategies of the national state (Kangas 2013). City-regionalism can hence be further conceptualized as a geopolitical process which brings together the state, city-regions and world politics (Jonas and Moisio 2018).

A geopolitical interpretation of city-regionalism examines the state/city-region interface and interrogates city-regionalism both as territorializing and de-territorializing spatial strategy. Its emphasis is much more on how city-regions enable the state to project its reach on an international stage than on how city-regions – especially global city-regions – somehow embody or enact processes of economic globalization (Jonas 2013). In such a perspective, city-regionalism is bound to a range of political-economic goals, geopolitical actors and political rationalities, which often make reference to academic constructs. We briefly interrogate some of these themes below.

As noted earlier, city-regionalism is often explained in economic geography and related fields as emanating from economic processes that underpin contemporary capitalist globalization. But theories generated by such academic endeavours can also be understood as forms of constitutive knowledge influencing the policy practices through which city-regionalism is produced. Scientific theories in the field of economic geography are therefore not only explanatory but also prescriptive, and these theories embody substantial policy relevance. As we have witnessed since the 1990s, scientific theories on the spatial organization of the 'new economy' (how the world is) have also often taken a normative form (concerning how the world should be). Let us take one example which highlights both the economic and political status of city-regionalism in the contemporary political-economic context.

Richard Florida's (2002) theory on the coming together of the creative class and creative economy is undoubtedly one of the most widely circulated and debated theories of urban and regional development in the age of the 'knowledge-based economy'. This theory is representative of a wider genre of academic writing on the generation of new knowledge and the related human creativity both as key factors of competitive advantage of nations and as inherently spatial-political phenomena (Moisio 2015). Indeed, it can be suggested that both the direct and more implicit politico-spatial implications of the purportedly 'knowledge intensive' processes of capitalism form the bedrock of contemporary interest in the geopolitics of city-regionalism. Florida's (2002) much-debated theory of the creative class is thus explicitly located within a purportedly post-industrial world in which creativity and knowledge are replacing the more traditional factors of production.

It is important to note that, along with his subsequent writings (Florida 2008), Florida's creative class concept celebrates, in effect, the rising importance of city-regions and metropolises. As such, it should also be read as a *geopolitical* metanarrative of the knowledge-based economy. Specifically, it tells a powerful story about the ways in which capitalism changes and is re-made through economic crises, and how new city-centered political geographies are being produced within the latest ruptures of capitalism.

One of the key messages of the theory is that following the demise of the previous capitalist era, which was construed around the so-called Keynesian national state, capitalism has remade itself around dynamic cities and larger city-regions. Florida further suggests that in this new geopolitical era city-regions have emergent class qualities which are regarded as crucial for facilitating creativity, innovation and economic growth and, as such, enhance the political and economic development of political communities.

Numerous state and local governments and planning offices have tailored local economic and urban development strategies around selective readings of Florida's theory along with related ideas, such as 'creative places' and 'smart cities,' and a range of consultant companies have put these ideas into motion in different geographical contexts. The widespread adoption of such academic ideas about the rise of city-regions by different state agencies suggests that the production of places – and in particular city-regions – having certain social characteristics is regarded to be a significant factor for the competitive advantage of nations. More generally, therefore, the relationship between city-regions and states has become one of the central dimensions of the contemporary geopolitics of city-regionalism. Many academics have argued that cities and major city-regions increasingly embody significant actorness in world politics and global governance (Taylor 2011) or that the enhanced political authority of 'global city-regions' indicates a weakened sovereign political autonomy of the territorial state (Soja 2011).

Moreover, such ideas about the rising importance of cities and city-regions in the new age of capitalism *and its new political condition* resonate with a set of other geopolitical writings that were presented in the early 1990s. One of the most telling was produced by Kenichi Ohmae, a Senior Partner of the consultant company McKinsey & Co and a prolific columnist. Ohmae's books and articles in the early 1990s not only mark a notable rupture in writings on the relationship between cities, regions and the nation-state but also embody the new geopolitical context.

First, these writings embody a historically contingent idea that, when compared with 'natural' creativity of city-regions, the nation-state is an inherently dysfunctional polity especially in the era of globalizing capitalism. The state should therefore be replaced by new kinds of spatial units: functional and increasingly cross-border economic mega-regions which consist of major urban agglomerations. The megaregion (on this concept, see Harrison and Hoyler 2015b) is a most interesting idea for the study of the geopolitics of city-regionalism. At the heart of this concept is a view of the world according to which significant urban agglomerations are more connected with each other than they are with the people and places in their national backyards (Ohmae 1993; Florida 2008, p. 7).

As first proposed by Ohmae in the early 1990s, the idea that metropolitan regions, not entire nation-states, are the unquestionable hubs of economic growth is part of a wider discursive and material visioning of the de-territorialization of the state and the associated restructuring of world politics that began in the 1980s. Whereas states are dysfunctional entities in spatial terms, major regions become the most effective units in the global economy. These 'region states' are more natural business units in part because they have the sufficient, correctly sized and scaled agglomerations of people and activities for tapping effectively into the global economy (Ohmae 1996): 'They are drawn by the deft but invisible hand of the global market for goods and services' (Ohmae 1993, p. 78).

Second, according to the logic above, if the state does not allow its city-regions to enter the global economy, the state as a whole is in danger of becoming a backwater. Ohmae's ideas on the ways in which the central forces of capitalism in the late 1980s began to produce a new region-based geopolitical order proved to be highly influential among consultants, planning gurus and even policymakers working within state apparatuses. Indeed, it has proven most efficacious in smaller countries lacking in a clearly dominant metropolitan agglomeration; the national governments of such countries have talked up the importance of their largest metropolitan areas as evidence of the need to exploit hitherto untapped assets, including skills, creativity and capital investment, with a view to the nation-state itself participating more effectively in the global economy (Jonas and Moisio 2018).

Third, Ohmae's ideas are notable for they opened up a new strand of scholarly writings in future-oriented urban and regional studies. We identify an ideational strand running from his arguments to, for instance, Richard Florida's (1995) treatise on 'the learning regions', to Allen Scott's (1996) 'regional motors of the global economy' as well as his later contributions on 'global city-regions', and to the influential work of Manuel Castells (1996) on the spatial nature of what he conceptualized as the network society.

Nonetheless, addressing the geopolitics of city-regionalism on a more general level touches upon the issue of the internationalization of the state. The geopolitical processes of city-regionalism bring together actors which are often difficult to define on the basis of the received international/national binary. In this capacity, city-regionalism can be understood as an instantiation of state power – a distributed authority which is constituted and re-made by private actors, formal state institutions, international organizations, management consultants, property and real-estate developers, urbanists, lobby organizations, and supranational political bodies (Sassen 2008). Accordingly, city-regionalism manifests itself as 'partial formations of private and public authority' (Allen and Cochrane 2010, p. 1078) and may well disclose the operation of 'transnational state apparatuses' (Demirović 2011, p. 39) as condensation of the relations of political forces that operate on the basis of particular internationalizing transnational priorities in the context of the state, cities and, crucially, capital.

Finally, the geopolitical processes of city-regionalism operate also in a supranational context. To illustrate, the European Union's (EU) nascent spatial planning system is predicated on an emphasis on market needs, the fundamentals of economic growth, and the idea of enhancing the international competitiveness and attractiveness of the EU as an investment landscape. Furthermore, the system emphasizes the role of particular 'global economic integration zones' (CEC 1999) as spaces of competitiveness. These demonstrate how just like individual nation-states the EU also seeks to 'megaregionalize' itself through a set of cross-border regions that are eventually collections of city-regions. European spatial planning is at least implicitly premised on an idea, which has particular currency in the USA (Wachsmuth 2015), that the megaregion is the most globally effective competitive urban form (Moisio and Luukkonen 2017).

23.5   CONCLUDING REMARKS

The recent resurgence of the city-region concept clearly captures some significant developments in the spatial patterning of urbanization at the global scale and represents the latest phase in a longer-term trend in the outgrowth of cities into their surrounding areas and political jurisdictions. This trend poses challenges for contemporary regional planning, urban policy, and sustainable urban development. It also threatens to undermine the assumed political authority of the nation-state. A materialist political economy interpretation highlights how city-regionalism has helped to shed light on broader shifts in the spatial and scalar configuration of capitalism and its supporting systems of societal regulation. Nonetheless, our aim has also been to suggest that city-regionalism often gets constituted as a set of geopolitical processes, which bring together the political and the economic in various state strategies that are instigated by different kinds of political actors (Jonas and Moisio 2018). Increasingly, city-regionalism is politically rationalized through all sorts of conceived challenges, risks and possibilities which touch upon both the security of a particular state and its population. Indeed, whether articulated as a politico-spatial strategy or as a technology of government in these contexts, we suggest that over the course of two decades or more city-regionalism has become one of the key geopolitical processes through which the internationalization and associated restructuring of the state is envisioned to take place.

From a geopolitical perspective, city-regionalism has major implications not only for the internationalization of the state itself but also how one approaches the internal reconfiguration of state territoriality. City-regionalism is often used to counterbalance uneven regional development and devolutionary tendencies within state territory. Since these political processes of state internationalization, on the one hand, and internal territorial redistribution, on the other, operate in tension with each other, it is necessary to recognize that the processes of city regionalism remain territorially bounded and that city-regionalism can be rationalized and mobilized through different kinds of geopolitical rationalities. Rather than juxtaposing territorial and relational aspects of city-regionalism in the context of the state, the challenge remains to study the complex coming-together of the relational and the territorial in the processes of city-regionalism. Indeed, the different ways the state and city-regions become entangled in efforts to manage the tension between, on the one hand, the state's international competitiveness and national redistribution, on the other, remains a compelling research question for spatially attuned social scientists.

23.6 ACKNOWLEDGMENT

Funding support from the Academy of Finland (RELATE CoE, grant 272168) and a Regional Studies Association Fellowship Research Grant is gratefully acknowledged.

23.7 REFERENCES

Allen, J. and A. Cochrane (2010), 'Assemblages of state power: topological shifts in the organization of government and politics', *Antipode*, **42** (5), 1071–1089.
Allmendinger, P. and G. Haughton (2009), 'Soft spaces, fuzzy boundaries, and metagovernance: the new spatial planning in the Thames Gateway', *Environment and Planning A*, **41** (3), 617–633.
Asheim, B. (2018), 'Learning regions – a strategy for economic development in less developed regions?', in A. Paasi, J. Harrison and M. Jones (eds), *Handbook on the Geographies of Regions and Territories*, Cheltenham, UK and Northampton, MA, USA: Edward Elgar Publishing, pp. 130–140.
Barber, B. (2013), *If Mayors Ruled the World: Dysfunctional Nations, Rising Cities*, New Haven, CT: Yale University Press.
Brenner, N. (2004), *New State Spaces: Urban Governance and the Rescaling of Statehood*, New York: Oxford University Press.
Castells, M. (1996), *The Rise of the Network Society*, Cambridge, MA: Blackwell.
CEC (1999), *European Spatial Development Perspective – Towards Balanced and Sustainable Development of the Territory of the EU*, Luxembourg: Office for Official Publications of the European Communities.

Cox, K. and A.E.G. Jonas (1993), 'Urban development, collective consumption and the politics of metropolitan fragmentation', *Political Geography*, **12** (1), 8–37.

Cox, K. (2009), '"Rescaling the state" in question', *Cambridge Journal of Regions, Economy and Society*, **2** (1), 107–121.

Cox, K. (2011), 'Commentary: from the new urban politics to the "new" metropolitan politics', *Urban Studies*, **48** (12), 2661–2672.

Demirović, A. (2011), 'Materialist state theory and the transnationalization of the capitalist state', *Antipode*, **43** (1), 38–59.

Florida, R. (1995), 'Toward the learning region', *Futures*, **27** (5), 527–536.

Florida, R. (2002), *The Rise of the Creative Class*, New York: Basic Books.

Florida, R. (2008), *Who's Your City? How the Creative Economy is Making Where to Live the Most Important Decision of Your Life*, New York: Basic Books.

Glaeser, E. and M. Resseger (2010), 'The complementarity between cities and skills', *Journal of Regional Science*, **50** (1), 221–224.

Hall, P. and K. Pain (eds) (2006), *The Polycentric Metropolis: Learning from Mega-city Regions in Europe*, London: Earthscan.

Hall, P. (2009), 'Looking back, looking forward: the city region of the mid-21st century', *Regional Studies*, **43** (6), 803–818.

Harding, A. (2007), 'Taking city-regions seriously? Response to debate on "City-regions: new geographies of governance, democracy and social reproduction"', *International Journal of Urban and Regional Research*, **31** (2), 443–458.

Harrison, J. (2007), 'From competitive regions to competitive city-regions: a new orthodoxy, but some old mistakes', *Journal of Economic Geography*, **7** (3), 311–332.

Harrison, J. (2008), 'Stating the production of scales: centrally orchestrated regionalism and regionally orchestrated centralism', *International Journal of Urban and Regional Research*, **32** (4), 922–941.

Harrison, J. (2010), 'Networks of connectivity, territorial fragmentation, uneven development: the new politics of city-regionalism', *Political Geography*, **29** (1), 17–27.

Harrison, J. (2014), 'Rethinking city-regionalism as the production of new non-state spatial strategies: the case of Peel Holdings Atlantic Gateway Strategy', *Urban Studies*, **51** (10), 2315–2335.

Harrison, J. and M. Hoyler (2015a), 'Megaregions: foundations, frailties, futures', in J. Harrison and M. Hoyler (eds), *Megaregions: Globalization's New Urban Form?* Cheltenham, UK and Northampton, MA, USA: Edward Elgar Publishing, pp. 1–28.

Harrison, J. and M. Hoyler (eds) (2015b), *Megaregions: Globalization's New Urban Form?*, Cheltenham, UK and Northampton, MA, USA: Edward Elgar Publishing.

Jacobs, J. (1961), *The Death and Life of Great American Cities*, New York: Random House.

Jacobs, J. (1984), *Cities and the Wealth of Nations*, New York: Random House.

Jessop, B. (2000), 'The crisis of the national spatio-temporal fix and the tendential ecological dominance of globalizing capitalism', *International Journal of Urban and Regional Research*, **24** (2), 323–360.

Jonas, A.E.G. and K. Ward (2007), 'Introduction to a debate on city-regions: new geographies of governance, democracy and social reproduction', *International Journal of Urban and Regional Research*, **31** (1), 169–178.

Jonas, A.E.G. (2011), 'Region and place: regionalism in question', *Progress in Human Geography*, **36** (2), 263–272.

Jonas, A.E.G. (2012), 'City-regionalism: questions of distribution and politics', *Progress in Human Geography*, **36** (6), 822–829.

Jonas, A.E.G. (2013), 'City-regionalism as a contingent "geopolitics of capitalism"', *Geopolitics*, **18** (2), 284–298.

Jonas, A.E.G., A.R. Goetz and S. Battarcharjee (2014), 'City-regionalism and the politics of collective provision: regional transportation infrastructure in Denver, USA', *Urban Studies*, **51** (10), 2444–2465.

Jonas, A.E.G. and S. Moisio (2018), 'City regionalism as geopolitical processes: a new framework for analysis', *Progress in Human Geography*, **42** (3), 350–370.

Kangas, A. (2013), 'Governmentalities of Big Moscow: particularizing neoliberal statecraft', *Geopolitics*, **18** (2), 299–314.

Khanna, P. (2016), *Connectography: Mapping the Global Network Revolution*, London: Weidenfeld & Nicolson.

Moisio, S. (2015), 'Geopolitics/critical geopolitics', in J. Agnew, V. Mamadouh, A. Secor and J. Sharp (eds), *The Wiley-Blackwell Companion to Political Geography*, Chichester: Wiley-Blackwell, pp. 220–234.

Moisio, S. and J. Luukkonen (2017), 'Notes on spatial transformation in post-Cold War Europe and the territory work of the European Union', in P. Vihalemm, A. Masso and S. Opermann (eds), *The Routledge International Handbook of European Social Transformations*, Abingdon: Routledge, pp. 224–238.

Morgan, K. (1997), 'The learning region: institutions, innovation and regional renewal', *Regional Studies*, **31** (5), 491–503.

Morgan, K. (2007), 'The polycentric state: new spaces of empowerment and engagement?', *Regional Studies*, **41** (9), 1237–1252.

OECD (2015), *Urban Development*, accessed on 27 September 2017 at http://www.oecd.org/gov/regional-policy/urbandevelopment.htm.

Ohmae, K. (1993), 'The rise of the "region state"', *Foreign Affairs*, **72** (1), 78–87.

Ohmae, K. (1996), *The End of the Nation-State: The Rise of Regional Economies*, New York: Free Press.

Peirce, N.R. (1993), *Citistates: How Urban America Can Prosper in a Competitive World*, Washington, DC: Seven Locks Press.

Porter, M. (2001), 'Regions and the new economics of competition', in A.J. Scott (ed.), *Global City-Regions: Trends, Theory, Policy*, Oxford: Oxford University Press, pp. 139–157.

Rodríguez-Pose, A. (2008), 'The rise of the "city-region" concept and its development policy implications', *European Planning Studies*, **16** (8), 1025–1046.

Sassen, S. (2008), *Territory, Authority, Rights: From Medieval to Global Assemblages*, Princeton, NJ: Princeton University Press.

Scott, A.J. (1996), 'Regional motors of the global economy', *Futures*, **28** (5), 391–411.

Scott, A.J. (2001), 'Globalisation and the rise of city-regions', *European Planning Studies*, **9** (7), 813–824.

Scott, A.J., J. Agnew, E. Soja and M. Storper (2001), 'Global city-regions', in A.J. Scott (ed.), *Global City-Regions: Trends, Theory, Policy*, Oxford: Oxford University Press, pp. 11–32.

Scott, A.J. and M. Storper (2003), 'Regions, globalization, development', *Regional Studies*, **37** (6–7), 579–593.

Scott, A.J. (2007), 'Capitalism and urbanization in a new key? The cognitive-cultural dimension', *Social Forces*, **85** (4), 1465–4582.

Scott, A.J. and M. Storper (2015), 'The nature of cities: the scope and limits of urban theory', *International Journal of Urban and Regional Research*, **39** (1), 1–15.

Soja, E. (2011), 'Regional urbanization and the end of the metropolis era', in G. Bridge and S. Watson (eds), *The New Blackwell Companion to the City*, Oxford: Wiley-Blackwell, pp. 679–689.

Storper, M. (1997), *The Regional World: Territorial Development in a Global Economy*, New York: Guilford Press.

Storper, M. (2013), *Keys to the City: How Economics, Institutions, Social Interaction, and Politics Shape Development*, Princeton, NJ: Princeton University Press.

Taylor, P.J. (2011), 'World city networks: measurement, social organization, global governance, and structural change', in M. Amen, N. Toly, P. McCarney and K. Segbers (eds), *Cities and Global Governance*, Farnham: Ashgate, pp. 201–216.

UN (2014), *World Urbanization Prospects: The 2014 Revision – Highlights*, New York: United Nations.

Wachsmuth, D. (2015), 'Megaregions and the urban question: the new strategic terrain for US urban competitiveness', in J. Harrison and M. Hoyler (eds), *Megaregions: Globalization's New Urban Form?*, Cheltenham, UK and Northampton, MA, USA: Edward Elgar Publishing, pp. 51–74.

Ward, K. and A.E.G. Jonas (2004), 'Competitive city-regionalism as a politics of space: a critical reinterpretation of the new regionalism', *Environment and Planning A*, **36** (12), 2112–2139.

24. Cross-border regions
Christophe Sohn

24.1 INTRODUCTION

What is the common denominator between a Euroregion, a bi-national metropolis adjoining the US–Mexico border and an Asian growth triangle? In all three cases, these are spatial region-based entities that straddle one or more state borders. Broadly defined, the three configurations refer to the concept of 'cross-border region'. Given the multiple realities it refers to and the contested nature of the notions it contains, this concept has all the appearances of a minefield. To the extent that cross-border regions can be considered as a specific type of region, let us circumscribe our object of study by attempting to define what we mean by 'region'.

In general, the concept of region corresponds to a particular area that constitutes a distinct entity. The delimitation of a region can be relatively precise and stable (especially when institutionalized as a territory) or blurred and shifting (as in the case of functional or imagined regions). Its degree of economic, political, cultural or historic cohesiveness is likely to vary considerably to the extent that it is not a prerequisite but the result of a historically contingent and evolutionary process (Keating 2004). Regions are actually social constructions in the making capable of having different degrees of 'regionness' (see notably Hettne and Söderbaum 2000; Paasi 1986, 1991). This chapter focuses on what are sometimes called 'micro-regions' and usually correspond to a sub-national entity, as opposed to 'macro-regions' (or transnational areas) which consist of more than one nation-state. In a cross-border context, a 'micro-region' is composed of several contiguous sub-national entities.

Indeed, the very existence of a cross-border region implies the presence of a border, understood as the boundary of a political entity. The type of political boundary generally considered is the state border which constitutes the external limit of a state's territorial power (Anderson and O'Dowd 1999). However, by definition, cross-border regions could equally consist of regions crossing infra-national borders, such as the internal borders of a federal state – for example, the US megaregions defined by the Regional Plan Association (2006) – or regional political boundaries – such as the city-region of Brussels.

More than the juxtaposition of the two notions, it is their articulation which is at the core of the concept of cross-border region and which should therefore be grasped. From a linguistic point of view, this articulation is specified by the use of the prefix 'cross' or 'trans' before the term 'border'. As highlighted by Taylor (1995), the prefix 'trans' means to 'cross' or 'span', but also, in a stronger sense, 'beyond'. This polysemy is not trivial and points to the existence of different ways of conceptualizing the relationships between regionalization processes and evolving state borders. These different conceptualizations and their impact on the meaning and scope of the concept of cross-border region are the focal point of this chapter.

First, the meaning of the concept of cross-border region is examined through a conventional view of the role of state borders that emphasizes the perspective of the nation-state.

The aim is to review the relevance of different conceptualizations that have marked the analysis of processes of cross-border regionalization. Second, a conceptualization that acknowledges the multiple and processual nature of borders is introduced and the notion of borders as a resource is discussed. The main idea is that cross-border regions do not only emerge in spite of the state borders they cross or undermine but also thanks to them. The third section is devoted to the analysis of the variety of configurations and trajectories of cross-border regionalism. This necessarily brief and incomplete presentation focuses on Europe, North America and South-East Asia. In the next section, the hypothesis of a specific trajectory for cross-border regions articulated around urban and metropolitan centres is considered. The last section concludes by underlying the role played by cities in the mobilization of border resources and the development of cross-border regions and outlines an agenda for further research.

24.2 THREE CONCEPTUALIZATIONS OF THE RELATIONSHIPS BETWEEN CROSS-BORDER REGIONS AND STATE BORDERS

The concept of cross-border region conveys different perspectives on the material role and symbolic significance of borders. Starting from the traditional meaning of state borders as the limit of the territorial sovereignty of a nation-state, three analytical categories that have structured much of the debates stand out. In reality, they refer to a motley collection of contingent practices and representations that may co-exist, combine or contradict each other.

The first relationship relates the emergence of regional entities to a putative dissipation of state borders. Historically, this radical perspective has accompanied the gradual opening of borders vis-à-vis the flow of capital, goods, services and, to a lesser extent, people, and was promoted during the 1980s and 1990s in different parts of the world. The emergence of functional economic regions in Europe, Asia and North America has notably been interpreted as a warning sign of the demise of nation-states (Ohmae 1990). Beyond such an absolutist interpretation of the impact of globalization on state territoriality, the vision of borders that retreat in favour of regional entities also nourished for a time the narrative of a 'Europe of regions' supposed to counterbalance the power of member states (Clark and Jones 2018). Of course, these predictions about the loss of significance of borders and the collapse of state territoriality proved overstated if not naïve. Although less radical in its interpretations, the perspective that cross-border regions are 'natural economic territories' that emerge from the opening of borders and the relativization of the role of states remains pivotal in conventional international relations and regional studies (Scalapino 2007). Similarly, in the European context, the reduction of border-related barrier effects continues to be closely associated with the emergence of Euroregions as policy-driven territorial entities in the making (see section 24.4.1 below).

The second relationship refers to the confrontation between two opposing forces: on one side, the formation of cross-border regional entities in search of identity and autonomy and, on the other, the persistence of the territoriality of nation-states. In this perspective, which emphasizes the dialectical relationship between the processes of deterritorialization and reterritorialization, the concept of cross-border regions is like an oxymoron, that is to say, a figure of speech that juxtaposes contradictory elements. Given the potential conflict between competing territorial logics, cross-border regions refer to initiatives that somehow emerge in spite of the resistance of state borders and the reluctance of central state institutions. They are subject to perpetual negotiations and their degree of regionness, often limited, reflects a precarious balance of power. In fact, this course of action seems to apply to many emerging cross-border regions that often face the anxiety of states losing their territorial sovereignty or are on the front line of national rivalries and historical animosities. The constrained development of many cross-border regions in Central and Eastern Europe illustrates this resistance of central states towards the emancipation of their border regions (see notably Popescu 2008, Soóz 2014). Such a conceptualization also points to the tensions between an economic debordering and a security-led state rebordering that whipsaw many cross-border cooperation initiatives and regions across the world (see the example of San Diego-Tijuana along the US–Mexico border below).

The third way of considering the relationship between the process of regionalization and state territoriality is based on the ideas of compromise or articulation. In some instances, states may have an interest in seeing the development of cross-border regions at their borders, up to a certain level of institutionalization which varies from one context to another. Instead of opposing it, state authorities can either adopt a laissez-faire attitude or promote consolidation. Various reasons can be cited. In some cases, it is a way of supporting the social and economic development of border regions, often historically disadvantaged, or to enable the management of common goods or negative cross-border externalities. The cases of Basel and Geneva, which benefit from the financial support of the Swiss Confederation for the development of their cross-border transportation infrastructures, are good examples of state support through specific national policies (Sohn and Reitel 2016). In other cases, states may actively promote cross-border regional growth dynamics based on complementarities in production factors through the creation of special economic zones (for example, the Mexican Border Industrial Program and the maquiladora industries). In addition, supporting cross-border regionalization is also sometimes a way for a state to keep the trajectory of peripheral regions with regionalist or ethno-national tendencies under control, as in the case of the Basque Eurocity that encompasses the cities of Bayonne (France) and San Sebastian (Spain) (Bayou 2008). In a context marked by tensions between economic liberalization and national securitization concerns, cross-border regions as new scales of governance can also represent a spatial fix to reconcile conflicting imperatives (that is, allowing trade and controlling mobility). Finally, cross-border regions may constitute relays and bridges for states seeking, as geopolitical actors, to extend their area of influence. China's economic cooperation initiatives in South-East Asia (see section 24.4.3 below), or the European Union's neighbourhood policy in North Africa and along its eastern borders (see Scott 2005), are good examples of these new manifestations of territorial power politics that operate through cross-border and transnational cooperation activities.

The common point to the three conceptualizations lies in their understanding of the territorial border of nation-states as political institutions, which, even though this may change, see states as the ultimate point of reference for understanding the functions and significance of borders. Though such a focus on national territorial borders remains a vital area of study, a decentred view on political borders that moves away from the tutelary position of the state may offer new and significant theoretical perspectives.

24.3 THE MULTIPLICITY OF BORDERS AND THEIR ROLE AS A RESOURCE FOR CROSS-BORDER REGIONS

In the last two decades or so, border studies have witnessed a dramatic expansion of new perspectives driven by the spreading and multiplication of border practices, effects and meanings at different levels of political and social action and in various spatio-temporal contexts (for an overview see Popescu 2012). The changing nature of borders has been interpreted as a shift from territorial dividing lines and political institutions towards socio-cultural practices and discourses (Paasi 1999). Indeed, as a political entity, a border always marks a limit between two territorial and social entities. According to their closed or open character, borders are part of practices of differentiation, protection and control, but also of openness, hybridization and inventiveness. As such, they convey a fundamental ambivalence. However, as social constructions the signification of borders cannot solely be derived from their supposed roles and functions. Borders mean different things to different people (Balibar 2002). The diversity of actors that contribute to the ways borders are imagined, shaped, contested and transformed in everyday life must therefore be accounted for (Rumford 2012).

In the context of cross-border regionalization marked by a relative opening of borders, a great variety of actors operating at different scales and in different registers of activity are likely to benefit, or seek to benefit, from cross-border interactions and promote other roles and meanings for state borders. This idea of borders as an opportunity or resource for other actors than states is not new. Several studies have contended that opening borders may serve as a resource for the economic, political or cultural development of border regions (see notably O'Dowd 2002; Van Geenhuizen and Ratti 2001). Based on a synthesis of various arguments, four forms of border resources are briefly introduced (Sohn 2014):

1. From the moment a border is open, border regions have a distinct advantage – that of being located close to the neighbouring area. This positional advantage can generate different benefits. First, the territorial gateway position which can be claimed by some border cities and regions enables the channelling of international flows, persons or goods. Second, the proximity to foreign markets – but also to critical mass in terms of labour, knowledge networks or other assets – represents key elements for fostering scale and agglomeration economies. Third, neighbouring cities and regions might benefit from positive externalities due to cross-border spillovers and the development of 'transbordering economies'.
2. Borders play an active role in differentiating society and space. One of the key potential benefits of border-induced differentiation rests on the exploitation of factor cost differentials such as labour, land, or differences in tax and regulations. Based on an international division of labour, the localization of low-cost industries in border areas represents a remarkable example of such a positive effect of border differential advantages (for example, the maquiladoras along the US–Mexico border). The exploitation of complementarities and 'related variety' constitutes another aspect linked to economies of scope. The establishment of cross-border production networks can be accompanied by a rise in cross-border labour flows.
3. As a place where ideas and different values are confronted, the border can also be a source of stimulation leading to hybridization and the invention of new ways of doing and thinking. The concept of hybridization refers to the production of new

social practices through the mixture of antecedents which were previously separated. The opportunity offered by the border relies on overcoming constraints and differences through a process of adaptation and mutual learning negotiated through daily exchanges. Various fields and registers of activities are likely to be affected by these processes. In Europe, increased cross-border cooperation in the field of urban development and territorial planning reveals a kind of 'institutional hybridization': the confrontation over the long term of different urban planning standards, procedures and 'administrative cultures' results in the development of innovative practices and workable arrangements that combine or reinterpret aspects from the national systems (Reitel 2006).

4. Finally, the mobilization of the border as an object of recognition allows display of the multicultural nature of some cross-border regions and the opportunities this represents to shape a regional identity or attract international businesses and talented workers in a context of global competition. The symbolic value of the border becomes involved in place-making strategies at the local and regional levels and refers to the establishment of public and club goods such as regional identity and territorial branding (OECD 2013). For political stakeholders, engaging in cross-border cooperation can also represent a means of gaining political recognition and generating leverage for coalition building at the regional level and beyond.

While there is little doubt that borders can represent, under certain circumstances that remain contextually contingent, a resource for actors engaged in cross-border region-building, the scope and significance of such a conceptualization remains to be clarified. The hypothesis considered in this chapter states that the capacity of cross-border regions to mobilize their border context as a resource is an important factor for their development and consolidation thanks to leverage effects (political, symbolic) and increasing returns. The exploitation of border-related resources does not simply derive from the opening (or the 'disappearance') of a border but depends on the ability of some actors to interpret and take advantage of a specific border context. Ultimately, this means that cross-border regions do not merely emerge in spite of the border or at its expense, but, above all, thanks to it. In order to provide some evidence supporting this hypothesis, the next part is devoted to an overview of cross-border regionalization trajectories in different macro-regional contexts.

24.4 DIVERSITY OF CONFIGURATIONS AND TRAJECTORIES OF CROSS-BORDER REGIONALISM WORLDWIDE

Over the past three decades, cross-border regions have emerged around the world in different ways and in varied configurations. The contextual convergence between the opening of borders vis-à-vis economic exchanges that took place from the 1980s, the rescaling of state spaces upwards, downwards and sideways, as well as the end of the Cold War, have rendered this phenomenon possible (Perkmann and Sum 2002). Beyond these global trends, the formation of cross-border regions stems from the specific and contingent actions of a wide variety of actors and the varying weight of the macro-regional, national and local contexts surrounding their implementation. A review of the rather extensive literature available points toward three main foci of cross-border regionalism, namely

Europe, North America, and South-East Asia, although other parts of the world are also implicated (for Africa, see Söderbaum and Taylor 2008). The goal is not to develop a comprehensive and detailed assessment of the dynamics of cross-border regionalization at work on three continents, but to bring to the fore context-sensitive evidence on the role of borders as resources in shaping cross-border regions.

24.4.1 Europe

The rise of cross-border regions in Europe is closely related to the process of European integration and, more specifically, to the regional policy of the European Union. Cross-border cooperation is seen as an appropriate way of promoting the idea of European unity and contributes to its economic, social and territorial cohesion. European institutions have notably developed specific policies and financial and regulatory instruments to support the emergence and consolidation of cross-border regions. Since its inception in 1990, the INTERREG Community Initiative has had the goal of strengthening the links between local and regional stakeholders along the borders of member states. Following the successive programmes (currently INTERREG V extends from 2014 to 2020), cooperation has intensified, the eligible areas have increased and the budgets grown. Various programmes specifically targeting 'external' borders and the border regions of the accession countries have complemented this institutional approach to regionalism.[1]

Beyond its policy-driven nature, cross-border regionalism in Europe is characterized by a wide variety of initiatives and cross-border cooperation structures that have followed different trajectories since the premises of the European integration process were made explicit (for a detailed view see Dominguez and Pires 2014; Wassemberg and Reitel 2015). The first experiences of cross-border cooperation emerged along the Dutch–German border (Euregio in 1958) and at the Franco–German–Swiss border in the Upper Rhine (Regio Basiliensis in 1963). These pioneering initiatives, involving the founding members of the European community and their neighbours, gave birth to the concept of Euroregion (Perkmann 2007). Subsequently, there has been a diversification of cooperative structures according to a logic that favours certain regional specificities. Thus, the 'Scandinavian' groups have emerged in the countries of Northern Europe (Öresundskomiten in 1964) and the 'working communities' appeared in the Alps (Arge Alp in 1972, COTRAO, the Western Alps Working Community in 1982) before spreading to other areas, including maritime spaces (Atlantic Arc in 1989, Arc Manche in 1995). This cross-border regionalism has gradually extended to the countries of Central and Eastern Europe following the fall of the Iron Curtain and the subsequent EU enlargements. It was during the 1990s and early 2000s that the creation of new structures of cooperation was the most intense, especially along the borders of Central and Eastern Europe. Today, there are about 130 regional cross-border cooperation structures (this excludes transnational cooperation areas) of which 80 are denominated Euroregions (or a related term).[2]

If the Euroregion has gradually become the emblematic figure of cross-border regions in Europe, it is above all a label that cross-border cooperation initiatives are free to adopt. In general, a Euroregion is a structure consisting of local and regional authorities on either side of a border, sometimes with a parliamentary assembly, secretariat and a technical and administrative team with their own resources (AEBR and EC 2000). They are established as legal entities under private law (for example, non-profit associations or foundations) or public law based on inter-governmental agreements such as the European Grouping of Territorial Cooperation (EGTC). In theory, a Euroregion is the result of a dynamic of territorialization and aims to build a bounded space within which public policies and projects are carried out (Medeiros 2011; Perkmann 2003). In practice, the vast majority of Euroregions cannot be considered regions from a symbolic, territorial or institutional point of view, to use Paasi's regional formation model (Paasi 1986). In many cases, the resistance of states remains strong (especially in Central and Eastern Europe). Moreover, the sense of belonging of the people in a cross-border region remains weak, even in the oldest and most active Euroregions such as the Oresund (Hospers 2006).

Among this diversity of experiences and trajectories, a type of cross-border region stands out. It has emerged out of cross-border cooperation initiatives centred on cities and metropolitan centres located close to borders and which mobilize their border-context to foster and legitimize the construction of new regional scales of governance. The formation of what is called 'cross-border metropolitan regions' can notably be witnessed around such European cities as Basel (Basel Trinational Eurodistrict/Trinational Metropolitan Region of the Upper Rhine), Geneva (Greater Geneva), Copenhagen–Malmö (Oresund Region), Lille (Eurometropolis Lille-Kortrijk-Tournai) or Strasbourg (Eurodistrict Strasbourg-Ortenau). Most of the aforementioned cross-border metropolitan regions use their border-context as a resource for their development, either from an economic point of view (mobilization of factor cost differentials to induce functional cross-border integration), politically (to legitimize the construction of a new scale of governance) or symbolically (to brand and promote the international or multicultural character of the region). As a matter of fact, these cross-border regions have managed to develop some of the most advanced forms of cooperation in the fields of urban planning, transport and economic development and some even managed to develop cross-border infrastructures (for example, a public square in Lille, tram or railway lines in Geneva and Basel, bridges in Strasbourg and the Oresund). In so doing, they have induced a shift of cross-border cooperation towards 'place-based strategies' that privilege economic competitiveness and the insertion of these regions into the international circuits of trade and investment through territorial branding. If the success of these strategies is extremely variable from one case to another, all these cross-border metropolitan regions evince a weak sense of belonging to a cross-border entity on the part of their inhabitants and, in some cases, as in Geneva, the growing of social resentment and political distrust vis-à-vis cross-border cooperation and the very idea of building a shared spatial imaginary or a common territorial identity (Herzog and Sohn 2014).

24.4.2 North America

In North America, the regional integration process is relatively new. The North American Free Trade Agreement (NAFTA) which brought together Canada, Mexico and the United States was inaugurated in 1994. Unlike the European case, the adoption of this agreement is not intended to establish supranational institutions that enjoy legislative power. Similarly, the implementation of transnational public policies to strengthen networks of regional actors and cross-border institutions is not on the agenda in North America. NAFTA is primarily an international treaty of an economic and financial order which aims to eliminate trade barriers and facilitate cross-border business between the three countries.

On the ground, North American cross-border regionalism is organized around informal strategies of promotion and economic development for mostly large geographic areas (Scott 1999). These strategies include a wide range of activities that impact the economic competitiveness of regions, particularly transport, but also environmental issues and quality of life. It is above all the existence of economic interdependence and the will to strengthen trade links that explain the emergence of cross-border cooperation initiatives. The rebordering which followed the events of 11 September 2001, however, had a major negative impact on many cross-border cooperation networks, local initiatives from border communities, and even on cross-border commuting.

Along the border between Canada and the United States, there are essentially two major cross-border regions: Cascadia, which includes the Canadian province of British Columbia and the US states of Washington and Oregon with, at its heart, the corridor Vancouver–Seattle and the Great Lakes–Heartland centred on the cross-border metropolitan area of Detroit–Windsor. In both cases, there is a variety of multi-level government agreements and functional organizations of cooperation focusing on trade and economic development (Brunet-Jailly 2008). The mobilization of the border as a resource is primarily discursive and seeks to promote the complementarities between Canada and the US. The case of Cascadia is a remarkable example of entrepreneurial rescaling that relies on discourses and imaginaries to invent and promote an ideational region in the globalized circuits of consumption and investment. As evidenced by Sparke (2002), Cascadia is a cross-border vision, a discourse and a state of mind.

For its part, the border between Mexico and the United States is characterized by the development of functional economic regions centred on the twin cities along the border, and in particular the largest of them, such as San Diego–Tijuana and El Paso–Ciudad Juarez. During the 1990s, the integration of industrial supply networks linked to the maquiladoras and the twin plants system, the development of trade relations and cross-border commuting for work, leisure or tourism have given credit to the idea that we were witnessing the emergence of cross-border metropolises, the emblematic case being San Diego–Tijuana (Herzog 1990). A multitude of initiatives and cross-border cooperation structures have sprung up to address urban planning and transport issues and the protection of the environment. Many of these initiatives, led by local and regional governments, businesses or civil society, have been halted following the rebordering measures taken after 9/11, and with them the projects they supported. Since the late 2000s, there has been a resumption of cooperation initiatives and the resurgence of a discourse arguing in favour of the border as a resource in order to depict the attractiveness of the cross-border metropolitan region. For instance, the Cali Baja Bi-National Mega Region Initiative launched in 2008 by regional economic development corporations highlights on its website the geographical proximity and economic complementarity between San Diego County (US) and Baja California (Mexico), the existence of differentiated wage, cost of living, and land cost structures, and the fact that the bi-national region is a gateway to Latin America (Cali Baja 2012; see also Harrison and Hoyler 2015 for a critical analysis of this case of megaregionalism). The construction and promotion of an imagined cross-border megaregion that mobilizes the border as a resource remains, however, hampered by the harsh reality of the security-led rebordering and the increasing militarization of the US–Mexico border.

24.4.3 South-East Asia

In South-East Asia, cross-border regionalism is an economic integration process orchestrated by states (Grundy-Warr 2002). The Association of South-East Asian Nations (ASEAN) is the largest alliance of nation-states, which promotes inter-regional and cross-border cooperation in view of attracting foreign investment and expanding exports. Despite their 'top-down' character, these are essentially pragmatic cooperation ventures that remain weakly institutionalized. The best-known instances of cross-border micro-regionalism are called 'growth triangles'.

Historically, it is around Singapore and Hong Kong that two areas of cross-border economic cooperation have emerged in East Asia. The SIJORI Growth Triangle is a partnership agreement between Singapore, the Malaysian state of Johor and the Riau islands of Indonesia that was formally established in 1994. The cooperation between the three constituent entities of the triangle – renamed since the Indonesia–Malaysia–Singapore (IMS) Growth Triangle – is based on existing economic complementarities between land and cheap labour in Johor and Riau and capital and connections in Singapore. Despite the pivotal mobilization of cross-border differentials in its growth strategy, the IMS triangle presents itself as an embodiment of a 'borderless world'. The persistence of geopolitical and postcolonial tensions around the management of migration flows and access to water resources highlights the idealized character of this regional construction (Sparke et al. 2004). The case of Hong Kong and the Pearl River Delta is characterized in turn by a spatial division of labour in which Hong Kong provides the necessary services to manufacturing industries located in Mainland China. The incorporation of Hong Kong and Macau as Special Administrative Regions in China has, however, blurred his triangle status (Breitung 2002). In both cases, one can witness the emergence of cross-border mega-city regions clustered around one larger metropolis and its border hinterland.

Various other regional cross-border configurations can be pointed out along the external Chinese borders. According to the United Nations, a vast cross-border urban corridor encompassing more than 97 million inhabitants stretches from Beijing (China) to Tokyo (Japan) via Pyongyang (North Korea) and Seoul (South Korea) (UN Habitat 2008). On the Chinese southern border, the cross-border activism of China within the Greater Mekong Subregion also draws attention. The development of Border Economic Cooperation Zones attracts labour-intensive manufacturing and trade and they are used as springboards towards South-East Asia (Chen and Stone 2013). The cross-border economic regions in the making take the form of growth corridors, structured around border towns such as Tengchong, and connected by transport infrastructures. Finally, the exceptional scale and pace of China's urbanization shows the emergence of metropolitan regions and mega-regions that transcend 'internal' borders, as in the case of the Yangtze River Delta region which straddles the provinces of Shanghai, Jiangsu and Zhejiang (Luo and Shen 2009).

24.5 TOWARDS A COUPLING BETWEEN CITY-REGIONALISM AND CROSS-BORDER REGIONALISM

Eurometropolises or eurodistricts, growth triangles, urban corridors, cross-border metropolitan regions or bi-national megaregions: many cross-border regions that mobilize borders as resources for their development and growth centre on cities and metropolitan areas. Before taking the interpretation of this 'urban factor' further, let us point out that there is no reason to suspect a Western-centrism at work, as the phenomenon does not seem related to a particular macro-regional context but embraces the entire globe, albeit according to singular arrangements (including in Africa and Latin America not covered in this chapter).

How, then, can we explain what amounts to an affirmation of cities, and especially the largest of them, as key drivers of cross-border regionalism? The most convincing arguments point to a coupling between two 'spaces of regionalism' – the cross-border region and the city-region (see Moisio and Jonas 2018). On the one hand, the border context offers to cities and metropolitan areas that are located nearby opportunities to engage in inter-scalar growth initiatives or 'glocalization' strategies (Jessop and Sum 2000). This relates to the various border resources previously analysed (see above, section 24.3). Of course, the intensity of this mobilization may vary, as well as its impact on the consolidation of cross-border regions. The mobilization of the border as a resource is not in itself a guarantee of success for a cross-border region and many other factors come into play, notably the attitude of the national governments involved. It should also be noted that the mobilization of various resources related to borders can have contradictory effects and an overall negative impact on cross-border cooperation. The Greater Region (a Euroregion straddling Luxembourg, France, Germany and Belgium) is a compelling example: on the one hand, strong differentials in wages and taxes have induced huge cross-border economic transactions (more than 180,000 French, German and Belgian workers cross the border into Luxembourg daily) and a cross-border metropolitan area that is functionally integrated has emerged; on the other hand, these sharp asymmetries have been a major obstacle to the establishment of a cross-border governance among the cities and the regions concerned (see Sohn et al. 2009). Due to their Janus-faced character borders are always both an interface that opens up opportunities and a barrier that emphasizes differences and inequalities.

On the other side, cities tend to concentrate specific skills and resources (as well as the capability of reaching and mobilizing remote resources) that allow them to benefit from border-related opportunities and work towards the emergence and consolidation of cross-border cooperation areas. In Europe, given the institutionalization of cross-border cooperation, it is obvious that the management capacities, the technical and financial resources available to urban authorities and their administrations, are an asset for mounting cooperation projects involving a multitude of actors and scales and securing INTERREG funding. More generally, the mobilization of economic elites and their networks, as well as civil society, is also an advantage, either because these milieus can stimulate public authorities to action (especially when public action does not seem to be up to the challenges) or, of course, because these actors can be very active and imaginative in the discursive framing of new cross-border regions and their promotion (such as the imagined megaregions of Cascadia or Cali Baja). Lastly, because (cross-border) metropolitan areas are often perceived as pivotal scales for inducing place-based growth strategies, they can benefit from the symbolic and sometimes financial support of states through specific national policies (for examples in Germany, France and Switzerland, see notably Harrison and Growe 2014; Sohn and Reitel 2016).

24.6 CONCLUSION

Beyond the bewildering variety of cross-border regions that have emerged in different parts of the world, the presence of a state border constitutes their common denominator and justifies their existence. The central question that this chapter has tackled points to the role these borders are likely to play. Based on a conceptualization that acknowledges the multiple and open-ended nature of borders, the hypothesis that borders are not necessarily barriers, but can also represent a resource for cross-border regions that have the skills and strategic capacity to mobilize them has been highlighted. The objective of such a conceptualization is not to replace other perspectives, but rather to provide a complementary approach. An overview of the various cross-border regionalization initiatives in different parts of the world suggests a specific role for cities and urban actors in mobilizing their border-context to their advantage. If border-related resources are able to constitute an asset for the development of cross-border regions, it is primarily the cities (especially the larger ones) that seem to have the capacity to activate and benefit from them.

Of course, further research is needed in order to identify more precisely the mechanisms at work and their actual outcomes. Two privileged fields of investigation outline an agenda for future research on cross-border regions. A first questioning concerns the urban factor identified in this chapter. So far, it is not possible to formally dismiss a possible urban bias in research on cross-border regionalism. More comparative analyses as well as meta-analyses in this domain would be welcome in order to pinpoint the specific role of cities, and under which conditions (geopolitical, economic, historical, urban) border resources are activated. Moreover, it remains unclear to what extent border-related advantages actually outweigh the disadvantages usually associated with the proximity of a border (for example barrier effects, marginalization, differentiation, exclusion) for cities and border regions. Finally, what are the outcomes of these long-term cross-border regionalization strategies in terms of spatial imaginaries, regional identities, governance arrangements or modes of production? These questions are not limited to cases of regions crossed by a state border, but also to the large number of cases, often less scrutinized, that involve the 'internal' borders of states, such as regional, administrative or ethno-territorial boundaries.

The second questioning concerns the impacts of the current shifting practices and meanings of state borders on cross-border regions and regionalization trajectories. As we discussed at the beginning of this chapter, cross-border regions do not arise simply from the (relative) opening of borders and the rescaling of states. They are above all social and historically contingent constructions. Given the diversity of regional configurations that have mushroomed since their emergence more than three decades ago, a critical assessment of their historical trajectories, in order to better understand why some cross-border regions tend to institutionalize and perpetuate whereas others decline or even become obsolete, appears timely. In the light of a shift in the framework conditions that prevailed at the time of the emergence of the phenomenon – in particular, rebordering dynamics driven by nationalism and/or security concerns – the question ultimately points to the impact of the hardening of borders on the existence of cross-border regions and their ability to demonstrate resilience.

24.7 NOTES

1. These include PHARE (Poland and Hungary: Assistance for Restructuring their Economies) launched in 1989 and TACIS (Technical Assistance to the Commonwealth of Independent States), which was inaugurated in 1991. Since 2007, the cross-border programmes from the Instrument for Pre-Accession Assistance (IPA CBC) target the countries of the former Yugoslavia as well as Turkey, while the cross-border programmes from the European Neighbourhood Instrument (ENI CBC) cover the eastern and Mediterranean borders of the EU.
2. These figures come from a critical review of the list of border cooperation structures provided by the Association of European Border Regions (AEBR, undated). These estimates should be approached with caution as lack of information makes it difficult to assess the relevance of some cross-border initiatives and structures.

24.8 REFERENCES

Anderson, J. and L. O'Dowd (1999), 'Borders, border regions and territoriality: contradictory meanings, changing significance', *Regional Studies*, **33** (7), 593–604.
Association of European Border Regions (AEBR) (undated), *Regions List*, accessed 25 September 2016 at www.aebr.eu/en/members/list_of_regions.php.
Association of European Border Regions (AEBR) and European Commission (EC) (2000), *Practical Guide to Cross-border Cooperation*, accessed 16 December 2016 at www.aebr.eu/files/publications/lace_guide.en.pdf.
Balibar, E. (2002), *Politics and the Other Scene*, London: Verso.
Bayou, C. (2008), 'L'Eurocité basque. Le rêve d'une métropole de rang européen', *La Documentation française*, n° 1, October 2008, accessed 16 December 2016 at http://www.ladocumentationfrancaise.fr/pages-europe/d000652-l-eurocite-basque.-le-reve-d-une-metropole-de-rang-europeen-par-celine-bayou/article.
Breitung, W. (2002), 'Transformation of a boundary regime: the Hong Kong and Mainland China case', *Environment and Planning A*, **34** (10), 1749–1762.
Brunet-Jailly, E. (2008), 'Cascadia in comparative perspectives: Canada–US relations and the emergence of cross-border regions', *Canadian Political Science Review*, **2** (2), 104–124.
Cali Baja Bi-national Mega-region (Cali Baja) (2012), accessed 12 October 2016 at http://calibaja.net/cbdb/p/.
Chen, X. and C. Stone (2013), 'China and Southeast Asia: unbalanced development in the Greater Mekong subregion', *The European Financial Review*, August–September, 7–11.
Clark, J. and A. Jones (2018), 'The "Europe of the Regions"', in A. Paasi, J. Harrison and M. Jones (eds), *Handbook on the Geographies of Regions and Territories*, Cheltenham, UK and Northampton, MA, USA: Edward Elgar Publishing, pp. 373–384.
Dominguez, L. and I. Pires (eds) (2014), *Cross-Border Cooperation Structures in Europe*, Brussels: PIE Peter Lang.
Grundy-Warr, C. (2002), 'Cross-border regionalism through a "South-east Asian" looking-glass', *Space and Polity*, **6** (2), 215–225.
Harrison, J. and A. Growe (2014), 'From places to flows? Planning for the new "regional world" in Germany', *European Urban and Regional Studies*, **21** (1), 21–41.
Harrison, J. and M. Hoyler (2015), 'Megaregions reconsidered: urban futures and the future of the urban', in J. Harrison and M. Hoyler (eds), *Megaregions: Globalization's New Urban Form?*, Cheltenham, MA and Northampton, MA, USA: Edward Elgar Publishing, pp. 230–256.
Herzog, L.A. (1990), *Where North Meets South: Cities, Space, and Politics on the United States-Mexico Border*, Austin: University of Texas Press.
Herzog, L.A. and C. Sohn (2014), 'The cross-border metropolis in a global age: a conceptual model and empirical evidence from the US-Mexico and European border regions', *Global Society*, **28** (4), 441–461.
Hettne, B. and F. Söderbaum (2000), 'Theorising the rise of regionness', *New Political Economy*, **5** (3), 457–472.
Hospers, G.J. (2006), 'Borders, bridges and branding: the transformation of the Oresund Region into an imagined space', *European Planning Studies*, **14** (8), 1015–1033.
Jessop, B. and N.-L. Sum (2000), 'An entrepreneurial city in action: Hong Kong's emerging strategies in and for (inter) urban competition', *Urban Studies*, **37** (12), 2287–2313.
Keating, M. (2004), *Regions and Regionalism in Europe*, Cheltenham, UK and Northampton, MA, USA: Edward Elgar Publishing.
Luo, X. and J. Shen (2009) 'A study on inter-city cooperation in the Yangtze river delta region, China', *Habitat International*, **33** (1), 52–62.
Medeiros, E. (2011), '(Re)defining the Euroregion concept', *European Planning Studies*, **19** (1), 141–158.

Moisio, S. and A.E.G. Jonas (2018), 'City-regions and city-regionalism', in A. Paasi, J. Harrison and M. Jones (eds), *Handbook on the Geographies of Regions and Territories*, Cheltenham, UK and Northampton, MA, USA: Edward Elgar Publishing, pp. 285–297.

O'Dowd, L. (2002), 'The changing significance of European borders', *Regional & Federal Studies*, **12** (4), 13–36.

OECD (2013), *Regions and Innovation: Collaborating across Borders*, OECD Reviews of Regional Innovation, Paris: OECD.

Ohmae, K. (1990), *The Borderless World: Power and Strategy in the Interlinked Economy*, London: HarperCollins.

Paasi, A. (1986), 'The institutionalization of regions: a theoretical framework for understanding the emergence of regions and the constitution of regional identity', *Fennia*, **164** (1), 105–146.

Paasi, A. (1991), 'Deconstructing regions: notes on the scales of spatial life', *Environment and Planning A*, **23** (2), 239–256.

Paasi, A. (1999), 'Boundaries as social practice and discourse: the Finnish–Russian border', *Regional Studies*, **33** (7), 669–680.

Perkmann, M. (2003), 'Cross-border regions in Europe: significance and drivers of regional cross-border co-operation', *European Urban and Regional Studies*, **10** (2), 153–171.

Perkmann, M. (2007), 'Construction of new territorial scales: a framework and case study of the EUREGIO cross-border region', *Regional Studies*, **41** (2), 253–266.

Perkmann, M. and N.-L. Sum (eds.) (2002), *Globalization, Regionalization, and Cross-Border Regions*, New York: Palgrave Macmillan.

Popescu, G. (2008), 'The conflicting logics of cross-border reterritorialization: geopolitics of Euroregions in Eastern Europe', *Political Geography*, **27** (4), 418–438.

Popescu, G. (2012), *Bordering and Ordering the Twenty-First Century: Understanding Borders*, Lanham, MD: Rowman & Littlefield.

Regional Plan Association (2006), *America 2050: A Prospectus*, New York: RPA.

Reitel, B. (2006), 'Governance in cross-border agglomerations in Europe: the examples of Basle and Strasbourg', *Europa Regional*, **14** (1), 9–21.

Rumford, C. (2012), 'Towards a multiperspectival study of borders', *Geopolitics*, **17** (4), 887–902.

Scalapino, R.A. (2007), 'The state of international relations in Northeast Asia', *Asia Policy*, **3** (1), 25–28.

Scott, J.W. (1999), 'European and North American contexts for cross-border regionalism', *Regional Studies*, **33** (7), 605–617.

Scott, J.W. (2005), 'The EU and "Wider Europe": toward an alternative geopolitics of regional cooperation?', *Geopolitics*, **10** (3), 429–454.

Söderbaum, F. and I. Taylor (eds) (2008), *Afro-Regions: The Dynamics of Cross-Border Micro-Regionalism in Africa*, Uppsala: Nordic Africa Institute.

Sohn, C., B. Reitel and O. Walther (2009), 'Cross-border metropolitan integration in Europe: the case of Luxembourg, Basel, and Geneva', *Environment and Planning C: Government and Policy*, **27** (5), 922–939.

Sohn, C. (2014), 'Modelling cross-border integration: the role of borders as a resource', *Geopolitics*, **19** (3), 587–608.

Sohn, C. and B. Reitel (2016), 'The role of states in the construction of cross-border metropolitan regions in Europe: a scalar approach', *European Urban and Regional Studies*, **23** (3), 306–321.

Soóz, E. (2014), 'Endeavours to establish EGTCs on Hungary's external borders', in L. Dominguez and I. Pires (eds), *Cross-Border Cooperation Structures in Europe*, Brussels: PIE Peter Lang, pp. 213–227.

Sparke, M. (2002), 'Not a state, but more than a state of mind: cascading Cascadias and the geoeconomics of crossborder regionalism', in M. Perkmann and N.-L. Sum (eds), *Globalization, Regionalization and Cross-Border Regions*, London: Palgrave, pp. 212–238.

Sparke, M., J. Sidaway, T. Bunnell and C. Grundy-Warr (2004), 'Triangulating the borderless world: geographies of power in the Indonesia–Malaysia–Singapore Growth Triangle', *Transactions of the Institute of British Geographers*, **29** (4), 485–498.

Taylor, P.J. (1995), 'Beyond containers: internationality, interstateness, interterritoriality', *Progress in Human Geography*, **19** (1), 1–15.

UN Habitat (2008), *State of the World's Cities 2010/2011: Bridging the Urban Divide*, London: Earthscan.

Van Geenhuizen, M.S. and R. Ratti (eds) (2001), *Gaining Advantage from Open Borders: An Active Space Approach to Regional Development*, Aldershot: Ashgate.

Wassemberg, B. and B. Reitel (2015), *Territorial Cooperation in Europe: A Historical Perspective*, Luxembourg: Publications Office of the European Union.

25. Comparing regionalism at supra-national level from the perspective of a statehood theory of regions
Luk Van Langenhove

25.1 INTRODUCTION

Region – and related concepts such as regionalism, regional security, regional cooperation or regional integration – are frequently used within the epistemic realm of International Relations (IR) and the study of world politics. The United Nations Charter – crafted in 1945 – for instance devotes a whole chapter to so-called 'regional arrangements'. Today, entities such as the European Union are referred to as a regional organisation. But, common as it might be used by policy-makers and scholars, it is not always very clear what actually is referred to when regions are mentioned in the framework of world politics. This chapter discusses how different literatures in and beyond IR have dealt with the notion of 'region' at the supra-national level. It will be argued that in order to advance scholarly understanding of such regionalisms, regions need to be looked at as governance entities with statehood properties. It will be claimed that supra-national regions are not states, but they can be regarded as actors that can behave *as if* they are states. Finally, the implications of such a position for the comparative study of supra-national regionalisms will be discussed.

25.2 THE PROBLEM WITH REGIONS IN INTERNATIONAL RELATIONS

The word 'region' derives from the Latin verb rego, which means 'to steer'. So, the original meaning of region was linked to governance and not to delimiting space by border. Later, it became associated with regere, meaning 'to direct' or 'rule'. Today, the concept is clearly polysemous as the term 'region' can refer – for instance – to geographical space, economic interaction, institutional or governmental jurisdiction, or social or cultural characteristics. Consequently, the number of definitions of 'region' is considerable. Within IR, there is for instance Nye's (1971, p. vii) classical definition that defines an international region as 'a limited number of states linked together by a geographical relationship and by a degree of mutual interdependence'. A somewhat similar definition, but without reference to states, is offered by Paasi (1986, pp. 105–146): 'A region is commonly regarded as a part of the earth's surface which possesses a quality of cohesion derived from a consistent relationship between associated features.' But such definitions do not seem to contribute a lot to the understanding of what a region is. This made Paasi (2011, pp. 9–16) more recently state that 'relatively little attention has been paid to such major questions as what is a region, how it "becomes", how diverging regions exist and how social power is involved in region-building processes'. Ten years earlier, Schultz et al. (2001, p. 252) already noted 'the problem of defining regions attracted a significant deal of attention during the first wave of regionalism, but the results yielded few clear conclusions'. So the problem seems to remain.

Indeed, most scholars seem to have given up looking for answers to that straight forward question 'what is a region?' The result is a conceptual vagueness that not only has consequences for the theoretical and empirical quality of the research, but also hinders policy-making. Without a clear view of what constitutes a region, it becomes difficult to analyse what regional integration is or to advise on how it is realised. It also becomes difficult to understand what is the relation between, for instance, the development of Europe as a region and the development of the 'Europe of the regions'. In sum, the region is a 'rubbery concept' stretching above and below the national state (Hooghe et al. 2010, p. 4). There is thus a clear need for some conceptual clarification as regions and 'regionalism' have not only become topics of concern for policy-makers, they are also hot academic topics studied by scholars from many social sciences disciplines. As Fawn (2009, pp. 5–34) said: 'Regions, regionalism and regionalisation matter.' For many years now, the mantra has been that a more rigorous theorising of regions is needed (Agnew, 1999; Schmitt-Egner, 2002; Neumann, 2010). Still, there is not yet a unified academic perspective on regions and therefore comparative studies of regions remain a problematic enterprise (De Lombaerde et al. 2010). In sum, regions are 'difficult to theorize, while making that also a necessity' (Fawn 2009, p. 33).

25.3   OLD AND NEW WAYS OF STUDYING SUPRA-NATIONAL REGIONS

Scholarly attention to regions in the field of IR focuses to a large extent on processes of regional integration (see, for instance, Farrell et al. 2005). Other scholars focus on cross-border regions or upon interactions between different kinds of regions (Shaw et al. 2012). Then come the economists, who study (supra-national) regional trade arrangements (see, for instance, Mattli 1999). Finally, there is a literature that focuses upon comparing regionalisms (De Lombaerde et al. 2010). Throughout these diverse literatures emerged the insight that 'regions are central to our understanding of world politics' (Acharya and Johnston 2007, p. 629). But it is striking to see that the concept of region itself is hardly problematised. Neither is there much attention paid to the development of a comprehensive theoretical framework for the study of regions.

There has been, and still is, much debate over what exactly constitutes a region, how the boundaries of a region may be drawn, and how regional projects are to be operationalised (Van Langenhove 2011; Fawcett 2013). This matter is complicated further due to the fact that those attempting to define a region often find that they are not statically situated or clearly defined, but rather find it is more often the case that regional boundaries are blurred, prone to adaptation and change, or may sometimes exist in an overlapping structure. According to Fredrik Söderbaum and Timothy Shaw, this problem of definition has been further exasperated by the various, and often competing, qualitative and quantitative approaches to regionalisation seeking to understand and measure its processes (Söderbaum and Shaw 2003, pp. 5–6). Considering these theoretical burdens, competing approaches, and problems of defining regionalism and regionalisation, it is perhaps most constructive for the purposes of this chapter to maintain a more open definition. To this end, following the succinct arguments put forth by Louise Fawcett, it may simply be put that for 'an increase in regional interaction and activity: regionalism refers to policies and projects, regionalisation refers to processes' (Fawcett, 2013, p. 5). A similar definition has been put forward by Van Langenhove (2013b) who, following Morgan (2005), distinguishes between regional *projects* (or dreams), regional *processes* (the acts that put the dreams into practice) and the regional *products* (the institutionalisation of the integration into treaties and organisations as well as into flows of goods, capitals, services and people).

With these underpinnings in mind, scholars have developed divided notions of regionalism into two main groupings, or what can be referred to as 'waves' of regionalisation: on the one hand, there is 'old regionalism' which is associated with the dominant theoretical thinking in the post-Second World War era that places state-based regional interaction at the forefront, and on the other, there is 'new regionalism' which has gained prevalence since the end of the Cold War and seeks to incorporate the formal and informal interactions between states and non-state actors.

Looking first at the school of thought associated with 'old regionalism', as was alluded to above, it may be said that the state and interstate interaction lies as its central focus. The early theoretical formulation of these integration theories were focused primarily on high politics, namely security and the survival of the State, as well as on increasing economic integration and interdependence. William H. Riker, one of the main contributors to the theory of federalism, argued that policy-makers would only be willingly to integrate and give up some degree of their national sovereignty in a process known as 'federal bargaining'. For Riker, there were only two circumstances in which states would be willing to join together and subvert their national sovereignty: in cases of an external threat (often military) or for the prospect of economic expansion (Riker 1964). In a similar vein, Karl Deutsch proposed the idea of a 'security community' whereby states would be bound together by mutual sympathy, trust, and common interests in order to resolve conflicts peacefully (Deutsch 1968). As well, Barry Buzan took this notion a step further with his proposed 'regional security complex theory', claiming that security concerns do not travel well over long distances and therefore should be organised and limited according to geographic region (Buzan 1986). In all three cases, ensuring and maintaining peaceful relations between states was thought to be the primary ambition.

Formulated in the late 1950s and early 1960s, mainly by the German economist Ernst Haas and American political scientist Leon Lindberg, neo-functionalism stresses the importance of autonomous supranational institutions in the formulation of organised interests, and emphasises the critical role technocrats may play in the decision-making process (Haas 1958; Lindberg 1963). Similar to regional economic integration theorists such as Bela Balassa and Jacob Viner, this mode of thinking views integration as a gradual process of state cooperation following a liner trajectory from preferential treatment, towards increasingly advanced stages of inclusiveness, until reaching an eventual complete level of integration (Viner 1950; Balassa 1961). For neo-functionalists, building and maintaining strong institutions as well as a competent bureaucracy will lead to the most positive and productive forms of integration.

The final theoretical approach which may be grouped among the 'old regionalism' theories is that of intergovernmentalism. This theory, originally proposed by Stanley

Hoffman and later expressed in its more liberal form by Andrew Moravcsik, maintains that national governments retain the ultimate authority over regionalisation and its decision-making, but recognises the capability of supranational institutions in enhancing the capacity of national governments through the development of mutually beneficial policies (Hoffman 1964, 1966; Moravcsik 1993). For Intergovernmentalists, engagement in regional integration projects can most accurately and concisely be understood as a series of rational choices undertaken by leaders within a specific institutional setting (Fioramonti 2014). Accordingly, if all three of these theories may be summarised together, 'whether more focus on agency (e.g. federalism and intergovernmentalism) or more concerned with institutional structures (e.g. neo-functionalism), these theoretical approaches understand regionalism as an eminently top-down process, dominated by technocratic and political elites' (Fioramonti 2014, p. 11). Or in other words, they are concerned solely with the regional interactions of state agents, while minimising the impact and influence of non-state actors or civil society actions.

Before the late 1980s and early 1990s, Regional Integration Studies had not been able to garner much support for itself as a distinct discipline (for an overview of the development of the discipline, see Shaw et al. 2012; De Lombaerde and Söderbaum, 2013). Only after the collapse of the Soviet Union, a growth in multilateralism, and a rapid expansion of regional integration projects did it become a separate field of study in its own right. Until this point, the nuances of regional integration were often subsumed within the field of International Relations, as well as confined to security and economic thinking. However, this new found scholarly attention, along with the litany of case studies to be examined, allowed for an innovation in thinking which sought to understand the increasing complexity of regional formations and their multi-level and multi-sectoral purposes (Fawcett and Hurrell 1995). Indeed, it would be difficult to find a contemporary scholar of regional integration that would disagree that regionalism should not be viewed as the exclusive domain of states but is more accurately understood as also encompassing the interactions between non-state actors, as well as among states and non-state actors (Shaw et al. 2012; Fioramonti 2013, 2014). In addition to the inclusion of non-state actors, Fioramonti argues that, 'there is also an increasing recognition, by and large prompted by the application of constructivism to the study of regionalism, that regions are not geographically "given" but are rather socially constructed through human interactions, political discourse and cultural evolutions' (Fioramonti 2014, p. 6). These constructivist-minded scholars believe that when undertaking an exercise of defining regions, one may be referring to a variety of elements, including a geographical space, economic interaction, institutional or governmental jurisdiction, or social or cultural characteristics (Van Langenhove 2013b). Similarly, Amitav Acharya maintains that regions are not predefined but transition and evolve over time depending on the prevailing political, economic and social discourses that are taking place in each society (Acharya 2009). Or, in other words, regions and regional thinking may transition to new formations and paradigms depending on social influences. This point on the transitions of societal discourse and the nature of integration has particular relevance in its applications to sustainable regionalisation and will therefore be returned upon again in the sections below.

25.4 A LINGUISTIC PERSPECTIVE ON REGIONS

When people speak about regions they always refer to a territorial space or to a certain characteristic of that territory. These regions can be small or large. They can be part of a single state or be composed out of different states. They can be well defined with sharp boundaries or be fuzzy. It looks like virtually every part of the geographical reality can be called a region, even areas around a sea (e.g. the Mediterranean region). But there is one type of geographical space that is difficult to label as a region: a state. While speaking of 'the region of Flanders' implies a reference to a clearly defined geographical area, speaking of 'the region of Belgium' does not refer to the territory inside the Belgian borders. It could only mean that one refers to Belgium and its surroundings. Otherwise stated, nobody refers to Belgium as a region because it is a state (e.g. a Kingdom). One can also observe that people have no difficulties in seeing the same geographical spot as being part of the different regions at the same time.

From these examples of first-order uses of the concept of region follows that regions are so much more than just geographic realities. Regions should therefore not only be defined by their surface or boundaries. They are a clear illustration of what Searle (1995) has called 'institutional facts': those portions of the world that are only 'facts' by human agreement. For instance, for a piece of paper to count as a five-euro bill one needs the existence of 'money' and a set of conventions about the value of that bill as well as a 'market' to trade it. Searle has labelled these facts 'institutional' because they require people and human institutions for their existence. As pointed out by Paasi (2002, p. 805), this holds for regions too: although being a geographical area, a region does not exist without people. A region is thus always an institutional fact and therefore also an idea. And because regions are ideas (be it with a geographical component), they are being talked about. So, in line with a social constructionist point of view, one can even say that it is not because regions exist that they can be talked about. It is because they are being talked about that they start existing! In other words, a region is always constructed through discourse. In such a view, the concept of 'region' can be regarded as a linguistic tool used by actors to talk about a geographical area that is not a state.

Accordingly, one may say that in principle every geographical area in the world that is not a state has the potential to be considered as a region. So, regions may be defined as what they are not: they are not sovereign states (De Lombaerde et al. 2010, p. 23). But regions, whilst not being a state, can, to some extent, be attributed statehood properties. For instance, a region can have its own regional innovation policy (just as there exist national innovation policies). Or it can raise taxes and have its own budget for the provision of certain public goods. Regions can also possess symbols or institutions (such as a flag or a parliament) that one normally associates with states. The concept of region seems therefore to be used in everyday language by people in order to refer to geographical spaces that whilst not being a state do look to some extent as if they are a state. Talking of regions can thus be regarded as a linguistic tool used to refer to something that is not a state but has some resemblances to a state.

Such linguistic devices can deal with areas inside, above and across states. Indeed, one can distinguish between regions at a sub-national, supra-national and cross-border level, and hence one can speak about regions at these three levels. First, there is talk about regions when referring to sub-national entities within existing states. The German Länder are a classic example but in many countries governance units such as Departments or Provinces are also often referred to as regions. The latter is, for instance, the case for Quebec, a 'provincial region' of Canada. But Quebec itself contains 17 administrative regions. Second, there are some cross-border regions that reach across national boundaries of two or more states which involve governance units below the national level of governance. The 'Euregions' are a good example thereof. Another example is the Georgia-Puget Sound, a cross-border region between Canada and the USA. Third, one can speak of regions when referring to two or more neighbouring states that have achieved a certain degree of 'integration'. Regional trade agreements fall under this category or regions with some form of institutional structure (the EU, the Benelux, etc.). But at the end of the day, even a continent can be referred to as a region – as is the case in the 'African Union', a continent-wide regional organisation.

25.5   A STATEHOOD THEORY OF REGIONS

The concept of region thus allows people to speak about all kinds of geographical spaces that are not a state but can be experienced as resembling a state. In that sense, talking about regions helps people organise places, spaces and institutions. This is illustrated by many references to 'regions' in everyday talk. Take for instance parliaments: for many years, this institution was associated with the democratic functioning of states. But today there exist parliaments that are not directly linked to a single state or to a state in its totality. Examples include the 'European Parliament' or the 'Flemish Parliament'. In both cases, these institutions are referred to as a regional parliament. Or take the issue of free trade. In principle, there are no quotas or tariffs to hinder trade within a single state. Therefore, a state can be considered as a single economic space or market. In contrast, trade between states is hindered by borders and the import and export rules that exist. Free Trade Agreements therefore try to reproduce the 'single market' at a level above single states by creating custom unions, etc. These agreements including two or more states are often labelled 'regional trade agreements'.

The statehood theory of regions, as presented in Van Langenhove (2013a, 2013b), builds upon the concept of a region that clearly links statehood to regions. It therefore takes as a point of departure the statehood properties of regions and the complex relations between states and regions. But using the concept of state in thinking about regions opens a kind of Pandora's box. There are many ways to conceptualise and theorise states. Here, the choice is made to look at states as if they were persons. There is a long tradition of thinking about the state as a person that started with Hobbes. In the Leviathan, he advanced the metaphor that actors in world politics can best be compared to persons as both persons and states can act autonomously and be regarded accountable for their deeds (Pettit 2008). Hobbes considered states as entities that can 'talk' on behalf of others. This idea was based upon his definition of actors as persons of whom the words can be considered as their own or as representing the words of someone else. For Hobbes, the notion of 'personality' fuses elements of authority, representation and the capacity to behave as one politically constructed actor. In that sense, personality according to Hobbes plays a crucial role in the establishment of the state as the sovereign power is seen as an artificial person (Pettit 2008; Ip 2010).

Recent discussions of this metaphor can be found in Wendt (2004), Franke and Roos (2010) and Luoma-Aho (2009). If one accepts the earlier introduced idea that regions can be compared to states and combines this with Hobbes' idea to assimilate states to persons, then it follows that one can metaphorically also compare regions to persons. Just as Alexander Wendt spoke about 'the state as a person', one can also speak about the region as a person. Indeed, both states and regions can be attributed 'actorness' in much the same way as to persons. This is reflected in 'first-order' utterances such as 'the EU has reacted angrily to. . .', 'Europe is behaving. . .', 'ASEAN warned. . .' or 'Flanders aims to. . .'. But of course, state and regions are only concepts and cannot actually say or do anything. As such, the statehood theory of regions is therefore different from the spatial fetishism approach in geography where causal powers are assigned to space per se (Soja and Hadjimichalis 1985). Only persons can speak and act, and certain persons can act on behalf of a state or a region. To the extent that persons, states and regions can all be regarded as actors with a power to act, such a metaphor should not be too surprising. After all, corporations for instance are in legal theory also metaphorically compared with persons. A so-called legal personality is said to be able to govern property, go broke or even be criminally indicted.

Looking at regions as if they are persons allows bringing in a specific conceptual apparatus to refine the thinking about regions. When people talk about persons, there are a number of concepts that are used. First there is personhood. In the English language, the suffix 'hood' refers to what distinguishes something from something else. Personhood, thus, refers to the general characteristics that distinguish all persons from non-persons. Such characteristics are common to all people. Although much conceptual confusion exists about individuality and personality (and related ones such as individual, self, persona and so on), there seems to be a consensus that a person is what each human being, given suitable biological and social conditions, is generally supposed to be. Second, personality is the term that should be used to designate individual persons (De Waele and Harré 1976). All persons can be said to have their own unique personality. Third, there is personification. This concept is used to refer to the processes of attributing personhood. People tend to treat other people as persons. But one can also attribute personhood to non-persons. Together these three psychological concepts can be treated as metaphors to talk about regions. This can be done by introducing three neologisms: regionhood, regionality and regionification.

First, regionhood is what distinguishes regions from non-regions. It points to what is common to all regions. Second, in analogy with the concept of personality, one can also speak of regionality. Just as personality refers to how an individual demonstrates his/her personhood by being unique, regionality can be regarded as referring to how regionhood occurs across different individual regions. The metaphor goes as follows: although all persons have personhood, no two persons are alike. Still, one can classify persons in categories (for instance, extroverts versus introverts). Mutatis mutandis: all regions have regionhood, but there exist many types of regions (such as sub-national, supra-national or cross-border regions) and regions within the same category can still be very different. Finally, there is the neologism of regionification, in analogy to personification, which is the process of ascribing personality to an actor. Regionification can be thought of as the discursive processes by which certain geographical entities are referred to as a region. Together, the concepts of regionhood, regionality and regionification allow us to talk about regions in a much more precise way. Armed with this conceptual toolbox, the following sections will now explore how regions can be theorised.

25.6   COMPARING REGIONS FROM A STATEHOOD PERSPECTIVE

Within the field of regional integration there seems to be a growing interest in comparative regional integration studies – sometimes also referred to as 'comparative regionalism' – as a scholarly sector performing scientific comparisons of regional integration processes (or regionalisms) across the globe and across time. It is generally regarded as an (interdisciplinary) academic field of research. However, as Sbragia (2008, p. 32) noted, 'the study of comparative regionalism is ill-defined and the boundaries of the field are permeable'. Nevertheless, as acknowledged by Söderbaum (2010, p. 477), there is virtually no systematic debate regarding the fundamentals of comparison, such as 'what to compare?', 'how to compare?' or 'why to compare?'. Nevertheless, comparative regionalism is a thriving sub-discipline of political science. Its focus is upon studying processes of regional integration and their comparison. But, the issue is what can be compared and what cannot. Answering that question can only be done if comparative regionalism better defines what its actual subject matter is while broadening its comparative perspective. This can be done by comparing regions with states.

One can consider region building from different analytical perspectives. First, regionalisation can be seen as a project performed by actors that drive region building. In many cases, these actors will be states, but they can also be part of civil society or industries pushing towards more regionalisation. Whatever the driving force, there will always be some kind of vision and telos behind the project. Second, region building is always a process. Regions are not constructed overnight: it is a step-by-step sequence with its own internal dynamics and a broad set of geopolitical and economic factors. Third, region building results in different outputs or products: regions that operate as actors and that are constituted in agreements, official documents, organisations, treaties and so on. Region building is thus a process based upon a project and results in a regional product.

The considerations outlined above translate into three distinct approaches for studying regionalisation. First, there is the study of the integration 'projects': the normative ideals and goals put forward by region-builders as the telos of what needs to be achieved by the integration. Second, there is the study of the integration 'processes', the actual step-by-step transformations leading to integration that are based upon discursive acts and interactions. Third, there is the study of the 'products' of integration, that is, the institutions, policies and practices emerging as outputs/outcomes of the process. Most comparative regional integration studies focus on the products and describe the varieties of regionalisation in terms of geographical mapping. For instance, regional organisations or agreements such as Mercosur or the Southern African Development Community (SADC) are listed as case studies of how regional integration manifests itself in different continents and sub-continents.

Most regional organisations have been formed under amiable circumstances, tending to either have been created to perform a specific function (e.g. resource management, conflict prevention, financial stability) or have been established as a 'general purpose' initiative (Fioramonti 2014). But after more than two decades operating under an increasingly multilateral system, many are beginning to wonder if these projects are working effectively. Are their goals and values still what was initially envisioned? Do they need to be adjusted? How may we remedy some of the common shortcomings and build a better path for the future? In this section, a pointed analysis will be presented outlining some of the major criticisms that have emerged concerning different regional formations in various sections of the globe.

The final case to be investigated deals not with a specific region per se, but addresses an increasingly common problem that is often associated with regional organisations – particularly economic organisations – operating in the developing world. The problem of so called 'zombie' regional organisations, as argued by Julia Gray, arises when an institution or agreement continues to persist despite its incapacity to produce any meaningful or tangible results. This can arise for such reasons as inability to retain quality staff or in a deficiency in its ability to garner the necessary resources to be effective (Gray 2013, p. 1). This phenomenon, which can occur on the international, regional, or local level, may develop in such cases as when it is judged to be too politically costly to withdraw from an agreement, or when a country views disbanding an organisation as an effective admission of failure. Whatever the case may be, the result of these 'zombie' institutions, which lack any form of organisational vitality, are extremely costly for the development of meaningful regional integration. They suck valuable resources from an already limited pool, particularly in developing countries, ignore or are unable to address their citizen's concerns, as well as exist only to sustain their own inward-looking bureaucracy.

The answer is that it provides a general framework that aims to allow a better understanding and comparison of different ongoing developments related to governance. We seem to be currently witnessing the transition from a state-dominated world order to a world system, in which not only states, but also regions at different geographical scales as well as networks of actors are major players. In such a neo-Westphalian world order, regions play, next to states (not instead of states!), an important role in international relations as well as in sub-national governance. This transition gives rise to complex geopolitical realities with, on the one hand, overlapping macro-regions in which states can be members of different regional integration schemes, and on the other hand, micro-regions that can be cross-border. Also, regional integration is clearly multidimensional as it implies cooperation along a number of different dimensions such as culture, politics, security, economics and diplomacy. As a consequence, regions are becoming increasingly important in understanding the present-day world. But studying regions has been characterised by a number of deficiencies related to (1) the fragmentation of the research over different (social sciences) disciplines and (2) the absence of unifying theoretical frameworks.

25.7 CONCLUSION

Many questions remain and there is a need to deepen our understanding of the processes that lead to the emergence of regional entities and the role that drivers towards integration and disintegration play in those processes. The basic questions are where, why and how do regions emerge? How do they function? What makes them sustainable and what drives regions or states into integration or devolution processes? Also, more knowledge is needed on the role that regions play in identity formation and how civil society can manifest itself in a more regionalised world. The statehood theory of regions aims to contribute to answering such questions. It is a theory that allows us to think about regions at different geographical scales and of different natures from a single perspective. By focusing on the formal aspects of regionhood and using personhood as a source of inspiration, this theory allows thinking about different types of regions within one single theoretical framework. The theory also allows us to underline the central role of discourse in the building of regions and can therefore be considered as a way to deepen the social constructionist approach in the study of regions.

25.8 REFERENCES

Acharya, A. and A. Johnston (2007), *Crafting Cooperation: Regional International Institutions in Comparative Perspective*, Cambridge: Cambridge University Press.
Acharya, A. (2009), *Whose Ideas Matter?*, Ithaca, NY: Cornell University Press.
Agnew, J. (1999), 'Regions on the mind does not equal regions of the mind', *Progress in Human Geography*, **23** (1), 91–96.
Balassa, B. (1961), *The Theory of Economic Integration*, Homewood, IL: R.D. Irwin.
Buzan, B. (1986), 'A framework for regional security analysis', in B. Buzan and G. Rizvi (eds), *South Asian Insecurity and the Great Powers*, London: Croom Helm, pp. 3–33.
De Lombaerde, P., F. Söderbaum, L. Van Langenhove and F. Baert (2010), 'Problems and divides in comparative regionalism', in F. Laursen (ed.), *Comparative Regional Integration: Europe and Beyond*, Aldershot: Ashgate, pp. 21–39.
De Lombaerde, P. and F. Söderbaum (2013), 'Reading the intellectual history of regionalism', in P. De Lombaerde and F. Söderbaum (eds), *Regionalism, Volume 1: Classical Regional Integration*, Farnham: Ashgate, pp. xvii–xlviii.
Deutsch, K.W. (1968), *The Analysis of International Relations*, Englewood Cliffs, NJ: Prentice Hall.
De Waele, J.P. and R. Harré (1976), 'The personality of individuals', in R. Harre (ed.), *Personality*, Oxford: Basil Blackwell, pp. 189–246.
Farrell, M., B. Hettne and L. Van Langenhove (eds) (2005), *The Global Politics of Regionalism*, London: Pluto Press.
Fawcett, L. and A. Hurrell (1995), *Regionalism in World Politics: Regional Organization and International Order*, Oxford: Oxford University Press.
Fawcett, L. (2013), 'The history and concept of regionalism', *UNU-CRIS E-Working Papers, W-2013/5*, http://cris.unu.edu/history-and-concept-regionalism (accessed 9 March 2018).
Fawn, R. (2009), '"Regions" and their study: where from, what for and where to?', *Review of International Studies*, **35** (S1), 5–34.
Fioramonti, L. (2013), *Civil Society and World Regions: How Citizens Are Reshaping Regional Governance in Times of Crisis*, Lanham, MD and New York: Lexington Books.
Fioramonti, L. (2014), 'The evolution of supranational regionalism: from top-down regulatory governance to sustainability regions?', *UNU-CRIS E-Working Papers, W-2014/2*, http://cris.unu.edu/evolution-supranational-regionalism-top-down-regulatory-governance-sustainability-regions (accessed 9 March 2018).
Franke, U. and U. Roos (2010), 'Actor, structure, process transcending the state personhood debate by means of pragmatist ontological model for international relations theory', *Review of International Studies*, **36** (3), 1057–1077.
Gray, J. (2013), *Life, Death, or Zombies? The Vitality of Regional Economic Organisations*, unpublished.
Haas, E. (1958), *The Uniting of Europe: Political, Social, and Economic Forces 1950–1957*, Stanford, CA: Stanford University Press.
Hoffmann, S. (1964), 'The European process at Atlantic cross-purposes', *Journal of Common Market Studies*, **3** (2), 85–101.
Hoffmann, S. (1966), 'Obstinate or obsolete? The fate of the nation state and the case of Western Europe', *Daedalus*, **95** (3), 862–915.
Hooghe, L., G. Marks, and A. Schakel (2010), *The Rise of Regional Authority*, London: Routledge.

Ip, E. (2010), 'The power of international legal personality', *CRIS Working Paper 2010/4*, http://cris.unu.edu/ power-international-legal-personality (accessed 9 March 2018).

Lindberg, L. (1963), *The Political Dynamics of European Economic Integration*, Palo Alto, CA: Stanford University Press.

Luoma-Aho, M. (2009), 'Political theology, anthropomorphism and personhood of the state: the religion of international relations', *International Political Sociology*, **3** (3), 293–309.

Mattli, W. (1999), *The Logic of Regional Integration: Europe and Beyond*, Cambridge: Cambridge University Press.

Moravcsik, A. (1993), 'Preferences and power in the European community: a liberal intergovernmentalist approach', *Journal of Common Market Studies*, **31** (4), 473–524.

Morgan, G. (2005), *The Idea of a European Superstate*, Princeton, NJ: Princeton University Press.

Neumann, R. (2010), 'Political ecology II: theorising regions', *Progress in Human Geography*, **34** (3), 368–374.

Nye, J. (1971), *Peace in Parts: Integration and Conflicts in Regional Integration*, Boston, MA: Little, Brown and Company.

Paasi, A. (1986), 'The institutionalisation of regions: a theoretical framework for understanding the emergence of regions and the constitution of regional identity', *Fennia*, **164** (1), 105–146.

Paasi, A. (2002), 'Place and region: regional worlds and words', *Progress in Human Geography*, **26** (6), 802–811.

Paasi, A. (2011), 'The region, identity, and power', *Procedia Social and Behaviourial Sciences*, **14**, 9–16.

Pettit, P. (2008), *Made With Words. Hobbes on Language, Minds and Politics*, Princeton, NJ: Princeton University Press.

Riker, W.H. (1964), *Federalism – Origin, Operation, Significance*, Boston, MA: Little, Brown and Company.

Sbragia, A. (2008), 'Comparative regionalism: what might it be?', *Journal for Common Market Studies*, **46**, 29–49.

Schmitt-Egner, P. (2002), 'The concept of region: theoretical and methodological notes on its reconstruction', *European Integration*, **24** (3), 179–200.

Schultz, M., F. Söderbaum and J. Ojendal (eds) (2001), *Regionalisation in a Globalising World*, London: Zed Books.

Searle, J. (1995), *The Construction of Social Reality*, New York: The Free Press.

Shaw, T., A. Grant and S. Cornelissen (eds) (2012), 'The Ashgate research companion to rationalism', *The International Political Economy of New Regionalisms Series*, Farnham: Ashgate.

Soja, E.W. and C. Hadjimichalis (1985), 'Between geographical materialism and spatial fetishism', *Antipode*, **17** (2–3), 59–67.

Söderbaum, F. and T. Shaw (2003), *Theories of New Regionalism: A Palgrave Reader*, Basingstoke: Palgrave Macmillan.

Söderbaum, F. (2010), 'Comparative regional integration and regionalism', in T. Landman and N. Robinson (eds), *Handbook of Comparative Politics*, London: Sage, pp. 477–496.

Van Langenhove, L. (2011), *Building Regions. The Regionalisation of World Order*, London: Routledge.

Van Langenhove, L. (2013a), 'The unity and diversity in regional integration studies', *Georgetown Journal of International Affairs*, **14** (2), 19–28.

Van Langenhove, L. (2013b), 'What is a region? Towards a statehood theory of regions', *Contemporary Politics*, **19** (4), 474–490.

Viner, J. (1950), *Customs Union Issue*, New York: Carnegie Endowment for International Peace.

Wendt, A. (2004), 'The state as a person in international theory', *Review of International Studies*, **30** (2), 289–316.

26. Regional urbanization: emerging approaches and debates
J. Miguel Kanai and Seth Schindler

26.1 INTRODUCTION: SCALAR DISJUNCTURE AND CONTESTED REINTEGRATION

After decades of disjuncture, the regional dimension seems to matter to urbanists once more, and it has acquired a richer, multi-scalar meaning when applied to urbanization processes taking place alongside economic globalization. If regional perspectives on cities, such as that of the 'conurbation,' have existed since at least the early twentieth century (Rodríguez-Pose 2008); and the mid-century regional science once confidently promoted itself as the field able to explain 'cities as systems within systems of cities' (Berry 1964), urban studies veered away from regional thinking beginning in the 1980s. Reasons varied: a growing interest for economic inequalities and their intersectionality with race, gender and other dimensions of social difference, as well as emergent theorizations of state and corporate power, and the rejection of technocratic tropes among a new generation of academic urbanists conjoined to produce a more epistemologically diverse and empirically vibrant field of urban studies focused squarely on the city. However, as more and more researchers opted for situated chronicles, they also began to disavow perspectives that would look on the city from above and flatten out 'the most immoderate of human texts' as de Certeau (1984) put it in his influential steering of urban research towards everyday-life practices and in critique of totalizing representations as the strategies of power.

Thus, the region began to be overlooked in urban theory as researchers stopped asking how regions matter for the historical and geographical constitution of cities and the shaping of urbanization as a globally integrated process of societal transformation. There is certainly much to agree with, to rather put it in the contemporary formulation of 'telescopic urbanism' (Amin 2013), in critiques of reductive views of cities from a distance as the latter selectively focus on elite 'city engines' full of economic promise, while blurring out 'the prosaic, jobbing, informal, making do, surviving, unkempt, hybrid spaces occupied by the majority population' (Amin 2013, p. 478). Yet a close engagement with the practices of the majority city may not be sufficient, as indispensable as this may be. The underlying dynamics that produce poverty, inequality and exclusion may not be identified properly if analyses focus exclusively on practices and experiences in the city. Furthermore, critical metropolitan and regional resources may be missed, a whole realm of possible interventions, such as inter-municipal coalitions, may be discarded inadvertently.

Edward Soja was one of the most prominent proponents of multi-scalar approaches to interpret contemporary urbanization, arguing that urban relationality should be conceptualized as extending outwards from the body and intimate city places to the regional and even global scales. This perspective began to develop in Soja's (1991, 1992) early critiques to studies of central cities that left out their metropolitan and regional contexts (such as, for example, research on economic development in Manhattan in isolation to developments at the Tri-State urban region, and thereby missed out on the 'post-metropolitan' commonalities that underlie even the most seemingly differentiated central-city trajectories – as, for example, development patterns of diffuse polycentrism shared between the Dutch Randstad and Southern California beyond idiosyncratic contrasts between central Amsterdam and downtown Los Angeles. Yet, his most recent work advances a more explicit definition of 'regional urbanization,' a concept that Soja (2011, p. 684) expresses as:

> [T]he emergence of a distinctive new urban form, the expansive, polynucleated, densely networked, information-intensive, and increasingly globalized city region . . . arising from the regionalization of the modern metropolis and involving a shift from the typically monocentric dualism of dense city and sprawling low-density suburbanization to a polycentric network of urban agglomerations where relatively high densities are found throughout the urbanized region.

Published shortly before his death, Soja's (2015, p. 372) latest work advances his perspective further, calling for more integration of urban and regional studies and praising the rise of a new regionalism in both the academic and policy worlds. Yet, Soja (2015) also departs from this literature in his conceptualization of the generative power of cities and regions. In his view, such spatial effects should not be reduced to 'superficial notions of economic clusters or creative cities' (Soja 2015, p. 373). Instead, urban-regional perspectives must be broadened beyond the thus-far dominant economist discourse as to also take stock of the negative consequences of urban agglomeration such as the creation of more acute social hierarchies and heightening of power asymmetries along class as well as other axes of social differentiation such as race and gender, but also the intensification of geographically uneven development in a worldwide system of increasingly integrated but also differentiated economic territories. The rest of this chapter reviews ongoing research on regional urbanization, focusing mainly on works such as Soja's that have privileged a geographically informed political economy perspective, and writings that are informed by postcolonial thought, and seek to broaden the theorization of global (regional) urbanization beyond its historically and geographically specific manifestations in EuroAmerica's modern metropolis and the world-class city model being promoted by global elites. The chapter will conclude with an argument on the need of both perspectives to conceptualize regional urbanization robustly but more open dialogue regarding respective blind spots is required before a synthesis can begin to be articulated.

26.2 FROM CITY-REGIONS TO THE URBANIZED WORLD: A POLITICAL ECONOMY OF RE-TERRITORIALIZED GLOBALIZATION

This section shows how the regional urbanization perspective constitutes a political economy of re-territorialized globalization and critical perspective on the so-called urban age. The section first addresses the rise of the global city-region construct in the late 1990s. Second, the section engages extensions to this perspective claiming that megaregions constitute globalization's new urban form (Harrison and Hoyler 2015). Finally, the section takes stock of the urbanization of the world and the debate that has emerged around the planetary urbanization perspective.

Globalization is more than the proliferation of economic flows amid worldwide market integration and growth. In fact, over the past few decades disciplines concerned with territorial development, such as urban planning and geography, have been at the forefront of the social-science critique to the thesis of globalization as deterritorialization and unrestrained economic mobility. This body of research demonstrates that insofar as transformative (oftentimes disruptive) globalization processes, such as, for example, industrial relocation overseas, spearhead certain forms of territorial and scalar restructuring (including deindustrialization and the need for wide-area regeneration based on new economic activities and partnerships across similarly affected local authorities), the overall functioning of the global economy as an integrated system is predicated upon the material moorings provided by relatively fixed and immobile forms of territorial organization (Brenner 1999) – these include industrially specialized urban-regional agglomerations servicing world markets; sunk investments in global transportation infrastructure such as state-of-the-art ports, airports, road- and railways; and the political/institutional architectures allowing certain jurisdictions the capacity to function extra-territorially (e.g. special economic zones not subject to home-country regulations).

Thus, seminal constructs such as the 'world cities' research paradigm (Friedmann 1986) and the 'global city' hypothesis began pointing to urban locations essential to globalization's existence due to their specialization in producing command-and-control functions for globally extended corporate activities (Sassen 1991). Based on an analysis of differential transaction and transportation costs (at different instances of both production and consumption), Scott (2001) extended these arguments to posit that globalization has heightened the territorial agglomeration of not only producer services in specialized city districts but rather includes a broader set of sectors clustering at the scale of the metropolitan area and even broader urban regions, some of which feature more than a single historical urban core. Thus, Scott (p. 814) defines such 'global city-regions' as:

> [D]ense polarized masses of capital, labour, and social life that are bound up in intricate ways in intensifying and far-flung extra-national relationships ... they represent an outgrowth of large metropolitan areas – or contiguous sets of metropolitan areas – together with surrounding hinterlands of variable extent which may themselves be sites of scattered urban settlements.

Furthermore, city-regions do not only exhibit an increased importance as economic territorial units in a globalized world, in perhaps the most controversial dimension of Scott's formulation (p. 813) they are also gaining political importance in the management of social life and 'with increasing autonomy of action on the national and world stages.'

Various other aspects of the emergence and functioning of global city-regions have been identified. For example, an edited book by Scott et al. (2001) includes contributions from several leading scholars in urban, regional and cognate fields of research. These interventions take stock of the emergence of multi-level governance at both the sub- and supra-national scales (including cases such as the European Union, NAFTA and ASEAN); the relation between 'global city' clusters of advanced producer services and other forms of industrial agglomeration present in the broader city-region; international and domestic flows of migration shaping the diverse populations of city-regions; issues of urban inequality and urban citizenship; and environmental sustainability. Whereas the city-region construct remains influential in both research and policy circles, for the latter city-regional policies in the UK and the Gauteng city-region of South Africa being the most explicit cases, it has also received a fair amount of critiques. These include arguments about the construct's reductive economism; fuzzy definitional boundaries both in historical (periodization of emergence, consolidation and diffusion) and geographical terms (where the city-region exactly begins and ends); and providing more practical use to legitimize elite projects (such as regionally funded provision of infrastructures favoring largely urban core populations) than to articulate inclusive alternatives (Camagni 2002; Jones and MacLeod 2004; Jonas and Ward 2007). Furthermore, recent approaches to urban-regional agglomeration indicate that the process's operative scale may exceed even the (post-)metropolitan realms on which the likes of Scott (2017) continue to focus their attention and put forward as empirical demonstration of their city-regional constructs.

Under conditions of globalization, economic activity is clustering within massive territorial formations that incorporate and functionally integrate multiple city-regions. Whereas these units may resemble what Gottmann (1961) once called the megalopolis, referring to the highly urbanized Northeastern Seaboard of the United States (or less formally the Bos-Wash corridor) in the mid-twentieth century, these units present new characteristics in a context of globalization, transnationalism and at times supra-national integration. For the latter case in the European Union, Hall and Pain (2006) posit the consolidation of networked, polycentric megacity-regions. Florida et al. (2008) take the argument further to argue that such massive units, within which the costs of reallocating capital and labor have become very low, have emerged worldwide (albeit with a highly uneven geographical distribution), and become the territorial cores of globalization, concentrating population, product, innovation and infrastructure (see also Florida et al. 2012). Yet, Harrison and Hoyler (2015, p. 2) suggest that caution is required before embracing this narrative whereby 'commentators appear convinced that the expansion of globalizing cities into larger cities is being superseded by trans-metropolitan landscapes comprising networked urban centres and their surrounding area.'

Whereas problems in boundary definition and differentiation of internal constitutive parts (its multiple urban cores and various forms of rural and other peripheral areas) plague the actual implementation of economic policies scaled to the megacity-region (Coombes 2014), Harrison and Hoyler (2014, p. 2249; see also 2015) explain that the megaregion has become one of the discourses whereby policy elites legitimize large-scale territorial development and infrastructure investment initiatives even if its analytics fail to provide substantive evidence 'to suggest these urban configurations actually function as large-scale urban economic entities, let alone any recognition of the complex geopolitical and trading relationships that exist across borders.' Giving urgency to this critique is the fact that megaregional settlements have emerged – and indeed, they are being actively produced – in a wide realm of world locations and across territorial conditions. Examples of megaregional interventions abound in China and the Asia Pacific region of rapid and dense urbanization (Oizumi 2011; Su et al. 2017). But also in contexts with sparser urban systems, such as the case of South America, territorially integrative approaches to consolidate development corridors are being pursued through investments in infrastructure networks (Kanai, 2016). In Chapter 28 in this Handbook, Schindler et al. (2018) show that this is a multi-level state project carried out jointly with global capital and in the framework of a resurgent regional planning that is now scaled at the world economy level and focuses more explicitly on urban cores and other internationally competitive components of what were once thought of as national space economies.

Soja and Kanai (2007, p. 54) have sought to theorize the implicated empirical phenomena: demographic growth in (and around) cities that is particularly fast in the global South; uneven global expansion of infrastructure space in city-centric networks; and widening urban footprints and spatial effects reaching ever further outwards into the 'rural countryside' and 'natural areas' in variously transformative dynamics. They called this the 'urbanization of the world,' also calling for dialectic understandings of urbanization and globalization whereby the former is not adjunct to the latter but rather 'its primary driving force, stimulating innovation, creativity and economic growth while at the same time intensifying social and economic inequalities and conflict filled political polarization.' The aim at the core of this work was to critique and influence the policy agenda emerging around these new processes of extensive urbanization and even more far-reaching territorial transformations, which is now known as the new urban agenda or global urban policy (Parnell 2016). This aim was advanced further in Brenner and Schmid's (2014, p. 750) critique of what they call the 'urban age' consensus, whereby, the authors point out, hegemonic understandings of global urbanization fail to recognize that the contemporary urban condition 'cannot be plausibly understood as a bounded, enclosed site of social relations that is to be contrasted with non-urban zones or conditions.'

Yet, further efforts to advance this alternative perspective, what is now called the planetary urbanization perspective (see Brenner 2013), have been met with a high level of disavowal from other academics engaged in critical understandings of global urbanization – a salient example can be found in Walker's (2015) unsympathetic critique of Brenner and Schmid's (2015) attempt to formalize their framework. Beyond the individual strengths and weaknesses in the work of these two senior urbanists (and even thornier questions pertaining to their positionality), for the purposes of the present discussion on regional urbanization, the most salient aspect of this pushback may well be a broader reaction to the overall political economy approach, with Marxian and Lefebvrian leanings, and its difficulties in opening its discourse up to other interpretive paradigms that have emerged in urban studies. Among these, the most relevance for the theorization of regional urbanization can be found among postcolonial perspectives and their influence on the re-emerging and reconfigured field of comparative urbanization. The next section turns to this important work.

26.3   REVALUING REGIONAL WORLDS OF URBANISM: THE EVOLUTION AND BLIND SPOTS OF POSTCOLONIAL URBAN RESEARCH

The postcolonial critique to the globalization paradigm in urban studies is longstanding (King 1990). Nevertheless, the past decade has witnessed a productive expansion in this literature, which has now evolved into a full-fledged research program on its own right. Subaltern urbanism and southern urbanism are other names commonly used to describe this body of work. Robinson (2016a, p. 187) appraises it as a reinvigorated form of comparative urban research aiming for more global urban studies, 'which can help to develop new understandings of the expanding and diverse world of cities and urbanization processes, building theory from different contexts, resonating with a diversity of urban outcomes but being respectful of the limits of always located insights.' While skeptical of the economistic regionality posited by theories of Marshallian industrial clustering and urban agglomeration, this literature has a regional dimension inasmuch as it is attuned to differentiated urban trajectories forged by geo-historical relations of power, through colonialism, imperialism and most recently global capitalism – whereas this regionalism may resemble that of (traditionally defined) area studies, its contributors explicitly clarify that the urban differentiations that they seek to take stock of should not be reified through fixed and often-times externally imposed geographical frameworks (such as reflected in ideas of, for example, the Latin American city as a single, monolithically and culturally driven entity).

This section begins by reviewing the postcolonial critique that (implicitly EuroAmerican) global urban studies have failed to substantively engage the world of cities in its entirety – and even the critical political economy strands with a planetary scope that were discussed in the previous section produce a form of epistemic peripheralization of the regional worlds of urbanism that they submerge in their privileged theoretical concepts (such as the dialectics of concentration and extension central to the planetary urbanization perspective). The section then reviews the programmatic consolidation of this new form of comparative urban studies. It will be argued that results have been uneven in terms of both the empirical work that has been conducted thus far to survey the world of cities under this perspective's aegis and the literature's overall theoretical development: the affinities of postcolonial urbanism tend to side with poststructuralist approaches such as that of assemblage urbanism rather than the systemic methods of political economy.

Global urban studies have long been suspected of a dual bias for the largest and wealthiest cities and for models of model metropolitan urbanism as it historically developed in the North Atlantic Basin. Bunnell and Maringanti (2010, p. 417) use the concept of 'metrocentricity' to formalize this critique, and explain that 'preference is given either to English-speaking urban worlds in which metropolitan-based scholars are able to operate comfortably and effectively, or else to topics that are amenable to research at a distance through the collection of secondary data.' Furthering this critique, Robinson (2002) has influentially argued that this spatial selectivity and geographical elitism left most of the world of cities in the dark or 'off the map' of urban global studies in the late twentieth century. Even more perniciously, Roy (2009) points out that the geographical imagination of Eurocentric urban research locates what could be called the 'properly urban' (from which theories of what cities and urbanization are about can emerge) in the limited realm of EuroAmerica, while the cities of the global South – which are overwhelmingly signified as vast, undifferentiated megacities containing infinitely precarious slums – are taken as 'interesting, anomalous, different, and esoteric empirical cases' (Roy 2009, p. 820). Thus, Roy (2009) expands her critique to the city-regional research agenda, which in her view functions as a normalized narrative that reproduces the asymmetrical ignorance of urban and regional studies in ways that cannot be remedied by simply '"adding" the experience of the global South to already existing frameworks of the city-region' (Roy 2009, p. 821).

Similarly, Roy (2016a) advances a critique of planetary urbanization's totalizing ambitions, particularly in what concerns the perspective's theorizing of urbanization without a constitutive outside. Whereas such affirmation is predicated on an overdetermined social world being transparent to onlookers with the required epistemic capabilities, Roy (2016a,

p. 821) posits that when it comes to the ontology of the urban (both in its socio-material and governmental dimensions) 'historical alternatives cannot be charted with certainty. There is instead an undecidability.' Such is the case for the three municipalities in West Bengal, India, which Roy presents as an empirical anchor to her arguments. For example, drawing attention to an old panchayat office that has been repurposed as municipal building in an area of mixed land-use conditions 'at the end of the world,' Roy (2016a, p. 822) explains that its dedication plaque can be read 'as a serendipitous anticipation and premonition of the urban yet to come but its rurality cannot be effaced or erased.' Furthermore, Roy (2016b, p. 200) admonishes that postcolonial urban perspectives as hers should not be confounded with an emphasis on empirical variation, but rather an attentiveness to 'historical difference as a fundamental constituent of global urbanism.' This stands as a critique to the assumed 'universal grammar of urbanism' (Roy 2016b, p. 205) which is composed of 'households, firms, market mechanisms, agglomeration, circulation' and other notional elements familiar to the EuroAmerican modern urban scene. Roy points out that these can prove of very little interpretive value for other regional worlds of urbanism and in fact impede 'a robust understanding of the present history of global capitalism and its urban futures' (Roy 2016b, p. 202).

With further encouragement to learn from the emerging issues in the urban South (Watson 2009) and the complex urban socio-materialities that have been left 'at the shadows of urban theory' (McFarlane 2008, p. 341), the postcolonial critique has consolidated into a vibrant and expansive literature animating urban global studies in the early twenty-first century. Robinson (2016b, p. 4) provides an optimistic account of this development, stating that 'surprises and new possibilities for thinking the urban emerge from many different sources: different cities, regions, trajectories, forms and practices press on taken-for-granted assumptions amongst scholars, "swerving" analyses, undermining the usefulness of concepts, turning them into something else, or inspiring quite different starting points,' which leads her to conclude that 'there is much work under way, therefore, which is establishing a more global urban studies.' Nijman claims (2015), however, that the overall field of urban global studies remains dominated by a select number of academics based in the West and overly focused on a relatively small number of urban locations worldwide. Kanai et al. (2017) point out that such assessments need to be evidence-based, and contribute a bibliometric analysis of published urban globalization research in the twenty-first century and its engagement with the world of cities. While cautiously optimistic about the growth of research on cities beyond EuroAmerica, this study draws attention to the sluggishness of the globalization paradigm to open up to cities of the global South, and calls for further assessments on the topical concerns animating urban research in different parts of the world.

Indeed, the rise of concerns with regionally differentiated worlds of urbanism seems to have occurred in parallel to, rather than in synergy with, interest for the worldwide phenomenon of regionally expansive urbanization dynamics. For example, with the exemption of consolidating studies of planetary urbanization situated in South America (Kanai 2014; Arboleda 2016; Wilson and Bayón 2016) – studies that have also been influenced by local (particularly Brazilian) frameworks of extensive urbanization and urbanization beyond cities such as Santos (2005), Becker (1995) and Monte-Mór (2011) – this perspective is yet to be systematically put to empirical testing throughout the global South. Furthermore, in a comprehensive counter-critique to the postcolonial turn Peck (2015) raises the issue that studies that privilege the singularities of urbanisms in the global South risk underestimating pan-urban pressures affecting all locations and regional urbanisms across the global North, South and East, and even pay little heed to macro-institutional factors directly affecting their study cities. Moreover, Peck (2015, p. 174) points out that the 'presumption of abruptly discontinuous geographies also runs the risk of severing relational connections, both across space and between scales, of constitutive significance.' Therefore, it is clear that whereas the postcolonial turn has helped to shed light on the shadows of pre-existing urban global research, and highlight the importance of (strategically essentialized) regional differences to better understand worldwide urbanization beyond the geo-historically specific experience of urbanism in the West, this approach is also creating its own blind spots, which may be particularly problematic for the understanding of the conditions and drivers of regional urbanization. Indeed, a recent critique by Schindler (2017, p. 51) argued that postcolonial urbanism highlights the shortcomings of the cannon of critical urban theory when applied in the global South, but 'postcolonial' remains somewhat of an empty signifier and 'when used as an adjective to modify a place name, "postcolonial" fails to signify a phenomenon or condition.'

26.4 CONCLUDING REMARKS

In this chapter, we have reviewed the resurgence of regional perspectives in urban studies, and paid particular attention to the rapprochement between urban and regional studies. This turn is perhaps all but expected given the expansive and relational character of urbanization processes in the global age. Cities have not only reached unprecedented population sizes and area extents, they are now also shown to be immersed in thick webs of dense functional linkages with contiguous as well as distantiated territories. While a consensus is still to be reached around the specific dynamics that sustain megaregional growth, let alone the internal coherence of this concept, it is clear that the urban question can no longer be defined solely by phenomena occurring in cities. We can even argue the specificities of such intra-urban concerns could be better understood with the support of more robust interpretive frameworks of urbanization as a comprehensive process. This process is not only behind the worldwide and highly uneven growth of cities but is also highly determined by, and determinant of, the workings and re-workings of the global economy. Furthermore, there are increasingly clearly defined settlements with city-like densities and intensities, with links to a multitude of different territories, whose conditions can no longer be written off as non-urban even if it may yet be problematic or premature to label them as urban.

Whereas the political economy approach has been particularly useful in establishing the theoretical basis of regional urbanization's global constitution and the need for explanatory frameworks at the worldwide and planetary scales, postcolonial perspectives have highlighted the importance of not confounding the geohistorically specific experience of regional urbanization in the global North for a universal process. In other words, this trajectory should not be expected to become the end game of urban-and-regional development in other world regions. Scholarship focused on the latter faces the critical challenge of advancing a fully-fledged alternative with the capacity of valuing regional worlds of urbanization while still being capable of theorizing the world of cities as a whole. The intersection between both approaches can be clearly promoted as a research aim for the field. Yet, the development of an integrative approach cannot be assumed to be a simple task resulting from a smooth additive process of, for example, inserting postcolonial concerns of difference and power as an additional dimension of a primarily political economy analysis, likewise political economic configurations around processes of urban regionalization cannot be simply treated as part of a contextual framework wherein situated practices provide the primary, and at times the sole, source of urban transformations to which the research field should attend. While such epistemological concerns are addressed, the field of urban globalization must also remain attuned to the rich empirical manifestations of regional urbanization worldwide.

26.5   REFERENCES

Amin, A. (2013), 'Telescopic urbanism and the poor', *City*, **17** (4), 476–492.
Arboleda, M. (2016), 'In the nature of the non-city: expanded infrastructural networks and the political ecology of planetary urbanisation', *Antipode*, **48** (2), 233–251.
Becker, B. (1995), 'Undoing myths: the Amazon – an urbanized forest', in M. Clüsener-Godt and I. Sachs (eds), *Brazilian Perspectives on Sustainable Development of the Amazon Region, Man and Biosphere vol. 15*, Paris: UNESCO and Parthenon Publishing Group, pp. 53–90.
Berry, B.J. (1964), 'Cities as systems within systems of cities', *Papers in Regional Science*, **13** (1), 147–163.
Brenner, N. (1999), 'Globalisation as reterritorialisation: the re-scaling of urban governance in the European Union', *Urban Studies*, **36** (3), 431–451.
Brenner, N. (2013), 'Theses on urbanization', *Public Culture*, **25** (169), 85–114.
Brenner, N. and C. Schmid (2014), 'The "urban age" in question', *International Journal of Urban and Regional Research*, **38** (3), 731–755.
Brenner, N. and C. Schmid (2015), 'Towards a new epistemology of the urban?', *City*, **19** (2–3), 151–182.
Bunnell, T. and A. Maringanti (2010), 'Practising urban and regional research beyond metrocentricity', *International Journal of Urban and Regional Research*, **34** (2), 415 420.
Camagni, R. (2002), 'On the concept of territorial competitiveness: sound or misleading?', *Urban Studies*, **39** (13), 2395–2411.
Coombes, M. (2014), 'From city-region concept to boundaries for governance: the English case', *Urban Studies*, **51** (11), 2426–2443.
de Certeau, M. (1984), *The Practice of Everyday Life*, Berkeley, CA: University of California Press.
Florida, R., T. Gulden and C. Mellander (2008), 'The rise of the mega-region', *Cambridge Journal of Regions, Economy and Society*, **1** (3), 459–476.
Florida, R., C. Mellander and T. Gulden (2012), 'Global metropolis: assessing economic activity in urban centers based on nighttime satellite images', *The Professional Geographer*, **64** (2), 178–187.
Friedmann, J. (1986), 'The world city hypothesis', *Development and Change*, **17** (1), 69–83.
Gottmann, J. (1961), *Megalopolis: The Urbanized Northeastern Seabord of the United States*, New York: Twentieth Century Fund.
Hall, P.G. and K. Pain (2006), *The Polycentric Metropolis: Learning from Mega-City Regions in Europe*, Oxon: Earthscan.
Harrison, J. and M. Hoyler (2014), 'Governing the new metropolis', *Urban Studies*, **51** (11), 2249–2266.
Harrison, J. and M. Hoyler (2015), 'Megaregions: foundations, frailties, futures', in J. Harrison and M. Hoyler (eds), *Megaregions: Globalization's New Urban Form?*, Cheltenham, UK and Northampton, MA, USA: Edward Elgar Publishing, pp. 1–28.
Jonas, A.E.G. and K. Ward (2007), 'Introduction to a debate on city-regions: new geographies of governance, democracy and social reproduction', *International Journal of Urban and Regional Research*, **31** (1), 169–178.
Jones, M. and G. MacLeod (2004), 'Regional spaces, spaces of regionalism: territory, insurgent politics and the English question', *Transactions of the Institute of British Geographers*, **29** (4), 433–452.
Kanai, J.M. (2014), 'On the peripheries of planetary urbanization: globalizing Manaus and its expanding impact', *Environment and Planning D: Society and Space*, **32** (6), 1071–1087.
Kanai, J.M. (2016), 'The pervasiveness of neoliberal territorial design: cross-border infrastructure planning in South America since the introduction of IIRSA', *Geoforum*, **69**, 160–170.

Kanai, J.M., R. Grant and R. Jianu (2017), 'Cities on and off the map: a bibliometric assessment of urban globalisation research', *Urban Studies*, online first, DOI: 10.1177/0042098017720385.

King, A.D. (1990), *Global Cities: Post-imperialism and the Internationalization of London*, London: Routledge.

McFarlane, C. (2008), 'Urban shadows: materiality, the "Southern city" and urban theory', *Geography Compass*, **2** (2), 340–358.

Monte-Mór, R.L. (2011), 'O que é o urbano, no mundo contemporâneo', *Revista Paranaense de Desenvolvimento-RPD*, **111**, 9–18.

Nijman, J. (2015), 'The theoretical imperative of comparative urbanism: a commentary on "Cities beyond compare?" by Jamie Peck', *Regional Studies*, **49** (1), 183–186.

Oizumi, K. (2011), 'The emergence of the Pearl River Delta economic zone – challenges on the path to mega-region status and sustainable growth', *Pacific Business and Industries*, **11** (41), 2–20.

Parnell, S. (2016), 'Defining a global urban development agenda', *World Development*, 78, 529–540.

Peck, J. (2015), 'Cities beyond compare?', *Regional Studies*, **49** (1), 160–182.

Robinson, J. (2002), 'Global and world cities: a view from off the map', *International Journal of Urban and Regional Research*, **26** (3), 531–554.

Robinson, J. (2016a), 'Comparative urbanism: new geographies and cultures of theorizing the urban', *International Journal of Urban and Regional Research*, **40** (1), 187–199.

Robinson, J. (2016b), 'Thinking cities through elsewhere: Comparative tactics for a more Global urban studies', *Progress in Human Geography*, **40** (1), 3–29.

Rodríguez-Pose, A. (2008), 'The rise of the "city-region" concept and its development policy implications', *European Planning Studies*, **16** (8), 1025–1046.

Roy, A. (2009), 'The 21st-century metropolis: new geographies of theory', *Regional Studies*, **43** (6), 819–830.

Roy, A. (2016a), 'What is urban about critical urban theory?', *Urban Geography*, **37** (6), 810–823.

Roy, A. (2016b), 'Who's afraid of postcolonial theory?', *International Journal of Urban and Regional Research*, **40** (1), 200–209.

Santos, M. (2005), 'A Urbanização Brasileira, v. 6', São Paulo: Edusp.

Sassen, S. (1991), *The Global City: New York, London, Tokyo*, Princeton, NJ: Princeton University Press.

Schindler, S. (2017), 'Towards a paradigm of Southern urbanism', *City*, **21** (1), 47–64.

Schindler, S., J. M. Kanai and D. Rwehumbiza (2018), 'The 21st century rediscovery of regional planning in the global South', in A. Paasi, J. Harrison and M. Jones (eds), *Handbook on the Geographies of Regions and Territories*, Cheltenham, UK and Northampton, MA, USA: Edward Elgar Publishing, pp. 346–357.

Scott, A.J. (2001), 'Globalization and the rise of city-regions', *European Planning Studies*, **9** (7), 813–826.

Scott, A.J., J. Agnew, E. Soja, and M. Storper (2001), 'Global city-regions', in A.J. Scott (ed.), *Global City-Regions: Trends, Theory, Policy*, Oxford: Oxford University Press, pp. 11–30.

Scott, A.J. (2017), *The Constitution of the City: Economy, Society, and Urbanization in the Capitalist Era*, London: Palgrave Macmillan.

Soja, E. (1991), 'Poles apart: urban restructuring in New York and Los Angeles', in J. Mollenkopf and M. Castells (eds), *Dual City: Restructuring New York*, New York: Russell Sage Foundation, pp. 361–376.

Soja, E. (1992), 'The stimulus of a little confusion: a contemporary comparison of Amsterdam and Los Angeles', in M.P. Smith (ed.), *After Modernism: Global Restructuring and the Changing Boundaries of City Life, Comparative Urban and Community Research vol. 4*, New Brunswick and London: Transaction Publishers, pp. 17–38.

Soja, E. and M. Kanai (2007), 'The urbanization of the world', in R. Burdett and D. Sudjic (eds), *The Endless City: An Authoritative and Visually Rich Survey of the Contemporary City*, London: Phaidon, pp. 54–69.

Soja, E. (2011), 'Regional urbanization and the end of the metropolis era', in G. Bridge and S. Watson (eds), *The New Blackwell Companion to the City*, Malden, MA and Oxford, UK: Wiley-Blackwell, pp. 679–689.

Soja, E. (2015), 'Accentuate the regional', *International Journal of Urban and Regional Research*, **39** (2), 372–381.

Su, S., Z. Liu, Y. Xu, J. Li, J. Pi and M. Weng (2017), 'China's megaregion policy: performance evaluation framework, empirical findings and implications for spatial polycentric governance', *Land Use Policy*, **63**, 1–19.

Walker, R. (2015), 'Building a better theory of the urban: a response to "Towards a new epistemology of the urban?"', *City*, **19** (2–3), 183–191.

Watson, V. (2009), 'Seeing from the south: refocusing urban planning on the globe's central urban issues', *Urban Studies*, **46** (11), 2259–2275.

Wilson, J. and M. Bayón (2016), 'Black hole capitalism: utopian dimensions of planetary urbanization', *City*, **20** (3), 350–367.

27. Extended urbanization: implications for urban and regional theory
Roberto Monte-Mór and Rodrigo Castriota

27.1 INTRODUCTION

Inherited categories such as the urban, the rural, the city and the countryside underwent a dramatic change of meaning throughout the twentieth century. These foundational concepts for urban and regional theory – as well as different theoretical apparatus mobilized in the past century – need to be revisited and critically re-interpreted if we are to understand contemporary sociospatial transformations.

Since its double process of 'implosion–explosion' (Lefebvre 1970 [2003]), what we used to call 'the city,' and particularly 'the metropolis,' lost its former attributes, as well as its epistemological power. Concepts such as the urban, the rural and the countryside, otherwise relationally defined against the city, gained other contours and dimensions. The urban and the rural lost their meanings as adjectives – as simple qualifiers of city and countryside as this latter duality is superseded. On the other hand, as nouns, these concepts are being constantly re-signified. The urban virtually gains planetary dimensions and accounts for the extension of the built environment (at various levels onto agrarian or forested regions) as well as for the social relations stemming from multiple urban centralities. The rural, instead, now free from the duality that previously defined it and embedded into the urban–industrial system, finds its novel meanings in various forms of articulation to the capitalist urban–industrial reality (Monte-Mór 2007).

In such a context, the extension of the 'urban' not only at metropolitan scale but beyond those limits and onto the 'region' itself – exemplified by the 'city-region,' among others such as conurbation, meta urbanization or postmetropolis – creates the conditions for total integration of social space under the auspices of the extension of the urban–industrial fabric. In this sense, industrialization created the conditions for the explosion of the urban forms beyond cities to encompass social space as a whole, reaching progressively all corners of the world, with a significant impact in incompletely developed spaces, such as peripheral countries like Brazil, and many others.

In Brazil, the conditions for a double process of urbanization and industrialization were created during the Vargas (1930–1945; 1950–1954) and Kubitschek (1956–1961) governments. Postwar urbanization and industrialization in the country saw a strong inflection as import substitution increased industrial scale and different sectors began to move to inland regions. Large infrastructure projects and major economic redefinitions entailed a rapid growth of urban agglomerations and population – although measuring 'the urban' and 'the rural' was (and has increasingly been) a contested issue. In Brazil we can clearly see this through critical assessments of the measurement of urban/rural population (Monte-Mór 2004), but also in accounts that are more global in their scope (see Brenner and Schmid 2014).

By 1970, Brazil's historical 'rural' character was already transformed. Even then, the city–countryside dichotomy remained rather clear. Urban and rural spaces, distinct in their sociospatial forms and sociocultural processes, were by no means confused. Contemporarily, however, the boundaries between these spaces are increasingly diffuse and sociospatial forms and processes are increasingly shaped by the 'urban–industrial' (Monte-Mór 1994) that organizes the whole 'social space' (Lefebvre 1974 [1991]).

How have the relations between city and countryside changed since then? How are these relations in contemporary Brazil? What does 'urbanization' currently mean in that country? In order to discuss these questions, we revisit the historical foundations of the city, the countryside, the urban and the rural, as well as the most influential attempts to theorization, especially in the twentieth century. We also present a 'geohistorical' (Soja 2000) account of the Brazilian national space, highlighting its urban and regional restructuring since the second half of the twentieth century and the redefinition of city–countryside relations in processes of territorial integration. The national context, although embedded within many political and sociocultural specificities, is articulated to the Lefebvrian hypothesis of the complete urbanization of society that, in Brazil, finds its counterpart in the 1960s implosion–explosion of the industrial city. We finally re-present the process of 'extended urbanization' (Monte-Mór 1988, 2004) – a crucial theoretical apparatus to understand the production of urban and regional space in the country – and its implications (for theory and practice) while thinking about social space in contemporary Brazil. Not only inherited categories are redefined to improve our understanding of sociospatial transformations, but also the sociocultural and political dimensions of the urban become crucial for concrete struggles and concerns around social reproduction and everyday life. Our aim is to emphasize that the broad sense of the Lefebvrian concept of the 'urban' needs to be clarified to avoid misunderstandings and possible anachronistic interpretations that may mask the nature of the 'urban–industrial' production of space in Brazil, in particular, and in the contemporary world, more generally.

27.2   THE CITY AND THE COUNTRYSIDE, THE URBAN AND THE RURAL

At first, there was the countryside and the city . . . or the city and the countryside, as some contemporary theorists emphasize.[1] Whether made possible by sanctuaries, caves, villages, fortresses and agricultural development (Mumford 1961) or built through the force of human agglomeration – or 'synekism' as Soja (2000) put it when recreating the Greek term *synoikismos* to refer to the creative synergy implicit in the urban agglomeration – before systematic agricultural production, the city always played a crucial role throughout history.

The city was first constituted as the space of concentration of the collective *surplus, of power* (dominant classes, decisions, politics), and of the *fête*[2] (Cunha and Monte-Mór 2000). This centrality concentrated the mechanisms of regulation, religious and cultural manifestations, monuments, market exchanges and collective services supporting everyday life (Lefebvre 1968 [1996]). Its existence, however, did not depend on the territory bounded by the *urbanum*, that is, the space enclosed by plow furrows drawn by the holy oxen. The city (*urbe*), magnified and symbolized by the *urbs* of Rome, gave a full meaning to the idea of civilization. It became the territory that materialized the society politically defined by the *polis* or *civitas* (from *civis*) (Monte-Mór 2007).

Originally, the city was the political and mercantile center that subordinated the countryside to its politico-ideological (and certainly military) domination. In many cases, the necessity to realize production in its marketplaces engendered radical transformations through the massive entry of industrial production into cityspace (Lefebvre 1970 [2003]). From the privileged space of collective surplus, power, and the *fête* – the three-dimensional *oeuvre* of civilization (*civis*) – the city has become the space of production itself that brings together dominant and dominated classes, and subordinated the countryside to its domination. It became the prime space of collective life and, at the same time, the territory of modern industry that concentrated the required conditions of production (and reproduction).

The 'countryside,' in turn, represented the circumventing natural space mostly referenced to a centrality. Formerly held as the privileged space of life and agrarian production, the countryside lost its potentially self-sufficient character after its complete subordination to the industrial city (Lefebvre 1970 [2003]), which encompassed not only the scope of production and its realization, but also its dependence to the creation of 'rural' products, services and technologies generated in the innovative centrality (Jacobs 1969).

Raymond Williams (1973, 1983) shows that the word 'city' (from the French '*cité*' and the Latin '*civitas*') paradigmatically appeared in the thirteenth century referring to ideal or biblical cities (against 'borough' and 'town') and qualifying representations of power: 'provincial city,' 'city-cathedral,' and so on (cf. Cardoso 1990 on the concepts of *polis*, *civitas*, and *urbs*). The word 'city' was later used to make reference to the financial center of London and became generalized only in the Victorian period as a contrast to the countryside.

The ideas of 'city' and 'countryside' were thus developed as antagonistic co-constitutive elements of human space. These substantive elements gave rise to their respective qualifications: the urban, proper of the city, and the rural, proper of the countryside (*rus-ruris*). The term 'urban' – an adjective lost for centuries and recovered in the Baroque period – started to designate features of the mercantile city and its inhabitants. In Portuguese, the 'urban' (adjective) was rescued in the sixteenth century and made reference to the city-empire. In English, it was recovered only in the seventeenth century to refer particularly to the main city of the British Empire under construction (Cayne 1987).

From the late nineteenth century onwards, the term 'urban' and the concrete world of urban life have grown to imply industrialization – either by the localization of industrial production within the territory of cities or by its influence in articulating industrial and service centers between cities and agrarian regions. Therefore, the imaginary of urban life surpassed the city to encompass industrialization, production and consumption as well as the reproduction of the capitalist relations of production formed and developed in the urban–industrial context (Lefebvre 1970 [2003]).

The agglomeration economies provided the synergistic economic articulations to the countryside and the formation of an urban–industrial culture. Also, as required by the productive (and reproductive) process of the industrial economy, agglomeration economies ensured the concentration of the *general conditions of production* – a Marxian concept that first referred to energy and transportation before being reviewed and amplified by French theorists Lojkine (1981) and Topalov (1979) amidst the debate of the contradictions of capitalist urbanization in the context of 'state monopolist capitalism.'

Within the Brazilian context, the meaning of the general conditions of production was subsequently extended to include infrastructure, state regulation, labor legislation and costs, social security, public and private services, among other 'urban traits,' and also making reference to urban–industrial conditions (Monte-Mór 2004).

In this context, the 'city' as a coherent urban–industrial agglomeration unit became the major theoretical and methodological target of scholars from several disciplines – especially for its putative potential in promoting 'progress' and 'development.' Agglomeration economies, for instance, were identified and studied by urban and regional economic theorists since August Lösch (1967).

In the beginning of the twentieth century, various attempts have been made in order to understand the modern transformations of 'urban' and 'rural' as *adjectives*, that is, qualifiers of city and countryside. The Chicago School, in its early sociological and economical approaches created one of the most influential theoretical frameworks for addressing urban–rural issues, one that informed regional science and the planning practices of the following decades. In an attempt to characterize and delimit the differences between city and countryside their authors proposed a continuum from rural to urban. They defined ways of life and analyzed patterns of consumption, forms of social organization and location, among other aspects of 'modern life.' The theory of modernization developed in the expansionist phase of twentieth-century capitalism was heavily inspired by Chicago's urban–regional sociology and economicist approaches based on what would later be critically understood as the expansion of capitalist relations of production in space.[3]

However, that perspective confused sociospatial processes with ecological forms and sociocultural characteristics. It was widely criticized by postwar neo-Marxists for the reification of spatial forms and the limitations implicit in their attempt to establish an 'urban science' or a 'spatial science' – see, for instance, Castells (1972 [1977]) and his critique of 'urban ideology.' The question of metropolitan transformation in the global North at the beginning of the century was much more related to forms of capitalist sociospatial organization than to 'ecological' and/or cultural practices of cityspace. These early attempts to attribute the cause and nature of spatial transformations to size, density, and heterogeneity did not resist systematic criticism.

Further attempts tried to understand the function of the city for capitalist accumulation. Manuel Castells (1972 [1977]) was very influential in his structuralist proposition that the city would be the privileged locus of collective reproduction of the labor force. It would particularly bring together the means of collective consumption, thus defining the prime function of the urban environment under capitalism. His critics then insisted that the agglomerative function of the city outweighed the 'urban question' of labor-force reproduction by adding to the production of complex use values linked to the 'general conditions of production' demanded by industrial capitalism (Lojkine 1981; Topalov 1979).

Henri Lefebvre proposed in broad lines after 1968 that the industry and its logic centered on exchange value had an effect of de-politicization over the city, formerly a privileged locus of *collective use values* (see Lefebvre 1968 [1996]). He denounced a class strategy to expel the working class from the urban centrality through the functional fragmentation of the city while emphasizing and anticipating the virtual resurgence of everyday life, the struggles over the right to urban life and the importance of social reproduction in the urban environment.

These questions, at first concerning the city, would then be extended to regional, national and virtually planetary scales together with the uneven extension of the urban–industrial fabric. The implosion–explosion of the industrial city extended not only the materiality of cityspace but also the urban condition expressed in the recreation of urban *praxis*, in the re-politicization of urban space around use value and in the tendency towards an *urban society* able to overcome the industrial logic.

In other words, the extension of infrastructure (proper of the *urbe*), service networks, legislation, organization of labor markets and land, capitalist relations of production entailed the extension of the germ of politics (*polis*) and citizenship (*civitas*). At the same time, it entails the extension of capitalist relations of production and the activation of landscapes that respond to the sociometabolic demands of larger urban agglomerations. It is in this sense that one can say that the urban environment ceases to be restricted to the space of the city and transforms itself into the total social space reaching planetary scales (cf. Brenner and Schmid 2014, 2015, on contemporary urban processes and epistemologies in the context of 'planetary urbanization').

The urban becomes then a metaphor to understand the contemporary social space penetrated by urban–industrial relations (Monte-Mór 2015). At the same time, the urban ends the long held epistemological dichotomy of city and countryside as it constitutes a third element in this formerly dual opposition (Monte-Mór 2007; see also Lefebvre (1974 [1991]) for the idea of dialectics of the triad, and Soja (1996) and Schmid (2008) for critical interpretations of the concept). In other words, this final stage of countryside subordination to the city together with the implosion–explosion of the latter gives rise to a third dimension in the countryside-city dialectic relation expressed by the urban.

City and countryside are thus redefined by the industrial logic of capitalist production and accumulation, losing much of their former substantive original traits. The urban and the rural as adjectives now represent remnants of the already disappeared substantive social spaces that are now transformed and integrated into the 'total space of our days' (Santos 1994). In this context, the concepts of city and countryside no longer express concrete and fully recognizable realities.

The 'urban' (as a noun) is now a level of social totality that mediates *global* processes (of state, capital, planning) and processes of everyday life. It expresses itself both in urban centralities and in the urban–industrial fabric that extends beyond cities in a process of 'extended urbanization' (Monte-Mór 1988, 1994, 2004) that contains the seeds of the Lefebvrian 'urban-utopia' (Monte-Mór 2015).

27.3 THE URBAN AND THE RURAL IN THE BRAZILIAN GEOHISTORICAL CONTEXT

The urban environment in Brazil was constrained to cities, centers of religious and civic festivals, arts, information centers and cultural manifestations at various scales. Cities were the headquarters of political power, apparatus of the state, privileged space of laws, organized land market, civil and military organizations. They concentrated local and regional collective surpluses manifested in the form of complex use values: urban and social services, monuments, collective facilities, financial, commercial and industrial capitals, and the few advanced support services of production and consumption. They were also marketplaces for commercializing products from the countryside as well as small manufacturing and a few industrial goods. They also concentrated wage labor in the more dynamic sectors of the economy.

The rural environment, on the other hand, was marked by family and kinship relationships present on farms and agricultural properties of varying sizes, mostly supported by pre-capitalist, familiar, and/or servile (partners, sharecroppers, settlers, among others) relations of production. It was the materialization of the export-oriented agrarian model that still dominates large portions of South America.

At the same time, the rural was the 'rustic,' the space of subsistence, of the excluded and the non-owners (since Brazilian rural oligarchies lived in cities or in small towns under their own control) and were thus represented as the space of illiteracy, of absence, popularly known for the lack of collective services, energy supply, transport and communications systems. It could be recognized by the 'non-integration' and 'non-access' to modern industrial goods. Roughly, the rural was *represented* as archaic, the non-modern, the territory of isolation and the space of non-politics. While symbolizing the 'primitive,' the rural also accounted for the majority of the Brazilian territory (in both statistical reports and popular imaginary) and therefore had to be superseded if the country were to overcome its putative condition of underdevelopment. Brazilian economist Celso Furtado (1983), for example, discussed the 'myth of progress and development' as well as the Brazilian condition of underdevelopment and technological dependency.

Getúlio Vargas, who came to power in 1930, was responsible for the so-called 'Brazilian bourgeois revolution,' implementing the beginnings of the industrialization process in Brazil. Using the economic surplus from the rural oligarchies, he created the conditions for both the emergence of an industrial class and the formation of regulated labor force, through a series of labor laws that only now, after the 2016 parliamentary *coup d'état*, is being disrupted. Vargas' first period, which became a dictatorship in 1937 (*Estado Novo*), focused on capital and intermediate goods industrial production, initiating the 'March to the West' which eventually led to the occupation of the Center-West and Amazonia. Ousted in 1945, Vargas was re-elected president in 1950, when he began to open Brazil for foreign capital to produce durable (Fordist) goods, particularly the metal-mechanic industry led by multinational corporations from those countries who lost the war and accepted his nationalist requirements in terms of nationalization of production and profit remittance.

However, it was only in the Kubitschek government (1956–1961) that imports substitution brought a more significant penetration of Taylorism and an incipient Fordism. From the 1950s, Brazilian planning grew to achieve regional and national scales in an attempt to promote territorial integration and reduce regional inequality – such as the creation of Sudene[4] and the construction of Brasília. However, this state-led process of industrialization (and urbanization) through imports substitution was spatially selective, restricted to larger cities and encompassed only modern sectors of the economy – industry, commerce, banking, technical services and public facilities. The penetration of foreign capital – at that time limited and closely controlled by the federal government – also produced a concentration of capital, labor, technology and possibilities of sociospatial transformation in big cities, and more particularly and strongly, in those commanding the process of industrialization.

This *concentration of development* reached large trading centers and regional political cities that led a still incipient process of industrialization. Brazilian geographer Milton Santos (1994) used the term 'urban archipelago' to describe this set of disarticulated cities in a fragmented and rural Brazil. These urban centers reunited the general conditions of production demanded by industrial capitalism – such as electricity and transportation infrastructure, communication networks, health and educational services as well as labor regulations, minimum wage and pensions, and social security programs. Since they concentrated the means of collective consumption, these centers were also the target of massive migration in the 1950s.

The military coup in 1964 inaugurated a new phase of urban–industrial transformation still grounded on the discourse of progress, economic development and industrialization. On the one hand, it promoted the economic and spatial concentration of growth – especially in the second phase of the military period when public investment aimed to fasten growth through industrial production. On the other hand, there was a process of de-concentration driven by the need to expand and integrate the Brazilian market of durable goods locally produced by foreign companies. Geopolitical requirements related to the interests of the military and its ideologies of national security were also responsible for the discourse and practice of economic integration beyond southeastern Brazil, the country's privileged regional industrial center.

Although in radically different conditions, the military's economic and geopolitical project ended up continuing the movement initiated by Vargas and Kubitschek towards national 'progress' and regional integration. It moved forward the process of integrating the Brazilian territory by extending transportation and communication infrastructure into Midwestern and Northern Brazil as well as into agricultural and national frontiers, such as Amazonia. In addition, the massive entry of foreign capital – this time with Fordist features and free from state regulation – transformed the Brazilian industrial profile. It was no longer focused on intermediate goods or capital goods under state control for nationalization of production and remittance of profits. Rather, it became open to foreign capital – particularly after the 1967 Constitution – mostly focused on durable goods.

Furthermore, the state was concerned with creating and extending the general conditions of production demanded by industrial capitalism to the country as a whole. The Second National Development Plan (II PND, 1975–1979) reinforced this inflection by developing policies for the production of space: transport and energy infrastructure to support production and construction of access and conditions for the exploitation of natural resources. It also comprised the creation and extension of social housing financing and its supporting infrastructure for the reproduction of the labor force while spreading labor legislation and social programs to the territory as a whole.

The massive investments both concentrated in the center of the major cities together with a scenario of fragmented urban and regional space produced the 'implosion–explosion' phenomena described by Lefebvre (1970 [2003]). Investments in transport infrastructure to meet the needs created by growing automobile production (freeways, elevated bridges, transportation plans) and public transportation (subways and complex bus systems) in the central areas of major industrial metropolises created the conditions for their restructuring.

On the other hand, the 'explosion' of the industrial metropolises over their immediate hinterlands led to the institutionalization of metropolitan regions forming urbanized regions and urban sub-centralities around the main cities of the country. Soon, regional middle-size cities received similar investments and extended their connections onto their hinterland. Industrial production was also under a process of de-concentration that began to be clear in the 1970s when São Paulo lost relative attractiveness and new industrial projects began to be distributed in other states and/or regions of the country. From the point of view of consumption, it meant extending the conditions for the consumption of Fordist goods to the national space in order to make viable the industrial park under construction.

In the 1960s and 1970s, this extension of capitalist relations of production and of the general conditions of production (and reproduction of the labor force) reached most of the national space. Brazilian influential economist Francisco de Oliveira (1978) stated that 'there are no agrarian problems in Brazil: all problems are now urban.' There was certainly a problem of interpretation: it was not that agrarian problems no longer existed. They continued to exist (and even grew since then), although they often changed their nature due to the process of industrialization in the countryside and the transformation of the relations of production in agriculture and resource extraction, among other issues. What seemed to no longer exist were the rural problems connected with rusticity, isolation, disarticulation, and exclusion from the countryside in relation to the modern world. Virtually, the 'rural' environment was totally integrated to Brazil's urban–industrial environment by the end of the 1970s.

It seems clear that this somewhat metaphorical interpretation did not correspond – or even intended to correspond – to the whole national reality. The important emphasis must be placed on the changing sociospatial dynamics in Brazil since the production of national social space was being dominated by urban and industrial movements. In other words, it means that the country's major questions, from then on, were refuted by and referred to an urban–industrial universe that broke the dichotomous forms of city and countryside and took over national space – whether in the metropolitan peripheries, the *cerrado* or the *caatinga*, or else even in indigenous reserve areas and in the Amazon as a whole, although more clearly in its urban–industrial agricultural and mining frontier (Monte-Mór 2004).

This interpretation finds its basis in the studies of Henri Lefebvre, in his understanding of the emerging urban society and of the urban revolution. It is a broad process of urbanization beyond cities that reaches the countryside and virtually all national space. It is a tridimensional dialectical synthesis that overcomes the city–countryside relation within a collective and political logic, centered on the struggle for everyday life and privileging the aspects of social reproduction. At the same time, it presents itself on a variety of densities, sizes and forms of sociospatial organization but all of it within an urban–industrial logic integrated by the general conditions of production (and reproduction). This contradictory logic and myriad of sociospatial forms is expressed in the process of *extended urbanization*.

27.4   EXTENDED URBANIZATION: URBAN PRAXIS AND URBAN EPISTEMOLOGIES

The contemporary question regarding sociospatial organization becomes as such: in a context of extended urbanization (virtual urban society, politicization of space and extension of capitalist relations of production), what happens to the city and the countryside – or equivalently, what happens to 'urban' and 'rural' as adjectives? What about the nouns? Can we still speak of 'rural' in a society and a territory that are virtually urbanized?

As elaborated here, the process of extended urbanization produces an overcoming of the city–countryside *dichotomy*. The analogous opposition urban–rural (as adjectives of city and countryside) has thus completely lost its explanatory power as epistemological categories. Under a complete urbanization of society, as the city–countryside opposition fades another opposition emerges, that of the centrality and the extended urban fabric accounting for both the built environment and the aforementioned political dimension. Since urbanization also entails the production of multiple centralities, the contemporary task for theory encompasses the unveiling of the relation between different urban centralities and the territories of extended urbanization. It also involves the production of a new vocabulary to differentiate social processes and spatial forms in a completely (although unevenly) urbanized society.

This seems to be the direction of the contemporary agenda on 'planetary urbanization' (Brenner and Schmid 2014, 2015; Brenner 2014): to put into question the foundational concept of the city while producing an ex-centric Lefebvrian point of view to understand sociospatial transformations.[5] This agenda encompasses a strong critique to the urban-adjective through the critique of the 'urban age discourse.'[6] It also entails a critique of 'methodological cityism' – the obsession of urban scholars with a supposedly privileged category and lens to understand urban processes (Angelo and Wachsmuth 2015). The city was left to a condition of ideology having lost its epistemological power (although maintaining its historical existence) and perpetuating itself as image or representation (Lefebvre 1970 [2003]; Wachsmuth 2014; see also Roy 2016a).

It is the role of theory to emphasize this ideological condition of the city and stress the importance of urban questions beyond the agglomeration since 'city' and 'countryside' will not cease to exist in both social imaginary and academic debates. Certainly, we can still identify, for instance, various forms of social and spatial organization typical of the old countryside at varying intensities in different Brazilian regions. However, these areas are, to some degree, extensively urbanized – in terms of spatial forms *and* social processes. The 'rural,' taken in its cultural sense evidently still exists. It is the meaning of what we call *roça* in Brazil: a displacement out of the urban centrality; a getaway to allotments (often small farms) where one can seek for a stronger presence of nature or for bucolic nostalgia; often a search for 'wilderness' as opposed to the material sophistication of the urban centrality; a (imaginary) break from urban–industrial life; a dream of being sequestered from a particular 'urban sensorium' (Goonewardena 2005) – noises, smells, landscapes, sensations, ideas.

This stronger presence of nature – also proposed in the modernist city, from New York to Brasilia – does not mean a 'ruralization.' It is the attempt to produce a particular sensorial environment for human (often upper classes) perception through a simulacrum of nature. It can be easily found in large urban agglomerations such as Rio de Janeiro, Belo Horizonte, and even in the concrete jungle of São Paulo or at its metropolitan peripheries. It is certainly to be found in large areas that developed from industrial cities such as London, Paris, Berlin or Chicago, or even areas that never were a 'real' city, such as the conurbation of Los Angeles that succeeded the *pueblo* and *missions* that congregated farmhouses and orange plantations.

Here, we are no longer speaking about the countryside or its qualifier. Rather, we emphasize *the* rural – an autonomous noun – that can be better understood as a relational concept as one identifies his or her own sense of *roça* in relation to a particular lived experience. In Tucumã, a very small Amazonian planned settlement in Southern Pará, twenty-five years ago, a taxi driver stated that, on weekends, he 'escapes from the confusion of the city and goes to the *roça*' (see Monte-Mór 2004). For him, it is very clear that his small town of six thousand inhabitants is distinct from his *roça* – his little farm where he draws milk from the cows and chews cane. A place where there is no electricity and piped water and no sound of horns or daily smoke from trucks. Where the clock does not rule his work. Where television (and now Internet) culture does not dominate social space. Where he can, even for brief moments, isolate himself from the urban–industrial reality – which even there may be hegemonic. Likewise, any taxi driver in Belo Horizonte knows that on Friday afternoon the 'road to the *roça*,' as popularly said in Brazil, is congested by the exit of the BR-040 highway towards the private condominiums, gated communities and weekend ranches (*sítios*) in the southern route of the metropolitan area. Of course, after many metropolitan dwellers chose to live in these condominiums in the past decades, the local municipalities around Belo Horizonte (and in other parts of Brazil) are striving to transform these 'rural spaces' into 'urban spaces' so that they can charge higher 'urban' taxes.[7]

The rural in Brazil, taken as a noun and not as a mere adjective for the countryside, is a relational concept and can be understood as 'interstitial spaces that remain relatively isolated from capitalist modernization and so everyday life still answers to the local dynamics that are not dependent on the rhythms of the urban–industrial reality' (Castriota and Monte-Mór 2016). Ultimately, although related to the urban, the existence of the rural is not an opposition to the (increasingly planetary) urban environment. In other words, the rural is not 'constitutive outside' of the urban (Brenner 2014). This is, of course, a contested issue subjected to debate within Brazilian scholarship. João Rua (2006), for instance, considers the 'rural' a crucial spatiality of contemporary capitalism that affects identities and territorialities at multiple scales. Urban extension beyond cities would thus constitute 'urbanities in the rural.'

Part of the categorical misunderstandings regarding urban and rural today is related to the confusion between the rural and the agrarian – briefly discussed by Milton Santos (2005). In Brazil, there are vast agrarian spaces that maintain the historical structure of land concentration, with large single-crop plantations supporting agribusiness for exports. However, the municipalities with an agrarian economic base are increasingly urbanized comprising what Milton Santos (2002) called the 'techno scientific informational milieu' – even if residences and economic activities remain in spaces with low density and strong 'green' base.

The relationship between the agrarian and the industrial has been changing significantly. Advanced industrial processes rely on agrarian processes: a pulp mill, for example, necessarily has a silviculture zone from which to extract its raw material. A number of other contemporary industries also have their inputs in forestry or agriculture. On the other hand, we are talking about increasingly mechanized agricultural processes organized by an industrial logic. The (otherwise rural) agribusiness and the agricultural economy focused on the exploitation of large capital and the production of commodities are increasingly integrated to the urban–industrial economy.

However, the intensification of the double process of industrialization and urbanization of the agrarian world is evident. If the rural as a landscape persists as a founding sense – as a myth – then, as the urban–industrial increases its intensity and extension onto the countryside, the myth becomes a simulacrum. It can be expressed in the 'cowboy,' businessperson and worker in pickup trucks playing loud 'country' or *sertanejo* songs informed by television practices. Comparably, it can be the simulacrum of a new rural naturalism, informed by the alternative and ecological sense gestated in the central and peripheral areas of the world's great metropolises.

In this way, rural spaces become everyday more the extensions of urban life. The so-called *novo rural* (new rural) in Brazil refers to the small farms, secondary country houses and refuges as above mentioned directly connected to everyday city life. In this sense, the contemporary rural submerges either in industrial processes (like agribusinesses) and their productive logic, or else in urban extensive processes focused on everyday life and the quality of collective reproduction.

So, what do city and country, and urban and rural mean today? How do these nouns and adjectives represent the complex reality of an integrated world with such extreme differences and manifestations of sociospatial settlements and arrangements for economic growth and for everyday life?

One can still think of modern (old) functional and cultural logics, but the hybridity and complexity of the myriad of sociospatial forms and processes will always show themselves present, making the attempts at dichotomous and rigid classifications look like highly reductionist and limited analytical artifices. As Lefebvre suggested, it is necessary to aim at the totality.

Totality is now linked to the virtuality of the urban society, we would argue (with Lefebvre). Nature has gained a new and definitive status and prominence in our globalized world. Our relations to economic growth, to development and to nature itself are being rapidly redefined, making room for radical criticisms and for the dismantling of established old practices and concepts. New approaches to contemporary life and to the future bring to the center of our debates radical societal restructurings that place our concerns about collective reproduction (of humanity itself) in the planet at levels of visibility not seen in centuries, at least in the so-called Western world. 'Is there a world to come?' ask Viveiros de Castro and Danowsky (2014). For them, we must learn to be indigenous quite quickly, if we are to survive.

Extended urbanization, seen from its transformative and utopian perspective, could be one of the innovative responses to critical industrialism. The extension of the urban onto social space as a whole, in its innumerous forms and intensities, dialectically recreates at various scales the most diverse sociospatial manifestations which, although under capitalist hegemony, combine with local and regional non-capitalist relations of production to produce different modes of social and economic integration. The urban – encompassing both the city and countryside, as well as the multiple centralities and (extendedly) urbanized regions – creates the sociospatial and political conditions for the materialization and the strengthening of those transformative social forms and processes. Of course, it also carries within it the most disruptive capitalist forces that extend decadent industrial processes as a dominant tendency within globalization, as it destroys peoples' territories and their different (or alternative) ways of living to give room to capital accumulation. Therefore, extended urbanization dialectically contains both the virus of old industrial days and the seeds of the urban epoch (announced by Lefebvre in his 'urban revolution') that may supersede it. The sociopolitical and territorial struggles should define multiple outcomes, particularly in the peripheries of globalized capitalism.

Indeed, the extension of the 'urban fabric' produces diverse sociospatial forms and processes that always carry within them the politicization of social space, stemming from urban centralities at all levels, from global cities to local hamlets. Politics (from *polis*) and citizenship (from *civitas*) reach everywhere along with the production of urban–industrial space. In so doing, to the relative astonishment of some and the hopes of others, it redefines social relations throughout the territory. In other words the urban, seen as the privileged locus of collective reproduction and of creative synekism, becomes the primary and most powerful mediation force in the contemporary world, from global cities to Indian villages. The possibilities raised by the extension of the 'techno-scientific and informational milieu,' described by Milton Santos (2002), have been equipping the territory with the infrastructure and objects required by the contemporary stage of capitalist development. How those peripheral spaces might draw alternatively from their own contexts and such a hyper modernization, is something to investigate thoroughly.

We are particularly interested in the process of politicization and construction of citizenship, and of self-awareness, democratic and non-alienated subjects, and people concerned with their lifespace, from local to planetary scales. Urbanization, both concentrated in cities and extended throughout the urban fabric, can be taken as a metaphor – or a metonymy – for the political organization of social space (taken in its broad and radical senses, towards self-managed lives). The urban, this virtuality of self-managed *differential spaces* in which urban life, produces the conditions for solidarity and creativeness in cities, towns, savannahs, forests, cultivated fields and social space as whole, eventually freed from the claws of capitalist *abstract space*.[8]

What's there left for theory, then? It seems that the urban perspective is a privileged point of view, a window from which to look at the contemporary, and the future of social space, while at the same time investigating its past (Roy, 2016b). Either we define lifespace as our central concern, or decadent industrialism will destroy our world, it seems quite clear. Lived space must be at the center of our everyday lives. The urban, thus, this concrete utopia that bears all the possibilities of collective reproduction at its best manifestations and of social appropriation of lifespaces, heralds the possible futures. Contemporary urban theory must, therefore, aim for totality while at the same time focusing on difference, on the myriad of new possibilities contained in such an extended process or urbanization.

Theory must also be critical and political, in the broadest and most radical sense of the self-managed polis, of citizenship as extended to social space as a whole, as well as inclusive enough to embrace the amplified diversities a globally integrated world presents to us. This seems to produce a transformation in the ways we have looked at urbanization and regional space, implying the focus on diverse and extended territories as opposed to the emphasis on concentrated processes in the downtown areas of major metropolises. It certainly seems to open new fields of inquiry and new windows from where to address contemporary urbanization.

27.5   NOTES

1.   The neolithic 'agrarian revolution' was preceded (or escorted) by an 'urban revolution.' The debate on the primacy of the city over the countryside was first put forward by Jane Jacobs (1969) and further discussed by Soja (2000) and Taylor (2012). Although criticized (see Smith et al. 2014), this view has very recently gained other contours with research in Amazonian archaeology (Heckenberger and Neves 2009) and forms of 'pre-Columbian urbanisms' (Heckenberger et al. 2008) and regional galactic clusters of towns and villages. Ultimately, increased evidences show that ancient spatial practices of Amerindian societies produced the

Amazon forest as we know it, including fertile soils on the top of previously infertile lands for agriculture and hyper-dominant plant species (Neves 2005).

2. The *Fête* is used by Lefebvre to refer to the cultural and sociopolitical dimensions of urban life, linked to festivities and the ludic appropriation of spaces of encounters.

3. Louis Wirth and Ezra Park are the most famous representatives of the Chicago urban sociology tradition while Robert Redfield, Ernest Burgess and Henry Richardson, among others, explored the economic dimensions of city form (Saunders 2003).

4. The Superintendency for the Development of the Northeast (Sudene) was created in 1959 to address problems of economic stagnation in that poorest region in Brazil, expanding the efforts in the late 1940s that created the São Francisco Basin Development Company (today, Codevasf) after the TVA experience in the United States.

5. For a thorough discussion of convergences and divergences between the contemporary agenda on planetary urbanization and the Brazilian literature on extended urbanization, see Castriota (2016a, 2016b).

6. Brenner and Schmid (2014) present a critique to the 'urban age discourse' derived from the UN-Habitat (2007) statement that human society crossed a putative urban threshold since more than 50 percent of the world's population would be living in cities from 2008. This is a clear example of how the urban-adjective can be instrumentalized rendering invisible crucial urban questions beyond 'the city' – although often produced by large urban agglomerations.

7. For a discussion of 'urban' and 'rural' as governmental categories, see Roy (2016b).

8. Lefebvre (1974 [1991]) uses various adjectives to qualify space as he discusses its production: *abstract space* is described as the space produced by industrial capitalism that tends towards homogeneity and fragmentation while *differential space* is produced by the social appropriation based on everyday life, the conditions for collective creativity and encounters that are at the basis of urban life.

27.6 REFERENCES

Angelo, H. and D. Wachsmuth (2015), 'Urbanizing urban political ecology: a critique of methodological city-ism', *International Journal of Urban and Regional Research*, **39** (1), 16–27.

Brenner, N. (ed.) (2014), *Implosions/Explosions: Towards a Study of Planetary Urbanization*, Berlin: Jovis.

Brenner, N. and C. Schmid (2014), 'The "urban age" in question', *International Journal of Urban and Regional Research*, **38** (3), 731–755.

Brenner, N. and C. Schmid (2015), 'Towards a new epistemology of the urban?', *City*, **19** (2–3), 151–182.

Cardoso, C.F. (1990), *A Cidade-Estado Antiga*, São Paulo: Editora Ática.

Castells, M. (1972), *The Urban Question: A Marxist Approach*, reprinted 1977 in Cambridge, MA: MIT Press.

Castriota, R. (2016a), 'Urbanização Planetária ou Revolução Urbana? De Volta à Hipótese da Urbanização Completa da Sociedade' (Planetary urbanization or urban revolution? Back to the hypothesis of the complete urbanization of society), *Revista Brasileira de Estudos Urbanos e Regionais*, **18** (3), 507–523.

Castriota, R. (2016b), *Urbanização Extensiva e Planetária: Formulações Clássicas e Contemporâneas (Extended and Planetary Urbanization: Classic and Contemporary Formulations)*, Belo Horizonte: Federal University of Minas Gerais.

Castriota, R. and R. Monte-Mór (2016), 'How inclusive is the urban? Which urban are we talking about?', *Regions Magazine*, **303** (1), 9–11.

Cayne, B. (1987), *The New Lexicon Webster's Dictionary of the English Language*, London: Lexicon Publications.

Cunha, A.M. and R. Monte-Mór (2000), 'A Tríade Urbana: construção coletiva do espaço, cultura e economia na passagem do século XVIII para o XIX em Minas Gerais' (The Urban Triad: collective construction of space, culture and economy in the passage from the eighteenth to the nineteenth century in Minas Gerais), *IX Seminário Sobre a Economia Mineira (Proceedings of the IX Seminar on the Mining Economy)*, Diamantina, Brazil, accessed March 1, 2018 from http://www.cedeplar.ufmg.br/diamantina2000/textos/CUNHA.PDF.

Furtado, C. (1983), *Accumulation and Development: The Logic of Industrial Civilization*, Oxford: Martin Robertson & Company.

Goonewardena, K. (2005), 'The urban sensorium: space, ideology and the aestheticization of politics', *Antipode*, **37** (1), 46–71.

Heckenberger, M.J., J.C. Russell, C. Fausto, J.R. Toney, M.J. Schmidt, E. Pereira, B. Franchetto and A. Kuikuro (2008), 'Pre-Columbian urbanism, anthropogenic landscapes, and the future of the Amazon', *Science*, **321** (5893), 1214–1217.

Heckenberger, M. and E.G. Neves (2009), 'Amazonian archaeology', *Annual Review of Anthropology*, **38**, 251–266.

Jacobs, J. (1969), *The Economy of Cities*, New York: Vintage Books.

Lefebvre, H. (1968), *The Right to the City*, reprinted 1996 in Oxford: Blackwell.

Lefebvre, H. (1970), *The Urban Revolution*, reprinted 2003 in Minneapolis, MN: University of Minnesota Press.

Lefebvre, H. (1974), *The Production of Space*, reprinted 1991 in Oxford: Blackwell.

Lojkine, J. (1981), *O Estado Capitalista e a Questão Urbana* (*The Capitalist State and the Urban Question*), Sao Paolo: Martins Fontes.

Lösch, A. (1967), *The Economics of Location*, New York: Wiley.

Monte-Mór, R.L. (1988), 'Urbanization, colonization and the production of regional space in the Brazilian Amazon', in *16th Interamerican Congress of Planning* (Sociedade Interamericana de Planificación), San Juan, Puerto Rico, August 22–26, 1988.

Monte-Mór, R.L. (1994), 'Urbanização extensiva e lógicas de povoamento: um olhar ambiental' (Extensive urbanization and settlement logics), in M. Santos, M.A, Souza and M.L. Silveira (eds), *Território, Globalização e Fragmentação* (*Territory, Fragmentation and Globalization*), São Paulo: Hucitec/Anpur, pp. 169–181.

Monte-Mór, R.L. (2004), *Modernities in the Jungle: Extended Urbanization in the Brazilian Amazonia*, PhD Thesis, Los Angeles, CA: University of California Los Angeles.

Monte-Mór, R.L. (2007), 'Cidade e campo, urbano e rural: o substantivo e o adjetivo' (City and Countryside, urban and rural the noun and the adjective), in S. Feldman and A. Fernandes (eds), *O Urbano e o Regional no Brasil Contemporâneo: Mutações, Tensões, Desafios* (*The Urban and the Regional in Contemporary Brazil: Mutations, Tensions, Challenges*), Salvador: EDUFBA, pp. 93–114.

Monte-Mór, R.L. (2015), 'Urbanização, Sustentabilidade, Desenvolvimento: complexidades e diversidades contemporâneas na produção urbano' (Urbanization, sustainability, development: contemporary complexities and diversities in the production of urban space), in G.M. Costa, H.S.M. Costa and R.L. Monte-Mór (eds), *Teorias e Práticas Urbanas: Condições Para a Sociedade Urbana* (*Urban Theories and Practices: Conditions for Urban Society*), Belo Horizonte: Com Arte Editora, pp. 55–70.

Mumford, L. (1961), *The City in History: Its Origins, Its Transformations, and Its Prospects*, New York: Harcourt, Brace & World.

Neves, E.G. (2005), 'Changing perspectives in Amazonian archaeology', in B. Alberti and G. Politis (eds), *Archaeology in Latin America*, London: Routledge, pp. 219–249.

Oliveira, F. (1978), 'Acumulação monopolista, estado e urbanização: a nova qualidade do conflito de classes' (Monopolistic accumulation, state and urbanization: the new quality of class conflict), in J. Moises (ed.), *Contradições Urbanas e Movimentos sociais* (*Urban Contradictions and Social Movements*), Rio de Janeiro: Paz e terra, pp. 65–76.

Roy, A. (2016a), 'Who's afraid of postcolonial theory?', *International Journal of Urban and Regional Research*, **40** (1), 200–209.

Roy, A. (2016b), 'What is urban about critical urban theory?', *Urban Geography*, **37** (6), 810–823.

Rua, J. (2006), 'Urbanidades no rural: o devir de novas territorialidades' (Urbanities in rural: the becoming of new territoriality), *Campo-Território: Revista de Geografia Agrária*, **1** (1), 82–106.

Santos, M. (1994), *Técnica, Espaço, Tempo* (*Technology, Space, Time*), São Paulo: Hucitec.

Santos, M. (2002), *A Natureza do Espaço: Técnica e Tempo, Razão e Emoção* (*The Nature of Space: Technique and Time, Reason and Emotion*), São Paulo: Edusp.

Santos, M. (2005), *A Urbanização Brasileira* (*Brazilian Urbanization*), São Paulo: Edusp.

Saunders, P. (2003), *Social Theory and the Urban Question*, London: Routledge.

Schmid, C. (2008), 'Henri Lefebvre's theory of the production of space: towards a three-dimensional dialectic', in K. Goonewardena, S. Kipfer, S. Milgrom and C. Schmid (eds), *Space, Difference, Everyday Life: Reading Henri Lefebvre*, London: Routledge, pp. 27–45.

Smith, M.E., J. Ur and G.M. Feinman (2014), 'Jane Jacobs "cities first" model and archaeological reality', *International Journal of Urban and Regional Research*, **38** (4), 1525–1535.

Soja, E.W. (1996), *Thirdspace: Expanding the Geographical Imagination*, Oxford: Blackwell.

Soja, E.W. (2000), *Postmetropolis: Critical Studies of Cities and Regions*, Oxford: Blackwell.

Taylor, P.J. (2012), 'Extraordinary cities: early "cityness" and the origins of agriculture and states', *International Journal of Urban and Regional Research*, **36** (3), 415–447.

Topalov, C. (1979), *La Urbanización Capitalista: Algunos Elementos Para Su Análisis* (*Capitalist Urbanization: Some Elements for its Analysis*), Mexico City: Edicol Editorial.

UN-Habitat (2007), *The State of the World's Cities Report 2006/2007*, Nairobi: UN-Habitat.

Viveiros de Castro, E. and D. Danowski (2014), *Há um Mundo por vir? Ensaio Sobre os Medos e os Dins'* (*Is there a World to Come? Essay on Fears and Purposes*), Florianópolis: Cultura e Barbárie.

Wachsmuth, D. (2014), 'City as ideology: reconciling the explosion of the city form with the tenacity of the city concept', *Environment and Planning D: Society and Space*, **32** (1), 75–90.

Williams, R. (1973), *The Country and the City*, New York: Oxford University Press.

Williams, R. (1983), *Keywords: A Vocabulary of Culture and Society*, London: Fontana Paperbacks.

28. The twenty-first century rediscovery of regional planning in the global south
Seth Schindler, J. Miguel Kanai and
Deusdedit Rwehumbiza

28.1   THE AGE OF INFRASTRUCTURE AND CONNECTIVITY

Regional planning has re-emerged as a key component of national development strategies in the global South. The UN Habitat's (2016) *New Urban Agenda* commits nation-states to territorial planning principles whose objective is to enhance connectivity across space and scales. To enable governments to develop territorial plans UN Habitat published the *International Guidelines on Urban and Territorial Planning*, which is meant to be 'a universally applicable reference framework to guide urban policy reforms' (UN Habitat 2015, p. 1). Importantly, this framework includes guidelines for transnational planning for cross-border city-regions, national urban and regional planning, city planning and neighbourhood planning. This is one of many examples of a global policy making institution that has rediscovered regionalism, and regional development strategies, yet it would be a mistake to interpret this trend as a top-down imposition. Instead, it is a manifestation of a growing consensus among policy makers at multiple scales regarding the role of the state in designing territory and articulating urban systems. Indeed, we are entering an age of state-driven territorial design and infrastructure enabled connectivity (Schindler 2015). For example, India has embarked on an ambitious corridor development strategy, the largest of which – the Delhi–Mumbai Industrial Corridor – integrates a network of investment regions and industrial areas into a contiguous territory that is criss-crossed by a dedicated freight corridor. The Chinese government has launched the much-heralded 'One Belt One Road' initiative which is a series of ambitious infrastructure projects that reorient trade networks towards China's hyper-global centres of manufacturing. A host of regional infrastructural projects that integrate cities and regions transnationally are also in various stages, such as the Lamu Port-South Sudan–Ethiopia-Transport Corridor, and Initiative for the Integration of Regional Infrastructure in South America.

This chapter narrates the collapse and rediscovery of regionalism in the global South. In the next section we begin with the post-independence period in which there was a consensus surrounding appropriate regional development strategies and the ability of the state to develop and implement territorial plans. We show how this consensus eroded after the neoliberal turn in the early 1980s when states' regional planning strategies were circumscribed. Finally, we show how regionalism was rediscovered in the early twenty-first century. We offer evidence from the UN Habitat's three urban agendas as well as other global policy documents that address city and regional planning. We conclude by proposing an agenda for future research in the age of territorial design.

28.2   CONSENSUS SURROUNDING REGIONAL DEVELOPMENT

In the early twentieth century regional planning in the United States emerged as a heterogeneous field that incorporated metropolitan development geared toward the management of sprawl, new-town building and river-basin development schemes. Policy makers and planners pursued a range of objectives, such as reducing regional inequality and establishing equitable city-rural linkages. Two schools of thought predominated, one centred in New York whose primary focus was metropolitan development, and the other in the southern states that was focused on safeguarding regional culture and economic autonomy in the face of perceived dominance from the industrialized north (Friedmann and Weaver 1979).

These two schools were consolidated out of necessity during the Great Depression, when the US government – under the auspices of the National Planning Board – launched a number of experiments in regional planning, most notable of which was the Tennessee Valley Authority (TVA). The TVA was a publicly owned regional development corporation meant to transform an underdeveloped region through scientific management, cutting-edge technology and democratic principles (see Lilienthal 1944). One US government agency announced that the 'Tennessee Valley [TVA] project has become a national laboratory as well as a regional planning and development scheme' (NRC 1935, chapter 9), yet the actual success of the project was modest. The TVA faced opposition from weary local elites and it was plagued by inter-organization rivalry (Molle 2009).

The TVA was never replicated in the US but in an exemplary case of 'policy mobility' (McCann and Ward 2011) the TVA model was exported by American aid and development initiatives throughout the so-called 'Third World' during the Cold War (Ekbladh 2002). It was a direct answer to Soviet and later Chinese infrastructure development projects. An article appearing in *Foreign Affairs* in 1961 lamented that 'the major Soviet triumphs at Aswan and Bhilai [where they built a dam and steel plant, respectively], along with several other projects, have helped to create the general impression that the Soviets are more adept at handling foreign aid than we in the United States' (Goldman 1961, p. 352). Similarly, the People's Republic of China achieved what was, according to Western donors, unachievable, when it built the Tazara Railway linking Zambia's copper mines to the Tanzanian coast (Monson 2009). Rivalry among superpowers during the Cold War led to an unexpected consensus surrounding regional development projects; there was a shared optimism in the state's ability to foster development, and there was an agreed-upon common sense in the virtues of undertaking large-scale projects in underdeveloped regions and linking them with more dynamic urban systems.

Fierce competition for influence during the Cold War led the superpowers to send skilled planners to undertake regional development projects in the global South. Most leading planners in developing countries were trained abroad, in the US and Europe, and many helped established planning departments in their home countries upon their return (Friedman 1973). John Friedman questioned the long-term impact of planners trained in the US, noting that they were adept at drafting plans but many countries lacked institutions capable of their implementation (Friedman 1973). However, American planning did have two noteworthy impacts in developing countries. First, American planners were particularly active in Latin America, and their presence presaged a shift from city planning to an emphasis on regional planning and territorial design (Almandoz 2010). Second, a number of flagship projects were implemented with long-term effort and commitment from domestic authorities. Perhaps the most illustrative example is what John Friedman calls the 'Guayana experiment' in Venezuela (Almandoz 2010, p. 275), in which a 'growth pole' (Friedman uses this term interchangeably with 'core region') was established to facilitate economic development in the Orinoco River basin. It was managed by the Corporacion Venezolana de Guayana, an organization with institutional similarities to the Tennessee Valley Authority, which was assisted by American planners and sought to foster the production of steel and other metals, as well as the petrochemical and machinery sectors. Importantly, as with other regional development projects Ciudad Guayana was not meant to be a welfare scheme for an underdeveloped region, but rather, planners anticipated that with the appropriate plans and sound administration, transportation links and urban services for the local population, its newly established industries 'would enjoy a comparative advantage and could compete successfully in foreign markets' (Rodwin 1969, p. 14).

In summary, newly independent countries across the global South enacted ambitious spatial development plans in the 1960s and 1970s informed by principles of regional planning whose aim was to produce and integrate sub-national urban systems typically through investments in infrastructure. There is not space to include an exhaustive list, but some examples include a series of new towns – so-called 'desert cities' – built in Egypt, Tanzania began the construction of a new capital city in Dodoma and embarked on a 'villagization' scheme to increase productivity in agriculture and foster light industry, Brazil built Brasilia and constructed highways to open the western Amazon to settlers, India built factory towns in so-called 'backward' regions, and Nigeria invested in transportation infrastructure to link Lagos with Abidjan and relocate the capital to Abuja.

This was a period of optimism in many newly independent countries, whose postcolonial thinkers – many of whom were directly involved in liberation struggles – envisioned state-led development strategies to lead societies 'from bondage to freedom, from despair to triumph' (Scott 2004, p. 166). As noted above, the superpowers were supportive of ambitious regional development projects in their attempts to win over allies. The result was a consensus that cut across the north and south, and communist and capitalist blocs, surrounding a set of core principles of regional development. These principles were enshrined in a series of global policy documents. For example, the United Nations Symposium on the Planning and Development of New Towns, held in the Soviet Union in 1964, concluded that:

> Comprehensive national and regional planning should include the planning and building of new towns to promote economic development. Such towns would accommodate new activities and could encourage and reinforce the incentives for such development, especially in the less developed or depressed regions of a country. New towns should be planned in relation to their region and integrated into a comprehensive regional plan.

Thus, the development of new towns, and the city planning that this entailed, was a cornerstone of plans to produce national urban systems with well-integrated regions. The World Bank's 1979 *World Development Report* echoes the call for balanced regional growth. It begins by noting that 'in most developing countries . . . it is extremely important to maintain balance between regions and between rural and urban development; hence some attempt to slow down the urbanization process and to spread economic development more evenly across regions may be politically necessary'. Rather than advocating a specific set of policies, however, the report endorsed 'policies required to improve the allocation of resources among regions and cities and to achieve a more balanced spatial development pattern differ across countries'. Thus, the report endorses 'the removal of national policies that bias the spatial pattern of development toward large cities' (World Bank 1979, p. 77). In summary, the World Bank report recognized the desirability for balanced regional growth, but it suggested this could be achieved through policies that steered investment and industrial activity away from large urban agglomerations. The UN Habitat's first urban agenda, passed in 1976, exhibits much more confidence in the ability of planners to implement territorial designs.

UN Habitat passed its first global urban agenda in 1976 in Vancouver, and it is comprised of *The Vancouver Declaration on Human Settlements* and *The Vancouver Action Plan*. The former establishes the role of the state as the penultimate arbiter of land-use and endorses state-led planning. It explains that:

> every state has the right to take the necessary steps to maintain under public control the use, possession, disposal and reservation of land. Every state has the right to plan and regulate use of land, which is one of its most important resources, in such a way that the growth of population centres both urban and rural are based on a comprehensive land use plan. (UN Habitat 1976, p. 6)

The *Declaration* goes so far as to state that 'it is the responsibility of Governments to prepare spatial development plans', that 'must seek harmonious integration or coordination of a wide variety of components, including, for example, population growth and distribution, employment, shelter, land use, infrastructure and services' (UN Habitat 1976, p. 6). The *Action Plan* outlines the policies whereby states can manage land to achieve 'balanced development for all regions' (UN Habitat 1976, p. 7), which include:

- 'The introduction of regions as an intermediate level of planning where local interest can be reconciled with national objectives' (p. 9).
- 'Development of a system of intermediate settlements with sufficient dynamism to counteract the attraction of the great metropolises' (p. 9).
- 'Development of growth poles for relatively undeveloped regions' (p. 9).
- 'The use of new settlements to improve and harmonize the structuring of national settlements network' (p. 12).
- 'Integrating the new settlements with regional and national plans, particularly with regard to the distribution of employment' (p. 12).

The influence of regionalism – in terms of planning and development strategies as well as the understanding that it is a scale at which state interventions should be made – was evident across the global South and enshrined in a series of global policy documents in the late 1970s. It is little wonder that regional theorists and planners felt triumphant and optimistic about the future of regionalism. Indeed, John Friedmann and Clyde Weaver (1979, p. 1) announced the establishment of 'a growing consensus about theory and doctrine' which translated into regionalism's accepted place as 'part of the established machinery of government'. The triumph of regionalism was short lived, however, as it was dealt a serious reversal of fortunes with the rise of neoliberalism in the 1980s.

The meteoric rise of neoliberal ideology came unexpectedly, including to its proponents who had hitherto been locked out of the most influential development institutions (see Leys 1996). This changing of the guard in governmental institutions in the North Atlantic and subsequently international organizations ushered in a sea-change in development policy. Rather than integrate sub-national urban systems and transform territory, governments redefined their role as custodians of markets. Thus, in the neoliberal period the remit of governments shrank to encompass a narrow set of instrumental activities designed to foster a positive business environment. The so-called 'Washington Consensus' was a set of ten policy recommendations that comprised comprehensive reform of state-led planning regimes, and it is telling that spatial planning of any sort was absent from the list (Williamson 1990). Thus, the design of territory and regional planning gave way to non-intervention in economic geography and states focused on 'getting the prices right'.

The absence of spatial planning from reforms advocated, and oftentimes imposed, by international institutions, did not mean that states ceased developing and implementing regional plans. Indeed, the role of governments was generally scaled back (e.g. price controls and subsidies were typically scrapped) and states reduced protection for domestic firms, but they also sought to manage domestic producers' relations with foreign investors. These efforts collectively amounted to an attempt to 'strategically couple' (Coe et al. 2004) industries and regions with global production networks in which investment not only had to be attracted, but it had to be 'embedded' (Hess 2004) and rooted in cities in regions in ways that allowed for the transfer of technology and capabilities. Fortuitous 'spillover effects' were meant to allow domestic firms to 'move up' value chains. Research has demonstrated that inducing 'spillover effects' required active governments and thoughtful policy (Phelps et al. 2009). One of the most common ways in which policy makers sought to attract foreign investment and strategically couple with global production networks was through the establishment of special economic zones and export processing zones (SEZ/EPZ).

Special economic zones are territories demarcated by governments in which country-specific barriers to investment are reduced. The Chinese government's experimental special economic zone established in Shenzhen led to the region's meteoric development. The astoundingly rapid rate of economic growth in Shenzhen overshadowed the nuanced policy in which Chinese authorities ensured foreign investment resulted in the fortuitous cycle of growth and development. Many policy makers in the global South sought to replicate the success of Shenzen by simply establishing an SEZ or EPZ, without the con-comitant institutions to foster what Coe et al. (2004) term 'strategic coupling' with global markets. The main premise behind SEZ/EPZs is that they must reduce context-specific barriers that inhibit investment, which range from poor infrastructure and prohibitive tax regimes, to strict environmental standards and well-organized labour unions. Thus, in theory SEZ/EPZs boast tailor-made investment-friendly governance regimes, but in reality they oftentimes became a rather blunt instrument in the hands of policy makers whose overriding objective became attracting investment at all costs. In many cases SEZ/EPZs were established without concomitant institutions that would have facilitated 'spillover effects', and the result has been that most SEZ/EPZs have failed to meet the ambitious expectations of planners. In some cases foreign investment simply failed to materialize, while in other instances they became enclaves from which there were few, if any, fortuitous spillover effects. For example, one six-country World Bank study of SEZs in sub-Saharan Africa notes that 'none of the programs studied show signs of zones having played any significant role in facilitating upgrading' (Farole 2011, p. 3).

The second UN Habitat urban agenda, known as the *Istanbul Declaration*, was adopted in 1996 and it is a product of the neoliberal period. State-led regional development schemes reminiscent of the Tennessee Valley Authority or Ciudad Guayana are predictably absent, and instead the *Istanbul Declaration* advocates the decentralization of governance and thereby seeks to empower municipal governments. The decentralization of governance is presented as the natural bedfellow of democratization, whose virtues are taken for granted given the recent collapse of the USSR. For example, the preamble states that 'democratization has enhanced such access and meaningful participation and involvement for civil society actors, for public private partnerships, and for decentralized, participatory planning and management, which are important features of a successful urban future' (section 6). Thus, the *Istanbul Declaration* exemplifies a subtle shift that occurred in the neoliberal period. Cities, rather than regions, became the appropriate scale at which plans were designed and implemented. However, the activities that municipal governments should undertake were circumscribed, and essentially included those that would foster a healthy business environment and the empowerment of civil society organizations. Thus, the central aim of the agenda is to provide 'adequate shelter for all', but rather than state-led housing development schemes, the agenda states that 'the actors who will determine success or failure in improving the human settlements condition are mostly found at the community level in the public, private and non-profit sectors' (section 56). The signatories of the *Istanbul Declaration* relinquished the responsibility to develop national urban plans and regional development strategies, yet regionalism is not entirely absent from the agenda. For example, the agenda states that 'governments at the appropriate level, including local authorities, should promote metropolitan-wide and/or regional planning, development and management strategies that address all aspects of urban activities in an integrated manner and that are based on agreed outcomes for the metropolitan area' (section 186). Thus, it is ambiguous which level of government should develop regional plans and whether these are meant to be vehicles of national or metropolitan development.

In conclusion, a consensus emerged in the post-independence period surrounding the national government's responsibility to enlist planners and adopt well-worn regional development strategies as part of national development schemes. Regionalism suffered a setback after the unexpected and rapid rise of neoliberal ideology, whose protagonists sought to shrink the state, decentralize governance and unleash markets. The rejection of state-led planning left regionalism in an ambiguous position, because it was unclear who should draft regional development plans and to what end.

28.3   REDISCOVERY OF REGIONAL DEVELOPMENT

In this section we chart the re-emergence of regional development strategies in the global South, which amount to an emergent regime of regionalism characterized by state-led planning of national urban systems and transnational connections among sub-national urban systems. Furthermore, transnational regional integration is achieved through the realization of large-scale infrastructure projects whose funding arrangements enrol private-sector funders in a range of novel ways. This regime draws together the state-led regionalism from the *Vancouver Declaration* and the imperative to enable private-sector activity from the *Istanbul Declaration*, and is exemplified by the third UN Habitat agenda

– known as the *New Urban Agenda* (NUA) – which was adopted in Quito, Ecuador, in 2016. It commits UN member states to the development of national urban development plans (section 49):

> We commit ourselves to supporting territorial systems that integrate urban and rural functions into the national and subnational spatial frameworks and the systems of cities and human settlements, thus promoting sustainable management and use of natural resources and land, ensuring reliable supply and value chains that connect urban and rural supply and demand to foster equitable regional development across the urban–rural continuum and fill social, economic and territorial gaps.

In addition to empowering national governments, the NUA recouples urban and regional development (section 96):

> Encourage implementing sustainable urban and territorial planning, including city-region and metropolitan plans, to encourage synergies and interactions among urban areas of all sizes, and their peri-urban, and rural surroundings, including those that are cross-border, and support the development of sustainable regional infrastructure projects that stimulate economic productivity, promoting equitable growth of regions across the urban–rural continuum.

The NUA was produced by a vast collection of stakeholders at numerous regional and thematic meetings. While this is reflected in the text in the sense that there is a role for many stakeholders in achieving the NUA, the role of central government authorities undoubtedly represents a recentralization of political power. For example, in contrast to the *Istanbul Declaration* and its reliance on municipal authorities for implementation, the NUA makes no mention of mayors. The national urban plans envisioned by the NUA are meant to be in conformity with the *International Guidelines on Urban and Territorial Planning* (UN Habitat 2015, p. 1), whose primary goal is to 'develop a universally applicable reference framework to guide urban policy reforms'. These urban and territorial plans should be national in scope, but incorporate plans at multiple scales, and it states that (UN Habitat 2015, p. 2):

> [S]ubnational regional plans could foster economic development by promoting regional economies of scale and agglomeration, increasing productivity and prosperity, strengthening urban–rural linkages and adaptation to climate change impacts, reducing disaster risks and intensity in the use of energy, addressing social and spatial disparities and promoting territorial cohesion and complementarities in both growing and declining areas.

The *International Guidelines* seek to universalize processes and principles rather than policies. For example, they acknowledge that planning is an iterative process that must involve a range of actors at multiple scales, yet there is an underlying assumption that these actors will share the universal vision of 'integrated cities and territories' (UN Habitat 2015, p. 23). Rather than an imposition of state-led development strategies on unwitting nation-states, however, this should be interpreted as a manifestation of a re-emerging consensus on the role of the state. In other words, nation-states have been developing urban development plans in recent years, and these have sought to integrate sub-national urban systems into transnational territorial systems.

What is striking about the emergent consensus is the rapidity in which it was established in very diverse political economic settings. For example, territorial design is a key component of China's urban development strategy at home and abroad. Governments at multiple scales seek to coordinate the country's urban transition, and manage and ameliorate the contradictions and struggles that inevitably arise (Liu and Dunford 2016a). The city-regional development plan of Chongqing, for example, seeks to integrate the metropolitan core with its regional hinterland in what it terms 'one circle' and 'two wings', and planning city-regions is part and parcel of China's attempt to foster domestic demand (Liu and Dunford 2016a). This will be achieved through national planning that relocates industry westward, and according to Liu and Dunford (2016a, p. 139) 'industrial transfer will permit a renewal of the competitiveness of labour-intensive industries, allowing east coast cities to upgrade, while the west affords a vast potential domestic market, and, with urbanization, massive potential increases in productivity and consumption'. Not only is China engaged in national and regional planning, but Chinese capital began to look for investment opportunities abroad after the 2008 financial crisis, as it shifts from 'a model/stage of growth characterized by intensive factor inputs and export orientation to a new one that involves exploring innovation, diversifying the economy, expanding the domestic market, embracing a more sustainable level of growth, distributing the benefits more evenly and deepening open development' (Liu and Dunford 2016b, p. 334). The key component of this strategy is the 'One Belt One Road' initiative, which is more of a flexible network than a contiguous territory, which consists of 'six major land transport corridors' and maritime connections (Liu and Dunford 2016b, p. 336).

African countries have embraced state-led regionalism as well. Transportation infrastructure accounted for 33 per cent of all large-scale infrastructure projects across Africa in 2016,[1] and significantly, 73 per cent of these projects were owned by the public sector (Deloitte 2016). The Lamu Port-South Sudan-Ethiopia-Transport Corridor (LAPSSET) is emblematic of the emergent regional development regime, as well as the challenges that are posed by complex multi-scalar stakeholder agreements. The plan calls for the integration of three 'resort cities' and a significant amount of territory through the construction of railways, highways, airports, a dam and other 'key infrastructure projects'.[2] The project has suffered a number of setbacks, however, such as Uganda's decision to re-route an oil pipeline south through Tanzania.[3] Furthermore, many of the projects have not attracted interest among investors that planners had anticipated. According to the LAPSSET Corridor Development Authority charged with executing the project, the three so-called 'resort cities' will cost approximately $1,242,000,000 and the financing plan states: 'The Resort Cities would be built by private investors once Government has put in place sufficient infrastructure to facilitate growth'.[4] National development strategies mirror this ambition and exhibit similar challenges. For example, the Tanzanian government's 2011 plan entitled *Integrated Industrial Development Strategy 2025* lists eight key policy measures, seven of which organize economic activity spatially. The key component of this strategy is the construction of a greenfield port, which was originally set to cost $10 billion and was slated to become the largest in Africa. However, the project is currently stalled, and appears to be the subject of high-stakes and non-transparent political rivalries.

South America provides another example of regional integration through infrastructure development. Since the creation of the Initiative for the Integration of Regional Infrastructure in South America (IIRSA) in the year 2000, South American nations have invested heavily in enhancing domestic and supra-national connectivity (Kanai 2016) – in contrast to the much slower advancement of similar initiatives in Mexico and Central

America, such as the schemes included in the original Plan Puebla Panama (PPP) and failed attempts to hemispheric market integration led by the United States such as the Free Trade Area of the Americas. Originally conceived as a decade-long forum for the region's twelve nations to coordinate infrastructure investments according to common priorities, IIRSA provided a vehicle for supra-national integration of infrastructure networks. Whereas a comprehensive approach was adopted to include the transportation, communications and energy sectors, the majority of actual projects focused on the development of cross-border roadway systems. With Brazil playing a leadership role in terms of territorial planning, capital provision and construction expertise, numerous projects were undertaken, such as the consolidation of the so-called Transoceanic Highway stretching from the Atlantic port hubs of Santos and Rio de Janeiro to Pacific counterparts in southern Peru. More generally, IIRSA's projects were structured geographically along ten 'axes of integration and development', which were drawn on the South American map to connect major cities, ports and resource-rich areas. Several of these are clear extensions of the 'national development axes' identified in Brazil to strengthen the country's infrastructure networks since the 1990s. Thus, the wealthy south and south-east have become more integrated through infrastructure networks to Uruguay, the core of Argentina and the Central Valley of Chile in the so-called 'Mercosur–Chile Corridor' and the extreme north portion of the Amazon has developed links with coastal areas in Venezuela and to a lesser extent the Guianas within the 'Guianese Shield Hub'. Overall, transnational connectivity in IIRSA was clearly aimed at enhancing the competitive access of South American nations to global markets, rather than promoting regional integration according to differential specializations and synergistically articulating a South American urban system (Chiarella Quinhoes 2011). The emphasis of reducing transportation costs, and thereby supporting corporate logistics and promoting competitive exports, has been maintained in the 2010s. Even if the region has gone through major geopolitical reorientations and domestic political shifts, IIRSA's territorial design was kept as a guiding framework in the Council of Ministers for Infrastructure Planning (COSIPLAN), which was created in 2009 as part of the Union of South American Nations (UNASUR). By 2016, COSIPLAN's portfolio had come to include 581 integration projects with an estimated investment of over $19 billion and of which 22 per cent had been completed (INTAL 2016). Such policy continuity is remarkable for a region which is rather characterized by its instability and historical deficits in connective infrastructure. Yet, if UNASUR now stands as an attempt to conceive regional integration in broader and more socially oriented terms, such aims are still to be reflected in how cross-border networks are developed throughout South America (Kanai 2016).

In conclusion, regional development has re-emerged as a key component of national development strategies but this time around it seeks to produce territories that can be easily plugged in to global value chains. These territories are articulated around connectivity-rich urban nodes but they are far from cohesive and exhibit high levels of uneven development. The NUA is a manifestation of the emergent consensus among national governments regarding this mode of territorial design in which regional planning features prominently once again. While a significant number of infrastructure projects are in the works aiming to integrate sub-national systems with one another across national borders, significant challenges threaten the ability of multi-scalar coalitions with diverse stakeholders to realize such territorial ambitions.

28.4 CONCLUSION

In this chapter we have demonstrated that regionalism has been rediscovered by national and international policy makers, and it is once again a core component in national development strategies in developing countries. This shift necessitates a reimagined role of the state, whose responsibility is once again devising and implementing national urban plans. To this end, states are once again embracing regional development strategies that include growth corridors, imposed regional divisions of labour, new town development and the establishment of satellite cities around metropolitan areas. In this concluding section we outline four directions for further research.

In this chapter we narrated the emergence of the regionalism consensus, its collapse and the subsequent rediscovery of regionalism. We have not gone beyond this historical narration to offer explanations as to why regionalism is once again centre stage. The first two parts in this movement are rather self-explanatory. In many cases post-independent states maintained active bureaucracies that had been created by colonial powers, hence the role of the state was inherently interventionist. Furthermore, while development economists disagreed on many aspects of development strategy, there was broad agreement on the importance of state-led planning. The reason for the collapse of state-led planning regimes after the neoliberal turn in the North Atlantic is also rather straightforward. Many formerly colonized states were in no position to resist the structural adjustments imposed by Washington-based international financial institutions, whose blind faith in the ability of markets to distribute goods and services and foster development has been researched extensively and critiqued at length. The rediscovery of regionalism that we narrated in the third section, however, remains under-theorized. Does it signal a profound rejection of the role of the state as outlined in the Washington Consensus, or is it an attempt to remake territory in ways that allow for the imposition of markets? In many cases sub-national systems are integrated with ambitious infrastructure projects whose funding involves the private sector in a range of ways. Thus, to what extent is the emergent regime of regionalism driven by global capital? In this chapter we focused on the main examples of regionalism's rediscovery, but an analysis of policy documents charting its origins may show that it is inextricably linked to the 2008 financial crisis.

The projects we highlighted in the third section, such as IIRSA, OBOR and LAPSSET foster transnational integration of sub-national systems. This is a subtle shift from the imperative in the post-independence period to integrate various sub-national systems into national urban systems. Thus, future research should focus on the subtle differences between the consensus surrounding regionalism that had taken root by the late 1970s, and the emergent regime of transnationally oriented regional development strategies. Quite simply, while the strategies may be the same – that is, national plans that include growth poles, corridor development strategies, satellite cities and metropolitan development plans, and new town developments – there are a number of significant differences. Thus, researchers should go beyond simply stating that both regimes seek to foster 'development', and ask whether they have different objectives. Second, do their subtle differences mean that the outcomes of the emergent regime will differ significantly from those of the previous regime? Research on outcomes should be done at multiple scales. First, does emergent regionalism influence national development outcomes? Second, the extensive infrastructure networks that serve to integrate sub-national systems are suddenly incorporating cities and regions that were hitherto rather isolated. How does the incorporation of a small or medium-sized city into transnational production and trade networks impact urbanization?

Finally, the emergent regional planning regime is unlike its predecessor with regard to the actors who are driving it, and producing the actual country-level strategies. While global consultants and international organizations remain heavily involved, there are a host of powerful new actors, such as Chinese firms, who are funding and building mega-infrastructure projects that concretize metropolitan and regional systems. While the previous regime witnessed a competition among superpowers to fund and implement infrastructure projects, the emergent regime has seen an abdication by the US government of this role. While the US remains a centre of academic expertise surrounding planning, China and other emerging powers are currently funding and building the new infrastructure networks that will integrate sub-national systems transnationally. To put this in perspective, Deloitte's 2016 report entitled *Africa's Changing Infrastructure Landscape: Africa Construction Trends Report* includes data on infrastructure projects valued at more than $50 million that broke ground in 2016 by 1 June. The largest funder is national governments (28.3 per cent) followed by private-sector domestic funders (14 per cent), international financial institutions (13.6 per cent), and then China (12.6 per cent). The US is quite far down the table, funding a mere 2.4 per cent of projects. China's role in the actual construction of African infrastructure is even more striking, as it is builds 22.4 per cent of projects compared with the United States' 2.8 per cent. Thus, the question is how China and other emerging powers are influencing the emergent regime of regionalism that is taking shape across the global South, in terms of strategies and outcomes.

In conclusion, regionalism is once again on the global policy making agenda, in a way that constitutes a new regime of territorial design and transformation, centred on urban nodes and aimed at participation in global value chains. While many of the strategies from the previous regime have been resurrected, there are some very important subtle differences that are worthy of scholarly investigation. By narrating the rediscovery of regionalism, we hope that this chapter can serve as a starting point for future research on the emergent regime of regionalism in the global South.

28.5   ACKNOWLEDGEMENTS

Seth Schindler would like to thank the Regional Studies Association for generous support to conduct research in Tanzania.

28.6   NOTES

1.   This is from Deloitte's report entitled *Africa's Changing Infrastructure Landscapes*, which included projects over $50 billion that had broken ground in 2016 by 1 June.
2   http://www.lapsset.go.ke/.
3.   http://allafrica.com/stories/201603070879.html.
4.   http://www.lapsset.go.ke/projects/resort-cities/.

28.7 REFERENCES

Almandoz, A. (2010), 'From urban to regional planning in Latin America, 1920–50', *Planning Perspectives*, **25** (1), 87–95.

Chiarella Quinhoes, R. (2011), 'Redes y territorios: la iniciativa IIRSA en foco', *Espacio y Desarrollo*, **23**, 5–29.

Coe, N., M. Hess, H.W. Yeung, P. Dicken, and J. Henderson (2004), '"Globalizing" regional development: a global production networks perspective', *Transactions of the Institute of British Geographers*, **29** (4), 468–484.

Deloitte (2016), *Africa's Changing Infrastructure Landscape: Africa Construction Trends Report 2016*, accessed 24 July 2017 at https://www2.deloitte.com/za/en/pages/infrastructure-and-capital-projects/articles/construc tion-trends-2016.html.

Ekbladh, D. (2002), '"Mr. TVA": grass-roots development, David Lilienthal, and the rise and fall of the Tennessee Valley Authority as a symbol for US Overseas Development, 1933–1973', *Diplomatic History*, **26** (3), 335–374.

Farole, T. (2011), *Special Economic Zones in Africa: Comparing Performance and Learning from Global Experience*, Washington, DC: World Bank.

Friedmann, J. (1973), *Urbanization, Planning and National Development*, London: Sage.

Friedmann, J. and C. Weaver (1979), *Territory and Function: The Evolution of Regional Planning*, London: Edward Arnold.

Goldman, M.I. (1961), 'A balance sheet of Soviet foreign aid', *Foreign Affairs*, **43** (2), 349–360.

Hess, M. (2004), '"Spatial" relationships?: Towards a reconceptualization of embeddedness', *Progress in Human Geography*, **28** (2), 165–186.

INTAL (2016), *UNASUR-COSIPLAN Project Portfolio 2016 – South American Infrastructure and Planning Council*, accessed 24 July 2017 at www.iirsa.org/admin_iirsa_web/Uploads/Documents/Cartera%202016_ web_eng.pdf.

Kanai, J.M. (2016), 'The pervasiveness of neoliberal territorial design: cross-border infrastructure planning in South America since the introduction of IIRSA', *Geoforum*, **69**, 160–170.

Leys, C. (1996), *The Rise and Fall of Development Theory*, Oxford: James Currey.

Lilienthal, D. (1944), *Tennessee Valley Authority: Democracy on the March*, New York: Penguin Books.

Liu, W. and M. Dunford (2016a), 'Urban–rural integration drives regional economic growth in Chongqing, Western China', *Area Development and Policy*, **1** (1), 132–154.

Liu, W. and M. Dunford (2016b), 'Inclusive globalization: unpacking China's Belt and Road Initiative', *Area Development and Policy*, **1** (3), 323–340.

McCann, E. and K. Ward (eds) (2011), *Mobile Urbanism: Cities and Policymaking in the Global Age*, Minneapolis, MN: University of Minnesota Press.

Molle, F. (2009), 'River-basin planning and management: the social life of a concept', *Geoforum*, **40** (3), p. 484–494.

Monson, J. (2009), *Africa's Freedom Railway: How a Chinese Development Project Changed Lives and Livelihoods in Tanzania*, Bloomington, IN: Indiana University Press.

National Resources Committee (NRC) (1935), *Regional Factors in National Planning and Development*, Washington, DC: United States Government Printing Office.

Phelps, N., J. Stillwell and R. Wanjiru (2009), 'Broken chain?: AGOA and foreign direct investment in the Kenyan clothing industry', *World Development*, **37** (2), 314–325.

Rodwin, L. (1969), *Planning for Urban Growth and Regional Development: The Experience of the Guayana Program of Venezuela*, Cambridge, MA: MIT University Press.

Schindler, S. (2015), 'Governing the twenty-first century metropolis and transforming territory', *Territory, Politics, Governance*, **3** (1), 7–26.

Scott, D. (2004), *Conscripts of Modernity: The Tragedy of Colonial Enlightenment*, Durham, NC: Duke University Press.

UN Habitat (1976), *Vancouver Declaration on Human Settlements and Action Plan*, Nairobi: UN Habitat.

UN Habitat (1996), *Istanbul Declaration*, Nairobi: UN Habitat.

UN Habitat (2015), *International Guidelines on Urban and Territorial Planning*, Nairobi: UN Habitat.

UN Habitat (2016), *New Urban Agenda adopted at Habitat III*, Nairobi: UN Habitat.

United Nations (1964), *United Nations Symposium on the Planning and Development of New Towns*, New York: United Nations.

Williamson, J. (ed.) (1990), *Latin American Adjustment: How Much Has Happened?*, Washington, DC: Institute for International Economics.

World Bank (1979), *World Development Report*, Washington, DC: World Bank.

29. African urbanization: will compact cities deliver shared and sustainable prosperity?
Ivan Turok

29.1 INTRODUCTION

Two interconnected transformations are underway which will have profound effects on social and economic systems and institutions across the world. First, the rise of so-called 'emerging economies' is shifting the balance of power away from North America and Europe towards the global South (Dunford et al. 2016). Alternative development models are evolving that are reshaping long-established geopolitical relationships and creating new territorial alliances, such as the BRICS. New tensions are also emerging that are destabilising the international order and creating heightened uncertainties within many nations and regions. Second, the swelling urban populations of Africa and Asia are reconfiguring domestic economies, consumption patterns and power relations.[1] The unprecedented rate, scale and character of urbanisation on these continents mean that African and Asian cities will also exert an increasing influence on the wider landscape of world development. There will be a mixture of desirable and undesirable consequences, depending on how the process unfolds (Miraftab and Kudva 2015).

International organisations such as the United Nations (UN) have recently recognised the necessity for urgent and effective action to ensure that burgeoning urbanisation in the south fosters social, economic and environmental progress, rather than disorder and despair. First, the 2015 Sustainable Development Goals set out a broad framework of measures to assist nation-states to reduce poverty and improve livelihoods. Goal 11 introduced an urban objective and targets for the first time: 'to make cities more inclusive, safe, resilient and sustainable' (United Nations Development Programme, 2015, p. 14). Second, the 2015 Sendai Agreement on disaster risk reduction proposed a range of actions required to make swelling urban populations less vulnerable to extreme weather events and other natural and human-made hazards (United Nations, 2015). Third, the Paris Accord on climate change pointed to the need to shift the trajectory of fast-growing cities in order to contain global warming by limiting future energy consumption and greenhouse gas emissions as they expand (United Nations Framework Convention on Climate Change, 2015).

The most recent and perhaps most relevant agreement for African urbanisation was the New Urban Agenda (NUA) adopted at Habitat III in October 2016. It spells out wide-ranging principles and guidelines for urbanisation to contribute to inclusive and sustainable development (UN-Habitat 2016). These imply a new paradigm for planning and managing cities to realise their productive potential, while minimising the detrimental impacts on the environment and social inequality. Urbanisation is embraced as a positive force for change in human development and a one-off opportunity to restructure national economies, promote social advancement, strengthen government and enhance environmental resilience. The key to unlock the transformative power of urban growth is a compact and connected spatial form that facilitates economic interactions, reduces infrastructure costs, economises on land and protects surrounding ecosystems and biodiversity. The NUA maintains that this can be achieved through careful urban planning and design, robust financial frameworks, responsive urban management, inter-governmental cooperation and active participation by civil society (UN-Habitat 2016).

The purpose of this chapter is to reflect on these bold propositions about urbanisation in the light of existing evidence about the situation on the ground in Africa. The core question posed is whether the UN's high-level proposals accord with current understanding of urbanisation processes and dynamics. In particular, does the idea of a denser and more integrated urban form get to the heart of the challenges facing African cities – would it create the foundation of well-functioning cities? Unfortunately, there is a dearth of systematic research on African urban growth, but much of the existing knowledge can be encapsulated within four broad narratives. These offer different perspectives through which the process of urbanisation and its effects can be understood.[2]

The simple message emerging from this brief review of recent arguments and evidence is that a more compact urban form would indeed confer important economic and environmental advantages, but there might be a social cost in terms of equity and inclusion because of how the land market operates to displace low income groups. There are also omissions in the UN's comprehension of political realities because of the somewhat technocratic nature of the NUA proposals. Finally, there are complications surrounding the timescales of the proposals, including uncertainties about the priorities and sequencing of actions to transform conditions for the better.

The next sections consider four particular narratives of African urbanisation in the following order: cities as social systems that tend to exclude vulnerable groups; cities as environmental entities that have hazardous consequences; cities as productive units whose performance has been indifferent; and cities as contested objects requiring better governance arrangements. Each interpretation has distinct implications for urban theory and policy. The conclusion reflects on the consistency between these perspectives and whether they can be reconciled with the UN's proposals for sustainable urban development.

29.2   ANTI-URBANISM AND SOCIAL EXCLUSION

The dominant narrative surrounding African urbanism is of concentrated poverty and social polarisation. Cities are arenas from which certain groups are consistently denied access to the opportunities available. In many countries, poor rural migrants were kept out of cities historically by restrictions imposed on urban residence by colonial authorities. Since independence, governments have removed these legal exclusions, but most have done little positively to correct past injustices by striving to accommodate in-migrants in decent and secure living conditions (African Development Bank 2011; Kayizzi-Mugerwa et al. 2014). This has resulted in the continuing marginalisation and indeed stigmatisation of poor urban households, mainly through the way the land market and government regulations work (or don't work). Anti-urban sentiments prevail among national decision-makers because of the challenges posed by spiralling urban populations, and pessimism about the possibility of managing urban growth more effectively (Smit and Pieterse 2014).

Consequently, 'governments have been fearful and neglectful of urbanisation' (Collier and Venables 2016, p. 408).

> [D]uring the first decades following independence, fear and loathing of cities nourished such strong intellectual, political and media currents that cities were long accused of every evil and seen as a burden and an obstacle to development. (UCLG Africa and Cities Alliance 2013, p. 10).

Investment in rural areas is favoured to mitigate overcrowded, congested and apparently chaotic urban conditions, and because national political elites are elected by rural majorities (Beall and Goodfellow 2014; Stren 2014). In addition, urbanisation is often linked in the mindsets of established leaders with undesirable changes in social norms and relationships. These include a weakening of community ties and a breakdown of traditional values, leading to more crime and other social ills. Meanwhile, many potential migrants have also been deterred from moving to cities by the shortage of land and housing and the higher cost of living in urban areas. These obstacles to urban inclusion are compounded by inappropriate and out-dated building codes and planning regulations that impose unrealistic standards on the construction of low cost accommodation and business premises (Watson 2009; World Bank 2013). These administrative procedures unintentionally reproduce and amplify existing social divisions and inequalities. Meanwhile urban elites seal themselves off from the masses of ordinary people in gated residential complexes, privatised shopping and business precincts, and new satellite cities (Cain 2014; Grant 2015; Watson 2014).

For these and other reasons, cities tend to be harsh and inhospitable environments for poor and powerless communities. Some 62 per cent of African urban residents live in 'slums', where dwellings are informal and lack tenure security and basic services (UN-Habitat 2014). These sprawling, single-storey shack settlements are vulnerable to natural and human-made disasters, such as the spread of fires and flooding. Women, ethnic minorities and undocumented foreign nationals are most at risk of discrimination, vilification and violent crime. Some 60 per cent of African urban inhabitants maintain precarious, survivalist livelihoods comprising casual employment or informal trading (Collier and Venables 2016). At best informality is ignored by public officials and political elites. Sometimes it is exploited and abused by powerful interests for financial gain (Henderson et al. 2016). At other times it is disparaged and criminalised, and periodic efforts are made to eradicate it. Governments undertake regular evictions of squatter settlements, harass informal traders and confiscate their goods and property because they are unauthorised and perceived to be illicit and a drain on city resources (Cirolia et al. 2016; Huchzermeyer 2011).

A notorious example was Operation Murambatsvina (literally 'Clear the Filth') in Zimbabwe, also officially known as Operation Restore Order. It was a major drive by the government during 2005 to forcibly expropriate and clear areas of unauthorised housing and informal commercial activity in cities across the country. This was supposedly to reduce the spread of infectious diseases and to promote physical renewal, under the auspices of the country's town planning legislation and by-laws. Approximately 700,000 people were directly affected by the police and army demolishing their homes and destroying their livelihoods. The United Nations (2005) criticised the crackdown as inhumane, unjustified and an indiscriminate effort to drive out large sections of the urban poor, who made up much of the political opposition to the Mugabe administration. They also slated the actions of the state for being indifferent to human suffering and representing a clear violation of international law.

A more recent example of the abuse of power to exclude marginalised groups occurred in Lagos in November 2016. Some 30,000 people from various ethnic minorities living in impoverished fishing communities around a lagoon in the east of the city were forcibly evicted from their makeshift homes using bulldozers to clear the area for up-market waterfront housing development (UN News Centre 2016). Four people died from the brutal treatment and the rest received no compensation for the loss of their livelihoods, homes and possessions. According to the UN, the evictions were carried out in disregard of a court order and ignored international human rights guidelines on forced evictions, which require affected communities to be consulted, alternative options to be explored and a resettlement plan to be put in place. The government appears to have supported the process because of the enhanced tax revenues to be generated from the redevelopment.

Summing up, cities are systems where outsiders are routinely marginalised and excluded in the interests of powerful elites and established urban residents. Poor households struggle to escape their precarious existence and to climb the ladder of urban opportunities because of their inaccessibility to land, basic services and other resources. The Lagos example illustrates a newer phenomenon of the reconstruction of well-located urban areas and displacement of vulnerable communities in the interests of commercial redevelopment. Potential responses are to extend human rights to the city to all citizens, to recognise and support informality, to increase popular participation and scrutiny of decision-making, and to progressively redistribute resources and legal safeguards to increase the well-being and security of hitherto impoverished and expendable groups.

29.3   URBANISATION AND ENVIRONMENTAL HAZARDS

A second and emerging narrative concerns many physical and environmental dangers posed by slum urbanism, now and into the future. Some of these hazards are acute and caused by destitute communities living in rudimentary dwellings crowded into unserviced settlements and exposed to water-borne and air pollution and untreated waste (Parnell et al. 2009; UNEP 2013; Buckley and Kallergis 2014). The impact of flooding and other disasters associated with extreme weather events is compounded by the physical concentration of people in particular places. Africa is already experiencing significant climate change, and two-thirds of countries are warming faster than the world as a whole, so its cities are exposed to greater threats than in many other places (Bishop 2017; Brahmbhatt et al. 2016). Other pitfalls relate to the growing scarcity of city dwellers' access to natural resources, such as water, fuel and food, also linked with urban growth and climate change (Cartwright 2015). The extensive physical form of urbanisation in turn has an impact on energy consumption and carbon emissions, with serious consequences for global warming.

Looking first at the problems of unplanned urbanisation, many hazards arise when large numbers of people live close together, with inadequate clean water supplies, sewers and storm-water systems, rubbish disposal and other essential infrastructure. The conditions of everyday life and public health suffer from cramped makeshift structures, poor sanitation and simple fuels such as wood and coal used for cooking. Household coping mechanisms are weak because of poverty and resilience to shocks is low, so there are high risks of infection, injury and mental stress from these 'neighbourhood effects'. Common contagious and life-threatening diseases in slums include tuberculosis, hepatitis, pneumonia, typhoid, cholera, hookworm and malaria. Premature deaths are relatively high and life expectancy is low. Children are especially vulnerable to a combination of malnutrition and recurrent diarrhoea, which stunts growth and damages cognitive development (Ezeh et al. 2016).

Retrofitting cities with underground water distribution networks, sewerage systems and drains is extremely costly and beyond the fiscal capacity of most African cities. This is particularly complicated in informal settlements because of the disruption to communities and the inevitable resistance encountered (Andreason and Moller-Jensen 2016). The same applies to access roads and other public spaces of circulation for people and goods, as well as the wider arterial network of paved roads. It is much more cost-effective to install these systems in advance of human settlement. Many squatter settlements also occupy 'left-over' land that is unsuitable for permanent residence because of the likelihood of flooding, subsidence and electrocution from power lines. In situ upgrading of these neighbourhoods may not be viable or sensible because of the environmental hazards involved. Considerable flexibility and ingenuity are required to resolve these problems.

The other set of dangers relate to the expansive form of urban growth and the impact on energy consumption, carbon emissions and the availability of natural resources, such as water, fuel, minerals and agricultural land for food production. They stem partly from the fact that the physical footprint of African cities is growing at a rate half as much again as the population (Angel 2016). Burgeoning cities that consume ever-increasing amounts of land struggle to sustain themselves because of the depletion of stocks of materials and resources of all kinds. Spontaneous, fragmented forms of urban development are most likely to damage the integrity and resilience of regional ecosystems, thereby exacerbating water scarcity and food insecurity (Jha et al. 2013; UN-Habitat 2014). Access to firewood, wild fruits and vegetables, fish and medicinal plants also sustains many poor urban communities (Schlesinger et al. 2015). Meanwhile, unplanned and dispersed physical growth worsens traffic congestion, overloads infrastructure and increases pollution (UNISDR 2012; UN-Habitat 2013). Without preventative action to plan their growth path, cities can get locked into dysfunctional trajectories which are extremely difficult to correct (Collier and Venables 2015).

Furthermore, if African cities reproduce the inefficient patterns of resource consumption and greenhouse gas emissions of wealthier cities in the global North, the consequences for the planetary environment will be dire (C40 Cities and Arup 2016). This is because the way cities grow has pervasive impacts on climate change through transport, buildings, energy and waste. Africa has contributed less than 4 per cent to the build-up of atmospheric greenhouse gases to date (Cartwright 2015) but having another 800 million people in its cities by 2050 will cause a step change. Some of the major threats include accelerating car ownership, increasing energy generation based on fossil fuels, forms of infrastructure and building techniques that embody high levels of non-renewable materials, and extensive use of land which exacerbates water scarcity, reduces agricultural output and increases food prices. It makes a sizeable difference whether cities grow through the construction of new settlements beyond the urban fringe, or through retrofitting and more intense redevelopment of existing settlements to increase population densities and improve access to amenities and public transport. A perfect storm would be created if climate change worsens droughts, cuts food production and accelerates rural-urban migration, while cities continue to expand in unsustainable ways.

Being only half way through its urban transition gives Africa a unique window of opportunity to change direction and introduce less hazardous and more resilient forms of urban development. The growth of new and existing cities needs to be decoupled from resource exploitation and environmental degradation (Swilling 2016). To leapfrog established urban forms would require embracing more resource efficient, cleaner technologies and novel urban designs and institutions, under the guise of the circular or green economy (Borel-Saladin and Turok 2013). Higher density, mixed-use, public transport-oriented development offers much potential (World Bank 2016). The same applies to green buildings and infrastructure using energy-efficient lighting and renewable energy generation (solar, wind, hydro and waste-to-energy power plants) (Brahmbhatt et al. 2016). Avoiding, reducing and recycling waste is also important. There is considerable scope for small-scale, decentralised investments in improved cooking stoves, solar water heaters, composting toilets, bio-digesters and off-grid solar energy systems for household appliances (Bishop 2017).

29.4   LOW INCOME, LOW INVESTMENT URBANISATION

A third narrative relates to an unusual feature of African urbanisation, namely its weak relationship with economic growth – 'urbanisation without growth' (Fay and Opal 2000; Jedwab and Vollrath 2015). This is linked to a fundamental difficulty that urbanisation is happening at much lower levels of GDP per capita than occurred elsewhere (Jedwab et al. 2015; World Bank 2015; Freire et al. 2015). In many African countries, economic development and job creation have consistently lagged far behind urban population growth (Henderson et al. 2014; UNDESA 2015). The apparently unproductive character of urban growth has wide-ranging implications for the prosperity of societies, the capacity fund public services, and for the ability of households to afford decent housing. The outcome of low income, low investment urbanisation includes extensive informal employment, shack settlements, overloaded infrastructure, intermittent electricity and social unrest (Collier and Venables 2015; Parnell and Pieterse 2014; Rossiasco 2015; Myers 2016).

The poor economic performance of African cities is partly a reflection of wider weaknesses in national economies. The long-term prosperity of African countries has suffered from their over-reliance on primary commodities, severe energy shortages, poor internal and external transport connectivity, low adult literacy and workforce skills, political instability and misgovernment (Brahmbhatt et al. 2016). Economic conditions improved between around 2004 and 2014 as a result of the global commodities boom and improvements in governance. However, infrastructure weaknesses and a lack of structural transformation continue to impede progress, and the commodity super cycle has come to an end. African economies are still dominated by low productivity sectors such as agriculture and informal trade (Collier and Venables 2015; Turok 2013). Shifting to high productivity sectors such as manufacturing, internationally traded services and the processing of minerals and agricultural products could make a valuable contribution to jobs and living standards.

Anaemic African urban economies also reflect local obstacles to private investment and business growth. These include bottlenecks in urban infrastructure, inadequate public services, parallel and contested systems of land ownership, ineffectual city governments and extensive rent-seeking (Turok 2016a). This produces relatively low density built environments with severe under-investment in multi-storey housing and business premises, as well as a patchwork of slums, formal suburbs and business/retail precincts scattered across the city (Henderson et al. 2016). The inefficient, spatially dispersed urban form results in chronic traffic congestion, long journey times for people and high operating costs for firms. Transport and housing costs are also high, so food prices are high, and wage pressures make it difficult for firms to compete in international markets (Collier and Venables 2016). Poorly functioning cities thereby undermine productivity, inhibit business formation and hinder job creation (Glaeser and Joshi-Ghani 2015; World Bank 2013).

The bulk of the revenues generated from extracting Africa's plentiful natural resources over the last decade have been spent on consumption activities in the cities and on transport connections between mineral deposits and seaports, rather than on investment to diversify production, or buildings and infrastructure for broader economic and social purposes (Collier and Venables 2016; Turok 2013). Urban infrastructure has been neglected by governments and international funders: 'infrastructure needs and financing options at the sub-national level, especially for growing urban areas, have been largely ignored' (Gutman et al. 2015, p. 3). Without state delivery, people devise self-help and informal solutions, but these impose huge strains on their time, energy and resources, and the outcome is inferior to properly planned public services (Andreason and Moller-Jensen 2016). The omnipresence of the informal economy is another symptom of low productivity, survivalist activity. The markets of informal enterprises are predominantly local, technologies are simple, barriers to entry are low, so competition is intense and incomes are low (La Porta and Schleifer 2014).

Evidence from elsewhere in the world indicates that cities have the potential to drive productivity, growth and structural transformation (Glaeser and Joshi-Ghani 2015; Turok and McGranahan 2013). A functional urban form helps to harness the positive externalities of large human settlements ('agglomeration economies'), including compact, connected and coordinated development (Collier and Venables 2016). As the ultimate scarce resource in cities, it is vital that land is used efficiently. This requires a well-functioning property market that enables smooth transactions and avoids prolonged disputes. Transparent land ownership and explicit land values also enable low density, under-utilised land and buildings to be converted to higher density, more valuable activities. An effective system of land registration and valuation permits local governments to tax landowners and thereby benefit from rising property values as cities grow and develop. This provides a vital revenue stream to fund the costly economic and social infrastructure that cities require.

Some means of coordinating the investment decisions of businesses, households and government departments is also important to ensure that the spatial arrangement of different activities across the city is efficient. This can be achieved through an effective land-use planning system that guides and regulates private investment decisions, underpinned by consistent public investment in infrastructure (Collier and Venables 2015; Turok 2016a). The alignment of planning and infrastructure decisions engenders confidence in the future form of the city and supports the patient, high risk private investment required in large and long-lived residential, industrial and commercial buildings. There is positive feedback at work as the city becomes a more attractive destination for investment, higher levels of activity raise productivity, and the city becomes an even more desirable place to do business and to live and work (Collier and Venables 2016).

29.5 WEAK URBAN INSTITUTIONS

The fourth narrative concerns the disempowered and fragile nature of the public institutions that govern African cities. This is partly a function of the limited legal status, formal roles and functions conferred on local authorities by many African governments (Buckley and Kallergis 2014; Smit and Pieterse 2014; Turok 2015), although this is changing with the gradual decentralisation of responsibilities over time. The weakness of city governments also reflects internal shortcomings related to aspects such as strategic leadership, technical capabilities, accountability and transparency. These deficiencies leave something of a vacuum for undemocratic actors and unelected gatekeepers to exert control, thereby perpetuating entrenched interests. Many national governments regard the weaknesses of local institutions, economies and tax bases as justification for maintaining central control over key functional responsibilities within cities.

Local government is the sphere of the state that is closest to the situation on the ground and better placed to respond to the needs of people and firms than regional and national authorities. However, the principle of subsidiarity is not widely observed and African municipalities typically have narrower functions, fewer competences and less autonomy than those on other continents (Gutman et al. 2015). They are often hamstrung by national governments under the control of dominant political parties or autocratic leaders who are reluctant to relinquish power and initiative to other entities (UCLG Africa and Cities Alliance 2013). One of the biggest obstacles is their limited capacity to generate their own revenues by borrowing or raising local taxes, so their resources often depend on transfers from the centre. This limits their discretion and ability to take their own initiatives.

In addition, municipalities are often handicapped by unsuitable and obsolete national legislation, such as inflexible land-use planning procedures, prescriptive zoning ordinances and unaffordable building standards for poor households (Parnell et al. 2009; World Bank 2013). Key decisions regarding different infrastructure projects tend to be made at national level based on the perspectives of separate sectoral departments. This inevitably neglects the understanding of essential local interactions and impacts – a transversal or cross-cutting perspective most feasible for local government (UCLG Africa and Cities Alliance 2013): 'African efforts at functional devolution of responsibility for services and fiscal decentralization of fiscal authority ... seriously lag behind other regions of the world' (Gutman et al. 2015, p. 4).

In the absence of a strong tradition of empowered local government, it is unsurprising that city authorities have not proved very attractive destinations for aspiring political and professional leaders. In many countries the culture of local government has been bureaucratic and control-oriented, which has often coincided with weak technical and managerial capabilities. This has inhibited the capacity of city authorities to provide strategic leadership and to coordinate the investment decisions of firms, households and other state entities. In addition, they have been unable to anticipate the future growth of the city, to prevent people from invading land owned by others and unsuitable for settlement, and to enforce planning decisions aimed at protecting land for future development. In the context of parallel land systems and uncertain rights, they have been unable to arbitrate between people with conflicting claims. Around 80 per cent of African court cases are about contested land ownership (Collier and Venables 2016). This is a source of serious delay and a major impediment to investment and development.

Transparency and accountability have also not featured prominently, with the voice of civil society typically directed more towards national government (UCLG Africa and Cities Alliance 2013). Similarly, creative problem solving has not been in high demand from municipal leaders, reinforced by the need to comply with inflexible national procedures. The widespread convention of statism means there is little experience of collaboration and working in partnership with other stakeholders, such as the private sector. African cities have been slow to develop shared visions and alliances among different interests to promote a common agenda of local development. Municipalities tend to lack the skills and experience to engage local communities in upgrading informal settlements, thereby missing an important opportunity to benefit from people's own knowledge and labour power (Cirolia et al. 2016).

29.6 CONCLUSION

There are formidable challenges surrounding the unprecedented rate, scale and character of African urbanisation in the period ahead. The social, environmental, economic and governance pitfalls are intertwined and difficult to disentangle in practice. Their cumulative and self-reinforcing effects at the scale of the city indicate the enormity of the predicament and the serious risks faced. International organisations such as the UN have only recently woken up to the situation. Their policy choices and tangible support for national and local governments could make a huge difference to the outcome. Under the right conditions, positive feedback could be created between changes in the economy, institutions, poverty and the environment, rather than a vicious cycle. There is clearly a great deal that needs to be done.

The big idea at the heart of the NUA is that a compact and connected urban form will contribute to social inclusion, environmental sustainability and economic prosperity. The main question addressed in this chapter is whether a more coherent and integrated built environment would produce these wide-ranging benefits. Put simply, would it create the foundation of a well-functioning city? The evidence from the dynamics of African urbanisation presented here suggests that more compact cities would indeed give rise to some of these advantages. Higher urban densities would improve economic interactions between firms and enhance workforce accessibility to jobs and amenities. This would raise productivity and thereby increase growth, employment and incomes over time. A smaller physical footprint would also reduce the impact on surrounding ecosystems and economise on the costs of transport and bulk infrastructure. This would help to safeguard water supplies and food security, and the cost savings would contribute to economic development.

Yet, there are also several important question marks and qualifications surrounding the propositions of the NUA. First, a more compact urban form would not automatically support social equity and inclusion directly. This is because the pursuit of higher densities would increase the demand for well-located land and buildings, and therefore put upward pressure on property prices and land values. Existing households with low and precarious incomes would be squeezed out of accessible areas towards lower-cost land on the periphery. The process would happen through market forces and might be inhumane, depending on the speed at which it occurred and whether there were forced evictions. The blow could be cushioned if the victims were compensated for their losses and offered alternative accommodation. Future poor households would be denied the opportunity to settle on well-located land. A more positive scenario would be for the state to find ways of cross-subsidising the accommodation of excluded groups from the income generated by developing market-related housing. This might be feasible only on a small scale until the general level of prosperity increased.

Second, there are complications around the timescales involved in achieving a compact urban form. This will inevitably be a slow process taking decades for the benefits to materialise and requiring households and decision-makers to show enormous patience and forbearance. The extensive hardship, suffering and other critical hazards faced will not disappear in the meantime. A wide array of other policy measures that have little to do with the built environment will be required to respond to these pressing needs and troubles in the interim. Sustaining the long-term vision of spatial transformation while managing the many everyday stresses and strains will be immensely difficult and require far-sighted political leadership, astute judgement calls and outstanding communication skills to build trust and understanding. This is an obvious stumbling block given the political pressures and governance weaknesses discussed in the previous section.

Third, there are doubts and uncertainties surrounding the priorities and sequencing of actions to deliver coherent cities. The simplest approach would be to start from scratch and focus on completely new cities and new extensions to existing cities. This is because preparing for the future and preventing unplanned urban growth is much more straightforward than trying to correct haphazard development after the event. This has been recommended by some observers and by UN-Habitat itself (Collier and Venables 2015; UN-Habitat 2013). Introducing innovative, green urban designs and low-carbon technologies is also easier with no vested interests to resist change. But what does this imply about all the existing informal settlements, older core urban districts and low density suburbs? Is it realistic to propose that they should be neglected while resources are diverted elsewhere? Would established communities tolerate, and would politicians be willing and able to sustain, a long-term commitment to invest in new urban areas with no voters at the expense of upgrading, maintaining and modernising existing neighbourhoods? This prospect seems remote considering that the funding to pay for the new developments would come from taxes paid by existing communities.

This raises a fourth point that programmes to build new urban areas will in all likelihood have to proceed in parallel with measures to renew, densify and redevelop existing urban areas so that they function better. Devising methods to upgrade and reconstruct established informal settlements is a particular challenge because of the combination of problems they face. This needs to be done by mobilising the energy of the communities themselves, rather than by imposing solutions from above, and without disrupting livelihoods and destroying the social fabric through physical relocation. Policies to renew existing urban areas require responsive forms of urban governance, whereas building new cities requires a more directive approach. This illustrates the political complexities and balancing acts required to shift the trajectory of African urbanisation. Such tensions are at the heart of dilemmas confronting many government plans for urban growth and housing development, reflecting underlying conflicts of interest between different stakeholders (Turok 2016b).[3] The NUA refers glibly to a new paradigm for planning cities that involves careful design, robust financing, responsive management, stronger cooperation across government and active public participation, but these are all very idealistic compared with current realities, and difficult to achieve in practice.

Summing up, it seems that progress is being made on the diagnosis of African urbanisation and on some of the strategic ideas required to transform conditions for the better. However, the outstanding challenges are formidable. They require a more nuanced understanding of how urbanisation is unfolding and a more grounded concept of how the process could be planned and managed more effectively into the future. The relationship between policies towards existing urban settlements and support for new greenfield developments presents particular difficulties.

29.7 NOTES

1. The population of African cities is expected to double over the next two decades and to triple to over 1.3 billion by 2050. This will be the fastest absolute growth of the urban population anywhere in the world (UNDESA, 2015). The projected increase of 800 million is about half of the expected increase in the urban population globally.
2. These perspectives still represent considerable simplifications of the diverse realities and subtle variations between urban development dynamics across a very large and differentiated continent.
3. For example, the Ethiopian government declared a six-month state of emergency in 2016 following violent protests arising from its plans to acquire land from minority communities to accommodate the future growth of Addis Ababa.

29.8 REFERENCES

African Development Bank (ADB) (2011), *The Bank Group's Urban Development Strategy: Transforming Africa's Cities and Towns into Engines of Economic Growth and Social Development*, Tunisia: ADB.

Andreason, M.H. and L. Moller-Jensen (2016), 'Beyond the networks: self-help services and post-settlement network extensions in the periphery of Dar es Salaam', *Habitat International*, **53**, 39–47.

Angel, S. (2016), 'Monitoring the share of land in streets', in G. McCarthy, G. Ingram and S. Moody (eds), *Land and the City*, Cambridge, MA: Lincoln Institute for Land Policy, pp. 62–101.

Beall, J. and T. Goodfellow (2014), 'Conflict and post-war transition in African cities', in S. Parnell and E. Pieterse (eds), *Africa's Urban Revolution*, London: Zed Books, pp. 18–34.

Bishop, R. (2017), 'African leadership in a time of climate risk', in A. Sy (ed.), *Foresight Africa 2017 Report*, Washington DC: Brookings Institution, pp. 78–79.

Borel-Saladin, J. and I. Turok (2013), 'The green economy: incremental change or transformation?', *Environmental Policy and Governance*, **23** (4), 209–220.

Brahmbhatt, M., R. Bishop, X. Zhao, A. Lemma, I. Granoff, N. Godfrey, and D.W. te Velde (2016), *Africa's New Climate Economy: Economic Transformation and Social and Environmental Change*, London and Washington, DC: New Climate Economy and Overseas Development Institute, accessed 1 March 2018 at http://newclimateeconomy.report/workingpapers/.

Buckley, R. and A. Kallergis (2014), 'Does African urban policy provide a platform for sustained economic growth?', in S. Parnell and S. Oldfield (eds), *The Routledge Handbook on Cities of the Global South*, London: Routledge, pp. 173–190.

C40 Cities and Arup (2016), *Deadline 2020: How Cities Will Get the Job Done*, accessed 1 March 2018 at http://www.c40.org/other/deadline_2020.

Cain, A. (2014), 'Africa's urban fantasies: past lessons and emerging realities', *Environment and Urbanisation*, **26** (2), 1–7.

Cartwright, A. (2015), 'Better growth, better cities: rethinking and redirecting urbanisation in Africa', Working Paper, Washington: The New Climate Economy, accessed 10 February 2016 at www.newclimateeconomy. net.
Cirolia, L., S. Drimie, M. Van Donk, T. Görgens and W. Smit (eds) (2016), *Upgrading Informal Settlements in South Africa: A Partnership-Based Approach*, Cape Town: UCT Press.
Collier, P. and A.J. Venables (2015), 'Housing and urbanisation in Africa: unleashing a formal market process', in E. Glaeser and A. Joshi-Ghani (eds), *The Urban Imperative: Towards Competitive Cities*, Oxford: Oxford University Press, pp. 413–436.
Collier, P. and A.J. Venables (2016), 'Urban Infrastructure for development', *Oxford Review of Economic Policy,* **32** (3), 391–409.
Dunford, M., A. Aoyama, C. Campolina Diniz, A. Kundu, L. Limonov, G. Lin, W. Liu, S. Park and I. Turok (2016), 'Area development and policy: an agenda for the 21st century', *Area Development and Policy*, **1** (1), 1–14.
Ezeh, A., O. Oyebode, D. Satterthwaite, Y.-F. Chen, R. Ndugwa, J. Sartori, B. Mberu, G.J. Melendez-Torres, T. Haregu, S.I. Watson, W. Caiaffa, A. Capon, R.J. Lilford (2016), 'The health of people who live in slums 1', *The Lancet*, **389** (10068), 547–558.
Fay, M. and C. Opal (2000), 'Urbanization without growth: a not-so-uncommon phenomenon', *Policy Research Working Paper Series 2412*, Washington, DC: The World Bank.
Freire, M.E., S. Lall and D. Leipziger (2015), 'Africa's urbanisation: challenges and opportunities', in C. Monga and J. Y. Lin (eds), *The Oxford Handbook of Africa and Economics, Volume 1: Context and Concepts*, Oxford: Oxford University Press, pp. 584–602.
Glaeser, E. and A. Joshi-Ghani (eds) (2015), *The Urban Imperative: Towards Competitive Cities*, Oxford: Oxford University Press.
Grant, R. (2015), *Africa: Geographies of Change*, Oxford: Oxford University Press.
Gutman, J., A. Sy and S. Chattopadhyay (2015), *Financing African Infrastructure: Can the World Deliver?*, Washington, DC: Brookings Institute.
Henderson, V., A. Storeygard and U. Deichmann (2014), '50 years of urbanisation in Africa: the role of climate change', *Policy Research Working Paper 6925*, Washington: The World Bank.
Henderson, V., A.J. Venables, T. Regan and I. Samsonov (2016), 'Building functional cities', *Science*, **352** (6288), 946–947.
Huchzermeyer, M. (2011), *Cities with 'Slums': From informal settlement eradication to a right to the city in Africa*, Cape Town: UCT Press.
Jedwab, R., L. Christiaensen and M. Gindelsky (2015), 'Demography, urbanization and development rural push, urban pull and . . . urban push?', *Policy Research Working Paper 7333*, Washington, DC: The World Bank.
Jedwab, R. and D. Vollrath (2015), 'Urbanization without growth in historical perspective', *Working Papers from The George Washington University*, Institute for International Economic Policy.
Jha, A.K., T.W. Miner and Z. Stanton-Geddes (2013), *Building Urban Resilience: Principles, Tools and Practice*, Washington, DC: The World Bank.
Kayizzi-Mugerwa, S., A. Shimeles and N. Yameogo (eds) (2014), *Urbanisation and Socio-Economic Development in Africa: Challenges and Opportunities*, London: Routledge.
La Porta, R. and A. Shleifer (2014), 'Informality and development', *Journal of Economic Perspectives*, **28** (3), 109–126.
Miraftab, F. and N. Kudva (2015), *Cities of the Global South Reader*, Abingdon: Routledge.
Myers, G. (2016), *Urban Environments in Africa: A Critical Analysis of Environmental Politics*, Bristol: Policy Press.
Parnell, S., E. Pieterse and V. Watson (2009), 'Planning for cities in the global South', *Progress in Planning*, **72**, 233–248.
Parnell, S. and E. Pieterse (eds) (2014), *Africa's Urban Revolution*, London: Zed Books
Rossiasco, P.A. (2015), 'Urban fragility and violence in Africa: a cross-country analysis', Washington, DC: World Bank Group, accessed 3 March 2016 at http://documents.worldbank.org/curated/en/2016/03/24862690/ urban-fragility-violence-africa-cross-country-analysis.
Schlesinger, J., A. Drescher and C. Shackleton (2015), 'Socio-spatial dynamics in the use of wild natural resources: evidence from six rapidly growing medium-sized cities in Africa', *Applied Geography*, **56** (1), 107–115.
Smit, W. and E. Pieterse (2014), 'Decentralisation and institutional reconfiguration in urban Africa', in S. Parnell and E. Pieterse (eds), *Africa's Urban Revolution*, London: Zed Books, pp. 148–166.
Stren, R. (2014), 'Urban service delivery in Africa and the role of international assistance', *Development Policy Review*, **32** (S1), S19–S37.
Swilling, M. (2016), 'Africa's game changers and the catalysts of social and system innovation', *Ecology and Society*, **21** (1), 37–49.
Turok, I. (2013), 'Securing the resurgence of African cities', *Local Economy*, **28** (2), 142–157.

Turok, I. and G. McGranahan (2013), 'Urbanisation and economic growth: the arguments and evidence for Africa and Asia', *Environment and Urbanisation*, **25** (2), 465–482.

Turok, I. (2015), 'Turning the tide? The emergence of national urban policies in Africa', *Journal of Contemporary African Studies*, **33** (3), 348–369.

Turok, I. (2016a), 'Getting urbanisation to work in Africa: the role of the urban land-infrastructure-finance nexus', *Area Development and Policy*, **1** (1), 30–47.

Turok, I. (2016b), 'South Africa's new urban agenda: transformation or compensation?', *Local Economy*, **31** (1), 9–27.

UN-Habitat (2013), *Urban Planning for City Leaders*, Nairobi: UN-Habitat.

UN-Habitat (2014), *State of African Cities 2014*, Nairobi: UN-Habitat.

UN-Habitat (2016), *HABITAT III. New Urban Agenda*, Outcome document adopted in Quito, October 2016.

United Cities and Local Governments of Africa (UCLG Africa) and Cities Alliance (2013), *Assessing the Institutional Environment of Local Governments in Africa*, Morocco. www.localafrica.org and www.citiesalliance.org.

United Nations (2005), 'Report of the fact-finding mission to Zimbabwe to assess the scope and impact of Operation Murambatsvina by the UN Special Envoy on Human Settlements Issues in Zimbabwe', New York: UN.

United Nations (2015), *Sendai Framework for Disaster Risk Reduction 2015–2030*, New York: UN.

United Nations, Department of Economic and Social Affairs, Population Division (UNDESA) (2015), *World Urbanization Prospects: The 2014 Revision (ST/ESA/SER.A/366)*.

United Nations Development Programme (2015), *Sustainable Development Goals*, Nairobi: UNDP.

United Nations Environment Programme (UNEP) (2013), *Integrating the Environment in Urban Planning and Management*, Nairobi: UNEP.

United Nations Framework Convention on Climate Change (2015), *Paris Climate Accord*, New York: UN.

United Nations News Centre (2016), 'Nigeria: UN expert seeks urgent answers on "brutal" eviction of 30,000 people in Lagos', 16 November, accessed 9 March 2018 at http://www.un.org/apps/news/story.asp?NewsID=55581#.WHO7bH0QtpY.

United Nations Office for Disaster Risk Reduction (UNISDR) (2012), *Making Cities Resilient Report 2012*, www.unisdr.org/campaign.

Watson, V. (2009), '"The planned city sweeps the poor away. . ." Urban planning and 21st century urbanisation', *Progress in Planning*, **72** (3), 151–193.

Watson, V. (2014), 'African urban fantasies', *Environment and Urbanisation*, **26** (1), 1–17.

World Bank (2013), *Planning, Connecting and Financing Cities – Now*, Washington, DC: World Bank.

World Bank (2015), *Stocktaking of the Housing Sector in Sub-Saharan Africa: Challenges and Opportunities*, Washington, DC: World Bank.

World Bank (2016), *Promoting Green Urban Development in African Cities*, Washington, DC: World Bank.

PART V

REGIONS AND REGIONALISMS IN CONTEXTS

30. The 'Europe of the regions'
Julian Clark and Alun Jones

30.1 INTRODUCTION

The 'Europe of the Regions' is a malleable phrase shaped by political-geographical concepts of territory, identity and power. It refers variously to everyday sub-national processes of identity formation across Europe; attempts to define regions by nation-states and latterly the European Union (EU) (regionalization); and to the hypothetical idea of a European political order based on regions, rather than nation-states. While it attracts considerable public policy and academic debate, the notion is also woven into the fabric of European civic life and it is only really possible to grasp its enduring significance by setting it within its historical-geographical context (Pagden 2002).

The premodern Europe of the thirteenth to late-sixteenth centuries was literally *a* 'Europe of the Regions' – a mosaic of local territorial spaces (city-states, bishoprics, and principalities) and practices (mercantilism and civic associationalism) that stretched from northern Italy through the Alps and southern Germany to the Low Countries, contextualized by the universalizing presence of the Catholic Church. Only dynastic monarchies stood out from this pattern. These local territories had diverse origins shaped by specific social and economic interactions with their surrounding hinterlands (Epstein 2002). Thus many northern European city-states' wealth was based on trade in locally produced goods, in contrast to the long-distance commercial relations and banking expertise typical in the south.

Gradually from the late-sixteenth century, nation-states emerged under the aegis of monarchical governments (often allied to Protestantism) which used their trading relations (and often warfare) to subsume these pre-modern spaces, in the process weakening Catholicism's grip in Europe. The resulting post-Westphalian reordering of space as 'national' during the seventeenth to the nineteenth centuries was strengthened by imposing nationwide languages and cultures and establishing capital cities; by asserting the discourses and practices of 'nationhood' over disparate communities to claim peoples and 'the nation' as one; by maintaining that the nation was best represented by the state; and perhaps most importantly by linking state formation with the evolution of capitalism. Through the nineteenth and twentieth centuries, pre-modern European boundaries, territories and identities seemingly disappeared in the face of the ensuing state-led drive towards industrialization and urbanization.

Latterly, with the establishment of the European Economic Community (EEC) in 1957, *the* 'Europe of the Regions' has emerged as the territorial-spatial praxis of European integration. The 'Europe of the Regions' is imbued with particular political-ideological conceptions of space from federalist thinkers including Denis de Rougemont, Guy Héraud, and Altiero Spinelli; Héraud (1974) for example argued for Europe as a federation of regions rather than a union of sovereign nation-states. While Héraud and Spinelli's ideas never materialized, arguably they found partial expression in EEC regional policy initiatives of the 1970s–1990s, piecemeal at first, based on social democratic principles of cohesion, partnership, solidarity, and (from 1992) subsidiarity.

The 'Europe of the Regions' as a social European political praxis came to prominence during the European Commission Presidency of Jacques Delors (1985–1995), now recognized as the high watermark of European integration, with the introduction of EEC Cohesion Policy. Sub-national policy interventions and the rhetoric of the region have since 'fallen out of favour' (Elias 2008, p. 483): certainly the original principles have undergone marked change over the last four decades in response to a rise in neoliberal orthodoxies and consequent changes in global capitalism and national economies.

However, it should be noted there were inherent tensions within the original concept. Thus on the one hand the 'Europe of the Regions' sought to privilege and empower the sub-national as a scalar category to work within (and possibly beyond) the political-administrative framework of EEC/European Union (EU) member states, even though Delors's aim was not to reawaken older sub-national identities to 'bypass the nation-state'. On the other, addressing the socio-economic and territorial disparities of the EU's c. 270 regions required progressive standardization of what a 'region' was by member states and the EEC, opening up differences between socially constructed local defined territorial identities, and the requirements of a new EUropean[1] taxonomy of political objects. Complicating this picture is the embedded power geometries between the national and the regional scales; as Paasi (2009, p. 123) notes the 'Europe of the Regions' conveys the 'idea . . . that nation-states are regarded as too small for global economic competition . . . while being too large and remote for cultural identification and participatory and active citizenship'. For despite federalist claims, as Keating (2008, p. 632) comments 'the EU does not provide an institutional space for anything other than states'. Most recently, these inherent tensions have multiplied and given renewed political impetus with secessionist moves in EU member state regions including Cataluña, Vascongadas, Scotland, Wallonia, Flanders, and Lombardia.

Academic scrutiny of the 'Europe of the Regions' has been undertaken from many disciplines using a variety of quantitative and qualitative approaches, including political administration (Le Galès and Lequesne 1998), spatial planning (Allmendinger and Haughton 2010), sociology (Bagnasco 2006), anthropology (Wilson 2012), as well as geography. Discussion of these extensive literatures is beyond the scope of the chapter, and here we confine our examination chiefly to relevant debates in geography and spatial planning, using the evolution of these debates to structure the argument as follows.

First, we chart how geographical work on regions changed during the mid-1980s from conceptualization as bounded territorial entities within nation-states, to understanding regions as collective sociospatial evolutionary constructions. We then apply this understanding to the 'Europe of the Regions' as EEC/EU spatial policy practice and focus of academic inquiry, outlining how EEC and latterly EU policy initiatives have been instituted supranationally and nationally, and the accompanying growth (in economic geography and regional/spatial planning particularly) in studies evaluating 'the EUropean region' as a policy object of socio-economic development, alongside work on regions as social constructions and sociospatial praxis. Following the thread of this argument takes us to recent work scrutinizing the Europe of the Regions as an historical-ideological mobilization between states and peoples through spatialized politics – that is as Europeanization. In turn, this work has informed the most recent tranche of research considered in the fourth section: the Europe of the Regions as contested ideological sociospatial processes that are being re-orchestrated as a singular EUropean territory. At the same time and in opposition to this trend, alternative imaginaries and practices for a Europe of the Regions have developed, and these are considered in section five. Finally, we assess what these different perspectives have to say about the Europe of the Regions as a territorial-spatial concept and lexical term in the twenty-first century, and conclude by identifying new research directions.

30.2 GEOGRAPHIES OF REGIONS

The region as ontological/epistemological focus has been a mainstay of geographical research. For many years, regions were regarded not only as one of geography's most salient intellectual contributions, but also as one of its main methodologies, defining sub-national territorially delimited/parcellated identities along myriad axes – including political-administrative, economic, ethnic, cultural, religious, and physiographic.[2] Thus during the early- to mid-twentieth century, geographers were at the forefront of scholarship theorizing the region (Hartshorne 1939). The so-called 'quantitative revolution', and the discipline's move towards systematic rather than territorially based analyses, saw these studies invigorated empirically but refocussed conceptually around positivist regional science-based approaches. Consequently, the region as a field of intellectual theorizing fell into abeyance.

It was only in the mid-1980s that the region again claimed geographers' attention. In particular, Paasi (1986) began reconsideration of the concept as social construction, based on its multiple discourses, practices and meanings. This gave rise to reconceptualization of regions as collective institutionalized spaces, reified by individual and community acts to produce territorial identities.[3] The region as institutionalization of collective ideas provided a much more nuanced interpretation of the sub-national, and moreover one that provided a new means of considering its inherent dynamism and scale-spanning qualities. Understandably therefore it was only a matter of time before geographers turned their attention to the social construction and practice of European regions. A crucial insight of this work has been recognition and empowerment of the sub-national as an autonomous scale-jumping category, working within (and possibly beyond) the political-administrative framework of the nation-state. Translated to the EEC/EU context, this reveals a tension that has always been at the heart of EU regional policy, as the following section shows.

30.3 THE 'EUROPE OF THE REGIONS' AS REGIONALIZATION AND FIELD OF ACADEMIC INQUIRY

During the 1980s–1990s, geography and spatial planning began to apply both mainstream positivist quantitative analyses and social constructivist understandings of the region to examine the 'Europe of the Regions' – that is EEC/EU spatial praxis aimed at the sub-national for socio-economic policy purposes. Initially informed by the social democratic orientation of the European political project, following the ascendancy of global economic neoliberalism in the 1980s–1990s a more hybridized template emerged in European policy, with member states emphasizing greater regional competition/competitiveness.

Tensions between social European and neoliberal ideologies have been matched by differing emphases placed over the last thirty years by EU institutions and member states on the region as a privileged scale of political intervention,[4] and by growth and enlargement in the EEC/EU redirecting the spatial emphasis of regional policy, particularly following the 2004 accession of ten member states. Economic geography and regional/spatial planning analyses have responded by evaluating the EUropean region as a spatial policy category with variable influence on economic development outcomes (Bachtler and Michie 1995), while political geographers have undertaken critical analyses of the ideas, institutions and interests mobilizing regional consciousness and identity formation across Europe.

30.3.1   The Europe of the Regions as Regionalization

The EEC instituted the European Regional Development Fund (ERDF) as one of the Structural Funds in 1972 to allow member states to address regional economic disparities and the conversion of declining industrial regions. Initially the ERDF was discretionary, relying on member states to instigate and fund schemes and, aside from entering EEC law, had limited supranational involvement. Nonetheless it established a mechanism for regionalization analogous to the already existing Structural Funds in agriculture, fisheries, and the European Social Fund. Calls for standardization of regional intervention in the 1980s resulted in greater EU institutional involvement, culminating in integration of national and EEC funds within targeted, multiannual 'Integrated Development Programmes'. This regionalization at supranational scale was given momentum by the global economic downturn of the late 1970s to early 1980s, resulting in high unemployment and an increased need to retrain workforces across Western and Southern Europe.

The main challenge for member states was thus to address the territorial effects of economic decline, with greater emphasis given to the ERDF and other Structural Funds to tackle the substantial interregional differences emerging over industrial competitiveness and levels of economic development. This commitment to what was termed 'Cohesion policy' was formalized in the Single European Act (SEA)(1986), and in 1988 the first regulation on Cohesion Policy was adopted. Five Objectives were introduced, including addressing the needs of lagging regions and tackling industrial decline, implemented in member states through local and regional actors working in partnerships, co-financing between the EEC and national governments, and funding over multi-annual (typically five-year) programmes. The goals of these Objectives were revisited in 2000 and again in 2007.

Cohesion policy has subsequently underwritten European networks on cross-border cooperation, transport, information and communication technology, nuclear energy, environmental policy, and investment in education and research. EUropean Treaties of Maastricht (1992), Amsterdam (1997) and Nice (2001) all reaffirmed Cohesion policy's importance; notably the Committee of the Regions, introduced under Article 198 of Maastricht, opened up new scale-jumping opportunities for sub-national actors by establishing channels of political representation between the regions and the EU Council of Ministers, alongside the principle of subsidiarity. The scope of Cohesion Policy was broadened under the Lisbon Treaty (2007) through new emphasis on European regions as 'territories' in their own right, with three specific qualities: economic and social cohesion; conservation and management of natural resources and the cultural heritage; and more balanced competitiveness of the resulting overall 'European territory'.

Alongside the European Commission and European Council's efforts to broaden the remit of Cohesion policy has been the influence of national governments of member states (in fact, the ERDF's introduction was partly to facilitate UK accession to the EEC in 1973 because of British concerns that its agricultural sector would be economically disadvantaged under the Community's Common Agricultural Policy). Later, Greece, Spain, Ireland and Portugal became the main beneficiaries of Cohesion Policy (to the point where they became known as the 'Cohesion Countries'), because of their comparative disadvantage under the criteria of the original five Structural Objectives. Similarly, the Finnish and Swedish accessions (1995) led to introduction of a new Structural Fund Objective providing financial assistance for so-called Arctic regions. Tellingly, the original social democratic focused aims of the Structural Funds (including assisting workers affected by technological change (old Objective 4), and regions affected by decline of traditional industries) had by the mid-1990s begun to be recast by the ascendance of neoliberal ideologies in European policymaking. This was formalized with agreement in 2000 of the 'Lisbon Strategy' by the European Council, with the Strategy's focus on growth, employment and innovation becoming the *leitmotiv* of EU regional policy. In effect, cohesion policy has been imbued with a particular discursive conception of 'economic region-building' based on neoliberal benchmarks of economic convergence and competitiveness metrics, grafted on to the pre-existing and more diffuse social European goals. More recent developments in cohesion policy under the *Europe 2020* programme have seen an intensification of these neoliberalizing trends through developing 'an economy based on knowledge and innovation', promoting 'a more resource efficient, greener and more competitive economy', and fostering 'a high-employment economy delivering economic, social and territorial cohesion' (CEC 2010, p. 10), set against the backdrop of tackling the legacy of the 2004 accessions. The net result has been regressive in achieving the balanced and sustainable development of European regions sought back in 1988. 'It is the development of a "Europe with the Regions", not the evolution of the "Europe of the Regions", that we have been witnessing in the past decade' (Borrás-Alomar et al. 1994, p. 51). Thus while more resources than ever are being spent under Cohesion Policy, in the EU-27 in 2014 one in three citizens – 170 million in total – live in its poorest regions. National economic and social disparities have significantly deepened with recent enlargements. At the regional scale, the difference is even larger: the wealthiest region is now inner London with 290 per cent of EU-27's per-capita income, while the poorest is Nord-Est in Romania with 23 per cent of the EU average.

30.3.2 The Europe of the Regions as Academic Enquiry

There was little appetite for evaluation of Cohesion policy in the European Commission until the mid-1990s, chiefly because of concerns that completion of the Single Market Programme might exacerbate regional differences across the Community. Nonetheless from the outset the regions have been the focus for economic geography analyses of the globalized economy. An enormous literature now exists providing quantitative spatial policy analyses of EU cohesion policy, with decidedly mixed findings. For example, Leonardi (1995) demonstrates the dramatic effects that the ERDF has had in boosting economic fortunes of specific localities in the Cohesion countries (specifically rural Ireland). Conversely in prosperous EU regions, Rodríguez-Pose and Fratesi (2004) show

how the effects of structural policy are muted as a result of agglomeration economies. These differing findings may also arise from standardizing datasets, and difficulties in establishing comparability of different data collection methodologies used by member states.

The most direct connection between the policy and academic worlds of the 'Europe of the Regions' is afforded through work on multi-level governance (MLG), proposed originally in 1993 by the political scientist Gary Marks (Marks 1993). MLG is concerned with establishing to what extent 'continuous negotiation' over particular policy aims between sub-national (Local Authorities (LAs), private and voluntary sectors) and supranational actors leads to collaboration, and how such collaboration affects existing patterns of decision making and taking nationally and regionally. Hence from this perspective the 'Europe of the Regions' is crucially about augmenting and enhancing regional decision taking powers, and the extent to which peoples might work together in new ways through EU cross-border and transnational programmes and networks.

Rising regional consciousness in the 1980s–1990s coincided with new opportunities for regional political representation at the supranational scale. This resulted in regions, Local Authorities, Lander and Autonomous Communities setting up offices and representations in Brussels, while other sub-national actors joined new trans-regional partnerships (Bartolini 2005). Some of these actors used the 'Europe of the Regions' as a political manifesto for regionalism– that is, a political campaign to secure sub-national control of political, economic and social affairs through new sub-national legislative powers (Loughlin 1996) – and for greater EUropean recognition of regions (Lynch 1996).

Yet the reality of the Europe of the Regions as regionalism has been more sobering. As long ago as 1994, prescient commentators observed how 'the automatism implied by the early writings about a 'Europe of the Regions' – more powers to Europe equals more powers to the regions – must be dismissed' (Borrás-Alomar et al. 1994, p. 49). The principle of subsidiarity, for example, introduced in 1992, has typically been applied to adjudicate legal competences between member states and the EUropean institutions rather than as a mechanism for devolving powers to the regions (van Hecke 2003). Indeed, nation-states have demonstrated great dexterity in redirecting regionalism for their own purposes (John 2000). Consequently 'By the beginning of the new millennium ... it quickly became clear that a "Europe of the Regions", still less a Europe *with* the Regions, had failed to materialize' (Greenwood 2003, p. 231; emphasis added).

Geographers have been very active in applying MLG to empirical examples, and in problematizing its differential dynamics between scaled actors across the EU (Jones and MacLeod 1999; Jones and Clark 2001; MacLeod and Jones 2007). This has run alongside the growth in studies of EU regions as social construction (van Houtum 2000; Paasi 2001). Taken together, such work has highlighted the ideological shift from a social European perspective based on reciprocity and support for lagging industrial and less favoured regions to a neoliberal drive for enhanced regional economic 'performance', whereby financial resource to regions is used to ramp up economic competitiveness. More significantly, it has highlighted the ways in which regions are constructed, sustained and mobilized as political entities sub-nationally (Brenner 2000), the intersection of these processes with the workings and operation of states (Gaberell and Debarbieux 2014), and the ways in which regional identities are made and remade through political technologies such as spatial planning, territorial governmentalities and policy programmes of one sort or another (Cochrane 2012). The consensus of geographical and spatial policy studies around these three findings has led to more detailed questioning of the mobilization of EUrope as a sociospatial category. In turn this has led scholars to reappraise the geographies of Europeanization, as opposed to European integration, as a means of developing fresh perspectives on the 'Europe of the Regions'. We consider this aspect next.

30.3.3 The Europe of the Regions and Critical Geographical Understandings of Europeanization

Over the last decade, geographers' interventions on Europeanization have deepened political science debates on this topic to provide a more nuanced understanding of the multifaceted relations between European (supranational) and national scales of political authority (Jones and Clark 2010; Moisio et al. 2013). Previously seen by political science as a contemporary, uniform routinized political-administrative process of 'uploading' and 'downloading' policies from/to Brussels to/from the nation-state, geographers have been in the vanguard of scholars arguing for a more forensic focus on Europeanization's geographically differentiated socialization and learning processes and how these 'have been configured over centuries by territorial propinquity and sites of government and power' (Clark and Jones 2008, p. 300).

It follows that manipulation of these continent-wide processes by political elites has been integral both to nation-building (including suppression of Medieval Christendom's 'Europe of the Regions') and latterly to the ideology of European integration, specifically taxonomies of European 'region-building'. Clark and Jones (2008, 2009) argue on this basis for examination of the under-researched scales and 'spaces of Europeanization', 'constituted from meetings / intersections between networks of relations stretching out across different scales . . . in which powerful individuals, groups and institutions seek to promote their own material and ideological visions of "Europe"'. These spatialized politics are shaped by factors including class, gender and ethnic divisions and the ways these link to EU identities; and the microgeographies of everyday working life, and how these structure social interaction. EUrope as a political category is therefore the sum of innumerable daily interactions across the sub-national, national and supranational scales that fashion a distinctive Europeanness both within and beyond its formal boundaries. Critically informed research on these Europeanization spaces has blossomed, with studies examining the regulated spaces of interaction governing EU geopolitical agency (Bachmann 2015), how EUropean diplomacy is prosecuted out with Europe (Bachmann 2016), and the use of pragmatic politics of Europeanization to position the sub-national relative to other political-geographic scales (Sellar 2013).

These studies are highly instructive in their own right, but coupled with analysis of the most recent developments in the unravelling of European integration they assume a new potency. For what is clear is the struggles over imaginaries, collective identities and ideas that underpin scalar politics across Europe are becoming ever more pronounced, as member states ('the national'), confronted by seemingly remorseless demands of global economic neoliberalism seek to assert their identity/authority by downplaying EUropean political significance to their electorates, while trying to contain restive sub-national political aspirations and new identity formations. Regionalism has thereby been greatly encouraged recently. The most significant implication of these developments for 'the

Europe of the Regions' is evident in new studies of the changing sociospatial politics of the sub-national as part of a mutable multi-level European polity; and in the emergence of alternative visions and imaginaries for the Europe of the Regions. We examine these aspects next.

30.4   THE 'EUROPE OF THE REGIONS' MEETS 'EUROPEAN TERRITORY'

Europeanization has been instrumental in informing the most recent tranche of research on the 'Europe of the Regions'. This seeks to develop political-geographic understandings of the refiguring of EUropean regions into an emergent 'EUropean territory' that expounds diverse knowledge economies as the latest instantiation of a hyper-competitive European economy. Central to this 'EUropean territory' is the role of spatial planning discourses and practices in corralling the sub-national within this novel framing, for as Paasi (2003, p. 110) comments 'territories are not frozen frameworks where social life occurs. Rather, they are made, given meanings, and destroyed in social and individual action'. Luukkonen (2015, p. 174) argues spatial planning is crucial here as *the* political technology with 'the capacity to fuse populations and geographical areas into manageable [territorial] entities'. Luukkonen and Moisio (2016) build on this insight to examine the EU's ESPON research programme as a distinctive activity space of EUropean territory, encompassing the activities of research institutes, universities, policy organizations and think tanks and their techniques of knowledge production to legitimize the knowledge economy as a new means of promulgating EUrope under global neoliberalism. The complex territorial dynamics these studies expose speak directly to contemporary sub-national mobilizations of territorial identity.

This work offers intriguing new insights into the Europe of the Regions in the twenty-first century in at least three ways. First is to expose the latent geopolitics in this framing process, specifically how a transnational community of politicians, policymakers, policy practitioners and academics sanction and authorise the sites and practices of underpinning the 'EUropean territory'. Second is to draw together theoretical insights on territory as a political technology of states (Elden 2010; Painter 2010), and the role of actors in reifying territory as a policy object which is produced in networked social practices (Schatzki 2010), to explore the supranational–sub-national–national nexus of political relations. And third is to problematize spatial planning as the principal sociospatial technology implicated in the dissolution of sub-national territories to fashion a 'singular [EUropean] territory' (Luukkonen 2015, p. 178).

30.5   ALTERNATIVE VISIONS OF THE EUROPE OF THE REGIONS

Alternatives to these hegemonic EUropean visions, imaginaries and practices of region-building have also emerged, some of them directly linked to EU policy. Thus Deas and Lord (2006) report on the ways in which the plethora of EU regional initiatives are being used by sub-national actors to develop their own relatively autonomous projects, in doing so subverting the 'Europe of the Regions' as functional policy object into a bewildering variety of polymorphous and polysemous forms, comprising among others multiple overlapping city regions, diverse polycentric (training, employment and technopole) designations, and transborder trading corridors. The result is an 'unusual regionalism' of 'confusing, overlapping boundaries, reflecting both the infancy of many of the initiatives, their often experimental nature and, in many cases, their continuing struggle to establish legitimacy and permanency' (Deas and Lord 2006, p. 1853). Clearly this 'unusual regionalism' has major implications for existing sub-national governance and state spatialities, not least in challenging established doings and sayings of territory. Different imaginaries of the scale of the region have also been advanced. For example Florida et al. (2008) draw attention to 'the rise of the mega-region', macro-spatial entities found around the world, including across Europe, that straddle national boundaries composed from city agglomerations and their hinterlands, which they identify based on aggregate economic output and underlying innovation processes. These authors claim mega-regions are 'new, natural economic unit[s] . . . with characteristics that are qualitatively different from those of [their] constituent cities' (p. 474). However, the methodologies used to define these complex spatial formations – including satellite imagery of night-time light emissions, and synthesizing miscellaneous quantitative datasets as proxies for innovation – tend to obscure, rather than reveal, the underlying rescaling and territorialization processes at work. While certainly deserving study, the phenomenon of European mega-regions thus demands closer scrutiny using critical social science perspectives.

30.6 CONCLUSIONS: THE SPACES AND TIMES OF 'THE EUROPE OF THE REGIONS'

In light of this discussion, the remark of Borrás-Alomar et al. (1994, p. 7) is still highly apposite: 'The question is whether the "Europe of the Regions" . . . can possibly be a meaningful term to describe, or even a helpful abstraction to analyse, the current phase of integration and regionalization in Western Europe'. By synthesizing the findings from the literatures considered here we are able to draw out some findings that help address this question.

First, the Europe of the Regions emerges as a malleable geohistorically contingent sociospatial category, reliant on processes of informal and formal institutionalization carried out at a variety of scales. Ironically as Keating (2008, p. 633) states, 'the most important avenue to the EU [for regions] has almost invariably been through the national government itself', rather than through regionalism or sub-national mobilization. Second, rationales and meanings attached to this concept are subject to shifting power relations between sub-national, national, and supranational scales, and how these are conditioned increasingly by neoliberalism. These power relations are evident in the changing appellations of 'the Europe of the Regions', 'Europe with the Regions', and 'a Europe for the Regions', discursive formulations that denote nascent rescaling opportunities for political actors within states relative to the multi-scaled polity of the EU. Third, irrespective of its nomenclature, the Europe of the Regions is likely to persist, albeit in new geohistorical forms. Thus continued instability following the 2008 crisis has meant new political-economic fault-lines are opening up in contemporary Europe between core and peripheral regions and states, city regions and their hinterlands, and between regional political aspirations for change and state-based narratives of stasis.

All this points to the need for further research exploring the differences, congruences and coherences between the literatures outlined here. In particular, greater awareness is needed of the historical-cultural antecedents of this sociospatial category, and how its underpinning latent Europeanness can be commandeered and redefined by powerful social fractions. Attention needs also to be focused on how regions intersect with globalized spaces of flows, for as Paasi (2009, p. 140) observes:

> within the EU, little is actually known about the meanings of regions as sources of identities, as constituents and motivators of social and economic life, and how these meanings work when regional structures, cultural influences and citizens are increasingly mobile. A question for future research [is therefore] what will be the role of regional identities in the globalising world which is characterised by mobilities: migration, immigration and tourism.

Closely related, how will the seeming multiplicity of new territorial identities, interrelations, bordering and boundary conditions made possible by social media give rise to new regional consciousness across EUrope? Another area requiring careful geographical analysis is how and in what ways underlying territorial inequalities have both contributed to, and amplified, the global recession, resulting in very different spatial impacts across European regions. Each of these areas we contend offer fresh perspectives on the reawakening of popular regional consciousness and its political expression as drivers for devolution, autonomy, secession, and independence. Such stirrings in the 'Europe of the Regions' could indeed be seen as a natural correction of a four-decade-old elite hegemonic regionalization project that has been less about empowering the sub-national, and more about 'efficient' and 'effective' state distribution of financial resources according to continually changing neoliberal prescriptions.

30.7   NOTES

1. 'EUrope' refers to the political identities and spatialities arising from the EU as the world's 'first truly postmodern international political form' (Ruggie 1993, p. 140).
2. cf. Keating (2004, p. 11): 'A region may have a historic resonance or provide a focus for the identity of its inhabitants. It may represent a landscape, an architecture or a style of cooking. There is often a cultural element, perhaps represented by a distinct language or dialect. Beyond this, a region may sustain a distinct civil society, a range of social institutions. It can be an economic unit, based either on a single type of production or an integrated production system. It may be, and increasingly is, a unit of government and administration. Finally, all these meanings may or may not coincide, to a greater or lesser degree.'
3. Thus Paasi (2009, p. 131) comments 'regions should be seen as complicated constellations of agency, social relations and power. Regions are institutional structures and processes that are perpetually "becoming" instead of just "being". They have a material basis grounded in economic and political relations. Various time scales come together in such processes.'
4. That the 'Europe of the Regions' is profoundly ideological is unsurprising. Borrás-Alomar et al. (1994, p. 27) comment that in the then EEC context, the phrase was 'promiscuously used to describe all types of activities which have some sort of relationship with sub-national entities, and not always with purely altruistic purposes. It has been brandished by national and regional movements and parties in their quest for a greater share of power or as a theoretical argument on which to base their demands for independence. Within the European Community, it is seen as a tool of the Commission in its confrontation with the Council of Ministers over the enlargement of its authority. It has finally been waved by some national governments in order to support their pleas for more European funding for their territories.'

30.8 REFERENCES

Allmendinger, P. and G. Haughton (2010), 'Spatial planning, devolution, and new planning spaces', *Environment and Planning C: Government and Policy*, **28** (5), 803–818.

Bachmann, V. (2015), 'Global Europa, ESPON and the EU's regulated spaces of interaction', *Journal of European Integration*, **37** (6), 685–703.

Bachmann, V. (2016), 'Spaces of interaction: enactments of sociospatial relations and an emerging EU diplomacy in Kenya', *Territory, Politics, Governance*, **4** (1), 75–96.

Bachtler, J. and R. Michie (1995), 'A new era in EU regional policy evaluation? The appraisal of the Structural Funds', *Regional Studies*, **29** (8), 745–751.

Bagnasco, A. (2006), 'Lo sviluppo locale: una risorsa per l'Italia', *Sociologia del Lavoro*, **101** (1), 63–69.

Bartolini, S. (2005), *Restructuring Europe: Centre Formation, System Building, and Political Structuring Between the Nation State and the European Union*, Oxford: Oxford University Press.

Borrás-Alomar, S., T. Christiansen and A. Rodríguez-Pose (1994), 'Towards a "Europe of the Regions"? Visions and reality from a critical perspective', *Regional Politics and Policy*, **4** (2), 1–27.

Brenner, N. (2000), 'Building "euro-regions" locational politics and the political geography of neoliberalism in post-unification Germany', *European Urban and Regional Studies*, **7** (4), 319–345.

Clark, J. and A. Jones (2008), 'The spatialities of Europeanisation: territory, government and power in "Europe"', *Transactions of the Institute of British Geographers*, **33** (3), 300–318.

Clark, J. and A. Jones (2009), 'Europeanisation and its discontents', *Space and Polity*, **13** (3), 193–212.

Cochrane, A. (2012), 'Making up a region: the rise and fall of the "South East of England" as a political territory', *Environment and Planning C: Government and Policy*, **30** (1), 95–108.

Commission of the European Communities (CEC) (2010), 'EUROPE 2020: a European strategy for smart, sustainable and inclusive growth', COM (2010) final, Brussels, 3 March 2010.

Deas, I. and A. Lord (2006), 'From a new regionalism to an unusual regionalism? The emergence of non-standard regional spaces and lessons for the territorial reorganisation of the state', *Urban Studies*, **43** (10), 1847–1877.

Elden, S. (2010), 'Land, terrain, territory', *Progress in Human Geography*, **34** (6), 799–817.

Elias, A. (2008), 'Introduction: whatever happened to the Europe of the Regions? Revisiting the regional dimension of European politics', *Regional and Federal Studies*, **18** (5), 483–492.

Epstein, S.R. (2002), *Freedom and Growth: The Rise of States and Markets in Europe, 1300–1750*, London: Routledge.

Florida R., T. Gulden and C. Mellander (2008), 'The rise of the mega-region', *Cambridge Journal of Regions, Economy and Society*, **1** (3), 459–476.

Gaberell, S. and B. Debarbieux (2014), 'Mapping regions, framing projects: a comparative analysis on the role of mapping in the region-building process of two European regions', *Geoforum*, **52** (2), 123–136.

Greenwood, J. (2003), 'Local governance in Western Europe', *West European Politics*, **26** (1), 250–251.

Hartshorne, R. (1939), 'The nature of geography: a critical survey of current thought in the light of the past', *Annals of the Association of American Geographers*, **29** (3), 173–412.

Héraud, G. (1974), *L'Europe des Ethnies*, Paris: Presses d'Europe, second edition.

John, P. (2000), 'The Europeanisation of sub-national governance', *Urban Studies*, **37** (5), 877–894.

Jones, A. and J. Clark (2001), *The Modalities of European Union Governance*, Oxford: Oxford University Press.

Jones, A. and J. Clark (2010), *The Spatialities of Europeanization: Power, Governance and Territory in Europe*, Abingdon: Routledge.

Jones, M. and G. MacLeod (1999), 'Towards a regional renaissance? Reconfiguring and rescaling England's economic governance', *Transactions of the Institute of British Geographers*, **24** (3), 295–313.

Keating, M. (ed.) (2004), *Regions and Regionalism in Europe*, Cheltenham, UK and Northampton, MA, USA: Edward Elgar Publishing.

Keating, M. (2008), 'A quarter century of the Europe of the Regions', *Regional and Federal Studies*, **18** (5), 629–635.

Le Galès, P. and C. Lequesne (1998), *Regions in Europe: The Paradox of Power*, London: Routledge.

Leonardi, R. (1995), *Convergence, Cohesion and Integration in the European Union*, New York: St. Martin's Press.

Loughlin, J. (1996), '"Europe of the Regions" and the federalization of Europe', *Publius*, **26** (4), 141–162.

Luukkonen, J. (2015), 'Planning in Europe for "EU"rope: spatial planning as a political technology of territory', *Planning Theory*, **14** (2), 174–194.

Luukkonen, J. and S. Moisio (2016), 'On the socio-technical practices of the European Union territory', *Environment and Planning A*, **48** (8), 1452–1472.

Lynch, P. (1996), *Minority Nationalism and European Integration*, Cardiff: University of Wales Press.

MacLeod, G. and M. Jones (2007), 'Territorial, scalar, networked, connected: in what sense a "regional world"?', *Regional Studies*, **41** (9), 1177–1191.

Marks, G. (1993), 'Structural policy and multilevel governance in the EC', in A. Cafruny and G. Rosenthal (eds), *The State of the European Community*, New York: Lynne Rienner, pp. 391–410.

Moisio, S., V. Bachmann, L. Bialasiewicz, E. dell'Agnese, J. Dittmer and V. Mamadouh (2013), 'Mapping the political geographies of Europeanization: national discourses, external perceptions and the question of popular culture', *Progress in Human Geography*, **37** (6), 737–761.

Paasi, A. (1986), 'The institutionalization of regions: a theoretical framework for understanding the emergence of regions and the constitution of regional identity', *Fennia*, **164** (1), 105–146.

Paasi, A. (2001), 'Europe as a social process and discourse considerations of place, boundaries and identity', *European Urban and Regional Studies*, **8** (1), 7–28.

Paasi, A. (2003), 'Territory', in J. Agnew, K. Mitchell and G. Toal (eds), *A Companion to Political Geography*, Oxford: Blackwell, pp. 109–122.

Paasi, A. (2009), 'The resurgence of the "region" and "regional identity": theoretical perspectives and empirical observations on regional dynamics in Europe', *Review of International Studies*, **35** (S1), 121–146.

Pagden, A. (2002), *The Idea of Europe: From Antiquity to the European Union*, Cambridge: Cambridge University Press.

Painter, J. (2010), 'Rethinking territory', *Antipode*, **42** (2), 1090–1118.

Rodríguez-Pose, A. and U. Fratesi (2004), 'Between development and social policies: the impact of European Structural Funds in Objective 1 regions', *Regional Studies*, **38** (1), 97–113.

Ruggie, J.G. (1993), 'Territoriality and beyond: problematizing modernity in international relations', *International Organization*, **47** (1), 139–174.

Schatzki, T. (2010), *The Timespace of Human Activity: On Performance, Society, and History as Indeterminate Teleological Events*, Lanham, MD: Lexington Books.

Sellar, C. (2013), 'Europeanizing Timisoara: neoliberal reforms, continuity with the past, and unexpected side effects', *GeoJournal*, **78** (1), 1–19.

van Hecke, S. (2003), 'The principle of subsidiarity: ten years of application in the European Union', *Regional and Federal Studies*, **13** (1), 55–80.

van Houtum, H. (2000), 'European perspectives on borderlands: an overview of European geographical research on borders and border regions', *Journal of Borderlands Studies*, **15** (1), 56–83.

Wilson, T. (2012), 'The Europe of regions and borderlands', in M.N. Craith, U. Kockel and J. Frykman (eds), *A Companion to the Anthropology of Europe*, London: John Wiley and Sons, pp. 163–180.

31. Mediterranean 'regionalism'
Michelle Pace

31.1 INTRODUCTION

The concept of the Mediterranean 'region' has been contested both theoretically and empirically time and again. But, what are its current meanings if any? Ranging from Malta to Syria's northwest part, the region often referred to as 'the Mediterranean' has historically been through unprecedented flows of people, goods, services, capital, criminal activities, cultural exchanges, environmental degradation, to mention just a few. While Malta holds the Presidency of the Council of the European Union during the first six months of 2017, Syria has been experiencing the worst humanitarian crisis of our time: Half the country's pre-war population – more than 11 million people – have been killed or forced to flee their homes (UNHCR 2016). Families are struggling to survive inside Syria, or to make a new home in neighboring countries. Others are risking their lives on the way to Europe, hoping to find a welcoming society and an opportunity to start their life anew. The effects of the conflict have become overwhelming. Since the toppling of Colonel Muammar Gaddafi, Libya has also experienced chaos in terms of its rival political factions: in recent years, it has also been a key springboard for migrants heading for Europe. Concerns have also been raised over the rise of Islamist militancy there (Ryan and Raghavan 2016). The Tunisian and Egyptian revolutions ended decades-long presidencies during 2011 but also led to widespread regional instability across the Middle East and North Africa.

In this contribution, I focus on the construction of regions, taking Wittgenstein's notion of 'meaning is usage' as the key frame for doing so. In his *Philosophical Investigations* (1953) Wittgenstein shifts from his earlier work of 1921 entitled the *Tractatus Logico Philosophicus*, where he saw language as a fixed structure imposed upon the world, to an approach to language as a fluid structure that is intimately bound up with our everyday practices and forms of life. When this frame is applied to how we can understand regions, it encourages us to explore the underlying meanings associated with this concept of a 'region.' Anssi Paasi (2010) highlights how words such as 'region' express various degrees of abstraction and challenge scholars to contest existing views and to develop new ones. Inspired by the work of Wittgenstein and critical scholars working across disciplines (and who are often labeled as 'post-structuralists'), my focus here is on how the meanings attached to the concept of 'region' – by diverse groupings – inform and constitute the practice of international politics and the patterns of socialization among states delineated within the borders of that same 'region.' I argue that it is through this border delineation – of who is in and who is out, who belongs to a particular region and who does not, that the Mediterranean has been carved out as a specific sub-global international society.

Conceptually, this may have some analytical clarity and grounds but empirically the Mediterranean is more fractured than ever. It is therefore the everyday practices and forms of life in today's Mediterranean that truly bring us back to question the universality of concepts such as 'region.' I am not disputing that there is a core meaning attached to the notion of region but in the case of the Mediterranean we do not have a common minimal agreement on how states within this territorially bounded space interpret their norm-abiding behavior within a global international society (Acharya 2011). Thus, the Mediterranean is the test case of how reference to this area of the world as even a minimal (sub-global) international society is not fulfilled, given that even diplomacy seems to have broken down as the only institution that can normally enjoy truly fully-fledged, common understandings and univocal meanings among the states composing that region. Empirically, I will do this by shedding light on the integrative failure of the project of pan-Arabism.

31.2   APPLYING WITTGENSTEIN'S NOTION OF 'MEANING IS USAGE' TO THE CONSTRUCTION OF THE MEDITERRANEAN

The keyword 'region' has traditionally been conceptualized in geographic terms as a natural, real entity. The world is often classified into regions. Within the discipline of international relations theories there are a number of approaches that focus on regionalism. What is important is to understand the underlying assumptions, shortcomings, limitations and expectations that these approaches on regional arrangements raise in order to better understand the 'substance' of regions. Theories of regionalism put forward the merits for taking the 'region' as a distinct level of analysis of world politics. So, what are the regular markers of regions, when does a region make sense and how is this concept then given meaning? Often states belonging to the same region are considered a homogenous group. The popular construction of a region is one in which 'sub-systems of states (are) linked by geographical relationship, mutual interdependence and subjective perception of belonging to a distinctive community.' And, that 'the sharing of common features brings about peculiar forms of political interactions among the countries of an international region' (Attinà 1996). Functionalism assumes a spill-over effect from political links to economic relations between states in the same region. Since the end of the Cold War, regionalism has been assumed to follow a smooth path through which states belonging to the same regional space progress together politically, economically and culturally.

The evolution of geographically, culturally and politically contested ideas about the Mediterranean can be understood along two different but broad representations of this region: one refers to the Mediterranean as a 'region' with sub-regions and the other refers to the Mediterranean as an interface between coherent regions (for example between Europe and Africa). Regarding the former, and geographically speaking, the Mediterranean embodies many sub-regions. These can be broadly classified as southern Europe, which incorporates southern EU member states (Malta, Cyprus, Italy, France, Greece and Spain/Portugal to an extent) and at least parts of Turkey; North Africa (Tunisia, Morocco, Algeria, Libya and Mauritania); and the Levant comprising the occupied Palestinian territories, Israel, Egypt, Jordan, Lebanon and Syria.

In spite of several controversies about which countries ought to be considered part of the Mediterranean 'region,' all Western institutions consider the Mediterranean in a holistic fashion, as a geopolitical unit that ties the countries around its rim with common 'concerns' and shared 'interests.' In 1994, the North Atlantic Council initiated NATO's Mediterranean Dialogue as a response to the post-Cold War security environment. During the 1950s and 1960s, the European Community flirted with ad hoc policies towards the Mediterranean. In the 1970s, it developed the Global Mediterranean Policy and in 1995 the Euro-Mediterranean 'Partnership' (EMP) was launched in Barcelona. The 2004 enlargement of the EU brought about an extension of the organization's borders to include seven new members from the so-called former Eastern Bloc, one from the former Yugoslavia and two small island states and former British colonies. The EU thus deemed it appropriate to develop its European Neighbourhood Policy with sixteen of its closest neighbors in order to 'prevent new dividing lines from emerging between the enlarged EU and its neighbours, and to strengthen the prosperity, stability and security of all' (COM 2004). Even the Organization for Security and Co-operation in Europe (OSCE) has developed special relations with six Mediterranean partners: Algeria, Egypt, Israel, Jordan, Morocco and Tunisia.

Various interdisciplinary studies also treat the Mediterranean as a 'region' due mainly to the interdependent nature of the political, economic and social issues affecting the area as a whole (Pace 2006). Critical security studies within the broad field of International Relations Studies have been pivotal in contesting existing views on the security of the Mediterranean (from a hard security perspective) and in incorporating the crucial element of human security in their theoretical tool box (Aliboni and Saaf 2010; Martin and Owen 2014; Volpi 2008).

If we understand the Mediterranean as a relational entity that is perpetually (re-)constituted through internal and external relations, then the English School or the Neo-Gramscian world order approach has a lot to offer in terms of conceptual tools that can shed light on the Mediterranean historically and on more contemporary notions of this space. Echoing Fred Halliday on the Middle East (2009), I would argue that the Mediterranean has a long history of interaction: military, political, economic, with the 'West' and in particular with the European state system. For Halliday the latter can be understood as 'the set of institutions and norms that have shaped modern, that is post-1500 and in particular post-1945 international relations' (Halliday 2009, p. 1). But, which dimension of International Relations (IR) does the Mediterranean represent? The English School has three core concepts that together represent the main components of IR. The first, *the international system*, refers to the 'macro side of the interactions that tie the human race together and more specifically to the interaction among states.' The international system can best be captured through realism, because of the power politics among states who interact within a political structure of international anarchy. There is interaction among the units of the system which are primarily states but there is no society in the international system (Buzan 2009, p. 25). The second dimension is *the international society* which refers to the institutionalization of shared interest and identity among states and puts the creation and maintenance of shared norms, rules and institutions at the center of international relations theory. Thus, within an international society there are rules and institutions that mediate the interaction between states. The third pillar of IR is *world society* which focuses on individuals, non-state organizations and the global population in general and as a whole since the focus here is global societal identities and arrangements (Buzan 2009). I would place the Mediterranean under the regional international society dimension since it is influenced by both the international system (realism) and world society (revolutionism).

With the Arab uprisings, the complexities of contemporary Mediterranean (and world) politics have been accentuated to such an extent that it is now more urgent than ever to sharpen our conceptual tools. Thus we need to rejoin the normative and structural elements of the English School as well as the intractable fuzziness of relations among states in the Mediterranean and with the outside world. By acknowledging that there are increasingly different regional societies within the international system, we can agree on the enlargement of the English School to incorporate the reality out there. Stivachtis (2013) argues that regional international societies consist of several sub-global regional social arrangements which can be differentiated one from another in terms of norms and institutions adopted, as well as in terms of 'access' and 'barriers' to membership (see also North et al. 2007). When applied to the construction of the Mediterranean this resonates with Wittgenstein's notion of 'meaning is usage.'

According to Buzan and Gonzalez-Pelaez (2009), regional international society (RIS) can be formed through one of three pathways: first, an RIS can come about when it adopts one or more institutions than those present at the global level; second, an RIS can be born when it rejects one or more institutions present at the global level; and third, an RIS can emerge when it adopts one or more institutions present at the global level but interprets them in a significantly different way. Thus, even those institutions that seem to be universally adopted and accepted may be seen as contested and subject to multiple interpretations. The Mediterranean falls within the third pathway of an RIS.

Since the outbreak of the revolution in Syria, which has culminated into an international conflict, the United Nations has issued eight resolutions concerning: the Syrian Civil War observer force resolution; the establishment of the United Nations Supervision Mission in Syria; the renewal of the mandate of the Syrian Observer Mission for 30 days; the Syrian Civil War: Framework for Elimination of Syrian Chemical Weapons; the Syrian Civil War: Access for Humanitarian Aid; the Syrian Civil War: Humanitarian Situation in Syria; the Establishment of a Monitoring Mechanism; the Syrian Civil War: Chemical Weapons in Syria; and, the Syrian Civil War: Cease Fire (Resolutions 2042, 2043, 2059, 2118, 2139, 2165, 2209 and 2254 respectively dated: April 14/21, 2012, July 20, 2012, September 27, 2013, February 22, 2014, July 14, 2014, March 6, 2015 and December 18, 2015). The ongoing conflict in Syria reveals the diverse interpretations of 'sovereignty,' of 'sovereignty as responsibility' of Mediterranean states and regional organizations such as the Arab League – which in July 2016 announced that 'thousands have been killed and millions displaced in addition to the destruction of the infrastructure of the country, as a result it is impossible for Bashar al-Assad to have any place in the future of Syria, especially since his hands are tainted with the blood of his own people' (Saudi foreign minister Adel al-Jubeir in AlJazeera, 2016).

But, according to Human Rights Watch (2017), throughout 2015, Saudi authorities themselves continued their practices of arbitrary arrests, trials and convictions of peaceful dissidents. Moreover, on March 26, 2016 a Saudi Arabia-led coalition began an airstrike campaign against Houthi forces in Yemen that included use of banned cluster munitions and unlawful strikes that killed civilians. Therefore, even 'sovereignty' or more specifically the practice of sovereignty – which is usually considered as the least problematic and most common institution of international society (Pascual and Benner 2012) shows a real rift in its interpretation and adoption particularly in the Mediterranean and wider Middle East and North African region. And even through membership of the world governing body – the United Nations – the Mediterranean countries show diverse interpretations of global institutions and their practices which shed light on the need to take into account the challenges in processes of norm diffusion and norm subsidiarity (Acharya 2004, 2011). This is why it does not make sense for the EU to speak of shared values and shared principles between the EU and its southern neighboring partners. Therefore, we should then rather speak of the Mediterranean as a 'minimal' rather than 'thin' regional international society since the so-called institutions, or norms of international society as treated by the English School are more ideal types rather than practices or patterns of durable relations (see Buzan 2004; Watson 1992).

In the Mediterranean, we simply do not find general acceptance and practice of the norms of international society, meant as 'principles of conduct.' This brings us to what Watson (1992) refers to as a pre-global international society, where different societies interacted via diplomatic means and were able to regulate their interactions with fairly shared relational procedures – despite sharing few or no common institutions. The Syrian conflict has however shed doubt even on the limited power of diplomacy as the only institution to enjoy common understanding – since diplomatic efforts have broken down several times in the span of the last six years or so of this seemingly intractable conflict. Needless to say, there are other conflicts in the Mediterranean that have shown the world the limited power of diplomatic efforts in this 'region' such as the Israel–Palestine conflict, the Cypriot conflict, the Western Sahara issue, to mention the main conflicts that have spanned over decades in this volatile region.

But is this a fair depiction of the Mediterranean today? Where do these underlying meanings associated with the Mediterranean today come from? In his famous work *Orientalism* (1978) Edward Said himself admits that it is impossible for a culture to grasp much about the reality of another, 'alien' culture without resort to categorization, classification, schematization and reduction – with the necessary accompanying distortions and misrepresentations: 'cultures have always been inclined to impose complete transformations on other cultures, receiving these other cultures not as they are but as, for the benefit of the receiver, they ought to be' (Said 1978, p. 67).

From the above theoretical analysis of the evolution of the geographically, culturally and politically contested ideas of the Mediterranean and its current meanings among contemporary supra-state regions, this contribution now moves on to the analysis of internal divisions and connections between Mediterranean countries themselves. The integrative failure of the project of pan-Arabism will be the main focus.

31.3 INTERNAL DIVISIONS: THE INTEGRATIVE FAILURE OF PAN-ARABISM

The idea of pan-Arabism, of the *Umma Arabiyya Wahida Dhat Risala Khalida* 'the one Arab nation with an immortal mission,' espouses the unification of the countries of the 'Arab world' assuming that Arabs constitute a single nation. Historian Bernard Lewis (1994) summed it up as follows: allegiance to the states was 'tacit, even surreptitious,' while Arab unity was 'the sole publicly acceptable objective of statesmen and ideologues alike.' Similar to Arab nationalism, the 'myth' of pan-Arabism could have resurrected the classical golden age of the Arabs had it not been for the lack of sufficient legitimacy of their states. States and their regimes lacked legitimacy since the early years of post-independence from colonial rule: the leaders of many Arab states faced challenges and threats of military coups. As a result of such threats, leaders depended, to a great extent, on traditional power bases, ranging from immediate clan members (the ruler's immediate tribal/sectarian clan) and the wider circle of power base including religious, sectarian, tribal or regional groups which were marginalized, discriminated against or felt threatened within the larger system or simply chose to be part of the political system and gain some of its spoils (Manea 2011, pp. 192–193). Moreover, in spite of several attempts, after the Second World War, to promote trade and policy cooperation in the Middle East and North Africa (MENA), economic interactions within the region remained limited.

On March 22, 1945, the Arab League was founded as part of a broad and ambitious political project that would lead to the creation of a single Arab state in the Middle East (Seabury 1949). In 1952, an Egyptian army officer and the second president of the Arab Republic of Egypt, Gamel Abdel Nasser, stepped forward to lead the drive for Arab unity, asserting a common history and the fact that Arabs share a common language. At the height of pan-Arabism, Arab states shared a common need to protect themselves from imperialism and colonialism. This also came at a time soon after the birth of the state of Israel (in 1948) when British forces still colonized most Arab states and imperialist Zionists posed a real threat to the existence of Arab states (Trabulsi 1969). For Adeed Dawisha, this Arab nationalism refers to the cultural and social similarities between Arabs (or Arabism) 'with the added element of a strong desire (and preferably articulated demands) for political unity in a specified demarcated territory' (Dawisha 2003, p. 13). Throughout its heydays, Arab nationalism faced several challenges, not least the authoritarian leanings of most Arab leaders and their lack of respect for their peoples' rights and freedoms, as well as a lack of a serious strategy for establishing and sustaining a politically, economically, culturally, socially and militarily unified Arab area. Further reasons for this failure include the already mentioned diverse interpretations of state sovereignty by very self-interested, power-thirsty Arab leaders who actually worked against Arab unity. A top-down ideology, inspired by despotic regimes, is bound to fail but the role that Western powers played against any hegemonic, unified Arab power from coming to fruition also played a major part in the demise of the Arab unity dream.

What more can explain why the ideal of Arab unity failed so miserably? Which factors damaged the credibility of pan-Arabism? The first 1948–49 Arab–Israeli war and the defeat by Israel in 1967 left a huge scar on the Arab consciousness (Ajami 1981). In fact, since 1945 the Middle East has not been immune from war and violence. As one of the most ethnically fragmented regions in the world (Peck 1998, p. 28), the region has also witnessed protracted civil wars and ethnic struggles with the resulting death and displacement of millions in Palestine, Lebanon, Iraq, Yemen and more recently Syria (see also Sarkees 2000). But, there has also been lack of economic growth and (for example in oil rich countries) fair wealth distribution in Arab states. The Arab League has thus been a 'failure' not only in preventing and managing regional conflicts but also in generating economic, political or military cooperation. The Arab states have also been marked by a high political economy of dependency (Alnasrawi 1991).

Or, are these factors simply a by-product of what is fundamentally a misguided alliance? This question comes at a time when alliance-building between major world powers is more important than ever. It is undeniably true that states gain strength in numbers and that a collection of united states – even if small ones – will always be more powerful than a collection of divided states. However, although a common language could facilitate international unity, it is by no means a guarantee or a catalyst for such unity. In fact, I would go as far as to argue that what makes a strong union is neither a common ethnicity, nor a common religion, or geographic proximity. Unions, like the European Community which later developed into the European Union, are formed out of a crisis situation or a need, and governments that agree to such a union must indeed wish to protect some common political agenda. In Europe, the six founding fathers of European integration swore to never again experience war as devastating as the two world wars had been between them. The need for peaceful relations was paramount. What brings NATO members together and what makes the alliance so strong is a shared understanding between its members that makes them prepared at any time to engage in a war if any member country is faced with a threat from outside. It is not a cultural, religious or geographic bond that established this alliance (Gordon 1997). In May 2011, when the Gulf states invited Jordan and Morocco to join the Gulf Cooperation Council (or GCC), it had nothing to do with their ethnicity or geography or religion: it was simply a need – in the wake of the Arab uprisings – to protect their political monarchies (Boukhars 2011).

Pan-Arabism, as an identity-restoration project, was at the time – as a minority movement under the Ottoman Empire to the dominating ideology of the Arab world by the 1950s – an essential *need* between the countries of the Arab world. But, the end of the Second World War brought to an end the threat of colonization and after the war, the British forces did not have the resources to maintain their Middle Eastern colonies. Thereafter, the process of decolonization commenced and lead to the independence of Arab nations. Moreover, the need for pan-Arabism was diminished with the end of the external threat of the Other – colonialism – and a lesser threat (at the time) of Israeli imperialism. Secularists – who originally championed the cause of pan-Arabism abandoned it for its lack of substantial results in terms of economic growth.

In the early 2000, there was some progress on the Arab-Israeli 'peace process' (Quandt 2005) and with a positive regional context there was increased attention to the economic potential of the MENA as a region per se. This attention came at a time of renewed global interest in regional arrangements, including those among so-called industrial countries (the European Union), industrial and developing countries (NAFTA or North American Free Trade Agreement and APEC or Asia-Pacific Economic Cooperation) or developing countries (Mercosur or *El Mercado Común del Sur*). On February 25, 2004, a Free Trade Agreement was concluded between Tunisia, Morocco, Egypt and Jordan. It was a first step towards social and economic integration in the Arab Mediterranean world and also a first step toward the implementation of a larger pan-Arab FTA. In addition, it was perceived as a step towards the promised goal of the EMP's Euro-Mediterranean FTA by 2010. The EU thus supported the Agadir process both financially and politically. In 2003, a four million euros program was initiated for the sole purpose of encouraging south to south trade integration in the Mediterranean area (EU Neighbourhood information centre, undated). But trade flows between the parties to the agreement remained dramatically low as a result of high trade costs: the Agadir Agreement in effect had only limited trade effects (Péridy 2005).

The outbreak of the Arab 'Spring' in 2010 to some extent kicked off the resurgence of Arabism: behind the varied motivations of the series of protests and demonstrations across the MENA, economic ones were crucial. The wave of initial riots, revolutions and protests addressed the impact of the global economic crisis (that had started to be felt most forcefully in 2007 but had long been coming), the profound social inequalities across the MENA region, the discrepancy between education and employability levels, especially among the youth of the region and the profound lack of civil and political rights of the people (Teti 2012). The combination of high unemployment figures and youth demographics, coupled with unrepresentative political systems and lack of civil–political and socio-economic rights increased the social unrest. Societal groups behind the making of the Arab Spring hoped for a prospective change in their countries' regimes, a rethink of state sovereignty and an Arabist platform that together could serve as a right step in the direction of a new bottom-up approach to a resurgent Arab nationalist movement that could correct past grievances in both theory and practice (Ansani and Daniele 2012). Unfortunately, the crisis situation in most Middle Eastern countries today – especially in terms of the humanitarian cost of the Arab 'Spring' and its aftermath to date – has shattered this imagined Arabist platform with devastating consequences for MENA societies.

31.4   CONCLUSION

This contribution has sought to critically problematize the notion of Mediterranean 'regionalism.' Conceptually, it did so through the use of Wittgenstein's notion of 'meaning is usage' which helped in framing how international organizations such as NATO, the EU and the OSCE have constituted the Mediterranean space in their strategic designs. It also operationalized the notion of a regional international society by testing this out against the region under examination here: the Mediterranean. Conceptually, it concluded that the Mediterranean may well have some minimal elements of a regional international society but what we observe in terms of practices and patterns of relations amongst states in this regional space are far from the ideal types of norms and institutions that govern such a society in theory. It takes this observation further by testing it out against the case of pan-Arabism. Empirically, it shows how the integrative efforts of Mediterranean Arab countries have failed because of various reasons. These include authoritarian leanings of most leaders in the region and their lack of respect for their peoples' rights and freedoms, as well as a lack of a serious strategy for establishing and sustaining a unified Arab area in the political, economic, cultural, social and military spheres. Mediterranean 'regionalism' thus represents at least a bleak experience of regional international society or possibly even a failed one. So is there any fresh space for future research on Mediterranean regionalism after this dismal account?

There is extensive research to date on the Mediterranean region: the complexities of its spatial politics (territorial and relational) as well as discursive and cartographic stratagems, which tell us a lot about how regional and external actors construct this space for their own interests.

But, since the start of the Arab uprisings, we have witnessed popular protests and dreams that have been crushed by the emergence of new rivalries between Arab countries. This series of events does not augur well for a revival of regional integration processes in the Arab world. Noticeably, the Arab League has been silent on the Syrian crisis, which indicates that many constraints remain before the organization can develop any meaningful, regional role.

What current events in and around the Mediterranean highlight once again is the importance of keeping an eye on Mediterranean voices and ways of thinking about the Mediterranean space, especially those that speak directly to some of the key theoretical preoccupations of human geography today. Thus, we should be asking: What lies ahead for future meaningful interactions between human beings and their environment in and around the Mediterranean? As Giaccaria and Minca (2011, p. 360) conclude in their discussion of the colonial/postcolonial dimensions related to the region, Mediterranean Studies require a critical space where 'geography learn(s) from such "liquid" spatialities – and . . . Mediterranean Studies learn from geography.' Thus, the study of Mediterranean regionalism requires disciplinary approaches that speak to each other in order to grasp a nuanced understanding of ongoing social processes and actions of non-state actors and groups in this geographical (albeit imagined) space. What is being suggested here is that we aim for a social science theory of the Mediterranean grounded in the every-day lived experiences and practices of the people that make up this region.

31.5 REFERENCES

Acharya, A. (2004), 'How ideas spread', *International Organization*, **58** (1), 239–275.
Acharya, A. (2011), 'Norm subsidiarity and regional orders: sovereignty, regionalism and rule-making in the Third World', *International Studies Quarterly*, **55** (1), 95–123.
Ajami, F. (1981), *The Arab Predicament: Arab Political Thought and Practices Since 1967*, Cambridge: Cambridge University Press.
Aliboni, R. and A. Saaf (2010), 'Human security: a new perspective for Euro-Med cooperation', February, Barcelona and Paris: IEMED and EUISS.
Aljazeera (2016), 'Syria, Iraq, Yemen, Libya top Arab League Summit Agenda', July 26, accessed March 5, 2018 at https://www.aljazeera.com/news/2016/07/syria-iraq-yemen-libya-top-arab-league-summit-agenda-160725132729802.html.
Alnasrawi, A. (1991), *Arab Nationalism, Oil and the Political Economy of Dependency*, New York: Greenwood Press.
Ansani, A. and V. Daniele (2012), 'About a revolution: the economic motivations of the Arab Spring', *International Journal of Development and Conflict*, **2** (3), 1–24.
Attinà, F. (1996), 'Regional cooperation in global perspective: the case of the "Mediterranean" Regions', *Jean Monnet Working Papers in Comparative and International Politics*, April 6.
Boukhars, A. (2011), 'Does Morocco have a place in the GCC?' May 25, Washington DC: Carnegie Endowment for International Peace, accessed December 23, 2016 at http://carnegieendowment.org/sada/?fa=44181.
Buzan, B. (2004), *From International to World Society?: English School Theory and the Social Structure of Globalisation*, Cambridge: Cambridge University Press.
Buzan, B. (2009), 'The Middle East through English School Theory', in B. Buzan and A. Gonzalez-Pelaez (eds), *International Society and the Middle East. English School Theory at the Regional Level*, Basingstoke Palgrave Macmillan, pp. 24–44.
Buzan, B. and A. Gonzalez-Pelaez (eds.) (2009), *International Society and the Middle East: English School Theory at the Regional Level*, Basingstoke: Palgrave Macmillan.
COM (2004), Commission of the European Communities, *'European Neighbourhood Policy Strategy Paper'*, Communication from the Commission, Brussels, May 12.
Dawisha, A. (2003), *Arab Nationalism in the Twentieth Century: From Triumph to Despair*, Princeton, NJ: Princeton University Press.
EU Neighbourhood Information Centre (undated), *'Agadir agreement – EU support project'*, accessed January 3, 2017 at http://www.euneighbours.eu/mainmed.php?id=14&id_type=10.
Giaccaria, P. and C. Minca (2011), 'The Mediterranean alternative', *Progress in Human Geography*, **35** (3), 345–365.
Gordon, P.H. (ed.) (1997), *NATO's Transformation. The Changing Shape of the Atlantic Alliance*, New York and London: Rowman and Littlefield Publishers.
Halliday, F. (2009), 'The Middle East and concepts of "international Society"', in B. Buzan and A. Gonzalez-

Pelaez (eds), *International Society and the Middle East: English School Theory at the Regional Level,* Basingstoke: Palgrave Macmillan, pp. 1–23.

Human Rights Watch (2017), '*World Report 2017*', USA: Human Rights Watch, accessed September 21, 2017 at https://www.hrw.org/sites/default/files/world_report_download/wr2017-web.pdf.

Lewis, B. (1994), *The Shaping of the Modern Middle East*, Oxford: Oxford University Press.

Manea, E. (2011), *The Arab State and Women's Rights: The Trap of Authoritarian Governance*, Abingdon: Routledge.

Martin, M. and T. Owen (eds) (2014), *Handbook of Human Security*, London and New York: Routledge.

North, D.C., J.J. Wallis, S.B. Webb and B.R. Weingast (2007), 'Limited access orders in the developing world: a new approach to the problems of development', *World Bank*, accessed December 23, 2016 at http://elibrary.worldbank.org/doi/abs/10.1596/1813-9450-4359.

Paasi, A. (2010), 'Regions as social constructs, but who or what "constructs" them? Agency in question', *Environment and Planning A*, **42** (10), 2296–2301.

Pace, M. (2006), *The Politics of Regional Identity. Meddling with the Mediterranean*, London: Routledge.

Pascual, C. and H. Benner (2012). 'Sovereignty's evolution: the role of regions–regional convergence in a transnational world', in P. de Lombaerde, F. Baert and T. Felício (eds), *The United Nations and the Regions. Third World Report on Regional Integration*, Dordrecht: Springer, pp. 17–25.

Peck, C. (1998), *Sustainable Peace: The Role of the UN and Regional Organizations in Preventing Conflict*, New York: Rowman and Littlefield Publishers.

Péridy, N. (2005), 'Toward a pan-Arab free trade area: assessing trade potential effects of the Agadir Agreement', *Developing Economies*, **43** (3), 329–345.

Quandt, W.B. (2005), *Peace Process: American Diplomacy and the Arab-Israeli Conflict Since 1967*, Washington, DC: Brookings Institution Press.

Ryan, M. and S. Raghavan (2016), 'US strikes Islamic State stronghold in Libya, expanding campaign against militant group', *The Washington Post*, accessed March 1, 2018 at https://www.washingtonpost.com/news/checkpoint/wp/2016/08/01/united-states-strikes-islamic-state-stronghold-in-libya-expands-campaign-against-militant-group/?utm_term=.a680dfd984f4.

Said, E. (1978), *Orientalism*, New York: Pantheon Books.

Sarkees, M.R. (2000), 'The correlates of war data on war: an update to 1997', *Conflict Management and Peace Science*, **18** (1), 123–144.

Seabury, P. (1949), 'The League of Arab States: debacle of a regional arrangement', *International Organization*, **3** (4), 633–642.

Stivachtis, Y.A. (2013), 'Shifting gears: from global to regional: the English School and the study of sub-global international societies', in R.W. Murray (ed.), *System, Society & the World: Exploring the English School of International Relations*, UK: e-International Relations, pp. 68–86.

Teti, A. (2012), 'The EU's first response to the "Arab Spring": a critical discourse analysis of the partnership for democracy and shared prosperity', *Mediterranean Politics*, **17** (3), 266–284.

Trabulsi, F. (1969), 'The Palestine problem: Zionism and imperialism in the Middle East', *New Left Review*, **I** (57), 53–90.

UNHCR (2016), *Syria Regional Refugee Response – Regional Overview*, accessed December 20, 2016 at https://data.unhcr.org/syrianrefugees/regional.php.

Volpi, F. (ed.) (2008), *Transnational Islam and Regional Security: Cooperation and Diversity between Europe and North Africa*, Abingdon: Routledge.

Watson, A. (1992), *The Evolution of International Society*, London: Routledge.

Wittgenstein, L. (1921), *Tractatus Logico-Philosophicus*, Annalen der Naturphilosophie. Published in English, London: Paul Kegan, 1922.

Wittgenstein, L. (1953), *Philosophical Investigations*, London: Macmillan.

32. Sovereignty and regionalism in Eurasia
Dmitrii Kofanov, Anton Shirikov and Yoshiko M. Herrera

32.1 INTRODUCTION: THE CONCEPT OF EURASIA AND SUPRANATIONAL INSTITUTIONS IN EURASIA

Since the fall of communism and the end of the Soviet Union, the question of what to call the region or regions of countries in Eastern Europe and the former Soviet Union has vexed scholars as well as regional-studies programs and centers. Is the region merely geographic, as in east of Paris, west of Alaska, and north of Cairo – somewhere between Europe and Asia and hence summed up in the name 'Eurasia'?

Originally, indeed, the term 'Eurasia' meant the combined landmass of Europe and Asia – names the ancient Greeks had given to the two parts of the world they knew. As etymological dictionaries suggest, the term first emerged as an adjective, 'Eurasian,' by which Europeans in the nineteenth century designated persons of mixed parentage, European and Asian (e.g. British and Indian). The term 'Eurasia' was entirely devoid of political meaning until the twentieth century, when empires collapsed and new nations sought ways to situate themselves in the world.

The tradition of 'Eurasianism,' developed by prominent Russian émigré figures in the 1920s, posited the existence of the unique Eurasian civilization, markedly distinct from Western democracy and capitalism (Laruelle 2008). Eurasianists envisioned a recreation of the Russian Empire as a commonwealth of Slavic and Asian nations.

After the collapse of the Soviet Union, Eurasianism experienced a revival in Russia, which was infused with elements of West-European right-wing ideology, and also in Kazakhstan (Mostafa 2013). It also gained a foothold in Turkey where it was crossbred with the ideas of pan-Turkism, so that Eurasia was imagined as a shared habitat for Turkic peoples (Erşen 2013; Sengupta 2014). In both cases, the Eurasian idea builds on contrasting the Eurasian space with Western European space, seeing these two spaces as proximate, but very distinct.[1]

The end of the USSR and communism generated chaos in the definition of the Eurasian region. During the Cold War, the communist system defined the communist bloc, a 'region' from East Berlin to Vladivostok; in addition, many academic centers focused on the linguistic (Slavic) aspect of the region for their self-definition. But in the 1990s and early 2000s, many of these centers formerly focused on Soviet, Russian, or Slavic studies relabeled themselves as 'Eurasian.' In this case, 'Eurasia' meant either Russia and its 'near abroad' (the republics of the former USSR), or, more broadly, the former Soviet sphere of influence, including nations of Central and Eastern Europe and Mongolia. Sometimes the label was also applied to all the countries in this post-communist space *except* for Russia. These definitions were criticized as arbitrary, inconsistent and insufficient (Gleason 2010), and alternative concepts, such as 'Central Eurasia' (Kotkin 2007), 'Northern and Central Eurasia' (Vinokurov and Libman 2012), or 'Inner Eurasia' (Christian 1994), were suggested, but have not yet gained prominence.

Alternatively, European social scientists and scholars are promoting the idea of a certain cultural and possibly political unity within the geographical borders of Eurasian continent (Hann 2016). This line of argument aims to overcome Western ethnocentrism and to recognize the presence of multiple centers of power on the continent. Hann (2014), for example, advocates greater economic integration in the Eurasian space as opposed to creating a free trade zone with North America.

32.1.1 Eurasian Institutions

Are the different conceptualizations of Eurasia reflected in economic and political integrative institutions of sovereignty in the post-communist space? The answer seems to be mixed. On the one hand, there are clear connections between Eurasianism and Russian-led projects of economic integration in the former Soviet space, highlighting growing antagonism between Russian elites and the West and the way in which Russia's leaders posit the uniqueness of their civilization. Russian President Vladimir Putin's most recent integration initiative is named the Eurasian Economic Union (EEU) and includes countries that Eurasianists thought to be pivotal for their project, such as Kazakhstan.

The EEU is clearly an attempt by the Kremlin to reestablish economic cooperation based on Russian dominance, a way for the Russian government to institutionally delineate its area of geopolitical influence and to leverage economic might in its foreign policy. However, Eurasianism as ideology, as opposed to a short-term Russian strategy, does not seem to be the basis of EEU integration (Laruelle 2015), although it is possible that Eurasianist ideas could be invoked sometime in the future.

As for Turkey's Eurasianism, it is pro-Russian in some ways (Akturk 2015), which might be linked to the recent Russo-Turkish rapprochement, especially since the prospect of Turkey joining the European Union now seems distant. But a Russian-Turkish tactical alliance does not yet imply any significant institutionalized integration. Turkey's president Recep Tayip Erdogan recently suggested that Turkey might join the Shanghai Cooperation Organization (created by Russia and China in 2001) instead of the EU, but so far this is only a symbolic gesture. It is also worth noting that Turkey promotes its own blend of Eurasianism, centered on imagining Eurasia as a shared habitat for Turkic peoples, via several supranational organizations, first of all the Turkic Council and the Organization of the Eurasian Law Enforcement Agencies with Military Status (TAKM).

On the other hand, some supra-national organizations can be associated with the ideological *rejection* of Eurasia as a sphere of Russian influence and an attempt to create sovereignty apart from Russia. In addition to the programs initiated directly by the European Union that are aimed at greater economic integration of parts of post-Soviet space into Europe – for example, the Eastern Partnership, the Transport Corridor Europe-Caucasus-Asia (TRACECA), and trade agreements with post-communist countries such as Georgia, Moldova and Ukraine – there are also supra-national institutions such as the Community of Democratic Choice or Baltic Assembly that were established by former Soviet republics and emphasize the pro-Western orientation of these newly independent nations.

Finally, in recent years, countries of Eurasia became more involved in new economic initiatives originating from China and South-East Asia. These programs – most notably 'One Belt, One Road' and the Asian Infrastructure Investment Bank – aim at economic and infrastructural development, but their implementation is inevitably linked to China's growing geopolitical influence in the region. And such massive economic undertakings could themselves lead to reinterpretation of sovereignty. For example, China is contemplating the deployment of its security forces along the states of the 'New Silk Road' throughout Eurasia, which has increased anxiety among the Central Asian nations. For now, China's initiatives are presented as parallel and complementary to Russia's regional integration efforts, and Beijing is eager to involve Russia and its other satellites as well, but this coexistence might gradually transform into a more direct competition.

The usage of 'Eurasia' as a single term may be compelling, but if Eurasia is a region, what makes it so?[2] One solution is to bypass this problem entirely by using multiple titles, for example, 'Russia, Eastern Europe, Central Asia, and the Caucasus' or some combination of those terms, and often with 'Eurasia' included as well. But if one rejects Eurasia, what regions should go in its place, and what is the basis for those designations?

32.1.2   The Concept of Eastern Europe

The concept of Eastern Europe seemed to gain prominence during the Enlightenment period when the Russian invasion of the Baltics and its growing influence in the European affairs made the old North–South distinction between parts of Europe obsolete (Wolff 1994). In the eighteenth century, there emerged the concept of Eastern Europe, a Europe's 'Other' coexisting with its counterpart in a mutually constitutive relationship (Wolff 1994; Neumann 1999 especially focuses on the 'otherness' of Russia). According to Wolff, the 'invented' Eastern Europe had a strong orientalist flavor: it was imagined as a land of 'barbarianism' and backwardness, associated with a lack of 'civilization.' At the same time, some intellectuals saw it as a tabula rasa – a place where the boldest social and political experiments could and should be performed. The notion of 'Eastern Europe' was very ambiguous from the beginning: on the one hand, it implied the 'Europeanness' of this territory, on the other – imagined it as inherently different.

The definition of its boundaries also posed a problem, and it was related to a broader and no less controversial issue: definition of the Eastern border of Europe (Heffernan 1998). In the eighteenth century, due to the influence of Peter the Great's Russia, the Ural Mountains became the commonly accepted geographical boundary of Europe in the East. Before that the antique notion of the Don River as the Eastern limit of Europe (which in some versions placed Moscow in Asia (Neumann 1999)) was prevalent (Wolff 1994). However, the 'imaginary,' or 'moral' geography (Moisio 2007) has always been at odds with this ostensibly neutral definition of Europe. According to Wolff's narrative, Eastern Europe initially included the Polish–Lithuanian Commonwealth, the Slavic and Hungarian parts of the Hapsburg and Ottoman Empires, and the European part of the Russian Empire.

Since then the concept remained very fluid: for example, during the Cold War the concept of Eastern Europe typically excluded the Soviet Union and encompassed Albania, Bulgaria, Czechoslovakia, East Germany, Hungary, Poland, Romania, and even Yugoslavia (Cassedy 2005). After the dissolution of the Eastern Block and USSR it is still common in the political and other social science literature to distinguish between former Soviet Union countries (excluding the Baltics which have recently been reclassified by UN as belonging to Northern Europe) and Eastern Europe. However, in some classifications, notably in the UN grouping of regions, Eastern Europe still includes Russia as well as Ukraine, Belarus and Moldova, but excludes Albania and former Yugoslavia countries which are placed in the Southern Europe.

32.1.3   Eastern European and European Institutions

Although communist-era borders proved to be very sticky in some respects, there were some important changes. Some of the sub-national borders became national as in the dissolution of Czechoslovakia, Yugoslavia, and the USSR, and the borders of some existing states (e.g. eastern borders of Central European states) became more meaningful as their sovereignty vis-à-vis Russia strengthened. At the same time, some borders became less meaningful, for example, among states entering the European Union. Herrschel (2011) argues that these processes in Eastern Europe demonstrated that 'borders are . . . inherently contradictory – doing both separating and bringing into touch neighboring territories and their "content"' (Herrschel 2011, p. 6).

The term 'Eastern Europe' still seems to bear some sense of inferiority and therefore has largely been abandoned politically (for example Zeigler 2002, Rupnik 1994): there are no international organizations which are based on this geopolitical concept. An alternative concept, which aims to carve out at least part of the countries usually associated with Eastern Europe and bring them to Europe proper is 'Central Europe.' This term alludes to the German *Mitteleuropa* which was used by some geographers-ideologues to delineate the sphere of German influence in territories mostly corresponding to former German and Austro-Hungarian Empires, and was almost irretrievably compromised after the two World Wars (Heffernan 1998; Neumann 1999; Hagen 2003). The idea of Central Europe was popularized in the 1980s by Eastern European intellectuals (especially Czechoslovak, Polish and Hungarian), who saw their countries as bearers of genuine European values and culture invaded by the civilizationally different Soviet/Russian Empire (Neumann 1999). The adherents of the Central Europe concept tried to distance themselves from Germany as well, and the often-used term 'East-Central Europe' (e.g. see Kuus 2004) strengthens this disambiguation.

The boundaries of Central Europe are also blurred, and its strongest political embodiment, the Visegrád group, includes only four countries: the Czech Republic, Poland, Hungary and Slovakia. In addition, some other institutional instantiations of Central Europe include the much wider Central European Initiative, which lists Austria and Italy among its founders, and the Central European Free Trade Agreement, as well as other broader initiatives such as the South-East European Cooperation Process or the Regional Cooperation Council.

Despite these integration efforts by Central European countries, EU accession was a much more important goal for many of the countries of 'Eastern Europe.' This process took place starting in the early 2000s and some aspects such as monetary union are ongoing. Thus, beyond the ideological underpinnings for the common 'return to Europe,' the concept of Central Europe seems to have almost no realization in sovereignty-aspiring institutions and little political, economic or identity impact. Some observers have even noted its decline as a concept as early as the early 2000s (Hagen 2003). On the other hand, it has to be acknowledged that the expansion of the European Union and of NATO into former Soviet space has once again emphasized the broader and persistent East–West division.

32.1.4   Central Asia and the Caucasus

Most commonly, Central Asia is understood today as a group of five former Soviet republics – Kazakhstan, Kyrgyzstan, Tajikistan, Turkmenistan, Uzbekistan – which reflects mostly the Soviet understanding of the region (Cummings 2012). However, earlier historical concepts of Central Asia were broader and fuzzier. In one reading, Central Asia was a space where 'two Eurasian civilizations, Islamic-Iranian sedentary and Inner Asian nomadic' coexisted (Sengupta 2002, p. 17). The Western concept of Central Asia emerged in the eighteenth and nineteenth centuries and comprised Iran, Afghanistan, western parts of China and the territories which later became the Soviet republics (Fuller 1990), and more recently parts of Mongolia, Pakistan, India, Turkey, and southwestern Siberia. Some authors suggest distinguishing between 'Soviet' Central Asia and a Greater Central Asia that includes more countries (Starr 2008); others advocate using the term 'Central Eurasia' instead, emphasizing this region's place at the heart of the continent.

But debates on Central Asia do not stop there. There are variations in Chinese, Indian, Iranian, and Japanese concepts of Central Asia (Rahul 1997; Azizov 2011). Laruelle (2011) notes that Central Asia can be viewed as Russia's southern area of influence, as part of the 'Greater Middle East' (and thus an area of the US influence), as China's 'Far West,' as 'Greater Central Asia' linked to South Asia, and as the 'Caspian Basin,' a buffer zone between Russia and Iran, and so on.

This uncertainty in terminology is matched by various and overlapping supra-national entities that operate in the region. The Russia-initiated EEU and CSTO are now complemented by Chinese integration initiatives, and the Turkey-sponsored intergovernmental programs are also at work. Central Asian countries are also typically included in broader Asian supra-national institutions such as the Asian Development Bank. Countries of the region are also attempting to create more local intergovernmental organizations such as the Central Asian Union proposed by Kazakhstan and Kyrgyzstan, but this initiative has not yet taken off. The sovereignty goals of these institutional initiatives, as well as effects on state and regional sovereignty of these initiatives, remain a work in progress.

The concept of the Caucasus is less debated in the pure geographic sense, but is rich with geopolitical interpretations. The Caucasus first emerged on maps in 1723 as the 'Caspian sea neighboring territories' and the subsequent transformation of this concept reflected various attempts of defining and redefining the limits of influence of Russians, Persians and Ottomans (Tsutsiev 2014). The Caucasus was essentially a buffer zone between these empires.

In the 1990s, these debates experienced a revival. Some Russian foreign policy experts viewed the countries of Transcaucasia – Armenia, Azerbaijan and Georgia – as its southern flank, while Iranian politicians contemplated the emergence of a new region comprising Transcaucasia, Central Asia, Afghanistan and Pakistan, where Tehran would play a central role. Policymakers and experts in Turkey, on the other hand, discussed potential integration of Turkic communities in Central Asia and the Caucasus under Ankara's umbrella (Coppieters 1996).

These political notions are still at work to some extent, which is evident in the spread of Russia-backed and Turkey-backed international organizations. But the Western European presence in the Caucasus is now more salient, with Georgia taking a clearly pro-Western and pro-EU course, rejecting Russia-sponsored organizations such as the CIS and the

Eurasian Union. Countries of the subregion are also involved in broader processes such as the Black Sea Economic Cooperation, which also includes some Eastern and Central European countries. At the same time, there are no attempts at Transcaucasian institutional integration.

Transcaucasia still seems not having overcome the status of the buffer zone, which makes it similar to the geopolitical standing of Central Asian nations. Some authors, noting these similarities, have even proposed another, unifying concept: Central Caucaso-Asia (Papava 2013). While this concept has not taken off, it is notable that in the Caucasus in particular, and to some extent in Central Asia, the main contemporary issues related to sovereignty have to do with threats to nation-state sovereignty at the sub-national level, rather than serious attempts at the creation of supra-national sovereign institutions.

32.2   THE SUB-NATIONAL LEVEL

The complexity of political identities in Eurasia is reflected in the proliferation of sub-national independence and autonomy movements. This problem became especially acute after the rise of nationalist movements in Europe in the nineteenth century, which linked sovereignty and the nation. There has always been a tension between the potential universe of nations and the existing political structure. There are quite a few 'dogs that didn't bark' (Gellner 1983) or potential nations that have thus far not made strong moves for greater sovereignty. Many of them still exist in the form of regionalist movements demanding autonomy or at least some distinctive regional identification. Hobsbawm (1990) posited the existence of 42 regionalist movements in Europe. The organization European Free Alliance, which is an organizational platform for European regionalist parties of 'progressive' (not far-right and xenophobic) orientation, currently lists 46 members of various statuses, with 10 of them being in Eastern Europe.

32.2.1   Eastern Europe

The aftermath of the First World War saw the emergence of many new states in the ruins of the Austro-Hungarian, German, Russian and Ottoman Empires. Despite the predisposition of Woodrow Wilson and other participants of the 1919 Paris Conference, universal implementation of the national self-determination principle proved to be unattainable (Bideleux and Jeffries 2007; Heffernan 1998). The newly created states still contained large ethnic minority groups (e.g. Germans in Poland and Czechoslovakia, or Hungarians in Romania, Czechoslovakia, and Yugoslavia (Brubaker 1996)).

The problem was that dominant ethnic groups in the new states (e.g. Poles in Poland, Serbs in Yugoslavia, Czechs in Czechoslovakia) posed threats to the rights of minorities (Bideleux and Jeffries 2007, pp. 324–325). Since the late nineteenth century, nationalism had increasingly been understood in ethnic terms (Hobsbawm 1990), and ethnically, linguistically and culturally homogenized national states were often seen as ideal, which in practice could be attained through assimilation, deportation or even mass killing of 'alien' groups. In practice, minority rights in the post-war states tended to be guaranteed (with limited success) through international treaties, rather than creation of ethnoterritorial autonomies (Mazover 1998). Even Yugoslavia and Czechoslovakia both were unitary, centralized states officially containing a single nation, and in the case of Yugoslavia the administrative divisions were not explicitly ethnic- or tradition-based (e.g. Bideleux and Jeffries 2007, p. 446).

The Second World War brought another mass movement of people and borders, which on the one hand resulted in a greater congruence of ethnic and state borders (e.g. the expulsion of Germans from East-Central Europe, and earlier Poles from the enlarged Soviet Ukraine and Belarus), but on the other hand weakened nation-states (e.g. invasion and incorporation of Baltic states by the Soviet Union, and the division of Germany). These processes were accompanied by large-scale mass violence and deprivation. Among the notable developments in sub-national structure during the communist period are the cases of Yugoslavia and Czechoslovakia (since 1969), which eventually turned into federations of national republics along the lines of the USSR (discussed below), but with a higher level of decentralization.

In the post-communist period in Eastern Europe, there was some rethinking of sub-national units in Eastern Europe and concomitant reshuffling of sub-national regional borders and hierarchies. Sagan and Lee (2005, p. 174) emphasize 'the significance of historically integrated and socially constructed spaces' in the success of regional policies in the Central European countries. For example, territorial reforms were implemented in the Czech Republic, Slovakia and Poland to foster decentralization, transition to market economy, and viable democratic self-governance. In Slovakia the 'super-regions' inherited from the Soviet times were eliminated, whereas in Poland the number of regions was reduced threefold. The legacies of Soviet era central planning that often ignored spatial logic and led to excessive industrial concentration were viewed as obstacles to more meaningful regional policies and to the development of interregional network connections.[3]

The limits of the practical application of a 'New Regionalism' in Post-Soviet conditions are also visible in the position of city regions. Herrschel and Newman (2005) distinguish between territory-based and policy-based regionalism. In the latter case, a region (called a 'virtual region' by the authors) is 'a temporal, repeatedly changing construct,' in practice outward-looking, and focused on economic development as opposed to just 'technocratic planning,' yet without abandoning its identity. The comparison of several cases shows that Prague, unlike Hamburg and Turin, did not become a virtual region: the level of co-operation with the newly created (and still weakly legitimate) encircling Central Bohemia region was minimal, and the city authorities were mostly interested in technocratic governance. The development of 'city-regions' – metropolitan areas which can transcend administrative-territorial borders, and can promote both local interests and national goals in global competition – is still a challenge for Eurasia and East European region.

32.2.2 The Soviet Union

Soviet Russia adopted a different solution to the 'national question.' Theoretical discussions as well as practical challenges to the Bolshevik leadership led the Soviets to conclude that the emergence of nations was an inevitable stage of modernization, and that incorporation of local nationalisms into the state structure could accomplish several goals: it would depoliticize nationalism and shift the focus to inter-class struggle, as well as contain the Russian nationalism – arguably the largest threat to the state unity (Martin 2001).

Therefore, the Soviet Union was organized as a federation of national territories with different degrees of autonomy and sovereignty.[4] Local elites were often recruited from the titular nationalities usually constituting the majority in their ethnoterritorial unit, and their identities, languages and cultures were promoted. The borders of the 'national' units were defined based on ethnic, economic and administrative considerations, and state mediation between conflicting ethnic groups was often required (Hirsch 2005). The authorities used ethnographic knowledge (taking into account self-reported nationality as well as linguistic and cultural criteria) along with other considerations to define the set of nationalities residing in USSR and decide which of them are worthy of separate administrative units.

To be sure, although the national autonomy was real, the Soviet state was highly centralized, controlled by the Communist Party, and often brutally repressive, especially with regard to nationalities whose loyalty was questioned by the authorities. In addition, since the late 1920s, there had been some important setbacks to the initial goals: some local nationalist tendencies grew too strong and had to be vilified, Russians increasingly became established as the dominant national group, and Russian language became the lingua franca. Yet, unlike every other constituent republic in the USSR, the Russian Federation within the Soviet Union was not supposed to be a 'Russian' national territory (Martin 2001).

Whether one thinks of the Soviet policy toward ethnic minorities as a type of 'affirmative action' targeting previously disadvantaged nationalities which gradually gained primordial overtones (Martin 2001) or a 'state-sponsored evolutionism' which developed nationalities only to dissolve them later in a new Soviet community (Hirsch 2005), administrative boundaries between ethnically and nationally based units, as well as individual nationalities recorded in passports (Brubaker 1996), remained in place and greatly nurtured territorial-based national identities, many of which have outlived the Soviet Union.

32.2.3   Post-Communist Sovereignty Movements

The Soviet Union was a multi-layered system of territorial units that included both ethnically defined units and non-ethnically defined units, sometimes nested within each other, for example, an ethnic republic, with a non-ethnic region in it, and an ethnic unit within that one. Since the late 1980s, claims for greater sovereignty started to appear at all levels of the USSR ethnoterritorial hierarchy, and this process continued in most of the new states, which inherited (and updated) the Soviet administrative structure.

One of the reasons for the 'parade of sovereignties' in post-communist states was that the end of the USSR and the end of the Cold War was such a shock that regional elites as well as populations at every level throughout the territory of Eurasia began to question their territorial unit's place in the world, in the system of states, as well as in federal contexts. Russia, to take one case, immediately faced the question of rights and levels of sovereignty of its 89 territorial units, and this questioning of sovereignty was not restricted only to non-Russian, ethnic units, but sparked regionalism even among Russian regions such as in the erstwhile movement for Urals republic.

There is a lot of scholarly work which sought to explain variation in the degree and timing of sovereignty demands in the USSR and Russia. Space constraints prevent a full discussion here, but the key arguments focused on nationalism (Beissinger 2002) and debate over the role of the economy in regional sovereignty movements. Some argued that material demands drove separatism, with the wealthier regions being most active (Hale 2000). Others argued that material concerns were subject to conflicting interpretations (Herrera 2004) and therefore that regional identities and material conditions interacted to produce demands for greater sovereignty (Giuliano 2006).[5]

In the context of our discussion of regional conceptualizations and concomitant attempts to institutionalize those concepts, one strand of the sub-national USSR/Russia sovereignty literature stands out, which is the focus on sub-national institutions as the driver of nationalist mobilization. Roeder (2007) observed that despite great variation in economic, identity, history, and security issues, the one variable that explains which regions became states following the end of the USSR and Yugoslavia is the status as a republic-level (highest sub-national level) region in the former state. Thus, although the post-socialist countries in general experienced a rise of sovereignty and autonomy movements at both the national and sub-national level, the relative positions on the sovereignty continuum were very much conditioned by the Soviet-era institutional structure.

Aside from the new states created out of the highest level sub-national units from the USSR, Yugoslavia, and Czechoslovakia, the majority of other regional sovereignty movements in Eurasia died out by the late 1990s, which corresponded to a settling in of statehood, borders, and federalism in most Eurasian states. A few cases, however, turned violent, for example, Nagorno-Karabakh in Azerbaijan; Abkhasia and South Ossetia in Georgia; Chechnya in Russia, and the civil wars in Tajikistan and Yugoslavia. Much of the violence however, also came to an end by the early 2000s, although some conflicts continued to spark occasionally or are 'frozen' as we discuss below.

32.2.4   Frozen Conflicts

A portion of Eurasian space is still contested or occupied by unrecognized territorial entities, giving birth to a new term in international relations – a 'frozen conflict.' In the foreign policy lexicon, frozen conflicts are territorial disputes where active military confrontation has stopped, but contestation continues, and different interpretations of sovereignty over a territory remain. Initially, it was applied to the breakaway territories in the former Soviet Union: Transnistria (a part of the former Moldovan Soviet Socialist Republic), Nagorny Karabakh, Abkhazia and South Ossetia. These conflicts are similar in their origin – they were projects of ethnic minority elites in the (former) Soviet republics – and exhibit similar patterns: short-term high-intensity conflict was replaced by low-intensity conflict over the longer term, the breakaway territories were sponsored by Russia, and are viewed as buffer zones by Russia.

Despite problems with this term (Broers 2015), frozen conflict remains a popular label for a state where there is no war, but also no peace. Occurring later, the Kosovo breakaway state was also referred to as a frozen conflict, and the recent war in the Eastern Ukraine has led to the emergence of two separatist enclaves, the Donetsk People's Republic and the Luhansk People's Republic, which is widely viewed as the beginning of another frozen conflict.

In the post-Soviet space, 'frozen conflicts' encompass a dual sovereignty issue: first, the sovereignty of the territory in question, and second, the sovereignty of the larger nations from which these states broke away, and the degree of sovereign external control, principally by Russia. The four breakaway states of the former USSR have established their own 'intergovernmental' organization, the so-called Commonwealth of Unrecognized States. This is not an integration project, but rather a symbol that emphasizes stability and 'frozenness' of these conflicts. This 'sustainable instability' gives Russia additional leverage over the countries of the region, and as the Donbas war has shown, serves as a warning to those nations who might go too far in asserting their own sovereignty.

32.3   CONCLUSION

Regionalism in the post-Soviet Eurasia and Eastern Europe has been marked by a range of sovereignty claims, movements and settlements, as well as by a wide array of institutions corresponding to different levels of sovereignty and administration. The imagined, or 'moral,' geographies that divide space along 'civilizational' lines (Europe versus Asia, West versus East, civilization versus barbarianism, and so on) have been prominent in shaping supra-national integration (or lack thereof) in Eurasia. While there are some real economic, political, and cultural differences across the region, the delineation of civilizational boundaries has led in some cases to what Bakić-Hayden called typical 'essentialist fallacies' and a proliferation of 'nesting orientalisms' – each nation's desire to portray itself as the Easternmost bulwark of Western or European civilization (Bakić-Hayden 1995). That said, the European idea turned out to be the most potent in terms of organization and identity. The European Union has become the most solid and cohesive supra-national institution encompassing post-communist countries, although the tension between the newly reinforced (or acquired) national sovereignty of post-communist states and the need to subordinate themselves to a new supra-national entity was also evident. The development of Eurasian supranational institutions remains a work in progress.

At the sub-national level, the dissolution of the Eastern bloc and the Soviet Union resulted in an initial avalanche of sovereignty movements and the increase in sovereignty of the existing sub-national units. While many of these have subsided, as the nations and territorial units converged on shared conceptualizations of space and rights, Eurasia has also contributed the concept of the frozen conflict for which there is no easy reconciliation of sovereignty and institutions on the horizon.

32.4   NOTES

1. This conceptualization may be one reason why Eurasian ideas did not take root, for example, in the Baltics or in China: the Baltic states were eager to be associated with Europe, while Chinese, as one author suggests, have never based their existence and historical role on their relation to Europe (Chan 2016).
2. See Shirikov et al. (2018) for an inductive analysis of what constitutes the Eurasian region. Our analysis shows that one can get several distinct partitions of 'Eurasian' countries into clusters depending on which political and socioeconomic criteria are chosen for their categorization. These clusters are also fluid over time, which makes customary Europe–Asia or East–West divisions even more problematic, revealing more complicated patterns than typically assumed.
3. Another important institutional development in Central Europe discussed by Sagan and Lee was the imposition of the Classification of Territorial Units for Statistics (NUTS) in European Union countries. Because economic aid from the EU Structural Funds was based on it, member countries had strong incentives to implement it. Still, the process of regional reconfiguration did not come easily. In some cases, it led to the

'disruption of local geographies' which created units lacking legitimacy and rooted historical traditions, for example in Hungary.
4. Hale (2000) lists 53 ethnically designated units within the Soviet Union alone.
5. Another argument focused on social institutions such as pre-communist literacy rates which might have affected the intensity of local nationalist feelings (Darden and Grzymala-Busse 2006).

32.5   REFERENCES

Akturk, S. (2015), 'The fourth style of politics: Eurasianism as a pro-Russian rethinking of Turkey's geopolitical identity', *Turkish Studies*, **16** (1), 54–79.
Azizov, U. (2011), 'Interpretation of the concept of Central Asia in foreign policy texts of Japan: theory and practice', *Journal of International and Advanced Japanese Studies*, **3** (1), 51–60.
Bakić-Hayden, M. (1995), 'Nesting orientalisms: the case of former Yugoslavia', *Slavic Review*, **54** (4), 917–931.
Beissinger, M.R. (2002), *Nationalist Mobilization and the Collapse of the Soviet State*, Cambridge: Cambridge University Press.
Bideleux, R. and I. Jeffries (2007), *A History of Eastern Europe: Crisis and Change*, New York: Routledge.
Broers, L. (2015), 'From "frozen conflict" to enduring rivalry: reassessing the Nagorny Karabakh conflict', *Nationalities Papers*, **43** (4), 556–576.
Brubaker, R. (1996), *Nationalism Reframed: Nationhood and the National Question in the New Europe*, Cambridge: Cambridge University Press.
Cassedy, S. (2005), 'Regions and regionalism, Eastern Europe', in *New Dictionary of the History of Ideas, vol. 5*, New York: Charles Scribner's Sons, pp. 2032–2035.
Chan, Y. (2016), 'The greater game: Qing China in Central Eurasia', *History Compass*, **14** (6), 264–274.
Christian, D. (1994), 'Inner Eurasia as a unit of world history', *Journal of World History*, **5** (2), 173–211.
Coppieters, B. (ed.) (1996), *Contested Borders in the Caucasus*, Brussels: VUB Press.
Cummings, S.M. (2012), *Understanding Central Asia: Politics and Contested Transformations*, New York: Routledge.
Darden, K. and A. Grzymala-Busse (2006), 'The great divide: literacy, nationalism, and the communist collapse', *World Politics*, **59** (1), 83–115.
Erşen, E. (2013), 'The evolution of 'Eurasia' as a geopolitical concept in post-Cold War Turkey', *Geopolitics*, **18** (1), 24–44.
Fuller, G.E. (1990), 'The emergence of Central Asia', *Foreign Policy*, **78**, 49–67.
Gellner, E. (1983), *Nations and Nationalism*, Oxford: Blackwell.
Giuliano, E. (2006), 'Secessionism from the bottom up: democratization, nationalism, and local accountability in the Russian transition', *World Politics*, **58** (2), 276–310.
Gleason, A. (2010), 'Eurasia: what is it? Is it?', *Journal of Eurasian Studies*, **1** (1), 26–32.
Hagen, J. (2003), 'Redrawing the imagined map of Europe: the rise and fall of the "Center"', *Political Geography*, **22** (5), 489–517.
Hale, H.E. (2000), 'The parade of sovereignties: testing theories of secession in the Soviet Setting', *British Journal of Political Science*, **30** (1), 31–56.
Hann, C. (2014), 'Imperative Eurasia', *Anthropology Today*, **30** (4), 1–2.
Hann, C. (2016), 'A concept of Eurasia', *Current Anthropology*, **57** (1), 1–27.
Heffernan, M. (1998), *The Meaning of Europe: Geography and Geopolitics*, London: Arnold.
Herrera, Y.M. (2004), *Imagined Economies: The Sources of Russian Regionalism*, Cambridge: Cambridge University Press.
Herrschel, T. and P. Newman (2005), 'Global competition and city regional governance in Europe', in I. Sagan and H. Halkier (eds), *Regionalism Contested: Institution, Society and Governance*, Aldershot: Ashgate Publishing, pp. 203–222.
Herrschel, T. (2011), *Borders in Post-socialist Europe: Territory, Scale, Society*, Farnham: Ashgate Publishing.
Hirsch, F. (2005), *Empire of Nations: Ethnographic Knowledge and the Making of the Soviet Union*, Ithaca, NY: Cornell University Press.
Hobsbawm, E. (1990), *Nations and Nationalism since 1780: Programme, Myth, Reality*, Cambridge: Cambridge University Press.
Kotkin, S. (2007), 'Mongol Commonwealth? Exchange and governance across the post-Mongol space', *Kritika: Explorations in Russian and Eurasian History*, **8** (3), 487–531.
Kuus, M. (2004), 'Europe's eastern expansion and the reinscription of otherness in East-Central Europe', *Progress in Human Geography*, **28** (4), 472–489.

Laruelle, M. (2008), *Russian Eurasianism, An Ideology of Empire*, Baltimore, MD: Johns Hopkins University Press.

Laruelle, M. (2011), 'Foreign policy and myth-making: great game, heartland, and silk roads', in M. Laruelle and S. Peyrouse (eds), *Mapping Central Asia: Indian Perceptions and Strategies*, Farnham: Ashgate, pp. 7–20.

Laruelle, M. (2015), 'Eurasia, Eurasianism, Eurasian union: terminological gaps and overlaps', *PONARS Policy Memo #366*.

Martin, T.D. (2001), *The Affirmative Action Empire: Nations and Nationalism in the Soviet Union, 1923–1939*, Ithaca, NY: Cornell University Press.

Mazover, M. (1998), *Dark Continent: Europe's Twentieth Century*, London: Penguin Books.

Moisio, S. (2007), 'Redrawing the map of Europe: spatial formation of the EU's eastern dimension', *Geography Compass*, **1** (1), 82–102.

Mostafa, G. (2013), 'The concept of "Eurasia": Kazakhstan's Eurasian policy and its implications', *Journal of Eurasian Studies*, **4** (2), 160–170.

Neumann, I.B. (1999), *Uses of the Other: 'The East' in European Identity Formation*, Manchester: Manchester University Press.

Papava, V. (2013), 'The Eurasianism of Russian anti-Westernism and the concept of "Central Caucaso-Asia"', *Russian Politics & Law*, **51** (6), 45–86.

Rahul, R. (1997), *Central Asia: An Outline History*, New Delhi: Concept Publishing.

Roeder, P.G. (2007), *Where Nation-States Come From: Institutional Change in the Age of Nationalism*, Princeton, NJ: Princeton University Press.

Rupnik, J. (1994), 'Europe's new frontiers: remapping Europe', *Daedalus*, **123** (3), 91–114.

Sagan, I. and R. Lee (2005), 'Spatialities of regional transformation in Central Europe and the administrative spaces of the EU', in I. Sagan and H. Halkier (eds), *Regionalism Contested: Institution, Society and Governance*, Aldershot: Ashgate Publishing, pp. 163–176.

Sengupta, A. (2002), *Frontiers Into Borders: The Transformation of Identities in Central Asia*, Delhi: Hope India Publications.

Sengupta, A. (2014), *Myth and Rhetoric of the Turkish Model: Exploring Developmental Alternatives*, New Delhi: Springer.

Shirikov, A., D. Kofanov and Y.M. Herrera (2018), 'What is the region? Making sense of Russia, the former Soviet Union, Eastern Europe, and Eurasia', *unpublished manuscript*.

Starr, S.F. (2008), 'In defense of Greater Central Asia', *Politique Étrangère*, **3**.

Tsutsiev, A. (2014), *Atlas of the Ethno-Political History of the Caucasus*, New Haven, CT: Yale University Press.

Vinokurov, E. and A. Libman (2012), 'Eurasia and Eurasian integration: beyond the post-Soviet Borders', *EDB Eurasian Integration Yearbook*.

Wolff, L. (1994), *Inventing Eastern Europe: the Map of Civilization on the Mind of the Enlightenment*, Stanford, CA: Stanford University Press.

Zeigler, D.J. (2002), 'Post-communist Eastern Europe and the cartography of independence', *Political Geography*, **21** (5), 671–686.

33. Chinese regionalism

Michael Dunford and Weidong Liu

33.1 CHINESE REGIONALISM

In a world divided into a series of nation-states the concept of regionalism has several meanings. At a national scale regionalism is associated with the identification of sub-national economic, political and cultural variation (social heterogeneity) and of the normative economic, political and/or cultural interests of sub-national entities. In some cases analyses of regionalism in this sense emphasize the importance of endogenous change, although in practice change is always a result of the interaction of external and internal factors. The identification of regional interests is also sometimes used to advocate decentralization, greater autonomy and even secession and independence. Centralists, conversely, see expressions of regional interests as particularistic, often associated with narrow sections of local societies, and obstacles to co-ordinated development and modernization. In cases where strong controversies arise, regionalism can moreover involve crises in the relations between the state and local societies (Dulong 1978). At an international scale regionalism is also an expression of shared identities and interests in this case between nations and is often associated with the creation of bilateral or multilateral institutions and moves in the direction of closer economic and political integration/co-operation. A consideration of Chinese regionalism involves these two dimensions.

33.2 CHINA'S SYSTEM OF NATIONAL AND TERRITORIAL GOVERNANCE

China is a continental-sized civilization state (Dynon 2014) with some 5,000 years of largely uninterrupted historical evolution, differing significantly from the Westphalian nation-state and the modern representative state. As a result of a recent wave of anti-imperialist struggle, state construction, late industrialization and cultural regeneration, a distinctive contemporary Chinese social model and Chinese path to economic and political modernization have emerged and continue to evolve. Economically China has developed a socialist market economy in which the state owns significant economic assets. Politically China is developing 'an effective system of government that fits the country's historical [and geographical] context and social conditions . . . [and] adequately addresses the functional requirements of voice and representation, accountability, conflict resolution, social integration, consensus building and goal attainment' (Chu 2013, p. 2).

Contemporary China is formally a multi-party state under the leadership of the Communist party of China (CPC) although the CPC is dominant. The system itself has been characterized in a number of ways. For Bell (2015) the Chinese political system is an imperfect system of 'vertical democratic meritocracy' combining grassroots electoral democracy, experimentation in the middle and meritocracy at the top, to which should be added elite consultation. This model reflects not just China's socialist heritage but also Confucius' advocacy of an orderly hierarchical society. In this system political legitimacy depends in part on traditional cultural concepts including benevolence, meritocracy and responsiveness to and responsibility for people's well-being (minben), as well as on perceived characteristics of the institutional system including adaptation, innovation, specialization, meritocracy and participation (Chu 2013).

As a civilization state the government has a twofold goal of (1) modernizing China's traditional and socialist heritage and (2) civilizing China's modernization, so as to offer a different Chinese path to modernity. Together these goals serve the material, spiritual and political functions of 'civilization maintenance' and 'power maintenance'. Material progress is an essential component of this dual strategy and contrives to make the Chinese state at times developmental and entrepreneurial.

The structure of the Chinese state gives the central government considerable influence over sub-national governments' powers to implement reforms and execute spatial governance, while also giving sub-national levels considerable scope to exercise economic development initiatives. The CPC is China's ruling party, but is not itself the Chinese government. The leading legislative body is the National People's Congress, and the main executive body is the State Council. All levels of government and all administration departments do however have a Party Committee as do many institutions and enterprises, with leadership groups at each level accepting the leadership of higher levels. In every administrative unit, the party secretary is 'number one'. The chief executive is 'second in command' and must discuss major questions with the department's party committee (Liu 2015). The great majority of senior officials are CPC members, and the Organization Department of the CPC operates a strict hierarchical cadre responsibility system to evaluate and appoint officials that is similar to the traditional Mandarin system. The CPC therefore enjoys powerful top-down strategic decision-making influence and power. This power is the main foundation of China's strong state system.

For most of its history China was a centralized state. The vertical administrative system of the new China resembles the old with five de facto tiers of sub-national government each made up of separate horizontal entities (kuai- kuai or horizontal blocks): (1) provincial (zhíxiáshì – Municipalities directly under the central government, shěng – Provinces, zìzhìqū – Autonomous regions and tèbié xíngzhèngqū – Special Administrative areas); (2) prefectural (Prefectures, Prefecture-level cities, Autonomous prefectures, Districts in a Municipality, and Leagues in Inner Mongolia); (3) county (Counties, Autonomous counties, County-level cities, Districts of a Prefecture-level city and Banners in Inner Mongolia); (4) township (Townships, Ethnic townships and Towns); and (5) village (administrative villages). In addition, special arrangements relate to cities that are capitals of provinces or Autonomous regions and Sub-provincial cities.

At the provincial level there are four Municipalities directly under the central government (Beijing, Chongqing, Shanghai and Tianjin), 22 Provinces, 5 Autonomous regions and 2 Special Administrative areas (Hong Kong and Macau reflecting the One China-Two Systems principle (Figure 33.1 which also records provincial Gross Domestic Product per capita in 2015). In addition, Taiwan is claimed as a Province of China, potentially affording a one-nation-three systems model. These entities are then sub-divided into different numbers of sub-tiers. The system is relatively complicated. In Municipalities and Hainan, for example, counties are second-tier divisions.

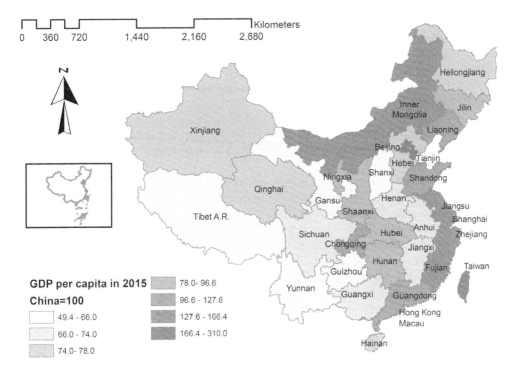

Kilometers, scale: 0 360 720 1,440 2,160 2,880

GDP per capita in 2015
China=100

49.4 - 66.0	78.0- 96.6
66.0 - 74.0	96.6 - 127.6
74.0- 78.0	127.6 - 166.4
	166.4 - 310.0

Source: Elaborated from NBS (2017).

Figure 33.1 China's provincial-level administrative divisions and GDP per head in 2015

Alongside normal administrative entities, special administrative units, such as Special Economic Zones (SEZs), Economic and Technological Development Zones (ETDZ), High-technology Development Zones (HTDZ), and state-level New Areas/New Districts were established and granted preferential policies and special privileges to carry out economic policy experiments as part of China's 'experimentalist' mode of governance. After fine-tuning and adjustment, measures that proved effective are implemented nation-wide. At first these zones were administered by special government agencies. More recently however they have been transformed from industrial zones to 'new urban' areas.

China's administrative arrangements grant different degrees of power and autonomy to different levels of government with considerable power reposing at the provincial level and in the four directly controlled municipalities that have provincial status. Administrative rank plays a very important role. Administrative rank also applies to major public institutions and State Owned Companies, and can cause problems as when large companies located in a city are managed by individuals with a higher administrative level than top local government officials.

Administrative status/grade relates not just to positions in the hierarchy but to the positions of the individuals occupying these different positions, which are themselves determined via a cadre responsibility system used to evaluate/appoint officials (similar to the traditional Mandarin system). Individuals recruited into civil service, state-owned enterprise (SOE) and social organization career tracks start at the lowest level (ke yuan).

After evaluation, the CPC Central Committee Organization Department can promote them up through six increasingly senior ranks (kē yuan, fù kē jí, kē jí, fù chù jí, chù jí, fù tīng jí, tīng jú jí, fù shěng jí, shěng bù jí, fù guó jí, guó jiā jí). Guó jiā serve as national leaders. Fù chù and chù serve as high-level officials. In 2012, there were 900,000 fù kē and kē, 600,000 fù chù and chù, and just 40,000 fù tīng and tīng jú. After the several decades required to reach the jú level, a few can reach provincial ministerial level positions, with yet fewer reaching the Central Committee and national leadership (Li 2013). Although a range of performance indicators are used, economic growth has played a predominant role in the cadre evaluation system and has led to intense competition to generate high GDP growth rates.

At the same time sub-national government is subject to supervision and inspection by the Central Commission for Discipline Inspection and the Ministry of Supervision and more specifically by their corresponding local discipline inspection and supervision departments. Government departments are also organized vertically ('tiao-tiao' or strips) so that every administrative tier has its own department that is subordinate to the department in the next tier up.

As of 2008, there were 27 State Council departments. Of these, the ones relating to spatial governance included the National Development and Reform Commission (NDRC), especially its Departments of Regional Economy, Western Development and Northeastern Region Revitalization, and the Ministries of Finance, Land and Resources, Housing and Urban Rural Development (MOHURD), Environmental Protection, Agriculture, Industry and Information Technology, Commerce, Water Resources, and Transport. These ministries all have their own vertical management systems, such that each administrative tier has its own subordinate department at the next level down, forming a vertical management chain. To carry out their work, these departments often have many operational units. These chains usually form interest groups.

This system gives rise to relatively serious block-strip co-ordination problems. The strips prioritize their own vertical arrangements and are reluctant to co-operate with other departments. The blocks are reluctant to co-operate with adjacent areas for reasons relating to the tax and the cadre evaluation systems, creating what is called an economy of feudal dukes and princes under an emperor (zhū hóu jīng ji), local protectionism and intense inter-area competition.

Although local government accepts national leadership and is subject to centrally controlled monitoring and supervision, the central government has at various times relaxed its control over local governments in an effort to promote decentralization and local initiative. With reform and opening-up, the main changes entailed: (1) granting greater autonomy to local governments in the areas of planning, administration, local and foreign investments, credit access, exchange control and foreign trade; (2) granting greater autonomy to enterprises by progressively reducing the level of central planning control; and (3) fiscal reform ending the centralized revenue and expenditure system in which all tax revenue was handed to the central government which then allocated funds to lower levels of government as it saw fit (Oi 1992).

In granting local government some tax authority, the central government allowed 'eating in separate kitchens' by providing local governments with the financial resources to carry out localized initiatives. Most public service responsibilities were also decentralized, and local government came to account for an increasing share of government expenditure

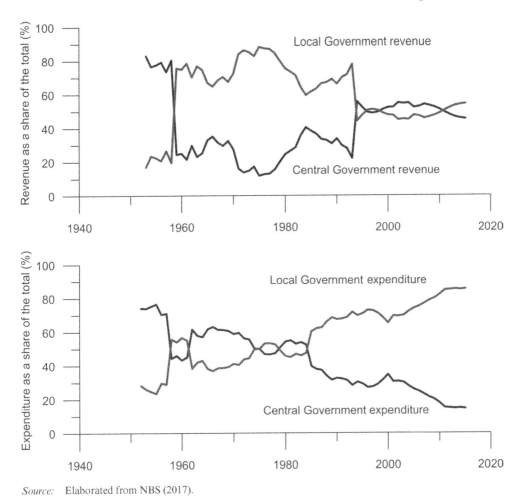

Source: Elaborated from NBS (2017).

Figure 33.2 National and local government revenue and expenditure, 1952–2015

reaching 85 per cent in recent years (Figure 33.2). As a result, sub-national government became responsible for local economic and social progress, and the performance, promotion and demotion of cadres was increasingly evaluated in these terms.

After the 1994 fiscal reform however local government directly received only about one-half of government revenue (Figure 33.2 and Dunford 2015). As the central government spends less than it receives, it makes fiscal transfers (Figure 33.3), with particularly high per capita net transfers to Tibet, Qinghai, Ning Xia and Xin Jiang. Government resources per capita nonetheless vary significantly with the highest values for revenue-rich Beijing, Shanghai and Tianjin and for the places with high net per capita transfers. As local government revenue falls short of its requirements, it is driven in the direction of seeking new sources of revenue particularly from the development of land for urban use: in 2013 sales of rights to state-owned land accounted for 61 per cent of the revenue for urban infrastructure maintenance and construction (Figure 33.4). Capital investment was

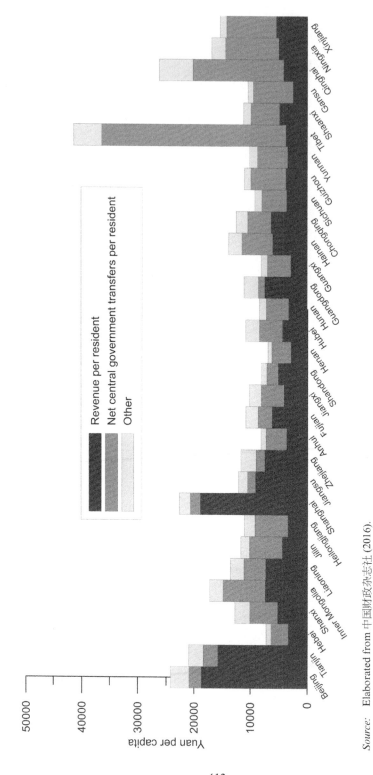

Source: Elaborated from 中国财政杂志社 (2016).

Figure 33.3 *Provincial government revenue and central-provincial fiscal transfers per resident, 2014*

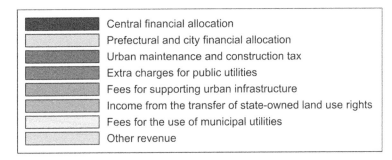

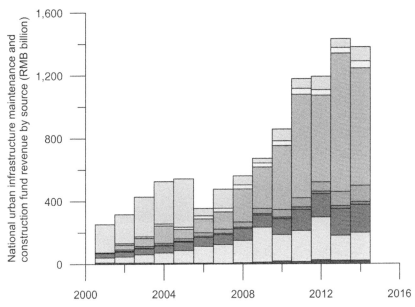

Source: Elaborated from NBS, City Construction Statistics Yearbook, various years.

Figure 33.4   *National revenue for the maintenance and construction of urban*
          infrastructure, 2006–14

mainly financed through the local government budget, domestic loans and self-raised
funds from local government commercial activities (Figure 33.5).

   In general, local governments can create new spatial governance policies through two
main channels. First, they can make use of existing powers to initiate regional economic
development. The suite of policies includes: (1) corporate tax relief/tax holidays/tax
rebates/production subsidies for companies locating in China's western provinces, in
various Tax-free Zones and in Developmental Zones and whose generosity relates to their
significance; (2) industrial land that is either free or offered in exchange for shareholder
equity; (3) the preparation of land, provision of infrastructure and supply of public services through programmes such as the so-called 'five (or seven) connections and one level-
ling', and the provision of affordable accommodation for workers, transport, inexpensive
utilities and energy; (4) the recruitment of a skilled but low-wage labour force possibly

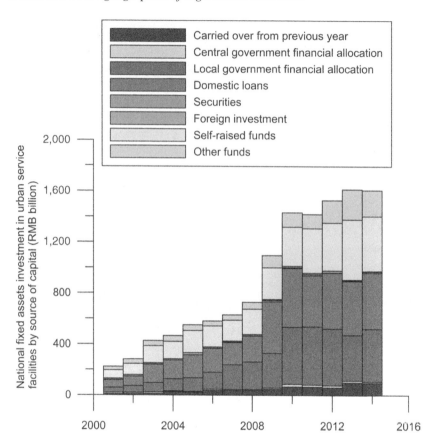

Source: Elaborated from NBS, *City Construction Statistics Yearbook*, various years.

Figure 33.5   National fixed assets investment in urban service facilities by source of capital, 2006–14

through relaxation of household registration policies to draw in workers from outside of the administrative area, assistance with the recruitment of skilled labour and continuous skills upgrading; and government subsidies to reduce production and logistic costs perhaps including cash subsidies. These powers vary however with administrative rank: the higher an area's administrative rank, the greater its powers and political resources, while in certain circumstances hierarchical dependencies allow higher ranked authorities to retain resources or to drain resources from lower ranked administrative entities.

Second, local governments quite often petition the higher levels of government for greater powers and for the establishment of special zones. Governments may, for example, request designation as a national-level ETDZs (of which there are 219 in China) or HTDZs (145 in number), Bonded Areas (15), Border Economic Cooperative Zone (16), Export Processing Zone (63) or Free Trade Zones, (4) which also have greater jurisdictional powers. Shenzhen, Shanghai Pudong, Tianjin Binhai, Chongqing Liangjiang and sixteen other areas have, for example, been designated as state-level New Areas with the aim of attracting foreign investment, earning foreign currency, acquiring technology and management expertise from foreign partners, opening up commercial channels to markets for Chinese produced goods and services, and diffusing economic development. Some local governments have approved provincial-level Development Zones. These designated zones enjoy special rights/preferential treatment in areas such as taxation, household registration, special capital grants and greater governance autonomy in the shape of a decentralization of decision making and greater regional discretion.

In all of these cases however rights and outcomes depend significantly on administrative rank and reflect the ability of key actors to negotiate agreements through their representation on powerful central policy forums and the impact of networks of personal allegiance that can accelerate or slow down specific proposals. Nonetheless at each level the ability of officials to adapt to circumstances, grasp opportunities and innovate also plays a significant role.

Governance flexibility has sometimes produced outstanding economic and social results. These results serve as a stick and a carrot: the economic results of local government programmes are a strong indicator of its capabilities which in turn determine the career path for the government officials concerned; and the possibilities for local initiative act as an incentive for local governments to compete vigorously for a share of central government largesse and for inward investment. These sticks and carrots result in significant power struggles among governments seeking to obtain favourable economic powers, although these powers depend to a significant extent on administrative rank. As a result, higher levels of government are usually much more likely to be selected as pilot regions for various economic programmes. For instance, more special zones were established in the four directly controlled municipalities than in other provinces, while provincial capitals have had more success than other cities.

The relationships between the central and local government are often more complicated than meets the eye. In notable cases, the central government deliberately handed-down infrastructure assignments to local governments without providing sufficient finance and resources to complete them. To seek to fulfil obligations to the central government, local government had to choose between subsidizing these projects and facing a negative assessment by central government in cases where projects were only partially or poorly executed.

'Superior has the policy, inferior has the countermeasure' is a common public policy phenomenon, with local governments sometimes working on the margins of the law to overcome financial constraints. An example involves the way sub-national governments have circumvented the lengthy approval process for land development: the 1986 Land Management Law stipulates that approval is required from the County Land Bureau if a land development involves more than 3 mu (0.2 hectares) of agricultural land or more than 10 mu (2/3 hectare) of non-agricultural land; rural governments responded by separating larger parcels into several smaller ones in order to avoid these lengthy approval processes (Gao et al. 2014).

33.3   CHINA'S TERRITORIAL DEVELOPMENT

In 1949 the newly established People's Republic of China was the poorest country in the world with a GDP of US $439 per head compared with US$619 in India and US$852 in Africa (Maddison 2001, p. 264). In 1952–77 GDP grew at 5.9 per cent per year on average

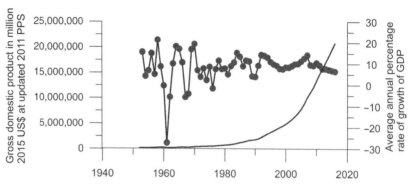

Source: Elaborated from The Conference Board (2015, TCB Original, Official).

Figure 33.6   Chinese economic growth, 1952–2015

(Figure 33.6). The economy grew on average at 10 per cent per year from 1978 to 2007, 9.7 per cent in the aftermath of the western financial crisis from 2008 to 2011 and at slower 'new normal' growth rates of 7.2 per cent from 2012 to 2015 (Figure 33.6). As a result, mainland China became an upper-middle income country and, at Purchasing Power Standards, the world's largest economy.

Real per capita disposable income increased rapidly in all parts of China and for virtually all sections of the population but at different speeds. These relative speeds of growth varied altering the geographical and social distribution of income. Overall growth was fastest: (1) in areas on the east coast rather than in the centre, northeast and west creating wide macro-territorial inequalities (Figure 33.7); (2) in some provinces rather than others resulting in an overall increase in inter-provincial inequalities (Figure 33.8); (3) in urban areas rather than rural areas increasing overall rural–urban inequalities (Figure 33.8); and (4) for some sections of the population rather than others increasing especially in recent years social inequality. In the recent past these disparities have started to diminish.

Figure 33.9 plots GDP per head in 2013 at a prefectural level. At this scale, it is clear that there is a concentration of economic development in a number of growth poles. Most of these growth poles are in eastern China especially in the Bohai Bay, Yangtze River Delta and the Pearl River Delta areas. Within many eastern provinces, however, there is a core-periphery structure. In the central and western interior, the provincial capitals have relatively high scores (Hebei, Shanxi, Henan, Hubei, Hunan, Jiangxi, Sichuan and Yunnan). The highest scores are for areas with high GDP per head due to the presence of resource extraction and resource-dependent industries (Ordos and Alxa League in Inner Mongolia stood at 435.9 per cent and 428.6 per cent of the national average) while the lowest was for Hetian in Xin Jiang (16.7 per cent).

In 1952–77 China introduced land reform, established a planned economy and embarked on industrial development located mainly in inland areas near natural resources especially in the northeast of the country (including coastal Liaoning). The 1958–62 Great Leap Forward designed to mobilize China's abundant labour to accelerate industrialization yet coincided with three years of natural disasters and famine (1959–62). In 1960 the Sino–Soviet split came into the open, and in the early 1960s US involvement in Vietnam

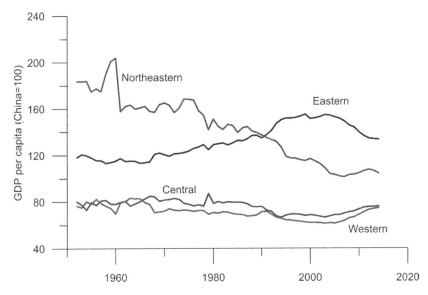

Source: Elaborated from NBS (2017).

Figure 33.7   *Comparative development of four main territorial divisions*

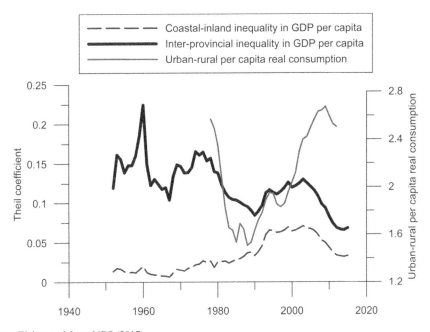

Source: Elaborated from NBS (2017).

Figure 33.8   *Inter-provincial and rural–urban disparities in China, 1952–2015*

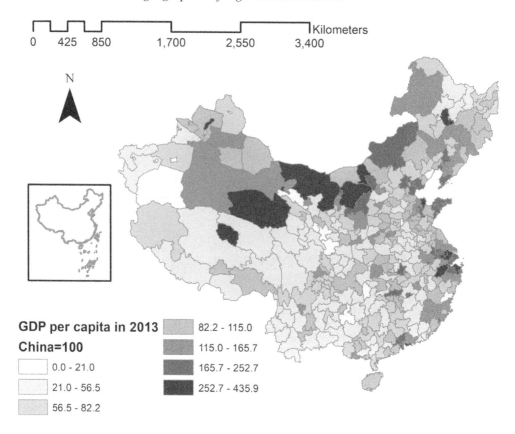

Source: Elaborated from NBS, various years.

Figure 33.9   Prefectural GDP per capita in 2013, China = 100

intensified. In the Third and Fourth Five Year Plan (FYP) periods China responded with an extensive Third Front construction programme relocating industry in central and western areas distant from potential US and Soviet incursions. The Cultural Revolution (1966–76) saw significant decentralization and emphasis on regional autonomy and self-reliance. In the Fifth FYP period (1976–80) the international situation improved and coastal development increased. In 1950–82 life expectancy rose from 42.2 for men and 45.6 years for women to 66.4 and 69.4 respectively. In 1952–78 the population increased from 552 million to 1,017 million. The share of the population that was illiterate declined from 80 per cent to 16.4 per cent. In the 1970s China therefore had a huge, youthful and educated population of which 80 per cent was rural. China was also a very egalitarian country although there was a rural–urban divide and a significant gap in GDP per head between the northeast and the rest of China (Figure 33.7).

In 1978 China embarked on a new course of reform and opening up to accelerate economic growth. In the first phase a Family Responsibility system in agriculture and the establishment of Township and Village Enterprises initially reduced the rural–urban divide (Figure 33.8). Opening-up however involved a prioritization of coastal development: Special economic zones, open cities and open economic zones established in the coastal areas formed a 0.3 million km² open coastal belt with 0.2 billion inhabitants, whose mission was specified in 1987 as the development of export industries with the aid of preferential financial, tax, credit and investment policies. The relatively rapid growth of coastal areas widened regional disparities and the urban–rural divide and saw the movement of migrant workers from rural areas to China's larger cities concentrated mainly on the east coast (Figure 33.8). At the time of the 2010 Census there were 260 million migrant workers. Of the cross-provincial flows of labour, some 90 per cent originated from central and western China.

In this context the Ninth National Plan (1996–2000) saw an early change in regional policies with the decision to adhere to co-ordinated regional economic development and gradually reduce regional development disparities. A series of policies to accelerate the development of the central and western regions including priority scheduling of resource development and infrastructure construction projects, more favourable prices for natural resource products and a normalized central fiscal transfer system were however not sufficient to prevent the continuing increase in regional disparities (Figure 33.8). In the late 1990s new measures were therefore prepared. In late 1999, the State Council launched the Western Development Strategy (xī bù dà kāi fā). These measures saw growth accelerate, although short-term efforts are far from adequate in the face of the development problems of the west which include the 'sān nóng' problems of agriculture, farmers and villages, environmental degradation as well as healthcare and education systems which still fall well behind those available in the eastern areas of China.

In 2003 the Revitalization of the Old Northeast Industrial Bases strategy (dōngběi lǎo gōngyè jīdì zhènxīng) was adopted. In the First Five-Year Plan (1953–57) northeast China received 58 out of 156 national production projects, and was subsequently a focus of further industrial development. The subsequent transition from a planned to a market economy and changes in the relative importance of different industrial sectors left northeast China with an industrial structure dominated by so-called rust-belt industries, resource-based cities whose natural resources were depleted, obsolete production equipment and outdated technologies and a predominance of struggling State Owned Enterprises (SOEs). These difficulties were associated with problems of dereliction and regeneration on the one hand and social tensions relating to social security and re-employment on the other.

A third element of the co-ordinated development strategy framework comprises policies for 'uplifting central China' (zhōng bù juéqǐ) adopted in 2004. The aim was to stop the tendency for Central China to 'sink' in a situation in which economic growth is led by coastal areas and the development of the northeast and west is supported. This policy covers six provinces including Shanxi, Anhui, Henan, Hubei, Hunan and Jiangxi. These areas play strategically important roles in the national economy as major grain production areas, centres for the exchange of materials and products and transport hubs. This new policy provides special support to enhance those roles by means of reinforcing the construction of an integrated transport system and energy and strategic material base, expanding markets in central China and strengthening competitive manufacturing and high technology industries.

In the Eleventh FYP (2005–10) a policy in favour of eastern development was put forward. The aim was to encourage the east coast to take the lead in development with a view to enhancing its capability of independent innovation, achieving structural upgrading and shifting from capital and resource-driven to innovation-driven growth, pushing forward its social and economic institutional transition, improving the socialist market economy, and driving central and western development. Special attention was to be paid to the four initial SEZs along with the Pudong New Area, the Binhai District in Tianjin and the West Coast of the Taiwan Straits identified as a dynamic area for co-operation with Taiwan. Emphasis was also placed on regional integration through metropolitan area development and urban agglomeration in the Pearl River Delta, Yangtze River Delta and Beijing-Tianjin-Hebei (Jing Jin Ji) area.

The Eleventh FYP also added a growth centre strategy as an alternative to a carpet-type regional development strategy. The aim was to support metropolitan areas that can act as engines of regional growth. The development of clusters of cities can be particularly effective. Access to urban cores is an important driver of integrated rural–urban development. In the west of China therefore there is a strong case for encouraging the development of provincial capitals such as Chongqing, Chengdu, Xi'an, Lanzhou, Urumqi, Kunming and Nanning as counterbalancing metropolitan areas and the improvement of inter-provincial communications. An important consequence is a reduction in the need for long-distance migration. This departure however questions concerning regional division and regional governance in China as a growth centre strategy involves planning for functional urban areas.

The Twelfth FYP, in a section on optimizing the structure, accelerating co-ordinated regional development and sound urbanization, reiterated the goals of western development, northeastern revival, the rise of the central region, and support for the leading role of the eastern region along with greater support for old revolutionary, ethnic minority and border areas. The Thirteenth FYP (2016–20) identified a Master Strategy for regional development, integration of Beijing, Tianjin, and Hebei, development of the Yangtze Economic Belt, support for Special Regions and widening the Blue Economy as priorities.

Some of these changes reflect the fact that growth has generated serious environmental problems and has placed pressure on critical resources (agricultural land, clean air, water and energy) whose limited availability in China are constraints on economic growth. In 2006 these considerations led the State Council to approve general proposals for functional zoning put forward initially in the Eleventh Five-Year Plan. The adoption of this strategy reflected a value re-orientation towards a 'Scientific Approach To Development Outlook' (kēxué fāzhǎn guān) and involved modification of narrow conceptions of regional economic performance to embrace a wider concern with the carrying capacity of the environment, the sustainability of development and an equalization of the provision of public services (with implications for the distribution of fiscal resources). Four types of area were identified: (1) optimized development zones (yōuhuà kāifāqū) with high density land development and a declining resource and environmental carrying capacity; (2) prioritized development zones (zhòngdiǎn kāifāqū) with relatively strong resource endowment and environmental carrying capacity as well as favourable conditions for the agglomeration of economic activities and people; (3) restricted development zones (xiànzhì kāifāqū) with weak resource endowment and environmental carrying capacity, poor conditions for the agglomeration of economic activities and people, and which are crucial to wider regional or national ecological security; and (4) prohibited development zones (jìnzhǐ kāifāqū) mainly comprising legally established nature reserves (Dunford and Li 2010).

Alongside regional development strategies spatial poverty reduction programmes were implemented. In 1994 592 poverty counties were identified. A 2001 revision identified 592 poverty counties (plus all 73 counties in Tibet) removing poverty counties in eight eastern provinces. These areas receive earmarked funds for enterprise support, construction and preferential loans and are given preferential treatment in the allocation of investment subsidies. A partnership system pairs each western province (except Tibet which is paired with all provinces) with an eastern province which is required to support poverty reduction programmes.

Most of China's residual poverty is found in fourteen mountainous rural areas in western and central China: some are former revolutionary base areas, many are inhabited by minorities, all are ecologically sensitive, often the physical environment is very harsh, the incidence of natural disasters is high, most are inaccessible and without good infrastructure, in many cases out-migration results in an ageing population, many are border areas or cross provincial borders and all are areas with unresolved problems of education, health and drinking water. In the 2011 China Rural Poverty Alleviation and Development Outline (2011–20) the government identified 14 'concentrated contiguous poor areas with special difficulties' (jí zhōngliánpiàn tèshū kùnnan dìqū) as the key battleground for poverty alleviation and development. In these areas, the aim is to deal with the problems of poor households and poor areas. As far as households are concerned, the aim is to achieve 'the two don't worries' (food and clothing) and 'the three guarantees' (basic health, education and housing). As far as area development is concerned, the solution entails the design and implementation of innovative regional development strategies, whose importance was increased by the commitment of the Chinese leadership at the 19th Congress of the CPC to eliminate poverty by 2020.

As these issues suggest, geography plays an important role in China's territorial development. China's regional economic development levels and population densities are almost inversely proportional to its relief which descends from west to east: the Qinghai-Tibet plateau standing at 4,000–5,000 metres above sea level, and much of the second tier of mountains, plateaux and basins lying between 1,000–2,000 metres are considered relatively unsuitable for development. Development potential is greatest in the third and most easterly tier of plains interspersed with hills and foothills lying at 500–1,000 metres above sea level. If a line is drawn from Aihui County in Heilongjiang Province to Tengchong County in Yunnan Province, the area north-west of this line is arid with a population density of 11 people per square kilometre. The area southeast of this line is very densely inhabited by 96 per cent of the total Chinese population. In all, only just over 1.8 million square kilometres are considered suitable for industrialization and urbanization. Arable land per capita is also extremely limited and increasingly strongly protected.

The other major feature of China's territorial development relates to the role of urbanization. In China in 2015 44 per cent of the population was rural, and 28 per cent were farmers (or other primary sector workers), although agriculture (and other primary sectors) accounted for just 9 per cent of GDP, helping explain low rural incomes (Figure 33.10). In the next 15 years the size of the urban population will increase by some 300 million people. The government has stressed the need to solve the 'three one hundred million people' (sān yī yì rén wèntí) by settling 100 million farmers in cities and towns, transforming the living conditions of 100 million people living in shanty towns and urban villages and urbanizing 100 million people in the Midwest.

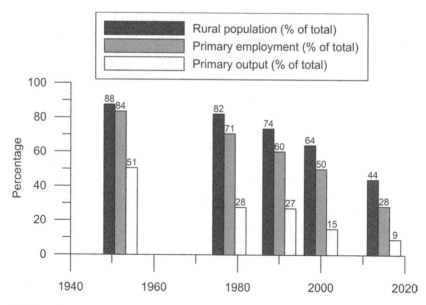

Source: NBS, various years.

Figure 33.10 *Evolution of the rural population and primary sector employment and*
output, 1952–2012

Agglomeration of economic activities acts as a source of productivity growth and innovation. Increased urbanization implies an increase in purchasing power, as urban incomes are far higher than rural incomes, massive investments in new infrastructure, housing and commercial and industrial property, significant increases in urban employment and urban services, increased social protection (health, pensions and social security) and reduced cautionary savings. This process will involve hukou reform and the integration of rural–urban migrants into urban life. It will also involve the transformation of the countryside as the number of farmers diminishes to increase rural productivity and feed the expanding urban population. These measures must however be carefully planned: rural property rights play a vital role in providing rural welfare and security, land is an important source of government revenue and the concentration of land use rights and social polarization should not be avoided. China's growth requires moreover the development of a new sustainable mode of consumption and way of life that can drive innovations that respect the environment and decouple increases in income and increased energy consumption.

33.4   MINORITIES, AUTONOMY AND REGIONAL CONFLICT

Over five millennia of evolution of Chinese civilization, China's borders have expanded and contracted and its people have evolved as a result of centuries of assimilation. At the time of the 2010 Census 91.81 per cent of the people of Chinese nationality (zhōnghuá mínzú) in mainland China were Han Chinese, and 8.19 per cent were members of 55 minorities. The officially recognized minorities include Taiwanese aborigines (gāo shān zú) who live mainly in mountainous areas in Taiwan, China (http://www.stats.gov.cn/english/Statisticaldata/CensusData/rkpc2010/indexch.htm). China's 55 minorities are located mainly in the south, west, and north of the mainland.

Areas in which minorities are relatively numerous are designated as autonomous regions (5 of the 33/34 first-tier administrative divisions), autonomous prefectures (30), autonomous counties (117) and autonomous banners (3). Of the first-tier administrative divisions only in the Tibet Autonomous Region and the Xin Jiang Uygur Autonomous Region do minorities account for the majority of the population, and only in Tibet does the designated minority account for a majority. All other first-tier provinces, municipalities, regions and special administrative districts of China have a Han majority. According to the PRC's Constitution and laws all ethnic groups have equal rights. However, a range of preferential measures promote the economic and cultural development of minority groups. Ethnic minorities were exempted from the population growth control measures of the former One-Child Policy and are represented politically at national and sub-national levels. Ethnic minorities that live in ethnic autonomous areas enjoy greater political autonomy, cultural rights and preferential economic policies (see also Figure 33.3 on fiscal transfers).

At present however in two parts of China there are small secessionist movements and there have been recent violent conflicts: one is Xin Jiang, and the other is Tibet and neighbouring Tibetan areas in Yunnan, Sichuan, Gansu and Qinghai provinces. The Xinjiang Uyghur Autonomous Region has land borders with Mongolia, Russia, Kazakhstan, the Kyrgyz Republic, Tajikistan, Afghanistan, Pakistan and India, and was a part of China at different times including well before the eighth century establishment of a Uyghur Empire and the ninth-century invasion of the area by Turkic Muslims. According to China's 2010 Census, the total population of Xinjiang was 21.8 million, of whom 45.8 per cent were Uyghur, 40.5 per cent Han, 6.5 per cent Kazakh, 4.5 per cent Hui and 2.7 per cent other ethnic groups. In the first census of 1953, 75 per cent of 5.11 million inhabitants were Uyghur and 6 per cent Han, though in 1800 Han people comprised about one-third. The Uyghur, Kazakh and Hui are all Muslim, while Uyghur and Kazakh are Turkic languages. The Hui have a Sino-Muslim identity. The cultural divide between the Uyghur and Kazakh and the Han is larger. Since the 1950s settlement by Han and other ethnic groups has continued to areas in Junghar Basin in northern Xin Jiang not settled by Uyghurs, while from 1954 the Xinjiang Production and Construction Corps (XPCC) administered newly established medium-sized settlements, farms and trading companies to develop, stabilize and protect frontier areas. This part of Xin Jiang developed rapidly and was from the 1980s an area also of economic migration by Uyghurs. Initially incited by the Soviet Union after the 1962 Sino–Soviet split, and at different times since the 1980s, Uyghur separatist movements have engaged in occasional and sometimes violent protest (and in the new millennium have sent supporters to the Middle East for military training and to help the Islamic State of Iraq and Syria establish a caliphate on the land it captured).

Tibet has had close relationships with China since the sixth century CE. In the seventh and eighth centuries a Tibetan Empire reached its heights. This empire was allied through marriage with the Tang Dynasty. In the 400 years after the Empire's collapse, Tibet fragmented and Tibetans spread into what are today parts of Yunnan, Sichuan, Gansu and Qinghai. In the mid-thirteenth century Tibet was incorporated into the Yuan Dynasty which exerted military and overall administrative control while granting Tibet a degree of political and cultural autonomy. Central control declined under the Ming Dynasty and increased under the Qing Dynasty which established a set of rules and regulations relating to overall political and administrative control. As the Qing Dynasty waned, Great Britain in particular extended its influence in Tibet, although the 1906 Convention between Great Britain and China with respect to Tibet reaffirmed Chinese possession of Tibet. Once the Qing Dynasty was toppled, however, the Dalai Lama declared himself ruler of an independent Tibet, although in the 1930s and 1940s the Guomindang Government extended its reach in the Tibet-Qinghai plateau.

In 1950 Tibet was incorporated into the PRC, and in 1951 a Seventeen Point Agreement for the Peaceful Liberation of Tibet granted Tibet autonomy and deferred reforms to Tibet's feudal social system. In 1959 a Central Intelligence Agency assisted rebellion demanding Tibetan independence failed, and the Dalai Lama fled to India, establishing a government in exile. At that point the Chinese government embarked on reform of Tibet's theocratic feudal order: a government composed of three groups of estate holders (upper-class lamas with monasteries, nobles and officials, comprising about 5 per cent of the population and owning almost all of the grassland, mountains, forests and water resources and most of the livestock), dominated serfs (the great majority of the population) and hereditary slaves (5 per cent) who faced high rents, interest on loans, taxes and corvée labour. Over 2.8 million mu of land was confiscated or redeemed from serf-owners, depending on whether they had or not participated in the revolt, and were distributed to 800,000 former serfs or slaves. Each of the former serfs and slaves received about 3.5 mu of land. Measures separating religion and the state and the implementation of religious freedom abolished theocracy. Government was reformed, and in 1965 the Tibet Autonomous Region was established.

In 1951 to 2008, state investment in infrastructure in Tibet exceeded 100 billion yuan. In 1959 to 2008 and in 2001 to 2008, respectively, 201.9 billion and 154.1 billion yuan from the central budget went to Tibet . . . and 154.1 billion yuan in the period 2001–08 alone. 'Since 1994, the Central Authorities have paired more than 60 central state organs, 18 provinces and municipalities, and 17 state-owned enterprises with the entities in Tibet, to help the latter's economic development' (Information Office 2009). Significant investment in transport, energy and telecommunications infrastructure and social overhead capital, the development of agriculture and animal husbandry, industrial activities and services saw GDP increase on average at 8.9 per cent per year from 1959 to 2008.

Although it speaks of a modern society in Tibet the regionalist movement headed by the government in exile and its supporters in some of the monasteries are in many ways a classic reactionary regional movement (Dulong 1975): a group representing a former elite, marginalized in this case by socialist modernization, appeals to traditional cultural and religious values and seeks to exploit grievances about Han settlement, economic disparities and the impact of modernity on traditional belief systems to re-assume power. In this case it is also a movement that actively cultivates support from nations with interests in the destabilization of China and the transformation of its economic and political system.

33.4.1   China and Eurasian Regionalism

Territorial integrity is a fundamental goal alongside sovereignty and independence. To deal with these regionalist issues domestically, China is deepening national integration and actively promoting economic development, in part through a Go West strategy dating from 2000. This strategy is itself a reminder that China's traditional centre of gravity, until the arrival of colonial powers in the nineteenth century, was in central and western China and not along the coast.

Internationally Go West is a part of China's new regionalism which involves a strategic reorientation to ensure that energy and product supply lines are unimpeded (to the Atlantic, Mediterranean and Indian Ocean), to develop trade and investment co-operation and economic assistance and to create a wider Eurasian community through improved infrastructural connectivity, cultural exchange and 'win–win' economic co-operation.

In the 1960s China was isolated from most of its neighbours. In 1971 China was finally recognized by the United Nations as the legal representative of China, and from the 1990s China has actively developed going-out strategies, participating in ASEAN (Association of Southeast Asian Nations) in East and South East Asia and advancing regionalism westwards across Eurasia and southwards towards the Indian Ocean. In 1991 China joined APEC (Asia-Pacific Economic Cooperation), in 2010 the China-ASEAN Free Trade Agreement (CAFTA) was completed, in 2001 the Shanghai Cooperation Organization (SCO) was established. In 2012 negotiations on the China–Japan–Korea FTA were started, and a regional comprehensive economic partnership (RCEP) was agreed in principle. China is a strong adherent of multilateralism and remains strongly committed to the World Trade Organization. In the trade arena, however, China's development of regional FTAs is a response to a swing away from multilateral to regional trade arrangements (which China views as possibly complementary with multilateral rules) and the potential trade diversion effects and impacts on rule-setting power of regional arrangements from which it is excluded.

As already indicated, the content of China's approach to regionalism has widened from trade and investment. In East Asia and the Pacific China has advanced the idea of an Asian community of 'common interest' and 'common destiny'. More generally, China has emphasized connectivity, the establishment of communities centred on historical, cultural and people to people linkages and a morality/justice-interest (yì and lì or in characters 义 and 利) concept of international relations (Zhang and Li 2014).

In 2013 President Xi Jinping proposed a Silk Road Economic Belt and a twenty-first century Maritime Silk Road. Other proposals saw the establishment of the Asian Infrastructure Investment Bank (AIIB), the BRICS New Development Bank (NDB) and the national Silk Road Fund. The BRI sets out China's new thinking about its globalization strategy, while AIIB and NDB are multilateral financial instruments (Liu and Dunford 2016).

The Chinese government has repeatedly stated that Chinese regionalism is open and inclusive. As its role increased, however, its relations with Japan, which wants to play a leading role in Asia, deteriorated, the United States announced its return to Asia and a number of unsettled territorial disputes with Japan and with Vietnam, the Philippines and a number of other countries in the South China Sea have intensified.

In the face of these difficulties Go West may mean that Eurasia may emerge as a more significant part of China's heartland. China's Belt and Road Initiative is driving infrastructure (roads, railways, ports, airports, telecommunications networks, pipelines, development zones and cities) and economic development, diversifying trade routes and reducing dependence on the Straits of Malacca and the South China Sea (though it remains vitally important). The US$46 billion China–Pakistan Economic Corridor (CPEC) connects the relatively underdeveloped, Uyghur dominated southern parts of Xin Jiang and neighbouring landlocked countries in Central Asia along the Karakoram Highway through northern Gilgit-Baltistan to the megaport of Gwadar on the Arabian Sea. Gwadar is just one of a string of economic and commercial nodes in the Indian Ocean rimland. Other corridors will connect western China with Myanmar, Bangladesh, Sri Lanka, the Maldives and West Africa, while others will connect it westwards with the rest of Eurasia.

33.5   CONCLUSIONS

China is a vast and diverse continental-scale country with some 5,000 years of continuous civilization. Territorially China is highly differentiated with much of its land mass not suited to modern industrial and urban development: development is therefore highly concentrated. As a result of many centuries of assimilation Han people predominate, but China is also an ethnically diverse country. After its failure to modernize and its humiliation at the hands of foreign powers in the 100 years from the First Opium War to the establishment of the new China in 1949, China has rapidly emerged as a leading economic power. In such a vast country territorial governance has played an important role in China's rise. At first highly egalitarian, the quest for sustained growth generated wide territorial, regional, rural–urban and social disparities in development which the Chinese government has sought to address. Modernization, its differential impact and its articulation with ethnic and cultural differences have generated some regional tensions that have varied in intensity but have been contained. Generally speaking Chinese development has lifted all boats but at different speeds and at considerable environmental costs. What remains to be seen is whether China can chart a more sustainable path in which Deng Xiao Ping's statement that 'some people will get rich first' does in fact mean that everyone else will eventually catch-up in a universal xiǎokāng society, and whether internationally Chinese regionalism can chart a new path of inclusive and sustainable globalization.

33.6   REFERENCES

Bell, D.A. (2015), *The China Model: Political Meritocracy and the Limits of Democracy*, Princeton, NJ: Princeton University Press.
Chu, Y.-H. (2013), 'Sources of regime legitimacy and the debate over the Chinese model', *China Review*, **13** (1), 1–42.
Dulong, R. (1975), *La Question Bretonne*, Paris: Presses de Sciences Po.
Dulong, R. (1978), *Les Régions, l'État et la société locale*, Paris: Presses Universitaires de France.
Dunford, M. (2015), 'Chinese economic development and its social and institutional foundations', in M. Dunford and W. Liu (eds) *The Geographical Transformation of China*, Abingdon: Routledge, pp. 1–21
Dunford, M. and L. Li (2010), 'Chinese spatial inequalities and spatial policies', *Geography Compass*, **4** (8), 1039–1054.
Dynon, N. (2014), 'Civilisation-state: modernising the past to civilise the future in Jiang Zemin's China', *China-an International Journal*, **12** (1), 22–42.
Gao, B., W. Liu and M. Dunford (2014), 'State land policy, land markets and geographies of manufacturing: the case of Beijing, China', *Land Use Policy*, **36**, 1–12.
Information Office of the State Council of the People's Republic of China (Information Office) (2009), *White*

Paper 2009: Fifty Years of Democratic Reform in Tibet, accessed 7 March 2018 at http://www.china.org.cn/government/whitepaper/node_7062754.htm.

Li, E.X. (2013), 'China and the end of meta-narratives', Press release, accessed 2 March 2018 at http://www.china.org.cn/china/2013-07/19/content_29474550.htm.

Liu, W. (2015), 'Governance, politics and culture', in M. Dunford and W. Liu (eds), *The Geographical Transformation of China*, Abingdon: Routledge, pp. 22–59.

Liu, W. and M. Dunford (2016), 'Inclusive globalization: unpacking China's Belt and Road Initiative', *Area Development and Policy*, **1** (3), 323–340.

Maddison, A. (2001), *The World Economy: A Millennial Perspective*, Paris: OECD.

NBS (2017), *National Bureau of Statistics of China*, accessed 2 March 2018 at http://www.stats.gov.cn/.

Oi, J.C. (1992), 'Fiscal reform and the economic foundations of local state corporatism in China', *World Politics*, **45** (1), 99–126.

The Conference Board (2015), *The Conference Board Total Economy Database™, November 2015*, accessed 2 March 2018 at http://www.conference-board.org/data/economydatabase/.

Zhang, X., and X. Li (2014), 'China's regionalism in Asia', *The Asan Forum*, **5** (6), accessed 7 March 2018 at http://www.theasanforum.org/chinas-regionalism-in-asia/.

zhōngguó cáizhèng zázhìshè [China Financial press] (2016), *zhōngguó cáizhèng niánjiàn 2015* [China Annual Finance Report, 2015], Beijing: zhōngguó cáizhèng zázhìshè [Beijing: China Financial Magazine].

34. The production of a trans-regional scale: China's 'One Belt One Road' imaginary

Ngai-Ling Sum

34.1 INTRODUCTION

This entry puts the production of China's new trans-regional scale known as the One Belt One Road (OBOR) initiative in its place in the post-2008 financial crisis conjuncture. Consistent with its largely investment-led mode of growth and responding to the socioeconomic challenges of falling exports and unemployment (Sum 2016a, 2016b), the Chinese leadership launched a four trillion Renminbi stimulus package (equivalent to USD 560 billion). This intensified the property, infrastructure and, later, financial asset bubbles in China between 2010 and 2015. This aggravated: (1) overproduction by property-infrastructure-related industries, leading to overcapacities in the engineering, construction, steel, cement and heavy-duty machinery sectors; and (2) mounting local government debts (Standard and Poor's 2015), as well as, later, encouraged by the 'China Dream', overinvestment in the stock market by retail (household) speculators in the hope of quick returns.

This crisis-prone period coincided with the transfer of leadership from President Hu and Premier Wen to President Xi and Premier Li in 2013. The Xi–Li leadership, anticipating falling growth rates in China, appropriated the 'new normal' discourse to explain recent below-average economic growth. Given the fluidity of this discourse, the leadership was able to subsume some old and new policy goals under this rubric. These included financial reforms (for example, the internationalization of the Renminbi, liberalization of interest rates, and greater exchange rate flexibility), increased household consumption, crack-downs on corruption, and promotion of the OBOR geostrategic initiative. Focusing on the latter, this chapter adopts a discursive-material approach (Sum and Jessop 2013) to examine its associated sociospatial changes in two parts. First, it examines the discursive production and negotiation of a new trans-regional scale in and through the construction and deployment of geoeconomic and geopolitical tropes and metaphors. Second, it examines how this truth regime and associated body of knowledge that accompany the OBOR initiative help to condense two inter-related governance configurations that underpin an emerging and contradictory infrastructural–infocommunication–finance complex in the shadow of global capitalism.

34.2 PRODUCING A TRANS-REGIONAL SCALE: CHINA'S 'ONE BELT ONE ROAD' INITIATIVE

The OBOR trans-regional spatial imaginary was co-produced by the Ministry of Foreign Affairs, the National Development and Reform Commission, and the Ministry of

Commerce. Its two spatial components aimed to connect China, Asia, the Middle East, Europe and Africa. 'One Belt' denotes the land-based 'Silk Road Economic Belt' and 'One Road' is the sea route of '21st Century Maritime Silk Road'. The terrestrial section was first officially announced by Xi in a speech at Nazarbavev University in Kazakhstan on 7 September 2013. He announced the maritime component in the Indonesian Parliament a month later, on 3 October. Faced with frightening domestic triple bubbles and geopolitical threats from the USA's military-cum-commercial 'Asia Pivot', the Chinese leadership swiftly reoriented its foreign policy rhetoric from promoting China's 'peaceful rise and harmonious world' (Shirk 2008; Lam 2009) to advocating 'peaceful development and Chinese Dream' (Yi 2014; Hartig 2016, pp. 22–28). This rhetorical shift frames China's recovery from 'a century of foreign humiliation' to become a nation able and willing to: (1) construct a new geopolitical power relation with the US; and (2) build friendly and mutually beneficial communities of interest with neighbouring countries. It is projecting and presenting this new geoeconomic imaginary nationally, trans-regionally and across urban scales (Wang 2014; Sorensen 2015).

34.2.1   Programming Geopolitical and Geoeconomic Imaginaries Via Cartographic Statecraft

Following Foucault's (1980) analysis of discourses and dispositives, OBOR can be interpreted as a sociospatial technology that projects China's geoeconomic and geopolitical imaginary abroad. This imaginary became official policy when it was incorporated into the *Decision of the Central Committee of the Communist Party of China on Some Major Issues Concerning Comprehensively Deepening the Reform* in November 2013 and into the State Council's 2014 *Report on the Work of the Government*. A major document, with the title *Visions and Actions on Jointly Building Silk Road Economic Belt and 21st Century Maritime Silk Road*, co-authored by the Ministry of Foreign Affairs, Ministry of Commerce and the National Development and Reform Commission, offered more details in March 2015. This new geostrategic vision intensifies the programming and ordering of China's future-oriented geoeconomic and geopolitical thinking. As an imaginary, the OBOR project partly reorders (inter-)subjectivities by appropriating and redirecting the invented historical and geographical metaphor of the 'Silk Road' that once stretched from China's old capital Xi'an to ancient Rome under the Han and Tang dynasties.

The initiative aims to translate the aura of the power, wealth, prestige and romance of an exalted antiquity into the present and future by reinventing the spatial connections between China, Asia, the Middle East, Europe and Africa. Specifically, the 'One Belt' envisions a land-based 'Silk Road' that will stretch from China via Central Asia to Turkey, Russia and Continental Europe. Complementing this is the 'One Belt', represented as the 'Maritime Route', which stretches from China via the Indian Ocean and Africa to the Mediterranean and Atlantic Seaboard. These multi-layered, trans-regional networks:

> … tap market potential, promote investment and consumption, create demand and job opportunities, enhance people-to-people and cultural exchanges, and mutual learning among the peoples of the relevant countries, and enable them to understand, trust and respect each other and live in harmony peace and prosperity. (Xinhuanet.com 2015, pp. 2–3)

As a priority geostrategic initiative, it is scripted to improve the spatial connectivity of trans-regional infrastructural construction plans by creating international high-speed train lines, seaways, ports, corridors, pipelines, information highways, fibre-optical lines, low-carbon arrangements, and so on. It is anticipated that service networks and industrial clusters would soon emerge along these traffic routes and then radiate into construction, energy, trade, finance, communication, logistics, and tourism. This project is mapped to cover 65 countries with a total population of 4.4 billion people with a disposable income of around US$ 21 trillion; it also accounts for 63 per cent and 29 per cent of global capacity respectively for the belt and road components (Wang 2015, pp. 94–98). This geostrategic imaginary, with its intertwined geopolitical and geoeconomic win-win stories, is supported by tools of statecraft and tradecraft, such as maps (see Figure 34.1), vision statements, press releases, think tank/investor reports, and so on that are produced and circulated widely in the diplomatic and business knowledge circuits (see Table 34.2).

The official Xinhua Agency published the OBOR map in Chinese and English to help popularize and lay the foundations to governmentalize this new multi-spatial imaginary and guide actions to extend it across time, space, place and scale. The two lines drawn on the map translate the abstract idea of OBOR into a simple visual representation. As cartographic statecraft, it gives authoritative meanings to space (Pickles 2004; Moore and Perdu 2014). This map fuses future hope and simplicity to make its geostrategic vision more readily communicable by official press, diplomats, think tanks, consultancy firms, business media, and other agents. These maps represent official spatial thinking and operate as a cartographic propaganda of the future. Like many such maps, the official OBOR version uses familiar techniques such as coloured lines (orange for the land-belt and blue for the maritime-road). These lines connect dots that represent places (here cities and ports). The monochrome Map 1 in this text cannot show the use of colour but both sets of dotted lines are depicted. These techniques signify the proposed land and sea modes and nodes that will bind space, place, scale and territory. These two hope-based and hopeful lines encircle a multi-scalar land-sea mass within which imagined place-based 'gateways' (e.g. Chongqing as the 'logistic gateway' to connect western China to Germany by the Yu-Xin-Ou Railway) and transnational 'corridors' (e.g. China–Pakistan Economic Corridor) will open up regions and enhance interconnectivity. As a cartographic construction, this map portrays a trans-regional imaginary that has it domestic roots with expansionary potentials.

34.2.2 Construction and Negotiation of Expansionary Geoeconomic and Geopolitical Tropes

This imaginary has its domestic roots in two earlier official strategies that started in the late 1990s under President Jiang. The 'Go West' strategy invested in infrastructure (e.g. ports, roads, hydropower plants, energy, and telecommunications) and promoted socioeconomic development (e.g. via education) in China's western provinces, notably Yunnan and autonomous regions such as Inner Mongolia, Xinjiang, and Tibet. The 'Go Out' strategy promoted investment abroad, especially by SOEs (state-owned enterprises), to diversify China's foreign reserves, exploit global opportunities, and develop new investment channels (on these strategies, see Wang 2013). With the onset of the 2008 North Atlantic financial crisis and its global contagion effects and the development of China's

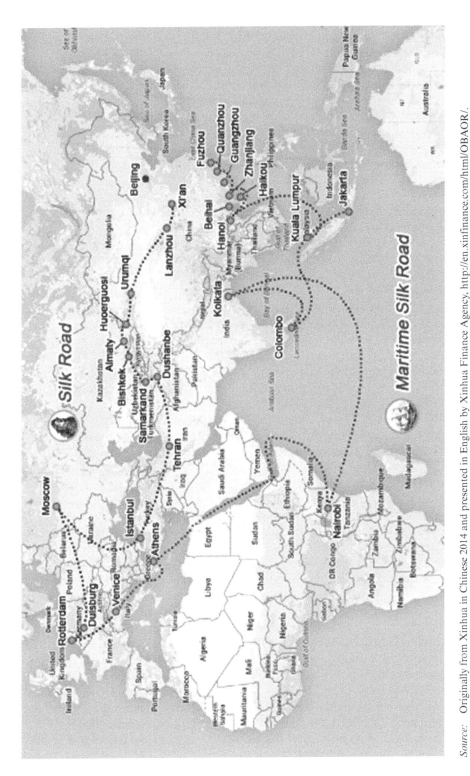

Source: Originally from Xinhua in Chinese 2014 and presented in English by Xinhua Finance Agency, http://en.xinfinance.com/html/OBAOR/.

Figure 34.1   The mapping of 'One Belt One Road' by Xinhua

own property, infrastructure and financial asset bubbles, the expansionary dreams acquired new geoeconomic and geopolitical meanings.

First, the 'Go Out' policy was framed in 2009 as 'Chinese Marshall Plan' by Xu Shanda, the former director of China's State Administration of Taxation. He presented this geoeconomic plan to the Ministry of Commerce and suggested that China's vast reserves be used to offer loans to developing countries that would enlist Chinese SOEs to build major infrastructural and construction projects. These roundabout subsidies to Chinese industry would sustain Chinese exports, underpin high GDP growth rates, and reinforce the legitimating ideology of GDP-ism (on the latter, see Sum 2013, 2016b). The 'Chinese Marshall Plan' trope triggered foreign interest in OBOR's geostrategic significance. American think tanks (for example Centre for Strategic and International Studies 2015), foreign relation journalists (such as Tiezzi from *The Diplomat* 2014) and global business media (for example *The Wall Street Journal* 2014) suggested that this 'Marshall Plan' would allow China to use its economic resources and capacities to secure its foreign policy goals as well as sustain its own economy.

Worried about the risks of translating American Cold-War security-domination images to the OBOR initiative, Chinese official media and diplomatic circles dismissed the relevance of the 'Marshall Plan' discourse to the OBOR project. For example, Foreign Minister, Wang Yi, speaking on 8 March 2015, stressed that this initiative was 'a product of inclusive cooperation, not a tool of geopolitics, and must not be viewed in the outdated Cold War mentality' (*China Daily* 2015a). For China, this was more a matter of mutual 'opportunities' than unilateral containment, that is, of infrastructural connectivity with 'win–win' benefits for national, regional and urban scales along the routes (see Table 34.1).

Second, the building of a geoeconomic imaginary is deeply intertwined with China's reorientation of its foreign policy rhetoric from promoting 'peaceful rise and harmonious world' (Shirk 2008; Lam 2009) to 'peaceful development and Chinese Dream' destinies/ destined to build a 'new type of great power relations' (Yi 2014; Hartig 2016, pp. 22–28). In response to the Obama Administration's intention, announced in 2011, to 'Pivot towards the Asia-Pacific', Wang Jisi, a leading Chinese expert, proposed in late 2012 to avoid confrontation with the USA by undertaking a 'March Westward' strategy (Clarke 2016, p. 19). This proposal and its subsequent reinvention of a Eurasia possibility is not without its analogous comparison with a key theme in classical nineteenth and early twentieth century geopolitics. Specifically, one of the 'fathers of geopolitics' and a fervent champion of the British Empire, Halford Mackinder, formulated his Eurasian 'Heartland Thesis' in 1904. By linking power to space, he suggested that the 'Eurasia' landmass is the most advantageous geopolitical location for military and industrial development. Countries that dominate this pivotal 'heartland' would possess the geopolitical and geoeconomic potentials to dominate the world. Similar themes were proposed in German geopolitical analyses (for example Ratzel, Haushofer and Kjellén), although these fell out of favour because of their association with Nazism. In contrast, Mackinder's heartland thesis has proved a popular geopolitical metaphor. It has provided a theoretical rationale for strategies of territorial-expansion and imperial governmental technologies (Morozova 2014). It is also counterposed to the main rival to the Eurasian heartland – the maritime sphere that includes Western Europe, North America, Maritime East Asia, Australia, and the Mediterranean littoral.

Table 34.1 Construction of the 'One Belt One Road': geoeconomic and geopolitical tropes and metaphors

Spatialized Knowledge	Discursive Construction and Negotiations	Spatial Imaginations (Tropes and Metaphors)
Geoeconomic tropes Reinvention of: • 'Go West' and 'Go Out' Policies • *Chinese Marshall Plan* Tropes of mutuality and inclusiveness	Extension of the 'Go West' and 'Go Out' Policies in the contexts of China's triple crises and the Xi's 'China Dream' and 'New Normal' Negotiation of OBOR's identity with reference to US Marshall Plan Focus on building infrastructural-oriented networks based on 'mutuality' and 'connectivity' (not domination as in the Cold War Marshall Plan)	Historical metaphor of the 'Silk Road' The use of cartographic statecraft such as maps, territorial lines and dots Joining these lines and dots to create the OBOR space to the west of China Mapping the 'One Road' and 'One Belt' as a land-sea mass that covers China, Asia, the Middle East, Europe and Africa Constructing mutuality and connectivity via the building of (trans-)regional infrastructure such as highways and ports Using geographical planning metaphors such as corridors and gateways to frame geographical connectivity (see Table 34.2)
Geopolitical tropes 'Eurasia' imaginary Trope of Mackinder's 'Heartland theory' Trope of 'community of common destiny'	Construction of 'West Pivot' in the contexts of China's more assertive 'Peaceful Rise' 'Pivot West' and the 'Eurasia' imaginary as offering opportunities Building community of common destiny with Central Asia, EU and Russia via infrastructure investment	Metaphors of mutuality and cooperation (and not imperial domination) Denouncing and distancing from Mackinder's space-conquering analogy in framing OBOR Disarticulating OBOR from Mackinder's theory and rearticulating the 'Eurasia' imaginary in mutual geoeconomic and geostrategic terms

Source: Author's own compilation.

Unsurprisingly, China's OBOR imaginary to create a contiguous Eurasian space by leveraging geoeconomic networks has been compared to Mackinder's analysis and its geostrategic implications. For example, Clarke, who wrote for *The Diplomat*, saw OBOR as 'a realization of Mackinder's vision' (Clarke 2015). *The Pacific Perspective* (2017) regarded it as an exercise of Chinese 'informal imperial power'. Such readings interpret OBOR as facilitating the creation of a Sinocentric Eurasian system that would be based on infrastructure investment rather than military conquest to enable China to build a land empire. Interestingly, the One Road could be seen as its Maritime equivalent. Worried about the connotations of transferring this space-conquering image to OBOR, the Chinese authorities have distanced themselves from this analogy. For example, Liu Xiaoming, the Chinese ambassador to Britain, argued that the OBOR initiative should not be seen as confirming Mackinder's thesis (Liu 2015). Apart from attempts to uncouple OBOR from the Mackinder's thesis, policy and academic efforts are devoted to rearticulate it as a global gift based on mutual cooperation and inclusive globalization (Wang 2015, pp. 103–107; Liu and Dunford 2016). Tropes of win–win and 'community of common destiny' based on flows and linkages are deployed to market/brand the 'Eurasia' imaginary.

34.3   THE CONDENSATION OF 'ONE BELT ONE ROAD' THROUGH AN EMERGING INFRASTRUCTURAL–INFOCOMMUNICATION–FINANCE COMPLEX

These geopolitical-geoeconomic tropes (and their contested negotiation) have pervaded policy and consultancy discourses since OBOR's official inception in September 2013. Official Chinese channels, commissions, business/investment consultancies, think tanks and diplomatic circles are all energetically engaged in producing, circulating, and normalizing OBOR as a policy object and defended it from criticisms.

34.3.1   The Making of OBOR Knowledge Products

On the promotional side, the OBOR identity and creation of a trans-regional land–sea mass is enthusiastically claimed to offer 'opportunities' to build a win–win and infrastructure-oriented community. *China Daily* (2015b), an official organ, hailed this on 6 May 2015 as the 'second biggest geographical discovery in human history after Mackinder's breakthrough in its Chinese version. The re-envisioning of this land–sea mass was praised as marking the re-awakening of 'Eurasia' from its 500-year slumber and facilitating China's return to centre stage. This imaginary was concretized through vision statements and a dedicated website with links to policies and OBOR news and activities: http://www.xinhuanet.com/english/special/silkroad/index.htm. This euphoria is echoed by some business-consultancy sources that praise it as a 'brilliant plan' (CLSA 2015) that could 'export China's [infrastructural] development blueprint to the world' (Swain 2014, p. 8) and 'stimulate world trade' (Tan 2015). The World Pensions Council has even seen it as a long-awaited response to a massive infrastructure gap created by neoliberal neglect of this key condition for world trade.

There are also critical discourses, however, especially in diplomatic circles. Contributors to *The Diplomat*, which is linked to the Centre for Strategic and International Studies (an influential American think tank), commented that the project was 'China-centred', 'at risk of failure' (Rudolf 2015) and represented as 'a geopolitical gamble' that competes with the US for allies (Yale 2015). The Ministry of External Affairs of India sees it as a 'national Chinese initiative' that should be opened up for more multilateral consultations (Madan 2016). One Taiwan source even interprets this initiative as China's endeavour to 'dominate Eurasia without a war' (Lin 2015). Nonetheless, in providing a policy focus, the OBOR imaginary is making the Belt-Road project more visible and encouraging actors to calculate how 'Eurasia' could lead to 'mutual benefit' and 'win–win' outcomes based on 'cooperation' and 'trust and respect' around cooperation and connectivity. This fits with official discourse about the scope for OBOR to align different local, regional, national, and trans-regional strategies and interests. These identities and calculations are staged and repeated in national and (trans-)regional official speeches, public forums (such as the 17th EU–China Bilateral Summit), cooperation intentions (for example the EU's Juncker plan, named after Jean-Claude Juncker when he was the European Commission President) and state visits (e.g. Xi's visit to Central and Eastern Europe in June 2016). By 2016, major think tanks, investment consultancies and the international organizations have produced their own knowledge products in the form of promotional/assessment reports and blogs on this scheme (see Table 34.2).

Table 34.2   Examples of 'One Belt One Road' knowledge products

Types of Institution	Names	Examples of Knowledge Products (Title and Year)
Think tanks	European Council of Foreign Relations (EU)	François Gôdement and Agatha Kratz (eds) *China's One Belt One Road: The Great Leap Outward* (2015)
	Chatham House (UK)	Tim Summers, *What Exactly is 'One Belt One Road'?* (2015)
	Konrad Adenauer Stiftung (Germany)	Patrick Bessler, *China's 'New Silk Road': Focus on Central Asia* (2015)
	Brookings Institute (USA)	David Dollar, *China's Rise as a Regional and Global Power: The AIIB and the 'One Belt, One Road'* (2015)
	S. Rajaratnam *School of International* Studies (Singapore)	*China's One Belt One Road: Has the European Union Missed the Train?* by Alessandro Arduino (2016)
International Organization	World Bank	*China's One Belt One Road Initiative*
Investment Consultancies	PriceWaterhouse Cooper McKinsey & Co.	*China's New Silk Road: the Long and Winding Road* (2016)
	BNP Paribas Investment Partners	*GII Beijing: Navigating One Belt One Road* (2015) *One Belt One Road: One Stone Kills Three Birds* (2015)

Source: Author's own compilation based on web research.

34.3.2   Two Emergent Governance Configurations Related to the OBOR Initiative

These ensembles of geoeconomic-geopolitical knowledge not only shape subjectivities but also contribute to building institutions and interest-related alliances that integrate various sites and scales more closely into the circuits of global capitalism. At the time of writing (July 2017), it has condensed institutionally in two inter-related governance configurations organized around various ministries, SOEs, SOBs (state-owned banks), and provincial governments in various alliances with private and regional/global institutions. The first is organized around infra- and info-structures and the second centres around finance (see Table 34.3). The former involves the governance of the infra- and info-structural setups that link China to emerging markets along the OBOR routes (for example, Yunnan as the 'transport corridor' to the Greater Mekong Sub-Region). This allows China to export its overproduction in engineering, construction, steel, cement, heavy-duty machinery, and so on to this trans-regional space. Construction, civil engineering, railway building, power generation, information technology, port operation and human resources can be used in OBOR projects such as the China–Pakistan Economic Corridor. These activities provide outlets for some of China's largest infrastructure-focused SOEs and large private firms like SANY and Huawei (see Table 34.3). For example, the China State Construction Engineering Corporation Limited, which is an infrastructure-building and power-generating conglomerate with ample project experience in 116 countries (Lam 2015), is expanding into other emerging markets, notably Central Asia and Russia. These expansionist crisis-management and displacement strategies can alleviate domestic over-capacity by opening (trans-)regional spaces for infrastructural projects and, in the longer term, should integrate China and other emerging markets further into global capitalism through trade in (semi-)finished goods, services and technologies.

Second, this production configuration is supported by and articulated to the financial one. With the development of the financial asset bubble and the widening of the funding gaps in China, existing and new practices are deployed and developed to plug the gaps with a long-term view to improve the usage of Renminbi and its internationalization (see Table 34.3). According to Xinhua Finance (2015), the OBOR initiative requires at least US$ 800 billion annually between 2015 and 2025. Apart from overseas direct investment from SOEs and private firms, loans from policy banks (e.g. China Development Bank), SOBs and the government-owned Silk Road Fund will provide the initial funding which enable SOEs or provincial/local governments to create overseas infrastructural demand for their growing excess capacities and development visions. This initial funding will form the basis to recruit non-public and inter-governmental inputs to plug the gaps and relieve the debt burden. These involve: (a) equity funds and bond issuances on different stock exchanges; (b) private–public partnerships (PPPs); and (c) three new financial institutions (for details, see Tables 34.3 and 34.4).

Three financial institutions have been established: the Silk Road Fund, the New Development Bank, and the Asian Infrastructure Investment Bank (AIIB) (see Table 34.4). Whilst the first is state-owned, the second is more BRICS-driven, and the third is even more multilateral. The AIIB was established in October 2014 with 77 countries signing onto the project by May 2017. Its authorized capital is US$ 100 billion with half coming from China. As an emergent multilateral infrastructure bank, it seeks to work with the World Bank and regional counterparts. It also mobilizes inter-governmental sup-

Table 34.3   Two emergent governance configurations related to the 'One Belt One Road'

Governance Configuration	Nature of the Configuration	Some Main National Institutions Involved	Some Private and Global Institutions Involved
Infra- and info-structural configuration that resolves domestic overcapacities by redirecting them abroad	Infrastructural construction abroad • roads, bridges, ports, harbours, airports, power generation, etc. Engineering and procurement Building materials • Steel, iron, cement, sheet glass, etc. High-speed and normal-speed railway construction Terrestrial telecommunication links • information technology (IT) equipment and telecommunication system (e.g. fibre optic cables, broadband, logistic networks, e-commerce) Infrastructure operation	Roads and bridges • *Ministry of Construction* • *China State Construction Engineering Corporation Ltd.* • *China Communication Construction Co. Ltd.* Engineering services • *China National Materials* Steel *Anshan Iron and Steel Group* Railway engineering and manufacturers • *China Railway Rolling Stock Corporation* Ministry of Communication Ministry of Commerce Port operation and cargo transportation • China Merchants Holdings International Co. Ltd.	Construction and heavy-engineering equipment • *SANY Heavy Industry Co. Ltd.* • *Zoomlion Heavy Industry* ICT products, services and solutions • *Huawei Technologies* • *ZTE* E-Commerce • *Alibaba* • *Tencent*
Financial configuration that mobilizes new funding to fill the funding gaps and relieve the debt burden	Outward direct investment Loans from policy banks and SOBs • Funding for infrastructural investment in ports, roads, rail and resources • Sovereign debt guarantees from borrowers	• *Ministry of Commerce* • SOEs (after mergers and acquisitions) • *State Administration of Foreign Exchange* • Policy banks (e.g. *Bank of China, China Development Bank, China Ex-Im Bank*)	• Private firms • Stock exchanges in Hong Kong, Shanghai, Shenzhen, New York, etc. • *Citibank Group, HSBC, Standard Chartered*, etc. • International brokerages (e.g. *JP Morgan*)

Table 34.3 (continued)

Governance Configuration	Nature of the Configuration	Some Main National Institutions Involved	Some Private and Global Institutions Involved
	• *Silk Road Fund* (see Table 34.4) New sources of non-public funding • IPO equity funds listed on stock exchanges (e.g. *Shanghai-Hong Kong Stock Connect*) • Bonds (e.g. **RMB bond, OROR** bond in Singapore and *China-Hong Kong Bond Connect*) • Private–public partnerships (PPPs). New sources of inter-governmental funds (see Table 34.4) Internationalization of Renminbi (RMB) • RMB as denominating currency in bond issuance • RMB in trade settlement • RMB swap mechanism	• SOBs and SOEs • Sovereign borrowers • *State-Owned Assets Supervision and Administration Commission* • *Bank of China* • *China Construction Bank* • *Silk Road Fund* • *Asian Infrastructural Investment Bank* • *New Development Bank* • *Ministry of Finance* • *State Administration of Foreign Exchange* • *Bank of China*	• RMB clearing centres worldwide • Offshore RMB centres

Source: Author's own compilation.

438

Table 34.4 A facet of the financial configuration: three new financial institutions

Name	Year and States Involved	Amount (US$)	Institutions	Nature
Silk Road Infrastructure Fund	December 2014 China	US$ 40 billion	State-owned by China Investment Corporation Loans issued by *China Development Bank, China Ex-Im Bank*	• Earmarked for OBOR infrastructural projects • An initial capital of US$ 10 billion • Another US$ 6.5 billion from China's foreign exchange reserves • Managed as China's sovereign wealth fund
Asian Infrastructure Investment Bank	Proposed in October 2014 and in operation in 2016 77 states (by May 2017)	Total capital of US$ 100 billion China's subscribed US$ 50 billion Paid-in capital around 20 per cent	Beijing-based inter-governmental development financing institution	• Funding for infrastructures that are not under sovereign credit • Promotion of PPP method in expanding funding (e.g. pension funds) • Managing projects by sharing risks and returns with the private sector • Enforcement of contracts (including user charges)
New Development Bank (former BRICS Development Bank)	July 2014	US$ 50 billion (10 billion from China)	BRICS countries (Brazil, Russia, India, China and South Africa)	• Infrastructural projects in BRICS as priority • Each country select its own infrastructural projects to be developed

Source: Author's own compilation based on Xinhua, Barclay Research, Ernst & Young China, and Central Policy Unit of Hong Kong SAR.

port conducive to raising semi-commercialized loans from sovereign funds, pension funds and private sector. To this end, public-private partnerships (PPPs) as a funding method is widely discussed and promoted to enable the sharing of risks and returns for the private sector (Jin 2015, p. 1) (Tables 34.3 and 34.4).

34.3.3   An Emerging Infrastructural–Infocommunication–Finance Complex and New Investment Consensus in the Shadow of Global Capitalism

These still emerging twin configurations are mobilizing trans-regional and inter-urban actors, resources and institutions. They are recruited from SOEs/SOBs related to infra- and info-structural building and banking, associated national/local government agencies, private firms, multilateral development banks (e.g. World Bank and regional counterparts), the UN (e.g. UNDP), IMF, G20 (e.g. its Global Infrastructure Initiative), G8, EU (e.g. the European Fund for Strategic Investment), commercial banks, credit rating agencies, investment consultancies, think tanks, research centres, transnational private corporations, national/multilateral development funds, investment and pension funds, development agencies, signatory central and local governments/actors, and so on.

These two configurations provide the basis for an emerging infrastructural–infocommunication–finance complex that rests on a still developing trans-regional, multiscalar and inter-urban articulation between geoeconomic and geopolitical strategies and infrastructural-financial development. Its manifestation involves constant organizational, functional and other connections across these different sites and scales that are gradually crystallizing into coordinating networks for exporting overcapacity, finding new funding/markets, relieving debt burden and developing infrastructural connections. For example, AIIB signed co-financing agreements with the World Bank, Asian Development Bank and European Bank for Reconstruction and Development signed in April and May 2016 to jointly develop projects and finance. Several mega programmes (e.g. Chinese–Pakistan Economic Corridor and Piraeus-Belgrade-Budapest Corridor), policy loans, intergovernmental investment funds (e.g. AIIB and New Development Bank) and financial instruments (OBOR bonds and PPPs) typify the formation of the complex. This provides a short-term basis for trans-regional and inter-urban alliance building to create hope and manage crisis-tendencies by redirecting overproduction abroad, relieving debt burden, finding new sources of private finance and rebuilding the geoeconomic-geopolitical landscapes in the shadow of global capitalism. Nonetheless, complexes of this kind do not develop on an equal footing but involve hierarchies of accumulation regimes and an uneven and combined development of trans-regional capitalism within and beyond countries. This makes them prone to contradictions, conflicts, and antagonisms.

In the case of the infra- and info-structural configuration, the attempt to resolve the generic overcapacity problems is undermined by the attempts of some sub-national governments to reinvest in OBOR-related infrastructure, thereby reproducing the overcapacity problems by investing in transport corridors, railways and heritage parks. Similar contradictions occur in the social realm. For example, the drive to export surplus Chinese (semi-)skilled labour also leads to segregations between Chinese and local labour, produces clashes in work ethics, and undermines workers' rights. This is exemplified by Greek dockers' protests against sweatshop practices (e.g. unpaid overtime and safety hazards) after Piraeus Port was bought in 2016 by China's COSCO Shipping Corporation

(Vassilopoulos 2016). Other social tensions range from community resentment towards Chinese migrant workers, dispossession due to land and resource grabs (Harvey 2009; Hall 2015), the displacement of fishermen in Gwadar Port in Pakistan, the repercussions of nationalist separatism in Tibet, and the onslaught of terrorism in Central Asia (Dawn 2017; Brown 2015).

As for the financial configuration, the promotion of PPPs by the Chinese leadership since 2014 encourages ties between governments and global/regional/national private funds to plan, fund, and build infrastructural projects. In 2016, the leadership even started to count PPP infrastructure investments by SOEs and state-backed financial institutions as 'private capital'. This adds infrastructure PPPs to the general growing global demand for PPP-related projects as a new 'asset class' that can be bundled, collateralized and traded by country, sector and region in global financial markets. This enables pension funds, hedge funds, venture capital, insurance companies, financial brokers and construction companies to extract fees and profits from these infrastructure PPPs (Alexander 2014, p. 7). This contributes to an emergent investment consensus (Tricarico and Sol 2015, pp. 2–3) that infrastructure offers new profit opportunities (e.g. public capital can collateralize PPPs to borrow further and private capital can gain from de-risked investment and low-risk bookable profits).

However, this emerging consensus also creates new conflicts of interest and contradictions. These arise because, in exercising their art of financial governance, PPPs (1) prioritize risk assessment in planning; (2) make the public sector responsible for de-risking infrastructural projects at early stages by offering subsidies, tax concessions, and other public resources; (3) allow SOEs and local governments to borrow from the shadow banking system as 'private capital'; and (4) turn infrastructure projects into a new 'asset class' that can be securitized. These practices blur the boundaries between borrowing, debt and investment. PPPs enhance infrastructural investment but also worsen and conceal the debt burden by moving debt 'off the books' (Alexander 2014). Further, allowing SOEs to use shadow banking loans (e.g. from wealth management funds) passes more risk onto individual investors in an already vulnerable, under-supervised sector (Wu et al. 2016). Instead of managing the crises, then, PPPs may exacerbate crisis-tendencies, especially as the RMB continues to depreciate and capital outflows from China have grown since mid-2015.

34.4   CONCLUDING REMARKS

This chapter has examined the discursive-material bases of China's new geostrategic imaginary of OBOR and its translation into specific economic initiatives. In response to the 2008 global financial crisis, a vast stimulus package and policies designed to increase liquidity have contributed towards the triple property, infrastructure and financial asset bubbles that have severely challenged China GDP growth rates. The new Xi–Li leadership went into a crisis-management mode. Discursively, it appropriated the 'new normal' rhetoric and constructed a trans-regional, multi-scalar OBOR imaginary. The latter expands China's 'Go West' and 'Go Out' policies in geoeconomic and geopolitical terms. Materially, they are condensing two sets of governance configurations that seek to displace China's overcapacities abroad by rearticulating sociospatial reorganization, infrastructure development, and financing mechanisms. An incipient infrastructural–infocommunication–finance complex is promoting an emerging trans-regional investment consensus. While this creates opportunities for further capital accumulation (e.g. through infrastructure building and finance), it also produces conflicts of interest, contradictions, and remakes rather than overcomes uneven economic, political and sociospatial development along both belt and road. The OBOR project is obviously still in its infancy and one cannot exclude perinatal morbidity.

34.5　REFERENCES

Alexander, N. (2014), 'The emerging multi-polar world order', Heinrich Böll Foundation, accessed 2 March 2018 at www.fahamu.org/file/1032/download?token=N6zok5wR.

Brown, R. (2015), 'Where would the Silk Road lead?', accessed 2 March 2018 at https://academiccommons.columbia.edu/catalog/ac:197926.

Centre for Strategic and International Studies (2015), 'Building China's "One Belt, One Road"', 3 April, accessed 2 March 2018 at http://csis.org/publication/building-chinas-one-belt-one-road.

China Daily (2015a), 'China's 2015 diplomacy focuses on "Belt and Road"', 8 March, accessed 2 March 2018 at http://www.chinadaily.com.cn/china/2015twosession/2015-03/08/content_19750295_2.htm.

China Daily (2015b), 'One Belt One Road can be said as the second biggest geographical discovery in human history after Mackinder's breakthrough', 一带一路" 构想堪称人类历 史上第二次地理大发现, 6 May, accessed 2 January 2017 at http://china.chinadaily.com.cn/2015-05/06/content_20633871.htm (in Chinese).

Clarke, M. (2015), 'Understanding China's Eurasian pivot', *The Diplomat*, 10 September, accessed 2 March 2018 at http://thediplomat.com/2015/09/understanding-chinas-eurasian-pivot/.

Clarke, M. (2016), 'Beijing's March West', accessed 2 March 2018 at https://www.psa.ac.uk/sites/default/files/conference/papers/2016/Clarke-PSA-2016-paper.pdf.

CLSA (2015), 'A brilliant plan: One Belt One Road', accessed 2 January 2017 at https://www.clsa.com/special/onebeltoneroad/.

Dawn (2017), 'Exclusive: CPEC master plan revealed', 15 May, accessed 2 March 2018 at https://www.dawn.com/news/1333101.

Foucault, M. (1980), *Power/Knowledge*, New York: Vintage.

Hall, D. (2015), *Why Public–Private Partnerships Don't Work*, Greenwich: Public Service International Research Unit, University of Greenwich.

Hartig, F. (2016), *Chinese Public Diplomacy: The Rise of the Confucius Institute*, London: Routledge.

Harvey, D. (2009), *The New Imperialism*, Oxford: Oxford University Press.

Jin, J. (2015), 'The true intent behind China's AIIB strategy', *Fujitsu Research Institute*, 25 August, accessed 2 March 2018 at http://www.fujitsu.com/jp/group/fri/en/column/message/2015/2015-08-25.html.

Lam, W. (2009), 'Hu Jintao unveils major foreign-policy initiative', *China Brief*, **24** (9), 2–4.

Lam, W. (2015), 'Stock market crash reveals serious flaws in the Xi Administration's economic policies', *China Brief*, **15** (14).

Lin, C.-P. (2015), 'AIIB and One Belt One Road: dominating Eurasia without war', *UDN News*, 21 April.

Liu, W. and M. Dunford (2016), 'Inclusive globalization: unpacking China's Belt and Road initiative', *Area Development and Policy*, **1** (3), 323–340.

Liu, X. (2015), 'New Silk Road is an opportunity and not a threat', *Financial Times*, 24 May.

Madan, T. (2016), 'What India thinks about China's One Belt, One Road initiative', New York: Brookings Institution.

Moore, A. and N. Perdu (2014), 'Imagining a critical geopolitical cartography', *Geography Compass*, **8** (12), 892–901.

Morozova, N. (2014), 'Can there be ethical politics? Rethinking the relationship between European Geopolitics and Russian Eurasianism', Moscow: National Research University, Higher School of Economics, WP BRP 08/IR/2014, accessed 2 March 2018 at https://www.hse.ru/data/2014/11/19/1101015101/08IR2014.pdf.

The Pacific Perspective (2017), 'Has China abandoned the pretense of a "peaceful rise"?', 3 February, accessed 2 March 2018 at https://thepacificperspective.wordpress.com/2017/02/03/has-china-abandoned-the-pretense-of-a-peaceful-rise/.

Pickles, J. (2004), *A History of Spaces: Cartographic Reason, Mapping, and the Geo-coded World*, New York: Psychology Press.

Rudolf, M. (2015), 'China's "Silk Road" initiative is at risk of failure', *The Diplomat*, 24 September, accessed 2 March 2018 at http://thediplomat.com/2015/09/chinas-silk-road-initiative-is-at-risk-of-failure/.

Shirk, S. (2008), *China: Fragile Superpower*, New York: Oxford University Press.

Sorensen, C. (2015), 'The significance of Xi Jinping's "Chinese Dream" for Chinese foreign policy: from "Tao Guang Yang Hui" to "Fen Fa You Wei"', *Journal of Chinese International Relations*, **3** (1), 53–73.

Standard and Poor's (2015), 'China's corporate debt looms large', accessed 2 March 2018 at http://www.finan ceasia.com/News/399907,china8217s-corporate-debt-looms-large.aspx.

Sum, N.-L. (2013), 'Rethinking "developmental state" via cultural political economy: neoliberal developmentalism and the case of China', paper presented to the 1st International Workshop on 'Geo-political Economies of East Asia', Seoul National University, 22 August.

Sum N.-L. and B. Jessop (2013), *Towards a Cultural Political Economy: Putting Culture in Its Place in Political Economy*, Cheltenham, UK and Northampton, MA, USA: Edward Elgar Publishing.

Sum, N.-L. (2016a), 'A regulationist and variegated capitalism approach to China since 1978: four stages of complex exportism in the world economy', in R. Boyer (ed.), *China and Regulation Theory*, Beijing: Beijing University Press, pp. 66–95, translated into Chinese.

Sum N.-L. (2016b), 'The makings of subaltern-diaosi subject: embodiment, contradictory consciousness and re-hegemonization of diaosi in China', *Globalizations*, **14** (2), 298–312.

Swain, M. (2014), 'Chinese views and commentary on the "One Belt, One Road" initiative', accessed 2 January 2017 at http://www.hoover.org/sites/default/files/research/docs/clm47ms.pdf.

Tan, W.Z. (2015), 'China's One Belt, One Road project could aid recovery in global shipping', 24 December, accessed 2 March 2018 at http://www.lloydsloadinglist.com/freight-directory/news/China%E2%80%99s-One-Belt-One-Road-project-could-aid-recovery-in-global-shipping/65190.htm#.VzzLS-TILaI.

Tiezzi, S. (2014), 'The New Silk Road: China's Marshall Plan?', *The Diplomat*, 6 November, accessed 2 March 2018 at http://thediplomat.com/2014/11/the-new-silk-road-chinas-marshall-plan/.

Tricarico, A. and X. Sol (2015), 'Mega-infrastructure as "structural adjustment 2.0"', *Heinrich Böll Foundation*, accessed 2 March 2018 at https://us.boell.org/2015/11/05/mega-infrastructure-structural-adjustment-20.

Vassilopoulos, J. (2016), 'Chinese completes majority purchase of Greece Piraeus port', accessed 2 March 2018 at https://www.wsws.org/en/articles/2016/09/02/gree-s02.html.

Wall Street Journal (2014), 'China's "Marshall Plan"', 11 November, accessed 2 January 2017 at https://www.wsj.com/articles/chinas-marshall-plan-1415750828.

Wang, J. (2013), 'North, south, east, and west – China is in the "middle": a geostrategic chessboard' (in Chinese), *World Affairs*, 1 November, 27–52.

Wang, Y. (2014), 'China's new foreign policy: transformations and challenges reflected in changing discourse', *The Asian Forum*, accessed 2 March 2018 at http://www.theasanforum.org/chinas-new-foreign-policy-transformations-and-challenges-reflected-in-changing-discourse/.

Wang, Y. (2015), 'China's "New Silk Road": a case study in EU-China relations', in A. Amighini and A. Berkofsky (eds), *Xi's Policy Gambles: The Bumpy Road Ahead*, Milan: Italian Institute for International Political Studies, pp. 93–110.

Wu, H., Y. Zhang and W. Han (2016), 'Public–private partnerships may have added to debt overhang', *Caixin Online*, accessed 2 March 2018 at https://www.caixinglobal.com/2016-10-28/public-private-partnerships-may-have-added-to-debt-overhang-101053081.html.

Xinhua Agency (2015), 'China's PPP financing may dominate Belt and Road Infrastructure investment', accessed 2 March 2018 at http://en.xinfinance.com/html/OBAOR/Analysis/2015/101877.shtml.

Xinhuanet.com (2015), 'Vision and actions on jointly building Belt and Road', accessed on 2 January 2017 from http://news.xinhuanet.com/english/china/2015-03/28/c_134105858.htm.

Yale, W. (2015), 'China's maritime Silk Road gamble', *The Diplomat*, 22 April, accessed 2 March 2018 at http://thediplomat.com/2015/04/chinas-maritime-silk-road-gamble/.

Yi, W. (2014), 'Peaceful development and the Chinese dream of national rejuvenation', China Institute of International Studies, accessed 2 March 2018 at http://www.ciis.org.cn/english/201403/11/content_6733151.htm.

35. Australasian regionalism

Andrew Beer

35.1 INTRODUCTION

Australasia – defined as Australia and New Zealand – has a distinctive regionalism that is a product of the relatively recent period of European colonisation, the legacy of British political institutions, the significant presence of Indigenous populations and long-running engagement with global markets and the associated production of commodities for export. Each of these factors is important: both nations were colonised by the British from the late eighteenth century to the mid-nineteenth century and this has meant distinctive regional cultures and identities have emerged only to a limited degree. At the same time, the British pattern of colonisation emphasised enduring political and institutional links to the United Kingdom, resulting in a legacy of relatively strong central government institutions. Settlement by the colonists was predicated on the production of primary goods for the British Empire, resulting in a commodified agricultural system, engagement with global markets; and patterns of urban settlement that were sparse relative to many other nations. Regionalism in both nations has also been affected by the ongoing presence and growth of pre-European peoples – the Maori in New Zealand and Aboriginal and Torres Strait Islanders in Australia. In both nations Indigenous people are over-represented outside the metropolitan areas, resulting in a distinctive regional pattern evident in any discussion of Maori or Indigenous Australian issues. Since the 1980s both nations have embraced neoliberal philosophies of government (Pusey 1991; Beer ct al. 2016) with subsequent impacts for regions and regionalism in each.

The strength of the similarities between regionalism in New Zealand and Australia must be acknowledged, but at the same time it is important to recognise the differences between the two antipodean nations. Physically the two nations are very different, with one a verdant, narrow strip of often mountainous land in the Pacific Ocean, while Australia is often described as a 'wide brown land'. Importantly, the systems of government vary significantly also: Australia is a Federation comprised of six states and two territories, while New Zealand has a unitary system of government. Both nations have local governments, but those in New Zealand have a wider range of powers and greater spending authority than their counterparts in Australia. There are significant differences also in their economies, with the Australian economy larger and wealthier and, while both nations largely depend on commodity production, mining is a major economic driver in Australia while New Zealand depends more heavily on agricultural and forestry production.

This chapter examines regionalism in Australasia and considers the ways in which it has – and continues – to develop. It outlines the history of regional thinking in the period 1945 to the 1980s, before moving on to consider more recent developments. The chapter uses an examination of policy and academic writing in Australia and New Zealand to develop a better understanding of how regionalism has developed over the past three decades, before speculating on likely developments in both nations.

35.2 REGIONALISM AND POLITICAL PROCESSES

Across Australasia regionalism has developed as a political, as well as a symbolic, entity. Most importantly, regionalism and regions in Australasia are equated with non-metropolitan places, and therefore stand in contrast with Europe where the terms 'regions' and regional policy are often used to refer to large metropolitan areas. The discourse of 'regions' as non-metropolitan places is both strong and pointed in Australia, Eversole (2016, p. 1) has argued forcefully that:

> In Australia, regions are not just a geographic category. They are also a cultural category . . . regions in Australia are geographic places with particular characteristics – just like regions anywhere in the world. On the other hand, *regions* in Australia carry layers of meaning that have nothing to do with the particularities of a particular geographic place. Indeed it is not uncommon for Australians to speak of 'living in the regions'. This does not mean they are living in multiple geographic places. Rather they are living in a cultural place: regional Australia.

Critically, the Australian understanding of regionalism rules out the possibility of metropolitan regions (Eversole 2016, p. 2). In part this reflects the nature of Australasian urban systems; both New Zealand and the Australian states have primate urban structures and non-metropolitan areas have been dominated by rural industries and their interests. In a very real sense 'Australia's regions were created as servants of the capital cities' (Eversole 2016, p. 3) and are 'simultaneously (economically) dependent and independent minded' (p. 4). This 'independence of mind' has increased greatly since the early 1990s as 'regional' areas have increasingly felt the impact of a deregulated and globalised economy.

Historically, the differences between metropolitan and non-metropolitan places have been formalised in rural-based conservative parties (the National Party in New Zealand and variously the Country Liberal Party or National Party in Australia) and they have served as the primary advocates for regions – and especially regional industries. In the immediate post-war years they drove a decentralisation agenda and more recently have lobbied for better services (broadband, education and health) and infrastructure investment (roads, dams, railways). Since the mid-1990s, their non-metropolitan mandate has been challenged by a raft of – often unstable – protest parties (One Nation) and independent Members of Parliament (Wilkinson 2013, p. 17). These alternative voices channel deep seated unease with the conventional, neoliberal, policies of the two major political forces in Australia (The Australian Labor Party and the Liberal/National Party coalition). Such representation reflects the growing voices of disenfranchised individuals who are either excluded, or occupy marginal positions, within the globalised labour market.

As noted earlier, Australia has a federal system of government whereas New Zealand is a unitary state, with a single parliament and relatively powerful local governments. Each governmental system generates its own political dynamic, in New Zealand overarching regional policies are clearly the responsibility of the national government – though local governments are important also and deliver many initiatives 'on the ground'. There is a more opaque set of arrangements in Australia. The Australian constitution reserves most areas of domestic policy for the states (with the exception of social security, Indigenous issues and the control of the Northern Territory and the Australian Capital Territory). It also includes a distinctive regionalism, one in which individual states are considered regions, despite the fact that the largest – New South Wales – accounts for one third of the nation's citizens while the smallest (Tasmania) has under three per cent of the land area and population. This broad-scale regionalism has been reinforced by the institutions of government, including a system of horizontal fiscal equalisation that seeks to balance economic outcomes across the various jurisdictions. This sense of regionalism and regions, however, has never enjoyed widespread acceptance or adoption by the Australian people, and, as Brown (2006) has noted, Australia's twentieth-century political landscape was marked by a series of political movements seeking to formalise a 'regional' level of government – even if these new entities had to be created as new states within the federation. Gray and Brown (2006) have provided evidence that the appetite for such reform has not entirely vanished. The constitutional reality of 'states-as-regions' has been further undermined by the processes of vertical fiscal imbalance: the Australian federation is marked by relatively weak and resource deprived sub-national units of government, with national government revenue raising and expenditures dominating public sector expenditures. Brown (2006) argued only Malaysia provides an example of a more centralised federation.

In Australia and New Zealand there is a long-standing preoccupation with issues of population growth and retention. In a policy landscape often bereft of hard-and-fast social and economic indicators, population growth and decline is often used as the barometer of regional performance. Poot (2005) has noted the importance of population change in measuring the well-being of New Zealand's regions, while McKenzie (1994), Beer and Keane (2000) and Hugo (2005) examined regional population loss in Australia and its implications for the sustainability of these places (see also Connell and McManus 2011). Such concerns are understandable, Australia and New Zealand have some of the most sparsely populated regions in the world, and there is both public and policy unease about the sustainability of services and quality of life in very small urban settlements distant from other population centres. In many ways this focus on the adequacy of regional populations to sustain communities is one of the distinctive features of regionalism in Australasia. While these issues have recently risen to policy attention in Europe, they are a long-standing feature of regional policy discourse in the antipodes and have been the focus of public sector programmes both recently and in the more distant past (see, for example, Government of Victoria 2004).

35.3 THE POLITICS AND POLICY OF REGIONALISM IN AUSTRALIA

Many established accounts of regionalism (Collits 2008, 2015) and regional policy in Australia have argued that engagement with regions has declined over time, with the withdrawal of policies and initiatives and the shift to a 'self-help' ethos (Cheshire and Lawrence 2005) that absolves governments of responsibility. Conventionally authors such as Beer (2000) and Collits (2008, 2011) have focussed on the establishment of Committees for Decentralisation and Development by the Curtin Labor government in 1949; the establishment of formal policies of decentralisation in a number of Australian states including NSW and Victoria in the 1950s and 1960s; a wave of regional and decentralisation initiatives introduced by the Whitlam Labor government in 1972, followed by a marked absence of significant commitments at the national level over subsequent decades. Scholars have noted (Collits 2015) that the Australian government in particular has displayed an episodic engagement with regionalism and regional policies, with periods of intense policy development interspersed amongst much longer periods of neglect (Higgins and Zagorski 1989; Forth 1996). By contrast, social democratic parties (such as the Australian Labor Party or the New Zealand Labour Party) have identified with their voting base in the major cities – immediately adding a party-political dimension to any discussion of regions or regional issues. There has therefore been a tendency under conservative governments in Australia to limit regional initiatives to their rural and remote areas. Collits (2015) has argued that at the national level Labor governments have been more likely to engage with regional issues than their conservative (Liberal/National Party) opponents, with the exception of the Howard Coalition government post 1998 and this new-found commitment to the welfare of the regions was a product of the rise of a more radical, rurally based rival.

There is a second important political dimension to regionalism in Australia: often regional policy and programmes are used by governments to achieve overtly party-political ends. Over a number of years, the reports of the Australian government's Auditor General (ANAO 2007, 2010) have noted that regional initiatives are more likely to be funded in government-held seats than those held by the opposition. In part these outcomes reflect the deliberate design of programmes and the priorities of government, but inevitably call into question the objective merit of all regional programmes (see Daley and Lancy 2011). Collits (2015) has observed that

> each of the main political parties has sought to take ownership of concern for non-metropolitan Australia. This often has meant that regional policy debate and political practice has descended into arguments over the size of one's commitment, rather than the quality or impacts of the policies . . . This is typically reflected in the perception amongst people outside the capital of an inequality of resources. (Collits 2015, p. 15)

It has also resulted in an emphasis on guaranteeing and funding services for non-metropolitan regions, rather than a more active strategy focussed on generating employment and economic growth locally.

Academic accounts of regional policies in Australia in particular have often been presented as a strange admixture of Ministerial announcements of new initiatives (Collits 2003) with often limited impact; relatively modest public sector investments in politically advantageous regions; and government promotion of a 'self-help' ethos for regional communities. As Collits (2003) has shown, the focus on providing Ministers with 'announceables' too often results in a triumph of form over substance: the resultant regional programmes are piecemeal and unlikely to exert a real impact in the recipient localities, policy objectives are subordinated to political goals, communities are encouraged to focus on lobbying politicians rather than taking substantive actions, and too great an emphasis is placed on public sector subventions over private sector investment. Overall, regional policy has lacked both a substantive evidence base and a focus on concrete outcomes, with Eversole (2016) noting that locally based regional development efforts in Australia often favoured the appearance of achievement over the reality of substantive improvements to community or regional well-being and economic performance. She observed that efforts to sustain small towns were commonly unsophisticated and directed toward mobilising community actions. Moreover:

> Definitions of success were enthusiastic and uncritical. Generating energy and community spirit in local towns was as valuable as generating infrastructure or jobs. (Eversole 2016, p. 16)

Contemporary accounts of regional policy and regionalism in Australia (Cheshire and Laurence 2005; Beer et al. 2005; Tonts 1995) have emphasised the rise of neoliberal policies within Australia since the mid-1980s and the associated globalisation of the economy (Pusey 1991). Similar analyses have been advanced for New Zealand where a regional 'self-help' focus has also been advocated (Dalziel and Saunders 2005). This argument suggests that beginning in the 1980s central governments in Australasia moved away from formal regional development policies and programmes, supplanting systematic approaches to place-based development with a philosophy of economic rationalism that prioritised national economic growth, and the efficient operation of markets, over the need for government engagement with the development of cities and regions. This perspective emphasised the role of communities – regions, cities and townships – in shaping their own future (McKinsey and Co 1994) with an economy re-invigorated by access to global markets and reduced government intervention.

Neoliberalism, of course, has had very uneven impacts on Australian society and, while it has contributed to rising national prosperity and increased average household incomes (Whiteford 2013), many within Australian society have fallen behind (Beer et al. 2016). Critically, communities and regions have been affected, with a number of authors noting the uneven geography of advantage and disadvantage in a restructured Australia and New Zealand (Baum et al. 2005). The larger cities – and especially their inner-city areas – have prospered on the back of an expanding services sector, while non-metropolitan Australia and the outer suburbs of the capitals have felt the hard edge of the shift to a post-industrial society. Critically, neoliberal policies mobilised resistance, with affected individuals and communities voting for independent Members of Parliament and minor political parties (Davis and Stimson 1998). These patterns of region-specific disillusionment have become entrenched in Australian political life, with the most recent federal elections (2016) recording a continuing shift to alternative political philosophies.

As noted above, the established narrative around regions and regionalism in Australia largely consists of four parts:

- first, Australia's formal – and significant – engagement with regional issues largely started after 1945 with the Chifley Labor government;
- second, at both the state and national level the commitment of central governments to regions has varied over time, with marked upswings and decline in activity as political interest has waxed and waned (Wilkinson 2013);
- third, Labor governments have tended to be more engaged with regional policies than their conservative Coalition opponents, largely because of their greater commitment to public sector intervention in the economy; and,
- finally, there has been an appreciable decline in government commitment to regional policy over the past 30 years, with central governments moving away

from well-founded policies and programmes to approaches that advocate self-help philosophies to communities.

The episodic nature of the engagement of Australian governments with regional issues has had a profound impact on the on-the-ground articulation of regional policy and the commitment to regionalism. Central governments have introduced waves of regional initiatives during periods of policy priority, often imposing new measures and agencies on top of already existing structures (Maude and Beer 2000). The negative impacts of this process of institutional accretion have been exacerbated by the potential for the duplication of effort as all three tiers of government seek to shape regional agendas and drive growth, resulting in a confused landscape of agencies and organisations, many with limited budgets or influence (Maude and Beer 2000). The complexity is such that much regional development effort in Australia is directed to co-ordinating the efforts of the various bodies at the regional scale (Beer et al. 2003; Buultjens et al. 2012) rather than achieving tangible outcomes. As a number of authors have observed (Buultjens et al. 2012), many regional development agencies report limited impact and/or effectiveness, difficulties in gaining traction with other public-sector agencies and setting a strategic agenda that is appropriate. More fundamentally, the interface between regional initiatives and the political process means that agencies are often under-resourced (Buultjens et al. 2012), and over-politicised (Maude 2004; Conway and Dollery 2009) for the task at hand.

Conway and Dollery (2009) were highly critical of regional development processes in Australia, and in particular the influence of party politics on the actions and decisions of individual regional development agencies. Their analysis of the Boards of regional development authorities in New South Wales and Queensland led them to conclude

> . . . regional development is incomprehensible . . . a 'myth or illusion' . . . regional development is principally driven by political motives and boards are regarded, at least by those within the boardroom, as instruments of political expediency. (Conway and Dollery 2009, p. 1)

Other research lends support to this interpretation of regionalism in Australia. For example, Sotarauta and Beer (2016) found significant gaps in regional leadership in Australia relative to Finland, and this deficit was the outcome of central governments retaining tight control over local governmental and political institutions. In Australia, the leadership of places – cities, towns and regions – often comes from outside government because formal institutions lack the independence and freedom to act if positive change is to be achieved (Beer 2014). Clearly, politics and the concerns of party political leaders cast a long shadow over regionalism and regional development in Australia.

In broad terms, this account of central government attitudes towards regions and regionalism is broadly similar for New Zealand. There has been an equivalent embrace of neoliberal policies and the adoption of a social and economic policies – such as Regional Partnership Programs – focused on regions that are broadly similar to those found in Australia.[1] In this sense, there is an identifiable antipodean or Australasian regionalism. One of the challenges with this account of regionalism in Australasia is that it is difficult to test empirically: while we can reflect upon earlier commentary and documentation (see, for example, Logan 1978), it is difficult to evaluate the import of these initiatives on the 1960s, 1970s and 1980s relative to contemporary programmes. In Australia this challenge is especially acute, as neither the national or state Treasuries report public sector expenditures by location, and there are nine central governments at the national level (six states, two territories and one national government) making the task difficult. Moreover, many 'regional' expenditures are buried within the outlays of sector specific agencies, such as health, police, social services and so on.

One indicator of engagement with regions and regionalism that is relatively easily measured is the level of political commitment, as reflected in the inclusion of a Minister with the word 'region' in their title, within government. Over time, there has been variation in the form of words used: in some periods such portfolios have been referred to as Ministers for Regional Development, Ministers for Regional Services or Ministers for Decentralisation and Regions. Such Ministries have been established at both the national and state levels. Data were collected for the period 1939 to 2015 on the presence of a 'regional' Minister in each Australian state and at the national level. These data were then quantified by enumerating the number of months each year a regional Minister was in place for each jurisdiction, and then creating an index by adding together the score across Australia as a whole. The outcomes of this index are presented in Figure 35.1. The interpretation of these data needs to acknowledge a number of factors: first, in no year was a regional Minister identified for Tasmania. On occasion, a Minister for State Development was included in the Tasmanian Ministry, and most likely had regional development responsibilities, but their focus was more likely to be on broader state development issues and therefore they were a zero return within the index. Second, the index has not been weighted, that is, it is a simple binary metric of the presence or absence of a regional Minister. It is important to acknowledge that there could be grounds for the imposition of weights, as the nomination of a Federal Minister into this portfolio area clearly indicates a greater commitment to regions and regionalism than a similar post in the South Australian, West Australian or Victorian government.

The index of regional engagement derived from the presence of regional Ministers in the

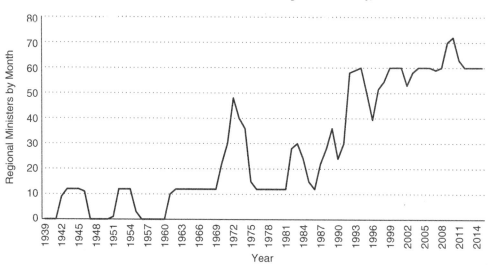

Source: The author based on state and Australian government gazettes.

Figure 35.1   Index of regional Ministers across Australia by year, 1939–2015

Australian governmental landscape presents a picture that is both familiar and unfamiliar to commentators on Australia's regions. In many ways the results conform with expectations: there are clearly identified episodes when political commitment to the regions waxes and wanes, and many of these episodes are synchronous with periods in which the Australian Labor Party has held office. Importantly, the variability in engagement appears to have increased over time, especially since 1990. Second, there are notable periods when the total engagement with regional issues has remained low, and this reflects the reality of uncertainties around where a regional agenda sits within a federation comprised of three tiers of government. Critically, the index also provides insights into political engagement with the regions that were not expected: the data clearly show that over the past 25 years Ministerial focus on regions has reached new highs and has been a sustained concern of governments over a prolonged period. In many respects, the contemporary era represents a 'golden age' of engagement with regional issues, not a period of governmental indifference as often portrayed in academic commentary and political discourse.

The mere presence of a regional Minister within a government does not, in itself, guarantee the adequacy of programmes or suggest a substantial commitment by governments to issues of spatial development. In the context of a discussion of regions and regionalism it is reasonable to question the impact of such appointments and ask: regional Minister – to what purpose, and to what effect? Have they ushered in substantial change or have they merely diverted criticism? In one sense, Ministers with a regional focus provide a focal point for debating questions of regionalism and highlighting government contributions to non-metropolitan regions. Over the last two decades, for example, Ministers have tended to release an annual budget statement (see, for example, Truss and Briggs 2015), which may, or may not, include major policy initiatives or new expenditure announcements. In one sense then, regional Ministers simply serve as a lightning rod for regional concerns and the development of new policies. And while their contribution to government processes and the people of non-metropolitan Australia may be more symbolic than substantive, their appointment is important, adding a regional 'voice' to the broader political landscape.

Finally, it is important to acknowledge an important shifting of emphasis in regionalism and regional policy over the past two decades: there has been a notable growth in the priority attached to regional services. Both Collits (2015) and Eversole (2016) have noted that since 1996 and the election of the Howard Coalition government the policy discourse has given greater attention to how basic services – health, banking, telecommunications, education, retailing and so on – are delivered outside the metropolitan areas. There are a number of key dimensions to this debate: first, there is an implicit 'deficits' model embedded within this policy theme, with governments called upon to overcome shortfalls created by the rationalisation of public and private sector services. Second, there is a sense in which the focus on regional services reflects a dimension of government intervention that is more 'acceptable' to governments: administrations unwilling to commit to the long-term and difficult task of ensuring economic growth in small rural or remote regions are more open to a discussion with communities on the adequacy of services. Importantly, these governments can acknowledge deficiencies in the market delivery of services to distant towns and communities while retaining a rhetoric of economic rationality. In many sectors governments either regulate to achieve minimum service levels in all regions – for example, telecommunications – or provide subsidies to achieve the same ends (health, transport and education). The ubiquity of this concern in regional policy in Australia was elegantly captured by Eversole (2016, p. 20) who observed:

> Equity and sustainability of services for 'the regions' are persisting leitmotifs in Australian regional policy.

And, it is likely they will remain prominent for decades to come as there will be an ongoing need to support services.

35.4   THE POLITICS AND POLICY OF REGIONALISM IN NEW ZEALAND

In some respects, the politics and policy of regionalism in New Zealand is less complex than for Australia and this greater simplicity reflects the unitary system of government. Within New Zealand's system of government, the national government sits over 16 local governments representing broad regions within the national landscape. Of these local governments, eleven are administered by regional councils (the highest level), while six are territorial authorities, representing a second tier within local government in New Zealand. The local governments were established in their current form by the Local Government Act 2002 and their enabling legislation requires them to promote economically, socially and culturally sustainable development. In this respect, local governments in New Zealand have an unambiguous role in regional development and regionalism not evident in Australia.

In common with Australia, the commitment of national governments to regionalism and regional programmes has varied over time as political priorities have shifted. Importantly, governments led by the New Zealand Labour Party have been willing to engage with formal regional policy, while conservative National Party Governments have had a lesser commitment in this area of government intervention. This political pendulum has been important, especially in a nation that experimented with radical forms of neoliberalism over the past forty years. Schollmann and Nischalke writing in 2005 observed that for New Zealand, 'regional development . . . [has] not been an important part of central government since the 1970s' (Schollmann and Nischalke 2005, p. 47). Both National Party and Labour Party led governments have sought to improve national and regional economic performance, while the former have adopted strategies intended to free up markets, the latter have acknowledged the need for direct action by governments in some areas.

Under Labour Prime Minister Helen Clarke, central government policies set out to:

- Address the impacts of central government activities on regional performance, including achieving better co-ordination across agencies and tiers of government;
- Provide leadership in strategy formation and in promoting a broader perspective on development issues; and
- Make better use of existing resources while simultaneously refocussing them on achieving sustainable development (Schollmann and Nischalke 2005).

Research by Dalziel and Saunders (2003) found that the regional partnership programs (RPP) introduced by the New Zealand government in this period varied considerably in their implementation, with some localities handing responsibility for programme delivery to specialist regional agencies, and others establishing regional working groups to deliver the outcomes of strategic plans.

More recent governments led by the National Party's Prime Minister Key have had a singular focus on boosting the nation's competitive advantage, with resulting policy frameworks boosting the growth of the largest city – Auckland – while provincial centres decline (EDANZ 2014). Moreover, many of the tensions evident in Australia's regions and regionalism, are observable also in New Zealand, especially issues around the aspiration to develop an overarching, coherent regional development policy; the devolution of decision making authority to local (regional) governments; and, strengthening the implementation of regional plans.

Regionalism in New Zealand is distinguished from Australia in the prominence given to Maori people and their well-being in national and regional development. As Davies et al. (2005) have noted, the development of Maori peoples in New Zealand is simultaneously an economic, cultural and political project. It is one with important regional implications as the Maori make up more than 25 per cent of the population in regions such as the southern part of the South Island, the top-most part of the North Island (Northland) and around the Bay of Plenty. Unlike Australia's indigenous peoples, the Maori retained significant tracts of productive land through colonisation and sustained significant rights under the Treaty of Waitangi of 1840. Critically, issues of Maori development have significant implications for regional well-being and advancement, while conversely regional programmes are significant for the Maori in turn.

35.5 CONCLUSION

This chapter set out to examine regions and regionalism in Australasia. It has argued that Australia and New Zealand have a distinctive, antipodean, regionalism that reflects the history of each nation, their forms of government, the ongoing presence of indigenous populations and Australasia's form of neoliberalism.

In many ways it is possible to identify two distinct periods in Australasian engagement with regionalism. From – broadly – 1945 to the late 1970s both Australia and New Zealand functioned as industrial societies with a strong reliance on Keynesian economic management. Both called upon a mix of primary industries and manufacturing industries to support their economies and implemented a suite of policies that sought to deliver both economic growth and a fair society. Regional policy and regionalism in this era was embedded within the wider liberal agenda of governments, with policies – such as subsidies for firms relocating to non-metropolitan places – simply one more dimension of public sector management of the economy. Since the early 1980s both nations have adopted neoliberalism and the use of monetary policies to manage the economy. These philosophies and instruments of government stand against specific support for regions and regional industries, creating conditions that have boosted the growth of the major metropolitan areas and overseen the decline of many non-metropolitan centres and regions in both nations.

In Australia in particular there is a fundamental irony evident within contemporary regionalism and regional policy: neoliberalism with its emphasis on spatially blind economic policies and limited government intervention in the economy, has created conditions that have escalated the politics of regionalism. Independent Members of Parliament and alternative political parties have garnered a wealth of support in outer metropolitan electorates and non-metropolitan regions. They have, in turn, driven a policy engagement with the regions that is focused on specific interests, often localised in its impacts and flexible in its broader political allegiance. In New Zealand this tendency has been less acute because of differences in methods of election and the unitary system of government. But many of the same tendencies remain evident, especially the episodic nature of central government involvement with regions, the greater willingness of Labour governments to embrace formal regional policies when compared with their conservative political opponents, and the cross-cutting lines with minor political parties and indigenous issues.

Looking to the future it is difficult to foresee a departure in Australasia from the trends evident over the past 20 years. While the major metropolitan areas will continue to strengthen economically – especially, Sydney, Melbourne, Brisbane, Perth and Auckland – globalisation continues to produce regions of relative disadvantage, resulting in ever more strident calls for ameliorative action by governments. Neoliberalism has not been the death of regionalism in Australasia; instead it has ushered in a new age of regional awareness and action.

35.6   NOTE

1. It would be wrong to assume that New Zealand policy settings simply follow Australian practice. While there is an ongoing exchange between the two nations, in many areas of programme development New Zealand has been more innovative than its larger neighbour, with many ideas first implemented there.

35.7   ACKNOWLEDGEMENTS

Thanks to Ms Sandy Horne for her assistance in the preparation of this chapter.

35.8   REFERENCES

Australian National Audit Office (ANAO) (2007), *Performance of the Regional Partnerships Program*, Canberra: ANAO.
Australian National Audit Office (ANAO) (2010), *The Establishment, Implementation and Administration of the Strategic Projects Component of the Regional and Local Community Infrastructure Fund*, Canberra: ANAO.
Baum, S., R. Stimson and K. O'Connor (2005), *Fault Lines Exposed: Advantage and Disadvantage in Australia's Settlement System*, Clayton: Monash E-Press.
Beer, A. (2000), 'Regional policy in Australia: running out of solutions?', in B. Pritchard and P. McManus (eds), *Land of Discontent*, Sydney: University of New South Wales Press, pp. 169–194.
Beer, A. and R. Keane (2000), 'Population decline and service provision in regional Australia: a case study of rural and remote south Australia', *People and Place*, **8** (2), 69–76.
Beer, A., G. Haughton and A. Maude (2003), *Developing Locally: Lessons in Economic Development from Four Nations*, Bristol: Policy Press.
Beer, A., T. Clower, G. Haughton and A. Maude (2005), 'Neoliberalism and the institutions for regional development in Australia', *Geographical Research*, **43** (1), 49–58.
Beer, A. (2014), 'Leadership and the governance of rural communities', *Journal of Rural Studies*, **34**, 254–262.
Beer, A., R. Bentley, E. Baker, K. Mason, K. Mallett, A. Kavanagh and T. LaMontagne (2016), 'Neoliberalism,

economic restructuring and policy change: precarious housing and precarious employment in Australia', *Urban Studies*, **53** (8), 1542–1558.

Brown, A.J. (2006), 'Federalism, regionalism and the reshaping of Australian governance', in A. Brown and J. Bellamy (eds), *Federalism and Regionalism in Australia*, Canberra: ANU E Press, pp. 11–32.

Buultjens, J., K. Ambrosil and B. Dollery (2012), 'The establishment of regional development Australia committees in Australia: issues and initiatives for the future', *Australasian Journal of Regional Studies*, **18** (2), 182–205.

Cheshire, L. and G. Lawrence (2005), 'Neoliberalism, individualisation and community: regional restructuring in Australia', *Social Identities*, **11** (5), 435–445.

Collits, P. (2003), 'Tyranny of the announceable and the scourge of economic development bingo', Paper presented to the Australian and New Zealand Regional Studies Association Annual Conference, Fremantle, unpublished.

Collits, P. (2008), 'The Howard government and regional development', *Australasian Journal of Regional Studies*, **14** (3), 287–212.

Collits, P. (2011), 'Country towns in a big Australia: the decentralisation debate revisited', in J. Martin and T. Budge (eds), *The Sustainability of Australia's Country Towns*, Bendigo: VURRN Press, pp. 82–96.

Collits, P. (2015), 'Regional policy in post war Australia: much ado about nothing?', in A. Hogan and M. Young (eds), *Rural and Regional Futures*, Abingdon: Routledge, pp. 19–38.

Connell, J. and P. McManus (2011), *Rural Revival: Place Marketing, Tree Change and Regional Migration in Australia*, Farnham: Ashgate.

Conway, M. and B. Dollery (2009), 'Constructing regional development in the boardroom, Centre for Local Government University of New England', *Working Paper 6*, Armidale.

Daley, J. and A. Lancy (2011), *Investing in Regions: Making a Difference*, Melbourne: Grattan Institute.

Dalziel, P. and C. Saunders (2003), *Regional Economic Development in New Zealand: Who Owns It?* Agribusiness and Economics Research Unit, University of Canterbury, unpublished.

Dalziel, P. and C. Saunders (2005), 'Regional partnerships for economic development', in J. Rowe (ed.), *Economic Development in New Zealand*, Aldershot: Ashgate, pp. 88–105.

Davies, P., R. Lattimore and K. Ikin (2005), 'Maori economic development: overview and prospects', in J. Rowe (ed.), *Economic Development in New Zealand*, Aldershot: Ashgate, pp. 107–126.

Davis, R. and R. Stimson (1998), 'Disillusionment and disenfranchisement at the fringe: explaining the geography of the one nation party vote in the Queensland election', *People and Place*, **6** (3), 69–82.

Economic Development Agencies of New Zealand (EDANZ) (2014), *Briefing Paper: Regional Development*, Auckland: EDANZ.

Eversole, R. (2016), *Regional Development in Australia: Being Regional*, Abingdon: Routledge.

Forth, G. (1996), 'Redrawing the map of regional Australia: The Commonwealth's Regional Development Program', *Australasian Journal of Regional Studies*, **2** (1), 75–86.

Government of Victoria (2004), *Beyond 5 Million: The Victorian Government's Population Policy*, Melbourne: Government of Victoria.

Gray, I. and A. Brown (2006), 'The political viability of federal reform: interpreting public attitudes', in A. Brown and J. Bellamy (eds), *Federalism and Regionalism in Australia*, Canberra: ANU E-Press, pp. 33–56.

Higgins, B. and K. Zagorski (eds) (1989), *Australian Regional Developments*, Canberra: Australian Government Publishing Service.

Hugo, G. (2005), *The State of Rural Populations*, Kensington: UNSW Press.

Logan, M. (1978), 'Regional policy', in P. Scott (ed.), *Australian Cities and Public Policy*, Melbourne: Georgian House, pp. 23–39.

Maude, A. and A. Beer (2000), 'Regional development agencies in Australia: a comparative evaluation of institutional strengths and weaknesses', *Town Planning Review*, **71** (1), 1–24.

Maude, A. (2004), 'Regional development processes and policies in Australia: a review of research 1990–2002', *European Planning Studies*, **12** (1), 3–26.

McKenzie, F. (1994), *Regional Population Decline in Australia: Impacts and Policy Implications*, Carlton: Bureau of Immigration and Population Research.

McKinsey and Co (1994), *Lead Local, Compete Global*, Sydney: McKinsey and Co.

Poot, J. (2005), 'The quest for people: population and economic development', in E. Rowe (ed.), *Economic Development in New Zealand*, Aldershot: Ashgate, pp. 31–46.

Pusey, M. (1991), *Economic Rationalism and Canberra: A Nation Building State Changes its Mind*, Melbourne: Cambridge University Press.

Schollmann, A. and C. Nischalke (2005), 'Central government and regional development policy: origins, lessons and future challenges', in E. Rowe (ed.), *Economic Development in New Zealand*, Aldershot: Ashgate, pp. 47–69.

Sotarauta, M. and A. Beer (2016), 'Governance, agency and place leadership: lessons from a cross national analysis', *Regional Studies*, **51** (2), 1–14.

Tonts, M. (1995), 'Some recent trends in Australian regional economic development policy', *Regional Studies*, **33** (6), 581–586.

Truss, W. and J. Briggs (2015), *Partnership for Regional Growth, 2015–16*, Canberra: Commonwealth of Australia.

Whiteford, P. (2013), *Australia: Inequality and Prosperity and their Impacts in a Radical Welfare State*, Canberra: Social Policy Action Centre, ANU.

Wilkinson, J. (2013), 'NSW parliamentary library research service', Briefing Paper No 13/03, Sydney.

36. African regionalism
Frank Mattheis

36.1 A SHORT HISTORY OF THE REGIONALISATION OF AFRICA

The late-nineteenth century saw the rise of Pan-movements in many parts of the world but none of them still persists in the way that Pan-Africanism does. Unlike other Pan-nationalist and Pan-regionalist movements (Snyder 1984) – for example, Pan-Germanism, Pan-Asianism – Pan-Africanism still represents a central vector for how African elites and societies position themselves in the global order.

When Pan-Africanism emerged as a Pan-movement in the early twentieth century, it was foremost an intellectual quest by descendants of slaves across the US and the Caribbean, as well as in European cities (notably London and Paris). As such, the movement was seemingly paradoxically chiefly fostered within the leading Western powers of that period. However, this ideology was precisely a product of the disruption between the proclaimed 'civic nationalism' of these powers, which bases citizenship on collective values on one side and the omnipresent racist exclusion on the other side. The Pan-African movement romanticised the common territory of origin in order to resolve the conflict between European and American assimilation and cultural autonomy. However, the ambition to reinvigorate links with the African continent proved difficult to materialise. The physical, social and cultural distance of Pan-Africans to societies on the continent confined Africa to a reference point rather than an active element. In addition to language barriers and a normative gap, Pan-African movements from within Africa only gradually emerged, such as in intellectual centres in West Africa.

The objectives that united Pan-Africans were directed towards the social position of slave descendants in North America and Europe in terms of reconciling assimilation with modern Western values with a cultural emancipation and political self-determination. Additional common objectives were geared towards the social and economic modernisation of an independent Africa. This emphasised the experience of slavery as uprooting as well as decolonisation as an overarching endeavour. The Pan-African focus on territory of origin was thus initially a movement to shape the self-perception of slave descendants. Its broad line of identification allowed for a variety of Pan-African definitions to emerge, each defining inclusion and exclusion differently. Under Pan-African reference points different political streams and identities emerged. One group of slave descendants, in particular in the US, sought a close linkage with the African people of their 'homeland'. Meanwhile, the slogan 'Africa for the Africans' embodied the anticolonial struggle based on cultural and political unity of the continent (Hill and Pirio 1987). In the Francophone world, Negritude comprised the ideal of equality of colonial inhabitants and their culture within a French system. Furthermore, racial and religious identities emerged, such as Pan-Negroism or a Pan-Africanism excluding North Africa. Further on, Pan-Africanism was also interpreted as being part of a broader anti-colonial solidarity movement that extended to Asia and parts of Latin America (Kahin 1956).

The 1950s and 1960s were a watershed for Pan-Africanism. The retreat of European powers from Africa as well as the United Nations values of self-determination and racial equality transformed Pan-Africanism from an ideal into a political reality. However, the achievement of political independence by most African colonies also exacerbated the fragmentation between the different streams of Pan-Africanism. As the joint enemy of colonialism faded, particularistic interests came to the fore. Even if the liberation struggle was characterised by transnational solidarity, the artificial colonial borders were largely maintained. The production of political power was based on sovereign nation-states in a Westphalian sense, to which federations or a territorial reorganisation of the continent represented a threat to national interests and stability.

The first post-colonial regional organisations in North and West Africa soon fell apart in the wake of nationalist state-building. Even colonial regional structures such as French Equatorial Africa fell apart into national states. An additional rupture line separated North and sub-Saharan Africa with autonomous regional projects emerging in the intellectual centres of Accra and Cairo. The divergence was expressed in a short-lived Pan-Arab state in the shape of a union between Syria and Egypt. At the same time, the bond between Francophone and anglophone countries respectively remained strong, expressed in Commonwealth membership and the Françafrique linkages.

As Pan-Africanism became a political ideology in postcolonial Africa, the composition of actors changed. Intellectuals debated the relevance of European discourses of liberalism and modernity vis-à-vis traditional African cultures. The resulting compromises reflected a localised adaptation of external concepts. African versions of socialism, nationalism and eventually regionalism emerged in a way to reflect their context. African socialism equated imperialism and capitalism while putting less emphasis on class struggle and atheism. African nationalism entailed national symbolism and political parties without overcoming tribal rule and ethnic division lines. Finally, African regionalism was inspired by the institutional forms of regional integration in post-war Europe but incorporated elements of both African socialism and nationalism. Free trade and neo-colonial division of labour were considered to be constitutive of an unequal global economic system. Therefore, a regional industrial development warranted protectionism and import-substitution. At the same time regionalism was seen as an enabling framework for states to acquire sovereignty, rather than pooling it.

The Cold War period witnessed a complex picture of regionalism in Africa. In 1963, the Organisation of African Unity (OAU) emerged as a Pan-African entity to support the liberation struggle in the remaining colonies on the continent (van Walraven 1999). The unifying paradigm of anti-colonialism was designed to incorporate all independent black-ruled states of the continent. This dimension covered all fragmentations mentioned above: between North and sub-Saharan Africa, between Francophone and anglophone countries, as well as between federalists and nationalists. However, the OAU depended on consensus, which severely curbed the prospect of African integration. The paramount importance given to non-interference and national sovereignty benefited authoritarian rulers rather than continental unity.

On a subcontinental level, several other organisations were created in the vein of African regionalism, notably the Economic Community of West African States (ECOWAS) and the East African Community (EAC). Through protectionism and state-led industrialisation these regions should be enabled to acquire economic autonomy from the former colonial centres and South Africa. Yet, externally driven regionalisms persisted in parallel. Since the 1960s, many Francophone countries in Africa share a common currency: the CFA franc. The monetary union is a legacy of French colonisation and comprises two distinct areas in West and in Central Africa, which are governed in the same way. A regional central bank is tied to the French finance ministry to ensure credibility and convertibility of the currency. The logic for the CFA franc is essentially of political nature to underpin the close entanglement of elites, coined as 'Françafrique' (Bovcon 2013). As no functioning common market to ensure the free movement of goods and people exists, economic demand for a transnational currency is limited. After having been pegged for decades to the French franc, the CFA franc is now pegged to its successor currency, the euro, but France retains its central role. Despite several depreciations, the CFA franc has proven to be a stable construct and is not challenged by its members. Rather than ending the colonial relationship, there have been signs of gradually emancipating the CFA franc, for example by accepting the Hispanophone Equatorial Guinea as a member or by envisaging an expansion into Anglophone West Africa. In Southern Africa an imperial regionalism solidified. The Southern African Customs Union (SACU) represented a tool for South Africa to control its neighbours economically and politically.

Many African states experienced a surge of national debt during the 1980s. In alignment with a global turn towards trade and capital liberalisation, previous economic paradigms of regionalism were abandoned in order to prevent a marginalisation. The overall concept of democracy also won recognition with the end of the Cold War, as many one-party states and apartheid were left behind. These watersheds also profoundly affected the interpretation of Pan-Africanism in African regionalism. Most organisations underwent institutional reform and paradigm shifts during the 1980s and 1990s.

While in 1980 the Lagos Plan of Action of the OAU still advocated a disentanglement from global markets to enable self-reliance, industrialisation and equal trade relationships within African Regional Economic Communities, the Abuja Treaty of 1991 introduced the paramount economic objective of creating common markets and monetary unions in view of upscaling them. This shift illustrated how the design and purpose of African regionalism moved from Third World developmentalism towards a mix of neoclassical economics and a European model of integration.

The ambitions to create economic communities have to date seriously lagged behind these plans and others that followed. The same can be said about participatory institutions such as regional parliaments and courts. By contrast, many regionalisms have increasingly dedicated themselves to peace and security, often as a reaction to violent conflicts (Francis 2006). Regional early-warning systems as well as regional standby forces and control mechanisms were developed to accompany externally led or multilateral missions. The Pan-African ideal of African solutions to African problems was set out to challenge the reliance on external involvement and was incorporated by some regional organisations. For instance, the members of the Southern African Development Community (SADC) claimed regional ownership of the political crises in Lesotho, Madagascar and Zimbabwe during the 1990s and 2000s and thereby legitimised themselves as primary or even sole parties to be involved.

The consolidation of postcolonial individual states in combination with a dominance of extra-regional economic relations reduced the opportunity for transnational social spaces to develop. As a consequence, not only did state-led regionalism struggle to produce a re-territorialisation but also non-state regionalism remained marginalised. Civil society groups stay confined to national arenas whereas cross-border interactions such as migration and trade tend to happen informally. Pan-African networks are highly dependent on funding from Europe or North America so that the regional connectivity of interest groups often requires external inducements. Nevertheless, political and intellectual movements maintain a tradition of Pan-Africanism that keeps the ambitions of African regionalism alive in the public discourse.

The development of regionalism in Africa has also fostered the idea of separating it analytically and politically as a single world region – as reflected in the structure of this volume. However, beyond the topographic categorisation, which also remains ambivalent with respect to diasporas, islands and overseas territories, numerous delineations between Africa and its other based on identity, paradigms and connections exist. Also within the continent there is no singular Africa. Even though the OAU's successor, the African Union (AU) claims to define Africa as a political, economic and social space, the continent is laced with fault lines. These lines are expressed by the manifold and incongruent overlap of regionalisms, by the mismatch between conceived regional organisations and informal lived regional spaced and by the ambivalence of regional leadership. The following section will deal with these themes individually.

36.2   PROJECTS OF REGION-BUILDING

Delineating Africa as a region is already a complex feat. Delineating regions within Africa is all the more challenging. There are multiple fragmentations of Africa into sub-regions and most of them remain very porous.

Since 2002, the continental and Pan-African project is embodied in the AU. Its institutional structure has grown considerably and the headquarters in Addis Ababa in Ethiopia now comprises a commission, a council of ministers and a general assembly. However, the autonomy of the AU remains limited, as the member states prefer an intergovernmental mode of governance. Under the umbrella of the AU, eight regional economic communities represent the subcontinental formal regionalisms. There is a considerable amount of overlap between these communities, both in membership and mandate. Though they were – in accordance with their acronym – created for economic purposes, most expanded into other policy fields such as chiefly peace and security (Oosthuizen 2006). In all regional communities member states remain in power of integration process, whereas the private sector and civil society remain marginalised actors in formally conceiving the region.

In addition to the regional economic communities several other regional institutions exist. Some fall within the Pan-African logic, such as the African Development Bank, while others represent a regional order that reflects structural power relations. The French central bank and finance ministry remain key actors in the monetary union of West and Central Africa. Despite a reform of the SACU in 2002 to provide smaller states with more voice, the institutional framework in practice consolidates their dependence on South African decisions.

The ascendance of regional powers in Africa has ambivalent effects on regionalism (Alden and Le Pere 2004). Since independence several heads of states have devoted themselves to the Pan-African ideal of a political continental union, notably Ghana's Nkrumah in Ghana and Libya's Gaddafi. The derived claim for them to lead such a regionalism could however not assert itself against the resistance of the majority of African governments that prefer a gradual process of cooperation as a model of regionalism. Countries that could play a leadership role due to their relative economic, military, territorial or demographic importance are either bogged down in domestic conflicts (for example Egypt, Democratic Republic of Congo, Kenya, Nigeria and Zimbabwe) or prioritise cooperation with non-African partners (for example Angola and Morocco). South Africa, the country with the biggest potential to achieve the status of a regional power has made Pan-African regionalism one of its main foreign policy pillars after apartheid. However, the country continues to be regarded with suspicion by many of its peers, which limits its capacity to project power into the region and continent. Even though South African enterprises are active in many African markets and South African troops take part in multilateral peace missions, it is not committed to lead the way for African regionalism in institutional terms.

National sovereignty is a norm that dominates the political culture in Africa since political independence. Regionalisms are designed in a way to conform with this norm (Welz 2013). The African Development Bank is an influential actor concerning functional cooperation such as infrastructure, but it does not have competences over fiscal or monetary policies. The Pan-African Parliament and other regional parliaments are at best occasional meeting venues for national deputies but they are not constituted and accountable through direct elections. Regional courts have a very limited mandate and can hardly stand up against national governments – or if they do they are cut down to size as in the case of the SADC Tribunal (Nathan 2012). Transnational economic projects to support industries based on natural resources and energy are generally designed as multi-country rather than regional projects.

Notable exceptions do exist, such as the authority of ECOWAS regarding peace and security, which at least in principle allows the organisation to intervene in member states even without their consent, or the Southern African Power Pool that has acquired autonomy with respect to the regional electricity grid.

Though the emphasis on national sovereignty considerably curbs the emergence of regional institutions as actors in their own right, regionalism is conversely instrumentalised in order to 'boost' national regimes (Söderbaum and Tavares 2013). Large parts of Africa are home to both a pronounced presidentialism and severely limited public administration. The resulting strong governments in weak states utilise regional organisations as a source of legitimisation and self-reassurance. Regional institutions reassert consensus-building and non-interference in domestic affairs and thus reinforce national sovereignty to the point of being able to shield countries from international intervention on the basis of regional legitimacy being paramount. Such dynamics have for instance unfolded in the case of SADC and Zimbabwe or the Indian Ocean Commission and Madagascar. In addition, regionalism is dominated by presidential summits that celebrate personified power over contribution and national sovereignty, and seldom entails the delegation of national powers to a regional body.

36.3   REGIONALISM BEYOND REGIONAL ORGANISATIONS

Beyond the politically driven intergovernmental regionalisms that aim to cover entire states, Africa is also home to numerous micro-regionalisms (Söderbaum and Taylor 2008). These cross-border projects only encompass parts of adjacent countries and are designed with a limited thematic and geographic scope. Local or issue-specific administrations as well as private actors play an important role in their creation. The subsequent appropriation of micro-regional spaces takes manifold forms. Chambers of commerce that join forces to facilitate cross-border trade promote the creation of export zones that are characterised by their exclusion vis-à-vis the remaining national territories. Infrastructure development and energy networks are running along functional lines between economic centres and natural resources. The so-called development corridors, which have been created in Southern and Eastern Africa to connect metropolitan areas in various countries, exhibit an expansive character that cuts across national borders. By contrast, transfrontier conservation parks, river basin commissions and ethnic separatist movements focus on the internal consolidation of delineations that precede national borders altogether.

Regionalisms are generally associated with the provision of regional public goods as well as with a contribution to prosperity and stability. This normative connotation distracts from the prevalence of regionalisms that are not created with such objectives in mind or undermine them in practice. The term shadow regionalism refers to processes that either occur below the facade of regional organisations or entirely outside the realm of states (Shaw et al. 2011). The first element implies the capture of regional organisations for particularistic interests, in particular the material gains of political elite networks. For instance, patronage and access to natural resources played a central role for the military intervention of SADC member states in the Democratic Republic of Congo at the end of the 1990s. The second element includes regions that are shaped by warlords or religious fanaticism. Such regionalisms are porous as often ephemeral but nevertheless capable to exercise control over territory and people and even create an identity. Examples for such regionalisms are 'Taylorland', an area in and around Liberia, which was ruled by the militia leader Charles Taylor, as well as the institutionalised dominion of Islamist gangs such as Boko Haram and Al-Shabaab. Shadow regionalisms are often shaped around their financial basis, such as blood diamonds, arms trafficking or oil smuggling and expand across borders into power vacuums.

36.4   OVERLAPPING REGIONALISM

The multitude of regionalisms in Africa produces a complex picture of overlaps that has been coined as a 'spaghetti bowl' in the literature on regional economic agreements (Baldwin 2006). Indeed, many African governments have subscribed to two or even more regional organisations that claim responsibility in the same policy fields, such as security or trade. The creation of new organisations and the expansion of existing ones produce additional overlaps. In some cases this leads to competition, such as between the Economic Community of Central African States (ECCAS) that has a Pan-African outlook and the Central African Economic and Monetary Community (CEMAC) that is closely entangled with the former colonial power France. In other instances overlaps trigger cooperation and harmonisation, such as in the case of the tripartite agreement under negotiation, which would unify EAC, SADC and the Common Market for Eastern and Southern Africa (COMESA). Once areas of free movement of goods and people overlap they de facto form one cohesive region. However, the lack of effectively binding obligations in most regional organisations means that free movement is seldom implemented. Overlaps do thus not automatically translate into a merger of regionalism. Multiple memberships are further facilitated by the lack of sanctions for not paying membership fees. As a consequence, governments are able to pick and choose on an ad hoc basis the regional organisation that is deemed most suitable for particular coalitions with regard to national security and economic interests. Overlapping regional organisations reflect the antagonisms that characterise the region as a whole. Since there is no shortage of regional organisations in Africa, new creations have become rare. Existing regionalisms are flexible enough to realign their raison d'être with new challenges. There is however a consensus that the African Union should comprise the entirety of the continent. Only European overseas territories and Morocco – which left the AU over the West Sahara conflict but is seeking re-accession – are formally excluded. Instead of making the adherence to specific rules or paradigms the main prerequisite for membership in the AU is rather tied to a topographic mapping. Conversely, the sub-divisions of the continent, for example Central or Southern Africa, are not clearly defined and thus facilitate different delineations that materialise in overlapping regional organisations

The high amount of overlapping regionalisms in Africa results in a number of specific challenges. One issue is the prioritisation for member states, be it with respect to financial contributions, delegation of personnel or implementation of regional policies. Regional projects in Africa are characterised by a high external financial dependency. Only a few organisations are able to autonomously cover a substantial amount of their expenses. The main donor is the EU which for instance funds large parts of the AU and SADC. One reason for this constellation is the combination of members being either unable or reluctant to pay their fees. The public budgets of many countries are only able to cover parts of their international obligations and regional contributions generally rank behind multilateral ones. Since regional organisations in Africa have few instruments to sanction defaulting member states and since external donors are willing to provide substantial financial support, the opportunities to freeride are clear-cut, even for solvent governments. Some countries thus continue to be in arrears with several regional organisations. The AU in particular has recognised this situation and is proposing reforms to ensure that at least the basic funding for African regionalism can be sustained internally. However, even if such reforms were to find favour with member states project funding, for instance in terms of providing regional security, would continue to stem from outside. External donors contribute to maintaining the financial dependency, as many of them adhere to the support of regional integration. The existence of capable regional organisations is thus a critical measure of success to legitimate regional development aid.

Another issue is to create regional organisations that are coherent with social and economic spaces. As a consequence, there are regular attempts to rationalise the multitude of organisations. A West African Monetary Zone is envisaged by the Anglophone West African countries so as to eventually merge with the Francophone West African Economic and Monetary Union in order to form a common currency that transcends colonial legacies. In the same postcolonial vein, CEMAC and ECCAS are working towards a merger. These endeavours indicate that existing regional delineations are the result of political logics and do not correspond to the realities of transnational social spaces. Additional pressure to rationalise stems from external donors, who have hitherto contributed considerably to the existence of regional organisations and are revising their policies so as to sponsor issue-oriented projects rather than static and otherwise under-funded institutions. However, rationalisation efforts face tenacious progress. Despite several attempts and announcements wholehearted consolidations are yet to materialise. As in many international organisations the bureaucracies of regional organisations are keen to preserve themselves and host countries are reluctant to give up the corresponding prestige and influence. Existing regionalisms also reflect balances of power or hegemonic relations, which reflect regional political structures that are resistant to external pressure.

36.5   INTERREGIONALISM

In addition to the relations between the numerous overlapping regional organisations within the continent, regionalism in Africa also features strong external ties, in particular with the European Union (EU) (Farrell 2005).

The economic relations between Europe and its former colonies in Africa, the Caribbean and the Pacific have since independence been organised through trade agreements offering preferential and unilateral access to the European common market. In addition, a privileged political dialogue has also been installed with these countries. The creation of the World Trade Organization (WTO) in 1994 required the end of these trade agreements in order to comply with non-preferential treatment. Accordingly, in 2000 the Cotonou Agreement set out seven new interregional trade agreements to be concluded between the EU and groupings in Africa, the Caribbean and the Pacific. The so-called Economic Partnership Agreements would establish more reciprocity by opening up the European agricultural market as well as ensuring access for European goods and services in the partner countries. The negotiations turned out to be very tedious and slow-moving. The seven sub-regions of the Economic Partnership Agreements added yet another layer to the overlapping regionalisms and created new delineations. The rearrangement occurred mainly in line with the diverse economic structures. Exporters of natural resources such as oil or the poorest countries that enjoyed WTO privileges already faced few tariffs and thus had little stakes in the agreements. Others, such as South Africa, had already concluded bilateral agreements with the EU. Only countries with a high share or potential for agricultural and manufactured exports had a strong economic interest in the agreements. The existing regionalisms in Africa thus faced another line of friction that the EU barely managed to mitigate with tied development aid and bilateral interim agreements. The future of the Economic Partnership Agreements as well as of the grouping uniting the former European colonies in Africa, the Caribbean and the Pacific thus remains unclear.

On a bi-continental level, the EU and the AU are entangled through a formal and multi-layered partnership, including a Joint Africa–EU Strategy. The EU also constitutes an important source of funding for the AU and serves as a model for certain institutional elements of regionalism. Other regional organisations such as SADC, ECOWAS, EAC and ECCAS also maintain a relationship with the EU, which is vital for many of their activities. The external link thus often plays a more relevant role than the intra-African interregionalism. However, the perception of the European integration process succumbing to a series of crises has tarnished the image of a role model and the EU funding to regional organisations, while still important, has decreased in many areas. Meanwhile, the increased presence of Latin American and Asian countries on the African continent has led to new interregional initiatives. Though countries such as China and Brazil focus on bilateral and multilateral foreign policy tools, they have started to cooperate with regional organisations. They are motivated by potential economies of scale, by promoting business interests and political coalitions more effectively than with each country individually.

These interregional ties between developing countries and their regional organisations are characterised by a political motivation concerning their position in the global order. They tend to start with non-committal dialogues to sound out common interests and turn into framework agreements, punctual fora and high-level demonstrations of commonality. Formal and permanent institutional linkages remain rare. North America has been a latecomer in terms of interregionalism, as Canada and the US have only gradually moved some of their development aid from national governments to regional organisations or projects.

Interregionalism has also faced setbacks. In several cases the initial enthusiasm for regionalism in Africa has led to a disenchantment. Countless formalised objectives, ranging from the free movement of people and goods to common currencies have not been implemented and continue to be postponed. Institutions expected to deliver participatory regionalism with the involvement of citizens, such as the ECCAS Parliament and the SADC Tribunal, only exist on paper or have been severely constricted. Most regional organisations have proven to be inactive in the face of human rights violations in member states. Only unconstitutional changes of government have in some cases brought organisations such as the AU and ECOWAS to the fore. The frustration with the limited capacity and leeway of regional organisations has resulted in many actors turning away. Civil society organisations and businesses, which have been initially keen to lobby on the regional level, have redirected their efforts to national or global arenas. Several donors, in particular from the UK and the US, refrain from engaging directly with many regional organisations that are perceived to be ineffective for their development agenda.

36.6   MARITIME REGIONALISM

Regions tend to be associated with territoriality and physical coherence. To delineate regions, oceans are considered frontiers rather than binding entities. This terra-centric approach is particularly prevalent in Africa where the continental vision of Pan-Africanism remains a dominant paradigm. Nevertheless, there are conceptions of region that challenge the dominant topographic categories. The Indian Ocean constitutes a cultural and economic space that has evolved over centuries and continues to be actively appropriated. Riparian countries and non-state actors are appropriating this maritime space as their own for political power projection or for economic ambitions, often embedded in blue economy plans. Two regional organisations are positioning themselves as maritime regionalisms: the Indian Ocean Rim Association and the Indian Ocean Commission. Whereas the former includes a vast number of countries and serves as negotiation space between emerging powers such as South Africa, China and India, the latter only comprises the Francophone island states as well as the French oversea territories in the Indian Ocean. As on the continent, the friction between overlapping regionalisms remains tangible off-shore.

From an African perspective, despite the historic slave trade the contemporary Atlantic Ocean is a maritime space with comparatively less economic and social density. The only organisation linked to African regionalism with an Atlantic focus – the Zone for Peace and Cooperation in the South Atlantic (ZOPACAS) – was created during the Cold War as a Third World antagonism against both the North Atlantic Treaty Organization and the apartheid government in South Africa. After a dormant phase after the end of the Cold War, ZOPACAS has been occasionally revived to foster South–South cooperation and for Brazil to appropriate the South Atlantic as an extension of its territory (Abdenur et al. 2016). On the African side, engagement with maritime regionalism has been very selective and largely confined to a response to security threats, in particular with the creation of the Gulf of Guinea Commission that is designed to tackle issues of piracy and offshore energy resources in collaboration with the existing external military presence. Apart from these specific issues, which occasionally extend to drug trafficking, fisheries and transport, a strategic approach to the Atlantic is lacking in Africa. Government policies and citizen identities remain dominated by a terra-centric paradigm.

36.7   OUTLOOK: AVENUES FOR RESEARCH ON AFRICAN REGIONALISM

Research on African regionalism has often been considered a topic for area studies rather than for broader efforts of conceptionalisation and theory-building in political geography and international relations. Three developments in the field of study are gradually changing that confinement.

First, the analytical work on regionalism on the African continent has produced concepts that are not reduced to an African phenomenon. In particular, studies on African regionalism have successfully questioned prevalent tacit normative assumptions about regionalism. Understanding the neo-patrimonial dynamics and particularistic logics underlying several regionalisms in Africa has countered the idea of regionalism being per se conducive to the creation of peace and prosperity (Bach 2016). The concept of sovereignty-boosting to describe how the status of national governments in Africa is enhanced by regionalism has questioned assumptions of regionalism as a phenomenon of pooling sovereignty with a view to supranational governance (Söderbaum and Taylor 2008). There is a compelling argument that such concepts have explanatory value for regionalism beyond the African case.

Second, the existence of a multitude of partly overlapping regionalisms in Africa has given rise to an interest in comparative regionalism and interregionalism within Africa. As a consequence, Africa is also receiving more attention in terms of transferring and adapting concepts so as to include the continent in global efforts of comparative regionalism and interregionalism. An area of particular interest is the finances of regional organisations in Africa, which is accentuated by political efforts to find sustainable budgetary mechanisms as well as by the current high interregional dependency on outside actors.

Third, the study of African regionalism is moving beyond the confinement to formal regional organisations with national governments as primary actors. The importance of forms of regionalisms, which are characterised by informality, periphery and ephemerality has been recognised for Africa and carries relevance for the broader research on borderlands and territoriality. This focus also allows for a dialogue with political geography and urban studies about the difference between perceived and conceived delineations of regions.

Studying regionalism in Africa does not only provide a fertile ground to deduct concepts with potential relevance for other regions and for theory-building. The way regionalism in Africa is predominantly studied also leaves important research gaps yet to be adequately addressed. The most important challenge to Africa's place in the study of regionalism – and by extension in social sciences at large – might still be reciprocity. While there is much research about the impact of the EU on African regionalism, there is little knowledge about the impact of African regionalism on European integration. Acknowledging the heterogeneity of regions across the globe without losing track of the mutual entanglement of multiple – sometimes contradicting – regionalisms is a crucial starting point but the recalibration of Africa's place in the world of regionalism is still far from being complete.

36.8   REFERENCES

Abdenur, A.E., F. Mattheis and P. Seabra (2016), 'An ocean for the global south: Brazil and the zone of peace and cooperation in the South Atlantic', *Cambridge Review of International Affairs*, **29** (3), 1112–1131.

Alden, C. and G. Le Pere (2004), 'South Africa's post-apartheid foreign policy: from reconciliation to ambiguity?', *Review of African Political Economy*, **31** (100), 283–297.

Bach, D. (2016), *Regionalism in Africa: Genealogies, Institutions and Trans-state Networks*, Abingdon: Routledge.

Baldwin, R.E. (2006), 'Multilateralising regionalism: spaghetti bowls as building blocs on the path to global free trade', *The World Economy*, **29** (11), 1451–1518.

Bovcon, M. (2013), 'Françafrique and regime theory', *European Journal of International Relations*, **19** (1), 5–26.

Farrell, M. (2005), 'A triumph of realism over idealism? Cooperation between the European Union and Africa', *European Integration*, **27** (3), 263–283.

Francis, D.J. (2006), *Uniting Africa: Building Regional Peace And Security Systems*, Aldershot: Ashgate.

Hill, R.A. and G.A. Pirio (1987), '"Africa for the Africans": The Garvey Movement in South Africa, 1920–1940', in S. Marks and S. Trapido (eds), *The Politics of Race, Class and Nationalism in Twentieth Century South Africa*, London: Routledge, pp. 209–253.

Kahin, G.M. (1956), *The Asian-African Conference, Bandung, Indonesia, April 1955*, Cornell: Cornell University Press.

Nathan, L. (2012), *Community of Insecurity: SADC's Struggle for Peace and Security in Southern Africa*, Farnham: Ashgate.

Oosthuizen, G. (2006), *The Southern African Development Community. The Organisation, Its Policies and Prospects*, Midrand: Institute for Global Dialogue.

Shaw, T.M., J.A. Grant and S. Cornelissen (2011), 'Introduction and overview: the study of new regionalism(s) at the start of the second decade of the twenty-first century', in T.M. Shaw, J.A. Grant and S. Cornelissen (eds), *The Ashgate Research Companion to Regionalisms*, Farnham: Ashgate, pp. 3–30.

Söderbaum, F. and R. Tavares (eds) (2013), *Regional Organizations in African Security*, Abingdon: Routledge.

Söderbaum, F. and I. Taylor (2008), 'Considering micro-regionalism in Africa in the twenty-first century', in F. Söderbaum and I. Taylor (eds), *Afro-Regions: The Dynamics of Cross-Border Micro-Regionalism in Africa*, Uppsala: Nordiska Afrikainstitutet, pp. 13–31.

Snyder, L.L. (1984), *Macro-nationalisms: A History of the Pan-Movements*, London: Greenwood Press.

van Walraven, K. (1999), *Dreams of Power. The Role of the Organization of African Unity in the Politics of Africa, 1963–1993*, Aldershot: Ashgate.

Welz, M. (2013), *Integrating Africa. Decolonization's Legacies, Sovereignty and the African Union*, Abingdon: Routledge.

37. North American regionalism
Michael R. Glass

37.1 INTRODUCTION

North American regionalism is best defined by its variegated character, and by the scope of real and imagined regions that proliferate across the continent. Perhaps this proliferation is because of the extensive land area available within North America, and the history of economic and political development that unfolded over time. Perhaps the number of regional governing spaces is due to the complicated multiscale governance arrangements that characterize the United States, Canada, Mexico, and international arrangements between the three countries, and the desire by planners and politicians to capture processes that spill over into adjacent areas. Or perhaps the configuration of North American regionalism can best be explained by the different stakeholder communities – private and public – that continue developing new spaces for governance that meet their specific needs and philosophies regarding land use and economic development. Regardless of the reason, the landscape of regionalism across North America is best conceived of in a multi-dimensional way because political, economic, and social dimensions all influence the historic and contemporary construction of regional spaces, and their efficacy is determined by the position of the observer.

This chapter provides a concise evaluation of regionalism across North America, although it is admittedly written from a United States-oriented perspective. The shape of regionalism in the United States is defined by the Federal political context, and by historic precedent that emphasizes the primacy of state rights in establishing other political spaces that cater to local needs. This context also fosters considerable suspicion about the motive and constitutionality of special regional spaces that are created to address specific problems. Canadian and Mexican regionalism is defined by different formal and informal relations between national and local scales of government, yet the dynamics are frequently similar. In Canada, the Federal government interacts with provincial governments that operate with considerable authority to set regional and local regional policy within their borders. The presence of special governments and debates over local autonomy resemble the dynamics found in the United States, yet are influenced by territorially specific state and local imperatives (Conteh 2012). The Mexican approach to regionalism is mediated by a centralized, Federal political framework that prioritizes national economic growth policies over development of regionally specific policies (Graizbord and Aguilar 2006). Consequently, scholars interested in understanding Mexican regionalism need to evaluate each state's mix of vertical relationships with the Federal government and horizontal relationships between state-level stakeholders. Whereas Mexico may be presumed as similar to the United States federal context, Rodriguez warns that the systems are highly distinct, with different approaches to local power and self-government (Rodriguez 1998).

The next section focuses on the United States, explaining how the Federal system and the country's economic expansion created a specific model of regionalism. I describe the history of regional planning to explain the bureaucratic philosophy that guides regionalist discourse, and then explain the difference between functional and structural regionalism. Focusing on urban areas, I will then describe how cross-border regionalism works, and then describe how regionalism is currently promoted as an opportunity to enhance equity. Shifting to the Canadian case, section 37.3 describes how national-provincial relations influence the form of regionalism, and also describe how national economic dynamics affect the development of particular regional spaces. Section 37.4 focuses on supranational regionalism, describing how Free Trade Agreements (CAFTA and NAFTA) create new spaces binding parts of the continent together. At more local scales, the uneven development of the Maquiladora belt created large economic gains for Mexico's border states, and exacerbated regional differences within Mexico (Graizbord and Aguilar 2006; Tamayo-Flores 2006). Recent post-2016 politics means that the potential landscape for regionalism at domestic and international scales is fraught with the prospects for regressive change. Therefore, the chapter closes with a turn to possible regional futures. These include the vexing tension in United States regionalism between localism and regionalism, and the contradictions between big plans for megaregional spaces and the pragmatics of the political. Beyond all of these debates, regions are experienced by individual people and communities; therefore, I close by describing how everyday regionalism matters to our conception of regionalism in North America.

37.2   US REGIONALISM

Regionalism should not be construed as a recent development in the United States. By the early twentieth century, different plans and organizations had arisen that sought to reconfigure the structural and functional boundaries of cities, suburbs, and their urban hinterlands. For example, the Regional Plan Association provided a comprehensive report for New York City in 1929, recommending that the region's governments and land uses be realigned to better reflect the city's regional scope, and to coordinate functions that were seen as beyond the capacity or purview of individual governments (Fishman 1992). In other cities, the National Municipal League and Bureaus of Municipal Research advocated the structural or functional consolidation of cities and their surrounding boroughs to provide greater efficiency and to modernize what were frequently described as anachronistic patterns of government and governance (Glass 2011, Teaford 1979). Similarly, public authorities arose as a good governance response to problems of service coordination and delivery across and within administrative boundaries. Emerging through the first half of the twentieth century in different areas of the country and in different sectors, public authorities in the United States and Canada created coordinated legal structures for managing public assets (including water infrastructure and transportation networks) that commonly overlapped established city borders and hence created forms of ad hoc regionalism (Lucas 2016; Radford 2013). These nascent forms of regionalism hence reflected the transformation of American society. As new social and technical infrastructures bound the fortunes of increasing territories, Progressive reformers and good government advocates sought to expand the scale of governance accordingly. They did so to avoid dysfunction in urban areas, and to bring emerging problems (such as pollution, transportation, and sanitation) under the control of a regional authority with the power to address them.

Regionalism's promise remained attractive in the second half of the twentieth century, and was advocated to reflect the changing geography of the United States. Jean Gottman's *Megalopolis* and James Vance's *Continuing City* each mapped the enlarging urban scale of cities in the United States during the period (Gottman 1961; Vance 1990). This new regional geography led to Federal policy responses including the Advisory Council on Intergovernmental Relations (ACIR) – a bi-partisan effort to develop new solutions to governing urban America in the post-Second World War era. Their 1962 report provided several recommendations for regional government, including structural reorganization of local government, and new districts for inter-governmental cooperation (ACIR 1962). ACIR was instrumental in keeping debates about regional governance active until the 1990s, though there was less evidence that their advocacy fostered large-scale changes to the practice of regional governance. However, regionalism remained significant as the century closed, with a 'new regionalism' emerging that saw interjurisdictional spaces as consequential for economic development, good governance, and regional equity.

In the past thirty years, significant studies have reasserted the real and rhetorical power of regional agglomerations for enhancing the economic competitiveness of their host countries (Saxenian 1994; Storper 1997; Scott 2012). While empirically distinct, these studies are connected by the conceptual argument that spatial propinquity of people and firms can influence economic growth at regional scales. The specific mechanisms that propel a region's economic growth are debated; possible explanations include growth via direct economic spillovers, specific economic policies, or because of less tangible characteristics such as regional culture. Regardless of the reason, the region became reified as a significant scale for economic development, with a burgeoning literature that sought to understand how governments and firms could leverage the power of regions to their advantage (Dunning 2000). Wachsmuth characterizes the post-1990 era as one dominated by a variety of strategies that use regionalism as a policy device to promote economic development (Wachsmuth 2017). Explaining that these economic development strategies occur at different scales in different political contexts, he suggests that the new experience of US regionalism conforms in certain ways to regional rescaling seen in different geographic contexts. Jonas and Ward's study of UK and US regional policies also found that significant sub-national variations in policy implementations and outcomes persist. They concluded that broadly similar territorial policies in both countries had dissimilar outcomes accruing from sub-national differences in governance and institutional histories, and in the US case because of what they term as the apparent 'variety of new regionalisms' (Jonas and Ward 2002, p. 397). These local political exigencies are an intractable feature of city-region governance, and hence must be regarded seriously when new regional planning reforms are considered.

Despite the alluring rhetoric of powerful and autonomous regionalism in the United States context, there are dangers to overstating the freedom with which US regions can act. Jonas and Ward note that it is more appropriate both conceptually and methodologically to understand the institutional and contingent character of city-region development (Jonas and Ward 2007). For instance, American city-regions are characterized broadly by constitutional and social preferences toward localism (Magnusson 2010), with politics and governance that differ across states based on the extent of powers granted by state governments to local jurisdictions (Miller and Cox III 2014). In addition, the political map of the United States is complicated by the influential role played by special governance districts (including school districts, utility districts, and planning jurisdictions). In 2007, there were 36,011 general purpose sub-county administrative units, consisting of municipalities, towns, and townships. By comparison, the United States had 37,381 special districts (special purpose administrative units, not including school districts) in the same year, representing an increase of 5,826 (or nearly 18.5 percent) since the 1992 Census of Governments. Therefore, there are more than double the total number of sub-county administrative units, and special districts account for 90 percent of the growth in local governments within the United States during the second half of the twentieth century (Miller 2002, p. 43). This situation implies both that American metropolitan regions are likely to be characterized by a complex political mosaic that makes either structural or functional changes in city-region governance both slow and uncertain of eventual success (Glass 2015).

Regional transportation policy provides an example of how the US Federal system generates variegated forms of regionalism. The Intermodal Surface Transportation Efficiency Act of 1991 (ISTEA) marked a neoliberal turn in Federal transportation policy by empowering local authorities to take responsibility for how Federal transportation funds would be allocated. This premise required the formation of Metropolitan Planning Organizations (MPOs) for all urbanized areas with populations of over 50,000 residents. State governors were responsible for establishing the form and structure of the MPO in each region, and so the composition of these governance structures varies across the country. More than half of all MPOs were either formed by having an existing COG assume the MPO role, or by creating a new structure that was separate from existing political units. Less frequently, MPO responsibilities were either allocated to one or more counties or were managed out of state government offices (Lewis 1998). Each MPO was governed by a board that represented the entire region, although there was no Federal guidance on how that representation should be allocated. Whereas the presumption was that these structures would create more flexibility for locally representative organizations to structure transportation funding that fits community needs, the results have varied. Some studies have found that their capacity to enhance regional cooperation is limited (Vogel and Nezelkiewicz 2002), whereas others are critical of the uneven representation on MPO boards (Sanchez 2006). The MPO example is akin to what Jonas et al. refer to as a 'top-down' territorial politics, wherein the Federal state shapes conditions for city-regionalism (Jonas et al. 2014). Just as in the empirical case that Jonas et al. describe, MPOs are generally shaped by 'bottom-up' territorial contingencies, meaning that both vantage points are necessary to understand how regionalism actually occurs.

The complexity of managing and planning for regionalism is exacerbated when the dynamism of borders at the local, state, and Federal scales are considered. For instance, at the local scale each state is comprised of minor civil divisions (MCDs – generally including counties, townships, municipalities, and cities). Each state is responsible for determining the geographic units contained within its territory, and for determining what powers are vested in each type of MCD. This investiture of powers is in many ways historically contingent, and varies considerably from state to state (Kinda 2001). Consequently, whereas the township becomes the primary form of local governance in the New England states, counties became more significant in the traditionally agrarian states of the Southern United States. Whereas the total number of MCDs expanded during the nineteenth century (because of formation by the states or through fragmentation of existing units), the shape and number of MCDs remained relatively stable over the twentieth century, and these units remain consequential as the political foundation of any new regional structures. However, regionalism will not arise from municipalities alone, because US states determine the allocation of MCD powers in what is now referred to as 'Dillon's Rule.' Named after Judge John F. Dillon of Iowa, his 1868 rulings found that municipalities only hold those powers explicitly provided by the state. The consequence for regionalism is that even if municipalities agree to create ad hoc regional structures through interjurisdictional arrangements, they would not possess legal authority to act without permission granted from the state legislature.

Whereas the political map of MCDs has remained relatively unchanged since 1945, broader patterns of metropolitan change necessitated new regional structures that overlay the traditional political geography of the United States. These new structures are responsible for the growth in special districts described earlier, as they can be assembled more easily than structural boundary changes. The complexity of managing and planning for city-regions is exacerbated when patterns of regional development spill over state borders. Domestically, the United States includes numerous examples of internal cross-border city-regions (such as the St. Louis region, spanning the Missouri–Illinois state line, the Kansas City region, spanning the Missouri–Kansas state line, and the Toledo region, spanning the Ohio and Michigan state line) that require inter-jurisdictional districts to coordinate planning functions. These interstate city-regions are typically coordinated by Councils of Government (COGs) or interstate planning agencies. Examples include the East–West Gateway COG (St. Louis), the Toledo Metropolitan Area COG, and the Delaware Valley Regional Planning Commission (Greater Philadelphia).

Another argument for regionalism coincides with its implementation in the United States as an economic development strategy or to administer inter-jurisdictional processes. At the vanguard of the 'new' regionalism in the 1990s were researchers and politicians concerned with increasing inequality within metropolitan regions (Benner and Pastor 2011; Rusk 1995). This focus is significant, as Benner and Pastor recently found that regions with higher rates of inequality, residential segregation, and political fragmentation were strongly (negatively) associated with the capacity to sustain job growth (Benner and Pastor 2015). An influential early contributor to this strand of 1990s regionalist thought was Myron Orfield, whose research in the Minneapolis region led to a broader agenda calling for regional mechanisms for social and economic equity (Orfield 1999, 2002). His early analysis found that restrictive planning practices and fragmentary governance were channeling urban growth into the wealthier geographic periphery of Minneapolis, whilst depriving the inner city and inner suburban areas of much-needed tax revenue. Because of these patterns of investment and growth, poorer communities were not benefiting from the conditions of prosperity that their taxes were underwriting. Orfield's policy solution to the inequalities that he described was metropolitan in nature; fair housing, equitable regional revenue sharing, and metropolitan government were all proposed as ways to solve the regional inequality challenge. His advocacy was met with opposition by certain stakeholder groups, yet the notion of regionalism provoked creation of a regional coalition and strategies to address local social polarization (Orfield 1997). Whereas the new regionalist approach to effecting social change is intellectually generative, Imbroscio argues that some aspects of the approach are rooted in liberal political ideology and claims that are empirically unproven (Imbroscio 2006). Niedt and Weir voice the separate concern that regionalist discourse has yet to develop a popular rhetorical framing to counter the arguments against asset sharing or the erosion of local controls inherent in some regionalist policy recommendations (Niedt and Weir 2010).

37.3 CANADIAN REGIONALISM

Regionalism is a profound and ingrained feature of Canada's political culture. This is because large inter-provincial variations in population and resources require significant coordination between Federal government and the provinces to overcome inequalities (Inwood et al. 2011). Unlike in Mexico, the Canadian political system provides significant decentralized power to provincial governments for establishing regionally appropriate policies and powers (Atkinson et al. 2013). This comparative autonomy has enabled different types of collaborative regional governance to emerge. For example, Wolfe describes the success of Waterloo, Ontario in forging a 'regionally resilient' governance model that protects the local R&D assemblage, with assistance from the provincial and Federal governments (Wolfe 2015). Lucas notes that special purpose governments (authorities, boards, and commissions) must also be considered when examining Canadian regionalism, given their consequential role in shaping governance within the provincial scale (Lucas 2016). At the Federal scale, Regional Development Agencies were created in 1987 with Ministerial-level authority to develop strategies for economic development tied to specific regional and local priorities in Western Canada (Western Economic Diversification Canada), the Atlantic Provinces (Atlantic Canada Opportunities Agency), Quebec (Canadian Economic Development for Quebec Regions), and Northern Ontario (FedNor) (Bradford 2010). As in other countries, the definition of region in Canada is contested. Cohen and Harris explore the construction of region in the context of Canadian water governance, arguing that attending to how regions are defined and practiced can provide analytical clarity on the formal and informal pathways that explain how regional politics actually functions (Cohen and Harris 2014).

The Canadian context is both similar yet distinct from the experience with regionalism in the United States. For instance, the countries are both highly urbanized with Federal systems that structure political life, and with deep social, economic, and political interconnections (Kent 2011; Rutherford and Holmes 2013). At the same time, claims for Canadian exceptionalism occur because of Canada's stronger preference for collectivism and governmental intervention, along with its reputation for efficient regional governance (Donald 2002; Goldberg and Mercer 1986). This seeming contradiction is explored by Nelles' evaluation of metropolitan governance across both countries (Nelles 2014). She agrees that political culture matters when analyzing regional governance, yet she finds no decisive difference in rates of metropolitan partnership formation between the two countries. These findings suggest that whereas context influences the shape of regionalism across North America, it is nevertheless possible to engage in cross-border theory building when it comes to explaining regional governance. For instance, Keil et al. find merit in comparing the Canadian experience with regionalism to the European case (Keil et al. 2016). Their analysis is based on a presumption of Canadian 'in-betweenness,' situated between the United States' robust market-oriented development paradigm and state-led development in European contexts.

37.4   SUPRANATIONAL REGIONALISM

When examined as a continental system, North America provides useful insights about the state's perspective toward regionalism. Different questions and contradictions become visible at this scale, whether it is the uneven transnational suturing created by free trade agreements, the cross-border regionalism created by the urban regions that cross the borders between the United States and Canada or Mexico, or because of the interjurisdictional governance spaces that govern specific environmental assets. In addition, political changes are also vividly captured at the transnational scale, as sudden swings in policy positions expose the fragility of interregional cooperation and cohesion.

One of the more prominent and controversial forms of supra-national governance in North America is the North American Free Trade Agreement (NAFTA). Enacted in 1994, the NAFTA was a classic neoliberal strategy that sought to enhance economic development by removing barriers to free trade in goods and services across the three North American countries. Witkowska concludes that the net benefits of the NAFTA remain modest yet positive (Witkowska 2016). Faber finds that Mexican sectors in the Northern border states with particularly strong export growth to the US between 1997 and 2003 grew at faster rates than in other areas of the country (Faber 2007), and yet free trade did not yield universally positive outcomes. Specific industries such as apparel and textiles experienced significant regional dislocation, causing economic decline for some regions and communities (Prince 2002). As with the economic results of integration, the influence of NAFTA on governance is decidedly mixed. Scott examined cross-border regionalism in both Europe and North America, finding that the stated policy objectives of cross-border legislation in the NAFTA did not foster universal cross-border cooperation. This was at least partly because of asymmetric power relations between Canada, the United States and Mexico, and because of concerns over losing sovereign authority precluded any rhetoric or policy that could lead to a borderless North America (Scott 1999). However, in select instances such as the Pacific Northwest, some targeted cross-border regionalism occurred relating to economic development (Artibise 1995).

The US–Canada border is the site of shifting relations in environmental governance and security. Norman and Bakker explored the presumption that water governance devolution along the US–Canada border would lead to greater empowerment of local actors (Norman and Bakker 2009). They found that whereas local stakeholders were increasingly present in discussions concerning transboundary water governance, their presence had not resulted in greater empowerment because of factors including a lack of resources. What their research concluded is that the rescaling of governance downwards should not be presumed as effective, since it can exacerbate power differences between stakeholders. In a separate example of shifting governance relations, the terrorist attacks on the United States in 2001 caused some relationships between Canada and the United States to change. The countries entered into new security partnerships that Kent examines as a reinterpretation of sovereignty, with Canada ceding specific aspects of border sovereignty through new partnerships intended to protect Canada's close interrelationships with the United States while the latter sought to enhance border security (Kent 2011). Despite these changes, the border spaces of North America continue to matter for governance and development, as governments and firms can leverage the uneven regulatory and economic landscapes to their benefit (Ramutsindela 2011; Rutherford and Holmes 2013).

37.5 REGIONAL FUTURES

Given the lengthy history and varied landscape of North American regionalism described in this chapter, it is easy to argue that the future is uncertain. Several initiatives are emerging to address new logics of economic development, infrastructure, and the changes wrought by globalization. One proposal – the megaregion – is based on presumptions that the scale of metropolitan life is expanding beyond the capacity of existing scales of regional governance (Florida et al. 2008; Lang and Knox 2009; Ross 2009; Sudjic 1992). While the megaregion is presently speculative in nature, it is studied and promoted by regional planning advocates such as the Regional Plan Association and their America 2050 program (America 2050, undated). The RPA considers these broad regional spaces fundamental for enhancing the cooperation and coordination necessary for tackling complex problems (Todorovich 2009). This certitude is based on the observation that United States megaregions account for over three quarters of the country's population and Gross Domestic Product (Hagler 2009). However, even advocates for megaregional planning admit that their concept is but the latest in a long history of speculative attempts to capture spatial processes within ever-expanding regional spaces; this history should indicate that new spaces are easy to consider, but much more difficult to implement (Glass 2015; Harrison and Hoyler 2015). Schafran's analysis of regional linkages in the Northern California 'megaregion' proposes how to distinguish the speculative from the specific (Schafran 2014). He distinguishes 'mega-regional space' (i.e. the expanding geographic envelope conceived by analysts) from 'spaces of the megaregion' that define areas where the tentative sinews of some nascent and spatially extensive regional formation are empirically evident.

What is particularly significant about critical approaches like Schafran's is that they remind us to avoid reifying regional spaces in ways that might be counterproductive for the notional goals of regionalist discourse such as economic development, good governance, or enhancing equity. For example, when confronted with a new spatial imaginary it pays to consider who will benefit from realization of the new space. In Western Pennsylvania, a large-scale regional visioning exercise was held that purported to determine citizen priorities for a regional advocacy space entitled the 'Power of 32' – named thusly because the area included 32 contiguous counties across four states (Glass 2014). The organizers for the Power of 32 collated community input through numerous community visioning sessions and online comments, intending to generate a cohesive set of regional priorities that the new region could promote. However, despite the open engagement at the start of the Power of 32 campaign, the priorities gradually came to reflect the priorities of the region's institutional funders – indicating that regional imaginaries are prone to capture by elite stakeholders and conservative visions of development, despite the inclusive rhetoric used to gain consensus for such spaces.

As North American regionalism proceeds into the twenty-first century propelled by real and presumptive spaces for planning and governance, it is also worth considering who regionalism is intended to help. Addie and Keil discuss this in the Toronto context, describing what they call 'real existing regionalism' (Addie and Keil 2015). This construct reminds us that while it is necessary to interrogate regulatory constructs for what they imply in an era of globalized regionalization, we must also consider what they mean to everyday flows and the lived experience of regions. This is hence a call to engage with regions through a multiscalar lens, since what regional thinkers see as problems might be experienced very differently by residents of the region (Glass 2018). Such enduring problems speak to the messiness of sociopolitical life that regional constructs attempt to simplify. As the examples in this chapter make clear, the landscape of regionalism across North America is highly varied and is therefore a useful representation of the continent's socio-spatial diversity.

37.6   REFERENCES

ACIR (1962), *A Commission Report: Alternative Approaches to Governmental Reorganization in Metropolitan Areas*, Washington DC: ACIR.

Addie, J.-P.D. and R. Keil (2015), 'Real existing regionalism: The region between talk, territory and technology', *International Journal of Urban and Regional Research*, **39** (2), 407–417.

America 2050 (undated), 'Megaregions' accessed May 10, 2017 at http://www.america2050.org/megaregions. html.

Artibise, A.F.J. (1995), 'Achieving sustainability in Cascadia: An emerging model of growth management in the Vancouver–Seattle–Portland corridor', in P.K. Kresl and G. Gappert (eds), *North American Cities and the Global Economy: Challenges and Opportunities*, Thousand Oaks, CA: Sage, pp. 221–250.

Atkinson, M.M., D. Beland, G.P. Marchildon, K. McNutt, P.W.B. Phillips and K. Rasmussen (2013), *Governance and Public Policy in Canada*, Toronto: University of Toronto Press.

Benner, C. and M. Pastor (2011), 'Moving on up? Regions, megaregions, and the changing geography of social equity organizing', *Urban Affairs Review*, **47** (3), 315–348.

Benner, C. and M. Pastor (2015), *Equity, Growth, and Community: What the Nation Can Learn from America's Metro Areas*, Oakland, CA: University of California Press.

Bradford, N. (2010), *Regional Economic Development Agencies in Canada: Lessons for Southern Ontario*, Toronto: Mowat Centre for Policy Innovation/School of Public Policy and Governance.

Cohen, A. and L. Harris (2014), 'Performing scale: watersheds as "natural" governance units in the Canadian context', in M.R. Glass and R. Rose-Redwood (eds), *Performativity, Politics, and the Production of Social Space*, New York: Routledge, pp. 226–252.

Conteh, C. (2012), 'Managing intergovernmental contracts: the Canada–Manitoba cooperation on regional economic development', *Canadian Public Administration*, **55** (2), 269–290.

Donald, B. (2002), 'Spinning Toronto's golden age: the making of a "city that worked"', *Environment and Planning A*, **34** (12), 2127–2154.

Dunning, J. (2000), *Regions, Globalization, and the Knowledge-Based Economy*, Oxford: Oxford University Press.

Faber, B. (2007), 'Towards the spatial patterns of sectoral adjustments to trade liberalisation: the case of NAFTA in Mexico', *Growth and Change*, **38** (4), 567–594.

Fishman, R. (1992), 'The Regional Plan and the transformation of the industrial metropolis', in D. Ward and O. Zunz (eds), *The Landscape of Modernity: Essays on New York City, 1900–1940*, New York: Russell Sage Foundation, pp. 106–125.

Florida, R., T. Gulden and C. Mellander (2008), 'The rise of the megaregion', *Cambridge Journal of Regions, Economy and Society*, **1** (3), 459–476.

Glass, M.R. (2011), 'Metropolitan reform in Allegheny County: the local failure of national urban reform advocacy, 1920–1929', *Journal of Urban History*, **37** (1), 90–116.

Glass, M.R. (2014), '"Becoming a thriving region" – performative visions, imaginative geographies, and the Power of 32', in M.R. Glass and R. Rose-Redwood (eds), *Performativity, Politics, and the Production of Social Space*, New York: Routledge, pp. 202–225.

Glass, M.R. (2015), 'Conflicting spaces of governance in the Great Lakes Megaregion', in M. Hoyler and J. Harrison (eds), *Megaregions: Globalization's New Urban Form?*, Cheltenham, UK and Northampton, MA, USA: Edward Elgar Publishing, pp. 119–145.

Glass, M.R. (2018), 'Navigating the regionalism-public choice divide in regional studies', *Regional Studies*, DOI: 10.1080/00343404.2017.1415430.

Goldberg, M.A. and J. Mercer (1986), *The Myth of the North American City: Continentalism Challenged*, Vancouver: University of British Columbia Press.

Gottman, J. (1961), *Megalopolis*, New York: The Twentieth Century Fund.

Graizbord, B. and A.G. Aguilar (2006), 'Regional differences and the economic and social geography of Mexico at the beginning of the twenty-first century', in L. Randall (ed.), *Changing Structure of Mexico*, New York, pp. 91–118, second edition.

Hagler, Y. (2009), *Defining American Megaregions*, New York: Regional Plan Association.
Harrison, J. and M. Hoyler (2015), 'Megaregions reconsidered: urban futures and the future of the urban', in J. Harrison and M. Hoyler (eds), *Megaregions: Globalization's New Urban Form?*, Cheltenham, UK and Northampton, MA, USA: Edward Elgar Publishing, pp. 336–387.
Imbroscio, D.L. (2006), 'Shaming the inside game: a critique of the liberal expansionist approach to addressing urban problems', *Urban Affairs Review*, **42** (2), 224–248.
Inwood, G.J., C.M. Johns and P.L. O'Reilly (2011), *Intergovernmental Policy Capacity in Canada: Inside the Worlds of Finance, Environment, Trade, and Health*, Montreal: McGill-Queen's University Press.
Jonas, A.E.G. and K. Ward (2002), 'A world of regionalisms? Towards a US–UK urban and regional policy framework comparison', *Journal of Urban Affairs*, **24** (4), 377–401.
Jonas, A.E.G. and K. Ward (2007), 'Introduction to a debate on city-regions: new geographies of governance, democracy and social reproduction', *International Journal of Urban and Regional Research*, **31** (1), 169–178.
Jonas, A.E.G., A.R. Goetz and S. Bhattacharjee (2014), 'City-regionalism as a politics of collective provision: regional transport infrastructure in Denver, USA', *Urban Studies*, **51** (11), 2444–2465.
Keil, R., P. Hamel, J.-A. Boudreau, S. Kipfer and A. Allahwala (2016), 'Regional governance revisited: political space, collective agency, and identity', in R. Keil, P. Hamel, and J.-A. Boudreau (eds), *Governing Cities through Regions: Canadian and European Perspectives*, Waterloo, ON: Wilfrid Laurier University Press, pp. 3–26.
Kent, J. (2011), 'Border bargains and the "new" sovereignty: Canada–US border perspectives from 2001 to 2005', *Geopolitics*, **16** (4), 793–818.
Kinda, A. (2001), 'The concept of "townships" in Britain and the British colonies in the seventeenth and eighteenth centuries', *Journal of Historical Geography*, **27** (2), 137–152.
Lang, R. and P.K. Knox (2009), 'The new metropolis: rethinking megalopolis', *Regional Studies*, **43** (6), 789–802.
Lewis, P.G. (1998), 'Regionalism and representation: measuring and assessing representation in metropolitan planning organizations', *Urban Affairs Review*, **33** (6), 839–853.
Lucas, J. (2016), *Fields of Authority: Special Purpose Governance in Ontario, 1815–2015*, Toronto, ON: University of Toronto Press.
Magnusson, W. (2010), 'Metropolitan reform in the capitalist city', *Canadian Journal of Political Science*, **14** (3), 557–585.
Miller, D. (2002), *The Regional Governing of Metropolitan America*, Boulder, CO: Westview Press.
Miller, D. and R. Cox III (2014), *Governing the Metropolitan Region: America's New Frontier*, Armonk, NY: M.E. Sharpe.
Nelles, J. (2014), 'Myths and legends: Exploring differences in regional governance and collective action in the North American city', *International Journal of Canadian Studies (Revue Internationale D'études Canadiennes)*, **49**, 159–203.
Niedt, C. and M. Weir (2010), 'Property rights, taxpayer rights, and the multiscalar attack on the state: consequences for regionalism in the United States', *Regional Studies*, **44** (2), 153–165.
Norman, E. S. and K. Bakker (2009), 'Transgressing scales: water governance across the Canada–US borderland', *Annals of the Association of American Geographers*, **99** (1), 99–117.
Orfield, M. (1997), *Metropolitics*, Washington, DC: Brookings Institution Press.
Orfield, M. (1999), *Pittsburgh Metropolitics: A Regional Agenda for Community and Stability*, Metropolitan Area Research Corp./Heinz Endowments.
Orfield, M. (2002), *American Metropolitics*, Washington, DC: Brookings Institution Press.
Prince, K. (2002), *Information Dissemination and Labor Response: The NAFTA and Central Pennsylvania Apparel Workers*, Dissertation, Pennsylvania State University, PA.
Radford, G. (2013), *The Rise of the Public Authority*, Chicago, IL: University of Chicago Press.
Ramutsindela, M. (2011), 'Experienced regions and borders: the challenge for transactional approaches', *Regional Studies*, **47** (1), 1–12.
Rodriguez, V.E. (1998), 'Recasting federalism in Mexico', *Publius: The Journal of Federalism*, **28** (1), 235–254.
Ross, C. (2009), *Megaregions: Planning for Global Competitiveness*, Washington, DC: Island Press.
Rusk, D. (1995), *Cities without Suburbs*, Washington, DC: Woodrow Wilson Press.
Rutherford, T. and J. Holmes (2013), '(Small) differences that (still) matter? Cross-border regions and work place governance in the Southern Ontario and US Great Lakes automotive industry', *Regional Studies*, **47** (1), 116–127.
Sanchez, T. (2006), *An Inherent Bias? Geographic and Racial-Ethnic Patterns of MPO Boards*, Washington, DC: Brookings Metropolitan Institute.
Saxenian, A. (1994), *Regional Advantage*, Cambridge, MA: Harvard University Press.
Schafran, A. (2014), 'Rethinking mega-regions: sub-regional politics in a fragmented metropolis', *Regional Studies*, **48** (4), 587–602.
Scott, A.J. (2012), *A World in Emergence: Cities and Regions in the 21st Century*, Cheltenham, UK and Northampton, MA, USA: Edward Elgar Publishing.

Scott, J.W. (1999), 'European and North American contexts for cross-border regionalism', *Regional Studies*, **33** (7), 605–617.

Storper, M. (1997), *Regional Worlds*, New York: Guilford Press.

Sudjic, D. (1992), *The 100-Mile City*, San Diego, CA: Harcourt Brace.

Tamayo-Flores, R. (2006), 'NAFTA-driven changes in the regional pattern of economic growth in Mexico: profile and determinants', in L. Randall (ed.), *Changing Structure of Mexico*, New York: Routledge, pp. 119–139, second edition.

Teaford, J.C. (1979), *City and Suburb: The Political Fragmentation of Metropolitan America, 1850–1970*, Baltimore, MD: Johns Hopkins University Press.

Todorovich, P. (2009), 'America's emerging megaregions and implications for a national growth strategy', *International Journal of Public Sector Management*, **22** (3), 221–234.

Vance, J.E. (1990), *The Continuing City: Urban Morphology in Western Civilization*, Baltimore, MD: Johns Hopkins University Press.

Vogel, R.K. and N. Nezelkiewicz (2002), 'Metropolitan planning organizations and the new regionalism', *Publius*, **32** (1), 107–129.

Wachsmuth, D. (2017), 'Competitive multi-city regionalism: growth politics beyond the growth machine', *Regional Studies*, **51** (4), 643–653.

Witkowska, J. (2016), 'Integration processes in the global economy: current state and prospects. The cases of the European Union, ASEAN, and NAFTA', *Comparative Economic Research*, **19** (4), 47–64.

Wolfe, D.A. (2015), 'Resilience and governance in city-regions: lessons from Waterloo, Ontario', in K. Jones, A. Lord, and R. Shields (eds), *City-Regions in Prospect? Exploring Points between Place and Practice*, Montreal: McGill-Queen's University Press, pp. 187–212.

38. Region building, autonomy and regionalism in South America
Pia Riggirozzi and Melisa Deciancio

38.1 INTRODUCTION

Over the last decade it became increasingly clear that a nationalist tone to global politics is challenging the role and vitality of regional integration as a political and economic project. Key gauges of the strength of nationalism vis-à-vis integration are the UK referendum to exit the European Union (EU) in June 2016, and subsequent declarations of President Donald Trump threatening to withdraw the USA from the Trans Pacific Partnership and to redefine the terms of contract with Canada and Mexico regarding the North American Free Trade Area in place since 1995. In this context, we ask, paraphrasing Dani Rodrik (1997), an imperative question: 'has regionalism gone too far?' While it might be too soon, and even intellectually futile, to declare the failure of supranational governance, these events open an opportunity to analyse empirical patterns of regional transformation revealing new nuances about the relationship between states and regional governance across the world. If any lesson is to be drawn from historical patterns in Latin America, and in South America in particular as this chapter will show, it is that regional governance is a dynamic process, a rebalancing act between the region and a series of individual responses to crises.

The discussion about regional governance and whether this is necessarily incompatible with a revitalisation of state power is not new in Latin America. In fact, what the region is, and what the region is for, has been historically contested as regionalisms unfolded. Aldo Ferrer, former Minister of Economy in Argentina, defended the thesis that, in the case of countries struggling against the long imperial arm or its heavy hand, regional integration was to be considered a governance tool supporting national states to support and coordinate 'construction of sovereignty' (Ferrer 1964). From this point of view, this construction does not rest upon the delegation of sovereignty to supranational communitarian institutions, nor does it rest on the transfer of sovereignty to supranational institutions. Constructing and supporting sovereignty through regionalism, from this perspective, rather rest on inter-governmental institutions and agreements set in place to help states to address in a coordinated manner economic and political challenges and gain leverage, for individual members and as a region, in the presence of asymmetries of power.

This is not to deny that tensions arise between national interest and regional governance. The chapter concentrates on South America because the way regional cooperation unfolded presents something of a paradox: regionalism in South America has not been seen as constraints to national sovereignty but rather, we argue, as a set of institutions enhancing rather than limiting national sovereignty and sovereign decisions. As we have expressed elsewhere in our writing, South American regionalism remains an effective and accepted inter-governmental modality of governance that while avoiding supranational rule, it enhances (some aspect of) state capabilities (Riggirozzi and Tussie 2017), particularly in relation to external influence from hegemonic states and external markets. The chapter looks at the process of region building and trajectories of regional governance in South America to claim that the region is another venue where politics happen beyond and above states, and that regional governance has been part and parcel of a constant search for autonomy in South America.

38.2   AUTONOMY AS IDENTITY: SOUTH AMERICAN REGIONALISM IN HISTORICAL PERSPECTIVE

What makes neighbouring nations a larger regional unit? What mystical qualities, paraphrasing Myrdal (1968, p. 39), explain why nations hang together beyond simply geographical proximity? The birthmark of Latin American regional integration traces back to the nineteenth century when the processes of independence and nation-building arose with the end of European colonialism and intervention (Rivarola Puntigliano and Briceño Ruiz 2013). Since then, an idea of 'region' started to develop in part as the struggles for independence and the coetaneous conformation of republics demanded joint efforts to leverage external influence (Deciancio 2016).

South American regionalism has been strongly marked by its topography. But what is truly distinctive of region building in South America is that nations considered themselves as part of a regional entity since the colonial times, sharing not only a common territory, cultural and historical ties, but more profoundly a pressing need to secure collectively a pathway to decolonisation, non-intervention, self-determination and international law (Fawcett 2005; Scarfi 2014). This is a distinctive birthmark, which also helps to explain the particular trajectory of South American regional institutions that evolved to a great extent respecting sovereignty of member states. Regional institutions were considered important features to deal collectively with the political and economic dilemmas that states by themselves found more difficult to address. But region building is about pragmatism (Tussie 2009). In postcolonial South America region building has mainly been conceived as an instrument to balance external influences – in a broader sense, that is US hegemony; and the pressures and impact arising from an incessant internationalisation of capital and trade. As independence became a continental goal, *continental unionism* was incorporated in many diplomatic declarations and endorsed by intellectuals, diplomats and policy makers who defended the notion that the economic and political destinies of each nation were to be guarded by a newly independent region through treaties and political arrangements (Deciancio 2016).

The liberation of Latin American territories from European dominion set the doctrinal bases for nineteenth-century regionalist projects tied to notions of self-determination and international law as instruments for nation-building (Fawcett 2005; Schulz 2014; Deciancio 2017). As Mace puts it, the political unity of Latin America was envisaged by founding fathers like Simon Bolivar 'as a means to de-fuse regional conflicts, to establish the predominance of a regional international law, and to reduce the vulnerability of the Latin American countries to the actions of the great powers, especially Great Britain and the US' (Mace 1988, p. 405).

In retrospect, there are two (competing) sets of ideas, values and motivations that historically embraced the struggles for independence – both at the birth of Latin American nation-states as independent political entities in the nineteenth century and more currently in the search for new socio-political and economic organisation. On the one hand, the idea of a united region has been embraced as a 'USA vision' born in the Monroe Doctrine and embodied in the Pan-American ideal that advocates Americas free from the influence of countries outside the Western hemisphere – yet guarded by the USA.[1] On the other hand, the 'Latin American vision' embraced by Simon Bolıvar's quest for a unified body of former Spanish colonies linked a vision of integration to culture, language and history. These two visions later evolved into modern manifest-ations of contrasting and competing models of economic and political governance, which dominated the twentieth century.

In practice, a perceived sense of common legacy together with a realpolitik calculus of cooperation against imperialist external rule, political and economic have been the drivers of different regional arrangements and integration projects. As openly put by Myrdal (1968, p. 39) 'there are no mystical qualities in geographical proximity that make neighbouring nations a unit in any real sense culturally, politically or economically'. This call for unity has been mainly conceived as an instrument to balance external influences – in a broader sense, that is USA hegemony, EU economic competitiveness, international capital and globalisation demands (Fawcett 2012). However, the breakup from Spanish and Portuguese colonial administrations left the continent with weak institutional frame-works that struggled to absorb and regulate economic and political conflicts (Rivarola Puntigliano and Briceño Ruiz 2013).

What followed was a complex process of state formation shaped by the pressures of (re)constructing markets and the insertion of new economies in the logic of international trade. As Colin Lewis (2013) puts it, South American nations transited a co-foundation process where states, and the construction of a domestic institutions and their capacity to regulate have been determined by the creation of market economies – and vice versa. Furthermore, the evolution of postcolonial national governance across the region tended to be highly captured and reproduced by elite politics. Increasingly export expansion, industrialisation, and infrastructure investment enhanced South America's insertion into the global division of labour and solidified the basis for elite-led 'order and progress' and 'peace and administration' (Lewis 2013).

Since the Great Depression and up until current developments, the USA and the Latin American visions reflected a debate of national and regional development defined in terms of statism versus liberalism. The ways in which this dichotomy was resolved had been inherently related to how Latin American nations managed autonomy vis-à-vis the regional power. As Riggirozzi and Tussie (2012, 2017) argue, regional projects unfolded as contestation, while the regional space became the locus for reworking regional arrange-ments that in philosophical, legal, and institutional terms gave expression to, and privi-leged many forms of, political and economic practices. Particularly in South America, the way regionalism unfolded reflected a variety of paths and paces, and overlapping and even competing projects, profoundly and indelibly shaped, from the nineteenth century onwards, by a need to offer national and regional responses to external economic and political pressures.

38.3 ECONOMIC REGIONALISM: THE SEARCH FOR AUTONOMY AND GLOBAL BELONGING

During the 1950s and 1960s trade agreements sought to enhance import substitution and fledgling closed markets at a regional scale. In this context, South American regionalism was driven by a quest for reducing external economic dependency through trade-based projects to protect and enhance the industrial bases of growth across the region. Two international organisations emerged from what became usually identified as the first wave of regional integration: the Economic Commission for Latin America and the Caribbean (ECLAC) and the Latin-American Free Trade Agreement (LAFTA) (Rosenthal 1991).[2] Under the leadership of Raul Prebisch and a coalition of technocrats and reformist politicians ECLAC became an advocator of economic cooperation as a means to reduce traditional dependence on primary commodity export trade (Malamud 2010). Prebisch put forward the first theoretical development calling for regionalism making a bold leap from the political, identity-bond unionism of the past, to large-scale projects of national economic development based on industrialisation and import substitution policies through the lenses of unfair terms of exchange between the core (the industrialised North) and the periphery (underdeveloped South) (Prebisch 1950). These core–periphery tensions set out a new understanding of North–South political economy and regionalism that gave way to an emphasis on regional economic development (Deciancio 2016).

After the signature of the Montevideo Treaty of 1960, LAFTA became the first vast trade-led regional bloc. LAFTA was the first attempt of South American countries to coordinate, without the US involvement, South American economic development (Magariños 2000). In many ways, ECLAC provided new practical and ideological impetus for thinking about the place that Latin America should adopt in the international system, both in terms of international insertion and strategies of economic development. It also provided new political economic foundations that contested, albeit not openly, Panamericanism as *the* way of organising Inter-American (economic and political) relations. At its centre was the notion of bounded sovereign states, largely able to control the nature of regional commitments and to protect their domestic producers from external competition via subsidies and tariffs (Chibber 2004; Lewis 2005). In this context, economic nationalism framed a new way of thinking and speaking about politics, economics and culture; while regionalism became a generalised reaction to the liberal rule.

LAFTA provided a distinctive political and normative economic framework, but failed due lack of policy coordination to assess regional asymmetries. In 1969 a split from LAFTA led Bolivia, Colombia, Chile, Ecuador and Peru to establish an institutionally ambitious common market project, the Andean Community, with an executive body with 'supranational' powers and mechanisms to promote an equitable distribution of benefits. Increasingly however the region became severely challenged by the ravages of debt, low growth and the warmongering mistrust of dictators affecting any sense of solidarity and common destiny (Haggard and Kaufman 1992). It was not until the end of the military dictatorships that regionalism was revisited with the emergence of the Latin American Integration Association (LAIA) in 1980 (Magariños 2000).

LAFTA, the Andean Pact and ALADI marked the first wave of nationalistic developmental projects that increasingly became unsustainable, while the severity of many years of political repression and military dictatorships that followed affected the spirit and the progress of close regionalism and any attempt to advance towards other areas of political union (Mattli 1999, Mace and Bélanger 1999). This decline in many ways meant not only a failure to tie the region closely in terms of its cohesion but critically a mitigation of its identity and autonomy.

As regional organisations lost dynamism, and as import-substitution strategies withered under the weight of debt crisis, a new approach to regional economic integration turned to the USA as gatekeeper to external finance, and standard-bearer of 'open markets', liberalisation and regionalism as a way to lock in market-oriented reforms through 'open regionalism'. This defined the second wave of regionalism in South America and the contours of region building in the 1990s (Estevadeordal et al. 2015).

The new wave of South American economic integration was therefore marked by 'new regionalism' strongly marked by trade liberalisation and the deepening of economic globalisation (CEPAL 1994). The increase in trade, foreign investment and financial fluxes marked the regional economies and led to new strategies in tune with the presence and power of multinational corporations that were gaining new space as processes of privatisation took over rapidly in the first half of the 1990s. In this context, the role of regional integration changed dramatically with respect to the early post-war period (De Lombaerde and Garay 2008).

The international context of trade negotiations epitomised in the conclusion of the WTO Uruguay Round of negotiations in 1994, which institutionalised – now globally – multinational trade liberalisation options through multilateralism. The establishment of the Common Market of the South (Mercado Comun del Sur, MERCOSUR, in Spanish) in 1991 grouping together Brazil, the largest economy in Latin America, with Argentina, Uruguay and Paraguay, and the North American Free Trade Agreement (NAFTA) signed between the US, Canada and Mexico in 1994, for instance, were premised on the notion of 'open regionalism' (CEPAL 1994). Both MERCOSUR and NAFTA were articulated as strategic responses to the imperatives generated by the globalisation processes aimed at enhancing markets, trade and investment (Phillips 2003). Increasingly trade grew significantly among regional partners as trade barriers went down from 40 per cent in the 1980s to 12 per cent by the 1990s; creating in many cases economic interdependencies among neighbours for the first time in modern history (IADB 2002).

Although, as Tussie (2009, p. 178) argues, open regionalism was 'triggered [by] panic reactions in a spate of excluded countries' the idea of open markets, neoliberal-led regionalism was highly contested from the outset across the region. The adoption of open regionalism became seen as the pursuit of economic growth through interaction with global markets. But adverse effects of economic integration on social cohesion and development contributed to deep disenchantment with neoliberal policies as they failed to deliver on their promises beyond controlling inflation.

The initial trust in market policies, mostly triggered by panic reactions in a spate of economically excluded countries, as put by Tussie (2009, p. 178), soon faced the challenges of delivering social promises beyond controlling inflation. After the economic crisis that started with Mexico in 1994 and continued in Asia in 1997, Russia in 1998, Brazil in 1999 and Argentina in 2001, the effects of neoliberal reforms evinced a clear lack of delivery. During the 'lost half decade' as Bértola and Ocampo (2011) called it, public debt in countries like Argentina and Ecuador reached up to 60 per cent of the GDP. Across the region, the number of people living in poverty was higher by the end of the 1990s than in

1980, while the percentage of people in poverty remained startlingly high going from 200 million people during the 1990s, to 220 million during the 2000s. Unemployment went from 6.4 per cent in 1990 to 13.2 per cent in 2002 (Bértola and Ocampo 2011). Mercosur went through its worst economic, institutional and social crisis. Brazil's devaluation in 1999 and Argentina's breakdown in 2001 led intra-zone trade to drop dramatically, up to 25 per cent in 1999 compared with the previous year (Informe Mercosur N°8 2001–2002). Trade measures hardly had an impact on structural and policy asymmetries. In fact, MERCOSUR has led to greater economic concentration. The increasing dissatisfaction of smaller partners in relation to the results of trade integration and the failure to address asymmetries led to a conception of a regionalism less focused on trade (Celli et al. 2011).

The failure of regional development projects, particularly through structural adjustment programmes adopted as part of conditional foreign aid packages but also as part of disciplining what regionalism should look like, failed to revert poor economic performance and to deliver well-being of those living within the confines of the region. As a consequence the economic rationale and even the morality of market-led development strategies at national and regional levels became under scrutiny across the developing world. This created an opportunity for regional organisations to redefine what development is and to develop a new 'political badge of identity' (Riggirozzi and Grugel 2015, p. 782).

38.4   REGIONALISM IN SEARCH FOR (POLITICAL AND SOCIAL) MEANING

New dynamics of political and social cooperation in South America since the early 2000s came up to fit the changing face of democracy in the region. As Acharya (2004) notes, changes to the form of national democracy profoundly affect the nature of regional governance. In the case of South America, after two decades of neoliberal democracy and market-based governance, the new leftists governments took office across the region – in Venezuela (1998), Brazil (2002), Argentina (2003), Uruguay (2004), Bolivia (2005), Ecuador (2006), Paraguay (2008) and Peru (2011) – promising mixed economies and a generally pragmatic combination of welfare and populist policies. This uncoupling of democracy from the market dramatically transformed what 'supporting' democracy and development at the regional level would mean. The era of 'post-neoliberalism' as it has been called (Grugel and Riggirozzi 2012; Sanahuja 2012), is characterised not only by a rejection of unmediated markets but also by a resurgence of nationalism through new leftist governments who reasserted equity and sovereignty as distinctive national and regional identities in South America.

The creation of the Bolivarian Alliance of the Americas (ALBA) in 2004 led by Venezuela and Cuba, the Union of South American Nations (UNASUR) in 2008, including the 12 South American nations; and the Community of Latin American and Caribbean States (CELAC), including all the nations of Latin America and the Caribbean, should be seen as manifestations in this direction. Both organisations exclude the US or Canada, and are another manifestation of increasingly diversified global engagement of Latin American and Caribbean countries with countries *outside* the region, particularly China, and growing diplomatic importance of alternative regional bodies fostering new compromises, institutions, funding mechanisms, policies and practices *within* the region in areas such as security, (political) rights, development, energy, infrastructure and security (Sanahuja 2012; Legler 2013; Serbin 2007).

In South America, UNASUR is the most recent attempt at regional governance and it follows on from two quite intense decades of, sometimes controversial, region-building based chiefly on principles of increasing inter-regional trade and market opening, alongside increase poverty and inequality as a consequence of economic crisis and austerity during the 1980s and 1990s.

At the First Summit of South American Presidents in 2000, which was to give rise to UNASUR a few years later, discussions turned to how to support regional democracies and encourage development by deepening contacts and flows of ideas, as well as material goods, across the region (Sanahuja 2012). After the creation of the Community of South American Countries in 2004 in Cuzco, Peru, the South American Union of Nations, UNASUR, was established in 2007 during the Energetic Summit in Margarita Island, Venezuela and set out three principal goals. Two were fairly standard: the promise to reinvigorate inter-regional collaboration and the commitment to the creation of physical infrastructure (roads, energy and communications) to support better regional development. But alongside these was a promise of greater political cooperation in poverty eradication, particularly in health (Riggirozzi and Tussie 2012). UNASUR's Constitutive Treaty explicitly declared the need to foster integration in ways that would support social inclusion and poverty eradication in ways that were based on the realisation of rights.[3] The duty to support rights-based social policy, delivered through member states, came to be framed as a 'regional' responsibility. Moreover, a democratic clause was added to the Constitutive Treaty in 2010, allowing for measures to be taken against a member state if the democratic process is put in danger.

In fact, since the early 2000s UNASUR became the scenario for contestation to the US-led regional governance, and the OAS, in what seems to show a determination to create a new sovereign space of governance at odds with the USA. Governing the regional crisis was for the first time addressed without USA involvement and by the coordination between South American leaders. This was put clearly as UNASUR acted in what at other times would have been the remit of the OAS: managing the political crisis in Bolivia in 2008; the coup d'état suffered by President Manuel Zelaya in Honduras in 2009; the USA intentions to settle military bases in Colombia in 2010; the crisis between Colombia and Venezuela in 2010; and the attempt to remove Ecuadorian President Rafael Correa in the same year. The management of these episodes confirmed the growing autonomy of South American countries to cope with their own crises and with their own tools, without the involvement of third actors (Serbin 2009).

For Riggirozzi (2014) UNASUR became a 'space for political action' as well as a space for reformulation of norms in support of the delivery of rights-based social provision in and through member states, in ways that would link the delivery of more inclusive social policy to the embedding and strengthening of social democracy (Riggirozzi and Grugel 2015). As such, UNASUR marks a profound departure from the early wave of new regionalism in the 1990s, where economic integration was so clearly in the driving seat.

In South America there has been a clear turn to more political entities addressing social policy, beyond trade, that is from defence and security (Battaglino 2012) and health (Herrero and Tussie 2015; Riggirozzi 2014; Riggirozzi and Tussie, 2018) to infrastructure and environment (Dabène 2012; Saguier and Brent 2015; Saguier 2012). These are new areas where regional organisations such as UNASUR, CELAC and ALBA developed new mandates and agendas. Yet the gap between what regional organisations can do and what they actually do still remains a matter of research.

These developments, and any manifestation of post hegemony, are undoubtedly challenged by current regional and global climate. Regionalism is in flux in dispute with more traditional forms of trade-based arrangements such as the Trans Pacific Partnership (TPP) initiative, which brings together 12 countries on the Pacific Rim, three of which are in Latin America (Quiliconi 2014a, 2014b). There are clear challenges as to what these organisations do and what they can actually do. Nonetheless, regional organisations such as UNASUR, ALBA and CELAC have certainly called into question, and quite successfully, the credibility of neoliberal governance. In the process, doors have been opened for regionalism to be reimagined as an instrument for more socially conscious development planning and a space for, in theory and practice, reinforcing the geography–identity nexus and the exercise of sovereignty through regional association.

38.5   CONCLUSION

The regional is a distinctive space of politics. In South America regional projects shaped and have been shaped by competing development models as well as a constant search for autonomous development and sovereignty. In practice, we argued, the construction of regionalism in South America, as a political and economic project, must be understood as a trans-border cooperation and practices of region building in South America have been in constant development as national actors found the regional space a place to (re)work consensus over social and economic resource sharing, regulations, planning and financial cooperation; most of which were tied to national goals seeking to enhance both autonomous development and sovereignty.

The relationship between region building, sovereignty and autonomous development as unfolded in South America is not only distinctive to this region but is an example of how newly independent nations assumed the defence of autonomy as a collective enterprise. This is not surprising, as the chapter shows, given the constant exposure to the pressures of particular sets of influences, political and economic, that distinguishes this region from other expressions of regionalism around the world. As Deciancio (2016, p. 11) argues, Latin American countries thought about themselves as a distinctive entity facing a common legacy of foreign interventions since the nineteenth century. This common factor not only united the nations but also determined their aversion to supranational institutional constriction. Nonetheless, as we also argued, it would be a mistake to claim that in the absence of supranational authority regionalism in South America failed: tackling common problems such as enhancing geographic and political autonomy and economic development in South America unfolded in different regional projects, in processes of dramatic, yet quiet and constant, transformation.

In this sense, the South American experience has a lot to add to the study of regionalism and International Relations. As such, the chapter calls to engage afresh with ideas and experiences of region building from the point of view of developing countries; rethinking how sovereignty can be constructed and supported through regionalism. This is particularly pressing in the current context where the re-emergence of nationalisms and tensions between integration and disintegration in Europe call into question the benefits and disadvantages of supranational regional integration.

38.6 NOTES

1. American President Henry Monroe articulated in 1823 what was then considered the main US policy towards the Americas. In his speech, Monroe warned European powers not to interfere in the affairs of the Western Hemisphere and set the ideological basis for US intervention in the region.
2. LAFTA was the first regional integration project including Latin American countries. It was later on replaced by the Latin American Integration Area (LAIA) with the signature of the Montevideo Treaty in 1970.
3. UNASUR Constitutive Treaty, at http://www.unasursg.org/uploads/0c/c7/0cc721468628d65c3c510a577e545 19d/Tratado-constitutivo-english-version.pdf (accessed 28 March 2014).

38.7 REFERENCES

Acharya, A. (2004), 'How ideas spread: whose norms matter? Norm localization and institutional change in Asian regionalism', *International Organization*, **58** (2), 239–275.

Battaglino, J. (2012), 'Defence in a post-hegemonic regional agenda: the case of the South American defence council', in P. Riggirozzi and D. Tussie (eds), *The Rise of Post-Hegemonic Regionalism. The Case of Latin America*, Dordrecht: Springer, pp. 81–100.

Bértola, L. and J.A. Ocampo (2011), '*Desarrollo, Vaivenes y Desigualdad. Una Historia Económica de América Latina Desde la Independencia*', Secretaría General Iberoamericana.

Celli, U., M. Salles, D. Tussie and J. Peixoto (2011), 'Mercosur in south–south agreements: in the middle of two models of regionalism', *Documento de Trabajo del Área de Relaciones Internacionales FLACSO*.

CEPAL (1994), *El Regionalismo Abierto en América Latina y el Caribe. La Integración Económica al Servicio de la Transformación Productiva con Qquidad*, Santiago de Chile: CEPAL.

Chibber, V. (2004), 'Reviving the developmental state? The myth of the "national bourgeoisie"', in L. Panitch and C. Leys (eds), *The Empire Reloaded*, London: Merlin Press, pp. 144–165.

Dabène, O. (2012), 'Explaining Latin America's fourth wave of regionalism. Regional integration of a third kind', Paper for delivery at the 2012 Congress of the Latin American Studies Association (LASA) panel 'Waves of change in Latin America. History and Politics', San Francisco, 25 May 2012.

De Lombaerde, P. and L.J. Garay (2008), 'El nuevo regionalismo en América Latina', in P. De Lombaerde, S. Kochi and J. Briceño Ruiz (eds), *Del Regionalismo Latinoamericano a la Integración Regional*, Madrid: Fundación Carolina – Siglo XXI, pp. 3–35.

Deciancio, M. (2016), 'International relations from the south: a regional research agenda for global IR', *International Studies Review*, **18** (1), 1–14.

Deciancio, M. (2017), 'Las Facultad de Derecho y Ciencias Sociales de la Universidad de Buenos Aires en la historia del campo de las Relaciones Internacionales argentinas', *Revista de Historia del Derecho*, **52**.

Estevadeordal, A., P. Giordano and B. Ramos (2015), 'Trade and economic integration', in J. Domínguez and A. Covarrubias (eds), *Routledge Handbook of Latin America in the World*, New York: Routledge, pp. 249–264.

Fawcett, L. (2005), 'The origins and development of the regional idea in the Americas', in L. Fawcett and M. Serrano (eds), *Regionalism and Governance in the Americas*, London: Palgrave Macmillan, pp. 27–51.

Fawcett, L. (2012), 'Between West and non-West: Latin American contributions to international thought', *The International History Review*, **34** (4), 679–704.

Ferrer, A. (1964), 'Modernización, Desarrollo Industrial e Integración Latinoamericana', *Desarrollo Económico*, **4** (14–15), 195–205.

Grugel, J. and P. Riggirozzi (2012), *Governance after Neoliberalism in Latin America*, Basingstoke: Palgrave Macmillan.

Haggard, S. and R. Kaufman (1992), *The Politics of Economic Adjustment. International Constraints, Distributive Conflicts and the State*, Princeton, NJ: Princeton University Press.

Herrero, M.B. and D. Tussie (2015), 'UNASUR health: A quiet revolution in health diplomacy in South America', *Global Social Policy*, **15** (3), 261–277.

IADB (2002), *Beyond Borders: The New Regionalism in the Americas*, Washington DC: IADB.

Informe Mercosur N°8 (2001–2002).

Legler, T. (2013), 'Post-hegemonic Regionalism and Sovereignty in Latin America: Optimists, Skeptics, and an Emerging Research Agenda', *Contexto internacional*, **35** (2), 325–352.

Lewis, C. (2005), 'States and Markets in Latin America: the Political Economy of Economic Interventionism', edited by LSE Department of Economic History, *Working Paper 09/05*.

Lewis, C. (2013), '"Colonial" industry and "modern" manufacturing: opportunities for labour-intensive growth in Latin America, c.1800–1940', in G. Austin and K. Sugihara (eds), *Labour-Intensive Industrialization in Global History*, Abingdon: Routledge, pp. 231–262.

Mace, G. (1988), 'Regional integration in Latin America: a long and winding road', *International Journal*, **43** (3), 404–427.

Mace, G. and L. Bélanger (1999), *The Americas in Transition: The Contours of Regionalism*, Boulder and London: Lynne Rienner Publishers.

Magariños, G. (2000), 'Proceso ALALC/ALADI', *Foro de política INTAL*.

Malamud, A. (2010), 'Latin American regionalism and EU studies', *European Integration*, **32** (6), 637–657.

Mattli, W. (1999), *The Logic of Regional Integration: Europe and Beyond*, Cambridge: Cambridge University Press.

Myrdal, G. (1968), *Asian Drama: An Inquiry into the Poverty of Nations*, London: Allen Lane Penguin Press.

Phillips, N. (2003), 'Hemispheric integration and subregionalism in the Americas', *International Affairs*, **79** (2), 327–349.

Prebisch, R. (1950), *The Economic Development of Latin America and its Principal Problems*, Geneva: United Nations Publication.

Quiliconi, C. (2014a), 'Competitive diffusion of trade agreements in Latin America', *International Studies Review*, **16** (2), 240–251.

Quiliconi, C. (2014b), 'Atlántico versus Pacífico: las alternativas en competencia de la integración comercial en América Latina', *Revista Relaciones Internacionales*, **23** (47), 165–184.

Riggirozzi, P. and D. Tussie (2012), *The Rise of Post-Hegemonic Regionalism: The Case of Latin America*, London and New York: Springer.

Riggirozzi, P. (2014), 'Regionalism through social policy: collective action and health diplomacy in South America', *Economy and Society*, **43** (2), 432–454.

Riggirozzi, P. and J. Grugel (2015), 'Regional governance and legitimacy in South America: the meaning of UNASUR', *International Affairs*, **91** (4), 781–797.

Riggirozzi, P. and D. Tussie (2017), 'Rethinking our region in a post-hegemonic moment', in J. Briceño-Ruiz and I. Morales (eds), *Post-Hegemonic Regionalism in the Americas: Toward a Pacific–Atlantic Divide?*, Abingdon: Routledge, pp. 16–31.

Riggirozzi, P. and D. Tussie (2018),'Regional governance in South America: supporting states, dealing with markets and reworking hegemonies', in P. Riggirozzi and C. Wylde (eds), *Handbook of South American Governance*, London: Routledge.

Rivarola Puntigliano, A. and J. Briceño Ruiz (2013),'Introduction: Regional integration: linking past and present', in A. Rivarola Puntigliano and J. Briceño-Ruiz (eds), *Resilience of Regionalism in Latin America and the Caribbean. Development and Autonomy*, London and New York: Palgrave Macmillan, pp. 1–18.

Rodrik, D. (1997), *Has Globalization Gone Too Far?*, Washington, DC: Institute for International Economics.

Rosenthal, G. (1991), 'Un informe crítico a 30 años de integracion en América Latina', *Nueva Sociedad*, **113**, 60–65.

Saguier, M. (2012), 'Socio-environmental regionalism in South America: tensions in new development models', in P. Riggirozzi and D. Tussie (eds), *The Rise of Post-hegemonic Regionalism. The Case of Latin America*, Dordrecht: Springer, pp. 125–145.

Saguier, M. and Z. Brent (2015), 'Regionalismo y economía social y solidaria en suramérica', *Estudios*, **48**, 133–154.

Sanahuja, J.A. (2012), 'Post-liberal regionalism in South America: the case of UNASUR', *EUI Working Papers* (Global Governance Programme).

Scarfi, J.P. (2014), 'In the name of the Americas: the Pan-American redefinition of the Monroe Doctrine and the emerging language of American International Law in the western hemisphere, 1898–1933', *Diplomatic History*, **40** (2), 189–218.

Schulz, C.-A. (2014), 'Civilisation, barbarism and the Making of Latin America's place in 19th-century international society', *Millennium: Journal of International Studies*, **42** (3), 837–859.

Serbin, A. (2007), 'Entre UNASUR y ALBA: ¿otra integración (ciudadana) es posible?', *Anuario de la Integración Regional de América Latina y el Gran Caribe* (CRIES), 183–207.

Serbin, A. (2009), 'América del Sur en un mundo multipolar: ¿es la Unasur la alternativa?', *Nueva Sociedad*, **219**, 145–156.

Tussie, D. (2009), 'Latin America: contrasting motivations for regional Projects', *Review of International Studies*, **35**, 169–188.

39. Arctic and Antarctic regionalism
Klaus Dodds and Alan D. Hemmings

39.1 INTRODUCTION

In this chapter, we develop two distinct strands of enquiry. At a conceptual level, our discussion is informed by a desire to better understand how 'territory' and 'region' are put to work discursively and acted out and upon geopolitically (see also Dodds and Hemmings 2015). Informed by the scholarship of authors such as Stuart Elden (2009, 2013) and Philip Steinberg and colleagues (2015), territory is something historically constructed and something that operates on a distinctly material register. In the polar regions the intersection of ice, rock and water is particularly distinct in terms of how territorial and regional management is expressed. Working off a volumetric rather than areal focus, recent work alerts us to how region-making projects have worked through height, depth and subterranean domains, none more so than in the Arctic and Antarctic.

Second, we address polar regionalism in general which then leads into separate sections on the Arctic and Antarctic. For the sake of brevity, the Arctic Council and the Antarctic Treaty System respectively will be the main areas of reflection. However, we are mindful of the fact that other organisations such as the Nordic Council, West Nordic Council, Barents Euro-Arctic Council and Conference of Parliamentarians of the Arctic Region are factors in Arctic regionalism (Exner-Pirot 2013). Multilateral instruments including regional fisheries management organisations operating immediately to the north of the Antarctic Treaty area of application are part of what we might term Antarctic regionalism. The Arctic Council is a circumpolar intergovernmental forum made up of the eight Arctic states (Canada, Denmark, Finland, Iceland, Norway, Russia, Sweden and the United States) while the Nordic Council, as the names implies, has a more regional membership composed of Denmark, Finland, Iceland, Norway, and Sweden. It is also axiomatic that the regional boundaries of the Arctic and Antarctic are fluid so that it is imperative that we appreciate that regional and international actors such as the European Union (EU) and UN agencies such as the International Maritime Organization (IMO) play a part in shaping polar regionalism in the water, air, and on the land. For instance, the IMO's Polar Code (entered into force on 1 January 2017) is an important legal intervention on the maritime environments of the Arctic and Southern Ocean. Alternatively, the EU is an ad hoc observer to the Arctic Council and major funder of Arctic and Antarctic science.

39.2 POLAR REGIONALISM

Any account of polar regionalism would have to acknowledge that the materiality of the Arctic and Antarctic plays an important role in the making and remaking of regional projects (Young 2005, 2012; Pincus and Ali 2015; Steinberg and Dodds 2015). Unlike other continents and islands, the interplay of sea and ice are critical in shaping the human and physical geographies of the Arctic and Antarctic. Both areas change markedly depending on seasonality, and historically have varied in extent depending on the distribution and thickness of land and sea ice. The (then) remoteness of the Antarctic arguably allowed the negotiators of the 1959 Antarctic Treaty (Saul and Stephens 2015, pp. 1–5) to include such path-breaking provisions as the prohibition of military measures, nuclear testing and waste disposal and to entirely ignore the question of potential future resource exploitation which was left to later development of the Antarctic Treaty System. In the case of the Arctic, sea ice and polar weather has played a pivotal role in deepening the work of the Arctic Council and arguably configuring a shared sense of the Arctic region as a *demanding space* needing regional cohesion when it comes to search and rescue, shipping, and oil response in the event of a shipping or oil/gas disaster affecting the Arctic Ocean. So there are discernible issues that contribute to the imaginative geographies of 'Arctic challenges'.

The geopolitics of the Cold War is a major factor in determining the how, where, who, why and what of regional co-operation. In the Arctic, the 'ice curtain' between the United States and the Soviet Union was clearly pivotal in shaping a lack of regional co-operation and collaboration as both sides feared that the other might engage in long-range bomber attacks and sneak submarine assaults. Where regional co-operation existed it was shaped by a security architecture including the United States and its regional allies such as the UK, Canada and Norway who were committed to patrolling the 'Northern Flank' and 'Northern Waters' of the Arctic and northern fringes of the Atlantic and Pacific Oceans (Archer 1988). Where there was a more regional even circumpolar co-operation, it was limited and tied to periods of relative détente. The most notable being the 1973 Polar Bear Agreement signed between Canada, Denmark, Norway, the US and Soviet Union,[1] which noted in the preamble that:

> Recognizing the special responsibilities and special interests of the States of the Arctic Region in relation to the protection of the fauna and flora of the Arctic Region . . . Recognizing that the polar bear is a significant resource of the Arctic Region which requires additional protection . . . Having decided that such protection should be achieved through co-ordinated national measures taken by the States of the Arctic Region.

What is significant here is the construction of the parties as 'States of the Arctic Region' and thus distinct from other Arctic states such as Iceland, Finland and Sweden because of the geographical scope of the polar bear itself. Thirty-five years later, these same states would be instrumental in re-imagining themselves as Arctic Ocean coastal states, in the sense of the UN Convention on the Law of the Sea (UNCLOS), when addressing the legal and maritime geographies of the Arctic Ocean – a within-region regionalism that privileges the Arctic Five (A5) over the Arctic Eight (A8).

The idea of the 'Arctic Region' as being distinct politically, ecologically and legally is embodied in the 1973 Agreement on the Conservation of Polar Bears. Looking south, the 1959 Antarctic Treaty identified and codified an Antarctic Treaty Area (south of 60 degrees South) in order to mobilise a new framework for shaping the present and future governance of the Antarctic. In both cases, these two instruments (an Agreement and a Treaty), one object-specific and another more wide-ranging, contribute to a regionalising process sensitive to prevailing geopolitical and legal geographies of the regions. In the Arctic, the five states invoked an 'Arctic region' for the purpose of polar bear conservation, which places limits on the killing of polar bears, consults with indigenous peoples, and encourages the sharing of polar bear-related research. In the Antarctic, the Antarctic Treaty signatories, although mindful of the contested sovereignty surrounding the polar continent and surrounding oceans, worked to create a regional architecture where states and other parties co-ordinate and integrate their activities above, across and below air, ice, rock and water.

Regional architectures are not just instrumental and legal-based, they are also iterative and declarative. As Judith Butler identified for categories such as 'gender', there is an inherent performativity to words such as 'Antarctic Treaty System' and 'Antarctic Treaty Area'. As Butler explains, 'Within speech act theory, a performative is that discursive practice that enacts or produces that which it names' (Butler 2011, p. 13). The Protocol on Environmental Protection to the Antarctic Treaty (Madrid Protocol) (Saul and Stephens 2015, pp. 104–137), for example, performs a powerful speech act in its Article 2:

> The Parties commit themselves to the comprehensive protection of the Antarctic environment and dependent and associated ecosystems and hereby designate Antarctica as a natural reserve, devoted to peace and science.

By endlessly repeating the Protocol and its provisions, the Antarctic Treaty Consultative Parties help to enact objects such as 'Antarctic environment', which then contribute to Antarctic regionalisms appearing both natural and necessary. The enactment of 'regional norms', although always artificial, have geopolitical and legal consequences, as well as subjectivities of those involved in the enforcement and monitoring of the Protocol.

Butler's emphasis on performativity and iteration has relevance for more critical engagements with polar regionalisms, through her interest in what she describes as 'petty sovereigns' (often state-sanctioned officials charged with security and border management) responsible for maintaining distinctions between security and insecurity (Butler 2006, pp. 56–60). What interests us is the role a medley of state-sanctioned diplomats, scientists, journalists and academics play in policing and monitoring 'polar regionalisms' and how distinctions made regarding 'the Arctic' and 'the Antarctic' have different implications for bodies, ideas, knowledges and activities. As Butler notes in her reading of sovereignty and sovereign power, 'petty sovereigns' are implicated in a managerial power that intervenes on how things are evaluated, implemented and judged. This might be most evident in areas such as: who gets to 'speak' of and for the 'Arctic' and 'Antarctic'? Which parties, and whose interventions in the Antarctic attract the most critical environmental scrutiny? Are there some actors who are more 'naturalised' than others when it comes to speaking and doing things in the Arctic and Antarctic? And, how far does the Arctic and Antarctic extend and stretch in area, height and depth?

The making and remaking of the region and regionalism as both a process and outcome is one riven with both large-scale and public interventions, variously labelled (e.g. treaties, conventions, declarations, and protocols) and perhaps more subtle 'little things' that help to determine the shape and scope of regional projects. In the Arctic and Antarctic, state parties have had to negotiate boundaries that are fluid rather than static (e.g. the Southern Ocean), limited political and economic agendas, uncertain sovereignties and/or where there is a complex interplay between the sovereign rights of coastal states and areas beyond national jurisdiction including international waters and the seabed beyond the continental shelf entitlements of coastal states. Depending on the issue and topic, there are different regional architectures and definitions at play, which contribute to multiple Arctic and Antarctic regional governance and geopolitical projects encompassing inter alia fish, whales, minerals, shipping and science. And as we have noted, they also touch upon who, where and what gets evaluated, monitored and judged.

39.3   ARCTIC REGIONALISM

While there is a wider history and geography to Arctic regionalism to be recorded (e.g. the use of terms such as Circumpolar North), the focus is here on the inter-governmental forum, the Arctic Council. Established in 1996, under the Ottawa Declaration,[2] the Council was intended to 'provide a means for promoting cooperation, coordination and interaction among the Arctic states, with the involvement of the Arctic indigenous communities and other Arctic inhabitants on common Arctic issues, in particular issues of sustainable development and environmental protection in the Arctic'. The identification of 'sustainable development' and 'environmental protection' as foci for the Arctic Council was rooted in the legacies and consequences of Cold War militarism and post-Cold War regional collaboration and confidence building as exemplified by the speech in Murmansk by Premier Gorbachev in 1987 calling for the Arctic to be a 'zone of peace' followed by the Arctic Environment Protection Strategy (AEPS) negotiated in 1991. And the lesson of that speech, alerts us to the important role that individual political leaders still play in geopolitical shifts – a not entirely comforting, if still necessarily speculative, realisation at the dawn of the US Presidency of Donald Trump.

The AEPS addressed common environmental challenges, acknowledged the agency of indigenous peoples and identified trans-national pollution such as lingering nuclear radioactivity and airborne contaminants as regional priorities. It did not specify an Arctic region per se. The Ottawa Declaration did not define the Arctic as region but rather identified eight Arctic states and six indigenous peoples' organisations as members and Permanent Participants of the Arctic Council.

As scholars such as Keskitalo (2004) recognised, the Ottawa Declaration emerged at a time of Arctic 'regional-speak', with multiple Arctic(s) in conversation with one another depending on geographical, ecological, legal and political criteria and registers. The working groups attached to the Arctic Council such as the Arctic Monitoring and Assessment Programme and the Conservation of Arctic Flora and Fauna adopt different Arctic boundaries with countries like Iceland occupying a liminal space between Arctic and near-Arctic and variation in how far the Arctic region should extend over the northern fringes of the Atlantic and Pacific Oceans (which as we will note below, has its analogue in the 'Greater Southern Ocean' today). So in terms of advancing the core agenda of the Arctic Council, the working groups and task forces addressing matters such as marine and scientific co-operation have co-opted different working definitions of the Arctic as region (Figure 39.1). Promoting a circumpolar perspective, and informed by this scientific-technical knowledge-producing architecture, the Arctic Council has been integral to producing the Arctic as a space of shared governance.

The regional agenda of the Arctic Council grew with a shared recognition that the

Figure 39.1   Definitions of the Arctic

Arctic coastal states of Canada, Denmark/Greenland, Norway, Russia and the United States were concerned about the ecological changes and challenges confronting the Arctic Ocean environment. Ranging from receding sea ice to ocean acidification, the A5 were drawn into closer co-operation on the basis of environmental change rather than say transnational capital and resource exploitation. The Arctic Ocean, unlike onshore Arctic regions, has largely avoided natural resource exploitation including oil, gas, coal, and fishing. While the coastal areas of the Arctic region have not escaped marine and mineral exploitation, the marine areas closer to the central Arctic Ocean have remained comparatively isolated. But these remoter areas have not been immune to geophysical and chemical changes affecting the Arctic.

In May 2008, the A5 issued the Ilulissat Declaration,[3] which declared that:

The Arctic Ocean stands at the threshold of significant changes. Climate change and the melting of ice have a potential impact on vulnerable ecosystems, the livelihoods of local inhabitants and indigenous communities, and the potential exploitation of natural resources. By virtue of their sovereignty, sovereign rights and jurisdiction in large areas of the Arctic Ocean the five coastal states are in a unique position to address these possibilities and challenges . . . Notably, the law of the sea provides for important rights and obligations concerning the delineation of the outer limits of the continental shelf, the protection of the marine environment, including ice-covered areas, freedom of navigation, marine scientific research, and other uses of the sea. We remain committed to this legal framework and to the orderly settlement of any possible overlapping claims.

The Declaration highlights both a shared ocean territory but also legal-judicial framework in the form of the 'Law of the Sea' in helping to manage and resolve present and future challenges including delimiting the outer limits of the continental shelves of coastal states. While other Arctic states such as Iceland registered their displeasure at this initiative, fearing a geopolitics of exclusion, the Arctic 5 established a regional bloc that while attentive to the regional was also keenly aware of national interests and their individual sovereign rights as coastal states.

State sovereignty and sovereign rights continue to be emphasised by all the Arctic states, and in particular by the A5. Article 76 of UNCLOS and the mechanism for the delimitation of outer limits of continental shelves encouraged substantial investment in oceanographic and geophysical mapping of the Arctic Ocean by the Arctic 5. With the exception of the United States, which has still not ratified UNCLOS, the four other Arctic Ocean coastal states have submitted materials to the UN Commission on the Limits of the Continental Shelf (CLCS). Environmental change coupled with the febrile reactions to the planting of a Russian flag being planted on the seabed of the central Arctic Ocean prompted the Declaration as a device intended to defuse speculation that the Arctic was thinly governed and about to be scrambled over (Dodds and Nuttall 2016). While the UNCLOS-related process has been 'orderly', it enables and constrains particular forms of regional co-operation. Denmark, Canada and Russia have, for example, consulted one another over their respective submissions to the CLCS and the A5 have initiated plans to work with other stakeholders about how to manage the central Arctic Ocean (international waters) should fishing become possible in the future. But the fact remained that the other Arctic states were unhappy with what they perceived to be exclusionary tactics and strategies.

Notwithstanding the common purpose of the A5 with regard to Arctic Ocean governance, the A8 were able to conjure up regional alignment by focussing on the prospect of future observers to the Arctic Council. The Ottawa Declaration made reference to:

Observer status in the Arctic Council is open to:

a. Non-arctic states;
b. inter-governmental and inter-parliamentary organisations, global and regional; and
c. non-governmental organisations.

The most challenging moment for the Arctic Council came at the Ministerial Meeting in 2013 when the Arctic states and Permanent Participants discussed the applications of six states and other applicants including Greenpeace and the Oil and Gas Producers Association. The six states (China, India, Singapore, Korea, Italy and Japan) were admitted at the meeting while others including the European Union (at the time an ad hoc observer) were not considered. The decision to admit five 'Asian' observers marked a shift from the existing pattern of state observers, which were overwhelmingly 'European' members including UK, Germany and Poland. At the same time the eight Arctic states agreed to a legally binding oil spill response agreement, which complemented an earlier agreement on search and rescue in the Arctic region (Steinberg and Dodds 2015).

As part of the expansion of state observers process, the Arctic Council revisited their guidelines (the so-called 'Nuuk criteria') for observers. Developed in 2011, they have been revisited in 2013 and revised again in 2016, but in essence they insist that observers respect the sovereignty, sovereign rights and jurisdiction of the eight states, that they contribute positively to the work of the Arctic Council and that they are not permanent observers. In effect, the guidelines stress that the contribution of observers will be assessed and evaluated mindful that the admission of additional observers carries with it transactional costs regardless of how substantial the contribution of an observer might be to the working groups and task forces of the Arctic Council.

The admittance of new observers to the Arctic Council in 2013 brought to the fore different projects – a regionalism shaped by the Arctic states and Permanent Participants and a vision of a global Arctic where states such as China were imagining themselves as 'near-Arctic' states. The Arctic as a region was imagined as possessing a stretchable quality where a medley of issues such as climate change, shipping, and living and non-living resources enable different Arctic(s) to become the basis for economic, political and legal governance. What makes Arctic regionalism interesting in recent years is how the materiality of the region itself is fundamental – as a transit zone, as a resource frontier, as a military zone, and the pressures that diminishing sea ice, ocean acidification and/or environmental perturbation place on the regulation of the Arctic.

The use, representation and regulation of the Arctic are integral to region building, but the Arctic Council does not enjoy exclusive sovereignty over that project. There are other forums that arguably participate in Arctic regionalism. Notably in October 2013 Iceland hosted an Arctic Assembly, which brought together an array of business, political, and non-governmental bodies and stakeholders together with Arctic and non-Arctic states. While this body and others such as the annual Arctic Frontiers conference do not pose a challenge to the authority and legitimacy of the Arctic Council, they serve as a reminder that the use, representation and regulation of the Arctic are not straightforward. And this became even more apparent in the aftermath of the Russian annexation of Crimea and the onset of crisis in Eastern Ukraine from 2014, and the confrontation in relation to Syria. Within months, commentators were expressing concerns that the regional co-operation engendered by the Arctic Council might be jeopardised by worsening relations between the EU, the West and Russia.

Two things have followed from the onset of a crisis in the West's relationship with Russia. First, the activities of the Arctic Council have endured but specific issues like the application of the EU for observer status has been abandoned for the moment as a consequence of EU sanctions against Russia. In retrospect, there was a period between 2008 and 2014 when the Arctic states were able to consolidate their collective regional interests, address growing extra-regional interest in the Arctic and cement their dominant role in Arctic governance. While the Arctic Council does not consider military and security matters, the Arctic states found ways of collaborating on matters of mutual interest such as search and rescue, oil spill response, coastguard and constabulary matters and avoided tension between the NATO member states and Russia.[4] The Arctic states arguably also agreed that the admittance of additional state observers such as China and Korea was a useful way of consolidating their sovereign authority (Steinberg and Dodds 2015). Second, as a consequence of sanctions, Russia has looked to other partners such as China and Vietnam to support its oil and gas sector and encouraged different stakeholder involvement as Western companies such as Exxon-Mobil and BP have pulled out of Russian partnership deals.

Until the Ukraine crisis and the consequential sanctions/travel restrictions placed on Russia and its officials, we might have concluded by stating that there is evidence of a 'regional community' forming around the Arctic region, and centred on the Arctic Council. There are degrees and levels of what might be termed 'region-ness' but we could point to a community of states and permanent participants working in a context characterised by working groups/task forces investigating the politics, ecologies and cultures of the Arctic region, supported by a permanent secretariat and working with an architecture characterised by ministerial meetings, permanent participants and Senior Arctic Officials attached to the eight Arctic states, and stakeholder engagement involving states, NGOs and IGOs. While the Ukraine crisis has led to some disruption in that overall process, Arctic regionalism has a resilient quality and secular scope to it that few would have imagined possible in the mid to late 1980s when President Gorbachev called for a new vision for the Arctic (Åtland 2008). Importantly, however, when the parties came together to negotiate an Ottawa Convention it seemed likely that very few anticipated that the 'Arctic region' would attract the kind of global interest that it does now. The last ten years have witnessed in short, an acceleration and intensification of Arctic regionalism, and serve as a reminder that there are temporalities and spatialities at play.

39.4   ANTARCTIC REGIONALISM

What is the region in the Antarctic context (Figure 39.2)? As a geographical area without any indigenous occupation, where permanent presence commenced just over a century ago – and for the first fifty years, discontinuously – the conception is essentially *political*. The arrival of exploring then sealing and whaling expeditions from the nineteenth century, and from the turn of the twentieth century of imperially driven scientific expeditions created a proto-Antarctic-regionalism. This was accelerated by the codification of territorial claims from the early to mid-twentieth century. When that project came up against the reality of near universal rejection, including by the post-Second World War superpowers of the United States and Soviet Union, a contingent internationalisation of Antarctica resulted. Contingent in the sense of only involving a subset of global states, and in representing only a limited abandonment of national autonomy in Antarctica by those states. But, Antarctica was now formally some sort of region; positively in the eyes of its principal actors, in a more passive manner for other states, including those emerging from colonialism. For these states, unless and until they were able to assert rights there too, Antarctic regionalism was at best moot, and at worst an ongoing demonstration

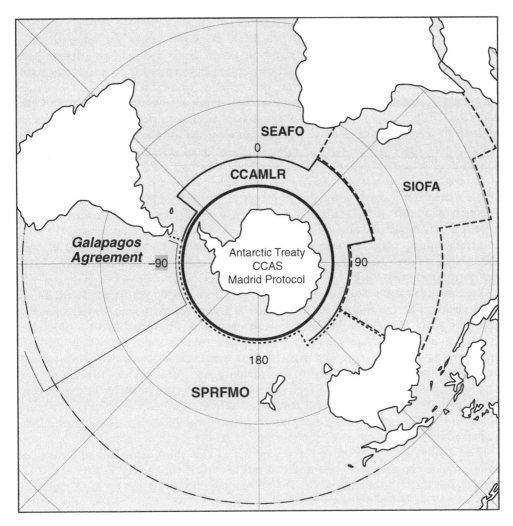

Figure 39.2 Antarctica showing the major regional instruments regulating the Greater Southern Ocean

of neo-colonialism. Later, in the 1980s, as part and parcel of the striving after a New Economic Order, Antarctica was indeed construed as such by the global South in the annual 'Question of Antarctica' in the UN General Assembly (Beck 2017).

But, across this modern period, during which a political Antarctic region has been in place the construct has changed several times. One thing that has *not* changed has been the global nature of regionalism in the Antarctic context – a seeming paradox. Most regionalisms necessarily coalesce around actors in and of the region, whether in the Mediterranean, the Baltic, West Africa . . .. There are of course hot-spots where a region, and often regional dysfunction, also involves extra-regional states. The South China Sea presently powerfully demonstrates this, but the Indian and (increasingly) the Arctic Ocean reflect this globalising reality too (on the latter see Hemmings 2016a). The

Antarctic is historically novel in that its regional structure was from inception a globally and not a regionally generated construct. There are states nearer the Antarctic than others, but Antarctica is not meaningfully in anybody's 'back yard'. The critical issue here is that inevitably, the Antarctic regional conception has evolved from a different base, and according to a different model, from most other geographical regions on the planet.

Political Antarctic regionalism has seen the dominant Antarctic states, and the Antarctic Treaty System which they created as a regime, exert considerable efforts to preserve their 'regional hegemony'. This was most evident in the 1980s, where the dual challenges of the environmental critique and Group of 77 through the annual UN 'Question of Antarctica' debates, galvanised then Consultative Parties to common action in defence of their regional management. Through a combination of the containment of the minerals resources issue (abandonment of the facilitating minerals convention, adoption in its place of the Madrid Protocol with its prohibition of minerals activities), a refocus on environmental protection with the Madrid Protocol, and opening of the ATS to membership by major global South states (notably Brazil, China and India), regional hegemony, only slightly diluted, was preserved, at least in the short term (Hemmings 2014, pp. 59–62; Hemmings 2017).

If we take 1959 as marking the birth of a modern and distinct politico-legal conception of the region, with the adoption of the Antarctic Treaty, we see that across the following almost 60 years, that region has progressively expanded. This expansion is *reflected* in the architecture of international governance (initially, but no longer exclusively, through the Antarctic Treaty System, important as that remains) but *driven* by the realities of geopolitical interest attendant upon the expanding menu of resource interests, in turn made possible by technological development. This last made possible the progressive overcoming of the natural physical barriers of Antarctica (continental and maritime) which had traditionally constrained, if not totally prohibited (see Hemmings 2015), human activity there.

Thus, despite the 1959 Antarctic Treaty applying to the entire area south of 60 degrees South latitude, the absence of marine harvesting activity in the area, apart from the whaling that was the responsibility of the 1946 International Convention for the Regulation of Whaling and its International Whaling Commission (IWC) (Saul and Stephens 2015, pp. 587–593), meant that until 1972, the Antarctic region as most active states understood it in practice applied to little more than the continent and islands.

With first the adoption of the 1972 Convention on the Conservation of Antarctic Seals (CCAS) (Saul and Stephens 2015, pp. 47–53), to manage any resumption of sealing, and then (more substantively, since no sealing has occurred) with the 1980 Convention on the Conservation of Antarctic Marine Living Resources (CCAMLR) (Saul and Stephens 2015, pp. 59–69), the Antarctic region expanded to include the huge oceanic area up to the Antarctic Convergence. This second stage in the conception of the Antarctic region was bolstered, but not materially altered, by the adoption, in 1991, of the Madrid Protocol – the last substantive instrument to be added to the Antarctic Treaty System (ATS).

Post-Madrid Protocol, Antarctic resource exploitation in the conventionally conceived Antarctic region – that is, the area subject to the instruments of this ATS – was essentially confined to marine harvesting (under CCAMLR) and tourism (not subject to any specific regional regulation beyond generic obligations under the Antarctic Treaty and Madrid Protocol). Minerals resource activity was prohibited under Article 9 of the

Madrid Protocol; and sealing (under CCAS) has not eventuated. The problematical issue of 'scientific' or 'special permit' whaling under the IWC (Fitzmaurice 2015), was now largely conducted close to the continent off East Antarctica and in the Ross Sea. But, as the recent case before the International Court of Justice has shown (Fitzmaurice and Tamada 2016), all parties went to lengths to insulate the Antarctic regime of the ATS from any role – and the corrosive effects of dispute – in relation to whaling there. In the late twentieth century, the only other harvesting activity occurring in high latitudes that was not managed directly under ATS auspices was fishing for southern bluefin tuna, managed by the taxa-specific (and not geographically delimited) 1993 Convention for the Conservation of Southern Bluefin Tuna (CCSBT) (Saul and Stephens 2015, pp. 603–609). Southern blue fin tuna occur, and have been harvested, within the CCAMLR area (although their main range appears to be north of it) and therefore it was anticipated that CCSBT and CCAMLR would have to coordinate, although this has proven very difficult in practice, notwithstanding a commonality of active tuna fishing states across the two conventions (Hemmings 2006).

But in the early twenty-first century, the huge and hitherto only slightly exploited band of ocean immediately north of the Antarctic Convergence became the focus for a further phase of institutional development, through a series of Regional Fisheries Management Organizations (RFMO) based on a set of new geographically delimited fisheries conventions across the south Atlantic, Indian and Pacific oceans, which each took the northern boundary of CCAMLR as their southern boundary. These RFMOs, comprising the South East Atlantic Fisheries Organisation (SEAFO), South Pacific Regional Fisheries Management Organisation (SPRFMO), and Southern Indian Ocean Fisheries Agreement (SIOFA) (Hemmings 2016b pp. 140–142) were adopted over just an eight-year period (2001–2009) and all in force by 2012. This is a very fast turnaround in international legal instrument terms, and has created an enormous new area across which marine harvesting is now regulated through international mechanisms. Individually and collectively they are positive in terms of fisheries management and the hoped-for wise management of marine ecosystems. Here our interest is in what they also represent in terms of an effective expansion of the Antarctic region.

For a large part of the circumpolar Antarctic, the Antarctic Convergence is a very long way south. From 150° E (to the south east of Tasmania) to 50° W (in the South Atlantic) – that is, across the entire Pacific sector of the Southern Ocean – the convergence, and the approximation to that codified in CCAMLR, is at 60° S, coincident with the boundary of the Antarctic Treaty, CCAS and Madrid Protocol. The choice of 60° S for the Antarctic Treaty boundary reflects 1950s political rationales, particularly in relation to the placement of the boundary in the South Atlantic. CCAS and the Madrid Protocol were essentially tied to that 1959 decision, and whilst CCAMLR had an ecologically based rationale for its choice of the Antarctic Convergence as its boundary, the South Pacific sector was not seen as presenting any immediate issues. But, it has been known for some time that a number of Antarctic species cross the 60° S boundary, and thus any RFMO that has 60° S as its southern boundary will inevitable have assumed control over some clearly high-Antarctic waters and species.

If it is incontrovertible that SPRFMO is substantively an expansion of the Antarctic region, because it exercises control over harvesting across such a huge swathe of the Southern Ocean and South Pacific at high latitudes, one may also argue expansion in the south east Atlantic and southern Indian Ocean areas through SEAFO and SIOFA respectively since here there is a greater northward extension of 'Antarctic' lands and waters, though the numerous sub-Antarctic islands that occur here, and the northward extension of CCAMLR to 55° S in the eastern Indian Ocean, 45° S in the western Indian Ocean and 50° S in the south east Atlantic Ocean. Since this boundary reflects the position of the Antarctic Convergence on this 'side' of the Antarctic, SEAFO and SIOFA, just as much as SPRFMO, 'collect' a good deal of Antarctic ecosystem. For these reasons, one must see these three new RFMOs in particular as substantially expanding the reality of the Antarctic region, contributing to a new maritime domain, best understood as 'The Greater Southern Ocean' (Hemmings 2016b, 2016c).

We appear to be seeing the building of a set of fisheries instruments extending from the coastline of Antarctica to the mid latitudes of the south Atlantic, Indian and Pacific oceans. These developments are largely driven by states which have territorial interests in the high Antarctic and sub-Antarctic littoral and/or global fishing interests. This may not seem remarkable, but it is striking in various ways. First in the relatively low representation of developing states – and the fact that amongst the small island states that are represented one is fairly confident that overseas developed-world fishing interests are in fact the prime movers. The United States is conspicuously absent, although it is one of four 'Cooperating non-Contracting Parties' to SPRFMO; except that of course the US is particularly well-placed through its global power.

It may be the case that the new RFMO architecture offers a basis for more rational and (one hopes) environmentally sustainable harvesting than an unstructured free-for-all would allow. Whilst much analysis of resource pressures and competition gravitates to discussion of scrambles for hydrocarbons and other minerals (in both polar regions, as elsewhere such as the South China Sea), less commonly remarked on is the competition for fisheries resources (Schofield et al. 2016). So, there are benefits to system and order but how those 'benefits' are articulated, disciplined and understood will remain controversial with plenty of scope for Butler's conception of 'petty sovereigns' to play a crucial role in deliberating on such distinctions.

39.5   POLAR REGIONALISM IN THE TWENTY-FIRST CENTURY

The Danish physicist, Niels Bohr, once quipped that 'Prediction is very difficult, especially if it is about the future' (quoted in Ellis 1970, p. 431) and followed up with a warning that, 'An expert is a person who has found out by his own painful experience all the mistakes that one can make in a very narrow field' (quoted in Coughlan 1954, p. 62). So our forecasting is by necessity cautious but rooted in a certain confidence that polar regionalism is going to be increasingly contentious, complex and creative. The resource potential of the Arctic and Antarctic will continue to attract regional and global attention, the prospect of further fishing in the Southern Ocean and possibly in the central Arctic Ocean remains alluring, and the management architecture erected to facilitate it may be a harbinger of further and broader regional management. We have no reason to think that resource pressures on both regions are going to diminish regardless of the efforts of campaign groups and celebrities to wish it were not so. Indigenous and northern communities in the Arctic region will continue to press their own demands for resource ownership and utilisation regardless, and the 'open' nature of the ocean areas beyond national jurisdiction around Antarctica poses challenges from a putative 'free-for-all' through a consensus-based international management, to a potential resource appropriation by the 'usual suspects'.

Physical and political complexity will not diminish (Lenton 2015). The regional and global architectures surrounding and intervening in both the Arctic and Antarctic are extraordinary in the way in which they overlap, intermingle and co-constitute one another. 'Petty sovereigns' in the Arctic Council and Antarctic Treaty System play a crucial role in deliberating and determining (where possible) how the boundaries of the regions are policed and monitored. Areas of future tension include the intersection between the UN Declaration on the Rights of Indigenous Peoples and the UN Law of the Sea Convention, and their impact on how indigenous peoples, coastal states and other actors negotiate mobility through the entire Arctic Ocean including coastal/historic waters. Diminishing sea ice will pose new challenges to existing bodies of international maritime law (notable Article 234 of UNCLOS). In the Antarctic, as we have noted, fisheries management provides a powerful insight into how multiple regional organisations, overlapping zones of resource management and a medley of actors with their own interests and wishes co-exist uneasily with one another.

Finally, what about the role of creativity in shaping regionalisms? In both cases, the Arctic Council (with regard to the role of indigenous peoples as Permanent Participants) and the Antarctic Treaty System (and its provisions on sovereignty, demilitarisation, peace and co-operation, and environmental protection) have been lauded as far-reaching and visionary. What will future iterations embrace and what will it take to secure new forms of consensual ideas and actions, in a world whose global order is changing before our eyes? Is there a role for further regional experimentation? Will further regional innovation emerge that is distinct because of the comparative remoteness and ongoing geophysical shifts affecting the polar regions? Our sense is that ideas associated with the twentieth century such as science diplomacy and ecosystem-based forms of resource management are becoming a little threadbare, even openly challenged in negotiations over fishing. In the case of the Southern Ocean, notwithstanding the apparent agreement to an amended Ross Sea MPA in October 2016, there was considerable opposition to longer-term resource management/prohibition. We expect polar regionalisms to become ever more contentious as multiple stakeholders engage with overlapping and cross-cutting policy themes, geophysical change, and the contested legacies of exploration, exploitation, colonialism and domination.

39.6   ACKNOWLEDGEMENTS

Our sincere thanks to Jen Kynaston at the Department of Geography at Royal Holloway University of London for redrawing the two figures used in our chapter.

39.7   NOTES

1. Canada, Denmark, Norway, USSR, USA – Agreement on the Conservation of Polar Bears. Adopted in Oslo 15 November 1973, entered into force 26 May 1976, 13 ILM 13.
2. The Declaration on the establishment of the Ottawa Convention, 19 September 1996, https://oaarchive. arctic-council.org/bitstream/handle/11374/85/EDOCS-1752-v2ACMMCA00_Ottawa_1996_Founding_ Declaration.PDF?sequence=5&isAllowed=y (accessed 5 March 2018).
3. Arctic Ocean Conference 'The Ilulissat Declaration' 29 May 2008, http://www.oceanlaw.org/downloads/ arctic/Ilulissat_Declaration.pdf (accessed 5 March 2018).
4. For example, Agreement on Cooperation on Aeronautical and Maritime Search and Rescue in the Arctic (2011), Agreement on Cooperation on Marine Oil Pollution, Preparedness and Response in the Arctic (2013), and Agreement on Enhancing Arctic Scientific Cooperation (2017).

39.8   REFERENCES

Archer, C. (1988), *The Soviet Union and Northern Waters*, London: Routledge.
Åtland, K. (2008), 'Mikhail Gorbachev, the Murmansk Initiative, and the desecuritization of interstate relations in the Arctic', *Cooperation and Conflict*, **43** (3), 289–311.
Beck, P. (2017), 'Antarctica and the United Nations', in K. Dodds, A.D. Hemmings and P. Roberts (eds), *Handbook on the Politics of Antarctica*, Cheltenham UK and Northampton, MA, USA: Edward Elgar Publishing, pp. 255–268.
Butler, J. (2006), *Precarious Life: The Power of Mourning and Violence*, London: Verso.
Butler, J. (2011), *Bodies that Matter*, London: Routledge.
Coughlan, R. (1954), 'Dr. Edward Teller's Magnificent Obsession', *LIFE Magazine*, 6 September.
Dodds, K. and A.D. Hemmings (2015), 'Polar oceans: sovereignty and the contestation of territorial and resource rights', in H.D. Smith, J.L Suárez de Vivero and T.S. Agardy (eds), *Routledge Handbook of Ocean Resources and Management*, London: Routledge, pp. 576–591.
Dodds, K. and M. Nuttall (2016), *The Scramble for the Poles*, Cambridge: Polity.
Elden, S. (2009), *Terror and Territory*, Minneapolis, MN: University of Minnesota Press.
Elden, S. (2013), *The Birth of Territory*, Chicago, IL: University of Chicago Press.
Ellis, A.K. (1970), *Teaching and Learning Elementary Social Studies*, New York: Allyn and Bacon.
Exner-Pirot, H. (2013), 'What is the Arctic a case of? The Arctic as a regional environmental security complex and the implications for policy', *The Polar Journal*, **3** (1), 120–135.
Fitzmaurice, M. (2015), *Whaling and International Law*, Cambridge: Cambridge University Press.
Fitzmaurice, M. and D. Tamada (eds) (2016), *Whaling in the Antarctic: Significance and Implications of the ICJ Judgement*, Leiden: Brill Nijhoff.
Hemmings, A.D. (2006), 'Regime overlap in the Southern Ocean: the case of southern blue fin tuna and CCSBT in the CCAMLR Area', *New Zealand Yearbook of International Law*, **3**, 207–217.
Hemmings, A.D. (2014), 'Re-justifying the Antarctic Treaty System for the 21st century: rights, expectations and global equity', in R.C. Powell and K. Dodds (eds), *Polar Geopolitics? Knowledges, Resources and Legal Regimes*, Cheltenham, UK and Northampton, MA, USA: Edward Elgar Publishing, pp. 55–73.
Hemmings, A.D. (2015), 'Commercial harvest in Antarctica', in D. Liggett, B. Storey, Y. Cook and V. Meduna (eds), *Exploring the Last Continent: An Introduction to Antarctica*, New York: Springer, pp. 413–428.
Hemmings, A.D. (2016a), 'The 1959 Antarctic Treaty and subsequent Antarctic Treaty system', in H.A. Conley (ed.), *History Lessons for the Arctic: What International Maritime Disputes Tell Us about a New Ocean*, Washington, DC: Center for Strategic and International Studies and Brzezinski Institute on Geostrategy, pp. 38–50.
Hemmings, A.D. (2016b), 'Southern horizons: South Asia in the South Indian Ocean', *Panjab University Research Journal Social Sciences*, **24** (1–2), 129–153.
Hemmings, A.D. (2016c), 'Evolution of the Greater Southern Ocean as a regulatory sphere', presentation at *9th Polar Law Symposium: The Rule of Law in Polar Governance*, Akureyri, Iceland, 5–6 October.
Hemmings, A.D. (2017), 'Antarctic politics in a transforming global geopolitics', in K. Dodds, A.D. Hemmings and P. Roberts (eds), *Handbook on the Politics of Antarctica*, Cheltenham, UK and Northampton, MA, USA: Edward Elgar Publishing, pp. 507–522.
Keskitalo, E.C.H. (2004), *Negotiating the Arctic: The Construction of an International Region*, London: Routledge.
Lenton, T. (2015), *Earth System Science: A Very Short Introduction*, Oxford: Oxford University Press.
Pincus, R. and S.H. Ali (eds) (2015), *Diplomacy on Ice: Energy and the Environment in the Arctic and Antarctic*, New Haven, CT: Yale University Press.

Saul, B. and T. Stephens (eds) (2015), *Antarctica in International Law*, Oxford: Hart.
Schofield, C., R. Sumaila and W. Cheung (2016), 'Fishing, not oil, is at the heart of the South China Sea dispute', *The Conversation*, 16 August 2016, http://theconversation.com/fishing-not-oil-is-at-the-heart-of-the-south-china-sea-dispute-63580 (accessed 5 March 2018).
Steinberg, P.E. and K. Dodds (2015), 'The Arctic Council after Kiruna', *Polar Record*, **51** (1), 108–110.
Steinberg, P.E., J. Tasch and H. Gerhardt (2015), *Contesting the Arctic: Politics and Imaginaries in the Circumpolar North*, London: I.B. Tauris.
Young, O.R. (2005), 'Governing the Arctic: from Cold War theatre to mosaic of co-operation', *Global Governance*, **11**, 9–15.
Young, O.R. (2012), 'Building an international regime complex for the Arctic: current status and next steps', *The Polar Journal*, **2** (2), 391–407.

40. Ocean regions
Kimberley Peters

40.1 INTRODUCTION

As this Handbook demonstrates, the 'region' has a special place in geographic study. In respect of the world's seas and oceans, the term 'region' has been long used to describe specific areas of water which are outside of, span beyond, yet also connect spaces and places (see Steinberg 2001, 2013). Indeed, the term 'region' lends itself neatly to the watery zones of the planet given the geophysical and geopolitical character of oceans where they fluidly link 'areas' together beyond typical spatial imaginaries, such as the nation-state (see Connery 1996). The world is typically divided into five oceanic regions: the Pacific, Atlantic, Indian, Southern and Arctic Oceans. But academics and policy practitioners have also used the term 'region' to describe other 'pockets' of maritime space: a Mediterranean region (Braudel 1966/1995), or a 'Western Seaways' region (Bowen 1972). As Jones and Paasi have noted (2013, p. 2) the term region is 'a vague category', that is 'interpreted and understood in many ways' – and this is evident in its application to maritime regions of connection as well as (more or less) 'landed', 'sub-states, supra-state and cross-border regions' (Jones and Paasi 2013, p. 1).

However, whilst the 'region' has a seemingly obvious application to the seas and oceans it has been on the fringes, or margins, of much work concerned with regional geographies. The seas and oceans, located on the very margins of land (Peters 2010; Ryan 2012) has resulted in a marginalisation of their study – in this sub-field and across geography per se (Anderson and Peters 2014; Steinberg 2001, Peters 2010). Yet the very origins of regional geography are linked to the seas and oceans. As Cloke et al. (1991, p. 6) have noted, regional approaches 'owed much to . . . classical times, and its later association with voyages of exploration and discovery', which were characterised by attempts to describe all that was specific about the new spaces and places that were visited, conquered and colonised. Indeed, driven by the opening of the world through oceanic connections 'grew a concern for *identification* and *description* of particular regions of the Earth's surface' (Cloke et al. 1991, p. 6, original emphasis). This task, 'focused on the causal relations between assemblages of phenomena which lend individuality to particular places', was – although spurred on by seas and oceans and journeys across them – almost entirely land-locked (Peet 1998, p. 16). In order to unpack the *differences* between regions, and the unique connections that produced that idiographic character of place, geographers had to focus on the *landscape* features that enabled such a differentiation to be observed and recorded. Within such a geographic approach, observation of the distinctiveness of the seas and oceans was limited, given the seas were simply, 'blue, flat and unchanging' – simply voids to be crossed for economic and political gain (Steinberg 2013, p. 159). As Levi-Strauss (pp. 338–339) has written, the diversity customary on land seems to me to be simply destroyed by the sea, which offers vast spaces and additional shades of colouring for our contemplation, but at the cost of an oppressive monotony and a flatness in which no hidden valley holds in store surprises to nourish my imagination . . . the sea offers me a diluted landscape.

The geophysical nature and social construction of the ocean (see Steinberg 2001) thus resulted in an abandonment of the seas with the emergence of a 'Regional Geography' in the 1950s, and it has remained side-lined in regional approaches since, with instead a focus on the (multi)scalar workings of the region for 'land-centred' activities such as industrial competitiveness, devolved governance, place-branding and so on. This is in spite of a growing body of work now attending to so-called 'maritime geography' (Anderson and Peters 2014; Steinberg 2001). That said, the idea of ocean regions has been popular in recent ocean-focused research in geography (Steinberg 2013), and also through the work of Historical Geographers and more broadly cultural theorists and international-relations (IR) scholars who have increasingly theorised the role of maritime 'regions' in the making of the contemporary world (see, for example, Ogborn 2008).

Accordingly, this chapter explores how the spatiality of the region has been thought of in the context of oceans, whilst also attending to what the oceans offer to geographic understandings of the region moving forwards. Indeed, the chapter makes suggestions for potential for future work in regional geography that is more keenly focused on ocean realms. This is not to argue the ocean is taken as a stand-alone space that should be conceived separately from the land (such a suggestion would run against both relational work in contemporary regional geographies (see Jones 2009) and efforts to dispel the land–sea binary in maritime-focused geographies (see Anderson and Peters 2014; Spence 2014; Steinberg and Peters 2015)), but the aim is to demonstrate the possibilities of thinking *with* and *about* the ocean in regional approaches (see also Peters and Brown 2017).

To begin the chapter will expand upon this introduction providing a context to the land-bias in geography and more specifically, regional geography. From here the chapter then 'goes to sea', charting how the spatiality of the region has been used in relation to understandings of seas and oceans, past and present, drawing on Braudel's historic theorisation of the Mediterranean region (Braudel 1966/1995), Gilroy's cultural 'Atlantic World' region (Gilroy 1993), and more recently the work of those interested in port logistics in the North Sea region (Lobo-Guererro 2012; Rodrigue and Notteboom 2010). In the final part, the chapter considers the limitations of this work, offering examples of how a regional approach – where the region is conceptualised not only as relational and globally connected, but three-dimensional and dynamic (Jones 2009; Steinberg 2013) – might provide both an *ungrounded* and *volumetric* focus for ongoing work (following Peters et al. 2018).

40.2 A 'DRY' GEOGRAPHY: REGIONS AS LANDLOCKED

Although the concept of the region has changed – from understandings that they are fixed, bounded 'units' or 'homogenous', 'contiguous entities' (Paasi 2010, p. 2297), to instead relational, globally connected and shaped by external factors (Allen and Cochrane 2007; Jones 2009; Paasi 1991), a consistent feature has been the stubbornly landlocked focus of regional studies. Even as regions are considered an organising multi-scalar spatiality that could encompass maritime spaces – and a spatiality of connectivity that involves traversing land and sea – much work has stayed firmly on dry land. Indeed, when students of geography are introduced to the idea of the region, they are most readily presented with grounded spaces: the traditional physical demarcation of intra-national spaces (the south-east or north-west region); to the devolved governmental regions of a country; or, even beyond the scale of the nation-state, international regions: the Western European region; the Polar region; the Middle-Eastern region and so on. Even analytic advances in regional thinking, which have provided geography at large with some of the most important contributions to spatial thinking, have nonetheless tended to focus on the workings of regions as somehow exclusively grounded spaces.

That regional geography is concerned with land is not unsurprising. Much of human geography is (Steinberg 1999a; Lambert et al. 2006; Peters 2010). As the sea does not geophysically present society with a space of 'permanent sedentary habitation' (Steinberg 1999a, p. 369) due to its (mostly) liquid form (see Steinberg and Kristoffersen (2017) for a discussion of sea ice) it has often become marginalised in discussions of social, cultural, economic and political life. The ocean's material fluidity makes typical forms of development (building, infrastructure and so on) impossible. As such, given the majority of human activities occur on land, it is perhaps unexpected that geographic scholarship has focused on the terrestrial sphere, at the cost of paying due attention to the oceans (Peters 2017).

Moreover, although approximately two-thirds of the Earth's surface consists of bodies of water – and around 90 per cent of trade (on average) is carried by ship across the liquid voids that separate land masses (George 2014) – it has failed to register as a site of interest and has rather been conceptualised as mere physical distance to be traversed to connect places that matter: on land (Steinberg 2001). Indeed, to look at a typical world map, the eye is trained to look at the land – continents, countries, counties – not that which surrounds it: the seemingly empty space of the sea. Philip Steinberg has noted how the map has thus been a political tool in emptying the ocean of significance (Steinberg 2013). Even where we depict the sea in more 'sophisticated maps' the ocean remains 'fundamentally presented as a series of latitude and longitude points' – reducing the character and qualities of the ocean to a flat, static, void 'between' the spaces that matter: land (Steinberg 2013, p. 159). This persistent idea, enshrined through mapping has worked hand-in-hand with the Western construction of the ocean in 1700s political-economic discourse as a void or empty space to be traversed only for capital gain (Steinberg 2001, p. 114). As Steinberg notes, 'the sea was constructed, like money or markets, as without social "roots" – beyond society, politics and other "artificial" constructs that could interfere with the "natural" free flow of capital' (Steinberg 2001, p. 114). As he describes,

> . . . (in) the mid-eighteenth century, the spatiality of capitalism underwent a transformation . . . At the root of this transformation in political economy were a host of new opportunities for investing in land space. Following from these opportunities, the industrial era's rationalist "development discourse" justified the reification of developable places and denigrated the spaces between . . . Thus the ocean became discursively constructed as removed from society and the terrestrial places of progress, civilisation and development . . . In general, the significance of marine space was diminished. (Steinberg 1999b, p. 409)

Rather than the sea being central to landed life, Steinberg argues it became separated, with new importance placed on the terrestrial sphere and on the development of pockets of land within the capitalist enterprise (Steinberg 1999b, p. 409). With such changes, philosophers and theorists have turned their attention inwards to towns and cities, making these the primary 'object(s) of critical reflection' (Parker 2004, p. 8). Indeed, there has (and remains) an emphasis on the study of social and cultural experiences, representations and practices within urban and rural, but nonetheless *landed* regional centres (see, for example, Bristow 2010; Ilbery and Kneafsey 1999; Goodwin et al. 2005). Such emphasis has created a demarcation between the land and sea; marginalising the sea and placing it 'outside of' what Steinberg describes as the traditionally studied 'world region' (Steinberg 1999a, p. 368).

This is not to say that geographers have avoided watery realms entirely. Human geographers have had a long interest in thinking with and about water (see Swyngedouw 2004), but less so with the vast liquid spaces of oceans and seas that separate (and also connect) continents. Sociocultural, economic, political and environmental geographers have explored issues of water flow (or lack thereof) in developing nations; irrigation systems; damming projects; flooding prevention; to name just a few engagements with what might be called 'hydro worlds'. The sea though, has been somewhere in the background (Steinberg himself argues that the sea is often seen as a static backdrop rather than dynamic agent in contemporary life, 2013). The issue of access looms large with geographers traditionally grappling with the difficulty (in terms of cost and safety) of researching a mobile, deep, liquid space. Yet although it may be 'easy to forget that our world is an ocean world' (Langewiesche 2004, p. 3) the oceans offer up a new space of geographical examination that is linked – albeit often invisibly – to our daily lives (Peters 2010).

Indeed, in recent years geography has experienced an 'oceanic' turn with a raft of work focused on water worlds and their broader connections to historic and contemporary life (see, for example, Steinberg 2001; Anderson and Peters 2014; Brown and Humberstone 2015). This work has been incredibly varied, focusing on the economic geographies of port and maritime industries (Notteboom and Rodrigue 2005; Rodrigue and Notteboom 2010); the social worlds of islands and those that develop aboard ships (Anim-Addo et al. 2014); the embodied and cultural experience of being in the sea (Peters and Brown 2017); the political-legal geographies of the ocean (Steinberg 2001; Steinberg et al. 2014); and the environmental impacts of a global industry through examples such as ship breaking (Gregson 2011). Geographers have not only explored the seas and oceans as an empirical focus though. The oceans also offer up new perspectives for thinking about core geographical concerns – space, time, movement, connection (Steinberg and Peters 2015). Likewise it can offer up new ways for thinking *with* and *about* the region. Accordingly then, as Steinberg notes (2013, p. 156), 'ocean-region based studies' are currently 'gain(ing) popularity'.

40.3 A 'WET' GEOGRAPHY: REORIENTATING REGIONAL STUDIES TOWARDS THE OCEANS

For Christopher Connery (1996), regions – as spatial concepts for making sense of ways of understanding, organising, and governing space – are not isolated to the land. We may also think of regions at sea – oceanic regions – which produce a radically different image of the world, no longer centred on nation-state territories, or indeed 'new regional' spaces at the sub-state level (Brenner 2004). The region, as a frame of reference that extends the traditional boundaries of the nation-state outwards, and allows for 'rescaling of state-hood' within national borders (MacLeod and Jones 2007, p. 1181), has much potential in the context of the seas and oceans. Indeed, relational approaches to thinking with and about the region have argued that 'an adequate understanding of the region and its futures can only come through a conception of places as open, discontinuous, relational and internally diverse' (Allen et al. 1998, p. 143, in Jones 2009, p. 492). The sea is the most radically 'free' and 'open' space on Earth (Langewiesche 2004). It is a fluid space mutating and discontinuous and changing borders as it ebbs and flows. It permits relations, links and connections across different scales of space (Lobo-Guerrero 2012). Its activities and materiality make the seas 'internally' distinct; yet always shaped by external processes too (Steinberg 2013).

The relevance of 'regional thinking' to scholars interested in the seas and oceans has not been lost. Historian Ferdinand Braudel's classic work on the Mediterranean (Braudel 1966/1995), for example, conceives of that part of the world as a *maritime region* of connection, shifting focus from the land to the relations forged *across* the seas. This work presents an alternative vision of the region, quite different to the version of regional geography 'centred on the community, the nation-state, or the continent, typically privileging settlements, place-based identities, and the development of stable social institutions, most notably those associated with state power' (Steinberg 2013, p. 157). Rather, Braudel's Mediterranean advocates an ocean-based regionalisation, able to 'give greater prominence to the cultural and economic *interchange* between societies that is the hallmark of historical and modern political economy' (Steinberg 2013, p. 157, emphasis added).

Braudel's broadly relational understanding of the ocean can be seen in the work of a range of thinkers for making sense of world-regional connections. For example, historians and also cultural theorists and IR scholars have considered the oceans as spaces of connectivity and exchange – that occur inwards (across the region) and outwards (making global links). Paul Gilroy's important text, *The Black Atlantic* (1993), for example, considers the 'Atlantic' as a region across which landed circuits of trade and commerce (of both tangible goods and of people as slaves) were enabled. For Gilroy, the Atlantic functions as a spatial concept for making sense of linkages that have formed and forged the contemporary world, building a triangular trade between Northern Europe, West Africa and the Americas (Armitage and Braddick 2002). The transatlantic slave trade cannot be conceptualised at the scale of the nation-state but through a series of relations spun from journeys around an Atlantic region, with that very region, in turn, shaping black cultural identities (Gilroy 1993).

The idea of ocean regions as spaces of connectivity has also been employed in more recent work on the functioning of ports, where it is possible to see new economic spatialisations occur at a supra-national, European regional scale around the linkages made possible through the 'strategisation of space' for maritime trade (Lobo-Guerrero 2012; Rodrigue and Notteboom 2010). For Lobo-Guerrero, the current success of Northern Europe has been tied to the 'connectivity of the port (of Hamburg)' and the 'economic activities' it brings to the region through 'transcending . . . sovereign practices'

(Lobo-Guererro 2012, pp. 311–312). Key to Lobo-Guerrero's analysis, however, is that the port itself does not enable connectivity per se, rather a set of *strategies* that shape regulations, mobilities and technologies are vital in enabling the 'regional' connectivity he describes, to occur. Also crucial to both Gilroy's cultural analysis of an Atlantic region and Lobo-Guerrero's economic and political investigation of the North-Sea European region is that such spaces are not *only* oceanic. They are not neatly bordered 'wet' ocean regions. Rather, they are 'domains of circulation' linking 'the land and maritime' together (Lobo-Guererro 2012, p. 311). This understanding chimes with the work of maritime geographers (Anderson and Peters 2014; Steinberg 2001) who although advocating a turn towards the sea (see Lambert ct al. 2006) dismiss a binary that separates the land and sea as somehow separate (see Peters 2010).

The notion of an ocean region of connectivity spanning land and sea to bring new sociocultural, political and economic relations has also been harnessed by policy makers in recognition that this scale and cross-oceanic linkages are vital in the contemporary world. The Interreg Scheme is a European Union initiative to tie together different pan-European government agencies to 'deliver better policy' (Interreg Europe, n.d.). Funded by the European Regional Development Fund (ERDF), it focuses on the role of the region for building pan-European cooperation. Part of the Interreg Scheme has been specifically focused on the North Sea Region – an economic, social and political space that brings together 43 rim areas of the North Sea, drawing these together, whilst helping (in creating a powerhouse 'region') greater global connections. Part of the power of oceanic regions is the specific regional *imaginary* they construct through envisaging cross-water links (see Connery 1996). Whilst the regions described thus far (the Mediterranean, Atlantic and North Sea) are physical spaces of connection, they are also powerful metaphors in creating 'ideas' about (dis)connection 'difference', 'unity', and so on (see Steinberg 2014, p. 28). The Interreg North Sea Region programme functions by linking landed spaces across the seas into a cohesive spatial unit that transcends typical categories of governance (notably the nation-state). Yet it also constructs a powerful regional imaginary connecting or unifying spaces across the North Sea as a means of producing integrative policies that build for a 'strong' regional identity and economy. The North Sea has traditionally been a space of European connection – but also contestation (particularly through fishing 'turf' wars). Interreg promotes the case that social, economic and environmental issues can best be tackled at the regional level that encompass coastal rim zones around the North Sea, a zone of commonality and connection (Interreg North Sea Region, n.d.).

40.4   REGIONAL LIMITS: DEEPENING STUDIES OF THE SEA

Whilst the 'ocean region' has offered much to historical and maritime geographers, cultural theorists, IR scholars, and policy makers as a geo-spatial concept and as a metaphor for connectivity (Lobo-Guerrero 2012; Steinberg 2014), its study and application to academic and policy arenas could be productively extended. First, there is a concern that ocean regions operate as mere metaphors – where the ocean itself remains dematerialised (Blum 2010). Steinberg problematises this understanding of ocean regionalisation (Steinberg 2013). He contends the sea lacks substance as an actual organising concept for flows, networks and connections. It is not so much the ocean that is the focus then, but the points on land that are held together by the ocean. This, Steinberg argues, works to marginalise the sea in geographic work – a space already marginal in much human geography (see also Peters 2010; Anderson and Peters 2014), and, in particular, in regional geography. The sea as metaphor or 'mere surface' (Steinberg 2013, p. 164) can be seen in Gilroy's conceptualisation of the Atlantic world-region (Gilroy 1993). For Gilroy, the concept of the region is a useful framework for unpacking the connections that persist *across* the ocean, resulting in a global African diaspora as cultural identity is forged beyond nation-state boundaries. What is evident though, is that for Gilroy the use of the Atlantic as a concept is centred on the ability of the sea to act as 'primarily a spatial signifier for processes of connection' (Steinberg 2013, p. 158). It is possible to see similar ways in which the ocean region is a mere metaphor in the work of historians and historical geographers who have built on Gilroy's work to argue not just for a 'Black' Atlantic (a region of connections made via race) but a 'white', 'black' *and* 'red' Atlantic region, representing respectively, the colonial, 'multicultural' and 'genocidal' character of the Atlantic (see Lambert et al. 2006, p. 481). Whilst this kind of conceptualisation is valuable as a tool for understanding a range of historical and cultural phenomena, there is a lack of attention to the sea itself as a geo-physical space (with qualities such as trade winds, currents and so on, that build the connections under examination). The 'actual' sea is oddly empty or dematerialised in such accounts. As Steinberg notes then, '[v]enturing into Gilroy's Black Atlantic, one never gets wet' (Steinberg 2013, p. 158).

Moreover, such work not only reduces the sea to a metaphor, it also flattens it – conceptualising the oceans as mere spaces of 'crossing' to connect-up spaces that matter: on land. Accordingly, the sea is 'emptied' of significance and becomes simply a space to be traversed, rather than being part-and-parcel of the very 'region' under examination (Steinberg 2001, p. 113). This can be seen in the policy approach of the Interreg programme, which centres attention on 'landed' policies (related to business, innovation, growth and so on), rather than the space in the middle – the sea itself (Interreg North Sea Region, n.d.). In the Interreg Scheme, the North Sea becomes simply a space of crossing, for facilitating the (landed) connections that are sought in the economic rationale of the programme. As Steinberg argues then, most often, 'the ocean region thus comes to be seen as a series of (terrestrial) points linked by connection', without a focus on what he calls, 'the actual (oceanic) space of connections' (Steinberg 2013, pp. 157–158).

However, Marcus Rediker in his historic study of the Atlantic takes up Steinberg's call to take seriously the relations that emerge regionally because of the sea itself (Rediker 2007). Rediker's work places special emphasis on the 'middle passage' and the centrality of the ship and sea to the process of transatlantic slavery (as well as the landed points either side: the West African coast and the American colonies). Rediker demonstrates how the ship and sea had a physical and material presence that is vital to grasping the *politics* of an Atlantic region world. Indeed, for Rediker it was at sea, on board ships, that the 'Atlantic region' gained its character as people were imprisoned, transformed to commodities, terrorised into submission, and put to work. This horror, occurring within the very space of the Atlantic Ocean, shaped slaves arriving to the colonies, in turn foregrounding the economic 'potential' of the Atlantic region as slaves were terrorised and forced into labour on the land, producing goods to be exported. For Rediker, it is vital to think of regions materially and not to reduce them to metaphors, at the risk of continuing the 'violence of abstraction' which has limited accounts of the Atlantic world region and the slave voyages that have forged the modern world (Rediker 2007, p. 12).

Finally, the region in the context of the ocean is not only reduced to metaphor, and/ or to an empty space of connection – it is also primarily 'areal' in its imaginary. Regions tend to relate to 'horizontal' plains and the lines of connection forged *across* these spaces. Although regional studies have often paid attention to the variable scalar dimensions of regions (Brenner 1998), the shift towards a geography 'without scale' (Marston et al. 2005) has flatted geographical imaginaries, which although opening up a relational and networked conceptualisation of space, has limited how we might understand watery regions. Indeed, in the context of the land, a flat ontology permits an understanding of relations tying spaces together where activities often happen 'on' land (Steinberg and Peters 2015). Yet the sea is a fluid, three-dimensional liquid space where activities happen 'in' and 'under' the sea. Accordingly, there are calls for academic and policy approaches which attend to ocean regions to take seriously not just the sea itself (and what happens in the 'middle'), but also the sea in all its three-dimensionality.

For example, the Indian Ocean Region (IOR) demonstrates how surface *and* sub-surface attention need to be paid to watery realms. On the one hand, the sea itself is an important space of surface connection as home to some of the most vital trade routes in the world, linking together the East and West, including some of the busiest shipping channels (such as the Straits of Malacca). Geographers and IR scholars have focused on the 'space between' and considered regional approaches to confronting the challenges in governing beyond the nation-state, where piracy has increased, threatening the flows that bring economic trade and wealth to the landed 'points' at the 'rim' of the region (see Bueger 2015). Yet whilst the IOR is a space of connection between major, emerging world powers – China and India – these connections are reliant in part on the physical properties of the oceanic region – fishing and whaling, mineral extraction and oil resources (Sharma 2015) – all of which lay beneath the surface of the sea. The sea is not then, just a surface space of connection. What is *in* the water and *under* it matters too. Accordingly, a study of ocean regions should consider how they are 'filled', with a 'perspective that takes the geophysicality of the ocean seriously' (Steinberg 2013, p. 164).

40.5 CONCLUSIONS

This chapter has mapped the concept of the region in the context of the oceans and seas. On the one hand, the chapter has demonstrated that whilst the terminology of the 'region' has had a relatively long-standing application to watery spaces in historical geographies and via the work of historians and cultural theorists, its history in regional geography specifically has been somewhat limited. This is characteristic of geography per se, with its preoccupation with the land as the primary space of sociocultural, political and economic life (Peters 2010). However, the chapter has, on the other hand, demonstrated a growing interest in ocean regions through theories of 'relationality' which configure the region as open, connected and networked. The sea, as a space traditionally traversed, thus works well within these newer conceptualisations (Connery 1996). Here the ocean functions as a spatial zone of connection permitting new ways of thinking, working and governing at a scale beyond the nation-state.

Yet whilst there has been an oceanic 'turn', there is still work to do to realise the potential of thinking *with* and *about* the seas and oceans in regional geography. First, to date – as this chapter has demonstrated – the sea has been a tool to think *with*, reducing it to a metaphor. There is a need to think about the oceans and seas as more than spatial devices that produce particular regional imaginaries, or which act as a signifier for 'rim' connections (in the Mediterranean, Atlantic, Indian Ocean, Arctic and elsewhere). How a region works is not just a product of what happens on land, at the points of connection facilitated by the seas and oceans. Things happen *at* sea, *in* ocean regions. Over-fishing, waste dumping, oil drilling, piratical activities, illicit migration, and so on, are phenomena happening within our oceans that will likely require regional responses – from collectives of cities, countries and local areas who all have a stake in these contemporary issues. Second, as the chapter has also demonstrated, when we think *about* the seas, we configure these regions as mere surface. There is a need to consider oceans as three-dimensional, fluid, mobile spaces and to look to what is below, as the sea extends down vertically. As the contentious issue of Deep Sea Mining (DSM) continues (see Sharma 2015), again there may be a need for regional approaches and interventions to properly address what areas of the seafloor are mined, by whom and with what considerations for the environment and for the future. This means recognising the sea as more than just a planar surface of connection, but a social, cultural, political, economic space of materiality and depth. This would answer the critique of Philip Steinberg that 'ocean regions studies undertheorize the ocean' (Steinberg 2013, p. 157).

Policy is already beginning to develop in such a way. In 2017 a joint report, published by the United Nations (UN) Environment Programme – a fund launched in 1973 to 'finance environmental programmes and initiatives' (UNEP, n.d.) – together with the European Commission, the executive body of the European Union, called for 'regional cross-sectoral institutional cooperation and policy coherence in respect of world oceans (UNEP report, 2017, p. 3). This report aims to provide a regional approach to 'monitoring and assessment' across world ocean regions, offering collaborative plans and contingency responses related to oil spills, coastal habitat management, marine litter and the making of legal and institutional frameworks (UNEP report 2017, p. 3). Given this onus on ocean regions in the governance and policy arena, arguably it may also be time for regional geography to follow other sub-fields of geography that have already taken the plunge, and begin to more fully shift the seas and oceans, 'from the margins to the centre of academic vision' (Lambert et al. 2006, p. 480).

40.6　REFERENCES

Allen J., D. Massey and A. Cochrane (1998), *Re-thinking the Region*, London: Routledge.
Allen, J. and A. Cochrane (2007), 'Beyond the territorial fix: regional assemblages, politics and power', *Regional Studies*, **41** (9), 1161–1175.
Anderson, J. and K. Peters (eds) (2014), *Water Worlds: Human Geographies of the Ocean*, Farnham: Ashgate.
Anim-Addo, A., K. Peters and W. Hasty (2014), 'The mobilities of ships and shipped mobilities', *Mobilities*, **9** (3), 337–349.
Armitage, D. and M.J. Braddick (eds) (2002), *The British Atlantic World, 1500–1800*, London: Sage.
Blum, H. (2010), 'The prospect of oceanic studies', *Proceedings of the Modern Language Association*, **125** (3), 670–677.
Bowen, E.G. (1972), *Britain and the Western Seaways*, New York: Praeger.

Braudel, F. (1966/1995), *The Mediterranean and the Mediterranean World in the Age of Philip II*, California: University of California Press.

Brenner, N. (1998), 'Between fixity and motion: accumulation, territorial organization and the historical geography of spatial scales', *Environment and Planning D: Society and Space*, **16** (4), 459–481.

Brenner, N. (2004), 'Urban governance and the production of new state spaces in Western Europe, 1960–2000', *Review of International Political Economy*, **11** (3), 447–488.

Bristow, G. (2010), 'Resilient regions: re-"place"ing regional competitiveness', *Cambridge Journal of Regions, Economy and Society*, **3** (1), 153–167.

Brown, M. and B. Humberstone (eds) (2015), *Seascapes: Shaped by the Sea*, Farnham: Ashgate.

Bueger, C. (2015), 'Learning from piracy: future challenges of maritime security governance', *Global Affairs*, **1** (1), 33–42.

Cloke P., C. Philo and D. Sadler (1991), *Approaching Human Geography: An Introduction to Contemporary Theoretical Debates*, London: Paul Chapman.

Connery, C.L. (1996), 'The oceanic feeling and regional imaginary', in R. Wilson and W. Dissanayake (eds), *Global/Local: Cultural Production and the Transnational Imaginary*, London: Verso, pp. 284–311.

George, R. (2014), *Deep Sea and Foreign Going: Inside Shipping, the Invisible Industry that Brings You 90% of Everything*, London: Portobello Book.

Gilroy, P. (1993), *The Black Atlantic: Modernity and Double Consciousness*, London: Verso.

Goodwin M., M. Jones and R. Jones (2005), 'Devolution, constitutional change and economic development: explaining and understanding the new institutional geographies of the British state', *Regional Studies*, **39** (4), 421–436.

Gregson, N. (2011), 'Performativity, corporeality and the politics of ship disposal', *Journal of Cultural Economy*, **4** (2), 137–156.

Ilbery, B. and M. Kneafsey (1999), 'Niche markets and regional speciality food products in Europe: towards a research agenda', *Environment and Planning A*, **31** (12), 2207–2222.

Interreg Europe (n.d.), 'What is Interreg Europe', accessed 23 October 2015 at: https://www.interregeurope.eu/about-us/what-is-interreg-europe/.

Interreg North Sea Region (n.d.), 'About the programme', accessed 23 October 2016 at: http://www.northsearegion.eu/about-the-programme/.

Jones, M. (2009), 'Phase space: geography, relational thinking, and beyond', *Progress in Human Geography*, **33** (4), 487–506.

Jones, M. and A. Paasi (2013), 'Guest editorial: Regional world(s): advancing the geography of regions', *Regional Studies*, **47** (1), 1–5.

Lambert D., L. Martins and M. Ogborn (2006), 'Currents, visions and voyages: historical geographies of the sea', *Journal of Historical Geography*, **32** (3), 479–493.

Langewiesche, W. (2004), *The Outlaw Sea: Chaos and Crime on the World's Oceans*, London: Granta Publications.

Levi-Strauss, C. (1973), *Tristes Tropiques*, London: Jonathan Cape.

Lobo-Guerrero, L. (2012), 'Connectivity as the strategization of space: the case of the Port of Hamburg', *Distinktion: Scandinavian Journal of Social Theory*, **13** (3), 310–321.

MacLeod, G. and M. Jones (2007), 'Territorial, scalar, networked, connected: in what sense a "regional world"?', *Regional Studies*, **41** (9), 1177–1191.

Marston, S.A., J.P. Jones and K. Woodward (2005), 'Human geography without scale', *Transactions of the Institute of British Geographers*, **30** (4), 416–432.

Notteboom, T.E. and J.P. Rodrigue (2005), 'Port regionalization: towards a new phase in port development', *Maritime Policy & Management*, **32** (3), 297–313.

Ogborn, M. (2008), *Global Lives: Britain and the World 1550–1800*, Cambridge: Cambridge University Press.

Paasi, A. (1991), 'Deconstructing regions: notes on the scales of spatial life', *Environment and Planning A*, **23** (2), 239–256.

Paasi, A. (2010), 'Commentary', *Environment and Planning A*, **42** (10), 2296–2301.

Parker, S. (2004), *Urban Theory and the Urban Experience: Encountering the City*, London and New York: Routledge.

Peet, R. (1998), *Modern Geographical Thought*, Blackwell: Oxford.

Peters, K. (2010), 'Future promises for contemporary social and cultural geographies of the sea', *Geography Compass*, **4** (9), 1260–1272.

Peters, K. (2017), 'Oceans and seas: physical geography', in D. Richardson, N. Castree, M.F. Goodchild, A. Kobayashi, W. Liu and R.A. Marston (eds), *International Encyclopedia of Geography*, USA: AAG-Wiley, pp. 1–5.

Peters, K. and M. Brown (2017), 'Writing with the sea: reflections on in/experienced encounters with ocean space', *Cultural Geographies*, **24** (4), 617–624.

Peters, K., E. Stratford and P. Steinberg (2018), *Territory Beyond Terra*, London: Rowman & Littlefield International.

Rediker, M. (2007), *The Slave Ship: A Human History*, London: John Murray.

Rodrigue, J.P. and T.E. Notteboom (2010), 'Foreland-based regionalization: integrating intermediate hubs with port hinterlands', *Research in Transportation Economics*, **27** (1), 19–29.

Ryan, A. (2012), *Where Land Meets Sea: Coastal Explorations of Landscape, Representation and Spatial Experience*, Farnham: Ashgate.

Sharma, R. (2015), 'Environmental issues of deep-sea mining', *Procedia Earth and Planetary Science*, **11**, 204–211.

Spence, E. (2014), 'Towards a more-than-sea geography: exploring the relational geographies of superrich mobility between sea, superyacht and shore in the Cote d'Azur', *Area*, **46** (2), 203–209.

Steinberg, P.E. (1999a), 'Navigating to multiple horizons: towards a geography of ocean space', *Professional Geographer*, **51** (3), 366–375.

Steinberg, P.E. (1999b), 'The maritime mystique: sustainable development, capital mobility, and nostalgia in the ocean world', *Environment and Planning D: Society and Space*, **17** (4), 403–426.

Steinberg, P.E. (2001), *The Social Construction of the Ocean*, Cambridge: Cambridge University Press.

Steinberg, P.E. (2013), 'Of other seas: metaphors and materialities in maritime regions', *Atlantic Studies*, **10** (2), 156–169.

Steinberg, P.E. (2014), 'Mediterranean metaphors: travel, translation and oceanic imaginaries in the "New Mediterraneans" of the Arctic Ocean, the Gulf of Mexico and the Caribbean', in J. Anderson and K. Peters (eds), *Water Worlds: Human Geographies of the Ocean*, Farnham: Ashgate, pp. 23–37.

Steinberg, P.E., J. Tasch and H. Gerhardt (2014), *Contesting the Arctic: Politics and Imaginaries in the Circumpolar North*, London: I.B. Tauris.

Steinberg, P.E. and K. Peters (2015), 'Wet ontologies, fluid spaces: giving depth to volume through oceanic thinking', *Environment and Planning D: Society and Space*, **33** (2), 247–264.

Steinberg, P.E. and B. Kristoffersen (2017), 'The ice edge is lost . . . nature moved it: mapping ice as state practice in the Canadian and Norwegian North', *Transactions of the Institute of British Geographers*, **42** (4), 625–641.

Swyngedouw, E. (2004), *Social Power and the Urbanization of Water*, Oxford: Oxford University Press.

United National Environmental Programme (UNEP) (n.d.), 'Regional seas', accessed 30 August 2017 at: http://www.unep.org/regionalseas/.

United National Environmental Programme (2017), 'Realizing integrated regional oceans governance: summary of case studies on regional cross-sectorial institutional cooperation and policy coherence', *UN Environment Regional Seas Reports and Studies*, **199**, accessed 30 August 2017 at: https://europa.eu/capacity4dev/unep/documents/realizing-integrated-regional-oceans-governance.

Index

accountability 86, 219–20, 222, 275, 316, 365–6, 407, 461
Acharya, A. 314, 484
actor-networks 72, 188
Acts of Union 245
Addie, J.-P. 475
Advisory Council on Intergovernmental Relations (ACIR) 470
aero-regionalism 14
Afghanistan 399, 423
African Development Bank 460–61
African regionalism 457–67
African Union 316, 460, 463, 465
African urbanization 358–68
Agadir Agreement 391
Agnew, J. 15, 37, 39, 54, 81, 84
agribusiness 341–2
agriculture 186, 212, 214, 242, 263, 333, 337–9, 341, 348, 362–3, 376–7, 410, 415, 418–21, 424, 444, 464
Airbnb 147
Airbus 112
al-Assad, B. 388
Albania 202, 397–8
Aldrich, H. 125
Algeria 386–7
Allen, J. 3–4, 30–31, 59–60, 84
Allmendinger, P. 86
Al-Shabaab 462
Amin, A. 59, 175, 226
Anglophone context 9, 15–16, 57, 458–9, 463
Angola 461
Antarctic regionalism 489–92, 496–501
Antarctic Treaty System 489–91, 498–9, 501
anthropology 1, 7, 25, 111, 268, 374
anti-colonialism 457–8
anti-globalization populism 256
anti-urbanism 359–61
apartheid 459, 461, 466
Apple 113
apps 147–8
Arab League 388, 390, 392
Arab Spring 206, 388, 391–2
archipelagic regionalism 14
architectural regionalism 14
Arctic Council 489–90, 492–6, 501
Arctic Environment Protection Strategy (AEPS) 492

Arctic regionalism 489–96, 500–501
area studies 1, 327, 466
Argentina 354, 479, 483–4
Aristotle 197
Armenia 399
Arnold, P. 222
artificial intelligence 142, 146, 148–50
Asheim, B.T. 130
Asian Development Bank 399, 440
Asian Infrastructure Investment Bank 396, 425, 436, 440
Asia-Pacific Economic Cooperation (APEC) 391, 425
Association of South East Asian Nations (ASEAN) 23, 37, 306, 324, 425
atavistic regionalism 44
Atkinson, J. 144
Augustine (St) 198
austerity 71, 222, 485
Australia 95, 214, 227
    Australasian regionalism 444–54
Austria 187, 189, 398
authoritarianism 390, 392, 458
autonomy 8, 11, 126, 199–200, 202, 214, 216–17, 220, 238, 243, 254, 256–7, 261, 288, 293, 324, 347, 365, 380, 400, 402, 410, 415, 418, 422–6, 457, 468, 473, 496
    in South America 479–87
Azerbaijan 399, 403

Baden-Württemberg 5, 10, 69, 95, 108, 159
Badinger, H. 188
Bailey, I. 190
Bakic-Hayden, M. 404
Bakker, K. 474
Balassa, B. 313
Baldersheim, H. 221
Balkans conflict 40
Bandura, A. 126
banks 63, 204, 436, 441, 459–60
Barber, B. 223–4, 238
Barents Euro-Arctic Council 489
Basque Country 220, 231–2, 234, 236–40, 300
Bavaria 220
Beal, V. 224
Becker, B. 328
Beer, A. 446, 449
behavioural economic geography 123–4, 127